Rural America in a Globalizing World

VOLUME ONE

IN THE WEST VIRGINIA UNIVERSITY PRESS

Rural Studies Series

Sponsored by the Rural Sociological Society

Mary Emery, Series Editor

VOLUME TWO

California Dreaming: Boosterism, Memory, and Rural Suburbs in the Golden State

Paul J. P. Sandul

Before 2012, the Rural Studies Series was published by Penn State University Press. Visit psu.edu to learn more about past volumes in this series.

Rural America in a Globalizing World

Problems and Prospects for the 2010s

Conner Bailey, Leif Jensen, and Elizabeth Ransom
Published in cooperation with the Rural Sociological Society

WEST VIRGINIA UNIVERSITY PRESS
MORGANTOWN 2014

First edition 2014 by West Virginia University Press
Printed in the United States of America

21 20 19 18 17 16 15 14 1 2 3 4 5 6 7 8

paper: 978-1-940425-10-8
epub: 978-1-940425-12-2
pdf: 978-1-949425-11-5

Library of Congress Cataloging-in-Publication Data
is available from the Library of Congress.

Cover design by Michel Vrana / Black Eye Design
Book design by Than Saffel / WVU Press

CONTENTS

DEDICATION

The editors would like to dedicate this volume to people who have been special in our lives. Conner Bailey would like to offer his dedication to daughters Rebecca Ann Bailey and Rachel Ann Bailey, young women with brilliant minds and good hearts. Leif Jensen wishes to dedicate the book to Maialisa Elin Jensen, intrepid and joyful. Elizabeth Ransom dedicates the volume to Matt Kleiman, a connoisseur of all things Humulus lupulus *and her biggest supporter. Finally, the editors join the Rural Sociological Society in dedicating this book to our friend and colleague, Dr. Ralph Brown, friend, professor, and executive director of the Rural Sociological Society, for all he has done to advance our field, to strengthen the RSS, and to share his unique joy of life with all whom he encounters.*

PREFACE

Roughly every ten years, the Rural Sociological Society (RSS) commissions, through its Rural Studies Series, a "decennial volume" designed to identify key issues facing rural people in North America and elsewhere in the world, take stock of the research that has been done on these topics, and identify issues and research needs that are likely to emerge over the next decade. We were chosen by the council of the RSS to serve as editors of this, the fourth decennial volume, and appreciate the confidence of our colleagues in being assigned this task. As editors, we worked as a team of equals and the order of names on the volume and the introductory chapter is merely alphabetic—an accident of birth.

The authors in this volume cover a wide range of topics, which reflect the scope of work done by rural sociologists and kindred scholars. In the early fall of 2011 we developed an initial list of substantive areas that needed to be covered and used our professional networks to identify authors who, in many cases, recruited others to join them. Initial drafts came to us during the spring of 2012. We reviewed these, made comments, and in some cases requested revisions before sending manuscripts out for the first set of double-blind reviews. We sent reviews to the authors, often with detailed comments of our own, and requested revisions. Once these revisions were complete we submitted the entire volume to the editor and editorial board of the Rural Studies Series during early spring 2013. This editorial board was established by the RSS to provide editorial expertise to West Virginia University Press, publisher of the Rural Studies Series. As editor of the series, Dr. Mary Emery organized a complete set of additional reviews of all chapters of this volume. These reviews led to further revisions over the summer of 2013 and final editing during early fall.

We would like to thank the many reviewers, as well as the editor and editorial board of the Rural Studies Series. The peer-review process contributed significantly to the quality of the chapters in this volume. To the authors who put up with editors who kept asking for revisions, we appreciate your patience. Finally, we appreciate the helpful assistance of Carrie Mullen, director of West Virginia University Press, who, despite initial alarm at the sheer length of the volume, worked with us to bring this volume to the light of day.

Conner Bailey, Auburn University
Leif Jensen, Pennsylvania State University
Elizabeth Ransom, University of Richmond
11 October 2013

Rural America in a Globalizing World: Introduction and Overview

Conner Bailey, Leif Jensen, and Elizabeth Ransom[1]

This is the fourth in a series of volumes produced roughly every ten years under the aegis of the Rural Sociological Society (RSS). Beginning with Dillman and Hobbs' (1982) *Rural Society in the US: Issues for the 1980s,* these decennial volumes have given readers a forward-looking, policy-relevant, state-of-the-art understanding of rural people and places and the challenges they face. Following the example of our predecessors Dillman and Hobbs (1982), Flora and Christenson (1991), and Brown and Swanson (2003), we asked authors to draw on current research without ignoring work of the past, to identify new and emerging issues related to their topic, and to discuss policy implications that emerge from their work. In a real sense, the decennial volumes have provided an opportunity for the RSS to take stock not only of conditions in rural America, but also of how we as scholars understand these conditions, identify needs for further research, and, where appropriate, recommend policies to address problems that have been uncovered.

Each decennial volume shares commonalities. First, they all focus geographically on North America, not because of some parochial vision of a separate destiny, but in deference to the enormity of the dynamics and complexities of rural change in just this one region. Also, a quick glance at the tables of contents of the four decennial volumes reveals a common concern for perennially important issues. Authors in each volume have grappled with problems in agriculture and natural resources, complex issues of community and population change, and how rural America relates to the rest of the world. Each volume has devoted considerable attention to questions of family, race and ethnicity, and rural health. These broad themes are repeated in this volume, providing a measure of continuity. Yet even within this continuity, the chapters in this volume reflect the dynamics of change sweeping contemporary rural North America. The subject of fracking—high-pressure fracturing of shale formations to release hydrocarbons—was a non-issue in previous decennial volumes, but has emerged as an important problem in several parts of the United States, as Kinchy and colleagues describe in chapter 14. Other new subjects that compelled our attention include the Hispanic immigration to rural North America and questions of vulnerability and resilience in small coastal communities. And of course structural changes in agriculture since the first decennial volume was published mean that the issues addressed today are not the same as those of the early 1980s. We recognize that the full range of topics—including topics near and dear to the hearts of the editors—did not make the cut, but we are confident that those covered represent the most current thinking on some of the most salient problems and prospects for rural North America.

Decennial Themes

North America in the second decade of the twenty-first century is a very different place than the early 1980s. During the 1970s the long decline in rural populations had reversed and there was a sense of a rural renaissance as commodity prices for food, energy, and other natural resources climbed to unheard of levels. Several authors in the Dillman and Hobbs (1982) volume drew attention to changes in the structure of agriculture but none predicted the economic recession of 1981 to 1982 and the ensuing farm crisis that swung the rural pendulum back away from growth in population and prosperity. At the beginning of the 1990s, Flora and Christenson (1991, 2–3) linked changing fortunes in rural North America to global trade and macroeconomic policies, but these themes were prominent in only a few chapters in that volume. The theme of rural restructuring and the impact of global forces came into sharper focus in Brown and Swanson (2003), with greater attention being given to the diversity of rural economies.

We believe that globalization and neoliberalism are forces having profound impacts on not only rural North America but also the rest of the world. We invited our authors to speak to these themes in their chapters. By globalization, we mean the increased global interconnectedness of social and economic life brought about by rapid changes in information and transportation technologies. The ideology of neoliberalism has created political conditions that favor deregulation of financial markets and consolidation of corporate power. In the context of globalization, the ideology of neoliberalism has been used to justify the removal of barriers to trade and the flow of financial capital. Few parts of the world are immune to these combined forces, which have changed the course of North American agriculture from a system based on family farms to global commodity systems dominated by multinational corporations and, in combination with government policies, have impacted agrifood systems globally. Neoliberalism and globalization have also led to the rapid decline in both rural and urban manufacturing employment over the past two decades, and have created increased inequalities in society. Not every author engages with these two themes to the same degree, but their pervasive qualities are evident in much of this volume.

Globalization and neoliberalism are hallmarks of the contemporary world. In asking our authors to consider how these forces influence their topics, we sought to establish a conceptual coherence to this volume without imposing intellectual uniformity. We believe setting a common conceptual framework has helped authors address underlying causal forces driving change in rural North America. In an increasingly globalized economy, rural textile workers compete on unfavorable terms—from the perspective of corporate decision-makers—with workers in the global South. The dramatic decline in manufacturing employment in the United States is as much a rural as it is an urban phenomenon, a reality that has largely been missed in most discussions of economic restructuring. At the same time, dramatic increases in production of agricultural commodities have been spurred by new opportunities for international trade.

Organization of this Volume

This volume is divided into five broad sections, detailed below. Each section opens with a framing chapter. These framing chapters are not meant as introductions to the rest of the chapters in the section, but rather as thoughtful overviews of important themes within each sub-field. We asked authors of these framing chapters to be provocative in their critiques of the existing research and to provide their vision of future research needs in their respective fields.

The Changing Structure of Agriculture

The first section addresses a long-standing concern of rural sociologists, the changing structure of agriculture. In his framing chapter, Alessandro Bonanno calls attention to five key themes that to varying degrees need further investigation and inquiry in rural sociological studies of the agrifood system: (1) the reorganization of time and space under globalization and the implications of these phenomena for the sector; (2) the crisis of the nation-state; (3) the increasing financialization and securitization of the sector; (4) the legitimation crisis of neoliberalism; and (5) the recent lack of scholarly attention given to agrifood laborers, which Bonanno observes has incongruously occurred as the conditions of workers worsened under globalization.

The next three chapters in this section outline the contours of how farming has changed in recent decades and what the sector looks like today. In chapter 1, Doug H. Constance, Mary Hendrickson, Philip H. Howard, and William D. Heffernan discuss concentration and vertical integration in the agricultural sector. Building on a thirty-year history of studies focused on the agrifood sector concentration, labeled the Missouri School, they reveal that fewer farmers are in the business because their choices of where they source their inputs and where they sell their commodities have become limited. Constance et al. argue that the consolidation of actors in the agrifood chain is better understood by focusing on power than on efficiency.

In chapter 2, Amy Guptill and Rick Welsh extend Constance and colleagues' discussion by demonstrating that in both the United States and Canada, midsized commercial farms continue to experience dramatic declines. Midsize farmers are usually those that earn anywhere from $10,000 to $250,000. Interestingly, compared to the United States, Canada has not seen as much growth in farm size below $10,000, but both the United States and Canada have seen a growth in the largest farms, defined as over $500,000. Echoing Constance et al.'s discussion, Guptill and Welsh emphasize that mid-level farms are not just losing ground numerically, but also are losing market power and government support. In chapter 3, rounding out the picture of what farming looks like today, Douglas Jackson-Smith and Peggy Petrzelka examine land ownership in US agriculture and the implications of changing trends for agricultural decision making, environmental behaviors, and local community. While national trends suggest that the total proportion of farmland that is owner-operated land has hovered near 60 percent since World War II, data from an Iowa study shows a pronounced decline in the proportion of land under owner operator status (dropping from 55 percent in 1982 to 40 percent in 2007). There has also been noticeable growth in the role of absentee farmland owners, and while we know very little about landowners in general, we know even less about absentee owners. Ultimately, Jackson-Smith and Petrzelka emphasize that there is a lack of data on land ownership and a significant opportunity for a new generation of rural sociologists to revisit theory and research traditions focused on the implications of land ownership patterns for farm structural change, rural community well-being, and environmental behavior.

In chapter 4, Eric B. Jensen focuses on Mexican-born farmworkers in US agriculture and engages with Bonanno's call for more research on agricultural laborers and directly links to Guptill and Welsh's discussion of declining mid-size farms. Jensen reveals that as farm size has grown, so too has the use of Mexican-born farmworkers across a growing range of agricultural commodities, the most recent of which is dairy. He explains declining availability of Mexican-born farmworkers as an issue caused by the confluence of factors, including increased return migration to Mexico, enactment of strict immigration laws, and increased employment of Mexicans in other sectors (e.g., construction). Jensen concludes with a series of important research topics for further study, including the challenges Mexican-born farmworkers arriving in new rural destinations face, the ways in which continued agricultural restructuring will shape demand for foreign-born labor, and whether country-of-origin composition of immigrant farmworkers will change if the availability of Mexican-born farmworkers continues to decline.

In chapter 5, Leland L. Glenna and Christopher R. Henke focus on the impact of agricultural technologies on the structure of agriculture. Despite longstanding rhetoric that connects agricultural science and technology with progress for farmers and society in general, they observe that reality has been more nuanced and even ironic. They detail the historically situated structures that have promoted the emergence of contemporary agrifood systems, while also considering forces that are accelerating past trends and perhaps promoting new ones. One of the trends they identify is erosion of the public sector's research and development (R&D) infrastructure in the midst of the dominance of the private sector's agricultural R&D. They note that the commercialization of science has exposed the fallacy of pure science, which may create opportunities to advocate for the democratization of agricultural research. Glenna and Henke conclude that intellectual property policies and flat funding may be stifling agricultural innovation in North America and that the biggest opportunities for innovation may exist in other parts of the world.

The final three chapters in the agricultural section look at reactions to the industrial agrifood system. Picking up on the theme of technology, in chapter 6 Michelle R. Worosz and Diana Stewart focus on the governance of our food safety system and call attention to the ways scholars have historically set about theorizing it. They observe that the changes in our food safety system have largely been "technological fixes" as opposed to solutions that recognize the problem with concentration in the industry—fewer sources of contamination impact a larger number of people. They emphasize that many significant changes in regulating food safety have occurred primarily to the detriment of small producers and processors, as the costs of compliance proves too much for small operators. Finally, they argue that future research should focus on previously ignored structures (subnational states) and actors, particularly the representation of less powerful actors (poor, women, elderly) and producers impacted, either directly or indirectly (loss of consumers), by foodborne illness outbreaks.

In chapter 7, Jeff Sharp and Dani Deemer analyze the rise of farm animal welfare legislation. Ohio is now one of nine states that have created livestock care standard boards, which are generally tasked with determining state standards for farm animal treatment. Sharp and Deemer observe that there may be a public ambivalence toward agricultural animal welfare, which means that the public tends toward an uneasy tolerance of modern farming so long as it is not provoked into a response (i.e., a video exposing farm laborers abusing animals). At the heart of Sharp and Deemer's analysis is the recognition of the interplay between the public, state, and capital interests in food system change and development. In the case of Ohio, the state may at times appear to act in the interests of industry; but there is also effective action by nongovernmental organizations that challenge the state to account for noncapital interests as well.

Finally, in chapter 8, Clare Hinrichs and John Eshleman explore the agrifood movements that have grown in visibility and diversity in the past two decades. They argue that individual action—in contrast to collective action—enjoys special openings and appeals in the context of global neoliberalization. Both conceptually and practically, individual action, especially when limited to market engagements, conflicts with classic understandings of social movements. Directly engaging with Bonanno's opening essay in this section, Hinrichs and Eshleman stress the lack of attention that workers in our food system have received in the context of the agrifood movements. They review the transformative impacts of various agrifood movements. They also identify promising areas for future research on agrifood movements including the need to improve our knowledge of current and historical agrifood movements in terms of accomplishments, as well as organizational declines and dead ends.

Natural Resources and the Environment

The sociology of natural resources and the environment represents a longstanding field of enquiry for rural sociologists, who in the early 1970s were the first professional social science society to organize a research interest group dedicated to the topic. In their framing chapter, Louise Fortmann, Merrill Baker-Médard, and Alice Kelly observe that in the decade to come the issues with which rural sociologists will grapple will surprise many of us. As they note, who could have foretold a decade ago that fracking, bioenergy, or even climate change would be many rural sociologists' central concerns? They argue that complexity and surprise are the hallmarks of contemporary change and that our ability to deal with change will depend on our ability to connect with the knowledge of others—not only credentialed scientists but also those whose sources of knowledge have nothing to do with universities, libraries, or books. Similar to the themes Bonanno raises, the authors identify several issues relevant to the next decade, including the financialization, global land grabs, and labor in the forestry, fishing, and mining sectors.

Lois Wright Morton and Tom Rudel address the subject of global climate change and how it might affect rural communities in North America in chapter 9. They describe climate change as being characterized both by slow incremental changes that "press" coupled human and natural systems and by more sudden and dramatic "pulse" events such as hurricanes, floods, and droughts that can rapidly change social and ecological systems. They illustrate the impacts of climate change using three case studies, including wildfires in the western United States, floods in the Midwest, and rapid temperature increases that affect indigenous populations in Alaska. Morton and Rudel raise concerns over rural communities resiliency as rural people dependent on farming and natural resources face direct threats to their livelihoods and may have fewer personal or institutional resources from which to draw while recovering from disaster. They argue that social scientists can make important contributions to such research to increase the resilience of rural people and communities in adapting to climate change.

In chapter 10, Courtney G. Flint and Naomi Krogman take on water, another big issue, and build on key ideas from the framing chapter by Fortmann and colleagues. Flint and Krogman open with the simple but powerful statement that "water captures the inseparability between society and nature," and note further that nothing lends itself to interdisciplinary research as much as water. They describe the commodification and privatization of water and the use of hydraulic technologies to dam and otherwise control water in generating power, both electrical and political. Water resources are of vital importance to the people of rural America, but control over these resources is often in the hands of powerful forces in urban centers. They conclude with a discussion of contending forces of globalization, privatization, and local governance of watersheds by civil society, suggesting that water-related issues are likely to become central foci of research for rural sociologists in the decade to come.

Resource dependency has been a consistent theme of rural sociological research, though as Richard S. Krannich, Brian Gentry, A.E. Luloff, and Peter G. Robertson point out in chapter 11, the nature of resource dependency has changed over time. They review literature detailing cyclical patterns of growth and decay that for decades have destabilized the social and economic fabric of resource dependent communities. They suggest that increased economic diversity in rural economies has reduced the pathological consequences of resource dependency in some parts of North America, but in other areas (e.g., associated with fracking) the nature of contemporary resource dependency bears striking resemblance to previous decades. Krannich and colleagues also foresee changing societal and political priorities favoring environmentally friendly technologies such as wind and solar power, representing new forms of resource dependency that will generate limited employment but may produce valuable income and tax revenues in rural areas. They conclude by noting the need for continued research on the impact of globalization and multinational corporations on ownership and production of natural resources.

Few regions in North America have the diversity of natural resources found along the northern Gulf of Mexico. Rural sociologists have tended to focus their energies on dry land and devoted limited attention to coastal peoples, communities, or resources. In chapter 12, Robert Gramling and Shirley Laska provide a broad overview of the Gulf coast and in so doing help us understand the relevance of coastal issues to rural sociology within the context of renewable natural resources, ecotourism, energy production, international trade, and exposure to natural and anthropogenic disasters. They show that the range of topics that remain underexplored by rural sociologists in the coastal United States is enormous.

The next three chapters focus on energy, a topic of increasing importance to rural sociologists. In chapter 13, Theresa Selfa and Carmen Bain examine the promises, pitfalls, and uneven local impacts of biofuels development. They document how government policies in the United States and elsewhere were instrumental in the rapid expansion of global ethanol production and that in general governmental mandates gave advantage to corporate investors instead of local biofuels developers. Selfa and Bain present case studies from Kansas and Iowa to describe employment and income benefits but also local concerns over water and other resources. They determine that the real beneficiaries of biofuels development have been large corn farmers, not the ethanol industry or the refineries' host communities. They conclude with a discussion of how sustainability standards might be incorporated into biofuels development to promote a broader rural and economic development impact.

Abby Kinchy and colleagues draw on the boomtown literature of the 1970s and 1980s to describe local enthusiasm for and opposition to natural gas development through fracking in chapter 14. Researchers who work on this unconventional form of natural gas development deal with a different institutional setting than in decades past. In previous decades governments were intent on developing and enforcing environmental regulations, but the regulatory will and resources of governments have now thinned. Landowners and local governments may benefit from income and tax revenues generated by fracking, but many residents may feel that environmental pollution and the rise of non-local energy companies have violated their sense of place. Kinchy and colleagues document the environmental and public health problems associated with fracking and suggest that researchers need to devote more attention to examining questions of environmental governance, equity, and land use conflict.

The rise of biofuels and fracking are relatively recent developments in the energy field, but the same cannot be said for coal. Coal has been the source of power for industrial development in Europe, the United States, and more recently China and India. In chapter 15, Suzanne E. Tallichet helps us understand how processes of globalization and neoliberalism affect the economics of energy and therefore the people and places that house these energy stores. She documents trends in coal production and employment, showing the rapid rise of surface-mined coal production in the West compared to Appalachia and coal beds stretching from Iowa to Oklahoma known as the Interior Basin. More recently, development of mountain top removal in the Appalachian region has replaced deep shaft mining while requiring far less labor. Tallichet describes human health impacts of coal mining, including black lung disease affecting underground miners, the impact of impoundments holding coal sludge or ash, which fail, as well as the environmental devastation of mountain top removal. She describes conditions of poverty in Appalachian coal communities and urges researchers to focus their attention on questions of ownership and power and to develop partnerships with coal mining communities that empower local people.

Population Change

The third section of this volume draws attention to population changes in rural North America. In the framing essay, David L. Brown places rural demography in global context by stressing how population change and dynamics are at once consequence and cause of other regional, national, and global forces. Of the myriad transformations at play in rural areas, Brown explores ongoing processes of industrial restructuring, the trend toward devolution of responsibility to lower levels of government, and the increasing intensity and asymmetry of global-local linkages to inform his treatment of three rural population dynamics: urban-rural population redistribution, rural population aging, and the shifting ethnoracial composition of rural America. A key message is not only that population dynamics and institutional change affect one another but also that institutional contexts from the local to the global level affect the impacts of demographic change.

The next two chapters set the stage by providing complementary overviews of key demographic trends. In chapter 16, Kenneth M. Johnson focuses on the 2000 to 2010 period and shows slower rural population growth compared with the 1990s when the economy was thriving. The abated growth was due principally to reduced migration, especially to rural counties adjacent to metropolitan areas, a reflection of the Great Recession. With migration contributing less, natural increase (the excess of births over deaths) was contributing proportionately more to rural growth, but even here Johnson points to the increasing prevalence of counties in a state of natural decrease. Finally, Johnson notes that while Hispanics and other minorities account for only 21 percent of the rural population, they contributed to 83 percent of overall rural population growth in the first decade of the twenty-first century.

Taking a more regional perspective, in chapter 17, John Cromartie and Timothy S. Parker detail nonmetro demographic trends within nine diverse regions of the United States, with emphasis on patterns in the most recent decades. They find that the attenuation of rural population growth in the first decade of the twenty-first century documented by Johnson is seen in all nonmetro regions, but that the South and West show greater growth than regions stretching from New England through the Plains. What rural growth there was within regions was fueled considerably by increases in the Hispanic population. Cromartie and Parker also document considerable regional diversity in elderly population dynamics, an issue Nelson elaborates on in this section. Finally, they reveal an intriguing and unprecedented regional convergence in rural population growth trends, with very little difference separating the fastest and slowest growing regions.

The remaining chapters in this section focus on rural families and households, children and youth, elders, and immigrants. In chapter 18, Jessica A. Carson and Marybeth J. Mattingly offer analyses of US Census Bureau data from 2000 to 2010 to describe household and family composition, size, and demographic characteristics. The authors take on the conventional wisdom that rural places, the rural United States included, represent a bastion for traditional family structure. They find that by 2010, the demographic character of families and households in rural areas increasingly resembled that found elsewhere, including a disconnect between marriage and childbearing, cohabitation, single headship, and same-sex partnering. Carson and Mattingly view this as a change, not a decline, in the rural family.

In chapter 19, Diane K. McLaughlin and Carla Shoff shine a spotlight on rural children and youth as we look ahead to 2020 and beyond. Rural children and youth tend to have higher poverty rates than those in urban areas, but were spared from the worst impacts of the Great Recession in this regard. A positive trend is the higher percentage of youth ages sixteen to nineteen still enrolled in school and the increase in the share of youth not enrolled who had completed high school between 2000 and the 2006 to 2010 period. Finally, McLaughlin and Shoff illustrate that rural places are experiencing the greatest losses of youth and young adults in recent years, an indication that ongoing problems of the brain drain of rural youth remain with us today.

The loss of youth inevitably raises concerns about the other end of the age distribution. Peter B. Nelson takes a geographic perspective in his analysis of 2010 US Census data in chapter 20. He finds that the rural parts of the Great Plains, South Atlantic, and Pacific census divisions have greater concentrations of elders than do other rural places, and that the most rural regions also are grayer. Nelson draws particular attention to the different forces (youth out-migration coupled with aging in place versus retirement in-migration) that give rise to elderly concentrations and how these vary by region.

Martha Crowley and Kim Ebert conclude this section in chapter 21 by focusing on new rural immigrant destinations. They examine the push and pull factors at play in the formation of rural immigrant enclaves, the impacts of these settlements as localities struggle to accommodate them, and the nature of inter-group (immigrant-native) relationships in new rural destinations. Crowley and Ebert chart a course for future research that needs to focus on the rural political landscape and exclusionary policies in particular, the circumstances of children of new rural immigrants, and the role of globalization as shaping the formation and nature of new immigrant destinations in rural areas.

Gender, Race, Ethnicity, and Class

Expanding on the demographic trends occurring in rural North America, the fourth part of this volume focuses attention on diversity, power, and inequality in rural North America. Carolyn Sachs sets the stage for this section by focusing on the impact of globalization and neoliberalism on diversity in rural communities, calling our attention to the possible future consequences of climate change and international human rights campaigns in rural locations. She reminds scholars that all rural places in the United States are not the same, and we therefore need to give further attention to how class, race, ethnicity, gender, and sexuality differentially shape people's lives. In particular, she notes the so-called benefits of globalization seem to have passed by many rural communities. Government cutbacks in particular have undermined possible solutions for reducing the high concentration of poverty found in the Southern Black Belt, as well as in rural spaces inhabited by Native Americans and Latinos.

The next three chapters examine changes affecting the status of African Americans by John Green, the impact of Hispanic migrants at state and local levels with illustrations from Idaho by J.D. Wulfhorst and colleagues, and Native Americans by Sarah Dewees. In chapter 22, using the livelihoods theoretical framework from development studies, Green explores the status of African Americans in the rural United States. Findings demonstrate that the presence of African Americans in rural areas continues to be a largely southern phenomenon. While published research shows some improvements in quality of life among rural African Americans, disparities remain relative to their counterparts in metropolitan places and whites in both metropolitan and nonmetropolitan areas. From the existing research, Green concludes that policies that seek to improve human capital through education and workforce development should continue, but are not sufficient for resolving structural and institutional factors that contribute to inequality and poverty. Moving forward, more place-based approaches, including regional initiatives, need to be advanced to overcome inequality and pursue justice.

J.D. Wulfhorst and colleagues provide both global context and a detailed case study to help us understand the impact of Hispanic migrant labor in chapter 23. They note that over the past decade, Hispanic migrants have spread out across the United States, from the South to the Mountain West. Increased visibility of migrant workers has led to political and cultural resistance. Wulforst et al. contrast popular media depictions of the social costs associated with new migrants with data showing that the impacts of migrant workers are complex, but have had an overall positive impact on the US economy. They present a case study of Hispanic workers in the dairy industry of southern Idaho, which is the third-largest dairy producing region in the United States. This industry is heavily dependent on migrant workers' willingness to do jobs that others in the local labor market would not.

With over 565 federally recognized tribal governments and many more non-federally recognized tribal communities in the United States, Dewees sets out to explain and explore reservation economic development. While Native American nations' internal governing powers have been recognized, their sovereignty has also been steadily curtailed. Due to their unique economic, cultural, and social organization, the policies of many Native nations continue to prioritize the collective (tribal government) over the individual (tribal citizen), which contrasts with neoliberal policies of scaling back government services. With Native Americans faring poorly by nearly all measures of economic and social well-being, Dewees overviews key reservation development strategies moving forward. She concludes that in the coming decade there will likely be an increasing emphasis on free-market economies among federal policy makers and Native American leaders.

Gender and sexuality are topics taken up in the next two chapters. Cynthia B. Struthers focuses attention on the changing status of rural women in chapter 25 while Julie C. Keller and Michael M. Bell address sexuality in rural America in chapter 26. Struthers reviews the major issues rural women confront based on previous decennial volumes. She then focuses on the contemporary issues rural women and their families face. Women's labor market activities have changed and there has been an increase of rural women engaged in alternative social movements, such as sustainable agriculture. Neoliberalism combined with the economic recession of the 2000s has reduced public services like education, health, and social services in rural areas. Ample research suggests that these cuts will disproportionately impact women. In conclusion, Struthers asserts that we know much more about rural places and rural women than we have in the past, but we have not seriously considered how to use research to advocate for rural places, rural people, and rural women.

Keller and Bell overview the history of work on rural sexualities, and then introduce conceptual terms for future studies focused on sexuality in rural spaces. They introduce the idea of the sexual rural and the rural sexual, the former being the material and grounded understanding of sex and sexualities in rural places, and the latter being the imaginative construction of the rural in sex and sexualities. Ultimately, they argue that a plural rural sexual approach means seeing the significance of both of the concepts and initiating conversations and intersections between the two.

Jennifer Sherman concludes this section in chapter 27 by examining the causes of and contributors to rural poverty. She looks at the roles of rural labor markets and deindustrialization in perpetuating poverty, as well as the impacts of in- and out-migration on poor rural communities. Sherman observes that given the depth of the Great Recession and its exacerbation of ongoing deindustrialization and globalization trends, it is likely that many of the problems in rural communities will not be resolved quickly. She concludes with a discussion of the unique challenges and opportunities that rural American communities pose for surviving unemployment and poverty with dignity.

Rural Economies, Community, and Quality of Life

The concluding section examines rural economic strategies, the communities in which rural people live, and the quality of life in those communities. In her introductory essay, Linda Lobao draws attention to four structural domains shaping the fortunes of rural people and places. These include the shifting structure of employment, the state at all levels, institutionalized relationships between actors vying for societal resources, and spatial processes that often disadvantage rural locales. Lobao calls upon scholars to examine such structural changes jointly, not independently, and proposes a political economy perspective as a unifying way to do just that. Drawing on this perspective, she sketches key realities of the early twenty-first century and their implications for rural social science generally, and the study of rural economies, community, and quality of life in particular.

Education is fundamental to individual and community economic well-being, but the challenges facing rural students, schools, and communities are always evolving. In chapter 28, Kai A. Schafft and Catharine Biddle examine the social, symbolic, and economic centrality of rural schools for the communities they serve. The key role of rural schools is challenged by rural out-migration, consolidation, poverty, and access to postsecondary schooling. They place these challenges in federal policy context, drawing out the implications of a neoliberal discourse that has come to dominate discussions and policy options today.

Ideally, education imparts human and cultural capital, and a reliable route to success in the labor market. In chapter 29, Tim Slack examines work in rural America. He traces changes in the national and rural labor markets in recent years and their implications for new challenges facing rural workers today. He then documents how these challenges are sharply manifest in recent patterns of underemployment, as global forces have conspired to render formal labor markets less able to provide ample work at a living wage. Slack concludes with a discussion of the informal economy and its role as an economic strategy among rural households.

Informal work often constitutes a self-help approach to economic survival and enhancement. Arguably, entrepreneurship is simply a more formalized, officially recognized, and advanced form of precisely the same strategy. In their chapter on rural entrepreneurship, Lori A. Dickes and Kenneth L. Robinson first explore why some rural localities are conducive to entrepreneurial development while others are not. They confront the tension between the traditional and get-rich-quick approach that emphasizes attracting outside businesses versus investments in local entrepreneurial infrastructures oriented toward longer-run benefits. They bring their arguments to life through both a case study and analysis of survey data from the rural South.

Creating a context that is conducive to entrepreneurship requires work within communities. In their chapter on community organization and mobilization, Cornelia Butler Flora and Jan L. Flora highlight the vulnerability of rural communities facing structural changes over which they have little control. They promote the community capitals framework as a conceptual model for enhancing local and community resiliency. The community capitals framework focuses attention on seven forms of capital (human, social, cultural, political, financial, natural, and built). They argue that intangible forms of community capital (human, cultural, social and political) are just as important as financial, built, and natural capital in community development. They present two case studies to illustrate this point. One case involves rapid population growth in a South Dakota community due to fracking. The second case involves an Iowa community dealing with the influx of migrant workers from Mexico and Central America. In both cases, small communities are forced to adapt to changes over which they have little control, but are shown to be resilient through effective use of social, cultural, and political capital.

In chapter 32, Todd L. Goodsell, Jeremy Flaherty, and Ralph B. Brown offer a conceptual discussion of the continued importance of community in light of processes of globalization that tend to erode the traditional underpinnings of this concept. They hold that processes of globalization are pervasive and, while not discounting communities as places where important functions and services are to be found, argue that place-based communities no longer play a central role in most people's lives. Community, to Goodsell and colleagues, may not be a place, much less a local place. For these authors, the key defining characteristic of community is moral proximity, which in the era of social media and global markets need no longer be restricted to a single physical space or even point in time. The increasing fluidity of human relationships and the increasing importance of the extra-local in our daily lives mean that moral proximity and the responsibility which we must accept for our actions is no longer determined primarily by place of residence. Goodsell, Flaherty, and Brown challenge us to rethink the concept of community in light of contemporary relationships and identities, and not simply accept that because a place exists it is the central social reality of those who live within it.

The final three chapters in this section concern issues related to quality of life among rural people. The most basic thing people need for a fulfilling life is food. But, as Keiko Tanaka, Patrick H. Mooney, and Brett Wolff point out in chapter 33, the historical connection of poverty and hunger has in many places been broken. Indeed, they are motivated by the fact that too often just the opposite is true—that poverty and obesity go hand in hand. Tanaka and colleagues are captivated by the contradictions of rising obesity and food insecurity coinciding in "places that make the United States the breadbasket of the world." After providing contemporary data on food insecurity and obesity, they situate both in a common framework that rests squarely on the four interrelated processes (economic structure, the state, institutionalized relationships, and spatial processes)

Lobao lays out in her framing essay. As such, they reconcile prevailing contradictions by showing how food insecurity and obesity are two manifestations of global forces shaping life in rural and urban America in the twenty-first century.

In her chapter about rural health, E. Helen Berry points out that standardized mortality rates are lower among rural than urban residents, but that such averages mask considerable diversity among rural populations. Some places defined as rural are in close proximity to urban areas where health services are readily available. Elsewhere, however, low population densities often constrain physical access to both physical and mental health care. Rural populations are also less likely to have health insurance. Chronic disease problems in rural areas, including obesity, are exacerbated by the lack of preventative care and the phenomenon of food deserts as rural populations decline and local grocery stores close.

In the concluding chapter, Katherine A. MacTavish, Ann Ziebarth, and Lance George describe the status and context of housing in rural America focusing on ownership, quality, and affordability—aspects of housing closely tied to quality of life. They examine the outcomes of market-driven approaches to housing development, and highlight the unequal housing opportunities that leave some people and places increasingly vulnerable while others are advantaged. Harkening back to the political economy perspective Lobao suggests, they conclude that the rural housing dilemma reflects socioeconomic and political processes that foster place-based persistent poverty and segregation of populations of color.

Concluding Remarks

Secretary of Agriculture Thomas Vilsak (2012) recently observed that rural America and its concerns are becoming less relevant in national political discourse because, with declining rural populations, few political leaders have an understanding of rural America. Vilsak pointed out, however, that rural America is a vital part of the United States, a statement that would hold true for Canada and almost any other nation. Rural areas are storehouses of energy and sources of food and fiber. Ecosystem services such as clean air and water depend on rural landscapes and the people who live there. Yet, because human populations in North America and most other parts of the world increasingly live in large urban settings, rural issues and concerns are marginalized in social and political discussions. As the chapters in this volume make clear, however, rural North America is not at all marginal in economic terms and is tied intimately to and shares a common fate with the larger society.

The trend toward urbanization in North America and elsewhere in the world has been in place since the days of the industrial revolution. Mechanization in agriculture has been one among a number of forces that have contributed to the decline in farm labor and out-migration to urban areas. Technological as well as policy changes over the past several decades have contributed to the increasingly global nature of our food supply. As documented in several chapters of this volume, these changes have been the driving force behind recent restructuring of agricultural production and the food system more generally. Globalization of food and agriculture has been made possible in part due to the development of new production and transportation technologies, but it has been the political ideology of neoliberalism and the emphasis of free trade unencumbered by tariffs and other regulatory restraints on trade that have allowed the penetration of industrial capital into the production, processing, distribution, and marketing of food on a global scale.

The anti-regulatory ideology of neoliberalism favors free market rationality which in an era of corporate consolidation has the effect of squeezing out family farms (the "disappearing middle" Guptill and Welsh describe) and either bankrupting smaller businesses or placing them into a status of dependence on more powerful economic actors. As Worosz and Stuart describe, even the operation of regulatory structures tend to serve the interests of corporate capital and not small businesses and family farms. The ideology of neoliberalism also impedes our abilities to address problems of climate change, create a rational energy policy, or effectively manage water resources.

There is no question that Secretary Vilsak on one level was correct in describing rural America as increasingly irrelevant in national affairs—an observation not limited to the United States or even to North America. The increasing concentration of people, wealth, and power in urban spaces is fact. What is less well understood is that urban populations and their wealth and power depend on rural people and communities. In some cases, as Jackson-Smith and Petrzelka as well as Tallichet note, rural resources are owned and controlled by urban interests, which directly draw wealth from rural to urban areas. In the case of agriculture and natural resources, the processing, distribution, and marketing of food, energy, and other resources are controlled by corporations based in urban areas.

Rural sociologists are well placed to help document these relationships, to help understand the importance of the rural part to the whole, and to tell the stories of rural people in an increasingly interconnected world. We have a long tradition of tracing demographic changes and how these affect access to health, education, and other vital social services. Rural sociologists also have long experience examining the impact of globalization on such fundamental societal building blocks as community, and more recently on how changes in the social and economic landscape are changing our understanding of gender roles and relationships. We recognize that we as rural sociologists are not alone in this quest for understanding, and that we have colleagues in related disciplines of geography, anthropology, and agricultural economics, among others, who have made important contributions to our understanding and who often take an active part in our annual meetings and intellectual life more generally. That said, members of the RSS consistently have sought to bring and maintain a focus on rural people and communities in North America and around the world, in order to understand the forces that bear on their lives and to ensure our research informs policies. The authors in this volume have been faithful to this disciplinary tradition.

Notes

1 The names of the editors are listed alphabetically. Each shared equally in editing this volume, working with chapter authors, and writing this introduction.

References

Brown, David, and Louis E. Swanson, eds. 2003. *Challenges for Rural America in the Twenty-First Century.* University Park: Penn State University Press.

Dillman, Don, and Daryl J. Hobbs, eds. 1982. *Rural Society in the U.S.: Issues for the 1980s.* Boulder, CO: Westview Press.

Flora, Cornelia B., and James A. Christenson, eds. 1991. *Rural Policies for the 1990s.* Boulder, CO: Westview Press.

Vilsak, Tom. 2012. Remarks by USDA Secretary Tom Vilsack at the 2012 Farm Journal Forum, Thursday, December 6, 2012, Washington, DC. News Transcript Release No. 0357.12. http://www.usda.gov/wps/portal/usda/usdahome?contentid=2012/12/0357.xml&navid=transcript&navtype=rt&parentnav=transcripts_speeches&edeployment_action=retrievecontent.

PART I

The Changing Structure of Agriculture

Agriculture and Food in the 2010s

Alessandro Bonanno

Introduction

Globalization and the accompanying ideology of neoliberalism can be considered the most defining features of society in the second decade of the twenty-first century. Research has underscored the growth of transnational chains of agrifood production and consumption and the power of the actors that control them. Similarly, it has shown that the creation of these transnational networks is supported by ideological claims about the efficiency of market-driven decisions and policies, the desirability of the free circulation of capital and labor, and the negative effects of state intervention. Employing this background, in the following pages I will discuss six items that are central for agrifood, both as social phenomenon and as areas in need of investigation. It is my contention that, despite their importance, these items have not been adequately researched and conceptualized in rural sociology. I will begin with a discussion of the reorganization of time and space under globalization and the implications that this phenomenon has for the sector and its analysis. Subsequently, I will briefly discuss the so-called crisis of the nation-state. Third, I will address the phenomena of financialization and securitization. Fourth, I will address the legitimation crisis of neoliberalism. Finally, I will briefly discuss the issue of labor in agrifood.

The Reorganization of Time and Space

Globalization has been defined as the "compression of time and space" (Harvey 2010; Bonanno and Cavalcanti 2011). This definition indicates that social relations unfold over a greater space and with enhanced speed than in the past. The agrifood sector offers an excellent example of the way in which the compression of time and space affects social relations. For instance, corporate supermarket chains operate systems that satisfy demand in the global North by controlling production processes in the global South. Simultaneously, laborers and farmers involved in these production processes are often unaware of the corporate strategies and distant actors that affect their daily work, yet their ability to maintain their employment and market their products depends on the careful execution of these corporate requirements. Finally, the quality of their work and products is certified and made acceptable to supermarkets and consumers by organizations that operate globally.

For the last two decades, many works on globalization of agrifood have stressed the global scope of production and consumption. Authors of such works underscored the novel characteristics of, and implications associated with, the enhanced transnational mobility of capital, commodities, and labor. Yet, they paid relatively less attention to the social creation of time and space and to the class dimension of this phenomenon. This is surprising given the fact that the global nature of production and its social and class dimensions are discussed in classical works. Marx, for instance, argues, "the need of a constantly expanding market for its products chases the bourgeoisie over the whole surface of the globe. It must nest everywhere, settle everywhere, establish connection everywhere" (Marx and Engels [1848] 1998, 39), and "the bourgeoisie, by the rapid improvement of all instruments of production, by the immensely facilitated means of communication, draw all, even the most barbarian, nations into civilization" (Marx and Engels [1848] 1998, 39). For Marx, the process of the compression of space is synonymous with the expansion of capitalism, as the growth of market relations requires the constant opening up of new spaces and the simultaneous reconfiguration of others. In this view, space is constantly transformed to fit the incessant requirement of growth that characterizes capitalism.

Max Weber also stresses the fundamental importance of the reorganization of space under capitalism ([1921] 1968, 313–16). Modern society, he contends, must organize its space in formal rational terms in order to meet the requirements of capitalism. This organization is functional to the growth of bureaucracies and authority structures that foster development. Paralleling Marx's argument, Weber stresses the necessary interdependence between the development of the capitalist enterprise and capitalism itself with the "professional administration" and rational law "made by jurists and rationally interpreted and applied" under the unified space of the nation-state system ([1921] 1968, 313). For Weber, this process of rationalization of space is central for the growth of capitalism.

Like space, time is also socially constructed. Marx maintains that it refers to the velocity with which capital is transformed from its money form into commodities that are then transformed again into money (Marx and Engels [1867] 1977, 247–57). The latter represents a greater quantity of capital that has been augmented by the profit obtained during this cycle (Marx and Engels [1867] 1977, 251). This velocity consists of the time necessary for the "turnover time of capital" that includes both production and consumption of commodities and the generation of profit. The faster the time in which capital completes this cycle, the greater the frequency of profit generation. Marx distinguishes between "working time" and "production time" (Marx and Engels [1885] 1992, 316–25). *Working time* is defined as "time during which capital is confined to the production sphere," and is the time in which labor transforms factors of production into commodities. *Production time*, conversely, refers to the "entire time in which capital exits in the production process" (Marx and Engels [1885] 1992, 316) and includes times in which capital is idle due to natural limits. The time necessary to complete a given production process—"the turnover period"—is not fixed. But it "can be often shortened to a greater or less extent by the artificial shortening of the production time" (Marx and Engels [1885] 1992, 3,170). Marx specifically discusses agricultural production as an example of the distinction between production time and working time. He contends that as natural barriers—such as the cold European winter—prevent farmers from working, agricultural production is confined to specific periods in which labor (working time) can be applied. For Marx, the rate of accumulation of capital in agriculture lags behind that of manufacturing because of the shorter working time within the overall production time.

In the case of the acceleration of time, Weber stresses that the rationalization of the use of time is one of the most fundamental aspects of the development of capitalism (Weber [1921] 1968). He contends that the most distinctive element of the capitalist enterprise is the efficient organization of the production process that is achieved through the use of formal rationality. The capitalist enterprise distinguishes itself from other enterprises by the constant search for the most rapid and cost-efficient way to achieve its production goals. Modern bookkeeping, Weber continues, allows modern capitalist enterprises to measure the cost of the acceleration of production and, consequently, to apply the most efficient production strategies. Ultimately, the general acceptance of modern bookkeeping and the consequent rationalization of the production processes defined the emergence of capitalist societies. For Weber, the monetarization of labor further allowed for rationalized forms of production that placed efficiency, calculability, and predictability as primary features of capitalism. Simultaneously, it allowed for the emergence of enhanced forms of control of labor, as labor processes are also standardized and organized following formal rationality.

These classical views of the social creation and compression of time and space under capitalism offer opportunities for contemporary critiques. The noted sociologist Anthony Giddens maintains that the compression of time and space is a constant of modernity but has accelerated under globalization. In his theory of "distanciation" (Giddens 1990, 21–27), he contends that the development of capitalism was characterized by a constant motion from "place," which is specific and original, to "space," which is homogenous and abstract. Social relations, he argues, were largely contained within confined locations (place) in early capitalism. As it developed, distant actors began to shape local social relations as time and space were progressively standardized as a result of market expansion. In contemporary global capitalism, the "disembedding" of social relations from the local defines society's functioning as distant actors and global integration affect the evolution of social relations. Agrifood is a typical example of this reorganization of time and space, as decisions that producers and consumers make are increasingly affected by the behavior of distant global actors such as input suppliers, supermarket chains, energy corporations, financial speculators, and certification agencies.

In the essay "Space as a Key Word," David Harvey (2006, 124; but also 2000, 22–25) critiques the understanding of time and space proposed by Marx. Harvey distinguishes three dimensions of space. First, *absolute space* is the fixed space represented by pre-existing structures such as the boundaries of a nation-state or a city. Second, *relative space* is the space experienced from the observer's point of view, and is relative to the observer's time and position. Accordingly, time and space may differ as the observer is located in one social or geographical location rather than another. Finally, *relational space* is defined by the process in which space exists. Space, in other words, is internal to that process. It follows that it is impossible to separate space from time. A particular space exists in so much as it exists in a particular time and vice versa. Harvey contends that the relational understanding of time and space is the way in which Marx understands these two concepts. However, Marx, he contends, employs a "linear" understanding of the spatial expansion of capitalism. For Harvey, Marx assumes a posture that contemplates a progressive and cumulative spatial expansion of capital that moves from the core—i.e., Europe—outward toward the rest of the world. Among other things, Harvey maintains, this tenet would not be able to explain situations like the emergence of networks of production that connect different social actors across the globe in ways that do not follow a trajectory from core to periphery. The current agrifood networks of production and consumption that connect locations in non-concentric ways exemplify this point. For instance, global supermarket chains purchase coffee directly from producers in Soconusco, Mexico, without involving any other locations or actors in North or Central America.

These accounts of the social creation of time and space under capitalism, their reorganization under globalization, and their non-linear evolution offer an opportunity to reflect on the often-employed approach of analyzing agrifood phenomena in spatially fixed terms. In particular, I am referring to the "scientific nationalism" that often characterizes studies in rural sociology. Research is based on data, cases, and narratives that are centered on the nation as if the social organization of time and space illustrated above is a fixed entity and could be contained within national borders and/or relations among nations. In essence, more often than not, research in agrifood reifies space and time and understands them as "things" rather than as socially constructed processes.

The Crisis of the State

The state is also socially constructed. However, this point has often been overlooked in rural sociology, resulting in a tendency to reify this concept. The state is viewed as a thing rather than as the product of social relations. Accordingly, the debate on the state has been characterized by the clash between arguments supporting the thesis that the state has lost most of its powers and those stressing its continuous relevance. In these analyses, the "state" refers to the nation-state. While the nation-state has been the most dominant form of the state in the modern era, other forms—such as the city-state of early capitalism (i.e., Venice and Florence) and the quasi nation-state (i.e., Holland)—preceded and/or coexisted with it. The nation-state, therefore, is only one historical form of the state. As capitalist economies expanded, they required homogenization, standardization, and regulation to foster the acceleration of the accumulation of capital. As Marx puts it: "Independent, or but loosely connected provinces, with separate interests, laws, governments and system of taxation, become lumped together into one nation, with one government, one code of law, one national class interest, one frontier and one custom tariff" (Marx and Engels [1848] 1998, 40). The nation-state is not only the product of the expansion of market capitalism but also creates culture and institutions that support the further growth of capitalism beyond its territory (Gramsci 1971).

The importance of the nation-state grew under Fordism. State intervention supported corporations, and firms' identification with their home nation-states solidified as they operated multinationally. Simultaneously, the nation-state legitimized social arrangements through the redistribution of wealth downward and the creation of social programs that benefitted the lower classes. The Fordist nation-state intervened to regulate all facets of agrifood including research, diffusion of innovations, production, consumption, commodity prices, and quality.

Labor was also reproduced and regulated through state intervention. Processes that enhanced workers' productivity and skills, maintained discipline, and buffered unwanted consequences of market fluctuations were fostered.

Under globalization, production was decentralized through the creation of transnational commodity networks while the adoption of neoliberal postures made national borders porous. Global sourcing became the primary corporate strategy as companies sought the most convenient factors of production and bypassed nation-state regulations. Nation-states' ability to enforce requirements that benefited labor and communities, protected the environment, and guaranteed product and production safety decreased. Corporate bypassing of nation-states was paralleled by neoliberalization of nation-states, which further weakened their power to regulate.

In this context, the identification of corporations with home countries became increasingly difficult. Companies invested, established operations, and carried out business decoupling their activities from national interests and priorities. As corporate profit remained high, unemployment increased and wages and employment stability decreased. Corporations searched for tax havens in which to locate their official headquarters. Coupled with reduced fiscal pressure, corporate mobility and the rare repatriation of profit exacerbated nation-states' fiscal crisis. The desirability of reduced state regulation and appeals to expand the free market economy characterized the ideology of political and corporate elites. Accordingly, nation-states not only reduced their control of corporate activities but also rolled back existing welfare programs and pro-labor and other measures that they viewed as obstacles to capital expansion and mobility. Simultaneously, the nation-states' capability to coordinate economy activities and promote corporate interests decreased as the scope and character of the globalized economy transcended their jurisdiction and powers. The result is that the "crisis of the state" is only the crisis of the Fordist nation-state. It is a historically specific crisis and it is evident in terms of the objectives and actions of the Fordist regime and the nation-state polity and socioeconomic equilibria in that context.

Attempts to create entities that are larger than nation-states have already emerged (e.g., the G20, the European Union, and free-trade treaties). Yet, none of these initiatives has generated institutions with the instruments and scope to adequately regulate and coordinate global capitalism. The gap between the space of economic relations and the scope of political institutions is one of the characterizing features of globalization. In this context, the regulatory space left by the crisis of the Fordist nation-state has been filled by neoliberal attempts to establish systems where no or limited regulation is required and by the proliferation of NGOs. In the case of the latter, governance—or the act of governing—has been privatized and removed from the public sphere. As Harvey (2006) argues, NGOs declare to represent all stockholders—and disenfranchised groups among them—yet this is not necessarily the case. To the merit of scholars in rural sociology, the consequences and implications of this process are among the major foci of their research. Yet, the view and practice that rural sociological studies ought to be framed in national, "international," or comparative terms remain recurrent dimensions in the discipline.

Financialization and Securitization

Financialization indicates the increased importance of financial capital over manufacturing and agricultural capital in determining the profit expected from investment as well as the increased subordination of investment to the demands of global financial markets. Financialization is accompanied by the phenomenon of securitization. *Securitization* refers to processes that tend to reduce all value produced into financial instruments. A *financial instrument* is any tradable asset in financial markets. Following neoliberal deregulation, corporate agents operated to produce new financial instruments by creating new assets or by combining new assets with existing ones and marketing these repackaged entities to investors. Financial actors increasingly affect corporations—but also larger entities such as nations—and their economic actions. Under neoliberal globalization, financial capital has become the most dominant form of capital.

The financialization of the economy has engendered a number of important consequences. First, profit has been transferred from the productive sector to the financial sector. This phenomenon has transformed the financial sector into the most profitable and powerful sector of the economy. Second, an intercapital conflict between financial and productive capital has emerged. Financial companies' short-term strategies and thinking now guide the evolution of the overall economy over the long-term objectives and stability preferred by productive capital. For companies involved in production, growth is largely determined by long-term market stability that allows sustained production and the availability of consumption markets. Financial actors, instead, prefer short-term strategies that allow the rapid creation and sale of financial products, derivatives, and credit arrangements. Third, wages have been decoupled from productivity growth, resulting in a stagnation of labor remuneration and rising income inequality. Income has shifted from labor to capital as a greater percentage of remuneration is allocated to profit. Forth, strategies and policies that assume that the growth of profit would translate into overall well-being of the economy, expanded employment, and socioeconomic stability are increasingly inadequate as they do not account for the fact that profit generation has been decoupled from job creation. Fifth, as wages and salaries stagnate or decrease, the level of household debt has grown significantly. The growing gap between household debt and income indicates the declining well-being of families and communities. Finally, financialization has increased the instability of the economy. At the outset, the creation of financial products tends to increase collateral value. This expanded value allows more borrowing that finances investment spending and fuels economic expansion. As collateral value decreases, borrowing and investment fall, triggering a downward spiral that results in a crisis. Attempts to address these recurrent crises normally consist of state-sponsored bailouts and/or austerity measures that strain nation-states' finances, create unemployment, and undermine social stability.

The evolution of agrifood over the last two decades is a clear example of the effects and functioning of financialization and securitization. Agricultural commodities as well as land have been employed as assets to be traded in financial markets. Increasingly, their value is decoupled from their productive uses and linked to their financial utility. In this context, speculative moves concerning agricultural commodities are considered among the primary sources of recent crises (e.g., food shortages, food insecurity, high food prices). Investment houses, private equity funds, hedge funds, and other financial actors have been active in agrifood commodity and land acquisitions and sales as forms of financial investment. As land and commodities are traded as financial assets, people's livelihoods, land-use patterns, food sovereignty, and the availability of natural resources are threatened.

Food giant Néstle's financial maneuvering, known as the Nestlé Model,[1] is a classical example of the manner in which financially driven value growth creates unemployment, wage stagnation, and economic instability. In 2006, Nestlé announced a 21 percent increase in net profit, a 12.5 percent dividend payout, and the allocation of $4 billion for a new round of share buy-backs. As investors were rewarded, Nestlé also downsized its labor force by 10 percent worldwide based on the direct elimination of existing jobs, outsourcing, and plant closing. A central element of this model is the understanding that, from the financial point of view, a better company is one that can produce more with less labor. A restructured company is a sound financial investment. Once restructured, the company market value increases on the expectation that it is more efficient. The net result is that the augmentation of the company's financial value creates added remuneration of stockholders and CEOs, but it increases unemployment and depresses wages. As unemployment and lower wages negatively impact consumption, overproduction is addressed by additional labor force downsizing and restructuring resulting in more employment and socioeconomic instability. Recent examples of the application of this model involve transnational food giants such as Kraft, Danone, and Heineken (Rossman and Greenfield 2006).

The rural sociology literature has discussed the characteristics and implications of financialization and securitization. However, the attention paid to these phenomena has not been commensurate to their importance and impact. It also does not equal rural sociologists' continuous focus on production and consumption actors and on concentration and centralization of production processes.

Neoliberalism and the Legitimation Crisis

Four decades ago, as Jürgen Habermas (1975) and members of the intellectual left argued that advanced societies could not fulfill their claims of economic growth, social stability, and political inclusion, the neoliberal critique of Fordism maintained that the politicization of the economy and social relations generated a number of negative consequences and, eventually, a systemic crisis. The market, proponents of that critique claimed, was clogged by big state and its misguided attempts to direct an economy that was not allowed to function autonomously. Rather than the politicization of the economy and society, the neoliberal proposal called for the free functioning of the market to decide political outcomes. The *economization of politics*—or the idea that what is good for the market is good for society—emerged as neoliberalism's defining message. Neoliberalism became the dominant ideology of globalization by promising that the application of unconstrained market mechanisms, the drastic reduction of the social and regulatory state, and the enhanced mobility of capital would generate economic expansion and social stability.

In the second decade of the twenty-first century, neoliberal globalization is experiencing a crisis of legitimation. Defining the financial crisis of 2008 as an epiphenomenon of the structural crisis of advanced capitalism, the French philosopher Gérard Raulet (2011) contends that the current situation is reminiscent of the legitimation crisis of Fordist capitalism that Habermas illustrates. Like in the case of the 1970s, under the current neoliberal global regime, the administrative system cannot meet the demands stemming from the economy and the expectations of the masses. The application of neoliberalism has magnified the unwanted consequences of the functioning of the market and diminished the socioeconomic well-being of many segments of society. As global capitalism enriched the top 1 percent of the economic spectrum and severely worsened the conditions of the lower and middle classes, its negative consequences were met by the upsurge of discontent and protest (Volscho and Kelly 2012; Harvey 2010).

These and like-minded authors call into question the adequacy of the dominant normative structures. They criticize the claims that neoliberal globalization brings about enhanced freedom, democracy, socioeconomic growth, and reliable instruments to achieve them. They also question the ability of global constituencies to substantively and democratically participate in decision-making processes, along with the proposition that providing economic and fiscal advantages to the rich would translate into jobs and economic prosperity for the rest of society. They increasingly view the unchecked dominance of private interests as a situation that strips the process of governance of necessary legitimacy. Ultimately, such authors see the contradiction between neoliberal claims about the effectiveness and desirability of market mechanisms and calls for state intervention to address frequent economic, social, and environmental crises as the system's delegitimizing factor.

Arguably, agrifood is one of the areas where the crisis of legitimation is most evident as free-market mechanisms do not meet many problems in production and consumption, such as economic and environmental sustainability, food quality, sovereignty, and availability. As the US Farm Bill is downsized, family farmers question whether market mechanisms could ever give them the safety net that has been their primary objective for decades. Similarly, consumers question the ability of market forces to generate a safe and just system of food distribution. A possible return to Fordist interventionism (neo-Fordism), however, appears problematic at best. The multifaceted crisis of the nation-state and the global scope of agrifood production and consumption prevent optimism about this solution. As discontent and protest persist, the extent and characteristics of the legitimation crisis and possible alternatives to neoliberalism constitute important areas of investigation. Recently, these themes have been researched. I hope that greater scholarly participation follows these few initiatives.

Labor

In the years between the mid-1970s and the end of the 1990s, rural sociological research paid significant attention to the theme of agricultural labor. Topics such as the proletarianization and class position of farmers, their role as reservoir of labor for the expansion of urban markets, and the marginalization of wage workers were frequently analyzed. In recent years, however, research in rural sociology has moved away from this traditional subject of investigation. Surprisingly, this trend evolved in a period in which labor relations were significantly altered and new and more serious forms of labor marginalization and control emerged. As the conditions of workers worsened under globalization, rural sociologists paid less attention to the theme of labor.

In a situation characterized by the enhanced mobility of commodities and capital, labor remains highly regulated as workers' ability to look for employment across national—and in some instances within domestic—borders is highly controlled by an upsurge of anti-immigration postures and measures. This is hardly a coincidence. Stricter mechanisms of labor control not only diminish the ability of labor to resist corporate actions but also allow for the faster acceleration of capital accumulation. In the past, labor was effectively controlled through labor market and institutional mechanisms. Historically, the assumption that high labor demand would generate higher wages and labor strength was often supported by empirical evidence. Simultaneously, the creation of labor surpluses—or reserve armies of labor—constituted one of the most effective tools to depress wages and contain workers' claims. Under Fordism, however, labor was most effectively controlled through state intervention and the so-called labor-management accord. This state-sponsored pact allowed the pacification of labor relations and promoted a steady growth in productivity, production, and wages, as well as relative employment stability. While agricultural labor maintained its distinctive characteristics—i.e., pluriactivity, part-time, seasonality of employment, spatial mobility, and out-migration—it followed these national trends.

Under globalization, the creation of transnational networks generated a demand for labor. Contrary to the past, however, this labor demand did not translate into labor strength. Corporate global sourcing placed production facilities and activities in regions where labor was abundant and politically docile. In effect, the availability and docility of labor have been among the most defining characteristics of global sourcing. Global sourcing also limited the power of stronger labor pools as these workers were placed in competition with those who were less expensive and less combative. As demand weakened in labor-rich regions, workers were forced to migrate. Because labor migration remained highly controlled, these migratory processes often took place through temporary immigration programs or illegal migration. In both cases, labor market mechanisms became secondary as legal-political mechanisms regulated employment opportunities. The net result is that globalization often signifies lower wages, unstable employment, and worsening working conditions.

The high vulnerability of immigrant labor is also reinforced by ideological mechanisms that stigmatize migrants. In the United States, dominant discourses identify immigrants as undesirable individuals who break the law, threaten community stability and national security, and take jobs from local workers. These discourses provide political fuel to the proliferation of repressive anti-immigrant laws. Simultaneously, the demand for immigrant labor continues to exist as enterprises in agrifood and other sectors are reluctant to halt the use of this inexpensive, efficient, and docile labor. This continuous desire of business to employ immigrants is contradictory to political pronouncements and moves to limit immigration. Nation-states, such as the United States, are caught between neoliberal claims of open markets and anti-immigration dominant political discourses. This contradiction is telling of the limits of state action and their repressive and class nature, and, ultimately, the importance of the analysis of agrifood labor under neoliberal globalization.

Conclusions

Significant changes are taking place in agrifood. Yet, their analysis has not found adequate space in rural sociology. Therefore, the invitation, but also the challenge, is twofold. First, investigation on these and related themes should be brought to a level commensurate to their importance. Second, efforts should be made to reconceptualize some of the assumptions that guided research in the recent past. The reification of concepts such time and space and the state requires immediate attention. The rich tradition of rural studies rests on researchers' ability to examine critically the conditions characterizing this substantive area and the assumptions employed to frame it. It is time, I believe, to return to this tradition and exercise this ability.

Notes

1 For more information on the Nestlé Model, see the documentation available on the International Union of Food Worker website at www.iuf.org/cms.

References

Bonanno, Alessandro, and Josefa Salete Barbosa Cavalcanti. 2011. *Globalization and the Time-Space Reorganization*. Bingley, UK: Emerald Publishing.

Giddens, Anthony. 1990. *The Consequences of Modernity*. Stanford: Stanford University Press.

Gramsci, Antonio. 1971. *Selection from the Prison Notebooks*. New York: International Publishers.

Habermas, Jürgen. 1975. *Legitimation Crisis*. Trans. Thomas McCarthy. Boston: Beacon Press.

Harvey, David. 2010. *The Enigma of Capital and the Crisis of Capitalism*. New York: Oxford University Press.

Harvey, David. 2000. *Spaces of Hope*. Berkeley: University of California Press.

Harvey, David. 2006. *Spaces of Global Capitalism*. London: Verso.

Marx, Karl, and Frederick Engels. [1867] 1977. *Capital*, vol. 1. New York: Vintage Books.

Marx, Karl, and Frederick Engels. [1885] 1992. *Capital*, vol. 2. London: Penguin.

Marx, Karl, and Frederick Engels. [1848] 1998. *The Communist Manifesto*. London, New York: Verso.

Raulet, Gérard. 2011. "Legitimacy and Globalization." *Philosophy and Social Criticism* 37 (3): 313–23. http://dx.doi.org/10.1177/0191453710389445.

Rossman, Peter, and Gerard Greenfield. 2006. "Financialization: New Routes to Profits, New Challenges for Trade Unions." *Labour Education* 142: 1–10.

Volscho, W. Thomas, and Nathan J. Kelly. 2012. "The Rise of the Super-Rich: Power Resources, Taxes, Financial Markets, and the Dynamics of the Top 1 Percent, 1949–2008." *American Sociological Review* 77 (5): 679–99. http://dx.doi.org/10.1177/0003122412458508.

Weber, Max. [1921] 1968. *Economy and Society*. 3 vols. Totowa, NJ: Bedminster Press.

CHAPTER 1

Economic Concentration in the Agrifood System: Impacts on Rural Communities and Emerging Responses

Douglas H. Constance, Mary Hendrickson, Philip H. Howard, and William D. Heffernan

Introduction

In this chapter we examine how the industrialization of agriculture has proceeded over the last thirty years, a process we argue has had negative consequences for farmers and rural communities. We apply a Missouri School of Agrifood Studies framework to the topic of economic concentration in agrifood to inform discussions regarding rural quality of life (Kleiner and Green 2009). Our method is to document economic concentration, provide a framework for interpreting its consequences, and to present accessible information to help farmers, workers, policy makers, and community members make sense of their lived experiences of agribusiness consolidation. We present concentration data for the input, production, processing, and retailing sectors. Our research reveals that the processes of vertical and horizontal integration accelerated during the latter half of the twentieth century, resulting in an oligopolistic market structure whereby a few firms dominate across several commodity sectors at the national and global levels. Vertical integration rationalizes the commodity chains, often to the detriment of producers, and horizontal integration limits producers' access to competitive markets. Agrifood system restructuring means some actors have more power to affect their life chances than other actors. As a result, rural quality of life decreases.

We are interested in farmers' concerns regarding restructuring in the United States and the world. As Bonanno notes in the introduction to this section, farmers and consumers have challenged neoliberal restructuring and consolidation in the agrifood system. Farmers' movements have resisted agribusiness market power by making claims on the government. The recent US Department of Agriculture and US Department of Justice (USDA/USDOJ) antitrust hearings are the latest examples. Despite these efforts, economic concentration continues.

Economic Concentration in Agrifood Systems

We have researched the relationship between economic concentration of agrifood systems and rural quality of life for forty years, beginning with Heffernan's (1972) study of poultry production in Union Parish, Louisiana. His goal was to understand how the structure of the industry impacted community in historically poor areas. Despite major investments from poultry growers and the largest agricultural sales in the state, Union Parish remained a persistent poverty county from the 1960s to 1999 (Hendrickson et al. 2008a). How could this happen? Horizontal and vertical integration in the food system reduced returns to communities as returns to capital and management flowed to corporate headquarters, thereby reducing rural quality of life (Heffernan 1982; 1984). Farmers were caught betwixt and between powerful input suppliers and processors (Martinson and Campbell 1980).

Agrifood consolidation accelerated during the 1980s as the government embraced neoliberalism and loosened antitrust enforcement activities. This shift created a surge of mergers and acquisitions across all sectors of the economy, but particularly in agricultural production and processing (Heffernan and Constance 1994; Heffernan, Hendrickson, and Gronski 1999). This trend toward increased vertical and horizontal integration diffused globally, resulting in a global poultry agrifood complex (Constance and Heffernan 1991), a pattern repeated in the hog industry (Bonanno and Constance 2006; Constance, Kleiner, and Rikoon 2003).

The Missouri School method is to document agribusiness concentration by reporting the market shares in major agricultural commodities in CR4 tables (CR4 is the combined market share of the top four firms in each market). We gleaned the data from trade journals, company annual reports, government reports, and financial newspapers, among other sources. As global concentration became apparent, our research expanded into a global network of rural social scientists loosely linked through the Agribusiness Accountability Initiative (Gronski and Glenna 2009).

We are interested in the top four firms in a specific market for two reasons. First, institutional economists generally agree that when four firms control more than 40 percent of a market the oligopolistic/oligopsonistic structure confers market power to those firms (Breimyer 1965; Connor et al. 1984). Second, the theory of small group behavior indicates that actors in small groups inform their own actions through observation of other actors, rather than through openly discussing actions with others (Olson 1965). We recognize that CR4 is an imperfect assessment of power relationships within a particular commodity (James, Hendrickson, and Howard 2013), but the value of the method is the documentation of the dominant players in and across particular commodities that helps people understand the reach of corporate actors. Until recently our CR4 tables were the only organized source of up-to-date statistics on the oligopolistic structure of agricultural markets. Due to pressure from agricultural groups, the USDA-Grain Inspection, Packers, and Stockyards Administration (GIPSA) now provides current information on CR4 ratios. Our major contribution remains the identification of the top firms by name to document the progress of cross-commodity integration. For instance, Table 1.1 reveals that Tyson provides a full array of protein—beef, pork, and broilers—while Cargill produces and processes meats, provides feed, and trades and processes corn and soybeans. Another major contribution of the Missouri School has been the documentation of concentration trends in alternative markets such as organics (Howard 2009a).

Horizontal Integration

We focused initially on major grain and livestock commodities, and then expanded to include input markets, food retailing, and organics. Over twenty years of CR4 data reveal clear trends. First, horizontal integration is a key component of agrifood system restructuring. Table 1.1 reveals that almost all commodities show increases in CR4 ratios from 1990 and 2011, which is primarily due to acquisitions and mergers among dominant players. We see the same process in grains and protein, where certain actors dominate across several commodities. For instance, in 1999 the top four beef packers were IBP (absorbed in 2001 by Tyson), ConAgra (now JBS, the world's largest meat company and top beef packer), Cargill, and Farmland National Beef Packing Company (a cooperative that has dissolved with packing operations, now just National Beef), with a CR4 of 79 percent. In beef, horizontal integration means that farmers and ranchers have fewer choices when they sell their cattle.

Farmers also have few options when they buy inputs such as fertilizers and seeds (Hubbard 2009; Moss 2011). Companies such as Yara, Potash Corp, Agrium, and Mosaic dominate the global fertilizer sector (Taylor 2010). Three cartels in potash and phosphorous account for about 70 percent of global trade (Blas 2010;

Etter 2008). Significant consolidation has occurred in the seed industry after the introduction of Round-up Ready seeds in 1996 (Howard 2009b). About 70 percent of the corn seed and 60 percent of the soybean seed in the United States is controlled by two firms, DuPont/Pioneer and Monsanto (Pollack 2010). In 2006, DuPont/Pioneer, Monsanto, Syngenta, and Limagrain controlled approximately 29 percent of global seed sales (UNCTAD 2006), including a CR4 of 53 percent for the global proprietary seed market, with Monsanto at 23 percent and DuPont at 15 percent (ETC Group 2008). Monsanto entered the seed industry in the mid-1980s and has since acquired more than fifty seed firms, some at a cost of over $1 billion. The numerous cross-licensing agreements carried out by the Big 6 chemical/seed companies create barriers to entry for non-Big 6 seed companies (see Howard's visual representation of seed industry consolidation at www.msu.edu/~howardp//seedindustry.html).

Vertical Integration and Global Reach

Vertical integration is also a key factor in agrifood restructuring. In 1999, the concept of the food chain cluster was developed from the integration of CR4 tables and research on firm strategies (Heffernan, Hendrickson, and Gronski 1999). Similar to Wilkinson's (2002) "netchains" concept, foodchain clusters are groups of dominant actors across input areas that have formal and informal agreements (e.g., acquisitions, joint ventures, or operating agreements) to operate from "seed to shelf." The clusters identified in 1999 (i.e., Cargill/Monsanto, ADM/Novartis, and ConAgra) appeared to operate with little competition within the vertically integrated cluster, but with quite dynamic competition between clusters.

The important point regarding clusters is that actors operate on a global scale and the global concentration ratios are difficult to document (McIntyre et al. 2009). The reorganization of space that Bonanno describes in the introduction to this section is thus aided by its increasingly opaque nature. Cargill operates significant processing enterprises around the globe with grain trading activities in all major ports. Tyson has significant broiler operations in Mexico and is expanding in China, India, and Brazil; Smithfield operates pork facilities in Brazil and Eastern Europe (Constance, Martinez, and Aboites 2010), and is being sought by a Chinese agrifood transnational corporation (TNC). Agrifood consolidation has generated a global food retail oligopoly with firms like Walmart (US), Tesco (UK), and Carrefour (France) acquiring or building supermarkets in Mexico, Brazil, China, and Southeast Asia (Burch and Lawrence 2007; Hendrickson et al. 2001; Reardon, Henson and Berdegué 2007; Wrigley and Lowe 2007). Walmart is the largest grocer in the United States and

Table 1.1

Comparison of 1990, 1999, and 2011 CR4 data

Industry Sector and Representative Firms	CR 4 (2011)	Industry Sector and Representative Firms	CR 4 (1999)	Industry Sector and Representative Firms	CR 4 (1990)
Beef Slaughter (Steer and Heifer)	82 percent	Beef Slaughter (Steer and Heifer)	79 percent	Beef Slaughter (Steer and Heifer)	69 percent
• Excel (Cargill)		• IBP		• IBP	
• Tyson Foods		• ConAgra		• ConAgra	
• JBS		• Excel (Cargill)		• Excel (Cargill)	
• National Beef		• Farmland National Beef		• Beef America	
Beef Production • JBS Fiver Rivers Cattle Feeding (838,000)	Top four had one-time capacity for 1,983,000 head	Beef Production • Continental Grain Cattle Feeding (405,000)	Top four had one-time capacity for 1,349,000 head	Beef Production • Cactus Feeders	Not reported
• Cactus Feeders [relationship with Tyson] (520,000)		• Cactus Feeders Inc. (350,000)		• ConAgra (Monfort)	
• Cargill Cattle Feeders LLC (350,000)		• ConAgra Cattle Feeding (320,000)		• J.R. Simplot Co.	
• Friona Industries (275,000)		• National Farms Inc. (274,000)		• Caprock (Cargill)	
Pork Slaughter • Smithfield Foods	63 percent	Pork Slaughter • Smithfield	57 percent	Pork Slaughter • IBP	45 percent
• Tyson Foods		• IBP Inc.		• ConAgra (SIPCO/Armour)	
• Swift (JBS)		• ConAgra (Swift)		• Morrell	
• Excel (Cargill)		• Cargill (Excel)		• Excel	
Pork Production • Smithfield Foods (876,804)	Top four had 1,618,904 sows in production	Pork Production • Murphy Family Farms (337,000)	Top four had 834,600 sows in production	Pork Production • Murphy Farms	Not reported
• Triumph Foods (371,000)		• Carroll's Foods (183,600)		• Tyson Foods	
• Seaboard (213,600)		• Continental Grain [inc. PSF] (162,000)		• Cargill	
• Iowa Select Farms (157,500)		• Smithfield Foods (152,000)		• National Farms	
Broiler Slaughter • Tyson Foods	53 percent	Broiler Slaughter • Tyson Foods	49 percent	Broiler Slaughter • Tyson Foods	45 percent
• Pilgrim's Pride (owned by JBS)		• Gold Kist		• ConAgra	
• Perdue		• Perdue		• Gold Kist	
• Sanderson		• Pilgrim's Pride		• Perdue Farms	

Table 1.1

Comparison of 1990, 1999, and 2011 CR4 data

Industry Sector and Representative Firms	CR 4 (2011)	Industry Sector and Representative Firms	CR 4 (1999)	Industry Sector and Representative Firms	CR 4 (1990)
Turkey Slaughter	58 percent	Turkey Slaughter	42 percent	Turkey Slaughter	31 percent
• Butterball (Smithfield/Goldsboro)		• Jennie-O (Hormel)		• Louis Rich (Philip Morris)	
• Jennie-O (Hormel)		• Butterball (ConAgra)		• Swift (Beatrice/ KKR)	
• Cargill		• Wampler Turkeys		• ConAgra	
• Farbest Foods		• Cargill		• Norbest	
Animal Feed	44 percent	Animal Feed	Unknown		
• Land O'Lakes Purina LLC		• Cargill (Nutrena)			
• Cargill Animal Nutrition		• Purina Mills (Koch Industries)			
• ADM Alliance Nutrition		• Central Soya			
• J.D. Heiskell & Co.		• Consolidated Nutrition (ADM and AGP)			
Flour Milling	52 percent	Flour Milling	62 percent	Flour Milling	61 percent
• Horizon Milling (Cargill/CHS)		• ADM		• ConAgra	
		• ConAgra		• ADM	
• ADM		• Cargill Flour Milling		• Cargill	
• ConAgra				• Grand Met (Pillsbury)	
Wet Corn Milling	87 percent	Wet Corn Milling	74 percent	Wet Corn Milling	74 percent
• ADM		• ADM		• ADM	
• Corn Products International		• Cargill		• Cargill	
		• A.E. Staley (Tate and Lyle)		• A.E. Staley (Tate and Lyle)	
• Cargill		• CPC		• CPC	
Soybean Processing	85 percent	Soybean Processing	80 percent	Soybean Processing	61 percent
• ADM		• ADM		• ADM	
• Bunge		• Cargill		• Cargill	
• Cargill		• Bunge		• Bunge	
• Ag Processing		• Ag Processing		• Ag Processors	
Grocery	42–51 percent	Unknown		Unknown	
• Walmart					
• Kroger					
• Safeway					
• Supervalu					

Sources: 2011 data (James, Hendrickson, and Howard 2013); 1999 data (Heffernan, Hendrickson, and Gronski 1999); 1990 data (Heffernan and Constance 1994).

Table 1.2
Changes in retail consolidation in the United States

1997: CR5 = 24%	2000: CR5 = 42%	2011: CR4 = 42–51%
Kroger Co.	Kroger Co.	Walmart
Safeway	Walmart	Kroger
American Stores	Albertson's	Safeway
Albertson's	Safeway	Supervalu
Ahold USA	Ahold USA	

Sources: 1997 and 2000 data is from Hendrickson et al. (2001). 2011 data is from James, Hendrickson, and Howard (2013).

Mexico, the second largest grocer in the United Kingdom and the third largest in Brazil, while Carrefour is the largest food retailer in France, the second largest in Brazil, and the third largest in China (Bauerova, Burritt, and Oliveira 2010; Datamonitor 2009).

In the United States, consolidation rose from a CR5 of 24 percent in 1997 to a CR4 of almost 50 percent at the time of writing (Table 1.2), with Walmart at three times the sales of its nearest competitor (Clifford 2011). Walmart changed food retailing when it entered the market in the late 1980s. Pressured by Walmart, in 1998 Kroger bought Fred Meyer and Albertson's bought American Stores to compete with Walmart. In 2006, after the brutal reorganization of food retail and Walmart's ascent, number two Albertson's abandoned the grocery business.

Walmart uses its market power to lower prices paid to producers, manufacturers, and workers, rather than forcing consumers to pay higher prices (Lynn 2009). This is an example of *buyer power*, which is not the mirror image of *seller power*, the usual focus of antitrust regulators (Chen 2008; Grundlach, and Foer 2008). Seller power takes effect in very highly concentrated markets (at 60 percent market share), while buyer power can be exhibited in relatively less concentrated markets (around 20 percent) (Foer 2010). Farmers are at the mercy of buyer power of highly concentrated processing firms, while those firms' selling power is no match for Walmart's buying power. For example, Tyson claimed that a changing food retail environment forced it to make acquisitions to provide the entire protein case, which prompted its purchase of pork and beef packer IBP in 2001.

Economists view increasing CR4 ratios as the natural result of economies of scale; larger firms are more efficient. Therefore, nothing should alter this fundamental process that serves best the needs of society. This is the position of most agricultural economists, industry leaders, and policy makers. However, as in the examples of Albertson's and Tyson above, very few of the acquisitions involved small, inefficient firms. It is more likely the acquired firms were so well-managed and with such great potential that their stock was undervalued. These transactions are better understood by focusing on power rather than efficiency. There are larger and fewer agrifood firms, while rural populations have declined. Farmers who remain have few choices in buying inputs and marketing commodities. A sharp increase in the concentration of food retail means those firms now force restructuring upstream through the system to the worker and farmer levels, all the while decreasing consumers' choice of where and what to shop.

Economic Restructuring and Impacts on Rural Communities

The idea that the industrialization of agriculture has negative impacts on rural communities has a long history in the rural social sciences. The Goldschmidt Hypothesis predicts that a middle-class structure of agriculture supports a higher quality of life for producers and their communities (Goldschmidt 1947; Lobao 1990; Lyson 2004). A meta-analysis by Lobao and Stofferahn (2008) on the relationship between agricultural structure and community well-being found industrial farming had detrimental effects on communities in 82 percent of fifty-one studies. These negative effects included greater income inequality; decreased retail trade and diversity of retail firms; population declines; and negative health effects of large livestock operations. In the Jeffersonian tradition, independent family farms that provide the management, capital, and labor make the best citizens because the autonomy of decision making on the farms carries into the civic arena (Breimyer 1965). With economic concentration and globalization, an agrifood system based on multiple horizontal linkages with multiplier effects at the community level is replaced with a system of vertical linkages organized as global commodity chains that send profits out of the community. Consolidation at the production level results in fewer family farms overall, combined with more of those farms linked in asymmetrical power relationships to agrifood TNCs that extract wealth from rural communities (Heffernan 2000; James, Hendrickson, and Howard 2013).

As noted above, horizontal and vertical integration are the two main mechanisms that confer power to agrifood corporations at the expense of producers. Horizontal integration leads to market concentration within a commodity sector. Rapid consolidation in the hog industry has resulted in fewer firms buying hogs from producers. Fewer buyers put the producers at a market disadvantage relative to processors, increasing the likelihood that pork packers will engage in predatory behavior (James, Hendrickson, and Howard 2013; Wise and Trist 2010). For grain farmers, this is especially problematic in the seed sector dominated by just a few firms; proprietary seeds and the required specialized inputs puts them in a dependency relationship (Hendrickson et al. 2008b; Howard 2009b). Both processes result in constrained choices in the face of market power for producers (Hendrickson and James 2005).

As horizontal integration increases, rural quality of life goes down. The trend toward fewer and larger input and output corporations is matched by a trend toward larger production units linked to these firms as part of global commodity chains, smaller farms servicing niche markets, and a decrease in mid-sized farms (see Guptill and Welsh in chapter 2 of this volume). Fewer middle-class farm units on the land exacerbates rural depopulation and increases inequality in the community, as the Goldschmidt Hypothesis predicts.

One example of the negative impact of agrifood restructuring on both farmers and communities is revealed by our research on the poultry industry (Constance 2001, 2008; Heffernan 1972, 1984, 2000; Hendrickson and James 2005; Hendrickson et al. 2008a). By the 1960s, vertical integration had replaced an independent system of poultry production. The early form of the broiler industry had positive influences on rural quality of life when there were many firms and many markets. As the industry consolidated through the 1980s, producers had fewer integrators to grow birds for, resulting in less-profitable contracts and extended debt. Poultry growers incur long-term debt when they mortgage their land to build single-purpose buildings, but the grow-out contracts with integrators tend to be short term. This system has been criticized as a transitional status between independent farmer and farm worker, referred to as "serfs on the land" (Breimyer 1965), "propertied laborers" (Davis 1980), and "debt slavery" (Wellford 1972). Integrators exert control over production without the responsibility and liability associated with formal labor relations and land ownership (Constance et al. 2013). Neighbors to the poultry complexes report reduced quality of life (Constance et al. 2003; Constance and Tuinstra 2005). As documented by Heffernan's thirty-year study in Louisiana, a county with the highest agricultural sales still remained a persistent poverty county in 1999 after three decades of investment in the poultry industry. Obviously, the poultry industry has had few positive—and mostly negative effects—for farmers and communities in Union Parish.

Contract poultry growers recently testified at hearings held by the US Departments of Agriculture and Justice (USDA/USDOJ 2010a). Growers reported a pattern of predatory practices as integrators use the threat of contract termination to force upgrades resulting in perpetual debt. The asset specificity of the single-purpose barns reduces the growers' negotiating power. As a result, growers are held up by the integrator through coerced compliance and less-lucrative contracts. Through a tournament ranking system, growers are threatened with contract termination if they don't improve their ranking (Constance et al. 2013). Growers are also embedded in place, and so are less likely to challenge integrator opportunism (James, Hendrickson, and Howard 2013). At the hearings, they called on the government to protect them from monopsony opportunism that produced a declining quality of life in poultry production regions experiencing horizontal integration.

It is important to note that what changed is growers' loss of choice in the marketplace. Even though poultry contracts were in place in the 1960s, growers reported some economic benefits to their household from poultry operations through the early 1980s. The vertical integration that yokes growers was exacerbated by horizontal integration, as the CR4 for broilers remained flat at about 18 percent from the 1960s until the mid-1970s, when it started to increase to its level of 53 percent in 2011 (GIPSA 2011). Both horizontal and vertical integration create dependencies that facilitate predatory behaviors through asymmetrical power relationships. Poultry growers are dependent on the integrators, livestock growers are dependent on a few packing companies, and grain growers are dependent on a few millers and seed/input suppliers (Heffernan 2000; James, Hendrickson, and Howard 2013). Our research on the pork industry reveals a similar pattern (Constance, Kleiner, and Rikoon 2003). In the 1990s, ADM colluded with Japanese and Korean agricultural input companies to fix lysine prices, exposing its philosophy that "the customer is our enemy" (Bonanno and Constance 2008).

In the 1973 study *Who Will Control American Agriculture*, agricultural economists concluded that further consolidation in agriculture did not increase efficiency and could negatively impact the quality of life (Breimyer, Guither, and Sundquist 1973). Breimyer (1965) warned that horizontal and vertical integration replace markets with bureaucracy and thereby reduce the economic democracy for producers. Globalization accelerates this process as the dominant firms diffuse this business model to capture global market share (Heffernan, Hendrickson, and Gronski 1999; Hendrickson et al. 2008b). Tyson's and JBS's global activities are evidence of the process. Today, Tyson and JBS are the two largest meat companies in the world (Hoovers 2012; JBS 2012). Following a pattern of horizontal integration through mergers and acquisitions, JBS, based in Brazil, is expanding rapidly in the United States, Mexico, Asia, and Europe, while Tyson continues its expansion in South America and Asia. Today, JBS controls 25 percent of the worldwide trade in beef.

As noted earlier, global grocers are also consolidating their positions. They construct global supply chains that source where they can obtain food cheaply and consistently, and sell into established and emerging markets. As Walmart exemplifies, these grocers become the point of contact with consumers, and use their buyer power to exert pressure upstream to lower costs on manufacturers, processors, workers, and farmers.

Powerful Actors and Fragmented Resistance

Periodically, increased economic concentration generates social movement resistance that attempts to change the system—what Polanyi (1944) calls a double movement. The market's attempt to separate itself from the bounds of society creates movements for social protectionism. Farmer social movement resistance emerged in the late nineteenth century in response to the economic power of the grain and railroad trusts (Mooney and Majka 1995). These movements were successful at securing legislation, such as the Packers and Stockyards Administration in 1921, designed to protect farmers from market power. New Deal policies institutionalized government support for farmers. As market concentration and globalization accelerated and as government protections contracted beginning in the 1980s, farmer social movement activity reemerged. The Farm/Debt Crisis of the 1980s demonstrated clearly the link between rural prosperity in the United States and globalization (McMichael 1996). Producer organizations such as the National Farmers Union again called for the government to protect producers from market power. The recent USDA/USDOJ antitrust hearings provide a good example of this form of resistance.

The Grain Inspection Packers Stockyards Administration (GIPSA) dates to the early 1900s, but its antitrust rules were not formalized until pressure by livestock producers regarding packer concentration pushed livestock competition titles into the 2002 and 2008 Farm Bills, resulting in hearings on concentration in agriculture. In 2010, the Agricultural Competition Joint task force of the USDOJ and USDA conducted five workshops on agrifood competition (USDA/USDOJ 2010b). Farmers and ranchers provided testimony on their disadvantaged position with corporations due to market concentration. Consumers, environmentalists, and labor unions worried about the negative impacts of economic power joined them. Although the hearings generated substantial testimony documenting the negative impact of concentration, as of the time of writing no new enforcement has emerged. Agribusiness lobbies rallied support against stricter antitrust enforcement and effectively split the producers into competing subgroups. In response to lobbying, Congress defunded any effective GIPSA rules or enforcement by the executive branch. The failed GIPSA rule-making process reveals that farmers are not a monolithic group, and that the nation-state is not in the position to represent the interests of farmers or other subordinate groups.

At the international level, La Via Campesina pursues a food sovereignty agenda to counter the dominant food security framework of agrifood TNCs and the World Trade Organization (WTO) (La Via Campesina 2012). La Via Campesina operates as 150 national and international organizations, and represents marginalized agricultural stakeholders against the negative impacts of corporate privilege, especially regarding proprietary seeds and land grabs. La Via Campesina has had some success in shaping international development institutions, especially in the recent International Assessment of Agricultural Science and Technology for Development (IAASTD) process, which laid out a development path embraced by the United Nations that focused on ensuring sustainable rural livelihoods as a solution to hunger and poverty (De Schutter 2011; McIntyre et al. 2009).

Another example of resistance to industrial agriculture is organics (Guthman 2004). As the ecological costs of chemical agriculture manifested, the organic food movement emerged as a counterpoint to the conventional system. In the United States, organics began as a diversified system of producers linked to progressive restaurants and retailers. Organic producers avoided participation in concentrated commodity markets by engaging in direct sales that rewarded quality over quantity. As demand outstripped supply, companies mobilized to service the growing market and capture the green premium (see Howard's visual representation of organic consolidation at www.msu.edu/~howardp//organicindustry.html). National and international standards rationalized organic production and major companies steadily increased their market share. Smaller firms now find it difficult to compete with the entrance of large concentrations of capital (Howard 2009a). Organics is increasingly taking on aspects of the dominant food system, a process termed *conventionalization*, whereby the majority of organic foods sold in supermarkets will be sourced through global value chains. Consolidation shrinks the organic premium and inefficient actors leave the market as global comparative advantage structures the commodity chains. This corporate takeover has forced more movement-oriented actors to create new alternative ecolabels that address values organic no longer embodies (Howard and Allen 2010).

Fair trade illustrates similar dynamics of an alternative agrifood system co-opted by agrifood TNCs (Jaffee and Howard 2010; 2012). The market success of this ecolabel has attracted corporations like Nestlé, J.M. Smucker, and Starbucks, albeit at token levels of participation. Nestlé is the largest coffee company in the world, but in 2008 less than .01 percent of its sales were fair-trade certified. Nestlé is allowed to prominently display the fair-trade seal in its marketing to burnish its image, a practice called "fair-washing." The appeal of increasing revenues through the participation of agrifood TNCs has led the major US fair trade certifier, Fair Trade USA, to weaken its standards. This weakening includes certifying coffee and cocoa from plantations, which the international certifying body does not allow. This trend has led more movement-oriented actors, such as 100 percent fair-trade firms, to align with alternative certifications (e.g., Fair for Life), thus bifurcating the fair-trade system.

Conclusions

In this chapter, we have documented the steady progression of vertical and horizontal integration, the emergence of a few agrifood TNCs that dominate markets across several commodity sectors, and the trend toward global food retailers driving the commodity chains. Tyson, JBS, Cargill, ADM, and other major agrifood TNCs are consolidating their market positions on the input, production, and processing sides, while Walmart and a few global firms exhibit growing monopsony power in the retail sector. A similar trend has been documented regarding agricultural intellectual property rights (Glenna and Cahoy 2009). The globalization of the agrifood system based on neoliberal restructuring has accelerated this process as the market is privileged compared to nation-states and subordinate groups (Bonanno et al. 1994; Bonanno and Constance 2008).

We have provided evidence of the negative community quality of life impacts of this process. Our research on the poultry industry illustrates the specific mechanisms by which the combination of horizontal and vertical integration creates a system of monopsony market power that marginalizes poultry producers. The poultry model, grounded in flexible forms of production, is a central feature of the globalization of the agrifood system and neoliberal restructuring. Our research in Mexico illustrates the process of nation-state reregulation away from a focus on indigenous producers and toward the interests of agrifood TNCs (Constance, Martinez, and Aboites 2010).

We have also shown that social movements challenge the advance of corporate agriculture. The capital accumulation strategies of the agrifood TNCs created legitimation crises and social movement resistance. These conflicts are mediated by the state, but more often than not to the advantage of corporate interests over citizens. An example from Texas is especially appropriate where state agencies, with the guidance of corporate agricultural interests, eliminated the public hearing process of Concentrated Animal Feeding Operation development (Bonanno and Constance 2006). Similarly, the government hearings on market concentration highlight the difficulty producer groups have in employing the nation-state to protect them from the negative impacts of economic concentration. At the global level, La Via Campesina fights for food sovereignty and against corporate domination of the agrifood system. While alternative agriculture movements, like organics and fair trade, deserve substantial credit for their successes, these initiatives are losing some of their emancipatory dimensions as they are incorporated into the mainstream agrifood system.

Our research reveals disturbing trends regarding producers' relationships with agrifood TNCs. Neoliberalism limits the nation-state's ability to protect producers from the negative effects of market power along global commodity chains. As economic concentration and contract production spreads to other commodities and countries, more producers will find themselves in asymmetrical power relationships with agrifood TNCs. As Walmart drives the global commodity chains, farmers and ranchers will increasingly perform the function of lowest-cost producers competing on a global scale. We do acknowledge that the impact of economic concentration is uneven across time and commodities—however, we argue the overall trend is toward producer marginalization in the agrifood system.

The US agrifood system was once the envy of the world, but increasing market concentration makes it economically unsustainable and exploitive of rural peoples and environments. Economic concentration violates the laws of economics, and creates market failure and asymmetrical power relationships between actors along the commodity chains. This structure of agriculture is not the result of a natural historical process and the invisible hand of capitalism, but rather the outcome of a competition between class interests to advance their political economic agendas.

The Missouri School of Agrifood Studies incorporates both research and praxis. We work with local, regional, state, national, and international social movements to bring about progressive social change and alternative agrifood systems (Hendrickson and Heffernan 2002). We embrace a public sociology grounded in praxis and the craft of sociology (Floro 2010). We call on rural social scientists to embrace social movement and policy intervention activities that simultaneously challenge the power of the agrifood TNCs and create a more sustainable and just alternative agrifood system. The task is daunting but necessary. We should not be surprised at the ability of conventional agriculture to sustain the unsustainable (Buttel 2006). It will take a commitment to transformative change to re-democratize the agrifood system and enhance rural quality of life.

References

Bauerova, Ladka, Chris Burritt, and Joao Oliveira. 2010. "A Three-Way Food Fight in Brazil." *Business Week*, 5 April, 70–71.

Blas, Javier. 2010. "End Looms for Fertiliser Cartels." *Financial Times*, 19 August.

Bonanno, Alessandro, Lawrence Busch, William H. Friedland, Lourdes Gouveia, and Enzo Mingione, eds. 1994. *From Columbus to ConAgra: The Globalization of Agriculture and Food.* Lawrence, KS: University Press of Kansas.

Bonanno, Alessandro, and Douglas H. Constance. 2006. "Corporations and the State in the Global Era: The Case of Seaboard Farms in Texas." *Rural Sociology* 71 (1): 59–84. http://dx.doi.org/10.1526/003601106777789819.

Bonanno, Alessandro, and Douglas H. Constance. 2008. *Stories of Globalization: Transnational Corporations, Resistance, and the State.* University Park: Penn State University Press.

Breimyer, Harold F. 1965. *Individual Freedom and the Economic Organization of Agriculture.* Urbana: University of Illinois Press.

Breimyer, Harold F., Harold D. Guither, and W.B. Sundquist. 1973. *Who Will Control American Agriculture: A Series of Six Leaflets.* Cooperative Extension Service. University of Illinois.

Burch, David, and Geoffrey Lawrence. 2007. *Supermarkets and Agri-food Supply Chains: Transformations in the Production and Consumption of Food.* Cheltenham, UK: Edward Elgar.

Buttel, Frederick H. 2006. "Sustaining the Unsustainable: Agro-food Systems and the Environment in the Modern World." In *Handbook of Rural Studies*, ed. Paul Cloke, Terry Marsden, and Patrick H. Mooney, 213–29. London: Sage Publications. http://dx.doi.org/10.4135/9781848608016.n15.

Chen, Zhiqi. 2008. "Defining Buyer Power." *Antitrust Bulletin* 53 (2): 241–49.

Clifford, Stephanie. 2011. "Groceries Fill Aisles at Stores like CVS." *New York Times*, 17 January.

Connor, John, Richard Rogers, Bruce Marion, and Willard Mueller. 1984. *The Food Manufacturing Industries: Structure, Strategies, Performance and Policies.* Lanham, MD: Lexington Books.

Constance, Douglas H. 2001. "Globalization, Broiler Production, and Community Controversy in East Texas." *Southern Rural Sociology* 18 (2): 31–55.

Constance, Douglas H. 2008. "The Southern Model of Broiler Production and Its Global Implications." *Culture & Agriculture* 30 (1–2): 17–31. http://dx.doi.org/10.1111/j.1556-486X.2008.00004.x.

Constance, Douglas H., Alessandro Bonanno, Caron Cates, Daniel Argo, and Mirenda Harris. 2003. "Resisting Integration in the Global Agro-Food System: Corporate Chickens and Community Controversy in Texas." In *Globalisation, Localisation, and Sustainable Livelihoods*, ed. Reidar Almas and Geoffrey Lawrence, 103–18. Burlington, VT: Ashgate Press.

Constance, Douglas H., and William D. Heffernan. 1991. "The Global Poultry Agrifood Complex." *International Journal of Sociology of Agriculture and Food* 1: 126–41.

Constance, Douglas H., Anna Kleiner, and J. Sanford Rikoon. 2003. "The Contested Terrain of Swine Regulation." In *Fighting for the Farm: Rural America Transformed*, ed. Jane Adams, 76–95. University Park: Penn State University Press.

Constance, Douglas H., Francisco Martinez, and Gilberto Aboites. 2010. "The Globalization of the Poultry Industry: Tyson Foods and Pilgrim's Pride in Mexico." In *From Community to Consumption: New and Classical Statements in Rural Sociological Research*, ed. Alessandro Bonanno, Hans Bakker, Raymond Jussaume, Yoshio Kawamura, and Mark Shucksmith, 59–75. Bingley, UK: Emerald Group Publishing Ltd. http://dx.doi.org/10.1108/S1057-1922(2010)0000016008.

Constance, Douglas H., Francisco Martinez, Gilberto Aboites, and Alessandro Bonanno. 2013. "The Problem with Poultry Production and Processing." In *The Ethics and Economics of Agrifood Competition*, ed. Harvey James, 155–75. New York: Springer Press. http://dx.doi.org/10.1007/978-94-007-6274-9_8.

Constance, Douglas H., and Reny Tuinstra. 2005. "Corporate Chickens and Community Conflict in East Texas: Growers' and Neighbors' Views on the Impacts of Industrial Broiler Production." *Culture & Agriculture* 27 (1): 45–60. http://dx.doi.org/10.1525/cag.2005.27.1.45.

Datamonitor. 2009. "Food Retail—BRIC (Brazil, Russia, India, China) Industry Guide." Market Publishers: Market Report Database. Accessed 13 October 2011. http://pdf.marketpublishers.com/datamonitor/food_retail_bric_brazil_russia_india_china_industry_guide.pdf.

Davis, John E. 1980. "Capitalist Agricultural Development and the Exploitation of the Propertied Laborer." In *The Rural Sociology of Advanced Societies*, ed. Frederick H. Buttel and Howard Newby, 133–54. Montclair: Allenheld, Osmun, and Co.

De Schutter, Olivier. 2011. "Towards More Equitable Value Chains: Alternative Business Models in Support of the Right to Food." Report presented at the 66th Session of the United Nations General Assembly by the UN Special Rapporteur on the Right to Food. Accessed 20 April 2012. http://www.srfood.org/images/stories/pdf/officialreports/srrtf_contractfarming_a-66-262.pdf.

ETC Group. 2008. Who Owns Nature? Corporate Power and the Final Frontier in the Commodification of Life. Accessed 17 December 2013. http://www.etcgroup.org/content/who-owns-nature.

Etter, Lauren. 2008. "Lofty Prices for Fertilizer Put Farmers in a Squeeze." *Wall Street Journal*, 27 May, A1.

Floro, George. 2010. "Applying Craft for Sociological Practice: Place in Odyssey." *Journal of Rural Social Sciences* 25 (1): 119–27.

Foer, Albert A. 2010. Agriculture and Antitrust Enforcement Issues in Our 21st Century Economy. Washington, DC: US Department of Agriculture and Department of Justice, 219–52. Accessed 11 July 2011. http://www.justice.gov/atr/public/workshops/ag2010/dc-agworkshop-transcript.pdf.

Glenna, Leland, and D.R. Cahoy. 2009. "Agribusiness Concentration, Intellectual Property, and the Prospects for Rural Economic Benefits from the Emerging Biofuel Economy." *Southern Rural Sociology* 24 (2): 111–29.

GIPSA. (USDA Grain Inspection, Packers, and Stockyards Administration). 2011. 2010 Annual Report of the Packers and Stockyards Program. Washington, DC: USDA Grains Inspection, Packers, and Stockyards Administration. Accessed 12 January 2012. http://www.gipsa.usda.gov/Publications/psp/ar/2010_psp_annual_report.pdf.

Goldschmidt, Walter. 1947. *As You Sow*. Glencoe, IL: The Free Press.

Gronski, Robert, and Leland Glenna. 2009. "World Trade, Farm Policy, and Agribusiness Accountability: The Role of Reflexive Modernization in Constructing a Democratic Food System." *Southern Rural Sociology* 24 (2): 130–48.

Grundlach, Gregory T., and Albert A. Foer. 2008. "Buyer Power in Antitrust: An Overview of the American Antitrust Institute's Invitational Symposium on Buyer Power." *Antitrust Bulletin* 53 (2): 233–40.

Guthman, Julie. 2004. *Agrarian Dreams: The Paradox of Organic Farming in California*. Berkeley: University of California Press.

Heffernan, William D. 1972. "Sociological Dimensions of Agricultural Structures in the United States." *Sociologia Ruralis* 12 (2): 481–99. http://dx.doi.org/10.1111/j.1467-9523.1972.tb00156.x.

Heffernan, William D. 1982. "Structure of Agriculture and Quality of Life in Rural Communities." In *Rural Society in the U.S.: Issues for the 1980s*, ed. Don A. Dillman and Daryl J. Hobbs, 337–46. Boulder, CO: Westview Press.

Heffernan, William D. 1984. "Constraints in the Poultry Industry." In *Research in Rural Sociology and Development*, vol. 1. ed. Harry Schwarzweller, 237–60. Greenwich, CT: JAI Press.

Heffernan, William D. 2000. "Concentration of Ownership in Agriculture." In *Hungry for Profit: The Agribusiness Threat to Farmers, Food, and the Environment*, ed. Fred Magdoff, John Bellamy Foster, and Frederick H. Buttel, 61–76. New York: Monthly Review Press.

Heffernan, William D., and Douglas H. Constance. 1994. "Transnational Corporations and the Globalization of the Food System." In *From Columbus to ConAgra: The Globalization of Agriculture and Food*, ed. Alessandro Bonanno, Lawrence Busch, William H. Friedland, Lourdes Gouveia, and Enzo Mingione, 29–51. Lawrence: University Press of Kansas.

Heffernan, William D., Mary K. Hendrickson, and Robert Gronski. 1999. "Consolidation in the Food and Agriculture System." Report to the National Farmers Union. 8 January. http://www.foodcircles.missouri.edu/whstudy.pdf.

Hendrickson, Mary K., and William D. Heffernan. 2002. "Opening Spaces through Relocalization: Locating Potential Resistance in the Weaknesses of the Global Food System." *Sociologia Ruralis* 42 (4): 347–69. http://dx.doi.org/10.1111/1467-9523.00221.

Hendrickson, Mary K., William D. Heffernan, Philip Howard, and Judith Heffernan. 2001. "Consolidation in Food Retailing and Dairy." *British Food Journal* 103 (10): 715–28. http://dx.doi.org/10.1108/00070700110696742.

Hendrickson, Mary K., William D. Heffernan, David Lind, and Elizabeth Barham. 2008a. "Contractual Integration in Agriculture: Is There a Bright Side for Agriculture of the Middle." In *Food and the Mid-level Farm*, ed. Thomas A. Lyson, G.W. Stevenson, and Rick Welsh, 79–100. Cambridge, MA: MIT Press. http://dx.doi.org/10.7551/mitpress/9780262122993.003.0005.

Hendrickson, Mary K., and Harvey S. James. 2005. "The Ethics of Constrained Choice: How Industrialization of Agriculture Impacts Farming and Farmer Behavior." *Journal of Agricultural & Environmental Ethics* 18 (3): 269–91. http://dx.doi.org/10.1007/s10806-005-0631-5.

Hendrickson, Mary K., John Wilkinson, William D. Heffernan, and Robert Gronski. 2008b. The Global Food System and Nodes of Power. Oxfam America. Accessed 3 January 2012. http://papers.ssrn.com/sol3/papers.cfm?abstract_id=1337273.

Hoovers. 2012. Tyson Foods, Inc. Accessed 19 December 2013. http://www.hoovers.com/company-information/cs/company-profile.Tyson_Foods_Inc.240048b607bbdb3c.html .

Howard, Philip H. 2009a. "Consolidation in the North American Organic Food Processing Sector, 1997 to 2007." *International Journal of Sociology of Agriculture and Food* 16 (1): 13–30.

Howard, Philip H. 2009b. "Visualizing Consolidation in the Global Seed Industry: 1996–2008." *Sustainability* 1 (4): 1266–87. http://dx.doi.org/10.3390/su1041266.

Howard, Philip H., and Patricia Allen. 2010. "Beyond Organic and Fair Trade? An Analysis of Ecolabel Preferences in the United States." *Rural Sociology* 75 (2): 244–69. http://dx.doi.org/10.1111/j.1549-0831.2009.00009.x.

Hubbard, Kristina. 2009. Out of Hand: Farmers Face the Consequences of a Consolidated Seed Industry. Washington, DC: National Family Farm Coalition. Accessed 22 December 2011. http://farmertofarmercampaign.com/out%20of%20hand.full!report.pdf.

JBS. 2012. "JBS is Now the World's Biggest Provider of Meat." Accessed 13 April 2012. http://www.jbssa.com/News/News.aspx.

Jaffee, Daniel, and Philip H. Howard. 2010. "Corporate Cooptation of Organic and Fair Trade Standards." *Agriculture and Human Values* 27 (4): 387–99. http://dx.doi.org/10.1007/s10460-009-9231-8.

Jaffee, Daniel, and Philip H. Howard. 2012. "Visualizing Fair Trade Coffee." *For a Better World* 4 (Spring): 8–9.

James, Harvey S., Mary K. Hendrickson, and Philip H. Howard. 2013. "Networks, Power, and Dependency in the Agrifood Industry." In *The Ethics and Economics of Agrifood Competition*, ed. Harvey James, 99–126. New York: Springer Press. http://dx.doi.org/10.1007/978-94-007-6274-9_6.

Kleiner, Anna M., and John J. Green. 2009. "The Contributions of Dr. William Heffernan and the Missouri School of Agrifood Studies." *Southern Rural Sociology* 24 (2): 14–28.

Lobao, Linda. 1990. *Locality and Inequality: Farm Structure, Industry Structure, and Socioeconomic Conditions.* Albany: The State University of New York Press.

Lobao, Linda, and Curtis W. Stofferahn. 2008. "The Community Effects of Industrialized Farming: Social Science Research and Challenges to Corporate Farming Laws." *Agriculture and Human Values* 25 (2): 219–40. http://dx.doi.org/10.1007/s10460-007-9107-8.

Lynn, Barry C. 2009. *Cornered: The Monopoly Capitalism and the Politics of Destruction.* Hoboken, NJ: John Wiley and Sons.

Lyson, Thomas. 2004. *Civic Agriculture: Reconnecting Farm, Food, and Community.* Medford, MA: Tufts University Press.

Martinson, Oscar B., and Gerald R. Campbell. 1980. "Betwixt and Between: Farmers and the Marketing of Agricultural Inputs and Outputs." In *The Rural Sociology of Advanced Societies: Critical Perspectives*, ed. Frederick H. Buttel and Howard Newby, 215–54. Montclair, NJ: Allenheld, Osmun.

McIntyre, Beverly D., Hans R. Herren, Judi Wakhungu, and Robert T. Watson, eds. 2009. Agriculture at a Crossroads: A Synthesis of the Global and Sub-Global IAASTD Reports. International Assessment of Agricultural Knowledge, Science, and Technology for Development. Accessed 19 December 2013. http://www.academia.edu/4564144/Agriculture_at_a_Crossroads_Global_Report.

McMichael, Philip. 1996. *Development and Social Change.* Thousand Oaks, CA: Pine Forge Press.

Mooney, Patrick, and Theo J. Majka. 1995. *Farmers and Farm Workers Movements: Social Protest in American Agriculture.* New York: Twayne Publishers.

Moss, Diana L. 2011. "Competition and Transgenic Seed Systems." *Antitrust Bulletin* 56 (1): 81–103.

Olson, Mancur. 1965. *The Logic of Collective Action: Public Goods and the Theory of Groups.* Boston, MA: Harvard University Press.

Polanyi, Karl. 1944. *The Great Transformation: The Political and Economic Origins of Our Time.* Boston, MA: Beacon Press.

Pollack, Andrew. 2010. "Monsanto's Fortunes Turn Sour." *New York Times*, 5 October.

Reardon, Thomas, Spencer Henson, and Julio Berdegué. 2007. "Proactive Fast Tracking Diffusion of Supermarkets in Developing Countries: Implications for Market Institutions and Trade." *Journal of Economic Geography* 7 (4): 399–431. http://dx.doi.org/10.1093/jeg/lbm007.

Taylor, C. Robert. 2010. "Fertilizer Cartels: Market Power and Sustainability Issues." Presentation at the annual meeting of the Organization for Competitive Markets. Omaha, NE. 11 August.

UNCTAD. 2006. "Tracking the Trend towards Market Concentration: The Case of the Agricultural Input Industry." Geneva: United Nations Conference on Trade and Development. Accessed 19 December 2013. http://unctad.org/en/docs/ditccom200516_en.pdf.

USDA/USDOJ (US Department of Agriculture/Department of Justice). 2010a. Public Workshops Exploring Competition in Agriculture: Poultry Workshop. Alabama A&M University. Normal, AL. 21 June. http://www.google.com/t&rct=j&q=&esrc=s&frm=1&source=web&cd=10&ved=0CGMQFjAJ&url=http%3A%2F%2Fmeetings.t.g%2Fwebupload%2Fcommupload%2FAT800006%2Frelatedresources%2FPoultryWorkshopTranscript.pdf&ei=KoKwUoSzK8O72QXD_oCADw&usg=AFQjCNHc_oXBYq4HPwWS5HnB1W8XXY0Yjw&bvm=bv.57967247,d.b2I.

USDA/USDOJ (US Department of Agriculture/Department of Justice). 2010b. *Agriculture and Antitrust Enforcement Issues in Our 21st Century Economy.* Washington, DC: US Department of Agriculture and US Department of Justice.

La Via Campesina. 2012. "What is La Via Campesina." Accessed 19 December 2013. http://viacampesina.org/en/.

Wellford, Harrison. 1972. *Sowing the Wind.* New York: Grossman Publishers.

Wilkinson, John. 2002. "The Final Foods Industry and the Changing Face of the Global Agrofood System: Up against a New Technology Paradigm and a New Demand Profile." *Sociologia Ruralis* 42: 329–47. http://dx.doi.org/10.1111/1467-9523.00220.

Wise, Timothy A., and Sarah E. Trist. 2010. Buyer Power in U.S. Hog Markets: A Critical Review of the Literature. Global Development and Environment Institute Working Paper No. 10–04, Tufts University.

Wrigley, Neil, and Michelle Lowe. 2007. "Introduction: Transnational Retail and the Global Economy." *Journal of Economic Geography* 7 (4): 337–40. http://dx.doi.org/10.1093/jeg/lbm025.

CHAPTER 2

The Declining Middle of American Agriculture: A Spatial Phenomenon

Amy Guptill and Rick Welsh

Introduction

The burgeoning food movement seems to herald an agricultural renaissance in the United States, Canada, and other countries of the global North. In the United States, small farms, particularly those with annual sales of less than $10,000, have grown steadily since 1992, and analysts note the surprising persistence of small farming in Europe, Australia, and New Zealand after decades of industrialization and growing corporate concentration (Aubert and Perrier-Cornet 2009; Swinnen 2009). This growth or persistence reflects, in part, increasing localized and direct marketing opportunities. In 1970, there were only about 340 farmers' markets in the United States (McKibben 2008, 81); by 2011, the US Department of Agriculture (USDA) counted almost 7,200 of them, marking a 17 percent increase over 2010. In the United Kingdom, the number of farmers' markets grew from only one in 1997 to 550 by 2006 (Kneafsey et al. 2008, 2). By 2012, farmers' market associations in Canada, Australia, and New Zealand counted over 500, 150, and fifty member markets, respectively. In the United States between 1992 and 2007, the number of farms selling direct to consumers grew 58 percent and the dollar value of all direct sales (adjusted for inflation) increased 77 percent (Low and Vogel 2011, 2).

However, the growing number and visibility of smaller farms masks the continued decline of the "agriculture of the middle": the farms, ranches, and related enterprises engaged in commodity-scale production largely outside of the corporate complexes that dominate the agrifood system (Lyson, Stevenson, and Welsh 2008). This middle sector is left in the gap as the agrifood system moves further toward a bifurcated structure, with the highly concentrated, corporate-controlled sector on one side and the growing localized, direct, and values-based food networks sector on the other. The value chains that mid-level farms traditionally anchored have uncoupled around them, leaving producers at loose ends, "too small to compete in the highly consolidated commodity markets, and too large and commoditized to sell in the direct markets" (Kirschenmann et al. 2008, 1). While farms of any scale can fall into this middle gap in market structure, researchers often track the declining middle by noting the shrinking number of farms in the United States selling between $10,000 and $250,000 per year, a category Hoppe, MacDonald, and Korb (2010, 5) call "small commercial."

Even with exciting developments in small-scale agrifood systems, there are good reasons to address the continuing crisis in the agriculture of the middle. First, mid-scale farms (broadly measured as $10,000 to $250,000 in annual sales) are a significant part of the farm population and resource base. In the United States such operations represent 36 percent of all farms, produce 22 percent of agricultural output, and steward 41 percent of the land in production (Hoppe et al. 2010, 6). Second, as demonstrated in an exhaustive literature, large numbers of mid-sized operations create healthy rural communities with positive effects for rural economies and rural residents in general (see Lobao 1990; Lobao, Hooks, and Tickamyer 2007; and Lyson, Torres, and Welsh 2001 for examples and reviews). Unlike the largest farms, which rely on vertical integration, and the smallest farms, which have little market power, mid-scale enterprises are the most likely to support a robust and diverse array of enterprises and community resources, contributing to a strong rural economy and vibrant community life (Lyson 2004). A third reason to direct more attention to the middle is the issue of farm succession. The operators of mid-level farms are overwhelmingly at or nearing retirement age, and there is a critical need for strategies to keep these farms viable in order to preserve the natural and social resources they provide (Kirschenmann et al. 2008). The unique contributions of mid-level farms have gained increased attention both within and beyond North America (Macken-Walsh 2011; Oosterveer and Sonnenfeld 2012).

Developing effective strategies to boost the viability, survival, and resurgence of mid-sized farming operations depends on a clear understanding of the dynamics that lead to the erosion of the middle and how those dynamics instantiate in space. This erosion has been well-analyzed (Duffy 2008; Kirschenmann et al. 2008), as have the kinds of value chains that offer promising opportunities for mid-level enterprises in the agrifood system (Gray and Stevenson 2008; Guptill and Welsh 2008; Stevenson and Pirog 2008). Less well-developed is inquiry into spatial factors such as urban/rural settlement and land-use patterns (Block and DuPuis 2001; Ling and Newman 2011) and state laws and regulations (Grow et al. 2003; Welsh, Hubbell, and Carpentier 2003). In this chapter, we first discuss the continued decline of mid-sized farms in the United States, with some comparisons to Canada. We next review emerging solutions to the problem of the disappearing middle, with a focus on value-chain approaches to rebuilding mid-level market structures. Following that, we explore the geography of the disappearing middle to demonstrate the need for nuanced spatial analyses of both the problem and potential solutions. Overall, we show that the decline of mid-sized farms continues to be an important food-system problem, one related to the increasing concentration of wealth in US society, and that potential solutions must take into account unique regional conditions.

The Disappearing Middle

While mid-level farms, as a category, are *scale-related* rather than *scale-determined*, we must use scale-based measures to make use of secondary statistics, and sales class has become the most often-used metric (Duffy 2008). USDA measures consider almost all mid-level farms "small" because they gross less than $250,000 in farm sales per year. In fact, over 90 percent of all US farms are considered small by this definition. A look at the trends among sales classes shows the inexorable decline of a broad agricultural middle in the United States.

Figure 2.1 shows the continued hollowing-out of agricultural structure: non-commercial farms (those selling less than $10,000 per year) and large farms (those grossing more than $250,000 per year) are growing in number, while all categories in between are shrinking. Strikingly, Figure 2.1 also shows that while large farms were far outnumbered by all other sales classes in 1982, they eclipsed all but the smallest farms by 1997. Paradoxically, the structural middle is now economically marginal.

Statistics from the United States and Canada show interesting comparisons (see Table 2.1 below). Both countries have seen the inexorable decline of mid-sized farms, and the most dramatic losses are among farms grossing at least $50,000 but less than $250,000 in sales. In Canada, farms in the $100,000 to $249,999 category declined 15.1 percent between 2001 and 2006; in the United States, the same approximate category shrunk by 11 percent between 2002 and 2007. Similarly, the largest farms—those grossing more than $500,000 per year—are growing the most dramatically in number, with a 26.7 percent growth (over five years) in Canada and 63.3 percent in the United States. A further breakdown shows that the largest of the large, those grossing more than $2 million annually, are growing the most dramatically in Canada: 36.7 percent between 2001 and 2006. The relatively small numbers of farms in these

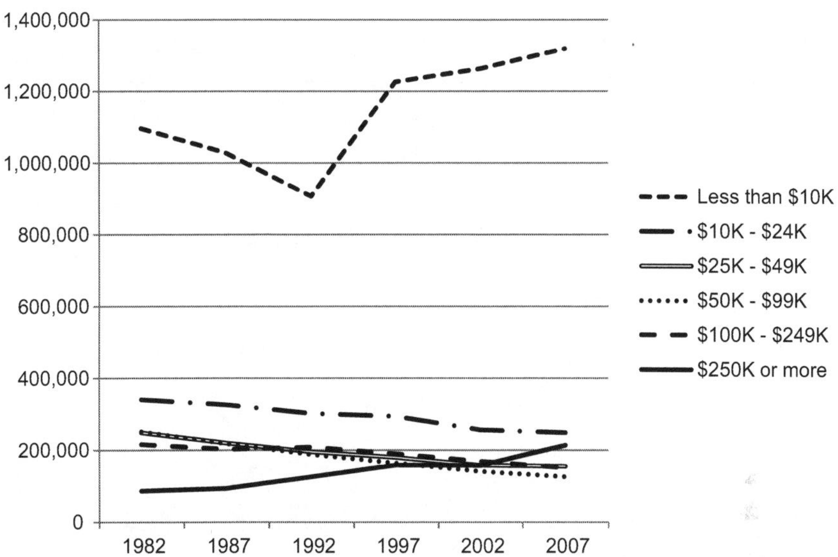

Figure 2.1. Trends in farm numbers by sales class, non-commercial, and commercial farms, 1982 to 2007. Sources: USDA Censuses of Agriculture 1987, 1992, 1997, 2002, 2007.

categories explains some of the dramatic percentages, but nevertheless, the cross-border parallels show a dominant trend that reflects shifts in the global agrifood system.

Interestingly, Canada and the United States differ on the fate of the smallest (non-commercial) farms. Canadian statistics show that farms grossing less than $10,000 per year shrunk 7.4 percent in number between 2001 and 2006, while those in the United States grew 4.4 percent between 2002 and 2007. This difference in non-commercial farm trends between Canada and the United States may reflect a relatively weaker growth in direct marketing outlets in Canada, perhaps due to shrinking land-base in peri-urban areas (Feagan, Morris, and Krug, 2004; Ling and Newman 2011). Alternatively, given that the majority (55 percent) of farms counted by the USDA are non-commercial, it may be that the smallest-scale producers in Canada have less access, or perhaps less motivation, to be counted as a "farm" in national statistics.

The 2010 data from Canada, the most recent available, indicate that these dual trends are only intensifying. Between 2006 and 2010 the number of farms in all sales categories below $500,000 per year shrunk, with an overall decline of 12 percent. Conversely, the number of farms with sales of $500,000 and

Table 2.1
Changing farm numbers by sales category in Canada and the United States

	Canada			United States		
	2006	2001	Percent Change	2007	2002	Percent Change
Total farms	229,373	246,923	-7.1	2,204,792	2,128,982	3.6
Less than $10,000	50,138	54,166	-7.4	1,319,160	1,263,052	4.4
$10,000 to $24,999	38,254	42,139	-9.2	248,285	256,157	-3.1
$25,000 to $49,999	30,608	34,145	-10.4	154,732	157,906	-2.0
$50,000 to $99,999	31,422	35,255	-10.9	125,456	140,479	-10.7
$100,000 to $249,999	39,971	47,079	-15.1	150,300	168,820	-11.0
$250,000 to $499,999	22,837	21,396	6.7	97,230	86,550	12.3
$500,000 or more	16,143	12,743	26.7	120,190	73,580	63.3
$500,000 to $999.999	10,241	8,380	22.2			
$1 million to $1.9 million	3,691	2,746	34.4			
$2 million or more	2,211	1,617	36.7			

Sources: USDA Censuses of Agriculture 1987, 1992, 1997, 2002, 2007; Statistics Canada, Farm Data and Farm Operator Data, 2006 Census of Agriculture, Catalogue No. 95-629-XWE. Ottawa: Statistics Canada.

above grew from 16,143 in 2006 to 23,570 in 2010, an astonishing 46 percent growth. The 2012 US Census of Agriculture will likely show that the crisis of the agricultural middle continues.

Explaining the Disappearing Middle

Mid-level farms are not just losing ground numerically; they are also losing market power and government support. Both the smallest and largest farms are growing in number, but only the largest farms are capturing a growing proportion of agricultural income and public resources. Small non-commercial farms (grossing less than $10,000 per year), now 55 percent of the 2.2 million farms in the United States, still account for only 1 percent of all agricultural production (Hoppe et al. 2010, 6). Conversely, the top 2 percent of farms, those grossing over $1 million, produce 47 percent of agricultural output by volume (Hoppe et al.,

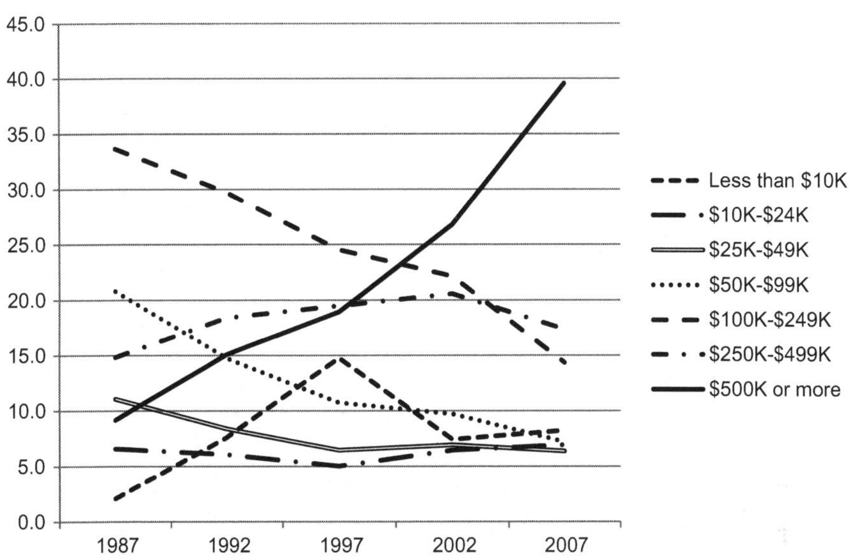

Figure 2.2. Percent of all government payments accruing to each sales class, 1987 to 2007. Source: USDA Censuses of Agriculture 1987, 1992, 1997, 2002, and 2007.

2010, 6). Almost all small farms depend on off-farm income to sustain operations, leading Lobao and Meyer (2001, 103) to characterize the ever-deepening crisis in agriculture as "the abandonment of farming as a livelihood strategy." Thus, the disappearing middle is not just the struggles of a particular sector. Rather, it reflects the ever-increasing dominance of the largest farming operations and the large agribusiness corporations through which they both source and market (Constance et al. in this volume; Hinrichs and Welsh 2003; Lobao and Meyer 2001; Lyson 2004).

Figure 2.2 shows that, in addition to sales, the share of government payments that accrue to the largest farms (those grossing $500,000 or more) has grown dramatically since the 1980s. The one exception is large farms grossing between $250,000 and $499,000; they saw their share of government payments rise until 2002 before falling in 2007. The most dramatic declines shown in Figures 2.2 are among farms grossing between $100,000 and $249,000 in sales. Those farms received the largest portion of government payments in the 1980s and 1990s, but have since been eclipsed by the largest sales classes.

A recent report published by the USDA's Economic Research Service reveals that as agricultural subsidies increasingly accrue to large farms, they also disproportionately benefit higher-income households (White and Hoppe 2012). They write (2012, 28):

> Half of commodity payments went to farms operated by households with incomes over $89,540, a quarter went to farms operated by households with incomes greater than $209,000 and 10 percent went to farms operated by households with incomes greater than or equal to $425,000. In 2009, the median household income among all US households was $49,777, practically the same as in 1991.

Comparatively, in 1991, half of commodity payments went to farms operated by households with incomes over $54,940 (in 2009 dollars), much closer to the US household median income of $47,453. White and Hoppe (2012, 8) further explain that because "64 percent of cropland is operated by someone other than the owner," and 94 percent of rented acres are owned by non-farmers, the higher land-rent prices that government subsidies enable mean that some of the value of those subsidies accrues to non-farming landowners. Kirwan (2009) estimates that non-farming landowners capture one quarter of the value of government agricultural subsidies.

In addition to benefiting disproportionately from public largesse, the largest farms are also best positioned to make use of financial risk-management products to profit even when production conditions are poor, leading one *New York Times* journalist to dub them "farming's own one percent" (Davidson 2012, para. 9). Not only are these farms at the apex of an increasingly concentrated industry, they also benefit from a broader economic shift from material production to finance as the driver of capital accumulation (Bonanno in this volume; Burch and Lawrence 2009). This financialization of agriculture and the food system marks an ongoing trend: the corporate concentration of the food system and the marginalization of most agricultural producers therein.

Rebuilding Mid-level Value Chains

One promising response to the disappearing middle focuses on "developing strategic business alliances among small and medium sized farms or ranches and other agrifood enterprises" that "(a) handle significant volumes of high quality, differentiated food products; (b) operate effectively at regional, multistate levels; and (c) distribute profits equitably among the strategic partners" (Stevenson et al. 2011, 27). Scholars call these arrangements "value chains" to denote both the high quality of the products and services, as well as the high priority given to enduring, mutually beneficial business relationships (Stevenson et al. 2011).

Some value chains focus on a single or small number of commodities, while others bring together many different products to serve retail and consumer markets. A prominent example of the former is Organic Valley, the brand name of the CROPP cooperative, which promotes its cooperative-produced dairy products by emphasizing organic production and family-scale farming (Day-Farnsworth and Morales 2011). Another commodity-based example is a value chain anchored by Country Natural Beef, a 120-member farm cooperative in the Northwest United States that maintains rigorous quality standards as well as enduring relationships with a custom feedlot, a mid-scale meat processor, and regional supermarket and hamburger restaurant chains (Stevenson and Pirog 2008). An example of a diversified chain is Red Tomato, a Boston-based nonprofit that forges links to get high-quality fruits and vegetables from the Northeast region into grocery stores and other outlets in ways that communicate the unique qualities of the products to consumers (Stevenson et al. 2011). All of these value chains begin with differentiated, but not niche, products and take shape in a relational business model that makes the conditions of production and trade more transparent to buyers (Day-Farnsworth and Morales 2011). Similar efforts seek to bring small-scale producers into mid-level market structures by coordinating products' aggregation, distribution, and/or collective marketing, either to institutions or direct to consumers. Examples include multifunctional food hubs (Schmidt et al. 2011), geographic indication systems that function as a collective inalienable brand (Giovannucci, Barham, and Pirog 2010, multi-farm CSAs (Berman 2011), farm-to-institution programs (Feenstra et al. 2011), and online local food markets (Guptill 2012).

Comparative studies of mid-level value chains indicate that their chief challenges are "aggregation, transparency and source identity throughout the supply chain, and fair pricing practices" (Day-Farnsworth and Morales 2011, 228). In its simple sense, aggregation is just gathering products from multiple growers. In the process of forging mid-level value chains, however, successful aggregation depends on "determining effective strategies for product differentiation, branding, and regional identity" (Stevenson et al. 2011, 31) and "employing farmers and ranchers as business representatives, storytellers, and listeners" (Lev and Stevenson 2011, 121). Maintaining "transparency and source identity throughout the value chain" (Day-Farnsworth and Morales 2011, 228) requires shared decision-making among producers and other value-chain partners that, in turn, depends on establishing and maintaining trust. A trust-based collaboration ensures consistent product quality, maintains logistical efficiency, and communicates "the deeper, more complex values" (Lev and Stevenson 2011, 121) associated with the product throughout the chain. The final challenge, appropriate pricing, must be met in order to sustain the value chain and its component enterprises within the broader food system. In these differentiated chains, prices are set to represent the true costs of production and the need for stability within the chain (Lev and Stevenson 2011; Stevenson et al. 2011). In contrast to conventional chains, value chains make sure that all participants understand such costs and needs.

Two features are notable about the value-chains approach to rebuilding an agricultural middle. First, while the people and organizations addressing the disappearing middle directly indict the government policies that accelerate agricultural concentration, the value-chains solution exists almost completely in the private sector. Concerned entrepreneurs and activists are first seeking to build a more autonomous agrifood system, and only secondarily making modest demands on the state to revise agricultural lending, regulation, procurement, and research-sponsorship practices to better support this rebuilding project (Ray and Schaffer 2008). Demands for more vigorous antitrust enforcement in agriculture, for example, has been muted (Carstensen 2008). The largely privatized value-chains approach has yielded notable successes, but the strategy raises important questions about the changing relationship between the public and the state and whether such shifts mark a capitulation to neoliberalism (Bonanno in this volume).

A second notable feature of the value-chains approach is that the conceptual framework is inherently spatial, yet to date little scholarly attention has been paid to how these agrifood market structures instantiate in place. On one hand, the very notion of a mid-level value chain rests on the idea of region as a space delineated by connections among natural and social features. The research reviewed above notes that many successful mid-level value chains engage with a regional identity in upholding a sense of values shared among producers, consumers, and all enterprise partners in between. Additionally, clearly the challenges of aggregation, transparency, and pricing all have critical spatial contexts. On the other hand, there is not yet a substantial body of literature comparing regions according to their distinct confluences of constraints and opportunities. In the following section, we explore the disappearing middle on both a national scale and through simple regional comparisons in order to demonstrate that bringing space to the core of the analysis would yield additional, nuanced insight into agrifood system change.

Exploring the Spatial Dimensions of Mid-level Agriculture

The maps in Figures 2.3, 2.4, and 2.5 show that different areas are seeing different trends in farm structure. Figure 2.3 shows that farms grossing between $10,000 and $99,000 per year, the smaller of Hoppe et al.'s (2010) small-commercial farms,[1] are declining throughout the Midwest and parts of the Great Plains as

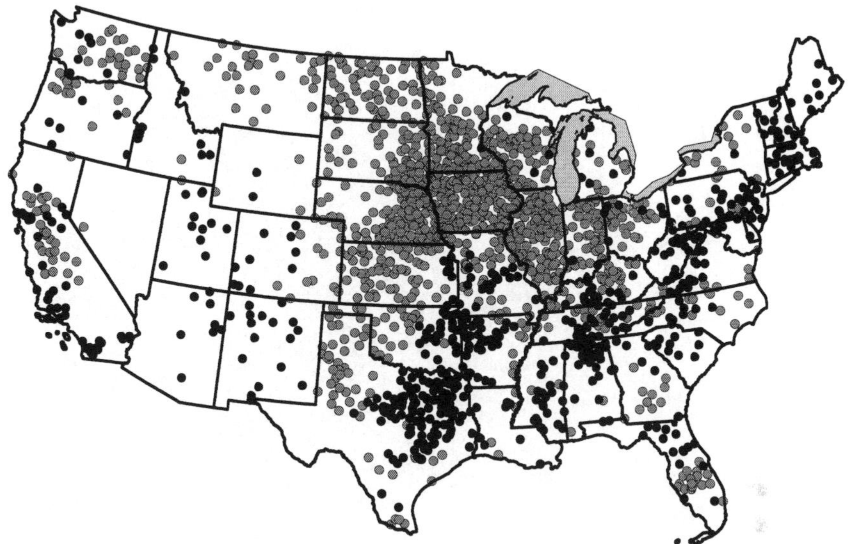

Figure 2.3. The growth (black circle) and decline (gray circle) of farms grossing $10,000 to $99,999 per year between 2002 and 2007. Each symbol represents fifty farms. Source: USDA Census of Agriculture 2002, 2007; 2010 Census of Population and Housing.

well as in California's Central Valley. Other notable clusters of farm loss in this category are found in Pacific coastal states and some areas within the South. At the same time, the numbers of farms in this category are growing in the Northeast, Appalachia, eastern Texas, the Ozarks, and the four-corners region, among other areas.

The map in Figure 2.3 illustrates how national trends are playing out in distinct regional patterns. Figures 2.4 and 2.5 provide a closer look at two regions, the Midwest and the South, and overlay the growth and decline of the same farm-size category onto county metropolitan status, as defined by the Office of Management and Budget in 2010. Figure 2.4, displaying the Midwest region, shows that while the decline of mid-scale farms is much more prevalent than their growth, the areas seeing growth are primarily in and around metropolitan statistical areas (MSAs). In contrast, Figure 2.5, depicting the South, shows a much more varied association between metropolitan status and growth of small-commercial farms. These farms are growing in metropolitan and peri-metropolitan areas, as in the Midwest, but also in some more rural areas. One plausible implication of this pattern is that agrifood entrepreneurs in more rural areas would do well to focus on commodity-based aggregation strategies

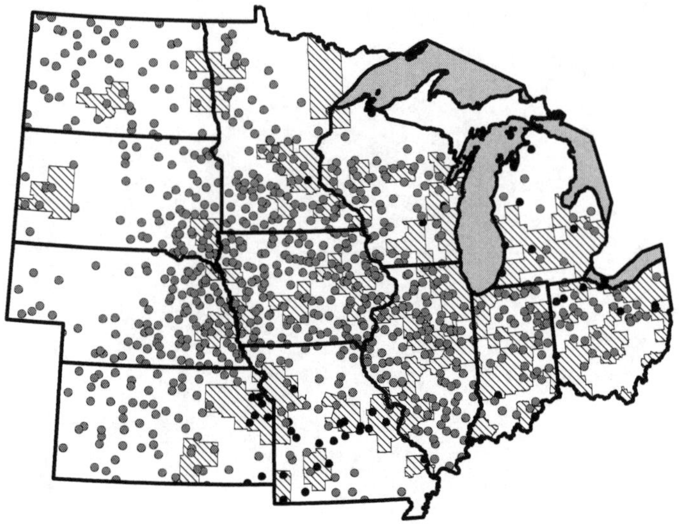

Figure 2.4. The gain (black circle) and loss (gray circle) of farms grossing between $10,000 and $99,999 per year, 2002 to 2007, and metropolitan counties in the Midwest. Each symbol represents fifty farms. Source: USDA Census of Agriculture 2002, 2007; 2010 Census of Population and Housing.

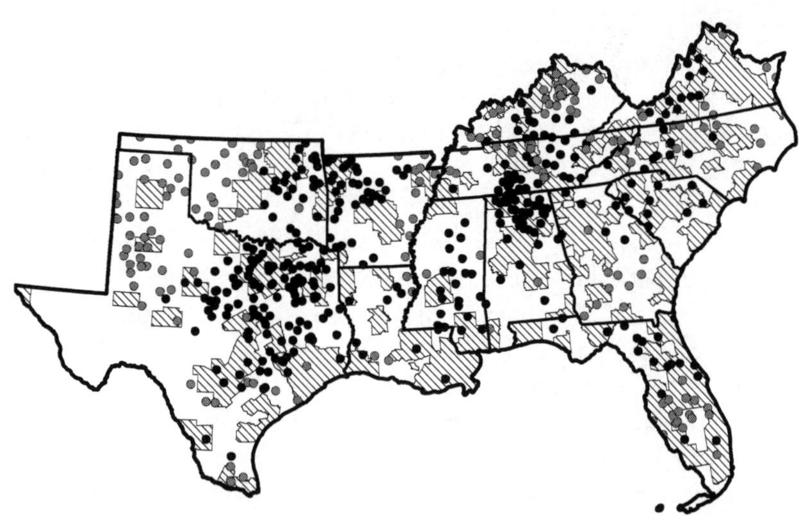

Figure 2.5. The gain (black circle) and loss (grey circle) of farms grossing between $10,000 and $99,999 per year, 2002 to 2007, and metropolitan counties in the South. Each symbol represents fifty farms. Source: USDA Census of Agriculture 2002, 2007; 2010 Census of Population and Housing.

to support and rebuild mid-level structures, such as agricultural cooperatives like those Gray and Stevenson (2008) and Guptill and Welsh (2008) profile. Those located in more peri-urban areas might better focus on mixed-product value chains that include prominent roles for retailers and consumers; for example, multifunctional food hubs (Schmidt et al. 2011) or farm-processor-restaurant chains such as the one anchored by Country Natural Beef (Stevenson and Pirog 2008). Clearly, much more research is needed, both to situate successful models more firmly in their geographic context and to elucidate the broader spatial patterns of changes in agrifood structure.

The Declining Middle in Spatial Perspective

The agriculture-of-the-middle movement—including scholarship, entrepreneurship, and activism—has made an invaluable contribution by bridging the large/small or local/global dualisms that have tended to dominate food systems thinking in recent years, and by renewing the claim that sustainable food systems must provide sustainable livelihoods (see Bonanno in this volume). Despite steep challenges and unavoidable contradictions, efforts to rebuild the middle can claim notable successes and an impressively diverse array of strategies. Careful studies of these cases have yielded important process-based insights about how the ties among participants are forged and maintained, as well as a robust conceptual foundation for understanding and evaluating these processes.

Now needed is a spatially informed and multi-scalar integration of these insights. The statistical and geographic profiles we provide here show that, despite promising cases, the problem of the disappearing middle is far from solved: mid-level farms continue to vanish, and their loss has a broad and negative impact on rural communities and society at large (Lobao et al. 2007; Lyson et al. 2001). Entrepreneurs and activists need a clearer picture of how the key features of their unique regional contexts may point to the most promising solutions. Just as small-scale alternative food efforts are scaling up to achieve greater stability and impact, scholars must scale up from insightful case studies to provide a more integrated picture.

The line of research reviewed here also suggests a need to reengage with the state to broaden the distribution of resources and power in the food system. While many organizations and businesses within celebrated value-chain cases have sourced small innovation grants from various USDA agencies (see Fitzgerald, Evans, and Daniel 2010), federal policy as a whole overwhelmingly exacerbates the growing concentration of power within a small number of agrifood corporations (Constance et al. in this volume), in part through the financialization of agriculture (Burch and Lawrence 2009). The entrepreneurialism of those rebuilding the agricultural middle is both admirable and politically compelling, but the national and global policy contexts cannot be ignored.

Notes

1 Ideally, we would include farms grossing up to $249,999 per year in this category, however, county-level census data aggregates all farms grossing $100,000 or more.

References

Aubert, Magali, and Philippe Perrier-Cornet. 2009. "Is There a Future for Small Farms in Developed Countries? Evidence from the French Case." *Agricultural Economics* 40 (s1): 797–806. http://dx.doi.org/10.1111/j.1574-0862.2009.00416.x.

Berman, Elizabeth. 2011. "Creating a Community Food System: The Intervale Center." *Journal of Agricultural & Food Information* 12 (1): 3–11. http://dx.doi.org/10.1080/10496505.2011.539527.

Block, Daniel, and Melanie DuPuis. 2001. "Making the Country Work for the City: Von Thünen's Ideas in Geography, Agricultural Economics and the Sociology of Agriculture." *American Journal of Economics and Sociology* 60 (1): 79–98.

Burch, David, and Geoffrey Lawrence. 2009. "Towards a Third Food Regime: Behind the Transformation." *Agriculture and Human Values* 26 (4): 267–79. http://dx.doi.org/10.1007/s10460-009-9219-4.

Carstensen, Peter. 2008. "The Prospects and Limits of Antitrust and Competitive-Market Strategies." In *Food and the Mid-level Farm: Renewing an Agriculture of the Middle*, ed. T.A. Lyson, G.W. Stevenson, and R. Welsh, 227–52. Cambridge, MA: MIT Press. http://dx.doi.org/10.7551/mitpress/9780262122993.003.0012.

Davidson, Adam. 2012. "Even Dairy Farming Has a 1 Percent." *New York Times*, 11 March.

Day-Farnsworth, Lindsey, and Alfonso Morales. 2011. "Satiating the Demand: Planning for Alternative Models of Regional Food Distribution." *Journal of Agriculture, Food Systems, and Community Development* 2 (1): 227–48. http://dx.doi.org/10.5304/jafscd.2011.021.020.

Duffy, Mike. 2008. "Appendix: The Changing Status of Farms and Ranches of the Middle." In *Food and the Mid-level Farm: Renewing an Agriculture of the Middle*, ed. T.A. Lyson, G.W. Stevenson, and R. Welsh, 257–83. Cambridge, MA: MIT Press.

Feagan, Robert, David Morris, and Karen Krug. 2004. "Niagara Region Farmers' Markets: Local Food Systems and Sustainability Considerations." *Local Environment* 9 (3): 235–54. http://dx.doi.org/10.1080/1354983042000219351.

Feenstra, Gail W., Patricia Allen, Shermain D. Hardesty, Jeri Ohmart, and Jan Perez. 2011. "Using a Supply Chain Analysis to Assess the Sustainability of Farm-to-Institution Programs." *Journal of Agriculture, Food Systems, and Community Development* 1 (4): 69–84. http://dx.doi.org/10.5304/jafscd.2011.014.009.

Fitzgerald, Kate, Lucy Evans, and Jessica Daniel. 2010. *The National Sustainable Agriculture Coalition's Guide to USDA Funding for Local and Regional Food Systems.* Washington, DC: National Sustainable Agriculture Coalition.

Giovannucci, Daniele, Elizabeth Barham, and Richard Pirog. 2010. "Defining and Marketing 'Local' Foods: Geographical Indications for US Products." *Journal of World Intellectual Property* 13 (2): 94–120. http://dx.doi.org/10.1111/j.1747-1796.2009.00370.x.

Gray, Thomas W., and G.W. Stevenson. 2008. "Cooperative Structure for the Middle: Mobilizing for Power and Identity." In *Food and the Mid-level Farm: Renewing an Agriculture of the Middle*, ed. T.A. Lyson, G.W. Stevenson, and R. Welsh, 37–54. Cambridge, MA: MIT Press. http://dx.doi.org/10.7551/mitpress/9780262122993.003.0003.

Grow, Shelly, Amy Guptill, Thomas A. Lyson, and Rick Welsh. 2003. "The Effect of Laws That Foster Agricultural Bargaining: The Case of Apple Growers in Michigan and New York State." In *Food and the Mid-level Farm: Renewing an Agriculture of the Middle*, ed. Thomas A. Lyson, G.W. Stevenson, and Rick Welsh, 179–202. Cambridge, MA: MIT Press.

Guptill, Amy. 2012. "Spatial Patterns of Local Food Marketing." Unpublished paper presented at the annual meeting of the Association of American Geographers. New York, NY.

Guptill, Amy, and Rick Welsh. 2008. "Is Relationship Marketing an Alternative to the Corporatization of Organics? A Case Study of OFARM." In *Food and the Mid-level Farm: Renewing an Agriculture of the Middle*, ed. Thomas A. Lyson, G.W. Stevenson, and Rick Welsh, 55–78. Cambridge, MA: MIT Press. http://dx.doi.org/10.7551/mitpress/9780262122993.003.0004.

Hinrichs, C. Clare, and Rick Welsh. 2003. "The Effects of the Industrialization of US Livestock Agriculture on Promoting Sustainable Production Practices." *Agriculture and Human Values* 20 (2): 125–41. http://dx.doi.org/10.1023/A:1024061425531.

Hoppe, Robert A., James M. MacDonald, and Penni Korb. 2010. *Small Farms in the United States: Persistence Under Pressure (EIB-63)*. Washington, DC: Economic Research Service, United States Department of Agriculture.

Kirwan, Barrett E. 2009. "The Incidence of US Agricultural Subsidies on Farmland Rental Rates." *Journal of Political Economy* 117 (1): 138–64. http://dx.doi.org/10.1086/598688.

Kirschenmann, Fred, G.W. Stevenson, Frederick Buttel, Thomas A. Lyson, and Mike Duffy. 2008. "Why Worry about the Agriculture of the Middle?" In *Food and the Mid-level Farm: Renewing an Agriculture of the Middle*, ed. Thomas A. Lyson, G.W. Stevenson, and Rick Welsh, 3–22. Cambridge, MA: MIT Press. http://dx.doi.org/10.7551/mitpress/9780262122993.003.0001.

Kneafsey, Moya, Lewis Holloway, Elizabeth Dowler, Laura Venn, and Helena Tuomainen. 2008. *Reconnecting Consumers, Producers and Food: Exploring Alternatives.* Oxford, NY: Berg.

Lev, Larry, and G.W. Stevenson. 2011. "Acting Collectively to Develop Midscale Food Value Chains." *Journal of Agriculture, Food Systems, and Community Development* 1 (4): 119–28. http://dx.doi.org/10.5304/jafscd.2011.014.014.

Ling, Chris, and Lenore Lauri Newman. 2011. "Untangling the Food Web: Farm-to-Market Distances in British Columbia, Canada." *Local Environment* 16 (8): 807–22. http://dx.doi.org/10.1080/13549839.2010.539602.

Lobao, Linda M. 1990. *Locality and Inequality: Farm and Industry Structure and Socioeconomic Conditions.* Albany: State University of New York Press.

Lobao, Linda M., Gregory Hooks, and Ann R. Tickamyer. 2007. *The Sociology of Spatial Inequality.* Albany: State University of New York Press.

Lobao, Linda, and Katherine Meyer. 2001. "The Great Agricultural Transition: Crisis, Change, and Social Consequences of Twentieth Century US Farming." *Annual Review of Sociology* 27 (1): 103–24. http://dx.doi.org/10.1146/annurev.soc.27.1.103.

Low, Sarah A., and Stephen Vogel. 2011. *Direct and Intermediated Marketing of Local Foods in the United States (ERR-128).* Washington, DC: US Department of Agriculture, Economic Research Service.

Lyson, Thomas A. 2004. *Civic Agriculture: Reconnecting Farm, Food, and Community.* Medford, MA: Tufts University Press.

Lyson, Thomas A., G.W. Stevenson, and Rick Welsh, eds. 2008. *Food and the Mid-level Farm: Renewing an Agriculture of the Middle.* Cambridge, MA: MIT Press. http://dx.doi.org/10.7551/mitpress/9780262122993.001.0001.

Lyson, Thomas A., Robert J. Torres, and Rick Welsh. 2001. "Scale of Agricultural Production, Civic Engagement, and Community Welfare." *Social Forces* 80 (1): 311–27. http://dx.doi.org/10.1353/sof.2001.0079.

Macken-Walsh, Aine. 2011. "The Potential of an 'Agriculture of the Middle' Model in the Context of EU Rural Development: An American Solution to an Irish Problem?" *Journal of Agriculture, Food Systems, and Community Development* 1 (4): 177–88. http://dx.doi.org/10.5304/jafscd.2011.014.018.

McKibben, Bill. 2008. *Deep Economy: The Wealth of Communities and the Durable Future.* Oxford, UK: Macmillan.

Oosterveer, Peter, and David A. Sonnenfeld. 2012. *Food, Globalization and Sustainability.* New York: Earthscan.

Ray, Daryll E., and Harwood D. Schaffer. 2008. "Toward a Pro-middle Farm Policy: What Will it Take to Ensure a Promising Future for Family Farming?" In *Food and the Mid-level Farm: Renewing an Agriculture of the Middle,* ed. T.A. Lyson, G.W. Stevenson, and R. Welsh, 147–64. Cambridge, MA: MIT Press. http://dx.doi.org/10.7551/mitpress/9780262122993.003.0008.

Schmidt, Michele C., Jane M. Kolodinsky, Thomas P. DeSisto, and Faye C. Conte. 2011. "Increasing Farm Income and Local Food Access: A Case Study of a Collaborative Aggregation, Marketing, and Distribution Strategy That Links Farmers to Markets." *Journal of Agriculture, Food Systems, and Community Development* 1 (4): 157–75. http://dx.doi.org/10.5304/jafscd.2011.014.017.

Stevenson, G.W., Kate Clancy, Robert King, Larry Lev, Marcia Ostrom, and Stewart Smith. 2011. "Midscale Food Value Chains: An Introduction." *Journal of Agriculture, Food Systems, and Community Development* 1 (4): 1–8. http://dx.doi.org/10.5304/jafscd.2011.014.007.

Stevenson, G.W., and Rich Pirog. 2008. "Values-Based Supply Chains: Strategies for Agrifood Enterprises of the Middle." In *Food and the Mid-level Farm: Renewing an Agriculture of the Middle,* ed. T.A. Lyson, G.W. Stevenson, and R. Welsh, 119–44. Cambridge, MA: MIT Press. http://dx.doi.org/10.7551/mitpress/9780262122993.003.0007.

Swinnen, Johan F.M. 2009. "Reforms, Globalization, and Endogenous Agricultural Structures." *Agricultural Economics* 40 (s1): 719–32. http://dx.doi.org/10.1111/j.1574-0862.2009.00410.x.

Welsh, R., Bryan Hubbell, and Chantal Line Carpentier. 2003. "Agro-food System Restructuring and the Geographic Concentration of US Swine Production." *Environment & Planning A* 35 (2): 215–29. http://dx.doi.org/10.1068/a352.

White, T. Kirk, and Robert A. Hoppe. 2012. *Changing Farm Structure and the Distribution of Farm Payments and Federal Crop Insurance.* Washington, DC: Economic Research Service, United States Department of Agriculture.

CHAPTER 3

Land Ownership in American Agriculture

Douglas Jackson-Smith and Peggy Petrzelka[1]

Introduction

One of the core cultural ideas that influenced the founding of the American republic was that a society with many independent property-owning farmers would serve as an important bulwark against tyranny and concentrated economic and political power. This distinctively American form of "agrarianism" held that landownership tied farmers to their local area and community and gave them a material stake in the decisions of local and national political institutions (Dalecki and Coughenour 1992). Relatively egalitarian patterns of landownership at the time reinforced the image of the United States as a nation of "family farmers" whose property interests demanded democratic approaches to governmental decision making. While scholars note that this agrarian idea was sometimes at odds with the realities of life in colonial America (Geisler and Popper 1984), the iconic image of the independent landowning family farmer remains a potent cultural and political idea (Browne et al. 1992). In this chapter, we review the theoretical arguments and empirical evidence surrounding trends in agricultural landownership in the United States. We discuss the implications of recent changes in landownership for farm decision-making, environmental behaviors, and local community well-being, as well as research and policy needs.

Landownership and Land Tenure in Social Theory

Sociologists have long recognized property (and particularly land) ownership as a critical determinant of social, economic, and cultural power in society. Feudalism, tenancy, and other inegalitarian patterns of landownership in Europe and Asia served as historical cases in the development of the critical sociological theories of Karl Marx and Max Weber. Similarly, the idea that private property rights are "natural" and the normative ideal of a society that consists of independent property-owning entrepreneurs fundamentally shaped the theoretical views of early liberal social theorists such as John Locke, Adam Smith, and John Stuart Mill (Macpherson 1978).

Modern property rights theorists argue that property rights are never "natural," but rather can only exist in the context of a society and state institutions that define and enforce the specific rights and duties associated with property ownership (Bromley 1991). They recognize a range of different forms of property-rights arrangements that include private property but also acknowledge the important role for communal and state-owned property in most societies (Dietz, Ostrom, and Stern 2003). Most contemporary scholars view ownership as a "bundle of sticks," combinations of which reflect the diverse relationships individuals have with their property under different societal arrangements (Honoré 1961). For example, the rights to acquire, possess, sell, and transfer property are distinct from the rights to use property in various ways, or the rights to prevent non-property owners from accessing or using property. People who lease property pay the owner a fee (rent) to obtain some of these rights (such as the right to use the property for agricultural production) for a specified time-period. While laws and legal institutions are important mechanisms for defining the nature and extent of property ownership in any society, a great deal of what influences and constrains property owners' behaviors is a reflection of cultural factors. For example, studies of farmers from different ethnic and nationality backgrounds in the United States suggest that similar legal arrangements can produce quite different patterns of land management, tenure, and intergenerational transfers across generations (Cross, Jackson-Smith, and Barham 2000; Salamon 1995).

There is a long history of interest in property rights and landownership in rural sociology. Studies of the penetration of capitalism into agriculture in advanced capitalist societies point to the rise of tenancy/rent and debt among farmers as evidence that landlords and bankers are extracting surplus value from farm households through exploitative rental and lending practices (Mooney 1988). However, the fact that social relationships over property are manifest in diverse ways across nations, cultures, and historical eras makes it difficult to argue that property ownership inherently involves the exploitation by owners of non-owners. There is growing appreciation that the locus of power may lie more in managerial control over land (use rights) than in fee-simple ownership (legal ownership rights). We discuss this in more detail below.

Trends in Land Ownership in US Agriculture

Tenure Status of Farm Operators

There are two overlapping approaches to classifying landownership patterns in agriculture. First, one can focus on the land tenure status of the farm operator. From this perspective, the relevant categories of landownership for farmers in a capitalist economy include *full owners* (who own all the land they operate), *part owners* (who own some, but not all, of their farmed land), and *full tenants* (who own none of the land they operate). Information about land tenure in the periodic US Census of Agriculture is obtained from surveys of farm operators, and census reports have long disaggregated results by these three land-tenure status categories.[2]

Approximately 922 million acres of US farmland (42 percent of the nation's land base) was operated in 2007.[3] Over one third of this farmland (37 percent) was operated by full owners, a group that comprised almost 70 percent of all farm operators and produced nearly 40 percent of all farm sales that year (USDA-NASS 2009). Meanwhile, part owners accounted for only one-quarter of US farms, but generated half of the total value of US farm sales. As a group, part owners owned slightly less than half of the total land they operated and dominated the market for rented farmland. Their importance in the US farm sector increased rapidly from the 1920s through the early 1980s, but has remained relatively constant since that time (Figure 3.1).

The rise of the part-owner farm category in the latter twentieth century reflects a dramatic shift from full tenancy to part ownership over the last eighty years (Figure 3.2). In the early twentieth century, full tenants operated most rented farmland in the United States, reflecting in large part the legacy of plantation agriculture in the South, with many former slaves working as share croppers for white landowners. The Great Depression and World War II brought the collapse of full tenancy and share cropping (and a dramatic decline in the numbers of non-white farm operators in US agriculture). Since that time, a growing share of people who rent farmland in the United States are part owners and an increasing proportion of farmland renters pay their rent in cash.

Interestingly, despite these changes, the overall proportion of land that is operated by the owner in the United States has not changed dramatically over the last seventy-five years (Figure 3.3). When one combines the land full owners operate with the owned land part owners operate, over 570 million acres (about 62 percent) of farmland was still owner operated in 2007 (USDA-NASS 2009). What has changed over the last century is the proportion of owner-operated

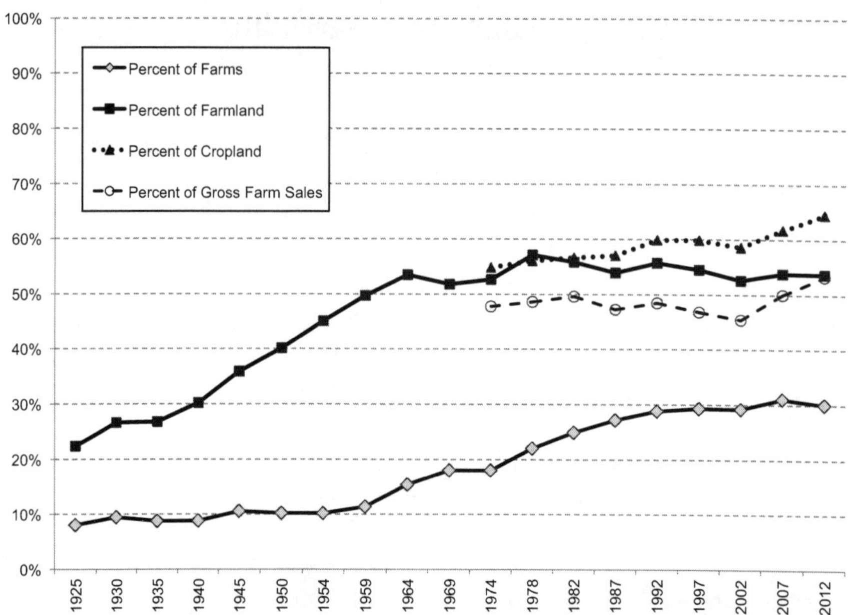

Figure 3.1. Importance of part owner farms in US agriculture, 1925 to 2012. Source: US Census of Agriculture, various years. Note: detailed information about cropland acres and farm sales by tenure status was not consistently reported prior to 1974.

land that part owners (who also lease additional acres) versus full owners own and operate.

While statistics for the nation tell the overall story, there is considerable regional variation in land-tenure arrangements. Figure 3.4 shows the proportion of farmland rented or leased by county. Several concentrated areas have a majority of farmland that was operated by someone other than the owner in 2007. As Nickerson et al. (2012) note, there are various explanations for this variation, including state laws that limit farmland ownership by corporations or non-US residents, and a tendency for higher rates of land leasing for the most commercially important agricultural areas.

Tenure Status of Farmland Owners

A second approach to tracking changes in agricultural landownership in the United States is to focus on the landowners. Initially, it is helpful to know if the landowner operates their own farmland (an *owner operator*), or if they lease it

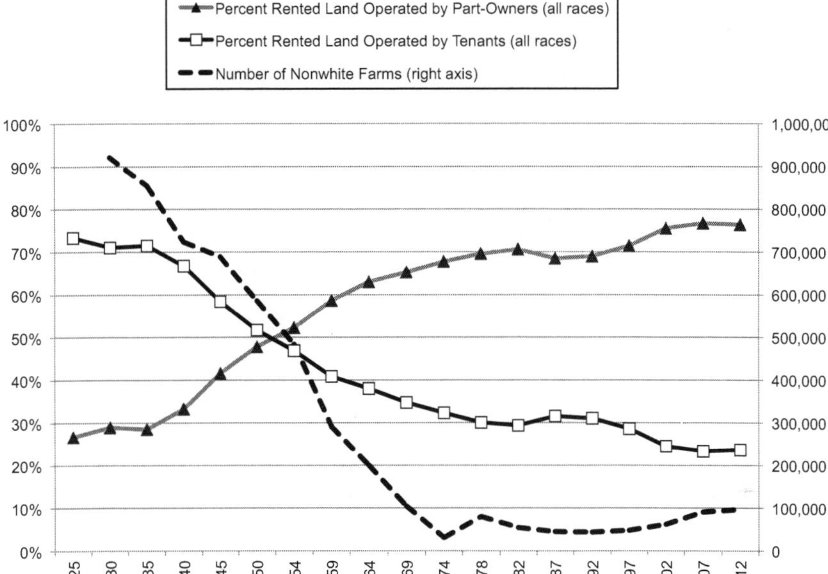

Figure 3.2. Percent of rented farmland, by operator tenure status, and number of farms operated by non-white farmers in the United States, 1925 to 2012. Source: US Census of Agriculture, various years. Note: some missing years were interpolated.

to someone else to farm (a *landlord* or *non-operator owner*). Both categories of landowners (owner-operators and landlords) include *resident landowners* (primary residence is on their farmland) or *absentee landowners* (primary residence is off their farmland). Farmland owners can also be differentiated by the distinctive goals they seek from the ownership of agricultural land. Most see their land as an input to be used for agricultural production, others own farmland as an investment based on their expectations of capital gains from the future sale of their asset, and still others value their land primarily as a place to live, to recreate, or for nature conservation.

Data on owners of US farmland is less available than information about US farm operators. The Census of Agriculture only reports information about owner-operators (full and part owners). Census information is not systematically collected from either landlords who rent out all their land to farmers or from other landowners who choose not to use their farmland in any way that qualifies as a farm according to the Census of Agriculture.[4] While agricultural census results indicate that just under 40 percent of agricultural land is non-owner operated (and thus must have a landlord), landlords' socio-demographic attributes are not included in the census tabulations.

An alternative source of national data on landowners in the United States is provided by the Agricultural Economic Land Ownership Survey (AELOS), which collects information from both landowners and tenants. The last two full AELOS surveys were conducted in 1988 and 1999[5] as follow-ups to the periodic Census of Agriculture (in 1987 and 1997, respectively). The 1999 AELOS results are based on surveys received from operators and landlords who were sampled from the National Agricultural Statistics Service (NASS) List and Area Frames. Because of the different years and sampling methodologies employed, the reported results in the 1999 AELOS are slightly different from those in the 1997 Census of Agriculture. Specifically, the AELOS estimates slightly fewer total acres of farmland than were reported in the census, and suggests a greater importance of part-owner farms and slightly higher overall levels of land renting in the United States.

AELOS also provides much greater detail about leasing arrangements and management decision making than the census. Table 3.1 presents summary information about landlords who leased out US farmland in 1999. As a group, most landlords did not operate their own farms. The vast majority were individuals and partnerships, with corporate landlords comprising just 3 percent of the total and providing just 6 percent of total rented land. Only 13 percent of private individual (or partnership) landlords lived on the farmland that they rented out, and about a third lived on any type of farm. The largest group of landlords reported residences in cities, towns, or urban areas, though they provided nearly 45 percent of the total rented farmland reported in the 1999 AELOS. More than half of US landlords were over age sixty-five, and three fourths were over age fifty-five. Those sixty-five and older provided 50 percent of all leased farmland in the United States. Most reported jointly owning their farmland, and female landlords were likely to lease out a larger fraction of the land they own.

Ultimately, the AELOS reports provide a profile of landowners in the United States for two points in time, which makes it difficult to infer trends or derive

(opposite top) Figure 3.3. Total acres and percent of acres by operator tenure status in the US, 1925 to 2012. Source: US Census of Agriculture, various years.

(opposite bottom) Figure 3.4. Percent of land in farms rented or leased in 2012. Source: 2012 US Census of Agriculture, Agricultural Atlas. Accessed 31 May 2014. http://www.agcensus.usda.gov/Publications/2012/Online_Resources/Ag_Atlas_Maps/Operators/Tenure/12-M116.php.

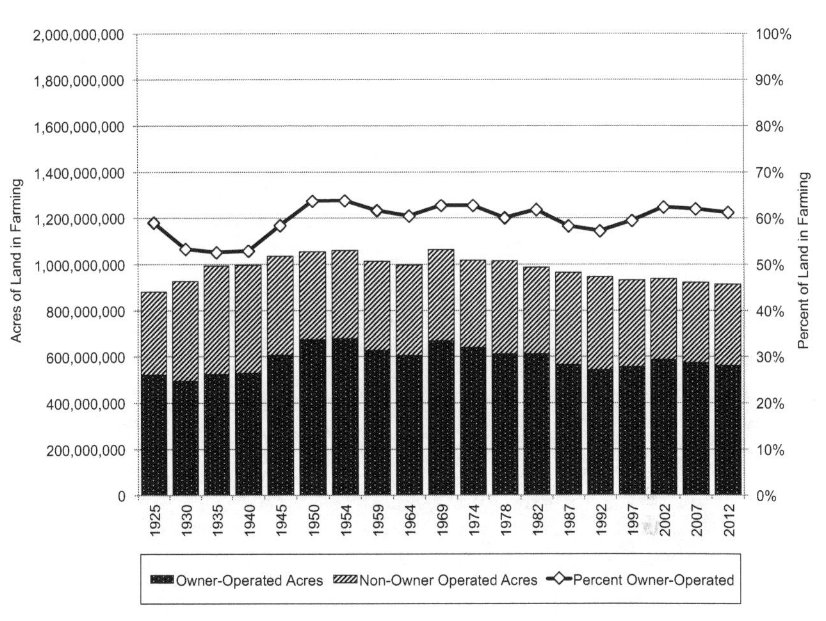
2,000,000,000
1,800,000,000
1,600,000,000
1,400,000,000
1,200,000,000
1,000,000,000
800,000,000
600,000,000
400,000,000
200,000,000
0
Acres of Land in Farming
100%
90%
80%
70%
60%
50%
40%
30%
20%
10%
0%
Percent of Land in Farming
1925
1930
1935
1940
1945
1950
1954
1959
1964
1969
1974
1978
1982
1987
1992
1997
2002
2007
2012
Owner-Operated Acres
Non-Owner Operated Acres
Percent Owner-Operated

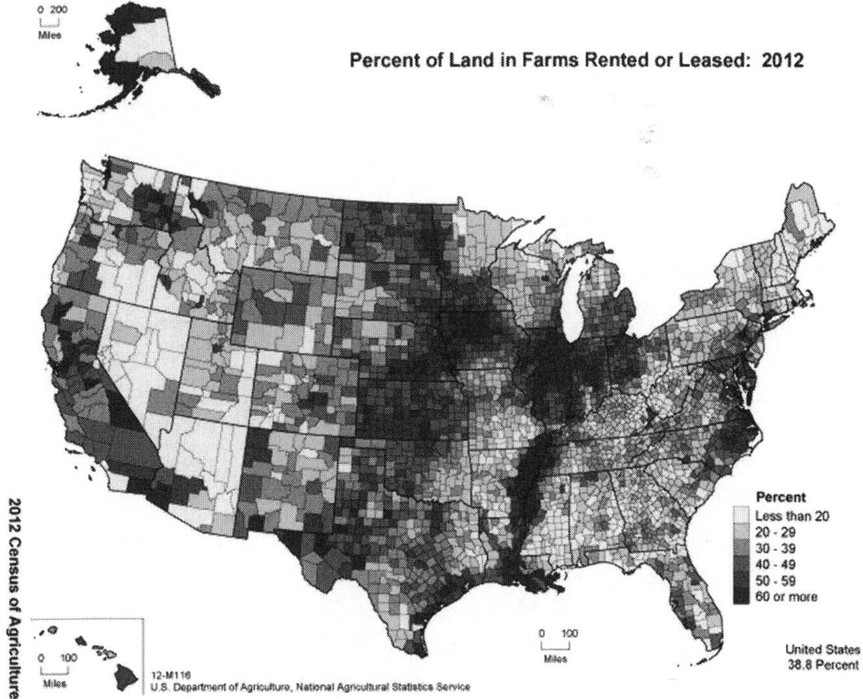
Percent of Land in Farms Rented or Leased: 2012
Percent
Less than 20
20 - 29
30 - 39
40 - 49
50 - 59
60 or more
United States
38.8 Percent
12-M116
U.S. Department of Agriculture, National Agricultural Statistics Service
2012 Census of Agriculture

Table 3.1
Characteristics of landlords who lease out farmland in the United States, 1999.

	Number of Land-lords	%	Total Acres Owned	%	Total Acres Rented Out	%	Percent Owned Land Rented Out
Overall	2,289,672		825,230,000		418,532,000		51
Public Landlords	31,915	1	n.a.		25,819,000	6	
Private Landlords							
Operating farms	263,611	12	221,804,000	27	49,538,000	12	22
Not operating farms	1,994,146	87	603,426,000	73	343,175,000	82	57
Private Subtotal	2,257,757	99	825,230,000	100	392,713,000	94	48
Private landlord characteristics							
Individuals or partnerships	2,150,630	94	654,282,000	79	345,117,000	82	53
Corporations	64,544	3	151,781,000	18	25,456,000	6	17
Total reporting	2,215,174	97	806,063,000	98	370,573,000	89	
Private Individual/partnership characteristics							
Landlords by place of residence							
On this rented farm	287,820	13	72,161,000	9	49,748,000	12	69
On another farm	437,855	19	159,650,000	19	59,549,000	14	37
In a rural area, not on a farm	518,634	23	93,975,000	11	50,515,000	12	54
In a city, town, or urban area	906,321	40	328,496,000	40	185,305,000	44	56
Total reporting	2,150,630	94	654,282,000	79	345,117,000	82	
Landlords by age group							
Under 25	3,141	0	377,000	0	196,000	0	52
25 to 34	33,602	1	7,205,000	1	3,467,000	1	48
35 to 44	176,315	8	36,365,000	4	18,243,000	4	50
45 to 54	324,732	14	109,326,000	13	46,239,000	11	42
55 to 64	451,215	20	139,312,000	17	67,740,000	16	49
65 and over	1,161,625	51	361,697,000	44	209,230,000	50	58
Total reporting	2,150,630	94	654,282,000	79	345,115,000	82	
Landlords by gender							
Male	547,952	24	158,743,000	19	82,603,000	20	52
Female	577,084	25	133,772,000	16	88,204,000	21	66
Joint ownership	1,025,594	45	361,767,000	44	174,308,000	42	48
Total reporting	2,150,630	94	654,282,000	79	345,115,000	82	

Source: 1999 Agricultural Economic Land Ownership Survey.

information about current land-tenure patterns. More detailed and recent analyses of such trends are only available for a few smaller geographies. One unique data set is the Iowa Land Ownership Survey (ILOS), which has collected panel data from a representative statewide sample of land parcels and landowners in Iowa since 1949 (Duffy and Smith 2008). While national trends suggest that the total proportion of farmland that is owner-operated land has hovered near 60 percent since World War II, the Iowa study shows a pronounced decline in the proportion of land under owner-operator status (dropping from 55 percent in 1982 to 40 percent in 2007). This is partly because of the aging of the farmland owner population in that state, where the share of land owned by persons over sixty-five increased from 29 percent in 1982 to 55 percent in 2007. This change is also reflected in the increased importance of older female landowners across the Midwest (Petrzelka and Marquart-Pyatt 2011).

There has also been noticeable growth in the role of absentee farmland owners. Absentee landowners include individuals such as retired farmers and ranchers who have moved away from their land, those who inherit land but live elsewhere, and those who buy land for recreational or investment purposes and live elsewhere (Petrzelka, Ma, and Malin 2013). While we know very little about landowners in general, we know even less about absentee owners. Information on absentee landowners derives from regional and state studies, which note that an "unprecedented level of absentee ownership" of rangelands occurred in the West in the latter part of the twentieth century (Haggerty and Travis 2006, 825), and that an increased number of farmland owners in the Midwest are no longer living on or near their land (Duffy and Smith 2008).

The majority of absentee landowners of farmland do not operate their land themselves. In a synthesis of research on absentee landowners of crop- and rangeland (Petrzelka, Ma, and Malin 2013), it was found non-resident landowners, as compared to resident landowners, are much more likely to live in urban areas (e.g., Constance, Rikoon, and Ma 1996; Redmon et al. 2004), are less dependent financially on the land, and are much more likely to own land for amenity reasons (e.g., recreation or vacationing) than production purposes (e.g., Constance, Rikoon, and Ma 1996; Gosnell, Haggerty, and Travis 2006).

Some absentee landowners purchase land primarily for investment goals. There is growing evidence that farmland around the world has become a target for global capital investors, particularly at a time when commodity prices are soaring and the worldwide recession has made traditional investment vehicles less profitable (Robertson and Pinstrup-Andersen 2010). These trends certainly affect prospects for food security and can foment political conflict in developing countries (Zoomers 2010), but can also compete with commercial farmers for prime farmland and bid up land prices in major agricultural production areas like the United States (Duffy 2011).[6] However, data to evaluate whether non-farm investor landownership is a significant new trend in US agriculture are difficult to find. While there has been steady growth since the early 1990s in ownership of Iowa farmland by people who say they hold land as an "investment" (Duffy and Smith 2008), data from both Iowa and Illinois indicate that existing farmers remain the primary purchasers of farmland, and the share of farmland purchased by investors actually declined between 2007 and 2010 as commercial farmers used increased net farm income to expand their land holdings (Duffy 2011).

Implications of Changes in Agricultural Land Ownership

In a 1993 *Rural Sociology* special issue on land tenure, Wunderlich (1993, 549) notes:

> The change in the structural relationship between farming and land ownership implies potential changes in who bears risk, makes production and investment decisions, protects the environment, and supports the community. Who, between farmer and landowners, decides whether farmland will go into a conservation reserve? Are non-operator owners less risk averse in production decisions than operator owners? Are absentee landowners as concerned about pesticide contamination of drinking water as resident owners? How are school budgets and community facilities affected by the level of absentee taxpayers?

The implications of changing landownership and tenure that Wunderlich posed in 1993 are even more relevant today, particularly with respect to land management decision making authority, agri-environmental behaviors, and impacts on local community well-being.

Control over Land Management Decisions

With the large amount of farmland rented, the [resident and absentee] landlord-tenant relationship clearly plays a significant role in US agriculture. The few empirical studies on this relationship in the United States show that tenants often have substantial managerial control over the land. For example, Gilbert and Beckley (1993) studied decision making in two Wisconsin townships and found landlords and tenants in agreement that the latter were the primary decision makers for operational decisions on the farm such as types of commodities to grow, application of particular soil conservation practices, and participation in specific federal programs. Constance, Rikoon, and Ma (1996) examined landlords' involvement on rented agricultural land in Missouri and found the vast majority of landlords gave decision-making control to their tenants—including decisions over crops grown, tillage practices, types of pesticides, pesticide application, and participation in soil conservation and water quality programs. These findings are consistent with AELOS (1999) data that show the tenant is generally the individual primarily responsible for making land-management decisions.

A growing share of farmland owners are women, primarily widows (Duffy and Smith 2008), and gendered power dynamics increasingly shape landlord-tenant relations. In his study of Iowa farmers, Carolan (2005, 402) found "all of the female landlords described inequitable power relations between themselves and their male tenants . . . [expressing] feelings of exclusion [and] alienation [from farm decision making]." Moreover, self-censorship occurred by female landlords who were reluctant to discuss implementing sustainable agricultural practices on their land with their tenants, fearing they would "scare away good tenants" (396). A study of landlords in four Great Lakes counties found female absentee landlords less likely to be involved in decision making on their land if they were older, retired, relied less on the land for income, inherited the land, co-owned the land with a sibling, or rented to a local farmer (Petrzelka and Marquart-Pyatt 2011). By contrast, for male absentee landlords, decision-making involvement was reduced only when a local farmer farmed the land. Thus, despite being owners of agricultural land, female landlords still found themselves in a disadvantaged position because of patriarchal structures in rural communities, as found in previous research (e.g., Sachs 1996).

Environmental Behaviors

Scholars studying the adoption of conservation practices in agriculture often assume that farm operators are more likely to make investments in conservation practices (particularly control of soil erosion) when they have secure long-term access to and personal ownership interests in their farmland (Caswell et al. 2001). While some widely cited recent studies suggest that landownership and rental arrangements can help explain variation in the use of some types of conservation practices (e.g., Soule, Tegene, and Wiebe 2000), recent reviews of the larger empirical literature suggests that there is little consistent support for this idea, with most studies finding no statistical significance for tenure variables and equal numbers finding positive and negative impacts on farmer conservation behaviors (Baumgart-Getz, Prokopy, and Floress 2012; Prokopy et al. 2008).

In addition, there is a growing population of absentee landowners who choose not to farm themselves or rent their land out, but rather manage their property for recreational, lifestyle, and amenity purposes (Duffy and Smith 2008). This group controls an increasing share of US farmland, and studies indicate a strong level of environmental concern and interest in conservation (e.g., Gosnell, Haggerty, and Travis 2006; Petrzelka, Buman, and Ridgely 2009; Petrzelka 2012).

As Bonanno states (in this volume), globalization processes can fundamentally alter important social relations by transcending locality. Farmland owners without strong ties to their local community may be less aware of or care less about the effects of land management on neighbors. Yung and Belsky (2007) find that absentee owners' management goals, such as increased wildlife, can result in detrimental environmental and economic impacts on nearby working farm and ranch operations.

As "non-traditional" owners increasingly own farmland, new ways of conducting outreach and providing resources to these landowners are needed. This presents both challenges and opportunities. In comparison to resident landowners, absentee owners are much less likely to have personal contact with local extension and natural resource agency staff, leading to lower levels of scientific and traditional management knowledge about local environmental conditions (e.g., Redmon et al. 2004; Petrzelka, Buman, and Ridgely 2009). The farther physically removed they are from their land, the more isolated they are from local social networks and contacts, both of which are well-established mechanisms for generating adoption of recommended land management practices. Further, they are less familiar with the traditional land and farming culture, and less attuned to conventional sources of information and agency.

The increase of female landowners provides additional challenges to those promoting land conservation goals. Governmental agencies and private nonprofit organizations that provide conservation services to landowners often take a "land as commodity" orientation when many female landowners (and others) hold a "land as community" orientation (Eells 2008, xi). These differences contribute to less interaction by the women with local natural resource agency offices and lower levels of involvement in state and federal government conservation programs.

These emerging new types of landowners also provide opportunities for conservation programs. They often depend less on their land for household income and more frequently desire high-amenity environmental quality outcomes. Farmland owners who inherited their land may also feel strong attachments to conservation of their land because of their family's agricultural heritage.

Community Well-Being

Some of the earliest research in the field of rural sociology directly examined the relationships between land tenure and rural community dynamics in the United States. In his classic study of Belleville, New York, pioneer rural sociologist Charles J. Galpin (1911) finds that tenant farmers were much less likely to be involved in community life. Many other community studies in the first half of the twentieth century found positive links between tenancy, low community well-being, and soil erosion (e.g., Benton 1918), though the impact was stronger in the South than in the North (Schuler 1938). The classic 1940s comparative study of two California farm towns by Walter Goldschmidt (1947) also highlights the role of landownership patterns on rural communities. Goldschmidt finds that the town with more egalitarian landownership patterns and smaller-scale farms had more vibrant community institutions and higher levels of local social and economic well-being. However, more-recent research suggests that the link between industrial-style agriculture and community well-being is primarily explained by the presence of large hired farmworker populations, not landownership or tenancy rates per se (Lobao and Stofferahn 2008). There is much less research on the role of absentee ownership on communities. Theoretically, absentee landowners may be expected to be less engaged in community activities (because of the distance they live from the land and/or a lack of strong social ties), but this has yet to be systematically examined.

Conclusions

In the 1993 special *Rural Sociology* issue mentioned earlier, Geisler (1993, 533) notes, "Despite the central place of private ownership in American life, ideology, and culture, little summary information is kept on who owns what land over time." Twenty years later, this statement still holds true, despite repeated calls for more data on landownership in the literature. In forestry, the National Woodland Owner Survey (NWOS) regularly surveys forest owners from across the country about: the forest land they own, their reasons for owing it, how they use it, if and how they manage it, sources of information about their forests, their concerns and issues related to their forests, intentions for the future of their forests, and demographics. The results of the NWOS are regularly used to design and implement programs and policies that affect forest owners by government agencies, landowner organizations, private service providers, forest industry companies, and academic researchers (USFS 2012). However, the federal government has not systematically collected comparable information on private farmland owners for over fifteen years. The data that do exist are dated and usually collected by state agencies or researchers working in limited geographical areas. Given that 42 percent of the US land base is in farmland, and the environmental and social implications of changing agricultural landownership, the provision of resources by Congress to collect land tenure data at the national level is of significant public interest.

Changes in agricultural landownership patterns have important (but largely unexplored) implications for social theory and broader societal processes. Widespread and egalitarian property ownership is still viewed as important to a well-functioning democracy and prosperous economy, but few scholars have successfully gathered empirical data to test the modern relevance of these relationships. Similarly, many scholars continue to assume that landownership is an obvious source of power in social and economic relationships, but the empirical evidence from recent studies suggests that power relationships between landlords and tenants are more nuanced. Contemporary research that explores how this power relationship is mediated by social relationships (gender, families, race or ethnic identity, and other direct social ties) and geography could help advance social theories of ownership, rent, and power.

There is also significant opportunity for a new generation of rural sociologists to revisit classic questions about the implications of landownership patterns for farm structural change, rural community well-being, and environmental behavior in the twenty-first century. Important research questions include: to what extent are absentee or investor landownership reinforcing or deflecting patterns of consolidation and industrialization in US agriculture? How do changes in landownership impact social ties and community dynamics? Does foreign or investor ownership of US farmland present a serious threat to US farmers and/or rural communities?

From an applied standpoint, there is a particular need for research on the role of new types of farmland owners (particularly women and absentee owners) and their tenant operators in agricultural conservation decision making (e.g., Constance, Rikoon, and Ma 1996). Some local groups have created programs to connect and facilitate the exchange of information and ideas between new landowners and experienced ranch managers (Yung and Belsky 2007). These and other efforts to work with new types of landowners would benefit from long-term research and monitoring to document their strengths and weaknesses. Results could guide the expansion of programs targeting these emerging categories of landowners.

Variation in access to land and patterns of land tenure were central topics of study for the first generation of self-described rural sociologists nearly a century ago. Given the rapid and fundamental changes occurring with landownership in the United States and abroad in recent decades, and their apparent implications for rural community dynamics and environmental behaviors, we believe the time is ripe to revisit these important questions.

Notes

1 The authors share first authorship.

2 The US Census of Agriculture is conducted roughly every five years. Historical reports are all available from the USDA website (www.agcensus.usda.gov).

3 These 922 acres are those census respondents reported as being part of an agricultural operation. There are also some (largely unknown) acres of farmland that are not actively farmed and thus not reported in censuses of agriculture.

4 To qualify as a farm for census purposes, an operation must be capable of producing at least one thousand dollars in farm products in any given year, even if not actually sold on the market.

5 A new AELOS was expected to occur in 2013—but has consistently failed to receive funding from Congress.

6 The most recent data show that direct foreign landownership remains a relatively small fraction of total US farmland. As of February 2009, only 1.7 percent of privately owned land in farms or forest (22.8 million acres) were under foreign ownership (Nickerson et al. 2012, 33).

References

AELOS. 1999. *Agricultural Economics and Land Ownership Survey*. Washington, DC: National Agricultural Statistics Service, United States Department of Agriculture.

Baumgart-Getz, Adam, Linda S. Prokopy, and Kristin Floress. 15 April 2012. "Why Farmers Adopt Best Management Practice in the United States: A Meta-Analysis of the Adoption Literature." *Journal of Environmental Management* 96 (1): 17–25. http://dx.doi.org/10.1016/j.jenvman.2011.10.006. Medline:22208394.

Benton, Alva H. 1918. *Farm Tenancy and Leases. Minnesota Agricultural Experiment Station Bulletin No. 178*. St. Paul: University of Minnesota.

Bromley, Daniel W. 1991. *Environment and Economy: Property Rights and Public Policy*. Cambridge: Blackwell.

Browne, William P., Jerry R. Skees, Louis E. Swanson, Paul B. Thompson, and Laurian J. Unnevehr. 1992. *Sacred Cows and Hot Potatoes: Agrarian Myths in Agricultural Policy*. Boulder, CO: Westview Press.

Carolan, Michael S. 2005. "Barriers to the Adoption of Sustainable Agriculture on Rented Land: An Examination of Contesting Social Fields." *Rural Sociology* 70 (3): 387–413. http://dx.doi.org/10.1526/0036011054831233.

Caswell, Margriet, Keith O. Fuglie, Cassandra Ingram, Sharon Jans, and Catherine Kascak. 2001. *Adoption of Agricultural Production Practices: Lessons Learned from the U.S. Department of Agriculture Area Studies Project*. Agricultural Economic Report No. 792. Washington, DC: USDA Economic Research Service.

Constance, Douglas H., J. Sanford Rikoon, and Jian C. Ma. 1996. "Landlord Involvement in Environmental Decision Making on Rented Missouri Cropland: Pesticide Use and Water Quality Issues." *Rural Sociology* 61 (4): 577–605. http://dx.doi.org/10.1111/j.1549-0831.1996.tb00635.x.

Cross, John A., Douglas Jackson-Smith, and Bradford Barham. 2000. "Ethnicity and Farm Entry Behavior." *Rural Sociology* 65 (3): 461–83. http://dx.doi.org/10.1111/j.1549-0831.2000.tb00039.x.

Dalecki, Michael G., and C. Milton Coughenour. 1992. "Agrarianism in American Society." *Rural Sociology* 57 (1): 48–64. http://dx.doi.org/10.1111/j.1549-0831.1992.tb00456.x.

Dietz, Thomas, Elinor Ostrom, and Paul C. Stern. 12 December 2003. "The Struggle to Govern the Commons." *Science* 302 (5,652): 1907–12. http://dx.doi.org/10.1126/science.1091015. Medline:14671286.

Duffy, Michael. 2011. "The Current Situation on Farmland Values and Ownership." *Choices: The Magazine of Food, Farm and Resource Issues* 26 (2). Accessed 25 September 2013. http://www.choicesmagazine.org/magazine/pdf/cmsarticle_24.pdf.

Duffy, Michael, and Darnell Smith. 2008. *Farmland Ownership and Tenure in Iowa 2007.* Ames: Iowa State University Extension PM 1983 Revised.

Eells, Jean C. 2008. *The Land, It's Everything: Women Farmland Owners and the Institution of Agricultural Conservation in the U.S. Midwest.* PhD dissertation, Department of Agricultural Education, Iowa State University.

Galpin, Charles J. 1911. "The Social Agencies in a Rural Community." *First Wisconsin Country Life Conference*, 12–18. Serial No. 472. General Series No. 308. Madison: College of Agriculture, University of Wisconsin.

Geisler, Charles C. 1993. "Ownership: An Overview." *Rural Sociology* 58 (4): 532–46. http://dx.doi.org/10.1111/j.1549-0831.1993.tb00510.x.

Geisler, Charles C., and Frank J. Popper, eds. 1984. *Land Reform, American Style.* Totowa: Rowman and Allanheld.

Gilbert, Jess, and Thomas M. Beckley. 1993. "Ownership and Control of Farmland: Landlord-Tenant Relations in Wisconsin." *Rural Sociology* 58 (4): 569–79. http://dx.doi.org/10.1111/j.1549-0831.1993.tb00513.x.

Goldschmidt, Walter. 1947. *As You Sow: Three Studies in the Social Consequences of Agribusiness.* Glencoe, IL: The Free Press.

Gosnell, Hannah, Julia H. Haggerty, and William R. Travis. 2006. "Ranchland Ownership Change in the Greater Yellowstone Ecosystem, 1990–2001." *Society & Natural Resources* 19 (8): 743–58. http://dx.doi.org/10.1080/08941920600801181.

Haggerty, Julia H., and William R. Travis. 2006. "Out of Administrative Control: Absentee Owners, Resident Elk and the Shifting Nature of Wildlife Management in Southwestern Montana." *Geoforum* 37 (5): 816–30. http://dx.doi.org/10.1016/j.geoforum.2005.12.004.

Honoré, Anthony M. 1961. "Ownership." In *Oxford Essays in Jurisprudence*, ed. A.G. Guest, 107–47. Oxford: Oxford University Press.

Lobao, Linda, and Curtis W. Stofferahn. 2008. "The Community Effects of Industrialized Farming: Social Science Research and Challenges to Corporate Farming Laws." *Agriculture and Human Values* 25 (2): 219–40. http://dx.doi.org/10.1007/s10460-007-9107-8.

Macpherson, Crawford B. 1978. *Property: Mainstream and Critical Positions.* Toronto: University of Toronto Press.

Mooney, Patrick H. 1988. *My Own Boss? Class, Rationality and the Family Farm.* Boulder, CO: Westview Press.

Nickerson, Cynthia, Mitchell Morehart, Todd Kuethe, Jayson Beckman, Jennifer Ifft, and Ryan Williams. 2012. *Trends in U.S. Farmland Values and Ownership.* EIB-92. US Department of Agriculture, Econ. Res. Serv. February 2012.

Petrzelka, Peggy. 2012. "Absentee Landowners in the Great Lakes Basin: Who They Are and Implications for Conservation Outreach." *Society & Natural Resources* 25 (8): 821–32. http://dx.doi.org/10.1080/08941920.2011.626511.

Petrzelka, Peggy, Thomas Buman, and Jamie Ridgely. 2009. "Engaging Absentee Landowners in Conservation Practice Decisions: A Descriptive Study of an Understudied Group." *Journal of Soil and Water Conservation* 64 (3): 94A–9A. http://dx.doi.org/10.2489/jswc.64.3.94A.

Petrzelka, Peggy, Zhao Ma, and Stephanie A. Malin. 2013. "The Elephant in the Room: Absentee Landowner Issues in Conservation and Land Management." *Land Use Policy* 30 (1): 157–66. http://dx.doi.org/10.1016/j.landusepol.2012.03.015.

Petrzelka, Peggy, and Sandra Marquart-Pyatt. 2011. "Land Tenure in the US: Power, Gender, and Consequences for Conservation Decision Making." *Agriculture and Human Values* 28 (4): 549–60. http://dx.doi.org/10.1007/s10460-011-9307-0.

Prokopy, Linda S., Kristin Floress, Denise Klotthor-Weinkauf, and Adam Baumgart-Getz. 2008. "Determinants of Agricultural Best Management Practice Adoption: Evidence from the Literature." *Journal of Soil and Water Conservation* 63 (5): 300–311. http://dx.doi.org/10.2489/jswc.63.5.300.

Redmon, Larry A., Greg M. Clary, Jason J. Cleere, Gerald W. Evers, Vincent A. Haby, Charles R. Long, Lloyd R. Nelson, Ron D. Randel, Monte Rouquette Jr., Gerald R. Smith, and Todd L. Thrift. 2004. "Pasture and Livestock Management Workshop for Novices: A New Curriculum for a New Clientele." *Journal of Natural Resources and Life Sciences Education* 33: 7–10.

Robertson, Beth, and Per Pinstrup-Andersen. 2010. "Global Land Acquisition: Neo-colonialism or Development Opportunity?" *Food Security* 2 (3): 271–83. http://dx.doi.org/10.1007/s12571-010-0068-1.

Sachs, Carolyn E. 1996. *Gendered Fields: Rural Women, Agriculture and the Environment.* Boulder, CO: Westview Press.

Salamon, Sonya. 1995. *Prairie Patrimony.* Chapel Hill: University of North Carolina Press.

Schuler, Edgar A. 1938. *Social Status and Farm Tenure—Attitudes and Social Conditions of Corn Belt and Cotton Belt Farmers.* Social Research Report No. IV. Washington, DC: Farm Security Administration and Bureau of Agricultural Economics Cooperating, US Department of Agriculture.

Soule, Meredith J., Abebayehu Tegene, and Keith D. Wiebe. 2000. "Land Tenure and the Adoption of Conservation Practices." *American Journal of Agricultural Economics* 82 (4): 993–1,005. http://dx.doi.org/10.1111/0002-9092.00097.

USDA-NASS. 2009. 2007 Census of Agriculture. Volume 1, Geographic Area Series Part 51. Washington, DC: USDA National Agricultural Statistics Service. Accessed 19 August. http://www.agcensus.usda.gov/index.php.

USFS. 2012. "National Woodland Owner Survey." Washington, DC: US Forest Service. Accessed 20 August. http://www.fia.fs.fed.us/nwos.

Wunderlich, Gene. 1993. "The Land Question: Are There Answers?" *Rural Sociology* 58 (4): 547–59. http://dx.doi.org/10.1111/j.1549-0831.1993.tb00511.x.

Yung, Laurie, and Jill M. Belsky. 2007. "Private Property Rights and Community Goods: Negotiating Landowner Cooperation amid Changing Ownership on the Rocky Mountain Front." *Society & Natural Resources* 20 (8): 689–703. http://dx.doi.org/10.1080/08941920701216586.

Zoomers, Annelies. 2010. "Globalisation and the Foreignisation of Space: Seven Processes Driving the Current Global Land Grab." *Journal of Peasant Studies* 37 (2): 429–47. http://dx.doi.org/10.1080/03066151003595325.

CHAPTER 4

Mexican-Born Farmworkers in US Agriculture[1]

Eric B. Jensen

Introduction

The demand for low-skilled farm labor has been vital to the history of Mexican immigration to the United States and continues to be an important factor in the contemporary migration processes of a large subset of immigrants. Beginning in the early 1900s, employers, labor contractors, and the US government actively recruited workers from Mexico to fill labor shortages in agriculture (Reisler 1976). From 1942 to 1964, nearly 4.5 million Mexican laborers migrated to the United States as part of the Bracero program, which was initially created to prevent farm labor shortages during World War II (Mitchell 1996). Even the restrictive Immigration Control and Reform Act (IRCA) of 1986 made special provisions for agricultural workers, which resulted in an additional 1.2 million undocumented immigrants receiving amnesty because of their status as farm laborers (Boucher et al. 2007). There has clearly been a strong connection between US agricultural labor and Mexican migration.

The global restructuring of agriculture has both increased the demand for immigrant farm labor in the United States and also changed the structure of this labor in substantial ways. For example, the industrialization of production that has taken place in nearly every region and type of commodity has resulted in a shift in the geographic distribution of Mexican-born farmworkers in the United States. Also, changes in the size and scale of production have led to a proliferation of immigrant labor into a diversity of commodities that have not historically employed immigrant laborers, such as the livestock and dairy industries. Finally, vertical integration in the food sector has included Mexican-born immigrants who work in both the production and processing of food and agricultural products.

However, even as the prevalence of Mexican-born labor in US agriculture has expanded, there have been dramatic changes in the supply of Mexican-born immigrants available to work in agriculture. In recent decades, an increasing number of Mexican-born immigrants are working in the construction, restaurant, and personal services industries rather than in agriculture. In addition, immigration from Mexico precipitously declined from 2000 to 2010 and, coupled with increased return migration to Mexico, the supply of immigrants is tenuous.

In this chapter, I explore both the impacts of agricultural restructuring on the demand for Mexican-born farmworkers in the United States and also the potential impediments to the supply of Mexican-born farmworkers to meet this demand. In the first section, I focus on the ways that agricultural restructuring has increased the demand for immigrant farm labor and simultaneously: (1) changed the geographic distribution of Mexican-born farmworkers in the United States, (2) expanded the need for Mexican-born farmworkers into new farm sectors, and (3) led to the vertical integration of farmworkers from the production to the processing of farm products. In the second section, I look at changes in the supply of Mexican-born farmworkers in the United States, including changes in the industrial composition of jobs that Mexican immigrants fill, the overall decline of immigration from Mexico, and the rising number of immigrants that are returning to Mexico.

Demand for Immigrant Farm Labor

The global economy is an economy that has the technological, institutional, and organizational capacity to coordinate production in real time on a planetary scale (Castells 1996). This coordination of production relies not only on the mobilization of capital but also on the international flow of labor. The global food system is a critical component of the global economy. That system, similar to other economic sectors, is experiencing rapid restructuring and transformation as input and output markets become vertically integrated, contract production increases, and traditional consumption patterns uncouple from local cultures (Morgan, Marsden, and Murdoch 2006). Historically, food and agricultural systems have retained certain characteristics that prevented local production from being completely co-opted by the global economy (Goodman and Watts 1994). For instance, agricultural production is embedded within the natural environment, which cannot be easily relocated or outsourced to other regions or countries. In addition, food consumption has traditionally been deeply embedded within culture, making local food systems less penetrable to world markets. Food production being embedded in ecology and culture hinders the free-flow of capital between regions and countries—a defining characteristic of globalization.

The processes of globalization have restructured agricultural production in other ways including increasing the demand for low-skilled agricultural labor in industrial societies. Farm labor in industrial economies are often among the most dangerous, dirty, and low-status jobs, and since farm labor is unattractive to native-born workers, these jobs are often filled by immigrant workers who have limited opportunities for employment in the primary sector.

The food and fiber system in the United States has undergone dramatic structural changes since World War II (Lobao and Meyer 2001). These changes include a decline in the number of farms, polarization by farm size, vertical integration of food production and processing, the industrialization of the livestock sector, the replacement of hired labor for family labor, and the replacement of native workers for foreign-born workers. In addition, farmers in the United States have had difficulty realizing profits as the costs of inputs steadily rise while at the same time commodity prices decline. Farmers often adapt to this cost-price squeeze by expanding their operations and intensifying production (Bell 2004). They also try to reduce their labor costs by adopting labor-saving technologies or employing low-skilled workers for low wages.

Since the early 1960s, the total number of farms has declined from just over 3.7 million to 2.2 million in 2007, a 40 percent decline (Albrecht and Murdock 1988; US Department of Agriculture 2009a). However, a greater indicator of structural change than just the loss of farms is the type of farm sector that remains. The trend until the 1970s was the consolidation of production as the number of farms declined but the size of farms increased. Beginning in the 1970s, the number of small farms also increased relative to mid-sized farms. Sociologists of agriculture refer to this phenomenon as the polarization of the farm sector, or the "disappearing middle" (Buttel and LaRamee 1991; Guptil and Welsh in this volume). The consolidation of production in agriculture is part of a larger trend toward the overall industrialization of the farming system. Large-scale operations, corporate or extra-local ownership, confined animal feeding operations (CAFOs), vertical integration, and large hired workforces are all characteristics of an industrialized farming system (Bell 2004).

The restructuring of agriculture has impacted farm labor in three substantial ways. First, through mechanization and the adoption of other labor-saving technologies, farmers have greatly reduced the need for labor for many commodities. Second, consolidation and industrialization of production have increased the demand for labor beyond what the farm household can supply. In 2007, there were over 482,000 farms employing over 2.6 million hired farmworkers (US

Department of Agriculture 2009b). The majority of these hired farmworkers, 65 percent, are seasonal (working less than 150 days a year) with the remaining 35 percent working year round. Farmworkers are also more likely to work in crop than livestock production, but the number working in livestock production has been increasing in recent years.

Third, farmers increasingly hire immigrants in place of native workers. While Mexican immigrants have long been used to prevent labor shortages in US agriculture, they were primarily employed in sectors where a large amount of low-skilled labor was needed for a short time period, such as harvesting perishable fruits and vegetables that cannot be harvested with machinery. In recent years, though, the prevalence of Mexican immigrants working other farm sectors such as dairy has increased dramatically (Harrison, Lloyd, and O'Kane 2009). There are several reasons farmers would hire immigrant workers in place of native workers. For instance, farmers may find the supply of native workers willing to do farm labor in their area limited, and therefore hire immigrant workers. Also, farmers may hire immigrant workers because of their previous experience or skill working in agriculture. Finally, farmers may hire immigrant workers, especially those who are undocumented, to control labor costs.

A large share of immigrant farm workers in the United States are undocumented or do not have legal status to reside and work within the United States. Data from the National Agricultural Workers Survey (NAWS) show that, in 2002, 53 percent of all crop workers in the United States were undocumented immigrants (Carroll et al. 2005). Harrison and Lloyd (2012) argue that for undocumented immigrants working in the Wisconsin dairy industry, workers' knowledge of their legal status and the fear of deportation makes them compliant and vulnerable to extreme working conditions and low wages.

The Geographic Distribution of Farm Labor

In recent decades, there has been a considerable shift in the geographic dispersion of Mexican immigrants in the United States (Massey 2008). Historically, Mexican-born immigrants were concentrated in relatively few large cities in California, Illinois, and throughout the Southwest. Today, many are either leaving these traditional gateway cities or bypassing them altogether and settling in new destinations, making Mexican immigration a national phenomenon (Durand, Massey, and Charvet 2000). Explanations for the recent growth of Mexican immigrant populations in new destinations focus on changes in immigration policy, the saturation of labor and housing markets in traditional settlement areas, and economic restructuring in new destinations (Light 2006; Crowley, Lichter, and Qian 2006). Restructuring in the food and agriculture sector has also shifted the geographic distribution of Mexican immigration, especially in rural areas (Kandel and Parrado 2005).

Table 4.1 reports the distribution of Mexican-born farmworkers by selected states from 1980 to 2010. The data for this table come from the 1980, 1990, and 2000 Decennial Census and the 2006 to 2010 American Community Survey. The table also reports the diversity index that measures the degree that Mexican-born farmworkers are spatially clustered or dispersed (Theil 1972). The index ranges from zero to one hundred with low scores indicating that observations are concentrated within a few geographic units and a high scores indicating that observations are equally dispersed across units.

In 1980, Mexican-origin farmworkers in the United States were clustered in a relatively small number of states along the West Coast and in the Southwest. In that year, California and Texas accounted for over 80 percent of Mexican farmworkers—65.5 and 14.8 percent, respectively—and over 90 percent of all Mexican farmworkers in the United States lived in just five states (California, Texas, Washington, Arizona, and Florida). With the exception of Illinois, Idaho, and Florida, all of the top-ten destination states were located in the Southwest and along the West Coast. In that year, the diversity index—which ranges from zero to one hundred with high scores indicating that values are evenly dispersed between units—was 34.2, meaning that the Mexican-born farmworker population was geographically clustered in just a few states.From 1980 to 1990, the total number of Mexican-born farmworkers in the United States more than doubled, in part because of amnesty provisions for seasonal farmworkers in IRCA that spurred the migration of over one million immigrants from Mexico (Martin, Fix, and Taylor 2006). However, there were only slight changes in the spatial distribution of Mexican-born farmworkers. California and Texas were still the destination states for 73.6 percent of all farmworkers, and the five states with the highest share remained the same but now accounted for 88.1 percent. By 1990, Georgia had become a destination for Mexican-born farmworkers. The diversity index increased to 40.5, suggesting that the overall population became more geographically dispersed. The greatest changes in the spatial distribution of Mexican-born farmworkers happened during the 1990s. From 1990 to 2000, the proportion living in California and Texas declined to 62.8 percent. Again, there was a drop in the percentage of Mexican-born farmworkers living along the West Coast and in the Southwest. Georgia was again a destination state and North Carolina emerged as one, too. The diversity index increased to 50.6, signaling greater spatial dispersion than in 1980 or 1990.

By the 2006 to 2010 time period, the share living in California and Texas declined to 56.9 percent. During that period, Washington became the state with the second highest percentage of Mexican-born farmworkers. The five states with the largest percentages were California, Washington, Texas, Florida, and Oregon, which accounted for 75.0 percent. Georgia and North Carolina continued to be destination states, as did Michigan. In addition, there were increases in the share of Mexican-born farmworkers living in Pennsylvania and Wisconsin, but these states were not among the top ten overall destination states and so are not included in Table 4.1. The diversity index increased to 56.2. Mexican-born farmworkers in the United States continue to be a very spatially clustered population; however, there has been considerable growth in the number of Mexican-born farmworkers living in new destinations.

Expansion into New Farm Sectors

Immigrant farm labor has historically been concentrated in the fresh fruits and vegetables (FFV) sector. This sector has high labor requirements, especially during harvest season when perishable products must be picked, packed, and shipped within a relatively short amount of time. While the majority of Mexican-born farmworkers still work in the FFV sector, restructuring in other farm sectors has created a demand for hired labor that Mexican-born workers often fill. For example, the dairy industry in the United States has undergone substantial restructuring in recent years, as the number of dairy farms has declined and many of the remaining farms have had to grow in size and efficiency to remain viable (Cross 2006). A 2009 survey of over 5,000 dairy farms in 47 states found that 50 percent of farms surveyed employ immigrant workers and 62 percent of the nation's milk supply comes from farms that employ immigrant workers (Rosson et al. 2009).

While Mexican-born farmworkers have worked on large dairies in California for decades, dairies in other states have employed significant numbers of immigrant laborers only recently. The structural changes in the dairy sector have transformed the demand for farm labor in Wisconsin, where labor had historically been supplied either from within the farm household or from local non-immigrant hired workers. In 2008, over 40 percent of all hired dairy workers in Wisconsin were immigrants, and the majority of these, 85 percent, were from Mexico (Harrison, Lloyd, and O'Kane 2009). The number of Mexican immigrants working in the dairy sector in New York has also increased dramatically in recent years (Maloney 2002).

In addition to the dairy industry, restructuring in other sectors has increased the demand for hired labor, much of which Mexican-born farmworkers have filled. The transformation of the apple industry in Washington State into a global supplier of fresh fruit has increased the demand for immigrant workers in

Table 4.1
Ten states with the highest percentage of Mexican-born farmworkers, 1980 to 2010

1980		1990		2000		2006–2010		
State	Percent	State	Percent	State	Percent	State	Percent	Margin of Error
California	65.5	California	60.7	California	54.1	California	50.8	0.9
Texas	14.8	Texas	12.9	Texas	8.7	Washington	7.7	0.4
Washington	4.9	Washington	5.6	Washington	6.7	Texas	6.2	0.3
Arizona	4.3	Florida	5.2	Florida	6.5	Florida	6.1	0.5
Florida	2.4	Arizona	3.7	Arizona	3.1	Oregon	4.3	0.4
Oregon	1.5	Oregon	2.5	Oregon	3	Arizona	2.6	0.2
Idaho	1.4	Idaho	1.6	Idaho	2.3	North Carolina	2.6	0.2
New Mexico	1.2	New Mexico	1.4	North Carolina	2.2	Idaho	2	0.2
Colorado	0.9	Colorado	0.9	Georgia	1.7	Georgia	1.7	0.2
Illinois	0.6	Georgia	0.7	New Mexico	1.3	Michigan	1.7	0.3
CA/TX	80.3		73.6		62.8		56.9	0.9
Top Five States	92.0		88.1		79.1		75.0	1.2
Top Ten States	97.6		95.1		89.5		85.5	1.3
Diversity Index	34.2		40.5		50.6		56.2	1.8
Population Estimate	107,875		238,558		333,236		499,563	10,069
Unweighted Sample	7,580		15,518		23,403		20,635	n/a

Source: 1% and 5% Public Use Census Microdata Samples (for 1980, 1990, and 2000); 2006–2010 American Community Survey (2006–2010)

that state (Jarosz and Qazi 2000). Also, restructuring in the tobacco industry in North Carolina has led that industry to become a destination for migrant farmworkers (Balderrama and Molina 2009; Griffith 2006). Agricultural restructuring is creating employment opportunities for Mexican-born immigrants in new commodities and new sectors.

Vertical Integration

Some farmers have combated the rising inputs prices and falling commodity prices in the agricultural industry (price-cost squeeze) by capturing additional value-added profits through processing their own farm products. Farmers are sometimes able to combine the harvesting, cleaning, and packaging of fresh produce into one vertically integrated system that relies on the same workforce for each stage of the process. As mentioned above, Mexican-born farmworkers have historically been concentrated in the FFV sector, the same sector that is undergoing this transformation to vertical integration.

This has long been the case for the lettuce industry in California, where the same farmworkers cut, wash, and wrap the produce (Friedland, Barton, and Thomas 1981). Restructuring in the Idaho potato industry in recent years—price volatility, a shift in consumer demand from fresh to processed potatoes, and prices falling below the cost of production—has led some growers to form processing cooperatives (Bolotova et al. 2008). These cooperatives often employ the same Mexican immigrants that worked to harvest the potatoes earlier in the year.

Supply of Mexican-Born Farm Labor

Despite the growing demand for immigrant farm labor in the United States, the supply of Mexican-born labor at the beginning of the 2010s is somewhat fragile. Recent estimates of the levels of immigration from Mexico indicate that fewer and fewer new immigrants are coming to the United States each year. At the same time, return migration to Mexico has been increasing. In addition to these emerging patterns in the migration flows between the United States and Mexico, the industrial distribution of Mexican immigrants is shifting away from agriculture to industries such as construction, food services, and personal services. Also, the context of reception for undocumented immigrants, who account for a sizable share of crop workers in the United States, is changing as some states enact strict immigration laws. All of these trends will have a substantial impact on the supply of Mexican-born farm labor in the coming decade.

Slowed Immigration from Mexico

Immigration from Mexico to the United States reached record levels during the 1990s. From 1990 to 2000, the Mexican immigrant population grew from 4.3 million to 9.2 million, a 114 percent increase (Malone et al. 2003). There were several factors, both in the United States and Mexico, that led to the unprecedented growth in Mexican immigration during this time period. The booming economy of the late 1990s increased the demand for low-skilled labor in the United States, which was a pull factor for Mexican migration. With the passage of IRCA in 1986, 4.5 million previously undocumented immigrants were granted amnesty and many of their spouses and children migrated from Mexico during the 1990s to join them (Massey, Durand, and Malone 2002).

During the 1990s, Mexico experienced tremendous economic and social instability, which pushed migrants to the United States. For instance, a currency crisis in 1994 led to an economic recession that greatly limited economic opportunities for Mexican workers. The implementation of the North American Free Trade Agreement (NAFTA) dramatically lowered the price of Mexican agricultural commodities, which created economic uncertainty in rural Mexico (McMichael 2005). Overall, the crisis of the nation-state that occurred in Mexico during this period was a significant push factor for migration to the United States.

However, from 2000 to 2010 Mexican migration slowed substantially. Figure 4.1 shows the total level of immigration during that period as well as the level of immigration from Mexico and from other countries. Total immigration to the United States peaked in 2001 with 1.4 million and dropped to its low in 2009 with just slightly over one million. Immigration from Mexico also peaked at the start of the decade with approximately 400,000 migrants after which it declined from 2001 to 2003 but then increased in 2004. From 2005 to 2010, immigration from Mexico to the United States declined significantly, with the annual total in 2010 dropping to less than half of what it was at the beginning of the decade (Figure 4.1).

Increased Return Migration to Mexico

The supply of Mexican-born workers is also impacted by the growing number of immigrants who returned to Mexico in the latter part of the last decade (Passel, Cohn, and Gonzalez-Barrera 2012). While much of the migration between the United States and Mexico is circular migration, the level of return migration from 2005 to 2010 was unprecedented (Figure 4.2). The 1990 Mexico Census measured 129,000 migrants who were living in the United States five years prior to the census date. In the 2000 Mexico Census, that number had increased to 337,000. Demographic surveys in 2005 and 2006 measured lower estimates of return migration, 246,000 and 274,000 respectively. Estimates from the 2010 Mexico Census show that return migration from the United States from 2005 to 2010 was roughly 985,000 (Figure 4.2).

The decline in the number of immigrants coming from Mexico coupled with the increasing number of return migrants has led some researchers to conclude that net migration between the United States and Mexico in 2010 was very close

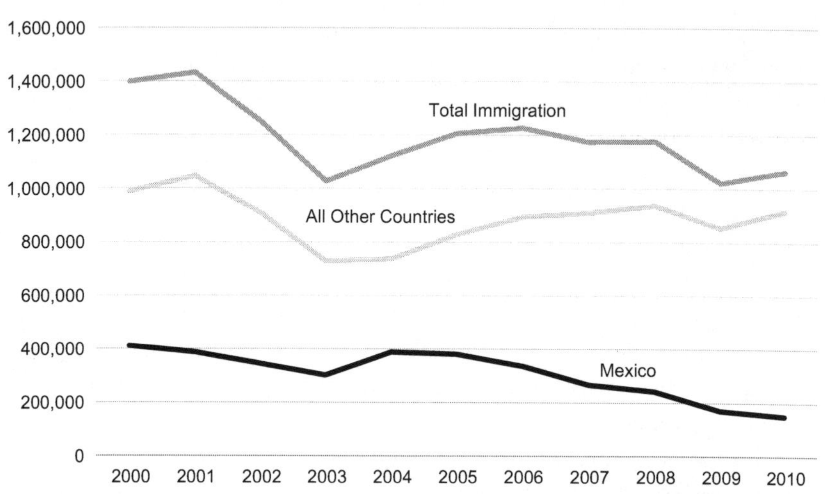

Figure 4.1. Annual immigration estimates, 2000 to 2010. Source: 2000–2010 Single-Year American Community Survey (ACS) files.

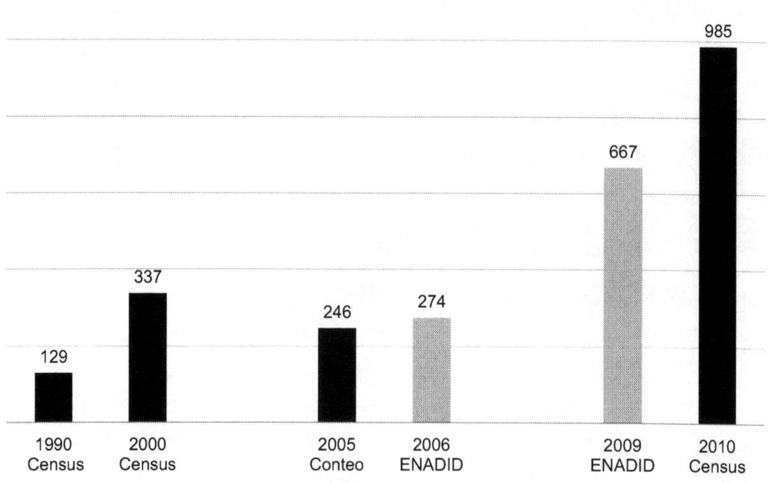

Figure 4.2. Return migration to Mexico for the population living in the United States five years prior to the census or survey (in thousands). Source: Passel, Cohn, and Gonzalez-Barrera (2012).

to zero (Passel, Cohn, and Gonzalez-Barrera 2012). The flow of immigrants from Mexico has not stopped, but the inflow of migrants is being offset by equally large outflows of return migrants. Either slowed immigration or return migration would reduce the supply of Mexican immigrant labor substantially and together they greatly decrease the supply of Mexican-born immigrants available to work in the farm sector.

Changing Industrial Distribution

Historically, more Mexican-born immigrants have worked in agriculture than any other industry. Figure 4.3 uses data from the 1% Public Use Microdata Samples (PUMS) of the 1930–2000 Decennial Censuses and data from the 2005–2007 American Community Survey (ACS) to illustrate the relative distribution of Mexican-born immigrants across select industries. These particular industries—agriculture, construction, restaurants, and personal services—all have high concentrations of immigrant workers. In 1930, roughly 18 percent of all migrants from Mexico worked in agriculture while less than 5 percent worked in restaurants, construction, or personal services combined. The percentage of Mexican-born immigrants working in agriculture increased dramatically with the establishment of the Bracero program, which lasted from 1942 to 1964. During that time, the share of Mexican-born immigrants working in agriculture peaked at nearly 30 percent in 1960 while the percentage working in restaurants, construction, and personal services remained relatively low (Figure 4.3). Since that time the percentage of Mexican-born immigrants working in agriculture dropped substantially as employment opportunities in other industries expanded. Even with this sharp decline, until 1990 there were more Mexican-born immigrants employed in agriculture than in any other single industry in the US economy.

The decline in the industrial concentration of Mexican immigrants working in agriculture corresponds with the beginning of one of the most substantial waves of immigration to the United States. The post-1965 era of immigration has been remarkable not only in its magnitude but also in its diversity (Portes and Rumbaut 1996). The foreign-born population in the United States increased from 9.6 million in 1970 to 31.14 million in 2000 (Gibson and Jung 2006). The substantial growth of the Mexican-born population in the United States during the 1990s has already been mentioned above. Beginning in 1990, the share of Mexican immigrants working in construction surpassed the share working in agriculture and has continued to increase while agriculture is declining. In 2007, only 5.5 percent of Mexican immigrants were working in agriculture compared to 19.7 percent in construction, 11.2 percent in food serviced, and 5.5 percent in personal services.

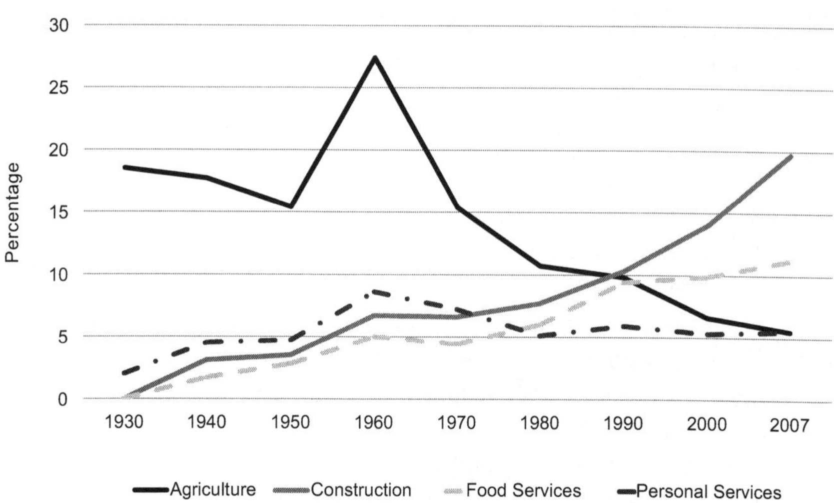

Figure 4.3. Relative industrial distribution of Mexican immigrants in the United States, 1930 to 2007. Source: 1930–2000 Decennial Census Data and 2007 American Community Survey.

Conclusions

The demand for agricultural labor has been vital to the history of Mexican migration to the United States. Since the early 1900s, many sectors within the agricultural industry have relied on immigrant labor. This relationship solidified with the establishment of the Bracero program in 1942, which over the subsequent twenty years brought millions of Mexican laborers to the United States to work in agriculture. Even with the enactment of strict immigration reform in 1986, there were special provisions made for farmworkers. There has long been a strong relationship between Mexican migration and agricultural labor in the United States.

Globalization and the restructuring of the United States agricultural sector have in many ways reshaped the relationship between the demand for agricultural labor and Mexican migration. For decades, immigrant farm labor in the United States was primarily used to harvest fresh fruits and vegetables in just a handful of states. Agricultural restructuring has created a demand for Mexican-born farmworkers that has substantially shifted their geographic distribution away from a few particular states (California and Texas) and into other regions. Restructuring in the dairy industry in the Midwest and Northeast has substantially increased the demand for workers, which has been filled by the dramatic expansion of immigrant farmworkers in these regions that are neither migrant nor seasonal. Finally, in response to agricultural restructuring, some growers are vertically integrating farm products' production and processing and employing the same immigrant workforce in both stages. As we begin this new decade, the demand for Mexican immigrants in US agriculture seems to be expanding.

Whether there will be the supply of Mexican-born farmworkers to meet this demand is questionable. The industrial distribution of Mexican immigrants has in recent decades shifted dramatically away from employment in agriculture to other industries such as construction and restaurants. Recent trends in immigration show that the overall flow of immigrants from Mexico has been declining since 2005. In addition, more and more Mexican immigrants living in the United States are returning home. It is unclear how long these emerging trends in Mexican migration will last, since they are responses to the struggling US economy, new restrictive immigration policies in some states, and changes in the Mexican economy and society—all trends that are likely to continue into the next decade.

In the coming years, as the trends in both the demand for farm labor and Mexican migration to the United States play themselves out, there will be ample opportunities for scholarship in this area. For instance, we know little about the specific challenges that Mexican-born immigrants face in new rural destinations. Research on the access of immigrant farmworkers to medical care and other services would provide an important insight into the well-being of immigrants in rural America. Also, research on the context of the reception Mexican-born farmworkers face will be important, especially given the changing climate in some states toward undocumented immigrants. Another area for research is the extent to which the dairy industry will continue to restructure, and whether its demand for immigrant labor will continue to grow. In addition, will there be an increase in the demand for immigrant farm labor in new commodity sectors within the food and agriculture system and what are the dynamics creating that demand. Finally, as migration from Mexico slows and the supply of Mexican-born farmworkers declines, it will be interesting to see whether the country-of-origin composition of immigrant farmworkers in the United States changes and immigrants from other countries replace Mexican-born farmworkers.

Notes

1 The views expressed are those of the author and not necessarily those of the US Census Bureau.

References

Albrecht, D.E., and H. Steven Murdock. 1988. "The Structural Characteristics of U.S. Agriculture: Historical Patterns and Precursors of Producers' Adaptations to the Crisis." In *The Farm Financial Crisis: Socioeconomic Dimensions and Implications for Producers and Rural Areas*, ed. F.L. Leistritz and S.H. Murdock, 29–44. Boulder, CO: Westview Press.

Balderrama, R., and H. Molina, II. 2009. "How Good Are Networks for Migrant Job Seekers? Ethnographic Evidence from North Carolina Farm Labor Camps." *Sociological Inquiry* 79 (2): 190–218. http://dx.doi.org/10.1111/j.1475-682X.2009.00281.x.

Bell, Michael. 2004. *Farming for Us All: Practical Agriculture and the Cultivation of Sustainability*. University Park: Penn State University Press.

Bolotova, Yuliya, Christopher S. McIntosh, Kalamani Muthusamy, and Paul E. Patterson. 2008. "The Impact of Coordination of Production and Marketing Strategies on Price Behavior: Evidence from the Idaho Potato Industry." *International Food and Agribusiness Management Review* 11 (3): 1–30.

Boucher, S.R., A. Smith, J. Edward Taylor, and A. Yúnez-Naude. 2007. "Impacts of Policy Reforms on the Supply of Mexican Labor to US Farms: New Evidence from Mexico." *Review of Agricultural Economics* 29 (1): 4–16. http://dx.doi.org/10.1111/j.1467-9353.2006.00327.x.

Buttel, F.H., and P. LaRamee. 1991. "The 'Disappearing Middle': A Sociological Perspective." In *Towards a New Political Economy of Agriculture*, ed. W.H. Friedland, L. Busch, F.H. Buttel, and A.P. Rudy, 151–69. Boulder, CO: Westview Press.

Carroll, D., R.M. Samardick, S. Bernard, S. Gabbard, and T. Hernandez. 2005. *Findings from the National Agricultural Workers Survey (NAWS) 2001–2002: A Demographic and Employment Profile of United States Farm Workers*. Washington, DC: Office of Programmatic Policy, Office of the Assistant Secretary for Policy, US Department of Labor.

Castells, Manuel. 1996. *The Information Age: Economy, Society, and Culture: Vol. 1: The Rise of the Network Society*. Oxford: Blackwell.

Cross, J.A. 2006. "Restructuring America's Dairy Farms." *Geographical Review* 96 (1): 1–23.

Crowley, M., D.T. Lichter, and Z.C. Qian. 2006. "Beyond Gateway Cities: Economic Restructuring and Poverty among Mexican Immigrant Families and Children." *Family Relations* 55 (3): 345–60. http://dx.doi.org/10.1111/j.1741-3729.2006.00407.x.

Durand, J., D.S. Massey, F. Charvet. 2000. "The Changing Geography of Mexican Immigration to the United States, 1910–1996." *Social Science Quarterly* 81 (1): 1–15.

Friedland, William H., Amy E. Barton, and Robert J. Thomas. 1981. *Manufacturing Green Gold: Capital, Labor, and Technology in the Lettuce Industry. The Arnold and Caroline Rose monograph series of the American Sociological Association*. New York: Cambridge University Press.

Gibson, Campbell, and Kay Jung. 2006. "Historical Census Statistics on the Foreign-Born Population in the United States: 1850 to 2000." Population Division Working Paper Number 81. Washington, DC: US Census Bureau. http://www.census.gov/population/www/documentation/twps0081/twps0081.pdf.

Goodman, D., and M. Watts. 1994. "Reconfiguring the Rural of Fording the Divide—Capitalist Restructuring and the Global Agrofood System." *Journal of Peasant Studies* 22 (1): 1–49.

Griffith, David Craig. 2006. *American Guestworkers: Jamaicans and Mexicans in the U.S. Labor Market.* University Park: Penn State University Press.

Harrison, Jill Lindsey, and Sarah E. Lloyd. 2012. "Illegality at Work: Deportability and the Productive New Era of Immigration Enforcement." *Antipode* 44 (2): 365–85. http://dx.doi.org/10.1111/j.1467-8330.2010.00841.x.

Harrison, Jill, Sarah Lloyd, and Trish O'Kane. 2009. "Overview of Immigrant Workers on Wisconsin Dairy Farms." Changing Hands: Hired Labor on Wisconsin Dairy Farms Briefing No. 1. UW-Madison Program on Agricultural Technology Studies.

Jarosz, L., and J. Qazi. 2000. "The Geography of Washington's World Apple: Global Expressions in a Local Landscape." *Journal of Rural Studies* 16 (1): 1–11. http://dx.doi.org/10.1016/S0743-0167(99)00028-5.

Kandel, W., and E.A. Parrado. 2005. "Restructuring of the US Meat Processing Industry and New Hispanic Migrant Destinations." *Population and Development Review* 31 (3): 447–71. http://dx.doi.org/10.1111/j.1728-4457.2005.00079.x.

Light, Ivan Hubert. 2006. *Deflecting Immigration: Networks, Markets, and Regulation in Los Angeles.* New York: Russell Sage Foundation.

Lobao, L., and K. Meyer. 2001. "The Great Agricultural Transition: Crisis, Change, and Social Consequences of Twentieth Century US Farming." *Annual Review of Sociology* 27 (1): 103–24. http://dx.doi.org/10.1146/annurev.soc.27.1.103.

Malone, Nolan, Kaari F. Baluja, Joseph Costanzo, and Cynthia Davis. 2003. *The Foreign-Born Population: 2000.* Census 2000 Brief, C2KBR-34. Washington, DC: US Census Bureau. http://www.census.gov/prod/2003pubs/c2kbr-34.pdf.

Maloney, Thomas R. 2002. "Management of Hispanic Employees on New York Dariy Farms: A Survey of Farm Managers." In *The Dynamics of Hired Farm Labour*, ed. J. Findeis, A.M. Vanderman, J.M. Larson, and J.L. Runyan, 67–78. New York: CABI Publishing.

Martin, Philip L., Michael Fix, and J. Edward Taylor. 2006. *The New Rural Poverty: Agriculture & Immigration in California.* Washington, DC: Urban Institute Press.

Massey, Douglas S. 2008. *New Faces in New Places: The Changing Geography of American Immigration.* New York: Russell Sage Foundation.

Massey, Douglas S., Jorge Durand, and Nolan J. Malone. 2002. *Beyond Smoke and Mirrors: Mexican Immigration in an Era of Economic Integration.* New York: Russell Sage Foundation.

McMichael, Phillip. 2005. "Global Development and The Corporate Food Regime." In *New Directions in the Sociology of Global Development*, 265–99. Research in Rural Sociology and Development, vol. 11. Bingley, UK: Emerald Group Publishing Limited. http://dx.doi.org/10.1016/S1057-1922(05)11010-5.

Mitchell, Don. 1996. *The Lie of the Land: Migrant Workers and the California Landscape.* Minneapolis: University of Minnesota Press.

Morgan, Kevin, Terry Marsden, and Jonathan Murdoch. 2006. "Networks, Conventions, and Regions: Theorizing 'Worlds of Food.'" In *Worlds of Food: Place, Power, and Provenance in the Food Chain*, ed. Kevin Morgan, Terry Marsden, and Jonathan Murdoch, 7–25. Oxford: Oxford University Press.

Passel, Jeffery, D'Vera Cohn, and Ana Gonzalez-Barrera. 2012. Net Migration from Mexico falls to Zero—and Perhaps Less. Pew Hispanic Center 2012 [cited April 2012]. http://www.pewhispanic.org/2012/04/23/net-migration-from-mexico-falls-to-zero-and-perhaps-less/.

Portes, Alejandro, and Rubén G. Rumbaut. 1996. *Immigrant America: A Portrait.* 2nd ed. Berkeley: University of California Press.

Reisler, Mark. 1976. *By the Sweat of Their Brow: Mexican Immigrant Labor in the United States, 1900–1940.* Westport, CT: Greenwood, Press.

Rosson, Parr, Flynn Adcock, Dwi Susanto, and David Anderson. 2009. The Economic Impacts of Immigration on U.S. Dairy Farms. Texas A&M University and the National Milk Producers Federation, June: Report prepared under contract for National Milk Producers Federation.

Theil, Henri. 1972. *Statistical Decomposition Analysis with Applications in the Social and Administrative Sciences.* Amsterdam: North-Holland Pub. Co.

US Department of Agriculture. 2009a. 2007 Census of Agriculture. Washington, DC.

US Department of Agriculture. 2009b. 2007 Census of Agriculture: Farm Numbers. Washington, DC.

CHAPTER 5

Agricultural Technologies and the Structure of the North American Agrifood System

Leland L. Glenna and Christopher R. Henke

Introduction

Technological innovation and change have had an immense impact on the history of agriculture, especially in the context of US agriculture during the last one hundred years. According to a US Department of Agriculture report, productivity increases are primarily responsible for the decline in farm numbers from a peak at just under seven million in 1935 to just over two million in the 1970s (Hoppe and Banker 2010). Although farm numbers have stabilized since the 1970s, productivity has continued to increase. As of 2007, just 12 percent of US farms accounted for 84 percent of US production (Hoppe and Banker 2010). When so few farms account for so much production, it is hard to deny the role that farm machinery, synthetic pesticides and fertilizers, biotechnologies, and other scientific and technological breakthroughs have had on the development of the contemporary North American agriculture and food (agrifood) system. At the same time, however, this focus on technological change can often lead to a narrow view of what technology is and how it affects farming and broader agrifood systems, leading to a kind of technological determinism and uncritical progressivism. When agricultural problems are portrayed as repeatedly being solved by the newest technology (e.g., Schlebecker 1975) or when attention is focused on the adoption rates of new technologies (e.g., Rogers 2003), primacy is given to technology. Such perspectives tend to reinforce ideological agendas and mask underlying conflicts and competing processes.

Work in science and technology studies (STS) has emphasized the contingency of technological development and implementation, especially the structures of interest, power, and conflict that shape what comes to be seen as discrete technological artifacts. In this view, technologies are systems of social and material relationships that cannot be easily disentangled (Bijker, Hughes, and Pinch 1987; Bauchspies, Croissant, and Restivo 2006; Glenna, Jussaume, and Dawson 2011a). STS analyses of farm technologies, such as hybrid corn (Fitzgerald 1993; Ramey 2010), tractors (Jellison 1993; Harper 2001), or integrated pest management (Warner 2007; McWilliams 2008) focus on how these technologies are embedded in larger institutional and organizational systems that shape technological developments and their ultimate integration into systems of agricultural production. This systems approach to technology is important in the case of agricultural technologies because, despite a long-standing rhetoric that connects agricultural science and technology with progress for farmers and society in general, the reality has been more nuanced and even ironic. Famers have often contested new technologies, and a deterministic view of technology may obscure the role of the state in pushing for the development and implementation of new farming machinery and methods in the context of a competitive political economy. Agriculture is a complex system of social and material relations, and the promise of any form of progressive change, technological or otherwise, depends on understanding the full extent of these relations.

In this chapter, we explore the role of science and technology in shaping the history and contemporary structure of US agriculture, focusing especially on the role of state and industry actors in emphasizing intensive agricultural production. Ramey (2010) uses "pushbutton cornucopia" to describe the way that technologies are promoted as quick fixes for an increasingly industrialized agrifood system. She borrows the term from a 1959 *Time* magazine article that praises agricultural technologies for enabling the application of "assembly line techniques" to agriculture that, at the time, were more characteristic of manufacturing. The pushbutton cornucopia is a way to frame our critique of the trends in the North American agrifood system. Indeed, the implementation of new mechanical, biological, and chemical technologies in agricultural production has led to higher agricultural productivity with the push of a button. However, that agricultural transformation has coincided with the neoliberalization of the North American agrifood system, especially in the form of increasingly concentrated food production and processing by fewer growers and agribusinesses integrated into global commodity chains (see Constance et al. in this volume).

In this chapter, we detail five key historical, political, and economic dimensions shaping the emergence and application of agricultural science and technology in the United States. These dimensions include: (1) the unique history of the US land-grant university system and the role of the capitalist state in sponsoring and promoting agricultural science and technology; (2) the cultural world of agricultural scientists and the influences of agribusiness on their work; (3) resistance movements that question the direction of agricultural research; (4) state policies that facilitate the hybridization of public and private agricultural research efforts; and (5) the ongoing tension between technological fixes versus more holistic management-oriented solutions to the problems of agriculture. For each of these factors, we emphasize the historically situated structures that have promoted the emergence of contemporary agrifood systems, while also considering forces that are accelerating past trends and perhaps promoting new ones.

The Land-Grant University System and the Science of Repair

The legislation that created the land-grant university (LGU) system had the explicit goal of applying science to boost manufacturing and to facilitate the industrialization of agriculture, and it created what would become the world's largest scientific research apparatus during the first half of the twentieth century (Friedland 1991). LGUs are often referred to as "the people's universities" because they were charged with making science and technology accessible to the public and applicable to agricultural and manufacturing progress (McDowell 2001). Early in the history of LGUs, however, there were already questions about the appropriate balance between research applied toward the practical production issues of specific farm communities and the kinds of questions that would advance the knowledge base of fields such as agronomy, agricultural chemistry, and other agriculturally relevant disciplines. Many of the first agricultural scientists that LGUs employed in the nineteenth century were trained in the German tradition laid down by Justus Liebig, which emphasized basic research focused on the fundamental processes of agriculture (Rossiter 1975). Perhaps even more crucially, scientists prioritized the goal of increasing the productivity of agriculture, believing, "to make two blades of grass flourish where one had before . . . was to act in an unambiguously moral fashion" (Rosenberg 1977, 403; Rossiter 1975; Marcus 1985; Henke 2008).

This focus on production has served as perhaps the single most consistent element of the LGUs' mission, despite criticisms that agricultural scientists have often acted as what Friedland (1974) refers to as "social sleepwalkers," developing new technologies and practices without considering the larger social consequences of increased agricultural production, especially the declining viability of small farms, the economic concentration of large agribusinesses, and the promotion of a resource-intensive and environmentally destructive agricultural system (see also Danbom 1979; Friedland 1991; Scott 1998; NRC 2002). Two examples illustrate the interactions of agricultural scientists, agricultural industrializers, and the state in promoting productivism.

First, the Country Life Movement was a Progressive Era social movement intended to modernize US agriculture and improve the lives of rural people. Danbom (1979) describes how the Country Life Commission and the larger Progressive Movement shared an uncritical focus on maximizing production outputs, which created a vicious cycle as supply exceeded demand. Farmers needed to increase production even more in an effort to increase their return on investment, which often had the paradoxical effect of reducing prices even more. Cochrane (1993) refers to this condition as the "technological treadmill." Through the uncritical emphasis on using agricultural science to increase yields, therefore, the commission, which consisted of prominent agricultural scientists and state and industrial representatives, contributed to dramatic structural changes in agriculture. Though its explicit intention may not have been the industrialization of US agriculture, the means by which it promoted productive efficiency had that ultimate effect (Henke 2008, chapter 4).

Second, as this cycle of overproduction became entrenched, the network of LGU agricultural scientists and extension agents formed what Henke (2008) calls a "technology of repair." The LGU system responded to production problems with technical fixes, which were shaped by the structure of the industrial agrifood system and ultimately perpetuated it. Although Cooperative Extension was ostensibly created to raise farm communities' standard of living in general through new techniques and technologies intended to improve agricultural productivity (as well as rural home efficiency through a system of "home demonstration agents"), the details of this mission were underspecified from the start (Danbom 1979; Marcus 1985; Henke 2008). Agents were typically trained with some level of postsecondary education in agricultural science, and thus their work with farmers was often most successful when the cultural and human capital of agent and farmer meshed most fully. This integration of farmers and extension agents was reinforced through the formation of the Farm Bureau system, which brought the wealthier and more politically conservative farmers into direct contact with Cooperative Extension agents (Henke 2008, chapters 2–3).

In the case of California's fresh produce industry, Cooperative Extension maintained the structure of the farm industry in the face of a wide variety of problems, including typical production-related issues such as the control of pests and the promotion of new technologies. When labor shortages emerged during World War II, Cooperative Extension was employed as a labor contracting service, eventually known as the Bracero program, which helped to coordinate migrant labor supply and even set local wages for farm work. Delegating the responsibility for farm labor management to the state repaired the industry's logistical and political challenges and proved so lucrative that it persisted well past the end of the war, ending only in 1965 (Henke 2008).

It would be an oversimplification to state that the agricultural industry completely coopted Cooperative Extension. In fact, there were instances of opposition, particularly in the case of the Bracero program. However, state and industrial actors were able to harness the structure of the industry and the practical tools and skills of Cooperative Extension, so that they worked in tandem to correct the growing pains of an industry that now supplies the majority of the fresh produce for the nation. In this way, Cooperative Extension provided the repair infrastructure that allowed the industry to consolidate its power relative to farm labor, through state-sponsored organizational expertise (Henke 2008).

The science of repair is useful for understanding the contemporary role of science and technology in applying stopgap solutions to systemic agricultural problems, particularly in the area of animal husbandry. Antibiotics are used for therapeutic purposes to keep animals alive in poor living conditions of concentrated livestock feeding operations (CAFOs). They are also used to enhance animal weight gain. As early as the 1950s, research demonstrated that antibiotics would "enhance the feed-to-weight ratio for poultry, swine, and beef cattle" (Marshall and Levy 2011, 718). Research indicates the widespread use of antibiotics in CAFOs has given rise to resistant strains of bacteria, including salmonella (White et al. 2001). The widespread use of anti-parasite drugs has also been linked to resistant parasites in cattle, sheep, and goats in Australia, Brazil, and the United States (Kaplan and Vidyashankar 2012). Furthermore, researchers now connect drug resistance in animals to drug resistance in humans, a problem world health organizations currently list as "one of the top health challenges facing the 21st century" (Marshall and Levy 2011, 718). These problems related to agricultural livestock management illustrate well both the systemic technological structure of agriculture, and how a relatively narrow focus on repair of certain elements within the system often leads to broader environmental and human health impacts. In this respect, though these impacts may even be anticipated and solvable, commitment to the system by industry actors promotes a pushbutton approach over structural change.

The Political Economy of Science and Technology

During the middle decades of the twentieth century, state-oriented efforts directing agricultural science and technology toward increasing productive efficiency expanded. One of the most prominently touted successes of the period was hybrid corn. Average corn yields in the early 1900s were in the area of twenty to thirty bushels per acre. By the first decade of 2000, corn yields had increased to 163 bushels per acre (Ramey 2010). The seeming success of hybrid corn, however, which is typically portrayed as a scientific and technical breakthrough, masks a constellation of political, economic, and cultural factors that also shaped corn yields. At least two points are important here. First, Berlan and Lewontin (1986) highlight a cultural obstacle to yield improvement by noting that corn breeding and selection in the early 1900s was primarily directed at improving the appearance of corn, not increasing yield. That changed when public and private investment in research to increase yield started in the 1920s. They note that such a political and economic mobilization would have likely increased yield even without hybridization. By way of comparison, Berlan and Lewontin (1986) observe that wheat yields increased even faster than corn, but without hybridization, between 1937 and 1945. They further note that increased corn yields coincided with mechanization, crop rotation, fertilizers, and public subsidies for production.

Second, hybridization paralleled efforts to gain intellectual property protection for agricultural research discoveries. Kloppenburg (2004) and Berlan and Lewontin (1986) argue that hybridization was chosen less for its contribution to yield than for providing a biological patent that would attract the private sector's involvement in plant breeding. Because it is not practical to successfully save high-quality seed from hybrid corn for the following year's planting, farmers who commit to using hybrid corn would need to purchase seed each year. Kloppenburg (2004) explains that hybrid corn was the initial step in privatizing seeds. The creation and strict enforcement of intellectual property protection for genetically engineered seeds is the latest step in that privatization effort.

The productivist agricultural research agenda has also had consequences outside the United States. First, the problem of overproduction and low commodity prices afflicting US farmers became a global problem through Public Law 480. This policy promotes the dumping of cheap, subsidized commodities on the global market, driving down commodity prices for small farmers around the globe (McMichael 2008). Second, crop and animal breeding programs intended to increase production in the United States became institutionalized through the Green Revolution in the Consultative Group on International Agricultural Research (McMichael 2008). Scholars have long questioned whether the Green Revolution was benign or universally beneficial, since it tended to be chemically intensive and focused on large-scale, capital intensive production (Araghi 2000; Freebairn 1995). After a thorough assessment of the Green Revolution, Evenson and Gollin (2003) conclude that large farmers disproportionately benefitted, while smallholder farmers tended to face negative social and economic impacts.

Applied Agricultural R&D and its Populist Challenge

In contrast to the National Science Foundation (NSF), which has focused on funding basic research, the USDA and LGU system was funded on the assumption that increased production would yield applicable public goods. During the 1970s and 1980s, however, the rationale behind publicly supported agricultural research and development (R&D) was attacked from two directions—one populist and the other neoliberal. The populist strain of critique was most evident in Jim Hightower's *Hard Tomatoes, Hard Times* (1973), a direct challenge to LGUs' research priorities. Hightower, an activist and former commissioner of agriculture for the state of Texas, claimed that LGUs had "become a handmaiden of corporate agribusiness" despite the intended role as "an institution of the people" (Hightower 1973, 8; Buttel 2005). This critique, which came to be known as Hightowerism, attracted public and US congressional attention, and coincided with the back-to-the-land and alternative food movements of the 1970s, as well as more general critiques of the industrialized food system (e.g., Berry 1977; Belasco 1989)

Buttel (2005) clarifies that Hightowerism was problematic from the outset, because it ostensibly attacked the LGU model for failing to live up to the ideal of the people's university when, in fact, LGUs have always emphasized higher yields and reduced labor costs over the broader interests of small farmers. More importantly, perhaps, Hightower's harsh critique of agricultural science and technology had elements of tragedy, since it coincided with a restructuring of agricultural R&D. The 1970s saw a decline in public support for agricultural research, a rise in private sector agricultural research, and a shift in agricultural colleges to more basic (molecularization) research (the NSF model). In addition to being premised on some flawed assumptions and lack of awareness of emerging trends, the Hightower movement, rather than coalescing around an effort to democratize agricultural R&D, bifurcated into (1) the sustainable/local food movement, and the (2) anti-genetically engineered crops movement, a split that undermined its impact (Buttel 2005).

Efforts to democratize agricultural R&D have been mixed. One prominent example is the lawsuit filed against the University of California (UC) system based on the claim that the research that contributed to the mechanization of tomato and lettuce harvesting served private interests at the expense of the public interest. Friedland (1991) explains that, between 1973 and 1978, a group of faculty, students, legal and rural advocacy groups, and other citizens coordinated with California Rural Legal Assistance to file a lawsuit to challenge the way the UC system works. A judge ruled that the Hatch Act requires that small or family farmers and consumers and rural communities must be beneficiaries of LGU research, that the UC system had failed to act accordingly in the development of the tomato and lettuce harvesting machines, and that the universities must establish a process to guarantee that these people are served. Despite the initial court victory, according to Friedland (1991), the reform efforts became complicated. First, they had to achieve a delicate balance between defending the autonomy of the public university and simultaneously claiming that agribusiness interests had captured the university when it should be influenced by the public interest. Second, a number of agribusiness-friendly groups, such as the Grange and the Farm Bureau Federation, claimed to represent the interests of small farmers. This led to the formation of a constituency group that was less well organized than the agribusiness groups (Friedland 1991). The experiment in democratizing the UC system ended when the initial court ruling was overturned on appeal.

The reasons for the lack of convergence between social movements and efforts to transform agricultural research may be due more to structural obstacles than to lack of creative thinking on the part of movement organizers. Kinchy's (2010a; 2010b) work on the anti-genetically engineered crops movements in Mexico and Canada demonstrates that genetic engineering in agriculture is framed by a high level of scientific discourse, which serves as an institutional barrier to the democratization of agricultural research, even in cases where the social movement is well-informed and sophisticated (Kinchy 2010a).

Despite the documented failures to democratize agricultural research, however, successful efforts to promote farmer-driven research should not be discounted. Studying organic and rotational grazing dairy farmers in Wisconsin, Hassanein (1999) describes the power relations implicit in agricultural R&D. Hassanein (1999) uncovers animosity toward the LGU system's information-generation and adoption-diffusion techniques among alternative agriculture proponents and practitioners. Still, she finds that the alternative agriculture organizations were open to inviting university experts to their meetings, as long as the outside experts entered the discussion on the farmers' terms and responded to research questions the farmers generated. Eshleman (2011) arrives at similar findings in a comparative study of conventional extension programs at the Pennsylvania State University (PSU), the Women's Agricultural Network, which is a less-conventional PSU extension program, and the Pennsylvania Association for Sustainable Agriculture, which is independent of PSU. He examined agricultural knowledge exchange in the context of livestock, crop, and machinery field days for the three distinct outreach programs. Using the concept of thought collectives, Eshleman (2011) explains that the social context in which the research question is generated and through which the information is diffused has important implications for understanding the diverse and complex relationships between the expert and layperson.

These examples of farmer-driven research are minor in terms of volumes of production and amount of research dollars when compared to the overall budgets of agribusiness and LGU research. However, there are hundreds of thousands of small farmers that these farmer-driven research efforts represent. Whether those farmer interests will be served is an open question. What makes Buttel's (2005) critique of Hightowerism insightful is that he highlights the need to recognize that populist efforts to reform agricultural research at LGUs occur within complex, flexible, and ever-changing contexts. Specifically, it is important to recognize that Hightower and other challengers to the LGU agricultural R&D model have coincided with broader political-economic transitions in national R&D. Slaughter and Rhoades (2004) describe how shifts, such as the end of the Vietnam War and the Cold War, undermined welfare-state coalitions in US Congress, which gave way to the rise of the economic-competitiveness coalition. As these political-economic transitions were taking place, the rationale for agricultural R&D was also shifting toward a neoliberal model.

The Neoliberal Challenge to Agricultural R&D

Agricultural R&D, and the larger landscape of public research funding in general, was subject to a neoliberal critique, beginning especially in the 1980s, that manifested most clearly in the form of the 1980 Bayh-Dole Act. Prior to 1980, few universities encouraged their scientists to pursue proprietary research. Few university scientists went through the time-consuming legal process of gaining the government's approval to patent publicly funded research discoveries. A series of policies beginning with the Bayh-Dole Act, however, streamlined the patenting process for universities by giving university scientists the right to patent their discoveries and by encouraging them to seek ways to pass those discoveries to the private sector (Slaughter and Rhoades 2004). By allowing universities to gain intellectual property protection, the state enabled private companies to leverage their investments in university research, even when the research is conducted in a publicly funded university laboratory (McSherry 2001).

The goals of the Bayh-Dole Act have fostered and reinforced other developments. Retiring public breeders have been replaced by molecular biologists unable to send their products directly to farmers (Knight 2003). The agricultural input and processing components of the agrifood system have become increasingly concentrated in the hands of a few companies (Glenna and Cahoy 2009). University scientists have found it necessary to collaborate with private companies to distribute their research to the public. Additionally, government funding increasingly promotes university-industry research collaborations (UIRs). These shifts are largely responsible for the rise of UIRs, university scientists' pursuit of private sector and competitive sector research funds, and university scientists' pursuit of intellectual property over the past four decades (Glenna et al. 2011b).

Glenna et al. (2007) argue that these shifts were supported by a neoliberal rationale that portrays public research as useless unless commercialized. They offer two equations to illustrate the shift from the NSF model for research to the neoliberal model in university plant and animal research that has implications for agriculture. Under the NSF and LGU/USDA rationales, the public good is considered the sum of public and private goods:

public goods + private goods = the public good

In contrast, under the Bayh-Dole model, the assumption is that public goods from the university are generally unused and a waste of public money unless used by the private sector. Therefore, public goods must be converted into private goods to contribute to the public good:

public goods → private goods >> the public good

Through interviews with university administrators, Glenna et al. (2007) find that many administrators who oversee UIRs have internalized the rhetoric of the Bayh-Dole Act and advocate for the privatization of university research. Universities are still expected to conduct basic research and other types of research that may not have immediate commercial applications. However, universities are also now expected to generate intellectual property and develop UIRs to explore commercial opportunities.

Some contend that the emphasis on privatizing university research has not had a discernible negative impact on the activities of university scientists in the form of reduced basic research or fewer journal publications (e.g., Thursby and Thursby 2011). Scientists may indeed be generating publications while also generating intellectual property. However, such a simplistic way of categorizing public- and private-interest science may be misleading. Journal publications fit into the category of public goods, but they are just one indicator of research serving the public interest, and not all publications serve the public interest equally.

This point can be illustrated through an analysis of transgenic crop research. Traditionally, universities have been responsible for conducting research on minor (orphan) crops, since they tend to have a high return on public investment but low return on private investment. Although university research in major crops is also expected, the rationale is that private sector research facilities already have an incentive to concentrate on major crops because of the potential for profit. Therefore, universities should primarily focus on minor crops.

Welsh and Glenna (2006) compare industry and university applications to conduct research on genetically engineered crops. They hypothesize that if university researchers were expected to focus on public-interest research, then agricultural crop research at universities would primarily be conducted on minor crops and minor traits. Private sector research, by contrast, would focus on major crops and major traits. What Welsh and Glenna (2006) find, however, is that university research on genetically engineered crops over time increasingly parallels private sector research. Therefore, although university scientists may be publishing more publically accessible research than private sector scientists, those journal publications are more likely to focus on the major crops and major traits that university scientists are now studying. This suggests there may be a crowding-out effect, as university researchers concentrate on the most commercially relevant crops and traits.

Glenna et al. (2011b) also find that funding source influences university scientists. Their analysis of a nation-wide survey of 912 plant and animal biotechnology scientists at sixty research universities reveals that industry funding is significantly associated with more applied and proprietary research. However, they also find that scientists' value orientations affect the amount of industry funding they receive, the proprietary nature of their discoveries, and the percentage of basic science research conducted in their laboratories. The findings suggest that strong incentives for public-science research along with adequate public-research funds to preserve the university's vital role in conducting basic and non-proprietary research are needed to complement private sector research investments at universities.

Conclusions

Agricultural science and technology have always been influenced by political, historical, and economic contexts. The neoliberal context that predominates today is simply the most recent manifestation. In his introduction to this section, Bonanno describes the increasing entrenchment and expansion of neoliberalism, which raises questions about future trends in agricultural R&D.

One prominent recent development is performance-based university research funding. In this system, funding for university research is directed to universities that are deemed to be achieving specified performance goals. Hicks (2012, 251) contends that although this strategy of "aiming for excellence" may shift resources to the most productive scientists and the most effective universities, it is also likely to undermine diversity and equity among universities. In the case of agricultural R&D, implementing such a program would likely exacerbate the challenges created by the shift from formula funds to competitive funds.

Neoliberalism and the associated trends in pursuing research that is likely to generate a revenue stream are having a discernible influence on LGU R&D. University research agendas focusing on biological pest control and noncommercial herbicide approaches to weed control are in decline (Warner et al. 2011; Davis et al. 2009). A group of LGU scientists recently sent a letter to the US Environmental Protection Agency claiming that intellectual property restrictions are preventing them from conducting important agricultural research. Twenty-six of those scientists asked that their names be withheld because they feared retribution from large agribusinesses (Pollack 2009). Although university researchers maintain organic and agroecological research agendas, agribusiness-driven transgenic crops continue to expand into greater percentages of crop acreage in the North America and the world. Genetically engineered crops, such as glyphosate resistance in crops, account for approximately 90 percent of US corn, cotton, and soybean acreage, even as weeds are developing resistance to glyphosate (NRC 2010). These trends suggest that the public sector's agricultural R&D infrastructure is being eroded as the private sector's agricultural R&D impact is becoming dominant.

Despite the neoliberal trend, however, agricultural R&D in universities and industries remains contested. As just one example, agricultural biotechnologies continue to be controversial (though with great variability) on a global scale. Because these technologies are being developed at specific research institutions and tested on particular plots of land, their locations offer up specific sites for protest and vandalism, providing a kind of target for protestors to direct their opposition to the structure of the food system (Henke and Gieryn 2008, 366–69). Therefore, the fact that farming will and must remain based in specific locations makes the future of agricultural science and technology in North America and around the globe anything but inevitable. The outcomes of the future conflicts will provide new opportunities to understand the intersection of political-economic context and agricultural science and technology.

Moore et al. (2011) argue that the emergence of the global knowledge economy has globalized the neoliberalization of science. They further argue that this raises important research questions about how university-industry relations will be shaped in the global knowledge economy, how emerging global regulatory regimes might shape the future of science and technology, and how these development will shape the relationship between science, technology, and social movements, as well as civil society more generally. Sharing an interest in the relationship between science, technology, and civil society, Lacy and Glenna (2005/2006) contend that one of the unintended consequences of the rise of the commercialization of science is that it exposes the fallacy of pure science. They further argue that this realization may create opportunities to advocate for the democratization of agricultural research, thus promoting the ideal of the people's science. Participatory plant breeding (PPB) and farmer-driven research agendas illustrate how LGU agricultural research agendas can be democratized, as well as how they might promote more holistic and sustainable approaches to agricultural R&D (Ervin, Glenna, and Jussaume 2011). PPB programs employ strategies that might be categorized according to various degrees of farmer participation. Glenna, Jussaume, and Dawson (2011a) describe a university wheat-breeding program that employed a survey to gain farmer feedback on program goals and projects. Although surveying farmers represents only modest farmer participation, there are examples of more intensive farmer participation. Mendum and Glenna (2010) analyze a PPB project that incorporated farmers into the process of setting the research agenda and in shaping dissemination strategies. Dawson and Goldberger (2008) explore farmer interest in a PPB project in which wheat breeders worked with farmers to develop their own new wheat varieties that would be more suitable for their diverse farming systems. Although these latter two PPB examples reflect intensive farmer participation, Mendum and Glenna (2010) document substantial intellectual property and funding obstacles that favor conventional agricultural knowledge generation and technology transfer approaches over participatory approaches.

Public and private investment in agricultural R&D has remained flat since 1975 (Fuglie et al. 2011). Social scientists argue that public support for agricultural research must increase to address problems in the United States and globally (Huffman et al. 2006). Similar developments have emerged in terms of international agricultural development funds. Public support has been in decline over the past few decades, while private foundations, industries, and nongovernmental organizations have become more involved in international agricultural R&D (Ransom and Bain 2011). Whether the US government and other governments recognize the need to fund agricultural R&D, the context necessary for innovation remains important area for research, since ironies are evident in these trends. Intellectual property policies and flat funding may be stifling agricultural innovation in the United States, but there may be new opportunities for agricultural R&D in other parts of the world. For example, Graff, Roland-Holst, and Zilberman (2006) argue that industrialized nations in the past achieved the greatest gains in agricultural R&D because of investments in research, favorable knowledge exchange policies, and development of human capital. Currently, emerging economies, including China, India, and Brazil, are making coordinated efforts to pursue these goals. As a result, some of the greatest agricultural innovations in the future are likely to emerge in these countries (Graff, Roland-Holst, and Zilberman 2006). After examining a range of agricultural development studies, the United Nations' Special Rapporteur on food concluded that world food production could be doubled by using agroecological practices and targeting smallholder producers (De Schutter 2010). Rural and development sociologists have been making similar arguments for decades, but the adoption of this position by the United Nations' Special Rapporteur on the Right to Food raises new questions about potential impacts. The most exciting future research opportunities on agricultural science and technology may be outside of the United States.

References

Araghi, Farshad. 2000. "The Great Global Enclosure of Our Times: Peasants and the Agrarian Question at the End of the Twentieth Century." In *Hungry for Profit*, ed. F. Magdoff, J.B. Foster, and F.H. Buttel, 145–60. New York: Monthly Review.

Bauchspies, Wenda K., Jennifer Croissant, and Sal Restivo. 2006. *Science, Technology, and Society: A Sociological Approach.* Malden, MA: Blackwell.

Belasco, Warren. 1989. *Appetite for Change: How the Counterculture Took on the Food Industry.* Ithaca, NY: Cornell University Press.

Berlan, Jean Pierre, and Richard Lewontin. 1986. "The Political Economy of Hybrid Corn." *Monthly Review* (New York, NY) 38: 35–47.

Berry, Wendell. 1977. *The Unsettling of America: Culture and Agriculture.* New York: Avon Books.

Bijker, Wiebe E., Thomas P. Hughes, and Trevor J. Pinch, eds. 1987. *The Social Construction of Technological Systems: New Directions in the Sociology and History of Technology.* Cambridge, MA: MIT Press.

Buttel, Fred. 2005. "Ever since Hightower: The Politics of Agricultural Research Activism in the Molecular Age." *Agriculture and Human Values* 22 (3): 275–83. http://dx.doi.org/10.1007/s10460-005-6043-3.

Cochrane, Willard W. 1993. *The Development of American Agriculture: A Historical Analysis.* Minneapolis: University of Minnesota Press.

Danbom, David B. 1979. *The Resisted Revolution: Urban America and the Industrialization of Agriculture, 1900–1930.* Ames: Iowa State University Press.

Dawson, Julie C., and Jessica R. Goldberger. 2008. "Assessing Farmer Interest in Participatory Plant Breeding: Who Wants to Work with Scientists?" *Renewable Agriculture and Food Systems* 23 (3): 177–87. http://dx.doi.org/10.1017/S1742170507002141.

Davis, A.S., J.C. Hall, M. Jasieniuk, M.A. Locke, E.C. Luschei, D.A. Mortensen, D.E. Riechers, R.G. Smith, T.M. Sterling, and J.H. Westwood. 2009. "Weed Science Research and Funding: A Call to Action." *Weed Science* 57 (4): 442–8. http://dx.doi.org/10.1614/WS-09-020.1.

De Schutter, Olivier. 2010. "Agro-ecology and the Right to Food." Report presented to the United Nations General Assembly Human Rights Council. Geneva, Switzerland: UN Human Rights Council. Accessed 2 April 2011. http://www.srfood.org/en/report-agroecology-and-the-right-to-food.

Ervin, David E., Leland L. Glenna, and Raymond A. Jussaume, Jr. 2011. "The Theory and Practice of Genetically Engineered Crops and Agricultural Sustainability." *Sustainability* 3 (12): 847–74. http://dx.doi.org/10.3390/su3060847.

Eshleman, John T. 2011. "Knowledge Co-production and Agricultural Field Days: A Comparison of Three Models." Unpublished master's thesis. The Pennsylvania State University Rural Sociology Program.

Evenson, R.E., and D. Gollin. 2 May 2003. "Assessing the Impact of the Green Revolution, 1960 to 2000." *Science* 300 (5,620): 758–62. http://dx.doi.org/10.1126/science.1078710. Medline:12730592.

Fitzgerald, Deborah. 1993. "Farmers Deskilled: Hybrid Corn and Farmers' Work." *Technology and Culture* 34 (2): 324–43. http://dx.doi.org/10.2307/3106539.

Freebairn, Donald K. 1995. "Did the Green Revolution Concentrate Incomes? A Quantitative Study of Research Reports." *World Development* 23 (2): 265–79. http://dx.doi.org/10.1016/0305-750X(94)00116-G.

Friedland, William H. 1974. "Social Sleepwalkers: Scientific and Technological Research in California Agriculture." Davis, CA: UC Davis, Department of Applied Behavioral Sciences, Research Monograph 13.

Friedland, William H. 1991. "Engineering Social Change in Agriculture." *University of Dayton Review* 21 (1): 25–42.

Fuglie, Keith O., Paul W. Heisey, John L. King, Carl E. Pray, Kelly Day-Rubenstein, David Schimmelpfennig, Sun Ling Wang, and Rupa Karmarkar-Deshmukh. 2011. *Research Investments and Market Structure in the Food Processing, Agricultural Input, and Biofuel Industries Worldwide. ERR-130.* US Dept. of Agriculture, Economic Research Service.

Glenna, Leland L., and Daniel R. Cahoy. 2009. "Agribusiness Concentration, Intellectual Property, and the Prospects for Rural Economic Benefits from the Emerging Biofuel Economy." *Southern Rural Sociology* 24 (2): 111–29.

Glenna, Leland L., Raymond A. Jussaume Jr., and Julie C. Dawson. 2011a. "How Farmers Matter in Shaping Agricultural Technologies: Social and Structural Characteristics of Wheat Growers and Wheat Varieties." *Agriculture and Human Values* 28 (2): 213–24. http://dx.doi.org/10.1007/s10460-010-9275-9.

Glenna, Leland L., William B. Lacy, Rick Welsh, and Dina Biscotti. 2007. "University Administrators, Agricultural Biotechnology, and Academic Capitalism: Defining the Public Good to Promote University-Industry Relationships." *Sociological Quarterly* 48 (1): 141–64. http://dx.doi.org/10.1111/j.1533-8525.2007.00074.x.

Glenna, Leland L., Rick Welsh, David Ervin, William B. Lacy, and Dina Biscotti. 2011b. "Commercial Science, Scientists' Values, and University Biotechnology Research Agenda." *Research Policy* 40 (7): 957–68. http://dx.doi.org/10.1016/j.respol.2011.05.002.

Graff, Gegory, David Roland-Holst, and David Zilberman. 2006. "Agricultural Biotechnology and Poverty Reduction in Low-Income Countries." *World Development* 34 (8): 1430–45. http://dx.doi.org/10.1016/j.worlddev.2005.10.014.

Harper, Douglas. 2001. *Changing Works: Visions of a Lost Agriculture.* Chicago: University of Chicago Press.

Hassanein, Neva. 1999. *Changing the Way America Farms: Knowledge and Community in the Sustainable Agriculture Movement.* Lincoln: University of Nebraska Press.

Henke, Christopher R. 2008. *Cultivating Science, Harvesting Power: Science and Industrial Agriculture in California.* Cambridge, MA: MIT Press. http://dx.doi.org/10.7551/mitpress/9780262083737.001.0001.

Henke, Christopher R., and Thomas F. Gieryn. 2008. "Sites of Scientific Practice: The Enduring Importance of Place." In *The Handbook of Science and Technology Studies.* 3rd ed., ed. Edward Hackett, Olga Amsterdamska, Michael E. Lynch, and Judy Wajcman, 353–76. Cambridge, MA: MIT Press.

Hicks, Diana. 2012. "Performance-Based University Research Funding Systems." *Research Policy* 41 (2): 251–61. http://dx.doi.org/10.1016/j.respol.2011.09.007.

Hightower, Jim. 1973. *Hard Tomatoes, Hard Times. A Report of the Agribusiness Accountability Project on the Failure of America's Land Grant College Complex.* Rochester, VT: Schenkman Books.

Hoppe, Robert A., and David E. Banker. 2010. "Structure and Finances of U.S. Farms: Family Farm Report, 2010 Edition." Economic Information Bulletin Number 66. Washington, DC: United States Department of Agriculture Economic Research Service.

Huffman, W.E., G. Norton, G. Traxler, G. Frisvold, and J. Foltz. 2006. "Winners and Losers: Formula versus Competitive Funding of Agricultural Research." *Choices* (New York, NY) 21: 269–74.

Jellison, Katherine. 1993. *Entitled to Power: Farm Women and Technology, 1913–1963.* Chapel Hill: University of North Carolina Press.

Kaplan, Ray M., and Anand N. Vidyashankar. 4 May 2012. "An Inconvenient Truth: Global Worming and Anthelmintic Resistance." *Veterinary Parasitology* 186 (1–2): 70–8. http://dx.doi.org/10.1016/j.vetpar.2011.11.048. Medline:22154968.

Kinchy, Abby J. 2010a. "Anti-genetic Engineering Activism and Scientized Politics in the Case of 'Contaminated' Mexican Maize." *Agriculture and Human Values* 27 (4): 505–17. http://dx.doi.org/10.1007/s10460-009-9253-2.

Kinchy, Abby J. 2010b. "Epistemic Boomerang: Expert Policy Advice as Leverage in the Campaign against Transgenic Maize in Mexico." *Mobilization (San Diego, CA)* 15 (2): 179–98.

Kloppenburg, J.R., Jr. 2004. *First the Seed: The Political Economy of Plant Biotechnology: 1942 to 2000.* Madison: University of Wisconsin Press.

Knight, Jonathan. 6 February 2003. "Crop Improvement: A Dying Breed." *Nature* 421 (6,923): 568–70. http://dx.doi.org/10.1038/421568a. Medline:12571562.

Lacy, William B., and Leland Glenna. 2005/2006. "Democratizing Science in an Era of Expert and Private Knowledge." *International Journal of Technology, Knowledge, and Society* 1 (3): 37–46.

Marcus, Alan I. 1985. *Agricultural Science and the Quest for Legitimacy: Farmers, Agricultural Colleges, and Experiment Stations, 1870–1890.* Ames: Iowa State University Press.

Marshall, Bonnie M., and Stuart B. Levy. October 2011. "Food Animals and Antimicrobials: Impacts on Human Health." *Clinical Microbiology Reviews* 24 (4): 718–33. http://dx.doi.org/10.1128/CMR.00002-11. Medline:21976606.

McDowell, G.R. 2001. *Land-Grant Universities and Extension in the 21st Century: Renegotiating or Abandoning a Social Contract.* Ames: Iowa State University Press.

McMichael, Philip. 2008. *Development and Social Change: A Global Perspective.* Los Angeles, CA: Pine Forge Press.

McSherry, Corynne. 2001. *Who Owns Academic Work: Battling for Control of Intellectual Property.* Cambridge, MA: Harvard University Press.

McWilliams, James E. 2008. *American Pests: The Losing War on Insects from Colonial Times to DDT.* New York: Columbia University Press.

Mendum, Ruth, and Leland L. Glenna. 2010. "Socioeconomic Obstacles to Establishing a Participatory Plant Breeding Program for Organic Growers in the United States." *Sustainability* 2 (1): 73–91. http://dx.doi.org/10.3390/su2010073.

Moore, Kelly, Daniel Lee Kleinman, David Hess, and Scott Frickel. 2011. "Science and Neoliberal Globalization: A Political Sociological Approach." *Theory and Society* 40 (5): 505–32. http://dx.doi.org/10.1007/s11186-011-9147-3.

National Research Council. 2002. *Publicly Funded Agricultural Research and the Changing Structure of U.S. Agriculture.* Washington, DC: National Academies Press.

National Research Council. 2010. *Toward Sustainable Agricultural Systems in the 21st Century.* Washington, DC: National Academies Press.

Pollack, Andrew. 2009. "Crop Scientists Say Biotechnology Seed Companies Are Thwarting Research." *New York Times.* 20 February. http://www.nytimes.com/2009/02/20/business/20crop.html.

Ramey, Elizabeth A. 2010. "Seeds of Change: Hybrid Corn, Monopoly, and the Hunt for Superprofits." *Review of Radical Political Economics* 42 (3): 381–86. http://dx.doi.org/10.1177/0486613410378005.

Ransom, Elizabeth, and Carmen Bain. 2011. "Gendering Agricultural Aid: An Analysis of Whether International Development Assistance Targets Women and Gender." *Gender & Society* 25 (1): 48–74. http://dx.doi.org/10.1177/0891243210392571.

Rogers, Everett M. 2003. *Diffusion of Innovations.* New York, NY: Free Press.

Rosenberg, Charles E. 1977. "Rationalization and Reality in the Shaping of American Agricultural Research, 1875–1914." *Social Studies of Science* 7 (4): 401–22. http://dx.doi.org/10.1177/030631277700700409.

Rossiter, Margaret W. 1975. *The Emergence of Agricultural Science: Justus Liebig and the Americans, 1840–1880.* New Haven, CT: Yale University Press.

Schlebecker, John T. 1975. *Whereby We Thrive: A History of American Farming, 1607–1972.* Ames: Iowa State University Press.

Scott, James C. 1998. *Seeing Like a State: How Certain Schemes to Improve the Human Condition Have Failed.* New Haven, CT: Yale University Press.

Slaughter, Sheila, and Gary Rhoades. 2004. *Academic Capitalism and the New Economy: Markets, State, and Higher Education.* Baltimore: Johns Hopkins University Press.

Thursby, Jerry G., and Marie C. Thursby. 2011. "Has the Bayh-Dole Act Compromised Basic Research?" *Research Policy* 40 (8): 1077–83. http://dx.doi.org/10.1016/j.respol.2011.05.009.

Warner, Keith D. 2007. *Agroecology in Action: Extending Alternative Agriculture through Social Networks.* Cambridge, MA: MIT Press.

Warner, Keith D., Kent M. Daane, Christina M. Getz, Stephen P. Maurano, Sandra Calderon, and Kathleen A. Powers. 2011. "The Decline of Public Interest Agricultural Science and the Dubious Future of Crop Biological Control in California." *Agriculture and Human Values* 28 (4): 483–96. http://dx.doi.org/10.1007/s10460-010-9288-4.

Welsh, Rick, and Leland Glenna. 2006. "Considering the Role of the University in Conducting Research on Agri-biotechnologies." *Social Studies of Science* 36 (6): 929–42. http://dx.doi.org/10.1177/0306312706060062.

White, David G., Shaohua Zhao, Robert Sudler, Sherry Ayers, Sharon Friedman, Sheng Chen, Patrick F. McDermott, Shawn McDermott, David D. Wagner, and Jianghong Meng. 18 October 2001. "The Isolation of Antibiotic-Resistant Salmonella from Retail Ground Meats." *New England Journal of Medicine* 345 (16): 1147–54. http://dx.doi.org/10.1056/NEJMoa010315. Medline:11642230.

CHAPTER 6

Food Safety and Governance of the Agrifood System

Michelle R. Worosz and Diana Stuart

Introduction

While the agrifood industry claims the United States has the safest food in the world, in any given year forty-eight million people suffer from foodborne illness, with 128,000 hospitalizations and 3,000 deaths (Scharff 2012). The public health cost is estimated between $10 billion and $83 billion annually (Nyachuba 2010). Foodborne disease outbreaks may have significant impacts on the structure of agriculture in terms of its influence on actors from production to consumption, the organization of the sector in question, and governance of the agrifood system at large.

A recent outbreak provides a good example. In the fall of 2011, 147 people from twenty-eight states became sick from cantaloupe infected with *Listeria monocytogenes.* Of these cases, there were 143 hospitalizations, one miscarriage, and thirty-three deaths, making it the deadliest outbreak in ninety years (CDC 2012; Tauxe 2011). The pathogen was traced to Jensen Farms, located near the small rural city of Rocky Ford, Colorado. While Jensen passed a third-party inspection (CDC 2012), state and federal investigators found questionable growing methods; sorting practices; and design of, and equipment, in its packing and cold-storage facilities (FDA 2011). In addition, they found that a subcontracted auditor conducted the inspection (Neuman 2011). Jensen, which labeled its cantaloupes Rocky Ford, recalled approximately 2.7 million melons. A processor in Kansas and another in New York that used Rocky Ford cantaloupes also issued recalls. Jensen has since been named in wrongful death suits along with its distributor and auditor, has filed for bankruptcy, and is under criminal investigation (Bloomberg News 2012).

Media covered the Jensen Farms outbreak extensively and consumers took notice; there was a 53 percent drop in cantaloupe sales nationwide (Karst 2011; Calvin 2003). High-profile cases have prompted some consumers to alter their buying habits, choosing foods grown according to specific practices (Wright, Ransom, and Tanaka 2005) and/or purchasing directly from producers, at least temporarily (Lockie 2006). Notable cases have also motivated sector reorganization. For instance, in hopes of reestablishing their reputations, others using the Rocky Ford label created a new grower association in which members undergo biannual state inspections (Booth 2012). Reacting to this case, and others, California cantaloupe handlers voted unanimously for a mandatory food safety program that will include certification and a government audit (Adler 2012). In addition, Jensen illustrates the breadth of actors that are now embedded in the day-to-day operation of the agrifood system such as media, food safety lawyers, and subcontractors. These types of actors contribute to the discourse on governance and prompt legislators to propose new laws and state and federal regulators to modify or reconsider existing rules (Fortin 2003; Worosz 2009). For instance, at the time of this writing, the US Food and Drug Administration (FDA) is considering new standards for audits and auditors (Neuman 2011).

As illustrated above, food safety has important implications for many actors in the agrifood system including consumers, food producers, and rural communities. In this chapter, we start with a brief discussion of food safety as an emerging social issue, with a focus on pathogenic organisms and the structure of oversight. In the next section, we highlight the primary sociological approaches that have been used to explore food safety and the implications of our contemporary food safety system. We also address the current controversies surrounding food safety governance and conclude with new directions for future work.

Safety as an Emerging Social Issue

Food safety is a multidimensional concept that includes, but is not limited to, concerns about filth and spoilage, new technologies, food constituents, pollutants and chemical residues, and infectious agents (Buzby 2001). However, it is mostly used in the context of pathogenic organisms, particularly pathogenic bacteria. For instance, approximately one thousand bacterial outbreaks occur annually (Gilliss et al. 2011). The health impacts of these outbreaks range from mild to life threatening (e.g., organ failure, death), with increased seriousness for "at risk" consumers—the very young, very old, pregnant, and immunocompromised.

Salmonella causes the greatest public health burden with 1,027,561 illnesses, 19,336 hospitalizations, and 378 deaths per year (Batz, Hoffmann, and Morris 2011). Other prominent pathogens include *Listeria monocytogenes*, Norovirus, *Escherichia coli* O157:H7, and *Campylobacter*. Poultry is the food most commonly associated with infection, and is responsible for 1,538,468 illnesses, 11,952 hospitalizations, and 180 deaths per year. Since the late 1990s, the overall incidence of foodborne disease has declined 23 percent, with little improvement in recent years (Batz, Hoffmann, and Morris 2011).

The most common explanations for foodborne illness are improper hygiene and food handling practices in the home. These claims tend to be based on unsystematic reports and a weak traceback system. They also fail to acknowledge the complexity of the agrifood system and how it contributes to the contamination of food products before they reach consumers (Jacob and Powell 2009). Some critics, for instance, point to the proportion of at-risk consumers; the volume of food prepared and consumed outside the home; and the emergence of new pathogens; as well as increasingly large-scale production, centralized processing, long-distance and global transport, and widespread distribution (Nyachuba 2010, 258; Mooney and Hunt 2009, 483). Industry spokespersons argue that current oversight is more than sufficient; while others argue that the US food safety system is archaic, overly specific, partial, redundant, fragmented, and both inefficient and ineffective (Robinson 2005; Dyckman 2004).

The modern food safety era is marked by the passage of the 1906 Pure Food and Drug and the Federal Meat Inspection Acts. These statutes were created at the behest of large-scale, highly industrialized stakeholders responding both to European allegations that foods from the United States were responsible for illnesses and the spread of diseases, and also to domestic allegations of unhygienic facilities, dubious practices, and contaminated products. Congress, committed to a free market, complied, and designed rules that protected industry as much as, if not more so, than consumers. For example, in *US v. Lexington Mill and Elevator Company* (1914), food additives, regardless of the substance, were presumed safe unless proven otherwise. Essentially, food manufactures were granted wide latitude in their production, processing, and marketing practices.

Today, fifteen agencies execute the requirements of at least thirty statutes. The two core agencies are the FDA's Center for Food Safety and Applied Nutrition (CFSAN), and the US Department of Agriculture's (USDA) Food Safety and Inspection Service (FSIS). CFSAN oversees most domestic and imported foods including fish and seafood; fruits, vegetables and nuts; cereals, flour, and bread; shell eggs and dairy products; game meat; canned foods and bakery goods; and snack food and candy. FSIS oversees domestic and imported red meat, poultry, and processed eggs. While each agency establishes a set of regulations for carrying out its mandates, federal authority is relatively limited. Neither CFSAN nor FSIS can block distribution or impose a sanction. Instead, they rely on the states to perform certain enforcement activities including product embargos, assigning penalties, and certain recalls (Fortin 2009). The states may also regulate food within particular boundaries and oversee production, processing, and sales within their borders.

Rule changes are generally reactionary. The most notable case occurred in 1993 when 732 people became sick, 195 were hospitalized, and four died from consuming hamburgers contaminated with *E. coli* O157:H7 at Jack in the Box restaurants. FSIS responded with the 1996 Hazard Analysis Critical Control Points (HACCP) regulation of slaughter and processing facilities. However, instead of prescribing specific rules, HACCP is an audit system that promotes self-regulation and keeps government at a distance. Thus, many view HACCP as a minimalist neoliberal policy that privatizes federal regulation for capital-accumulating enterprises (Juska et al. 2003, 4). Similarly, the 2011 Food Safety Modernization Act (FSMA), modeled after HACCP, was a response to a series of domestic outbreaks—including those related to leafy greens, peanuts, and eggs—that occurred in the late 2000s. Unique to FSMA is that the FDA has the authority to mandate a recall; to regulate on-farm produce handling, holding, and packing; and to require the implementation of science-based HACCP plans (Ribera and Knutson 2011). Of particular concern is the nature of inspections. Federal inspectors are charged with determining whether or not an entity is in compliance with the rules. This narrow function tends to create an antagonistic relationship with small-scale farmers and processors wary of inspectors who may have little knowledge of their industry (Ten Eyck et al. 2006). FSMA also keeps the state at a distance as powerful industry actors have, by law, the ability to design their own food safety program with little direct oversight.

Food safety rules have also been altered in response to outbreaks associated with global sourcing. In 2003, for instance, a dairy cow was diagnosed with bovine spongiform encephalopathy (BSE, also known as mad cow disease) (Wright, Ransom, and Tanaka 2005). Investigation found that the animal originated from Canada. During the following year, the National Animal Identification System (NAIS), administered by the USDA Animal and Plant Inspection Service, was put in place to track cattle from farm to slaughter. At the slaughter and processing level, FSIS instituted new regulations that included banning "specified risk materials" (e.g., brain, spinal cord, vertebral column) and non-ambulatory cattle from the human food chain (Cohen 2004). In sum, increasing globalization can have far-reaching effects on a wide range of agrifood system actors including, but not limited to, regulations, producers, and domestic and international consumers.

Using Social Theory to Explore Food Safety

Rural sociologists and related scholars have applied a variety of theories to explore food safety as an emerging social issue. These theories include political economy, risk and reflexive modernization, and actor-network theory.

Political Economy

Political economy has been used to make significant contributions to the study of food safety at the institutional level. Drawing on Marx, this approach examines how modes of production shape relationships, as well as the role of political institutions, economic systems, and power relations. Scholars have used this approach to link specific outbreaks and oversight decisions to political and economic trends. For example, Stuart (2011) and Stuart and Worosz (2012) show how strategic decisions to maximize profitability in large-scale food processing result in outbreaks with widespread impacts. Juska et al. (2000) illustrate how government rule making can be plagued by coercion from corporate interests and may result in negative impacts to marginalized groups (cf. Gouveia and Juska 2002). Moreover, scholars show that the state has consistently overlooked the impacts of food safety rules on small-scale businesses (DeLind and Howard 2008; Worosz, Knight, Harris, and Conner 2008).

This approach also highlights the backstage rule making that takes place outside of government (Konefal, Mascarenhas, and Hatanaka 2005). Scholars have illustrated the power of agribusiness to shape the day-to-day practices intended to ensure food safety, and have identified who gains and who loses when new rules are created. As Gouveia and Juska (2002, 372) state, "increased corporate power to mold and re-mold production and consumption relations and regulatory initiatives is an undeniable fact in contemporary capitalism." For example, decision makers for supermarkets and restaurant chains tend to be far removed from the sites of production, yet have increasing power to stipulate growing practices and safety standards (Hatanaka and Busch 2008; Hatanaka, Bain, and Busch 2005) that can be quite difficult for producers to meet when faced with complex regional and site-specific challenges (Stuart 2009).

Risk Society and Reflexive Modernization

Adam (1999, 235) points to the invisible relationships between science, production, and politics that form the foundation of "modern" agriculture and serve as the source of present-day food scares. Work on risk and modernization has been useful for exploring these relationships. Beck's (1992) "risk society" posits that we can no longer escape the consequences of modernization as externalities resurface through a "boomerang effect"; society is the perpetrator, but also the victim. Beck links these events to the prioritization of capitalist production. Numerous food issues illustrate how the emphasis on productivity has overshadowed what might otherwise be discernible risks.

In the risk society, the side effects of modernization are no longer invisible, resulting in a growing public awareness and the rise of "reflexive modernization" (Beck 1992; Beck, Giddens, and Lash 1994; Beck, Bonss, and Lau 2003). Reflexive modernization suggests that society is increasingly mindful of risks and is actively reshaping systems to address these risks. In terms of food safety, reflexivity requires changes in priorities, seeking "out of the box" solutions, and adapting systems and/or reorganizing industrial production as new conditions emerge. While some consumers have raised concerns, governance regimes and industry groups have not responded to outbreaks in ways that constitute reflexive change (Stuart and Worosz 2012). Instead, commodity representatives opt for quality claims that deny or downplay threats and exude confidence in an effort to secure public trust (Wright, Ransom, and Tanaka 2005). Firms "deny responsibility, place blame on others . . . resist changes in their production or processing" practices, and/or advertise new technologies so as to deflect attention (Stuart 2008, 177).

Actor Network Theory

Actor network theory (ANT), as brought forth by Latour (1999), Law (1992), and Callon (1986), is a methodological approach that allows for a more complex view of the roles of, and interactions among, humans and nonhumans. ANT has been used to explore foodborne outbreaks, network instability caused by outbreaks, and the renegotiation of relationships among actors (Stuart 2011; Stuart and Worosz 2013). Attempts to overcome or avoid biological limits while maximizing profits have led to pushback from nonhuman actants (e.g., pathogenic bacteria). This notion echoes Beck's (1992) "boomerang effect," exemplifying the consequences of attempts to reshape ecological systems.

ANT has also been used to look beyond monolithic corporate actors to examine the relationships that shape food safety standards (Busch and Juska 1997; Juska et al. 2000) and to facilitate a deeper understanding of overlooked struggles (Stuart 2010). The approach challenges the "black boxes" associated with the creation and implementation of new food standards. Latour (1999, 183) describes "black boxing" as "a process that makes the joint production of actors and artifacts entirely opaque." It masks the processes and interactions that lead to specific relationships and outcomes. Located within are taken-for-granted networks that often remain unexplored (Callon 1986). Goodman (1999, 29) claims, "food scares open black boxed agro-food networks to reveal the hybrid collectives in which daily food habits and practices are enrolled." With increasing examples of neoliberal governance, and the use of private standards, Marsden (2000) argues that new black boxes in agrifood governance have been created.

Combining Theories

More recently, scholars have explored combining theoretical approaches to address possible weaknesses found in individual frameworks. Many scholars have critiqued political economy for having a narrow focus on structural explanations and being inattentive toward the role of nature and consumption (Busch and Juska 1997; Goodman 2001; Lockie and Kitto 2000; Whatmore and Thorne 2008). Adding ANT to political economy is thought to provide a more comprehensive way to investigate the role of nonhumans in profit-oriented production systems (Juska et al. 2000). This additional approach also helps to address the limitations of political economy by offering relational ontologies and post-structural insights that forge together production and consumption (Goodman 1999; Gouveia and Juska 2002; Murdoch 2000). These combined theories have been used to explore, for instance, the emergence of BSE (Goodman 1999) and *E. coli* O157:H7 (Stuart 2011), revealing overlooked connections between nonhuman actors and advanced capitalist food production systems. They have also revealed how actors black-box food safety standards, and establish their authority and credibility in doing so, by drawing upon the norms and values of technoscience (Bain, Ransom, and Worosz 2011).

Controversies

While US consumers generally trust agrifood system actors (Knight, Worosz, and Todd 2009), they are less trusting of large-scale production technologies (Vanderpool, Ten Eyck, and Harris 2004). They also view government as most responsible for oversight (Knight et al. 2008a). Correspondingly, scale and governance are key controversies that scholars have addressed.

Food Safety and Scale of Production

Before World War II, most US food processing took place in small, dispersed facilities. Today, processing tends to resemble the high-efficiency production found in other industries. To increase returns on capital investments, production systems have become increasingly centralized and concentrated with fewer manufacturers producing the majority of our food. However, these large-scale industrial processing systems have been associated with widespread outbreaks of foodborne disease (Altekruse, Cohen, and Swerdlow 1997; Nestle 2003). For instance, intensification and concentration in ground beef production led to the blending of meat and trim from an increasing number of domestic and international sources and to the production of larger lots of meat processed with the same machinery. At the plant level, these characteristics foster the rapid amplification of small amounts of contamination (Juska et al. 2003), and to an expanding volume of contaminated meat (Armstrong, Hollingsworth, and Morris 1996, 45). Meanwhile, industry consolidation led to a larger number of hamburger patties coming from a smaller number of processors. Thus, when contamination occurs, many consumers across a wide geographic area are at risk (Stuart and Worosz 2013). This concern is not limited to ground beef. In 2009, *Salmonella*-tainted peanuts from the Peanut Corporation of America (PCA) were confirmed to have sickened 714 people, nine of who died, across forty-six states (CDC 2009). PCA's peanuts were used by 361 manufacturers in 3,918 food products (FDA 2009). Concentration and consolidation have also created rigidity, making it difficult for a sector to make rapid changes in response to contamination (Juska et al. 2003).

Legislative, regulatory, and industry responses to outbreaks have avoided significant deviation from the dominant principles and organizational strategies of large-scale industrial food production. Instead, they rely on technological fixes (Juska et al. 2003; Stuart 2008) that foster industry resilience, creating an image of change in response to negative claims but without transformative change (Worosz, Knight, and Harris 2008). Moreover, these technological fixes ignore the consequences for the small-scale sector (Stuart and Worosz 2012). Commodity associations, for instance, favor large-scale producers when they design industry-wide food safety protocols and traceback systems that require specific production practices, new equipment, and third-party audits. These types of investments are problematic for small-scale producers who need to spread the cost of production over a smaller volume of output (Calvin 2003, 92). The unit cost for equipment and the associated paperwork was a key reason that small producers and ranchers rejected NAIS (Neuman 2010).

Scholars argue that reorganizing production to better protect consumers would entail transitioning to a more decentralized system that avoids large-scale cross-contamination (DeLind and Howard 2008). While foodborne illness has been associated with products from small-scale businesses, such incidents affect significantly fewer consumers. Processing smaller volumes of food and doing so at slower speeds can increase the effectiveness of inspection and testing, reduce cross-contamination, and allow for more adaptive capacity as problems emerge (cf. Hennessy 2005). Furthermore, shorter supply chains may facilitate quicker and easier traceback.

Food Safety Governance

The government's ability to oversee food safety is increasingly overshadowed by industry groups, corporations, and third-party certifiers with their own food safety standards. Industry influences the regulatory process via extensive representation during rule-making, as was the case with HACCP (Juska et al. 2000). This contrasts with the small-scale sector that typically has little influence, if any, on rule development or approval (Ten Eyck et al. 2006). The power of industry is illustrated by its ability to lobby against efforts to grant government the authority to recall (Fortin 2003), to manipulate science in the construction of standards, and to obscure or obstruct alternatives (Anderson 2004). In response to limited government involvement, at least four groups who are engaged in nongovernmental food safety standards setting have emerged: consumers, commodity groups, restaurant chains, and supermarket chains. Each of these groups is briefly discussed below.

Generally, there are weak market incentives for private investment in food safety technologies (Golan et al. 2004) and individual firms are unlikely to invest if a problem cannot be traced to them (Fortin 2003, 578). Thus, as Bonanno (in this volume) suggests, consumers have begun to "question the ability of market forces to bring about a safe and just system of distribution." When consumers exit and/or loose confidence in the market, profits decline. For instance, in 1996, the California strawberry industry lost $16 million in revenue in one month when it was falsely implicated in a large *Cyclospora* outbreak that was eventually linked to Guatemalan raspberries. As Calvin (2003, 93) states, "anyone producing a product for the U.S. market, including U.S. growers, may be caught in the consumer backlash."

Commodity groups have sought greater legitimacy and protection by distancing themselves from problematic growers and international sources of contamination. They have also rethought their relationship with the state. Not willing to surrender power, new arrangements to govern food safety have emerged where the state is recruited to enforce standards created by industry groups (e.g., those related to leafy greens or cantaloupe). As seen in the fresh produce sector, these arrangements create the perception of government oversight, while the most powerful stakeholders determine the standards (Stuart 2010).

Responding to outbreaks has been further influenced by the rise of corporate global restaurant and supermarket chains that favor downstream buyer interests (Flynn, Marsden, and Smith 2003; Busch and Bain 2004). Large chain restaurants rely on product branding to establish market identity, and tend to reward suppliers who meet particular standards. Following the Jack in the Box case, restaurants such as McDonald's sought to diminish their liability by requiring their suppliers to use HACCP during production and to verify practices via product testing and process audits (Ollinger and Mueller 2003). Consolidation has resulted in retail oligopolies that include Walmart, Kroger, and Safeway. These transnational supermarket chains (TSC) bypass nation-states' rules and create food safety standards that are stricter and outside the realm of public discourse and democratic decision-making (Calvin 2003). Although effort is focused on maintaining consumer confidence, the standards adopted often enhance an entity's reputation, profits, and competitive advantage, while also reducing liability should a food safety crisis arise (Konefal, Mascarenhas, and Hatanaka 2005; Hatanaka, Bain, and Busch 2006).

Neoliberal trends have clearly emerged in food safety governance. Since the 1980s, there has been an emphasis on governance "characterized by strong private property rights, free markets, and free trade" (Harvey 2005, 2). This movement includes deregulation and an overall "roll-back" of government involvement (Peck and Tickell 2002). This can be seen throughout US public policy as "new governance" emphasizes flexibility, market mechanisms, and public-private partnerships (Fiorino 2004; Salamon and Elliott 2002). The development of HACCP, and more recently FSMA, left food companies in charge of self-monitoring while the government focused on paperwork (Nestle 2003). Budget allocations consistently lack funds for extensive site visits, monitoring, and enforcement. The industry and its congressional and regulatory allies have strongly opposed attempts to strengthen statutes and/or regulations or add funds for surveillance. Instead, accountability is increasingly market based (Busch and Bain 2004). Like TNCs, US food retailers use their own standards and demand the use of third-party certifiers (Hatanaka, Bain, and Busch 2005). Especially problematic for small growers is the fact that different companies and certifiers use different standards with no public oversight (Calvin 2003).

Scholars have increasingly criticized the role of private industry in food safety governance for several reasons. First, the standards are black boxed (Busch and Bain 2004). They are created behind closed doors (Konefal, Mascarenhas, and Hatanaka 2005; Busch 2007) without transparency regarding how they are created, the use of science, or the role of politics and economics. Second, the process of creating private standards is far from democratic (Busch 2003). Those that powerful actors create often ignore the concerns of specific and/or less powerful interests. Uneven participation reshapes relationships, resulting in clear winners and losers, which often has ripple effects in rural communities. For instance, new food safety requirements and marketing agreements have the potential to create financial hardship for small and medium producers and processors, which further contributes to industry concentration and consolidation (DeLind and Howard 2008; Worosz, Knight, Harris, and Conner 2008; see Constance et al. and Guptill and Welsh in this volume). Lastly, neoliberal governance and the use of private standards may contradict programs intended to support other public health and/or social goals (Stuart 2010).

Future Directions for Food safety Scholarship

Food safety issues have contributed to the shaping and reshaping of the agrifood system. As illustrated above, industry influences government decision making, including the development of rules that further consolidation and large-scale production, facilitate market access, provide product assurance, and promote capital accumulation over other values. While research on food safety reveals new and important insights related to the structure of the agrifood system, more attention ought to be given to local actors, additional state functions, other forms of contaminates, and a broader range of impacts to individuals and communities.

Much attention in the food safety literature has focused on public and private governance schemes, but there has been little attention directed toward a more comprehensive understanding of the role of subnational states. As Herbert-Cheshire and Lawrence (2002) claim, there are ontological questions of what we mean by the "state" that remain unaddressed or assumed to be self-evident. Further studies are needed to explore state involvement at subnational levels including legislative barriers and constraints in local governance. Actors at the local level, for instance, have somewhat different interests than those at a distance (Worosz, Knight, and Harris 2008). Consequently, subnational actors may be more receptive to the cultural values and moral imperatives of a community (Juska et al. 2000), particularly those in rural areas.

In addition, there are fundamental questions about the role of the state, whether national or subnational, that have yet to be addressed, including what ought to be its role in protecting the safety of food, how it should determine risk acceptability, and to what extent it is appropriate to protect all consumers from all potentially hazardous foods regardless of perceived benefits. For example, the FDA is adamantly opposed to the consumption of raw dairy as it is highly susceptible to pathogenic bacteria, and at least twenty-eight states have made selling raw dairy products illegal. Yet, some consumers value the supposed nutritional benefits of raw fluid milk, some chefs value the characteristics of raw-milk cheese, and some producers value the perceived quality of their products and seek a premium price. This case, and others, raises questions about how food safety decisions should be made, in what ways fairness and democratic values should be incorporated (Ten Eyck et al. 2006), and whether or not alternative governance schemes should be adopted (cf. Knight et al. 2008b).

A myriad of contextual questions have yet to be explored and continue to limit our understanding of the relationship between food safety and the structure of the agrifood system. While a number of works focus on pathogens, there has been less attention to other dimensions of food safety (e.g., food security, food constituents), and little invested in elucidating the role of other social actors, particularly those that may contribute to contamination. For example, further studies could explore the role of consumer advocacy organizations, as well as the consequences of non-participation in both standards-setting and determining risk acceptability (Worosz and Wilson 2012).

By focusing on the global agrifood system and the state, our studies tend to overlook individuals and communities. Nearly absent from the rural sociology literature on food safety to date are the impacts on those who are most germane to the core of our discipline—vulnerable populations such as the very young, the very old, the sick, and the poor, as well as the most disenfranchised producers including women and minorities. This gap remains despite our acknowledgment of food deserts and the problems of access and choice in these regions (Adam 1999), the importance of producer and consumer trust in institutional actors and their voice in policy discourse (Sapp et al. 2009), and our awareness of the disparities among producers and consumers and between urban and rural communities (e.g., Pothukuchi, Mohamed, and Gebben 2008).

A growing body of work in nutrition, child development, and other behavioral sciences is beginning to identify and address some of these issues. To contribute, rural sociologists ought to examine the distribution of food safety risks focusing on both social (race, class, gender) and geospatial (urban, rural) inequalities. More attention should focus on agricultural producers that suffer hardship and loss from food safety scandals and scares that are unrelated to their own production system. As illustrated above, outbreaks associated with producers in one state can impact those in another. Likewise, outbreaks linked to foreign products may alarm consumers and negatively impact the livelihoods of rural communities dependent on the production of that commodity. It may also be worth exploring how new food safety standards encourage outsourcing and foreign food production in order to avoid challenging or costly requirements. Overall, understandings of food safety would benefit from more research on these possible linkages, including how minority and/or small-scale producers grapple with changing markets and standards and the related impacts to rural communities.

References

Adam, Barbara. 1999. "Industrial Food for Thought: Timescapes of Risk." *Environmental Values* 8 (2): 219–38. http://dx.doi.org/10.3197/096327199129341806.

Adler, Steve. 2012. "Melon Growers Inaugurate Food-Safety Plan." *AgAlert*, 5 September. http://www.agalert.com/story/?id=4569.

Altekruse, S.F., M.L. Cohen, and D.L. Swerdlow. July–September 1997. "Emerging Foodborne Diseases." *Emerging Infectious Diseases* 3 (3): 285–93. http://dx.doi.org/10.3201/eid0303.970304. Medline:9284372.

Anderson, Paul Nicholas. 2004. "What Rights are Eclipsed when Risk is Defined by Corporatism? Governance and GM Food." *Theory, Culture & Society* 21 (6): 155–69. http://dx.doi.org/10.1177/0263276404050460.

Armstrong, Gregory L., Jill Hollingsworth, and J.G. Morris Jr. 1996. "Emerging Foodborne Pathogens: *Escherichia coli* O157:H7 as a Model of Entry of a New Pathogen into the Food Supply of the Developed World." *Epidemiologic Reviews* 18 (1): 29–51. http://dx.doi.org/10.1093/oxfordjournals.epirev.a017914. Medline:8877329.

Bain, Carmen, Elizabeth Ransom, and Michelle R. Worosz. 2011. "Constructing Credibility: Using Technoscience to Legitimate Strategies in Agrifood Governance." *Journal of Rural Social Sciences* 25 (3): 160–92.

Batz, Michael B., Sandra Hoffmann, and J. Glenn Morris. 2011. *Ranking the Risks: The 10 Pathogen-Food Combinations with the Greatest Burden on Public Health.* Gainesville, FL: Emerging Pathogens Institute, University of Florida.

Beck, Ulrich. 1992. *Risk Society: Towards a New Modernity.* Trans. M. Ritter. London: Sage.

Beck, Ulrich, Wolfgang Bonss, and Christoph Lau. 2003. "The Theory of Reflexive Modernization." *Theory, Culture & Society* 20 (2): 1–33. http://dx.doi.org/10.1177/0263276403020002001.

Beck, Ulrich, Anthony Giddens, and Scott Lash. 1994. *Reflexive Modernization: Politics, Tradition and Aesthetics in the Modern Social Order.* Stanford, CA: Stanford University Press.

Bloomberg News. 2012. "Colorado Cantaloupe Processor Investigated by U.S. Attorney General's Office." *Denver Post*, 14 August. http://www.denverpost.com/nationworld/ci_21306055/cantaloupe-processor-investigated-by-u-s-attorney-generals?source=pkg.

Booth, Michael. 2012. "Jensen Farms Files Bankruptcy in Wake of Cantaloupe Listeria Deaths." *Denver Post*, 25 May. http://www.denverpost.com/breakingnews/ci_21345110/rocky-ford-canteloupe-growers-hold-eating-event-bolster.

Busch, Lawrence. 2003. "Virgil, Vigilance, and Voice: Agrifood Ethics in an Age of Globalization." *Journal of Agricultural & Environmental Ethics* 16 (5): 459–77. http://dx.doi.org/10.1023/A:1026383727365.

Busch, Lawrence. 2007. "Performing the Economy, Performing Science: From Neoclassical to Supply Chain Models in the Agrifood Sector." *Economy and Society* 36 (3): 437–66. http://dx.doi.org/10.1080/03085140701428399.

Busch, Lawrence, and Carmen Bain. 2004. "New! Improved? The Transformation of the Global Agrifood System." *Rural Sociology* 69 (3): 321–46. http://dx.doi.org/10.1526/0036011041730527.

Busch, Lawrence, and Arunas Juska. 1997. "Beyond Political Economy: Actor Networks and the Globalization of Agriculture." *Review of International Political Economy* 4 (4): 688–708. http://dx.doi.org/10.1080/09672299708565788.

Buzby, Jean C. 2001. *Effects of Food-Safety Perceptions on Food Demand and Global Trade. Changing Structure of Global Food Consumption and Trade.* WRS01–S1. Washington, DC: US Department of Agriculture, Economic Research Service.

Callon, Michel. 1986. "Some Elements of a Sociology of Translation: Domestication of the Scallops and the Fishermen of St. Brieuc Bay." In *Power, Action, and Belief: A New Sociology of Knowledge?*, ed. John Law, 196–223. London: Routledge & Kegan Paul.

Calvin, Linda. 2003. *Produce, Food Safety, and International Trade: Response to U.S. Foodborne Illness Outbreaks Associated with Imported Produce.* Agricultural Economic Report. Washington, DC: US Department of Agriculture Economic Research Service. 828.

Centers for Disease Prevention and Control (CDC). 2009. "Investigation Update: Outbreak of Salmonella Typhimurium Infections, 2008–2009." Department of Health and Human Services. Accessed 21 April 2010. http://www.cdc.gov/salmonella/typhimurium/update.html.

Centers for Disease Prevention and Control (CDC). 2012. "Multistate Outbreak of Listeriosis Linked to Whole Cantaloupes from Jensen Farms, Colorado." Accessed 28 August 2012. http://www.cdc.gov/listeria/outbreaks/cantaloupes-jensen-farms/082712/index.html.

Cohen, Steven. 2004. "USDA Issues New Regulations to Address BSE." USDA Food Safety Inspection Service. Accessed 11 September 2012. http://www.fsis.usda.gov/wps/portal/fsis/newsroom/news-releases-statements-transcripts/news-release-archives-by-year/news-release-archives-by-year-2004/!ut/p/a1/jzddcojaeeafpqdydlzn9fik8ycvicz2jrbydmfuvax7-psujernroy5h4czthgcace6kbjwlaxlx5mqv4hajbojbmgzfjibbmvascew2w7azqlozatikprme7raxpmfkqow8u4kgvt7pp9iwre2q6j4ldgp-ktbnc85azhi9t0thw_qruc9z_xcgkkacj5joludgxpqhxxbdwtw1f_gz2--wpzx1fouva82cmfyfaa3q59h/?1dmy¤t=true&urile=wcm%3apath%3a%2ffsis-archives-content%2finternet%2fmain%2fnewsroom%2fnews-releases-statements-and-transcripts%2fnews-release-archives-by-year%2farchives%2fct_index81.

DeLind, Laura B., and Philip H. Howard. 2008. "Safe at Any Scale? Food Scares, Food Regulation, and Scaled Alternatives." *Agriculture and Human Values* 25 (3): 301–17. http://dx.doi.org/10.1007/s10460-007-9112-y.

Dyckman, Lawrence J. 2004. "Federal Food Safety and Security System: Fundamental Restructuring is Needed to Address Fragmentation and Overlap." Testimony before the Subcommittee on the Civil Service and Agency Organization, Committee on Government Reform, House of Representatives. GAO-04–588T. Washington, DC: US Government Accounting Office.

Fiorino, Daniel J. 2004. "Flexibility." In *Environmental Governance Reconsidered: Challenges, Choices, and Opportunities*, ed. Robert F. Durant, Daniel J. Fiorino, and Rosemary O'Leary, 393–426. Cambridge, MA: MIT Press.

Flynn, Andrew, Terry Marsden, and Everard Smith. 2003. "Food Regulation and Retailing in a New Institutional Context." *Political Quarterly* 74 (1): 38–46. http://dx.doi.org/10.1111/1467-923X.00510.

Fortin, Neal D. 2003. "The Hang-up with HACCP: The Resistance to Translating Science into Food Safety Law." *Food and Drug Law Journal* 58 (4): 565–93. Medline:15027451.

Fortin, Neal D. 2009. *Food Regulation: Law, Science, Policy, and Practice.* Hoboken, NJ: Wiley & Sons, Inc.

Gilliss, Debra, Alicia Cronquist, Matthew Cartter, Melissa Tobin-D'Angelo, David Blythe, Kirk Smith, Sarah Lathrop, Guthrie Birkhead, Paul Cieslak, John Dunn, et al., and the Centers for Disease Control and Prevention (CDC). 10 June 2011. "Vital Signs: Incidence and Trends of Infection with Pathogens Transmitted Commonly through Food—Foodborne Diseases Active Surveillance Network, 10 U.S. Sites, 1996–2010." *Morbidity and Mortality Weekly Report* 60 (22): 749–55. Medline:21659984.

Golan, Elise, Tanya Roberts, Elisabete Salay, Julie A. Casewell, Michael Ollinger, and Danna Moore. 2004. Food Safety Innovation in the United States: Evidence from the Meat Industry. 831. Washington, DC: US Department of Agriculture, Economic Research Service.

Goodman, David. 1999. "Agro-food Studies in the 'Age of Ecology': Nature, Corporeality, Bio-politics." *Sociologia Ruralis* 39 (1): 17–38. http://dx.doi.org/10.1111/1467-9523.00091.

Goodman, David. 2001. "Ontology Matters: The Relational Materiality of Nature and Agro-food Studies." *Sociologia Ruralis* 41 (2): 182–200. http://dx.doi.org/10.1111/1467-9523.00177.

Gouveia, Lourdes, and Arunas Juska. 2002. "Taming Nature, Taming Workers: Constructing the Separation between Meat Consumption and Meat Production in the U.S." *Sociologia Ruralis* 42 (4): 370–90. http://dx.doi.org/10.1111/1467-9523.00222.

Harvey, David. 2005. *A Brief History of Neoliberalism.* Oxford: Oxford University Press.

Hatanaka, Maki, Carmen Bain, and Lawrence Busch. 2005. "Third-Party Certification in the Global Agrifood System." *Food Policy* 30 (3): 354–69. http://dx.doi.org/10.1016/j.foodpol.2005.05.006.

Hatanaka, Maki, Carmen Bain, and Lawrence Busch. 2006. "Differentiated Standardization, Standardized Differentiation: The Complexity of the Global Agrifood System between the Local and the Global in Research." In *Rural Sociology and Development*, ed. Terry Marsden and Jonathan Murdoch, 39–68. Bingley, UK: Emerald Group Publishing Limited.

Hatanaka, Maki, and Lawrence Busch. 2008. "Third-Party Certification in the Global Agrifood System: An Objective or Socially Mediated Governance Mechanism?" *Sociologia Ruralis* 48 (1): 73–91. http://dx.doi.org/10.1111/j.1467-9523.2008.00453.x.

Hennessy, David A. 2005. "Slaughterhouse Rules: Animal Uniformity and Regulating for Food Safety in Meat Packing." *American Journal of Agricultural Economics* 87 (3): 600–609. http://dx.doi.org/10.1111/j.1467-8276.2005.00750.x.

Herbert-Cheshire, Lynda, and Geoffery Lawrence. 2002. "Political Economy and the Challenge of Governance." *Journal of Australian Political Economy* 50 (December): 137–45.

Jacob, C.J., and D.A. Powell. November 2009. "Where Does Foodborne Illness Happen—In the Home, at Foodservice, or Elsewhere—and Does it Matter?" *Foodborne Pathogens and Disease* 6 (9): 1121–23. http://dx.doi.org/10.1089/fpd.2008.0256. Medline:19694555.

Juska, Arunas, Lourdes Gouveia, Jackie Gabriel, and Susan Koneck. 2000. "Negotiating Bacteriological Meat Contamination Standards in the US: The Case of *E. coli* O157:H7." *Sociologia Ruralis* 40 (2): 249–71. http://dx.doi.org/10.1111/1467-9523.00146.

Juska, Arunas, Lourdes Gouveia, Jackie Gabriel, and Kathleen P. Stanley. 2003. "Manufacturing Bacteriological Contamination Outbreaks in Industrialized Meat Production Systems: The Case of *E. coli* O157:H7." *Agriculture and Human Values* 20 (1): 3–19. http://dx.doi.org/10.1023/A:1022416727626.

Karst, Tom. 2011. "Outbreak Dings all Melon Sales." *Produce Retailer*, 2 December. http://www.produceretailer.com/produce-retailer-news/Outbreak-bruises-entire-melon-category-134904698.html.

Knight, Andrew J., Michelle R. Worosz, Maria K. Lapinski-Lafaive, Toby A. TenEyck, Craig K. Harris, Ewen C.D. Todd, Leslie D. Bourquin, Tom Dietz, and Paul B. Thompson. 2008a. "Consumer Perceptions of the Food Safety System: Implications for Food Safety Educators and Policy Makers." *Food Protection Trends* 28 (6): 27–32.

Knight, Andrew J., Michelle R. Worosz, and Ewen C.D. Todd. 2009. "Dining for Safety: Consumer Perceptions of Food Safety and Eating Out." *Journal of Hospitality & Tourism Research*, 33 (4): 471–86. http://dx.doi.org/10.1177/1096348009344211.

Knight, Andrew J., Michelle R. Worosz, Ewen C.D. Todd, Leslie D. Bourquin, and Craig K. Harris. 2008b. "Listeria in Raw Milk Soft Cheese." In *Global Risk Governance: Concept and Practice Using the IRGC Framework*, ed. Ortwin Renn and K. Walker, 179–220. Dordrecht: Springer Press.

Konefal, Jason, Michael Mascarenhas, and Maki Hatanaka. 2005. "Governance in the Global Agro-food Systems: Backlighting the Role of Transnational Supermarket Chains." *Agriculture and Human Values* 22 (3): 291–302. http://dx.doi.org/10.1007/s10460-005-6046-0.

Latour, Bruno. 1999. *Pandora's Hope: Essays on the Reality of Science Studies*. Cambridge, MA: Harvard University Press.

Law, John. 1992. "Notes on the Theory of the Actor-Network: Ordering, Strategy, and Heterogeneity." *Systems Practice* 5 (4): 379–93. http://dx.doi.org/10.1007/BF01059830.

Lockie, Stewart. 2006. "Capturing the Sustainability Agenda: Organic Foods and Media Discourses on Food Scares, Environment, Genetic Engineering, and Health." *Agriculture and Human Values* 23 (3): 313–23. http://dx.doi.org/10.1007/s10460-006-9007-3.

Lockie, Stewart, and Simon Kitto. 2000. "Beyond the Farm Gate: Production-Consumption Networks and Agri-food Research." *Sociologia Ruralis* 40 (1): 3–19. http://dx.doi.org/10.1111/1467-9523.00128.

Marsden, Terry. 2000. "Food Matters and the Matter of Food: Towards a New Food Governance?" *Sociologia Ruralis* 40 (1): 20–29. http://dx.doi.org/10.1111/1467-9523.00129.

Mooney, Patrick H., and Scott A. Hunt. 2009. "Food Security: The Elaboration of Contested Claims to a Consensus Frame." *Rural Sociology* 74 (4): 469–97. http://dx.doi.org/10.1526/003601109789864053.

Murdoch, Jonathan. 2000. "Networks—A New Paradigm of Rural Development?" *Journal of Rural Studies* 16 (4): 407–19. http://dx.doi.org/10.1016/S0743-0167(00)00022-X.

Nestle, Marion. 2003. *Safe Food: Bacteria, Biotechnology, and Bioterrorism*. Berkeley: University of California Press.

Neuman, William. 2010. "U.S.D.A. Plans to Drop Program to Trace Livestock." *New York Times*, 5 February. http://www.nytimes.com/2010/02/05/business/05livestock.html.

Neuman, William. 2011. "Listeria Outbreak Traced to Cantaloupe Packing Shed." *New York Times*, 19 October. http://www.nytimes.com/2011/10/20/business/listeria-outbreak-traced-to-colorado-cantaloupe-packing-shed.html?_r=1.

Nyachuba, David G. May 2010. "Foodborne Illness: Is It on the Rise?" *Nutrition Reviews* 68 (5): 257–69. http://dx.doi.org/10.1111/j.1753-4887.2010.00286.x. Medline:20500787.

Ollinger, Michael, and Valerie Mueller. 2003. Managing for Safer Food: The Economics of Sanitation and Process Controls in Meat and Poultry Plants. Washington, DC Agricultural Economic Report No. 817.

Peck, Jamie, and Adam Tickell. 2002. "Neoliberalizing Space." *Antipode* 34 (3): 380–404. http://dx.doi.org/10.1111/1467-8330.00247.

Pothukuchi, Kameshwari, Rayman Mohamed, and David Gebben. 2008. "Explaining Disparities in Food Safety Compliance by Food Stores: Does Community Matter?" *Agriculture and Human Values* 25 (3): 319–32. http://dx.doi.org/10.1007/s10460-008-9132-2.

Ribera, Luis A., and Ronald D. Knutson. 2011. "The FDA's Food Safety Modernization Act and its Economic Implications." *Choices: The Magazine of Food, Farm & Resource Issues.* Accessed 5 September 2011. http://www.choicesmagazine.org/choices-magazine/submitted-articles/the-fdas-food-safety-modernization-act-and-its-economic-implications.

Robinson, Robert A. 2005. "Overseeing the U.S. Food Supply: Steps Should Be Taken to Reduce Overlapping Inspections and Related Activities." Testimony before the Subcommittee on the Federal Workforce and Agency Organization, Committee on Government Reform, House of Representatives. GAO-05-549T. Washington, DC: US General Accounting Office.

Salamon, Lester M., and Odus V. Elliott. 2002. *The Tools of Government: A Guide to the New Governance.* Oxford: Oxford University Press.

Sapp, Stephen G., Charlie Arnot, James Fallon, Terry Fleck, David Soorholtz, Matt Sutton-Vermeulen, and Jannette J.H. Wilson. 2009. "Consumer Trust in the U.S. Food System: An Examination of the Recreancy Theorem." *Rural Sociology* 74 (4): 525–45. http://dx.doi.org/10.1526/003601109789863973.

Scharff, Robert L. 2012. "Economic Burden from Health Losses Due to Foodborne Illness in the United States." *Journal of Food Protection* 75 (1): 123–31. http://dx.doi.org/10.4315/0362-028X.JFP-11-058. Medline:22221364.

Stuart, Diana. 2008. "The Illusion of Control: Undustrialized Agriculture, Nature, and Food Safety." *Agriculture and Human Values* 25 (2): 177–81. http://dx.doi.org/10.1007/s10460-008-9130-4.

Stuart, Diana. 2009. "Constrained Choice and Ethical Dilemmas in Land Management: Environmental Quality and Food Safety in California Agriculture." *Journal of Agricultural & Environmental Ethics* 22 (1): 53–71. http://dx.doi.org/10.1007/s10806-008-9129-2.

Stuart, Diana. 2010. "Science, Standards, and Power: New Food Safety Governance in California." *Journal of Rural Social Science* 25 (3): 111–40.

Stuart, Diana. 2011. "'Nature' is Not Guilty: Foodborne Illness and the Industrial Bagged Salad." *Sociologia Ruralis* 51 (2): 158–74. http://dx.doi.org/10.1111/j.1467-9523.2010.00528.x.

Stuart, Diana, and Michelle R. Worosz. 2012. "Risk, Anti-reflexivity, and Ethical Neutralization in Industrial Food Processing." *Agriculture and Human Values* 29 (3): 287–301. http://dx.doi.org/10.1007/s10460-011-9337-7.

Stuart, Diana, and Michelle R. Worosz. 2013. "The Myth of Efficiency: Technology and Ethics in Industrial Food Production." *Journal of Agricultural & Environmental Ethics* 26 (1): 231–56. http://dx.doi.org/10.1007/s10806-011-9357-8.

Tauxe, Robert. 2011. "Deadly Listeria Outbreak Halted in Record Time." Centers for Disease Control and Prevention. Accessed 24 August 2012. http://www.cdc.gov/24-7/savinglives/listeria/.

Ten Eyck, Toby A., Donna Thede, Gerd Bode, and Leslie Bourquin. 2006. "Is HACCP Nothing? A Disjoint Constitution between Inspectors, Processors, and Consumers and the Cider Industry in Michigan." *Agriculture and Human Values* 23 (2): 205–14. http://dx.doi.org/10.1007/s10460-005-6107-4.

US Food and Drug Administration (FDA). 2009. "Peanut Butter and Other Peanut Containing Products Recall List." Accessed 28 March 2012. http://www.accessdata.fda.gov/scripts/peanutbutterrecall/index.cfm.

US Food and Drug Administration (FDA). 2011. "Environmental Assessment: Factors Potentially Contributing to the Contamination of Fresh Whole Cantaloupe Implicated in a Multi-state Outbreak of Listeriosis." Accessed 24 August 2012. http://www.fda.gov/Food/RecallsOutbreaksEmergencies/Outbreaks/ucm276247.htm.

Vanderpool, Christopher, Toby Ten Eyck, and Craig Harris. 2004. "Legitimation Crisis: Food Safety and Genetically Modified Organisms." In *Biotechnology Unglued: Science, Society, and Social Cohesion*, ed. Michael D. Mehta, 101–30. Toronto: University of Toronto Press.

Whatmore, Sarah, and Lorraine Thorne. 2008. "Nourishing Networks: Alternative Geographies of Food." In *Reading Economic Geography*, ed. Trevor J. Barnes, Jamie Peck, Eric Sheppard, and Adam Tickell, 235–248. Oxford, UK: Blackwell Publishing Ltd.

Worosz, Michelle R. 2009. "Small Scale Agriculture, Large Scale Rules." Paper presented at the annual meetings of the Rural Sociology Society, 31 July to 2 August, Madison, WI.

Worosz, Michelle R., Andrew J. Knight, and Craig K. Harris. 2008. "Resilience in the Red Meat Sector: The Role of Food Safety Policy." *Agriculture and Human Values* 25 (2): 187–91. http://dx.doi.org/10.1007/s10460-008-9127-z.

Worosz, Michelle R., Andrew J. Knight, Craig K. Harris, and David S. Conner. 2008. "Barriers to Entry into the Specialty Red Meat Sector: The Role of Food Safety Regulation." *Southern Rural Sociology* 23 (1): 170–207.

Worosz, Michelle R., and Norbert L.W. Wilson. 2012. "A Cautionary Tale of Purity, Labeling and Product Literacy in the Gluten-Free Market." *Journal of Consumer Affairs* 46 (2): 288–318. http://dx.doi.org/10.1111/j.1745-6606.2012.01230.x.

Wright, Wynne, Elizabeth Ransom, and Keiko Tanaka. 2005. "The 'All-American Meal': Constructing Confidence in the Case of BSE." *Illness, Crisis & Loss* 13 (2): 95–115.

CHAPTER 7

Changing Animal Agriculture and the Issue of Farm Animal Welfare

Jeff Sharp and Dani Deemer

Introduction

Since the 1970s, the evolving structure and character of livestock farming in the United States has attracted considerable attention from rural sociologists. Recently, farm animal welfare has emerged as a significant issue, engaging citizens/consumers, farmers, business, and the state in a complex process of balancing the diverse and often-conflicting goals of these food-system stakeholders. In this chapter, we reflect on how farm animal welfare is being contested and addressed through the state, with special attention to the case of Ohio. To inform this review, we draw on scholars who work in the sociology of agriculture and food systems as well as on our own work and first-hand observations of the farm animal welfare issue in Ohio. We also approach this matter with an appreciation for the observations Bonanno offers in the introduction to this section, particularly in regards to the interplay of public, state, and capital interests in food-system change and development. We observe a variable role of the state that may at times appear to act in the interests of industry; but we also see effective action by nongovernmental organizations (NGOs) that challenge the state to account for noncapital interests as well.

In the following sections we address these matters in more detail, but first we offer a brief overview of rural sociology's contribution to animal agriculture research. We divide this body of work into three literatures: an early focus on structural changes in livestock production, later inquiries into public attitudes toward livestock welfare, and an emerging focus on state intervention in animal agriculture. These literatures scaffold our discussion of the interplay of the livestock industry, the public, and the state.

The Changing Structure of Livestock Production: Rural Sociology's Early Focus

One of the earliest and continued foci of sociological research related to animal agriculture has been an examination of how and why the structure of livestock production has been changing. Heffernan (1972; 1984) was one of the first to attend to this matter with his study of poultry production in a Louisiana parish. He observed not only an increase in the size of poultry operations and an associated decline in the number of operations, but also fundamental changes in the organizational structure of production. Specifically, he described a shift from the independent family farm model to an integrated system in which the farmer is contractually integrated into a larger corporate or corporate farmhand system where a corporate firm directly employs the farm labor and management. Heffernan's fieldwork also began to investigate some of the consequences of these changes, including how the changing economic organization impacts the power and control of growers over their production (Heffernan 1984) as well as the community consequences of replacing independent family farmers with corporate farmhands.

Documentation of these organizational and structural changes in livestock production has continued, including descriptions of how the process of industrialization and integration have occurred in other livestock sectors, including pork and dairy (Constance 2002; Jackson-Smith and Barham 2000; Welsh 1996). Technological changes in production facilities, advances in disease control, and other innovations in on-farm production processes have allowed for increasing scale and concentration of production—but more importantly, changes in the economic organization of a particular commodity chain, particularly at the processing level, has been identified as an important driver of farm-level changes (Constance 2002; Heffernan 2000; Welsh 1997).

In addition to documenting and seeking to explain the course of structural change in livestock production, there has also been considerable focus on identifying the farm, community, and environmental impacts of the increasing scale of livestock production. One of the most significant physical manifestations of structural change in livestock production is the confined animal feeding operation (CAFO). The US Environmental Protection Agency defines a large CAFO as one that has at least 700 dairy cattle, 1,000 beef cattle, either 2,500 or 10,000 pigs depending on their size, and either 30,000 or 125,000 broilers depending on the manure management system. Federal environmental regulations impact CAFOs once they are above these thresholds, but despite this environmental oversight, extensive work has identified a variety of possibly negative consequences from

CAFO sites. Some scholarly work in this area is standard impact assessment that seeks to identify strategies for ameliorating potential negative consequences (Salant et al. 2009; Schwab 1998), while other work seeks to justify alternative livestock sector development strategies that may not have the negative impacts associated with CAFOs (NCRCRD 1999).

The Social Basis of Livestock Animal Welfare Attitudes and Beliefs

Increasing concern for animal welfare has arguably gone hand in hand with structural transformation in animal agriculture. A recurring narrative in the animal welfare literature is that industrialization has violated an "ancient contract" embodied in traditional husbandry practices that arose with civilization, in which humans treated farm animals with care because they were intimately reliant on livestock for food, fiber, and draft power (Bonney 2008; Niman 2009; Rollin 2008; 2010; Scully 2002). As the story goes, humans are no longer reliant on farm animals because of the industrial revolution and so are no longer required to care about their well-being. As industrial technologies have been applied to animal agriculture in this moral vacuum, animal well-being has been defined by capitalist productivity goals, transforming animals into expendable machine parts (Rollin 2008). But consumer pushback against commodification of farm animals has emerged even as the CAFO production system comes into its own. The public increasingly conceptualizes animal welfare in terms of output and mortality as well as in terms of social and emotional well-being (Hewson 2003).

Sociologists and related social scientists have sought to understand how attitudes about farm animal welfare are distributed throughout society (starting with Kellert and Berry 1980 and Kellert 1989). A nascent but slowly formalizing subfield of study labeled animals and society has emerged. While much of the early attitudinal work in this field focused on lab animals, pets and wildlife, attention to public attitudes toward farm animals became a focus of the society and animals literature in the late 1990s and 2000s. Research on farm animal welfare attitudes has largely consisted of an effort to gauge respondents' preferences for specific food attributes, attitudes toward common husbandry practices, and general perceptions of the meat industry (Bennett, Anderson, and Blaney 2002; Deemer and Lobao 2011; Hall and Sandilands 2007; Kendall, Lobao, and Sharp 2006; Prickett, Norwood, and Lusk 2010; Tonsor, Olynk, and Wolf 2009; Verbeke 2009). A smaller body of work also gauges respondents' preference for alternative livestock housing systems (Bennett, Anderson, and Blaney 2002; Frewer et al. 2005). The findings associated with these studies are consistent with previous findings regarding non-food-animal welfare, with similar demographic and socioeconomic characteristics linked to both farm animal welfare concerns and also general animal welfare concern. For example, women are likely to have a higher level of farm animal welfare concern compared to men (Deemer and Lobao 2011; Heleski, Mertig, and Zanella 2006; Herzog 2007; Prickett, Norwood, and Lusk 2010). There is also evidence that higher income individuals are less likely to report concerns about farm animal welfare (Prickett, Norwood, and Lusk 2010), and that individuals experiencing financial worry or structural disadvantages are more sympathetic toward farm animals (Deemer and Lobao 2011; Kendall, Lobao, and Sharp 2006).

Probably the most salient application and extension of farm animal welfare attitudinal research is investigation of how these attitudes impact consumer shopping choices. One weakness of attitudinal studies, though, is the fact that attitudes do not always correlate with behavior. For instance, concern about livestock welfare seems to be at an all-time high, but levels of meat consumption remain steady overall (Horowitz 2006). While several studies indicate that consumers would be willing to pay more for humanely produced meat products (Prickett, Norwood, and Lusk 2010), there is still a need to understand this preference in relation to consumers' many other food preferences. In their recent work, Howard and Allen (2010) begin to shed light on this matter. Their study of paired comparisons of different ecolabels extends choice modeling methods from economics, finding that consumers significantly preferred local and humane ecolabels over other labels and preferred local over humane by a narrow margin.

The fact that consumers may more frequently have to accept some trade-offs among valued food attributes (for instance, having to choose between organic or local or humane) may be the new reality of food consumption in modernity, as the management of risks and the achievement of social goals is increasingly left to consumer preference rather than state intervention (Hatanaka, Bain, and Busch 2005; Hatanaka and Busch 2008; Raynolds, Murray, and Heller 2007). Interestingly, there may also be some ambivalence among consumers. In their survey of Dutch consumers seeking to determine their views of modern dairy farming practices, Boogaard et al. (2011) find consumers to be not only sympathetic to the plight of animals, but also appreciative of the modern day farming practices that farmers must employ to sustain their businesses. Boogaard et al. (2011, 260–61) describe this ambivalence on the part of society as reflective of the two sides of modernity: "on the one hand there is increasing criticism about modern animal farming practices, such as the way farm animals are treated and used for production. On the other hand, people appreciate certain aspects of modern animal farming, such as food quality and food safety and low cost products." In practice, this may mean the public tends toward an uneasy tolerance of modern farming, but has the potential to react if the context evokes a stronger response. The possibility of this reaction becomes more apparent in the next section.

The State and Animal Agriculture

A third sociological approach to livestock agriculture has sought to not only describe the structural changes and identify the community impacts of livestock production, but to also examine the state's role in facilitating these developments and communities' potential to resist. Bonanno and Constance (2006; Constance 2002) effectively explore the states' capability to restrict or direct the actions of transnational corporations (TNCs) that have developed the capacity to quickly and easily shift their capital investments from one particular place to another depending on the location that offers the greatest benefit. In this era of globalization, where capital fluidly moves within and between nations, Bonanno and Constance (2006) identify three different ways the TNC and nation-state might interact. One view is that the nation-state is no longer able to control and direct TNCs' actions. From another perspective, the state retains some power to direct TNCs' actions, such as through the formulation of international governance structures, but TNCs retain the power to circumvent some of the local and regional governance structures through their nimble movement. From a third perspective, the nation-state is under threat, but continues to have some capacity to resist global capital—organized efforts of various groupings of citizens and their active engagement in the political process can motivate the nation-state to actively regulate or guide the actions of capital to the extent possible in the era of globalization. In Bonanno and Constance's (2006) examination of the behavior of Seaboard farms' quest to locate a second "hog pyramid" in one of the US plains states, they find evidence of all three state-capital perspectives (see also Glenna and Mitev's 2009 analysis of a CAFO in Bulgaria).

This literature highlights the multiple roles of the state and points to the limited applicability of the political economy approach to studying the relationship between the state, society, and capital. Specifically, it appears that *subnational* states play an important regulatory role in animal agriculture. This role is not entirely predictable within a political economy framework, since state intervention reflects the interests of several diverse stakeholder groups rather than just those of the public or private capital. State intervention also appears to involve a regulatory back and forth, as these stakeholders use the state as a vehicle to challenge state intervention. In other words, the state is dynamic, contested, and contingent. In extending the state literature to the issue of animal welfare regulation, it follows that a "nuts and bolts," or case study, approach to state intervention is called for in the style of Bonanno and Constance (2006).

The State and Farm Animal Welfare: The Case of Ohio

In this section, we extend rural sociology's inquiry into the state's role in livestock agriculture to the issue of farm animal welfare, focusing on the case of Ohio. The most salient animal welfare strategy employed by pro-animal welfare movement actors in the 2000s has been the use of state ballot initiatives. California's Proposition 2 is one of the foremost examples of this strategy being employed, where 63 percent of voters in 2008 approved a ballot initiative to create a state statute stipulating that all veal calves, laying hens, and sows must be confined in ways that allow them to lie down, turn around, stretch their limbs, and stand up. Similar ballot measures have also passed in Florida, Arizona, Oregon, and Colorado. This success in achieving certain food quality goals through direct democracy is a quite new phenomenon in food politics and warrants further investigation into how the issues were framed in the public discourse and how policies were ultimately implemented.

Further investigation of the counteracting efforts of industry in response to the pro-animal welfare movement is needed. While anti-confinement and pro-animal welfare ballot measures have been strategically pursued by animal welfare advocates in several states, the creation of livestock care standard boards (LCSBs) has been a pre-emptive state-level strategy executed by industry to try to nullify the need or appropriateness of these anti-confinement ballot initiatives. Some argue that LCSBs serve as vehicles for powerful livestock industry interests to enact standards that codify or sympathetically modify current husbandry practices on factory farms (Vick 2011; Allen 2010). LCSBs now exist in Ohio, New Jersey, Illinois, Indiana, Kentucky, Louisiana, Utah, Vermont, and West Virginia, and are generally tasked with determining state standards for farm animal treatment. They are often composed of appointed members including state officials, experts in various fields that concern animal care and food safety, and ordinary consumers. Alternatively, existing committees or state agencies have been called upon to also act as their state's LCSB.

In the state of Ohio, an interesting interplay has developed between the pro-animal welfare movement and the livestock industry and allies as both have pursued statewide ballot initiatives to amend the state's constitution to achieve their ambitions. Ohio has a large and diverse livestock industry with both very large CAFOs and small-scale operations generating over $3.6 billion in economic output and employing nearly forty-six thousand people (Battelle Memorial Institute 2008). Fearing restrictions on livestock production similar to those in California, Ohio's livestock industry successfully introduced State Issue 2 onto the 2009 election ballot, which ultimately passed with 63 percent of the vote. State Issue 2 directly amended Ohio's constitution and created the nation's first LCSB with the purpose of establishing standards governing the care of livestock and poultry. This ballot initiative and the board it created quickly became a model for other states, with Kentucky set to adopt Ohio's standards altogether for reasons of expediency (Vick 2011). Supporters of the Ohio measure framed it in a way that appealed simultaneously to consumers and producers, and argued it was needed to ensure food safety and affordability as well as to "protect Ohio's farms and families" from radical out-of-state animal rights interests that would purportedly weaken the agricultural sector (Ohio Department of Agriculture 2011).

The Ohio constitutional amendment created a thirteen-member LCSB, including the director of the Ohio Department of Agriculture, two family farmers appointed by the speaker of the House and the president of the Senate, and ten additional members appointed by the governor, including two licensed veterinarians and a dean of a college of agriculture. Vick (2011) points out that the vague qualifications for many of the board members leaves open the possibility for the appointment of board members representing special interests. For example, owners of even the largest CAFOs could be considered for appointment as representatives of family farmers. However, to date this board has appeared to operate openly and transparently, even holding a series of listening sessions to gather public input. In fact, the passage and subsequent execution of the LCSB has engaged some alternative Ohio farm organizations, such as the Ohio Ecological Food and Farming Association (OEFFA), in policy processes that they have not historically actively participated in. OEFFA organized members to speak on behalf of the needs of small livestock producers as well as serve on board subcommittees. Such organized input and participation has the potential to ensure that proposed standards do not favor factory farms over small-scale livestock farms.

The standards created by the LCSB were approved by the Ohio General Assembly and went into effect on 29 September 2011. At this early stage, it is unclear to what extent the standards have had a meaningful impact on farm animal welfare practices or whose interests the standards best serve, but further monitoring of outcomes is warranted to understand the complex ways that capital interests, public interests, and the state interact.

Another sociologically interesting question to explore in Ohio and other states where state-level ballot initiatives have been pursued is in-depth examination of how the public was persuaded to support the various initiatives. Interestingly, the California public supported relatively aggressive restrictions on some farm animal production practices, but the Ohio public expressed strong support for a farm animal welfare approach that was more sympathetic to the interests and needs of industry and farmers. While the state-level context might account for some variability, it may also reflect the public ambivalence that Boogaard et al. (2011) report concerning modern farming practices. On the one hand, there is sympathy for farm animal welfare, but on the other hand, there is an appreciation that farming is a business. How the public can hold both views and how the policy sector must accommodate both interests is in need of further exploration.

One additional footnote to the Ohio experience is that the passage of the constitutional amendment that created the LCSB has not deterred farm animal welfare lobbyists from seeking further restrictions on farm animal welfare practices in Ohio. In response to what the farm animal welfare lobby saw as a weakening of animal welfare protection in the state (HSUS 2010), Ohioans for Humane Farms collected over 500,000 signatures to introduce a ballot measure onto the November 2010 election that would further amend the state constitution. The measure would have prohibited "extreme confinement" for sows and laying hens, ended the slaughter and sale of downer cattle, and mandated humane euthanasia for farm animals (HSUS 2010). But before the signatures could be turned over to the Ohio statehouse for validation, then-Governor Ted Strickland negotiated a deal between the advocacy groups and nine agricultural organizations, including the Ohio Farm Bureau, to implement legislation and policies related to animal welfare without having to amend the constitution. Many of the tenets embodied in the proposed constitutional amendment, including phasing out veal crates by 2017 and gestation crates by 2025 and bans on inhumane euthanasia and transport of downer cattle, were included in the negotiated deal. Provisions were added for outlawing cockfighting, puppy mills, and acquisition of exotic animals (HSUS 2010). A moratorium on new battery cages for laying hens was also instituted, and existing facilities would be required to meet a minimum space per hen requirement by 2016 (Ohio Department of Agriculture 2011).

Even before the agreement could be implemented, some animal welfare advocates argued that it did not go far enough since it allowed for what could be seen as a generous phase-out period for some practices and permitted the continuation of others in existing hen confinement facilities. New hen facilities could also use cages, as long as they were "enriched cages" with a minimum of sixty-seven square inches per bird to allow for some natural behaviors like perching and grooming (Ohio Department of Agriculture 2011). Welfare advocates' fear that the livestock industry, through the Ohio LCSB's welfare rules-setting functions, would dilute or protect their own interests seemed warranted at one point when the standards board overrode elements of the negotiated agreement by deciding to allow the extreme confinement of veal calves after veal farmers complained about the proposed changes (Harding 2011a). In the end, though, the LCSB decided that veal confinement would transition to group housing by 2017 as initially negotiated. Overall, the standards, which became effective on 29 September 2011, appear faithful to the 2010 agreement, and the CEO of the Humane Society of the United States (HSUS), Wayne Pacelle, voiced his approval for the standards (Harding 2011b).

Ohio's effort to legislate animal welfare policy brings the intersection of the state and capital in guiding the shape of agricultural industry into sharp relief. Like the case of Seaboard Farms in some of the plains states (Bonanno and Constance 2006), the case of Ohio suggests that the state can be a proponent of capital at the same time it can restrict it. The mechanism that enables this dual agency lies in Ohio's state constitution, which allows for a high degree of direct democracy. Ohio is one of eighteen states where citizens can introduce constitutional amendments and one of twenty-five states where citizens can initiate referendums to overturn state statutes (Ballotpedia 2013). This means that well-funded private interests like livestock associations (e.g., Ohio Pork Producers, the Ohio Poultry Association, and the Ohio Beef Council) can propose constitutional amendments that protect and promote the interests of capital (like the creation of the LCSB), but it also means that organized citizen action can use the same processes to institute restraints on the actions of capital and even potentially overturn successful industry-sponsored initiatives. The effectiveness of citizen action in challenging the agricultural industry and prompting a negotiated settlement is contrary to what might be expected in a state where the industry has well-funded agricultural interest groups and strong legislative advocates. However, the state of Ohio has substantial urban populations to whom the animal welfare issue may have some salience. In addition, context can be extremely important as the impact of only one or two extreme incidents of farm animal abuse, albeit very rare, may quickly coalesce ambivalent public opinion into supporting some sort of action. In Ohio, two incidents in the span of eighteen months garnered substantial state (and even international) attention that heightened public awareness of animal welfare issues and probably put the livestock industry on the defensive, forcing them to be more cooperative in drafting and implementing some standards. In one case, a pro-animal welfare organization, Mercy for Animals, conducted an undercover investigation, which revealed some extreme farm animal abuse and led to the conviction of one farmhand on animal abuse charges (Zachariah 2010). The next year, the release of fifty-six exotic animals in Zanesville, Ohio, forty-nine of which law enforcement officers shot, also spurred public support for stricter exotic animal regulations (Johnson 2012).

While state-level ballot initiatives or the threat of initiatives remain a viable mechanism for contesting farm animal welfare in some states, there is some indication that a strategic shift may be occurring in how the farm animal welfare issue will be resolved in the future. Legislating farm animal welfare at the state level can ultimately lead to compromise and cooperation, but not without protracted, bitter, and highly labor- and capital-intensive campaigns, as was the case in Ohio. State measures have also been seen by many as overly burdensome on livestock farmers, who are often already heavily indebted by their investment in production facilities. As a result, an alternative policy and legislative strategy circumventing cumbersome state ballot initiative processes may be emerging. The presidents of the HSUS and United Egg Producers, "bitter adversaries," recently decided to set aside costly and unproductive media campaigns and started working together to lobby Congress for changes to welfare standards for laying hens. The standards still endorse cages, but "enriched" cages with more space and perches (Charles 2012). While critics may accuse these leaders of compromising their core values, this path of negotiating and discovering common ground may be a more fruitful option for a balanced outcome that respects the public's ambivalence on the issue. The leaders in these processes are often seen as authorities to their constituents, and their alliance presents a powerful message to federal lawmakers that might prompt action among entrenched constituencies unaccustomed to seeking consensus or common ground. Future food-system research will need to explore the implications of this shift in strategies.

Conclusions

We have sought to provide a brief overview of rural sociology's attention to animal agriculture, with considerable focus on the issue of state intervention in farm animal welfare. Our review and discussion has not been exhaustive, focusing on the interplay of public attitudes, industry, and the state, with limited attention to the production side of the equation that includes the individual farmer or animal handler. We have identified several opportunities for further examination of farm animal welfare, particularly questions about how the issue is being managed through state and market mechanisms and to whose benefit. In these conclusions, we suggest research themes we believe warrant more attention.

In general, the process of balancing the needs of the livestock industry with the public's desire for farm animal welfare has been impacted by context and, from a bird's-eye vantage, appears to be quite ad hoc. We expect the approaches and responses to this issue to continue to be piecemeal and somewhat unpredictable for the foreseeable future. The United States, with its powerful agricultural lobbies, is not likely to follow the European Union, which has undertaken animal-welfare reform in a largely top-down manner (Moynagh 2000). While many advocates might like to see the United States legislate standards in a similar fashion, there is probably equal worry that federal intervention could water down standards the same way the US Organic Certified label was seen as corrupting organic farming (Guthman 1998; Raynolds 2004). Whether a consensus eventually emerges, or whether industry and farm animal welfare movement organizations continue to variably contest the issue at local and state levels, warrants ongoing monitoring by rural sociologists and fellow food-system scholars.

One question for further investigation concerns the issue of public ambivalence. The social psychological questions about how consumers or the public cognitively balance what can be contradictory views of the livestock sector warrant more investigation. It is possible that the dynamism of Ohio's experience in seeking to regulate the farm animal welfare issue is in part a result of the fact that the public is sympathetic to both the interests of farmers and agriculture and to the welfare of farm animals. There is a need for further investigation of the balance of those sympathies, and there may be useful insights that can inform our understanding of other complex food-system issues in the postmodern era. Work in this area might build on social-psychological literature associated with biotechnology and organics, but there are also opportunities to explore how sympathy for farm animal welfare might parallel sympathy for other social justice issues, an association that many have noted (Deemer and Lobao 2011; Kendall, Lobao, and Sharp 2006; Nibert 1994; Verbeke 2009). More conceptual research is needed to understand why and how these "constellations" of attitudes are formed both socially and psychologically, and how they drive consumption behaviors or impact voting preferences.

A third area of future research should examine the role of large-scale retailers, who have deftly responded to consumer animal welfare concerns and are poised to have substantial upstream influence on the future of meat production. Chipotle is one franchise that has successfully built its reputation around what it claims is a rigorous meat sourcing regimen. Other large retailers including McDonalds, Wendy's, and Burger King have participated in auditing their beef slaughterhouses for over a decade to achieve a more humane slaughtering system (Grandin 2005). As Bonanno points out in the introduction to this section, private capital is increasingly able to act independently of the state—and indeed, farm animal welfare seems to be a clear case in which the private sector is opting to bypass state action. Retailers are well positioned to respond to calls for increased oversight of farm animal welfare (preemptively to preserve their brand quality, or strategically to capture whatever market premium there may be with animal welfare) and are able to do so with the flexibility and efficiency that is often absent from state regulation. However, the adequacy of retailer standards remains largely unclear. While the state-level legislative process undertaken in Ohio followed a pluralist model and appears to have synthesized the interests of industry, consumers, NGOs, and small livestock producers, it remains to be seen how these same stakeholder interests are privileged or restricted in the private sector.

Finally, the preponderance of attention in the study of livestock and farm animals has either been producer focused or consumer focused in evaluating state and market processes. Many other important actors in the livestock commodity chain have interests that also warrant attention. In terms of the commodity chain in general, questions about labor have been understudied, with some attention to meat packing (Grey, Devlin, and Goldsmith 2009; Eisnitz 1997) but with many interesting sociological questions remaining, such as labor in the CAFOs themselves. Another important actor in the livestock commodity chain that we have become aware of in regards to investigating the farm animal welfare question are the people working in veterinary and animal health. We have observed a very sincere interest on the part of professionals in this field to identify production systems that are animal-welfare friendly. The interesting challenge, though, may be that systems that minimize animal stress and maximize animal welfare may not conform to the vision of livestock production that many members of the concerned public hold. We need to better understand the social-psychology of the issue, and we posit that some aspects of farm animal welfare concern may be conflated with an agrarian bias for small farm animal production, which is not inherently more animal welfare friendly, nor even realistic given the size of demand for animal agriculture products. While some claim that small-scale livestock production is "inherently" more humane (Niman 2009, 246), this is not necessarily true. In some ways, industrial husbandry techniques are more humane than those in alternative livestock operations, and industrial slaughter is probably the quickest and most painless death available to farm animals (Purcell 2011). One promising new multidisciplinary research effort, The Socially Sustainable Egg Production Project discussed by Swanson, Mench, and Thompson (2011), aims to improve animal welfare in industrial production through a collaboration between social and animal scientists that seeks to appropriately measure and weigh different views and harmonize to the extent possible public concern and best welfare practices, while also balancing the economic considerations of producers.

In conclusion, we find livestock and farm animal welfare to be a quite dynamic area of activity that has received and should continue to receive attention from rural sociologists. In many ways, the contemporary challenges associated with addressing farm animal welfare concerns is a logical outcome of the earlier era of structural change in the scale and character of livestock production. While we should not assume earlier eras of livestock production were animal-welfare friendly, we argue that the industrialization of livestock production and the increasingly Fordist, factory-like character of livestock production does not conform to the agrarian imagery that has historically been associated with farming and farm animals. While much early research on livestock agriculture illuminated how capital interests were motivating structural change, it seems that contemporary discussions of animal welfare illuminate the public's power to restrict the practices of capital to certain publicly desired performance standards—or at least demand that they follow those standards. Whether this continues to be the case as global sourcing and capital mobility persist remains to be seen, but the industry currently appears to be increasingly willing to moderate its activities at the behest of the public's decisions at the ballot box.

References

Allen, Laura. 2010. "States Are Empowering Industry Boards to Decide Farm Animal Care." *Animal Law Coalition*, 4 June. http://animallawcoalition.com/states-are-empowering-industry-boards-to-decide-farm-animal-care.

Ballotpedia. 2013. "States." Last modified 31 July. http://ballotpedia.org/states.

Battelle Memorial Institute. 2008. "The Ohio Livestock Industry's Economic Impact on the State of Ohio." Accessed 25 April 2012. http://www.yumpu.com/en/document/view/6927372/the-ohio-livestock-industrys-economic-impact.

Bennett, R.M., J. Anderson, and P. Blaney. 2002. "Moral Intensity and Willingness to Pay Concerning Farm Animal Welfare Issues and the Implications for Agricultural Policy." *Journal of Agricultural & Environmental Ethics* 15 (2): 187–202. http://dx.doi.org/10.1023/A:1015036617385.

Bonanno, Alessandro, and Doug H. Constance. 2006. "Corporations and the State in the Global Era: The Case of Seaboard Farms and Texas." *Rural Sociology* 71 (1): 59–84. http://dx.doi.org/10.1526/003601106777789819.

Bonney, Roland. 2008. "The Business of Farm Animal Welfare." In *The Future of Animal Farming: Renewing the Ancient Contract*, ed. Marian Stamp Dawkins and Roland Bonney, 63–72. Malden: Blackwell.

Boogaard, Birgit K., Bettina B. Bock, Simon J. Oosting, Johannes S. C. Wiskerke, and Akke J. Zijpp. 2011. "Social Acceptance of Dairy Farming: The Ambivalence between the Two Faces of Modernity." *Journal of Agricultural & Environmental Ethics* 24 (3): 259–82. http://dx.doi.org/10.1007/s10806-010-9256-4.

Charles, Dan. 2012. "Coop D'Etat: Farmers, Humane Society Partner on Chicken-Cage Revolution." *NPR*, 26 January. http://www.npr.org/blogs/thesalt/2012/01/26/145900751/ex-foes-stage-coop-detat-for-egg-laying-chickens.

Constance, Doug H. 2002. "Globalization, Broiler Production, and Community Controversy in East Texas." *Southern Rural Sociology* 18: 31–55.

Deemer, Danielle, and Linda M. Lobao. 2011. "Public Concern with Farm-Animal Welfare: Religion, Politics and Human Disadvantage in the Food Sector." *Rural Sociology* 76 (2): 167–96. http://dx.doi.org/10.1111/j.1549-0831.2010.00044.x.

Eisnitz, Gail. 1997. *Slaughterhouse: The Shocking Story of Greed, Neglect and Inhumane Treatment inside the U.S. Meat Industry*. Amherst: Prometheus.

Frewer, L.J., A. Kole, S.M.A. Van de Kroon, and C. de Lauwere. 2005. "Consumer Attitudes towards the Development of Animal-Friendly Husbandry Systems." *Journal of Agricultural & Environmental Ethics* 18 (4): 345–67. http://dx.doi.org/10.1007/s10806-005-1489-2.

Glenna, L.L., and G.V. Mitev. 2009. "Global Neo-liberalism, Global Ecological Modernization, and a Swine CAFO in Rural Bulgaria." *Journal of Rural Studies* 25 (3): 289–98. http://dx.doi.org/10.1016/j.jrurstud.2009.01.001.

Grandin, Temple. 1 February 2005. "Maintenance of Good Animal Welfare Standards in Beef Slaughter Plants by Use of Auditing Programs." *Journal of the American Veterinary Medical Association* 226 (3): 370–73. http://dx.doi.org/10.2460/javma.2005.226.370. Medline:15702685.

Grey, Mark A., Michele Devlin, and Aaron Goldsmith. 2009. *Postville, USA: Surviving Diversity in Small-Town America*. Boston: Gemma Media.

Guthman, Julie. 1998. "Regulating Meaning, Appropriating Nature: The Codification of California Organic Agriculture." *Antipode* 30 (2): 135–54. http://dx.doi.org/10.1111/1467-8330.00071.

Hall, C., and V. Sandilands. 2007. "Public Attitudes to the Welfare of Broiler Chickens." *Animal Welfare (South Mimms, England)* 16: 499–512.

Harding, Dave. 2011a. "Ohio Livestock Care Standards Board Overrides Portion of Strickland Animal Welfare Agreement." *Progress Ohio Blog*, March 2. http://www.progressohio.org/blog/2011/03/ohio-livestock-care-standards-board-overrides-portion-of-strickland-animal-welfare-agreement.html.

Harding, Dave. 2011b. "A Milestone For Ohio Farm Animals: Ohio Livestock Care Standards Board Finalizes Welfare Standards." *Progress Ohio Blog*, 20 April. http://www.progressohio.org/blog/2011/04/a-milestone-for-ohio-farm-animals-ohio-livestock-care-standards-board-finalizes-welfare-standards.html.

Hatanaka, Maki, Carmen Bain, and Lawrence Busch. 2005. "Third-Party Certification in the Global Agrifood System." *Food Policy* 30 (3): 354–69. http://dx.doi.org/10.1016/j.foodpol.2005.05.006.

Hatanaka, Maki, and Lawrence Busch. 2008. "Third-Party Certification in the Global Agrifood System: An Objective or Socially Mediated Governance Mechanism?" *Sociologia Ruralis* 48 (1): 73–91. http://dx.doi.org/10.1111/j.1467-9523.2008.00453.x.

Heffernan, William D. 1972. "Sociological Dimensions of Agricultural Structures in the United States." *Sociologia Ruralis* 12 (2): 481–99. http://dx.doi.org/10.1111/j.1467-9523.1972.tb00156.x.

Heffernan, William D. 1984. "Constraints in the U.S. Poultry Industry." *Research in Rural Sociology and Development* 1: 237–60.

Heffernan, William D. 2000. "Concentration of Ownership and Control in Agriculture." In *Hungry for Profit: The Agribusiness Threat to Farmers, Food, and the Environment*, ed. Fred Magdoff, John Bellamy Foster, and Frederick H. Buttel, 61–75. New York: Monthly Review Press.

Heleski, C.R., A.G. Mertig, and A.J. Zanella. 2006. "Stakeholder Attitudes toward Animal Welfare." *Anthrozoos* 19 (4): 290–307. http://dx.doi.org/10.2752/089279306785415439.

Hewson, C.J. June 2003. "What is Animal Welfare? Common Definitions and Their Practical Consequences." *Canadian Veterinary Journal* 44 (6): 496–9. Medline:12839246.

Herzog, H.A. 2007. "Gender Differences in Human-Animal Interactions." *Anthrozoos* 20 (1): 7–21. http://dx.doi.org/10.2752/089279307780216687.

Horowitz, Roger. 2006. *Putting Meat on the American Table: Taste, Technology, Transformation.* Baltimore: Johns Hopkins University Press.

Howard, Philip H., and Patricia Allen. 2010. "Beyond Organic and Fair Trade? An Analysis of Ecolabel Preferences in the United States." *Rural Sociology* 75 (2): 244–69. http://dx.doi.org/10.1111/j.1549-0831.2009.00009.x.

Humane Society of the United States (HSUS). 2010. "Landmark Ohio Animal Welfare Agreement Reached among HSUS, Ohioans for Humane Farms, Gov. Strickland, and Leading Livestock Organizations." 30 June. http://www.humanesociety.org/news/press_releases/2010/06/landmark_ohio_agreement_063010.html.

Jackson-Smith, Douglas, and Bradford Barham. 2000. "Dynamics of Dairy Industry Restructuring in Wisconsin." In *Research in Rural Sociology and Development*, vol. 8. ed. Harry K. Schwarzweller and Andrew P. Davidson, 115–39. New York: Elsevier Science. http://dx.doi.org/10.1016/S1057-1922(00)80008-6.

Johnson, Alan. 2012. "Senate Panel Unanimously Approves Exotic-Animal Rules." *Columbus Dispatch*, 25 April. http://www.dispatch.com/content/stories/local/2012/04/25/tamer-exotic-animal-bill-provides-for-exceptions.html.

Kellert, S. 1989. "Perceptions of Animals in America." In *Perceptions of Animals in American Culture*, ed. R.J. Hoage, 5–24. Washington, DC: Smithsonian Institution.

Kellert, S., and J.K. Berry. 1980. *Knowledge, Affection and Basic Attitudes toward Animals in American Society.* Washington, DC: United States Department of the Interior, Fish and Wildlife Service.

Kendall, Holly A., Linda M. Lobao, and Jeff S. Sharp. 2006. "Public Concern with Animal Well-Being: Place, Social Structural Location, and Individual Experience." *Rural Sociology* 71 (3): 399–428. http://dx.doi.org/10.1526/003601106778070617.

Moynagh, J. 2000. "E.U. Regulation and Consumer Demand for Animal Welfare." *AgBioForum* 3: 107–14.

North Central Regional Center for Rural Development (NCRCRD). 1999. *Bringing Home the Bacon*. Poteau: The Kerr Center.

Nibert, D.A. 1994. "Animal Rights and Human Social Issues." *Society & Animals* 2 (2): 115–24. http://dx.doi.org/10.1163/156853094X00135.

Niman, Nicolette H. 2009. *Righteous Porkchop*. New York: Harper Collins.

Ohio Department of Agriculture. 2011. "Ohio Livestock Care Standards." Accessed 1 April 2012. http://www.agri.ohio.gov/LivestockCareStandards/.

Prickett, R.W., F. Bailey Norwood, and J.L. Lusk. 2010. "Consumer Preferences for Farm Animal Welfare: Results from a Telephone Survey of U.S. Households." *Animal Welfare* (South Mimms, England) 19: 335–47.

Purcell, N. 2011. "Cruel Intimacies and Risky Relationships: Accounting for Suffering in Industrial Livestock Production." *Society & Animals* 19 (1): 59–81. http://dx.doi.org/10.1163/156853011X545538.

Raynolds, Laura T. 2004. "The Globalization of Organic Agro-food Networks." *World Development* 32 (5): 725–43. http://dx.doi.org/10.1016/j.worlddev.2003.11.008.

Raynolds, Laura T., Douglas Murray, and Andrew Heller. 2007. "Regulating Sustainability in the Coffee Sector: A Comparative Analysis of Third-Party Environmental and Social Certification Initiatives." *Agriculture and Human Values* 24 (2): 147–63. http://dx.doi.org/10.1007/s10460-006-9047-8.

Rollin, Bernard. 2008. "The Ethics of Agriculture: The End of True Animal Husbandry." In *The Future of Animal Farming: Renewing the Ancient Contract*, ed. Marian Stamp Dawkins and Roland Bonney, 7–20. Malden: Blackwell.

Rollin, Bernard. 2010. "Farm Factories: The End of Animal Husbandry." In *The CAFO Reader: The Tragedy of Industrial Animal Factories*, ed. Daniel Imhoff, 6–14. Berkeley: Watershed Media.

Salant, P., J.D. Wulfhorst, S. Kane, and C. Dearien. 2009. *Community Level Impacts of Idaho's Changing Dairy Industry*. Moscow: University of Idaho College of Agricultural and Life Sciences.

Scully, M. 2002. *Dominion: The Power of Man, the Suffering of Animals, and the Call to Mercy*. New York: St. Martin's Press.

Schwab, J. 1998. *Planning and Zoning for Concentrated Animal Feeding Operations*. Washington, DC: American Planning Association.

Swanson, J.C., J.A. Mench, and P.B. Thompson. January 2011. "Introduction—The Socially Sustainable Egg Production Project." *Poultry Science* 90 (1): 227–28. http://dx.doi.org/10.3382/ps.2010-01266. Medline:21177464.

Tonsor, G.T., N. Olynk, and C. Wolf. 2009. "Consumer Preferences for Animal Welfare Attributes: The Case of Gestation Crates." *Journal of Agricultural and Applied Economics* 41: 713–30.

Welsh, R. 1996. *The Industrialization of US Agriculture: An Overview and Background Report*. Greenbelt, MD: Henry A. Wallace Institute for Alternative Agriculture.

Welsh, R. 1997. "Vertical Coordination, Producer Response, and the Locus of Control over Agricultural Production Decisions." *Rural Sociology* 52: 491–507.

Verbeke, W. 2009. "Stakeholder, Citizen and Consumer Interests in Farm Animal Welfare." *Animal Welfare* (South Mimms, England) 18: 325–33.

Vick, Lindsay. 2011. "Comment: Confined to a Process: The Preemptive Strike of Livestock Care Standards Boards in Farm Animal Welfare Regulation." *Animal Law* 18: 151–74.

Zachariah, Holly. 2010. "Former Dairy Worker Will Spend Four More Months in Jail for Animal Abuse." *Columbus Dispatch*, 24 September. http://www.dispatch.com/content/stories/local/2010/09/24/animal-abuse-plea.html.

CHAPTER 8

Agrifood Movements: Diversity, Aims, and Limits

Clare Hinrichs and John Eshleman

Introduction

Social and civic movements addressing food and agriculture—agrifood movements—are not new, but they have grown in visibility and diversity of focus through the 1990s and 2000s. Across North America, initiatives and practices that seek to change human connections to food and agriculture now capture public attention. In this chapter, we examine the emergence, patterns, and sociological significance of North American agrifood movements within the context of a globalizing world where neoliberal ideologies and policies increasingly shape the options. By *agrifood movements*, we refer to a broad field of social action that can be seen as challenging the status quo of the now-prevailing agrifood system (Friedland 2010). This definition is marked first by its topical focus—the wide arena including both agricultural production and food consumption and encompassing environmental, economic, social, political, and cultural concerns about those activities. It is plural because, as yet, there is no comprehensive or integrated "movement" that gathers together and coordinates the myriad sub-issues and sometimes fractious actors into one united force.

The increasing visibility and cachet of agrifood movements comes at a crowded historical juncture. The period since the 1990s has been punctuated by food safety crises around everyday products like hamburger, peanut butter, and leafy greens; anti-globalization demonstrations; and spikes of civil unrest around the globe in response to food price increases that began dramatically in 2008. Behind catalytic "shocks" are slower burning social issues, from public concern about the rising rates of child obesity and diabetes to debate about the climate and environmental impacts of current agricultural and dietary practices. Public, consumer, and citizen disquiet and the rise of these agrifood movements can be seen as responses to the growing global neoliberalization of the agrifood system. In some cases, the emergence of new agrifood movements represents a direct response to the growing power transnational agrifood capital wields in shaping the structure and performance of the agrifood sector to privilege market priorities and profits over social or environmental goals. In other cases, cultural malaise and unease with the commodification of land and food prompt personal searches for "reconnection" to food that can be seen as more indirect forms of resistance (Kneafsey et al. 2008). Broadly, then, agrifood movements can be understood as sociologically differentiated responses to the neoliberalization of the agrifood system.

We begin by providing some conceptual tools for considering the forms and aims of agrifood actions and movements. We draw on sociologists Snow and Soule's (2010) work on social movements to highlight the analytical distinction between individual and collective action that is crucial in the field of agriculture and food. We also incorporate Snow and Soule's (2010) distinction between making direct and indirect challenges to further characterize contemporary agrifood action and movements. This question of strategic aim speaks to ongoing debate about the transformative potential and politics of agrifood movements. We next use these conceptual touchstones to anchor our discussion of context and trends in North American agrifood movements. Focusing on the period from about 1990 through 2012, we trace key emphases as well as growing diversity in agrifood movements and action. Finally, we identify several controversies and tensions in the field and suggest some promising directions for future research on North American agrifood movements.

Agrifood Action and Movements: Some Conceptual Tools

The umbrella term *agrifood movements* captures a diverse set of issues, initiatives, and organizations, which together reflect widening disenchantment with conventional corporatized agriculture and food. Organic agriculture, farmers' markets, community food security, agribusiness accountability, farm-to-school programs, food policy councils, fair trade, food justice, anti-genetically engineered (GE) crops and food, animal welfare, food sovereignty, and urban agriculture suggest some of this varied discursive terrain. Although academics, practitioners, and activists sometimes lump all such manifestations together as agrifood movements, there is debate about the meaning and depth of "alterity" (i.e., "alternativeness") within and across these manifestations (Maye, Holloway, and Kneafsey 2007).

Indeed, most academic research has focused more on such debates about alterity than on examining actual social movement processes and the outcomes of new agrifood initiatives and practices. With a few notable exceptions (e.g., Munro and Schurman 2008; Schurman and Munro 2009), research on agrifood movements has not been in close conversation with the broader literature on social movements, which by traditional definition involve some form of collective action. Snow and Soule (2010, 6) state, "social movements are *collectivities* acting with some degree of organization and continuity, partly outside institutional or organizational channels, for the purpose of challenging extant systems of authority, or resisting change in such systems, in the organization, society, culture or world system in which they are embedded." In emphasizing collective action, such a definition seems to preclude analytical consideration of many less explicitly collective manifestations of cultural and behavioral change among agricultural producers, food consumers, citizens, and others in the agrifood system.

We adapt the conceptual framework Snow and Soule (2010) develop to categorize and relate forms of agrifood action and probe the movement character of those actions. Strictly understood, social movements involve collective action, but Snow and Soule's (2010) framework recognizes that people often engage in individualized, even independent action in response to concerns they have about their experiences and environments. This is an important point for agrifood movements. In a context of global neoliberalization of the agrifood system—a situation privileging individual choices and responsibility within increasingly market-driven and privately regulated social spaces—individual action enjoys special openings and appeals. Even as the instances of collective action related to food and agriculture in North America increase and diversify, individual unorganized action by food consumers now voting with their wallets at farmers' markets and in the organics section of their supermarkets remains central. But both conceptually and practically, such individual action, especially when limited to market engagements, jars with classic understandings of social movements. Increased consumer purchasing of organic food at the supermarket or more shopping at farmers' markets are noteworthy economic and cultural trends in food and agriculture, but under what conditions can these consumer behaviors be understood as a "social movement"? This analytical distinction between individual and collective action offers one important touchstone for thinking about agrifood movements.

Snow and Soule (2010) further distinguish between the types of challenges people may make (whether acting individually or collectively) in response to some situation in public life that concerns them. Collectively undertaken direct challenges to prevailing authority and power are perhaps exemplified by classic social movement repertoires, including protests and occupations. Explicit claims and demands for change by organized groups through lobbying or litigation represent direct challenges, too. But collectively undertaken indirect challenges, as seen, for example, in secessionist or separatist efforts that constitute withdrawal from the problematic or contested social context, are also, according to Snow and Soule (2010), the stuff of social movements. Development of alternative agrifood institutions, such as community-supported agriculture projects, public procurement initiatives, regional food hubs, and values-based food supply chains, can be seen as involving some measure of collective endeavor while constructing food economies that re-embed social, community, civic, and ecological values (Hinrichs 2003; Lyson 2004). From this standpoint, collective action centered on constructing alternative institutions that indirectly challenge the status quo can be considered within an agrifood movements frame.

These two axes of (1) individual-collective action and (2) direct-indirect challenge help to anchor thinking about agrifood movements and action now evident in the first decades of the twenty-first century. They offer purchase for some of the main debates and questions in the field. Furthermore, they echo concepts put forward by other researchers. For example, agrifood sociologist Patricia Allen's distinction between more "oppositional" and more "alternative" strategies of agrifood initiatives corresponds to the direct-indirect challenges axis (Allen et al. 2003). While an oppositional politics involves organizers and activists directly confronting and working to change structural inequalities in the current agrifood system, an alternatives-focused politics emphasizes constructing food, farming, and economic institutions that offer different models. Concepts of political consumerism (Micheletti 2003), sustainable and ethical consumption (Cohen, Comrov, and Hoffner 2005), and the citizen-consumer (Johnston 2008) further highlight the tensions, limitations, and sometimes-nascent promise in market-based individual action related to food and agriculture.

Agrifood Movements: Context and Themes

Given the diversity and emergent quality of agrifood movements, their full history has yet to be written. In this section, we can only sketch some central orientations, organizations, and evolving issues of the field from about 1990 through 2012. We focus on the United States, with some attention to its larger North American and international context. The roots of contemporary agrifood movements stretch back to early interest in organic farming and the 1960s counterculture (Belasco 1993) and Jim Hightower's (1973) blistering critiques of agribusiness and the land grant university system. However, developments in the late 1980s and early 1990s set the stage for an upwelling and diversification of agrifood movement ideologies and activities. Activist pressure helped to launch the USDA's Sustainable Agriculture Research and Education (SARE) program in 1988. Despite its small budget and early concentration on agricultural production systems, SARE's regional projects and initiatives through the 1990s and beyond opened up symbolic and practical space to develop broader constituencies for sustainable food and agriculture (Allen 2004). A sharp uptick in organic food sales by 1990 marked growing consumer interest in alternatives to conventionally produced food (Friedland 2010), while numerous food safety crises and agri-environmental incidents reinforced public and activist doubt about the ascendant neoliberal agrifood regime (Bonanno in this volume). Furthermore, new market-liberalizing policies and institutions, including the 1994 North American Free Trade Agreement and the World Trade Organization starting in 1995, anchored state and corporate commitments to globalization. Some US-based nongovernmental organizations (NGOs), such as the Institute for Agriculture and Trade Policy, specifically linked the global context and operation of neoliberal agrifood policies to outcomes for US producers and consumers, as well as those in other countries. Taken together, multiple developments through the 1990s made agriculture and food ever more compelling terrain for social action and social movements, a trend that has intensified in the first decade of the twenty-first century. Keeping Snow and Soule's (2010) framework in mind, we take up the question of individual action later and focus next on collective action directly challenging the perceived harms and inequities of the prevailing agrifood system.

Resistance to Industrial Farming and Food Technologies and Practices

Collective direct challenges to the mainstream, industrialized agrifood system have been prompted by concerns about environmental and health impacts, corporate concentration and control, and social injustices. Actions have included classic targeted protests such as consumer boycotts, farmers' tractorcades, and most recently activist calls to "Occupy Big Food" (Wartman 2012). The 1970s and '80s legacy of US activist concern about "agribusiness accountability" anticipated contemporary critiques of global neoliberalization in food and agriculture. However, agrifood movements making direct, organized challenges to current patterns and practices in the agrifood system now focus more on the priorities, operations, and power of private corporations and much less on the role of public research and the land grant university system (Buttel 2005). Here, we briefly present two specific areas of contention that represent collective direct challenges to the prevailing agrifood system—community-based responses to large-scale confinement animal feeding operations (CAFOs) and nationally organized opposition to GE crops and food.

With dramatic consolidation in livestock sectors such as swine and poultry, increased vertical integration, and geographic concentration of animal production through the 1990s and 2000s, some local rural communities have organized to oppose such agricultural development altogether or to reduce its potential harms. In some rural places, local concerns about air and water quality impacts as well as potential community disruption from new and proposed intensive livestock operations have galvanized grassroots community opposition groups. DeLind (1998) recounts local resistance to proposed "hog hotels" in Parma, Michigan, where citizen groups targeted state policymakers to better regulate and manage such industrial agricultural development. In Texas, although local opposition to CAFO development grew into "a statewide organization with an active legislative agenda and political strategy," the state's acquiescence to global corporate and capital interests constrained the long-term success of such direct challenges (Bonanno and Constance 2008, 143).

Opposition to the development and use of agricultural biotechnologies and GE organisms offers a second example of collective, direct challenge to the dominant agrifood system. Although US activists had been concerned about GE before commercialization, rapid growth of the agricultural biotechnology sector since the late 1980s and increasing consolidation in the "life sciences" industry through the 1990s and 2000s fanned concerns about the democratic threats and environmental risks with GE crops. Munro and Schurman (2008, 171) observe that the US anti-GE movement began not as a mass movement, but rather as an emergent network of seasoned, well-educated activists, who marshaled scientific and legal expertise and pursued coordinated direct "tactics that were relatively 'professional' and nonconfrontational in character." Though limited in its capacity to mobilize broader US public support, this early anti-GE movement still generated valuable counter-knowledge and information that other related agrifood movements would use in their own efforts for GE labeling, GE-free ordinances, and the like, thereby broadening the initial movement. Overall, however, challenges by the US anti-GE movement have lacked the efficacy of anti-GE organizing in Europe and elsewhere. These uneven patterns highlight links, but also contrasts in the context for agrifood movements across geographic space. Schurman and Munro (2009), for example, argue that the unique cultural and economic construction of the highly concentrated UK food retailing sector in the 1990s and 2000s created openings and opportunities for UK anti-GE activists that did not apply in the United States. National regulatory systems, media coverage, and consumer priorities on quality versus price and convenience also differed between the United Kingdom and the United States, underscoring that specific national, regional, and local conditions can shape the outcomes of agrifood movements within broad-brush patterns of global neoliberalization in the agrifood system.

Constructing Production and Marketing Alternatives

Collective indirect challenges to the agrifood system are not necessarily divorced from the issues or tactics we discuss above. However, indirect challenges tend to emphasize the design, organization, and implementation of preferred alternative models more than battles with the state or corporations over practices in the prevailing agrifood system. Kloppenburg, Hendrickson, and Stevenson's (1996) foodshed principles of self-protection, secession, and succession underlie the orientation of current agrifood movements that aim to build production, marketing, and consumption alternatives through sustainable local food systems. The very weaknesses of the dominant globalizing agrifood system offer strategic opportunities for those organizing and building alternative food system initiatives based on ascendant quality attributes such as "local" or "sustainable" (Hendrickson and Heffernan 2002). Here we explore the collective action of agrifood movements centered on organics, local, and fair trade as alternatives to the dominant agrifood system.

Organics is an important early agrifood movement, although it has changed markedly over the past half-century. With connections to the radical politics of the 1960s and the "back-to-the-land" movement, it began as a farming (and gardening) centered movement that drew energy from Sir Albert Howard and J.I. Rodale's criticisms of synthetic chemicals in agriculture in the 1940s, Rachel Carson's *Silent Spring*, and the DDT scare of 1969 to 1972 (Goodman, DuPuis, and Goodman 2012). Small-scale, often countercultural farmers produced foods according to evolving organic and agro-ecological practices. They networked (and learned) with nearby organic farmers and began to certify their organic products through regional organizations, such as Oregon Tilth. Building these small alternative organic food systems depended on economic links and ideological connections to small alternative food retailers, such as cooperatives and health-food stores (Belasco 1993).

As consumer demand for organic food slowly grew through the 1970s and '80s and a handful of agricultural scientists began to pay attention to organic farming, a more "technologically-led vision" emerged, now aspiring to greater institutional legitimacy of organic agriculture within the USDA and land grant university system (Buttel 1997, 355). By the 1990s, this newer, more market-oriented organic vision spawned heated public debates about whether and how to standardize US organics. The USDA's initial draft of standards in 1997, heavily influenced by agribusiness interests that wanted to capitalize on the "organic" label, included use of GE organisms, sewage sludge, and irradiation as acceptable organic practices (DeLind 2000). When the USDA invited public comment on the proposed rules, organic agriculture activists responded by mobilizing grassroots public response. Some 250,000 comments were submitted in opposition to the draft rules, resulting in final standards more aligned with organic activists' wishes (Friedland 2010).

But the very existence of any federal organic standards has heightened the concerns of activists and critics, who see codified national "rules" as a way to commandeer the original vision on behalf of agribusiness interest in a growing base of organic food consumers (DeLind 2000). Once the province of small counter-cultural farmers and hippies dedicated to ecological and local well-being, organic food has become a sophisticated, profit-focused global industry. According to the Organic Trade Association (2011), sales of organic products in the United States grew from $1 billion in 1990 to $26.7 billion in 2010, with mass-market retailers comprising over 50 percent of all sales.

Standardization and signs of conventionalization in the success of organics, as well as divisions around the meaning of an organics movement, coincided with and appeared to stimulate new interest in constructing alternative, direct markets centered on local foods. Through the 1990s and 2000s, local food initiatives emphasizing direct exchanges between proximate farmers and consumers burgeoned in the United States, Canada, and Europe. Touted as spaces revitalizing civic engagement and regional economies (Lyson 2004), direct local food markets offer multiple advantages over conventional food retail exchange, chief among them "food with a face." For many farmers, they foremost represent an opportunity for access to higher-value consumer markets, while for consumers, the strongest appeal of direct markets lies in access to high quality, fresh, and often distinctive foods (Ostrom and Jussaume 2007).

Although farmers participating in direct local markets often use sustainable, if not certified organic, farming practices, the local food movement has turned more on constructing and invigorating sites for alternative exchange, including farmers' markets, community-supported agriculture (CSA), and farm-to-school programs. A lively mix of local farmers, individual champions, and NGOs has mobilized to increase local food activity. The USDA reported that the number of farmers' markets in the United States increased from 1,755 in 1994 (the earliest available data) to 5,274 in 2009, and that community-supported agriculture farm projects had increased from 761 in 2001 to 1,144 in 2005, an estimate that many consider conservative (Martinez et al. 2010). By 2012, the National Farm to School network website reported farm to school programs in all fifty states and in over 12,000 schools.

As the word *locavore* joined the lexicon and local food interest burgeoned, the local food movement explored different tactics and strategies in the late 2000s, which have led to expansion and, potentially, mainstreaming. For example, local food practitioners and activists have developed overarching Buy Local Food campaigns, premised on generic marketing and messages, to increase local food purchasing and solidify farmers' markets and CSAs (Hinrichs and Allen 2008). They have also targeted institutions such as schools, hospitals, and colleges as local food buyers, a move that has increased the penetration of local food, but also revealed the logistical limitations of local food's signature "direct" exchange. The interest in local procurement, in turn, has increased efforts to organize and establish "local food infrastructure"—including new distribution structures and local/regional food hubs (Bloom and Hinrichs 2011). However, with supermarkets and even Walmart now eager to capitalize on local food, some movement activists ask whether the local food movement's successes have caused it to stray from its core commitments to place and community, reducing its potential to contribute to a regenerative agrifood system (DeLind 2011).

The movement for fair trade in agrifood products has grown dramatically since the 1990s, somewhat parallel to the local food movement. Centered originally on handicrafts and led mostly by faith-based groups and charities in its early days, fair trade is now associated most famously with products like coffee, tea, and bananas produced in the global South that have significant markets in the wealthier global North. Broadly, the fair trade movement seeks to develop alternative trade channels and product labeling to improve the livelihoods and welfare of marginalized food producers who are disadvantaged in a global agrifood system undergirded by neoliberal free trade principles (Shreck 2008). Certified fair trade product sales burgeoned to some US$5.8 billion worldwide in 2010, with the United Kingdom followed by the United States being the two countries with the largest value of fair trade consumer purchases (Raynolds 2012).

Where the local food movement has sought to reduce *spatial* distance between producers and consumers, the fair trade movement has emphasized reducing *social* distance between producers and consumers, thereby helping consumers to exercise knowledge and care in their purchase of fair trade products and in the process become more engaged global citizens (Raynolds 2012). The construction of such alternative, fairer, more equitable marketing and trade relations is central to collective fair trade work and activism, according well with Snow and Soule's (2010) framework of social movements prioritizing indirect challenges to prevailing systems of authority and economic rules.

A key tension as the fair trade movement has evolved is its relative balance between "social movement" and "market" priorities. Jaffee (2012) sees the growing reliance of international fair trade movement organizations on private regulation via voluntary certification and labeling as a tipping toward "market" that structures the possibility of corporate co-optation of the fair trade movement. In 2011, shifts in the commitments and policies of Fair Trade USA, the dominant fair trade certification body in the United States, had the effect of weakening fair trade product standards so that they better align with the interests of corporate partners and interests (Jaffee 2012). However, Raynolds (2012) asserts that a "capture narrative" for fair trade paints too stark a picture. Instead, she argues that through a durable and ongoing process of "social regulation," the interactions of "NGOs, movement groups, activist producers, and politicized consumers continue to support economic alternatives and resist Fair Trade's cooptation" (Raynolds 2012, 278).

Organics, local, and fair trade movements are prominent, illustrative examples of the range of contemporary agrifood movements. All involve promoting and developing alternative production practices and market initiatives that challenge, albeit indirectly, economic, environmental, or social detriments of the prevailing agrifood system.

Multiplying Frames

Beyond the multiple issues and engagements that prompt agrifood movements, it is also useful to consider briefly the various and evolving frames agrifood movement actors now use to situate and shape their work. Frames do more than statically describe a movement's goals and orientations; instead, movement actors use frames to shape, interpret, represent, and position their agrifood movement activity (Snow and Soule 2010). As Allen (2004) shows, in the 1990s, sustainable agriculture and community food security provided important frames for agrifood movements, emphasizing concern with ecological protection and greater community food self-reliance respectively. In the 2000s, frames invoking food democracy, food justice, and food sovereignty have offered new touchstones.

The multiplying frames now evident in the agrifood movement field suggest dynamism, but also the absence as yet of a coherent, unifying aim for agrifood movements overall. *Community food security*, as evident in work of the US Community Food Security Coalition between 1996 and 2012, emphasizes local community development, local agriculture, and empowerment of low-income people rather than traditional anti-hunger approaches to food access problems (Allen 2004). Other activist organizations in the United States have stressed *food democracy*, emphasizing that citizen power develops as people participate in food practices and shape the food policies that affect them (Hassanein 2003). *Food justice* is a related and ascendant frame for US agrifood initiatives, particularly in urban settings. A direct descendent of environmental justice, food justice stresses the need to redress inequalities in the "benefits and risks of where, what, and how food is grown and produced, transported and distributed, and accessed and eaten" (Gottlieb and Joshi 2010, 6). Finally, *food sovereignty* represents a frame that emerged in the global South in the mid-1990s and is now seeing growing uptake in the global North. Introduced by the international peasant movement Via Campesina, food sovereignty issues a more radical challenge to neoliberal globalization of the agrifood system, stressing "the right of nations and peoples to control their own food systems," from production to markets to the cultural context of consumption (Wittman, Desmarais, and Wiebe 2010).

Controversies and Tensions

Many issues about agrifood movements merit further discussion, but two related concerns are particularly important, given central themes in this volume. These are the place of labor within agrifood movements and the actual transformative impact of agrifood movements.

Agrifood Labor

The lack of attention to farm workers and other food system workers within many contemporary agrifood movements is a longstanding tension and critique of the field. Concern about the difficult, dangerous, and highly disadvantaged situation of farmworkers motivated social movement activity in the 1960s and '70s (Mooney and Majka 1995). Nonetheless, as Bonanno (in this volume) notes, global neoliberalization and the obstacles posed by current immigration policies and politics have generally worsened labor conditions and increased worker vulnerabilities throughout the agrifood system. Until recently, farm labor hardly registered on agendas of agrifood movement organizations concerned with local or organic foods. Allen (2004) observes that although environmental protection efforts of sustainable agriculture initiatives and movements may have reduced farmworkers' direct exposure to pesticides, such movements were initially reticent about incorporating social equity concerns related to wages and working conditions for farmworkers into their agendas. Harrison's (2011) account of pesticide drift politics and policies in California and her invocation of an environmental justice frame further highlight the tensions surrounding labor's place and priority in the work of agrifood movements.

Just as an environmental justice frame refocuses attention on vulnerable agrifood field workers, the ascendance of fair trade models has stimulated greater attention to labor processes and outcomes in the agrifood system. Indeed, the extension of fair trade scholarly research and the diffusion of fair trade concepts to North American movement actors have helped to energize social justice and equity perspectives on the place of labor and work in the agrifood system. In "Bringing the 'Moral Charge' Home," Jaffee, Kloppenburg, and Monroy (2004) argue that as northern domestic agrifood initiatives take up fair trade principles, they can improve working conditions and outcomes for US small farmers and farmworkers. Shreck's (2008) scholarship on the fair trade banana initiative in the Dominican Republic usefully informed her subsequent research on "social sustainability"—how California organic farmers were addressing (or resisting) improved conditions and wages for farm labor (Shreck, Getz, and Feenstra 2006).

In the 2000s, national level agrifood movement organizations like the Comité de Apoyo a los Trabajadores Agrícolas/Farmworker Support Committee have addressed ongoing US farm labor issues in the context of immigration reform, while the Agricultural Justice Project has developed social justice standards and certification specifically aimed at protecting people laboring on sustainable and organic farms. New tactics and even new targets reveal that agrifood movement action addressing labor issues has moved well beyond the farm. For example, new organizations like Restaurant Opportunities Centers United target low wages, inadequate benefits, and poor working conditions for workers at the other end of the food system—the restaurants where Americans eat out. A recent Food Chain Workers Alliance study found that food system workers use food stamps at double the rate of the overall US workforce (Food Chain Workers Alliance 2012). The financial crisis of 2008 and the subsequent Great Recession have only increased the need for academic and activist attention to how the agrifood system is undergirded not just by marginalized farm labor, but also by vulnerable workers in food processing, food retail, and the food service sector.

Transformative Impacts

Perhaps the most prominent and persistent tension concerning agrifood movements centers on their transformative impacts. What exactly can agrifood action and movements change? This question points back to the action-challenges framework discussed earlier. Under what conditions does individual action related to the agrifood system create meaningful change? Wright and Middendorf (2008) invoke a shift to "mindful eating," where reflexivity about consumption choices and practices can foster wider engagement with the agrifood system. Levkoe (2011) suggests that transition from individual action to "collective subjectivities" is necessary for a "transformative food politics."

The notion of the citizen-consumer sits at the heart of these debates about contemporary agrifood movements. Here consumers galvanized by the popular injunction to "vote with their dollars" are positioned as viable and important agents for social change (Johnston 2008). With the ascent of neoliberalism and the ubiquity of markets, this social movement strategy of individual consumers making responsible, ethical, and sustainable market choices has arguably superseded other forms of political contention. The citizen-consumer role resonates within many agrifood movements, particularly those that emphasize various forms of "reconnection" (Kneafsey et al. 2008) between food producers and consumers as the logical and necessary response to a globalizing agrifood system.

The abundant collective efforts now to organize and coordinate initiatives such as farmers' markets and CSAs often create important social and economic alternatives within the existing system, but they remain predicated on individual acts of consumer patronage, which may occur with little social or political engagement beyond the activity of shopping. Even as it has been celebrated, the citizen-consumer notion has also been criticized for so readily casting individual consumer choices and behaviors as political engagement and withdrawing any expectation of more deliberate, collective opposition to powerful institutions now shaping the agrifood system. As Roff (2007, 512) asserts, "much contemporary scholarship and food activism is geared towards changing the *daily* practices of *individuals* and in this way making the alternative foods 'market friendly'" (emphasis original). This very market friendliness then allows the products of alternative agrifood movements to be appropriated by the consumer marketplace and more readily conventionalized by mainstream corporate agrifood interests (Goodman, DuPuis, and Goodman 2012). Such mainstreaming and corporate appropriation of attributes such as organic, local, and fair trade raise questions about whether gains by agrifood movements are being sustained.

Thus, questions remain about the power and effect of individual action, particularly in the form of individual consumer behavior. On the one hand, the citizen-consumer notion points to Snow and Soule's (2010) individual-indirect form of social action, neither engaging collectivities nor identifying specific strategic targets, suggesting a more limited form of contention. But on the other hand, the individual action of the citizen-consumer can be seen as part of a "lifestyle movement," where identity work in crafting a deliberate way of life and participating in related informal networks serves a larger process of social change (Haenfler, Johnson, and Jones 2012). And as Friedland (2008) claims, individual action has the potential to become social when a critical mass of consumers applies pressure on hegemonic corporate powers. However, the question of what constitutes adequate pressure remains.

Beyond the individualized sphere of the citizen-consumer or collective efforts to build alternatives, it is important to note that agrifood movements have also pursued collective action targeting state institutions to influence the national agenda or spur policy change. Returning to Snow and Soule's (2010) framework, lobbying and policy advocacy can support either direct or indirect challenges to the prevailing agrifood system. In the United States, through the 1990s and 2000s, agrifood movements have engaged ever more actively with the Farm Bill, the sweeping legislation that is renegotiated and authorized approximately every five years and addresses agriculture, food, nutrition, conservation, rural development, and other areas. Prominent, though not alone among these efforts, has been advocacy and analysis by the National Sustainable Agriculture Coalition (NSAC), launched in 2009 as product of a merger between two earlier sustainable agriculture coalitions started in the 1980s and 1990s. The NSAC has worked on multiple issues in farm and food policy, including commodity program payment limitations to address directly the present structural incentives for industrial, monocrop agriculture. Such a direct challenge to the current agricultural political economy has met far less success than indirect challenges, which have included efforts to bolster preferred practices and alternatives, such as cost-shares for organic transition, programs to support and train new and beginning farmers, and the farmers' market nutrition programs. Even though agrifood activists have had limited success achieving deeper structural reforms of the agrifood system, their presence and role in shaping recent important federal legislation, such as the 2010 Child Nutrition Reauthorization Act and the 2011 Food Safety Modernization Act, cannot be discounted.

Conclusions

In this chapter, we have presented some of the diversity in early twenty-first century agrifood movements, using Snow and Soule's (2010) action-challenges framework as a guidepost. We have focused on the US context, while recognizing that globalization is both the source of grievances for many agrifood movements and the larger context for any social action. Despite its heuristic value, our framework has limitations as a tool for empirically classifying agrifood action and movements. Forms and practices of agrifood action are dynamic within a field that is subject to continual rearrangement, realignment, and redefinition.

For example, how well does an action-challenges framework account for indirect challenges that people first make at an individual level (e.g., a private decision to buy more local foods), but over time situate more socially and politically by shopping, volunteering, and even working in collective endeavors such as community food enterprises? Does it capture agrifood movement organizations whose strategic leanings encompass making both direct and indirect challenges to the agrifood system? Hard-won skills in policy work, for example, can be applied to directly challenging inequitable structures of the prevailing agrifood system (e.g., commodity payments limitations) and to challenging indirectly by gaining resources and technical support to construct alternatives (e.g., community food projects, regional food hubs).

In this chapter, we point to promising areas for future research on agrifood movements. To conclude, we briefly mention four. The first two relate to the tensions discussed earlier. First, what is the character of participation in new agrifood movements centralizing concerns about the conditions and welfare of agrifood labor, and what obstacles or opportunities does this present for linkages to other agrifood movements? Second, to what degree have different agrifood movements achieved their intended effects on the agrifood system? And what have been some of the unintended effects of agrifood movements and action, whether beneficial or not? A third question concerns the implications of agrifood movements for rural people and places. Under what conditions do agrifood movements incorporate work on bridging rural and urban interests and how effective are such efforts?

A final overarching question arises from the present diversity and florescence of agrifood movements. While the agrifood movement field now seems tumultuous and exciting, we are clearly witnessing many food movements rather than one united or cohesive food movement. As agrifood movements topics continue to mainstream into public view (now via multiple media platforms), finding a more convergent path forward while honoring the movements' diversity will present challenges. Can agrifood movements become a more robust, coherent, and effective collective response to the current agrifood system? More systematic analysis of the many agrifood movement organizations' claims, operational and political resources, and strategic aims and outcomes would improve our knowledge of current and historical agrifood movement alignments and accomplishments, as well as patterns of organizational decline, dead-ends, or disappearance. Such research can help us to anticipate and possibly inform the role and impact of agrifood movements in changing the agrifood system in the decades to come.

References

Allen, Patricia. 2004. *Together at the Table: Sustainability and Sustenance in the American Agrifood System.* University Park: Penn State University Press.

Allen, Patricia, Margaret FitzSimmons, Michael Goodman, and Keith Warner. 2003. "Shifting Plates in the Agrifood Landscape: The Tectonics of Alternative Agrifood Initiatives in California." *Journal of Rural Studies* 19 (1): 61–75. http://dx.doi.org/10.1016/S0743-0167(02)00047-5.

Belasco, Warren J. 1993. *Appetite for Change: How the Counterculture Took on the Food Industry.* Ithaca, NY: Cornell University Press.

Bloom, J. Dara, and C. Clare Hinrichs. 2011. "Moving Local Food through Conventional Food System Infrastructure: Value Chain Framework Comparisons and Insights." *Renewable Agriculture and Food Systems* 26 (1): 13–23. http://dx.doi.org/10.1017/S1742170510000384.

Bonanno, Alessandro, and Douglas H. Constance. 2008. *Stories of Globalization: Transnational Corporations, Resistance and the State.* University Park: Penn State University Press.

Buttel, Frederick H. 1997. "Some Observations on Agro-food Change and the Future of Agricultural Sustainability Movements." In *Globalising Food: Agrarian Questions and Global Restructuring,* ed. Daniel Goodman and Michael Watts, 344–65. London: Routledge.

Buttel, Frederick H. 2005. "Ever Since Hightower: The Politics of Agricultural Research Activism in the Molecular Age." *Agriculture and Human Values* 22 (3): 275–83. http://dx.doi.org/10.1007/s10460-005-6043-3.

Cohen, Maurie, Aaron Comrov, and Brian Hoffner. 2005. "The New Politics of Consumption: Promoting Sustainability in the American Marketplace." *Sustainability: Science, Practice and Policy* 1: 58–76.

DeLind, Laura B. 1998. "Parma: A Story of Hog Hotels and Local Resistance." In *Pigs, Profits and Rural Communities,* ed. Kendall M. Thu and E. Paul Durrenberger, 23–38. Albany: SUNY Press.

DeLind, Laura B. 2000. "Transforming Organic Agriculture into Industrial Organic Products: Reconsidering National Organic Standards." *Human Organization* 59: 198–208.

DeLind, Laura B. 2011. "Are Local Food and the Local Food Movement Taking Us Where We Want to Go? or Are We Hitching Our Wagons to the Wrong Stars?" *Agriculture and Human Values* 28 (2): 273–83. http://dx.doi.org/10.1007/s10460-010-9263-0.

Food Chain Workers Alliance. 2012. "The Hands That Feed Us: Challenges and Opportunities for Workers Along the Food Chain, June 6 report." Accessed 15 February 2013. http://foodchainworkers.org/wp-content/uploads/2012/06/Hands-That-Feed-Us-Report.pdf.

Friedland, William H. 2008. "Agency and the Agrifood System." In *The Fight over Food: Producers, Consumers, and Activists Challenge the Global Food System,* ed. Wynne Wright and Gerad Middendorf, 45–67. University Park: Penn State University Press.

Friedland, William H. 2010. "New Ways of Working and Organization: Alternative Agrifood Movements and Agrifood Researchers." *Rural Sociology* 75 (4): 601–27. http://dx.doi.org/10.1111/j.1549-0831.2010.00031.x.

Goodman, David, E. Melanie DuPuis, and Michael Goodman. 2012. *Alternative Food Networks: Knowledge, Practice and Politics*. London: Routledge.

Gottlieb, Robert, and Anupama Joshi. 2010. *Food Justice*. Cambridge: MIT Press.

Haenfler, Ross, Brett Johnson, and Ellis Jones. 2012. "Lifestyle Movements: Exploring the Intersection of Lifestyle and Social Movements." *Social Movement Studies: Journal of Social, Cultural and Political Protest* 11 (1): 1–20. http://dx.doi.org/10.1080/14742837.2012.640535.

Harrison, Jill L. 2011. *Pesticide Drift and the Pursuit of Environmental Justice*. Cambridge: MIT Press. http://dx.doi.org/10.7551/mitpress/9780262015981.001.0001.

Hassanein, Neva. 2003. "Practicing Food Democracy: A Pragmatic Politics of Transformation." *Journal of Rural Studies* 19 (1): 77–86. http://dx.doi.org/10.1016/S0743-0167(02)00041-4.

Hendrickson, Mary, and William Heffernan. 2002. "Opening Spaces through Relocalization: Locating Potential Resistance in the Weaknesses of the Global Food System." *Sociologia Ruralis* 42 (4): 347–69. http://dx.doi.org/10.1111/1467-9523.00221.

Hightower, Jim. 1973. *Hard Tomatoes, Hard Times: A Report of the Agribusiness Accountability Project on the Failure of America's Land Grant College Complex*. Cambridge, MA: Schenkman.

Hinrichs, C. Clare. 2003. "The Practice and Politics of Food System Localization." *Journal of Rural Studies* 19 (1): 33–45. http://dx.doi.org/10.1016/S0743-0167(02)00040-2.

Hinrichs, C. Clare, and Patricia Allen. 2008. "Selective Patronage and Social Justice: Local Food Consumer Campaigns in Historical Context." *Journal of Agricultural & Environmental Ethics* 21 (4): 329–52. http://dx.doi.org/10.1007/s10806-008-9089-6.

Jaffee, Daniel. 2012. "Weak Coffee: Certification and Cooptation in the Fair Trade Movement." *Social Problems* 59 (1): 94–116. http://dx.doi.org/10.1525/sp.2012.59.1.94.

Jaffee, Daniel, Jack R. Kloppenburg Jr., and Mario B. Monroy. 2004. "Bringing the 'Moral Charge' Home: Fair Trade within the North and within the South." *Rural Sociology* 69 (2): 169–96. http://dx.doi.org/10.1526/003601104323087561.

Johnston, Josée. 2008. "The Citizen-Consumer Hybrid: Ideological Tensions and the Case of Whole Foods Market." *Theory and Society* 37 (3): 229–70. http://dx.doi.org/10.1007/s11186-007-9058-5.

Kloppenburg, Jack R., John Hendrickson, and George W. Stevenson. 1996. "Coming into the Foodshed." In *Rooted in the Land*, ed. William Vitek and Wes Jackson, 113–23. New Haven, CT: Yale University Press.

Kneafsey, Moya, Rosie Cox, Lewis Holloway, Elizabeth Dowler, Laura Venn, and Helena Tuomainen. 2008. *Reconnecting Consumers, Producers and Food: Exploring Alternatives*. Oxford, New York: Berg.

Levkoe, Charles Zalman. 2011. "Towards a Transformative Food Politics." *Local Environment* 16 (7): 687–705. http://dx.doi.org/10.1080/13549839.2011.592182.

Lyson, Thomas A. 2004. *Civic Agriculture: Reconnecting Farm, Food and Community*. Medford, MA: Tufts University Press.

Martinez, Steve, Michael Hand, Michelle DaPra, Susan Pollack, Katherine Ralston, Travis Smith, Stephen Vogel, Shellye Clark, Luanne Lohr, Sarah Low and Constance Newman. 2010. *Local Food Systems: Concepts, Impacts and Issues*. United States Dept. of Agriculture, Economic Research Service. No. 97. May.

Maye, Damian, Lewis Holloway, and Moya Kneafsey, eds. 2007. *Alternative Food Geographies: Representation and Practice.* Oxford, Amsterdam: Elsevier.

Micheletti, Michelle. 2003. *Political Virtue and Shopping: Individuals, Consumerism, and Collective Action.* New York: Palgrave Macmillan.

Mooney, Patrick H., and Theo J. Majka. 1995. *Farmers' and Farm Workers' Movements.* New York: Twayne.

Munro, William A., and Rachel A. Schurman. 2008. "Sustaining Outrage: Cultural Capital, Strategic Location, and Motivating Sensibilities in the U.S. Anti-genetic Engineering Movement." In *The Fight over Food: Producers, Consumers, and Activists Challenge the Global Food System,* ed. Wynne Wright and Gerad Middendorf, 145–76. University Park: Penn State University Press.

Organic Trade Association. 2011. "Industry Statistics and Projected Growth." June. http://www.ota.com/organic/mt/business.html.

Ostrom, Marcia Ruth, and Raymond A. Jussaume. 2007. "Assessing the Significance of Direct Farmer-Consumer Linkages as a Change Strategy in Washington State: Civic or Opportunistic?" In *Remaking the North American Food System: Strategies for Sustainability,* ed. C. Clare Hinrichs and Thomas A. Lyson, 235–59. Lincoln: University of Nebraska Press.

Raynolds, Laura T. 2012. "Fair Trade: Social Regulation in Global Food Markets." *Journal of Rural Studies* 28 (3): 276–87. http://dx.doi.org/10.1016/j.jrurstud.2012.03.004.

Roff, Robin J. 2007. "Shopping for Change? Neoliberalizing Activism and the Limits to Eating Non-GMO." *Agriculture and Human Values* 24 (4): 511–22. http://dx.doi.org/10.1007/s10460-007-9083-z.

Schurman, Rachel, and William Munro. July 2009. "Targeting Capital: A Cultural Economy Approach to Understanding the Efficacy of Two Anti-genetic Engineering Movements." *American Journal of Sociology* 115 (1): 155–202. http://dx.doi.org/10.1086/597795. Medline:19852188.

Shreck, Aimee. 2008. "Resistance, Redistribution and Power in the Fair Trade Banana Initiative." In *The Fight over Food: Producers, Consumers, and Activists Challenge the Global Food System,* ed. Wynne Wright and Gerad Middendorf, 121–44. University Park: Penn State University Press.

Shreck, Aimee, Christy Getz, and Gail Feenstra. 2006. "Social Sustainability, Farm Labor and Organic Agriculture: Findings from an Exploratory Analysis." *Agriculture and Human Values* 23 (4): 439–49. http://dx.doi.org/10.1007/s10460-006-9016-2.

Snow, David A., and Sarah A. Soule. 2010. *A Primer on Social Movements.* New York: W.W. Norton.

Wartman, Kristin. 2012. "Occupy's Message to the Food Movement: Bridge the Class Divides." *Tikkun* 27 (2): 34–35, 64. http://dx.doi.org/10.1215/08879982-2012-2013.

Wittman, Hannah, Annette Aurélie Desmarais, and Nettie Wiebe, eds. 2010. *Food Sovereignty: Reconnecting Food, Nature and Community.* Halifax, Winnipeg: Fernwood.

Wright, Wynne, and Gerad Middendorf. 2008. "From Mindful Eating to Structural Change." In *The Fight over Food: Producers, Consumers, and Activists Challenge the Global Food System,* ed. Wynne Wright and Gerad Middendorf, 273–82. University Park: Penn State University Press.

PART II

Natural Resources and Environment

Connections[1]: The Next Decade of Rural Sociological Research on Natural Resources and the Environment

Louise Fortmann, Merrill Baker-Médard, and Alice Kelly

In the next decade the range of natural resource issues that rural sociologists should address will doubtless surprise many of us. Who a decade ago foresaw the explosion (sometimes literally in kitchen sinks) in fracking? Who would have imagined the series of crises in the Gulf of Mexico? Who in the last century would have imagined corn production as a center of controversy? Then water, as the new gold was a fresh idea. Now we struggle with its reality.

In this chapter, we identify some likely natural resource and environmental issues of the next decade and consider methods and approaches needed for effective research and analysis. We emphasize questions of the nature of knowledge production because the issues of the next decade will be even more characterized by complex interconnections. Remember, the chief feature of complexity is surprise.[2] We will need more and better tools that enable us, our students, and the rural communities we work with to grapple with connections, complexity, and surprise.

Surprise is only part of our profession's future. The other part has always been better recognized: to explain the operation and effects of power and those who exercise power at increasingly wide scales. We already know the local is global and the global, local.[3] When the atmosphere carries pollution, volcanic ash, and other particulate matter from there and deposits it here, other countries' environmental problems become our environmental problems. Water, too, is a transboundary medium, be it oil spilling onto our shores from a Gulf of Mexico oil exploration platform or farm runoff carried downstream by the Mississippi River into the Gulf of Mexico dead zone. In short, our exercise of power in distant places can come back to bite us via natural processes. This is one lesson of climate change. Thus, although this volume focuses on North America, we have included examples and issues from Europe and the global South. Not only are we affected by socio-ecological phenomena elsewhere, but all too often North American institutions are culpable for adverse social and ecological effects outside North America. We need to focus our analytical lens on those connections and their effects, not just on those in our own backyard (cf. Stonich and Bailey 2000).

On the face of it, power and surprise seem strange bedfellows since the operation and effects of power seem depressingly predictable. But perhaps this is a function of our analytic lens. The tools we need must be able to zoom in, out, and across the various levels of analysis that matter to rural communities. What is clearly the exercise of power at one level is connected all too often with surprises that emerge at another level. We try to tease out some of the important issues around such a lens in the remainder of this chapter.

Part I:
What Will Require Our Attention in the Next Decade?

The issues we discuss below are by no means discrete, simple problems suitable for puzzle solving. Rather, they are complex and interconnected and call for the kinds of analytical approaches we will discuss in the following section.

Financialization

Financialization is often defined as the increasing percentage of GDP contributed by the financial sector. In the rarefied world of derivatives, credit default swaps, hedge funds, and math that very few people actually understand, it is easy to forget that financialization has its roots in the nitty-gritty world of US commodity markets and futures. Research in the next decade will need to tack more knowledgeably between the nitty-gritty (deep and informed attention to concrete technical and social detail, as Lohmann (2011, 664) puts it) and the economically and technically abstract. Such research will focus on the processes of commodification, marketization, and privatization of what had been and possibly still are public goods and their multi-scalar effects on ecological and social well-being embedded in diverse contexts.

Carbon trading[4] is a particularly visible manifestation of financialization in the natural resources sector.[5] Indeed, other issues we discuss below are linked to it. Carbon trading shifts attention away from palpable local instances of carbon emissions and the effects of climate change toward the carbon molecule that is seen as equivalent and interchangeable across time and place. That is, it homogenizes the problem and thereby implies an undifferentiated solution. It draws focus from actual reductions in emissions to hypothetical "avoided emissions" that are then treated as if reductions had actually occurred somewhere. It shifts attention and action from the project of reducing/eliminating the extraction and use of fossil fuels to mitigating the effects of their continued use on a global (disembedded) scale. It undermines social movements for global and locally embedded ecologically and socially sustainable energy and climate action. It benefits rich investors, not—despite claims to the contrary—the poor or local institutions.

Carbon trading is not just an issue in the global South. Frequently carbon trading does not work as it is purported to, as seen in the case of the European Emissions Trading Scheme. Carbon trading makes it financially rational to delay reduction in emissions now in order to benefit later (Lohmann 2012). In the European case, too many permits were issued, which led to low prices that "defeated the scheme's original purpose; moreover [as a result], coal imports into Europe have been rising" (Morrison 2007).[6] Parfitt's (2011)[7] account of the irregularities associated the British Columbia's Pacific Carbon Trust carbon credit scheme suggests that the kind of carbon scams criticized in the global South are happening in North America as well. California, which in 2006 instituted an instate carbon cap and trade program modestly titled The Global Warming Solution Act, held its first auction of greenhouse gas allowances on 14 November 2012 (Air Resources Board 2012). And the practice of California forestry already is showing the effects of the cap and trade experiment (Barringer 2012). The effects of this carbon trading program in rural California and the effects of programs in other states that are bound to follow are clearly foci for new rural sociological research.

Green Land Grabs

The term *global land grab*[8] refers to the rapid rise in national and transnational commercial land transactions and speculations (Borras and Franco 2012). Karl Marx's concept of "primitive accumulation" will be useful to rural sociologists in analyzing this phenomenon. According to Marx, "the so-called primitive accumulation . . . is nothing else than the historical process of divorcing the producer from the means of production. It appears as primitive, because it forms the pre-historic stage of capital and of the mode of production corresponding with it" (Marx 1906, 431–34). Primitive accumulation is a violent, ongoing process that encloses the commons and affects both economic and social mechanisms (Kelly 2011). Land grabs often follow a similar trajectory—enclosing land, water, and underground minerals, and dispossessing local people of access to them (Borras and Franco 2012).

Scholarship has generally focused on land grabbing in the global South for food production by food-insecure countries, but it is focusing increasing attention on "green land grabs," the rapidly accelerating commoditization of "nature" and its appropriation in the name of 'conservation' and 'sustainability' (Fairhead et al. 2012). Green land grabs follow the same principles of primitive accumulation—resulting in enclosure, dispossession, violence, and capitalist markets' expansion (Kelly 2011). They also occur in North America.

Conservation practices (particularly in the form of protected areas) may seem at odds with the concept of primitive accumulation, in that they technically take land and resources out of the market and create public property rather than the private property of classic cases of primitive accumulation. However, following Igoe and Brockington's (2007) description of neoliberal conservation as the commoditization and control of nature through regulation and the collaboration of state, NGOs, and for-profit organizations that work to exclude local populations or drastically alter rural people's livelihoods and lifestyles, we begin to see that protected areas may be doing the same kind of work (Kelly 2011). Following the trend of other forms of primitive accumulation, protected area creation is a violent, ongoing process that alters social relations and practices and can be defined by the enclosure of land or other property, the separation of local people from land and resources, and the establishment and maintenance of conditions for capitalist production that allow a select few to accumulate wealth (Kelly 2011).

Subterranean minerals in the United States have long been subject to large-scale land grabs. By actively producing the legal, fiscal, and proprietary conditions for large-scale domestic and foreign capital accumulation from mineral exploitation (Emel et al. 2011), the state is complicit in this type of land grabbing, which dispossesses locals from previous claims on mineral and non-subterranean land. The phenomenon of national ownership, in which the "default" state of subterranean property rights divests local people from claims they previously had on the resources, is common in many countries in both the global North and the global South. Such underground divestments and dispossessions are most familiar in the United States in relation to fracking (Sakmar 2012), uranium mining, and oil exploration and extraction.

While mineral extraction often follows a classic model of primitive accumulation through the direct dispossession of people from their land, operations like fracking expand the means by which dispossession and accumulation can take place. Fracking, the process in which drilling horizontal wells into shale or coal deposits forces previously inaccessible natural gas to the surface, has led to a large energy boom in the United States (Soeder 2010; Kinchy et al. in this volume). While fracking does not directly dispossess local populations of their lands—ostensibly allowing people to live very close to the wells because it causes very little surface disruption—new means by which dispossession take place are emerging. Fracking, following the paradigm of primitive accumulation, causes the dispossession of people from their land, homes, and natural resources but in a more obscure way, as it poisons their drinking water, air, and soil (Schmidt 2011).

In addition to studying land grabbing in North America, rural sociologists should also analyze the involvement of North American corporations, NGOs (particularly environmental NGOs), and other institutions in land grabs beyond US borders. The allegedly unwitting near-involvement of Iowa State University in an 800,000-acre land grab in Tanzania provides a cautionary tale (Guebert 2012; Wintersteen 2012).

Labor

Labor in the forestry, fishing, and mining sectors requires attention to a number of arenas. The kind of corporate and governmental negligence and wrongdoing that led to the Upper Big Branch Mine disaster in West Virginia is neither confined to the Massey Energy Company (Urbina 2010; Ward 2012) nor to the coal industry nor to the US Mine Safety and Health Administration. Particular attention should be paid to "invisible" labor, particularly undocumented immigrants who work in fishing and forestry. Migrant laborers who do not speak the local language, are very far from home, and are afraid of immigration authorities can neither easily leave their jobs nor make common cause with local people. The plight of immigrant laborers in forestry has been documented in the US South and Pacific Northwest (McDaniel and Casanova 2003; Sarathy 2012). Modern slavery has been documented in US agriculture (Bowe 2008; Carter and Tamura 2011) and in international fishing fleets (CdeBaca 2011). More research needs to be done on modern slavery in North American fishing, forestry, and mining, and on the complicity of North American firms in modern slavery in natural resource sectors elsewhere.

Part II: Epistemathingies and Questions of Methods

After listening to card-carrying philosophers for an entire morning at the sixth International Conference on Environmental Future in Newcastle, United Kingdom, in July 2011, graduate students in the biophysical sciences came up with the term *epistemathingy*. Epistemathingy basically means, "we know there's something about knowledge and how we get it that is important in how we do science but it's pretty squishy and hard to understand." Indeed!

So let us begin with epistemathingies. Mercifully, most rural sociologists have left behind the extremely silly debate over whether quantitative or qualitative methods provide accurate knowledge, as the obvious answer is, "it depends on your question." But there is plenty of room for asking other epistemathingy questions. How is knowledge acquired? What are the sources of knowledge? What constitutes credible evidence? These questions necessarily involve multiple scales and units of analysis that we must address if we are to do good research, particularly good policy-relevant research, over the next decade.

Specifically, while notable exceptions exist, much research on natural resources by rural sociologists has tended (1) to focus primarily on social or socioeconomic phenomena, (2) to be framed within distinct social science disciplinary perspectives, and (3) to be undertaken by credentialed academics, or those seeking to be. Putting aside the issue of whether these approaches were ever suitable even for simple questions, they are manifestly problematic for the complex issues of the next decade. Rural sociologists should need little reminding that, as Funtowicz and Ravetz (1993, 744) write about post-normal science, our research has to be better tailored to "contexts in which the facts are uncertain, values are in dispute, stakes are high, and decisions are urgent." Before we can determine whether or not we are using the intellectual tools and methods needed to work in such circumstances, we must define the challenge ahead more specifically. We are suggesting that rural sociological research on complex natural resource and environmental issues, such as those discussed above, will increasingly have three characteristics: (1) a focus on socio-ecological units, (2) interdisciplinary frameworks (note the term is plural), and (3) the use of transacademic methods. This is required if we are to zoom in, out, and across in our research. As we will show below, these characteristics are to varying degrees interconnected themselves.

Biophysical and Social Connections: Socio-ecological Units of Analysis

It is not surprising that rural sociologists focus on social phenomena—that literally comes with the name of our discipline. But in the arenas of natural resource use and management and of the environment more generally, where social and biophysical entities and processes are interdependent, such a focus is too narrow and unproductive. There actually has been a long tradition of recognizing what are now generally called "socio-ecological systems." Early on, Walter Firey (1978) recognized the importance of the society-nature interconnection, stating that the well-being of the soil and of agricultural communities were interdependent. In their foundational political ecology text, *Land Degradation and Society*, Blaikie and Brookfield (1987, 4, 19) posit "that damage to the land and damage to certain classes in society are interrelated." Socio-ecological systems are characterized by a set of dependencies and interdependencies within and among social and ecological elements (by which we mean actors/actants, structures, and processes). To understand such systems, we must analyze them using units that encompass this interaction of dependence and interdependence, that is, their socio-ecological units and levels of analysis.

We offer three very brief descriptions of analytical approaches that attempt to do this and that might strengthen rural sociological research: political ecology, ecofeminism, and Ostrom's SES approach. Political ecology has always focused on social-ecological relationships. Political ecologists analyze environmental phenomena in the contexts of different scales (including a focus on micro-politics), historical perspectives, differentiation, and representation (cf. Robbins 2012). While the field as a whole is attentive to distributive justice, feminist political ecologists (cf. Rocheleau et al. 1996) have highlighted questions of gender that are often overlooked in other natural resource studies. Ecofeminist scholars also are attentive to social-biophysical interrelationships. Ecofeminist approaches tend to be characterized by the understanding of relationships of humans and nature as web-like and by an ethic of caring. Ostrom and Cox (2010, 451), in their criticism of "overly simplified institutional prescriptions" to environmental problems or what they call "the panacea problem," proffer a further framework for analyzing socio-ecological systems. Their analytical approach is less normative than political ecology or ecofeminism, and hence less prescriptive about what variables should be analyzed in a framework. The framework is good to think with, but may be frustrating for the neophyte researcher.

Disciplinary Connections: Interdisciplinary Research

If we are to research complex socio-ecological units, we can only do so in collaboration with researchers from other disciplines, that is, through practicing interdisciplinary research.

Only those who have never done it think that interdisciplinarity must be simple—that all that we need do is to ensure that good and well-trained people bring something to the research from their own disciplines, collaborate as a team by putting the pieces together, and, lo and behold, the puzzle solving is a success! Disciplinary training may lead us to think that interdisciplinarity is rather like a discipline, that is, a singular phenomenon. These presuppositions are mistaken.

First, there is no gold standard, capital-I Interdisciplinarity. Rather, there are diverse and fluid interdisciplinarities. They vary in terms of the disciplines and sub-disciplines that are involved, disciplinary and national research cultures, and the multitudinous research approaches that can be taken. Nor is interdisciplinary research in any way a straightforward combination of disciplines (cf. Öberg 2010; Öberg et al. 2013; Sievanen et al. 2012). As Léle and Norgaard (2005, 967) point out, "shared interests . . . do not translate into a research plan with predetermined bridges between the disciplines," nor even the same problem definition. Interdisciplinary research requires learning other disciplinary languages. It means convincing academic institutions, including journals, funding agencies, and tenure committees, that it is a legitimate form of research. It may require what Wallner (2011) calls "strangification," viewing one's discipline from the viewpoint of another discipline and thereby revealing its underlying assumptions, including assumptions about what constitutes credible evidence. It means giving up assumptions about other disciplines. Interdisciplinary research involves recognizing that what seems fascinating from one's own disciplinary perspective can be crashingly boring or irrelevant from the viewpoint of another. All these negotiations and processes of co-learning take time that may exceed what is budgeted in the typical research project.

Ostrom and Cox's (2010, 460) summarize these points well in their call for moving beyond overly simplistic models of environmental and social processes and accompanying recommendations for relatively simple blueprint property-rights systems as "the" way to solve environmental problems. To do the social-ecological work necessary will require knowledge and perspectives from scientific disciplines that are frequently isolated from one another. It will also require a novel integration of methodologies to study social and environmental processes. Enabling scholars from multiple disciplines to share a common framework for diagnosing the sources of diverse environmental problems will take time and effort within a dedicated research program.

While interdisciplinarity is becoming more common, we need to practice even more of it. This means not only starting to think collectively with colleagues from other disciplines but also working within our own institutions to make interdisciplinary thinking and research possible.

Academy-Community Connections: Transacademic Research

Transacademic research "engages with individuals and institutions outside academia" (Öberg et al. 2013).

It is not uncommon for academics to insist on the importance of "pure" research without any "interference" from nonacademics, including but not limited to the people they study. This stance is based on the beliefs that expertise resides in disciplinary credentials (cf. Fricker 2007 on epistemic injustice) and that the involvement of nonacademics introduces bias and weakens analytic rigor.

Funtowicz and Ravetz (1993) suggest an alternative view in their discussion of post-normal science, in which they invoke the concept of an "extended peer community." In their words, "the relevant peer community is extended beyond one particular research community to include users of all sorts, and also managers." They also contend that local knowledge can be essential in identifying strong and relevant data as well as policy issues (1993, 753). This interaction goes well beyond community advocacy and into actual co-framing, co-managing, and co-analyzing research. Funtowicz and Ravetz's stance is echoed in Scott's (1998) observation that "'practical knowledge' that is learned through practice is *locally* superior to general knowledge that often does not apply well to specific situations." It is also consistent with Haraway's (1988) concept of "situated" knowledge, which holds that all knowledge is partial and situated, that is, embedded in time, geographical space, and social position. Credentialed researchers will create and hold some partial knowledge. Nonacademics will create and hold other partial knowledge. Fortmann (2008, 8) argues for the term *civil scientist* to denote nonacademic research partners on the grounds that they create knowledge using experimentation and observation just as conventional scientists do.

While there is a considerable body of research demonstrating the importance of extended peer communities, civil scientists, and the practice of transacademic research in the natural resources and environment (cf. Ballard and Huntsinger 2006; Belsky 2011; Bethel et al. 2011; Buruchara 2008; Fortmann 2008; McSpirit, Faltraco, and Bailey 2012; Parotta and Trosper 2012), such research remains far less common than conventional science. In practice, a conventional-science-only approach to research cuts researchers off from the important body of knowledge held by civil scientists and other nonacademics and may stall the generation of knowledge. Hence, in some circumstances it is not an effective research practice. Doing rigorous research in the next decade is clearly going to require much more transacademic research.

Paul Robbins (2004) describes political ecology as being both a critical hatchet and also a seed portraying the possible. His metaphors serve well for the tasks ahead of us. We have an obligation to do critical research investigating the actors, structures, and processes leading to adverse social and ecological outcomes, both those that occur in North America and also those that North American actors perpetrate elsewhere. And we have an obligation to make visible and tell the stories of alternative structures and processes that might lead to better outcomes. These are the challenges of the next decade.

Notes

1 Dedicated to the memory of Elinor Ostrom (1933–2012). Thanks to Conner Bailey, Ignacio Chapela, Dennis Baldocci, Dick Krajeski, Larry Lohmann, Matt Potts, and most especially Emery Roe for helpful comments, insights, and information.

2 See Roe (1998) for an insightful analysis of complexity.

3 Young et al. (2006) argue that a central feature of socio-ecological systems is globalization.

4 In this section, we draw heavily on Lohmann (2011 and 2012), who gives excellent introductions to this issue. The inquisitive should consult the websites for the Chicago Climate Exchange (2012) and the European Union Emissions Trading Scheme (European Commission 2012).

5 See also Gunnoe and Gellert's (2011) analysis of financialization of the forestry sector.

6 Emery Roe brought this example to our attention.

7 Bill Stewart brought this case to our attention (cf. SCS Global Services 2011).

8 The World Bank report on land grabs (Deininger et al. 2011) is available at http://siteresources.worldbank.org/INTARD/Resources/ESW_Sept7_final_final.pdf. Grain (2010) critiques this report.

References

Air Resources Board, California Environmental Protection Agency. 2012. "California Air Resources Board Quarterly Auction 1." http://www.arb.ca.gov/cc/capandtrade/auction/november_2012/auction1_results_2012q4nov.pdf.

Ballard, H.L., and L. Huntsinger. 2006. "Salal Harvester Local Ecological Knowledge, Harvest Practices and Understory Management on the Olympic Peninsula, Washington." *Human Ecology: an Interdisciplinary Journal* 34 (4): 529–47. http://dx.doi.org/10.1007/s10745-006-9048-7.

Barringer, F. 2012. "A Grand Experiment to Rein in Climate Change." *New York Times*, 14 October. http://www.nytimes.com/2012/10/14/science/earth/in-california-a-grand-experiment-to-rein-in-climate-change.html.

Belsky, Jill. 2011. "Discussion." Paper presented at the 6th International Conference on Environmental Future. Newcastle, UK, 19–22 July.

Bethel, Matthew B., Lynn F. Brien, Emily Danielson, Shirley B. Laska, John P. Troutman, William M. Boshart, Marco Giardino, and Maurice A. Phillips. 2011. "Blending Geospatial Technology and Traditional Ecological Knowledge to Enhance Restoration Decision-Support Processes in Coastal Louisiana." *Journal of Coastal Research* 27: 555–71. http://dx.doi.org/10.2112/JCOASTRES-D-10-00138.1.

Blaikie, Piers, and Harold Brookfield. 1987. *Land Degradation and Society*. London: Methuen & Co. Inc.

Borras, Saturnino M., Jr., and Jennifer C. Franco. 2012. "Global Land Grabbing and Trajectories of Agrarian Change: A Preliminary Analysis." *Journal of Agrarian Change* 12 (1): 34–59. http://dx.doi.org/10.1111/j.1471-0366.2011.00339.x.

Bowe, John. 2008. *Nobodies: Modern American Slave Labor and the Dark Side of the New Global Economy*. New York: Random House.

Buruchara, Robin. 2008. "How Participatory Research Convinced a Skeptic." In *Participatory Research in Conservation and Rural Livelihoods: Doing Science Together*, ed. Louise Fortmann, 18–35. Oxford: Wiley-Blackwell.

Carter, Chelsea J. and Traci Tamura. 2011. "Feds File Human-Trafficking Suit against Farm Labor Contractor." *CNN Freedom Project Blog*, April 21. http://thecnnfreedomproject.blogs.cnn.com/2011/04/21/feds-file-human-trafficking-suit-against-farm-labor-contractor/.

CdeBaca, Luis. 2011. "The Trafficking in Persons Report 2011: Truth, Trends, and Tier Rankings." Statement before the Subcommittee on Africa, Global Health, and Human Rights of the House Foreign Affairs Committee. 27 October 2011, Washington, DC.

Chicago Climate Exchange. 2012. Accessed 26 January 2012. https://www.theice.com/ccx.jhtml.

Deininger, K., and D. Byerlee, with J. Lindsay, A. Norton, H. Selod, and M. Stickler. 2011. *Rising Global Interest in Farmland: Can It Yield Sustainable and Equitable Benefits?* Washington, DC: World Bank.

Emel, Jody, Matthew T. Huber, and Madoshi H. Makene. 2011. "Extracting Sovereignty: Capital, Territory, and Gold Mining in Tanzania." *Political Geography* 30 (2): 70–79. http://dx.doi.org/10.1016/j.polgeo.2010.12.007.

European Commission. 2012. "Emissions Trading System. EU ETS." Accessed 26 January 2012. http://ec.europa.eu/clima/policies/ets/index_en.htm.

Fairhead, James, Melissa Leach, and Ian Scoones. 2012. "Green Grabbing: A New Appropriation of Nature?" *Journal of Peasant Studies* 39 (2): 237–61. http://dx.doi.org/10.1080/03066150.2012.671770.

Firey, Walter. 1978. "Some Contributions of Sociology to the Study of Natural Resources." In *Challenges of Societies in Transition*, ed. M. Barnabas, S.K. Hulbe, and P.S. Jacob, 162–74. Delhi: Maxmillan Company.

Fortmann, Louise, ed. 2008. *Participatory Research in Conservation and Rural Livelihoods: Doing Science Together.* Oxford: Wiley-Blackwell.

Fricker, Miranda. 2007. *Epistemic Injustice: Power and the Ethics of Knowing.* Oxford: Oxford University Press. http://dx.doi.org/10.1093/acprof:oso/9780198237907.001.0001.

Funtowicz, Silvio O., and Jerome R. Ravetz. 1993. "Science for the Post-Normal Age." *Futures* 25 (7): 739–55. http://dx.doi.org/10.1016/0016-3287(93)90022-L.

Grain. 2010. "World Bank Report on Land Grabbing: Beyond Smoke and Mirrors." 8 September. http://www.grain.org/article/entries/4021-world-bank-report-on-land-grabbing-beyond-the-smoke-and-mirrors.

Guebert, Alan. 2012. "Iowa State May Want Shy from [sic] African Lands." *Farm and Dairy*, January 12. http://www.farmanddairy.com/columns/iowa-state-may-want-shy-from-african-lands/33267.html.

Gunnoe, Andrew, and Paul Gellert. 2011. "Financialization, Shareholder Value, and the Transformation of Timberland Ownership in the US." *Critical Sociology* 37 (3): 265–84. http://dx.doi.org/10.1177/0896920510378764.

Haraway, Donna. 1988. "Situated Knowledges: The Science Question in Feminism and the Privilege of Partial Perspective." *Feminist Studies* 14 (3): 575–99. http://dx.doi.org/10.2307/3178066.

Igoe, J., and D. Brockington. 2007. "Neoliberal Conservation: A Brief Introduction." *Conservation & Society* 5: 432–49.

Kelly, A.B. 2011. "Conservation Practice as Primitive Accumulation." *Journal of Peasant Studies* 38 (4): 683–701. http://dx.doi.org/10.1080/03066150.2011.607695.

Léle, Sharadchandra, and Richard Norgaard. 2005. "Practicing Interdisciplinarity." *Bioscience* 55 (11): 967–75. http://dx.doi.org/10.1641/0006-3568(2005)055[0967:PI]2.0.CO;2.

Lohmann, Larry. 2011. "Capital and Climate Change." *Development and Change* 42 (2): 649–68. http://dx.doi.org/10.1111/j.1467-7660.2011.01700.x.

Lohmann, Larry. 2012. "Financialization, Commodification and Carbon: The Contraditions of Neoliberal Climate Policy." *Socialist Register* 48: 85–107.

Marx, Karl. 1906. *Capital A Critique of Political Economy*. New York: Charles H. Kerr and Company.

McDaniel, J., and Vanessa Casanova. 2003. "Pines in Lines: Tree Planting, H2B Guest Workers, and Rural Poverty in Alabama." *Southern Rural Sociology* 19: 73–96.

McSpirit, Stephanie, Lynne Faltraco, and Conner Bailey, eds. 2012. *Confronting Ecological Crisis; University and Community Partnerships in Appalachia and the South*. Lexington: University Press of Kentucky.

Morrison, K. 2007. "Next Carbon Trading Phase Promises to Clean up Anomalies." *Financial Times*, February 7, 22.

Öberg, Gunilla. 2010. *Interdisciplinary Science Studies: A Primer*. Oxford: Wiley Blackwell. http://dx.doi.org/10.1002/9781444328486.

Öberg, Gunilla, Louise Fortmann, and Timothy Gray. 2013. "Is Interdisciplinary Research a Mashup?" IRES Working Paper Series 2013-02. Vancouver: University of British Columbia, Institute for Resources, Environment and Sustainability.

Ostrom, Elinor, and Michael Cox. 2010. "Moving beyond Panaceas: A Multi-tiered Diagnostic Approach for Social-Ecological Analysis." *Environmental Conservation* 37 (4): 451–63. http://dx.doi.org/10.1017/S0376892910000834.

Parfitt, Ben. 2011. "Darkwoods, the Murky World of Carbon Credits and a 'Carbon Neutral' BC Government." *CPA Monitor*, July 26. http://www.policyalternatives.ca/publications/commentary/darkwoods-murky-world-carbon-credits-and-%E2%80%9Ccarbon-neutral%E2%80%9D-bc-government.

Parotta, John A., and Ronald L. Trosper, eds. 2012. *Traditional Forest-Related Knowledge: Sustaining Communities, Ecosystems, and Biocultural Diversity*. New York: Springer.

Robbins, Paul. 2004. *Political Ecology: A Critical Introduction*. Oxford: Blackwell.

Robbins, Paul. 2012. *Political Ecology: A Critical Introduction*. 2nd ed. Oxford: Blackwell.

Rocheleau, Dianne E., Barbara P. Thomas-Slayter, and Esther Wangari. 1996. *Feminist Political Ecology: Global Issues and Local Experiences*. New York: Routledge.

Roe, Emery. 1998. *Taking Complexity Seriously: Policy Analysis, Triangulation and Sustainable Development*. Boston: Kluwer Academic Publishers.

Sakmar, S.L. 2012. "Natural Gas Production—International/Cross-Border: Rest of World Learning from US Shale Gas Experience." *Natural Gas & Electricity* 29 (2): 7–11. http://dx.doi.org/10.1002/gas.21629.

Sarathy, Brinda. 2012. *Pineros: Latino Labour and the Changing Face of Forestry in the Pacific Northwest.* Vancouver: University of British Columbia Press.

Schmidt, C.W. August 2011. "Blind Rush? Shale Gas Boom Proceeds amid Human Health Questions." *Environmental Health Perspectives* 119 (8): A348–53. http://dx.doi.org/10.1289/ehp.119-a348. Medline:21807583.

Scott, James. 1998. *Seeing Like a State: How Certain Schemes to Improve the Human Condition Have Failed.* New Haven: Yale University Press.

SCS Global Services. 2011. "SCS Verifies Canada's First VCS Forest Carbon Offset Project." June 10. http://www.prweb.com/releases/carbonoffset/darkwoods/prweb8560364.htm.

Sievanen, Leila, Lisa Campbell, and Heather Miles. 2012. "Challenges to Interdisciplinary Research in Ecosystem-Based Management." *Conservation Biology* 26 (2): 315–23. http://dx.doi.org/10.1111%2Fj.1523-1739.2011.01808.x.

Soeder, Daniel J. 2010. *Shale Gas Development in the United States.* Advances in Natural Gas Technology. InTech. Accessed 12 March 2013. http://www.intechopen.com/books/advances-in-natural-gas-technology/shale-gas-development-in-the-united-states.

Stonich, Susan, and Conner Bailey. 2000. "Resisting the Blue Revolution: Contending Coalitions Surrounding Industrial Shrimp Farming." *Human Organization* 59: 23–36.

Urbina, Ian. 2010. "Inspector General's Inquiry Faults Regulators." *New York Times*, 24 May. http://www.nytimes.com/2010/05/25/us/25mms.html?pagewanted=all.

Wallner, Friedrich. 2011. "Nature and Science: The Hidden Relation or How to Protect Nature against Science." Paper presented at the 6th Conference on Environmental Future. Newcastle, UK, 19–22 July.

Ward, Ken, Jr. 2012. "Feds Looking into Report MSHA Tipped off Massey." *Sunday Gazette-Mail*, April 12. http://wvgazette.com/News/201204120272.

Wintersteen, Wendy. 2012. "Dean Wintersteen Ends Advisory Role in Tanzania Plans. A Message from Dean Wendy Wintersteen." Iowa State University College of Agriculture and Life Sciences. 10 February 2012. Accessed 17 December 2013. http://www.ag.iastate.edu/features/2012/dean-wintersteen-ends-advisory-role-tanzania-plans/.

Young, Oran R., Frans Berkhout, Gilberto C. Gallopin, Marco A. Janssen, Elinor Ostrom, and Sander van der Leeuw. 2006. "The Globalization of Socio-ecological systems: An Agenda for Scientific Research." *Global Environmental Change* 16 (3): 304–16. http://dx.doi.org/10.1016/j.gloenvcha.2006.03.004.

CHAPTER 9

Impacts of Climate Change on People and Communities of Rural America[1]

Lois Wright Morton and Tom Rudel

> Three great patterns dominate the earth and are of tremendous importance to man-the pattern of climate, the pattern of vegetation, and the pattern of soils. When the three patterns are laid one upon the other, their boundaries coincide to a remarkable degree because climate is the fundamental dynamic force shaping the other two . . . the fourth pattern laid upon the three is that of human culture, or civilization. (USDA Climate and Man Yearbook 1941, 98)

The year 2011 saw fourteen extreme weather events in the United States costing more than $1 billion each and with carnage that represented a devastating "new normal" in a global context of increasingly extreme weather events (Coumou and Rahmstorf 2012; Hansen, Sato, and Ruedy 2012). Rural people have always assessed changing weather conditions—evaluating the shape and color of the clouds as predictors of an early snowfall, sniffing the moisture in the air to predict rain and make planting and harvest decisions, and scanning green-tinted skies in the calm before a tornado touches down. Despite the unpredictability of where lightning will strike, how long a drought will last, and when the first frost will occur and the last snows will melt, rural peoples have used past weather patterns to guide their daily behavior.

In an era of climate change, weather events seem even more fraught with uncertainty. The Intergovernmental Panel on Climate Change (IPCC) assessments for North America document increases in annual mean air temperature since 1955, with the greatest warming occurring in Alaska, substantial warming in the continental interior, and modest warming in the southeast (IPCC 2001; 2007; Field et al. 2007). Spring and winter temperatures have changed the most, with daily minimum (nighttime) temperatures warming more than daily maximums (daytime). Earlier spring warming has lengthened growing seasons, with an average increase of two days per decade since 1950. Annual precipitation

Box 9.1: Key North American and US findings on climate change effects adapted from the 3rd and 4th Assessment Report on Climate (Field et al. 2007) and USDA Climate Change and Agriculture in the United States: Effects and Adaptation (Walthall et al. 2012).

Resources and Ecosystems

- In western snowmelt-dominated watersheds, shifts in seasonal runoff, with more in winter.
- Increased regional and seasonal variability in availability and management of water resources, including rain-fed and irrigated agriculture.
- Changes in pressures associated with weeds, diseases, and insect pests, and with the timing and coincidence of pollinator lifecycles.
- Changes in the abundance and spatial distribution of species important to commercial and recreational fisheries.
- Increased production costs and productivity loses associated with animal products (e.g., meat, eggs, and milk) with prolonged exposure to extreme temperatures.
- Benefits from warming for food production but with strong regional differences.
- Increases in the productivity of forests.
- More pervasive disturbances in forest ecosystems, with longer fire seasons and wider areas subjected to high fire danger.
- Likely losses of cold-water ecosystems, high alpine areas, and coastal and inland wetlands.

Human Settlements

- Less extreme winter cold in northern communities, and more extreme heat.
- Heightened risk of storm surges (e.g., Hurricanes Katrina and Sandy), water scarcities, and floods.
- Increased frequency and severity of heat waves leading to more illness and death, particularly among the young, elderly, and frail. Respiratory disorders may be exacerbated by warming-induced deterioration in air quality.
- Expanded ranges of vector-borne and tick-borne diseases.
- Increased weather-related losses since the 1970s, with rising insured losses reflecting growing affluence and movement into vulnerable areas.
- Coverage, since the 1980s, by disaster relief and insurance programs of a large fraction of flood and crop losses, possibly encouraging more human activity in at-risk areas.
- Reduced availability of disaster insurance from insurers.

has increased particularly in northern regions, but has decreased in the southwestern United States. Although effects vary among regions of the United States, all production systems dependent upon precipitation and reliable water sources are affected to some degree by changes in climate (Walthall et al. 2012). In Box 9.1 we summarize many of the key North American findings on how temperature and precipitation changes have affected ecosystems and rural human settlements to date.

While climate has always shaped both natural and human communities (USDA Climate and Man Yearbook 1941), its influence now seems much more uncertain with records and models of temperature, precipitation, and atmospheric conditions indicating increased variability and more frequent extreme events (Hatfield et al. 2011). The vulnerabilities and risks associated with these uncertainties present new challenges that people of rural places must recognize and plan for in order to adapt, survive, and thrive.

People do not always see these challenges in the same way. Despite Intergovernmental Panel on Climate Change (IPCC) reports over the last twenty years that document climate change, a great deal of disbelief and uncertainty persists among the general US population (Donner 2011; McCright and Dunlap 2011; Weber and Stern 2011). The natural variability of local weather conditions from day to day and year to year is a significant barrier to public recognition of human impacts on the global climate. Climate changes occur over the course of decades and centuries, sometimes in incremental ways, so it is easy for this long-term signal to get lost in the midst of weekly and seasonal fluctuations in weather (Gleick 2012).

The challenges of understanding and responding to climate change have been amplified by controversies over the legitimacy of climate change science. While more than 90 percent of publishing climate scientists agree that climate change is occurring and caused primarily by human activities, in 2011 only 15 percent of the American public believed there is a high degree of scientific agreement (Leiserowitz et al. 2011). The agricultural community illustrates this skepticism, and at its 2010 national conference the Farm Bureau established, as its official position, that "there is no generally agreed upon scientific assessment of the exact impact or extent of carbon emissions from human activities, their impact on past decades of warming or how they will affect future climate changes" (Winter 2010). At its 2012 conference, it reiterated its position that climate change is not human induced (Clayton 2012). Fossil fuel producers, worried about the threat to their livelihoods by efforts to reduce fossil fuel use, have sought through misinformation campaigns to discredit the consensus view of climate change among scientists (McCright and Dunlap 2011). Until recently, the press amplified the voices of climate change denialists through its desire to present all sides of the controversy, without regard to the very large differences in the rigor of science underlying different positions (Boykoff 2011).

A social-ecological framework of press-like processes of incremental change and pulse-like processes of sudden, event-driven changes provides a useful way to understand the interactions among climates, rural peoples, their natural resource bases, and their livelihoods. Case studies of wildfires in the western mountain states, flooding in the Midwest, and warming in Inuit coastal communities in Alaska exemplify the ways climate change has begun to impact rural peoples. The differences in impacts and perceptions of risk have created different discourses. Programs of planned adaptation vary from isolated individuals and households living in poor rural communities to highly capitalized communities of interest like agribusiness and forestry. The former people are especially vulnerable to climactic disturbances as natural resource dependent populations with few resources.

Press-Pulse Dynamics in Coupled Human and Natural Systems

The human-dominated landscapes of North America represent a coupled human and natural system (CHANS) that changes through a mix of press and pulse processes. *Press processes* alter the structure of a system in small increments, while *pulse events* transform social and ecosystem functions suddenly through "shocks" (Collins et al. 2011). Population growth, agricultural and forestry expansion, yield increases, and coastland erosion represent typical press processes that are less visible than pulse processes, which occur suddenly and make structural changes highly visible. Pulse events transform rural places, livelihoods, and quality of life in short intervals of time. For Americans, pulse events are more salient than press events. They foresee deaths and injuries due to pulse events such as floods, hurricanes, winter storms, and wildfires, but are less concerned about press threats to water resources, plants and animals, public infrastructure (roads, schools, sewer systems), and crop productivity (Leiserowitz et al. 2011).

Press-pulse dynamics entail a recursive dimension in which humans adapt to the perturbation. These responses include actions to sustain flows of goods and services and to bolster the resilience of communities (Jackson et al. 2010). Adaptation often begins with efforts to resist and attempts to manage change, such as building new or strengthening existing levees and seawalls to protect towns, businesses, and farmland against hurricanes, sea level rise, and flooding.

Adaptation strategies focused on resilience try to increase the capacity of the rural community to be more flexible and cope without changing the baseline structure—e.g., shifting the types of agricultural crops grown or diversifying the community's economic or social infrastructure to be prepared for warmer, wetter, or drier conditions, but not changing the basic nature of land uses or rural livelihoods. Transformative adaptive responses might include moving settlements out of coastal regions facing rising sea levels (see Gramling and Laska in this volume), returning floodplains and bottomlands to seasonal wetlands rather than levee protected agricultural uses (Morton and Olson 2013), or creating public policies that incentivize agrobiodiversity and the creation of different livelihoods congruent with changing conditions.

Weather refers to day-to-day temperature and precipitation, whereas *climate* refers to the average temperature, precipitation, and atmospheric conditions over longer periods of time. These short- and long-term patterns influence how rural people chose livelihoods and create desirable places to live. Changes in these patterns can represent threats to economic, physical, and social well-being, particularly when temperature and precipitation vary considerably from human expectations and preparedness. When changes in the frequency, intensity, and variation of temperature, precipitation, and atmospheric conditions (pulses) occur, they inevitably intersect with the steady presses of human activity and land use changes. Given the intense use of the natural resource base—row crop cultivation, cattle grazing, mining, fishing, and building on floodplains—these systems have little redundancy built into them so unanticipated events like drought can quickly compromise their capacities.

Pulse events such as floods, droughts, and tornados are highly visible, dramatic events that grab media headlines and pose immediate threats to human livelihoods. During the southwestern United States drought of late 2011 and early 2012, newspapers headlined, "Texas Rice Farmers Lose Their Water" and reported that the $394 million Texas rice industry would suffer a shortage of water for irrigation if the Lower Colorado River (Texas) Authority cut off water to farmers for the first time in seventy-eight years (Koppel 2012). A climate pulse occurred in March 2012 in the interior United States when meteorological conditions spawned a series of unusually powerful tornados from the Gulf of Mexico to the Great Lakes. This event left behind fourteen dead in Indiana and twelve dead in Kentucky, leveled small towns, transformed rural homes into piles of debris, flattened a fire station, and ripped roofs off of schools and prisons, leaving survivors without power and emotionally stunned (Associated Press 2012). Rural communities and outlying homes without good warning systems are particularly vulnerable. Further, strong winds, hail, and heavy rains increase water runoff and loss of nutrients and soil in agricultural regions, with effects on annual and future yields when they occur during the growing season. Totaling up the various types of extreme weather events from the first half of 2011, the National Oceanographic and Aeronautics Administration (NOAA) declared that the year had already become one of the most extreme weather years in history (Morello 2011).

Water problems originate through press processes. The IPCC documents decreased stream discharge in the Colorado River Basin since 1950, and warming trends that have reduced the amount of winter snow in the mountain headwaters of the Colorado River and the timing of snowmelt (one to four weeks earlier in 2002 than in 1948). As the fraction of annual precipitation falling as rain rather than snow increases (an increase of 74 percent in the US western mountain states from 1949 to 2004), landslides and flooding occur more often. When more rapid rain-based runoff replaces slow release from snow melt, there is an increased need for greater reservoir capacity to capture and hold water for the dry season, which in turn complicates the availability of water for agricultural production, population and economic growth, and mining industries.

Climate disasters in one rural region may create opportunities for another rural region (Lal, Alavalapati, and Mercer 2011). The increase in the growing season, warmer temperatures, higher levels of CO_2, and more precipitation have increased agricultural productivity in the upper Midwest and Pacific Northwest, leading to record yields of corn, wheat, and soybeans. At the same time, other agricultural regions, like northern China, have experienced crop failures due to droughts and flooding. While price volatility in commodity markets is not unexpected, economists find that the volatility of the last few years seems attributable to an unusual mix of market inelasticities associated with public policies, scarcity of global land supply, and grain supply shortfalls caused by adverse weather events in major agricultural regions of the world (Diffenbaugh et al. 2012).

Persistent drought, high temperatures, and loss of forage have caused declines in cattle herds in the southwestern United States, giving a competitive advantage to northeastern US cattle and dairy producers who have experienced more precipitation, lower heat intensities, and abundant forage. Some analysts suggest that more intense heat in southern regions may shift crops northward, with pork and chicken production moving from the Southeast to the Northeast, and fruit tree production shifting from crops such as apples and pears, which require cold dormancy, to peaches, nuts, and vegetables. This might be beneficial to northeastern rural communities engaged in agriculture and forest related activities. The Southwest and Southeast may continue to experience water scarcity and increased energy costs as temperatures rise and precipitation patterns shift.

Similar dynamics of regional losses and gains appear to be affecting non-farm, amenity-rich rural areas in the United States. The loss of southern ski areas in New England has arguably benefited ski areas in northernmost New England and the Colorado Rockies (Hamilton, Brown, and Keim 2007).

Climate Impacts on Three Rural Places

Although climate scientists agree that the world is getting warmer, they are not certain about how global patterns impact local and regional conditions. Some parts of rural America are experiencing drought and heat stress; other parts are too wet from unprecedented flooding; and still others have had their town infrastructure as well as homes and lives destroyed by tornados, hurricanes, and melting permafrost. The following three case studies illustrate the range of variation in climactic impacts across different rural regions.

Wildfires in the Western Mountain States

The western United States has experienced a significant increase in wildfires during the summer months. Geographical analyses of the fires' locations have tied the increase in fires to smaller snowpacks at the higher elevations in the Rocky Mountains. More fires have begun at high elevations because with the smaller snowpack, these places have, in a press-like process, become drier and more prone to fire than they were during years with longer, colder, more snow-abundant winters (Westerling et al. 2006). Prolonged drought conditions have also accompanied the warming trends, and together they have contributed to substantial increases in the numbers of fires. The annual area burned has increased from less than 500,000 hectares prior to 1985 to more than 1,200,000 hectares after 2005 (Riley 2009). The number of large fires, pulse-like events, has also increased over the same two decade period at a rate of about seven fires a year. The increasing size of the fires stems in part from the drier conditions in which ignition events like lightning strikes occur.

The growing size of the fires stresses the firefighters who struggle to contain them. The firefighters, usually young men from rural backgrounds, work in small teams of five to fifteen people with responsibility for limited areas of forest. When large fires break out, forest service dispatchers bring in teams of firefighters from elsewhere in an attempt to bring the blazes under control before they destroy homes and endanger lives. In 2002, hundreds of firefighters from around the Southwest fought to subdue the Rodeo Chediski fire for several weeks. They brought it under control only after it burned almost 200,000 hectares of forest and destroyed 400 homes. The Wallow fire of 2011 burned for more than a month and consumed even more forest than the Chediski fire. Fires along the front range of the Rockies in Colorado during June and July 2012 destroyed comparable amounts of forests and hundreds of homes. The growth in the size of fires and the organizational demands of throwing together teams of unacquainted firefighters to fight large fires has exposed increased numbers of firefighters to dangerous situations (Desmond 2007). Even experienced teams are exposed to danger. In August 2013, nineteen members of one specially trained team of firefighters were killed in Arizona.

Cairo, Illinois, Levees, and the New Madrid Floodway

River flooding along the Mississippi and Ohio rivers is a pulse process that impacts adjacent agricultural lands and port infrastructure; exacerbates poverty, unemployment, and declining rural populations of the river towns; and heightens the racial tensions embedded in their social-political histories (Gellman and Roll 2011). Cairo, Illinois, situated at the confluence of the Ohio and Mississippi rivers, marks the divide between the Upper and Lower Mississippi River and is surrounded by an extensive system of levees and floodwalls. Formerly a vibrant river city and transportation hub with a population of 15,203 in 1920, Cairo in 2011 has a declining (2,900 inhabitants), aging (18 percent are sixty-five and older living alone), and impoverished (more than one-third of residents living below the poverty line) population.

The Mississippi and Ohio river bottomlands were historically riparian forests, transition ecosystems between the river and uplands that experienced the seasonal pulse of flooding with little damage to human settlements or activities (Morton and Olson 2013). These rivers also represented physical, social, economic, and symbolic divides between slave and free states, the opposing sides in the Civil War, and opposed positions about minority civil rights. Over 2.5 million acres of agricultural bottomlands in Missouri and Arkansas are protected by hundreds of miles of levees on the western border of the Lower Mississippi River south of Cairo.

Heavy snowmelt and rainfall ten times greater than average across the eastern half of the Mississippi watershed (~200,000 mi^2) in spring and summer of 2011 produced a flood to rival the destructive 1927 and 1937 floods and strained the capacity of the entire levee system (Camillo 2012; Olson and Morton 2013). On 2 May 2011, the USACE deliberately breached the Birds Point fuse plug levee in the New Madrid Floodway to protect the town of Cairo and other downstream cities from levee failures and loss of human life by diverting floodwaters into the agricultural lands of the Floodway. This decision reignited racially charged and class-based tensions between agricultural landowners and urban populations.

The 2011 Floodway decision altered agricultural lands as the force of the water rushed through the breaches and created hundreds of acres of deep gully fields and crater lakes, displaced tons of soil, and damaged irrigation equipment, farms, and homes.

Stream flows in the eastern United States have increased 25 percent in the last sixty years (Field et al. 2007) with increasing flows in winter and spring. While opening the Floodway reduced the water pressure on the Cairo levee system and enabled it to withstand the record flood, more than a year later depressions and sink holes in roads and on private properties remain; weakened levees and the floodwall require significant re-engineering and repair in preparation for future flood events; and the social and economic life of the rural town is struggling to recover. As a single 100- or 500-year event, the floods of 2011 might be considered a once-in-a-century or five-century event, except many of these rural communities have experienced one-hundred-year floods in both 2007 and 2008, suggesting a pattern of frequency and unpredictability not experienced before.

The Inuit in Alaskan Coastal Communities

Climate change exposes some North American populations to particularly large stresses. For example, the indigenous peoples of North America exhibit a special vulnerability to climate change. In disproportionate numbers, they reside in rural areas and engage in natural resource dependent occupations like fishing, trapping, or hunting, so markets with sources of supply all over the world do not buffer the impacts of climate change for American Indians as they do for urban residents. Further, a large proportion of them live in poverty, so they have fewer personal resources to draw upon in trying to cope with climate change. Some American Indians, like the Inuit, are particularly vulnerable to the effects of climate change given that the magnitude of change increases in the high latitudes where they live. Parts of Alaska have experienced an increase of four degrees Fahrenheit in average temperatures over the past thirty years.

The climate-related misfortunes visited upon the Inuit have come in various forms. Severe storms and melting permafrost have damaged the infrastructure in Inuit communities. Houses, roads, boardwalks, and even entire villages have begun to sink into the melting permafrost on which they were built. Ocean storms have eaten away at coastal shorelines and destroyed houses, docks, and fish-drying racks in coastal villages. Marine-based livelihoods have changed dramatically. Hunting and fishing regimens have been disrupted by thinning ice that has made it too dangerous to venture forth on the winter ice floes (Alaska Native Science Commission 2010) to fish or hunt for seals. Invasive species like spruce beetles have begun to decimate forests at higher rates. More generally, climate change has jeopardized the rural poor by destroying natural resources, like seal populations and fisheries, vital to Inuit livelihoods.

Climate change has had social as well as physical effects on American Indian communities. As one Inuit observer puts it, "the seasons are getting very fast and are all mixed up . . . These seasons are in too much of a hurry now." Another remarks, "Our elders tell us that our earth is getting old and needs to be replaced" (Alaska Native Science Commission 2010). These changes, occurring more or less simultaneously, have sharpened problems of food security in Inuit households as they have disrupted seasonal routines for obtaining foodstuffs (Ford and Beaumier 2011). Attachment to place among the Inuit has also declined with disruptions in subsistence routines and changes in landscapes brought about by melting permafrost (Willox et al. 2012). More generally, climate change has disabled the habitus surrounding Inuit activities, and, in so doing, has ushered in a period of rapid social change (Bourdieu 1977). These misfortunes test the resilience of Inuit communities. Because the Inuit do not have as much social and economic capital to draw upon as other populations, they have become more dependent on outside aid, with its complications, for their survival.

The Many Faces of Climate Change: Varying Perceptions of Vulnerability and Risk

The varying forms that climate change takes in different locales coupled with the different scales at which people experience and visualize climate means that groups of people in different places perceive the threats very differently. The discourses surrounding climate change reflect these regional disparities in impacts. Discussions have focused on specific local experiences and emergency responses as well as planning to minimize future damages. Farmers in the upper Midwest have invested in measures to cope with unusually large spring floods while ranchers in the southern Great Plains have explored ways to cope with historically unprecedented drought conditions, and residents of the western mountain states have expressed concern about the large increase in the number and scale of forest fires during the summer months. At a national scale, officials and academics have begun thinking in more concerted ways about extreme weather events and efficacious ways of addressing them.

Much of the discussion concerns the vulnerability of people to the adverse effects of climate change. A community's vulnerability varies with the magnitude of events, types of events, rates of change, community exposure, sensitivity to events, and adaptive capacity (Lal, Alavalapati, and Mercer 2011; Howden et al. 2007). In this highly variable context, climate scientists face major challenges when they try to communicate with non-specialist audiences about the risks and uncertainties associated with climate change (Pidgeon and Fischhoff 2011). The concept of risk means different things to different people. Expert judgments of risk stem from technical estimates while lay judgments of risk are sensitive to everyday perceptions of catastrophic potential, controllability, and threat to the future (Slovic 2009).

New discursive currents have entered agricultural communities. Many officials in larger agricultural NGOs now acknowledge the reality of climate change and assert the need to plan for it. The 25x'25 Alliance, a national organization of voluntary agricultural and forestry organizations with a goal to provide 25 percent of the nation's energy by 2025, has created a Climate Change Sub-committee to develop adaptation strategies to achieve its goal (Yoder 2012). Foresters may perceive the opportunity to sequester carbon and proactively engage in mitigation discussions and actions. Row crop agronomists have been more reticent to acknowledge climate change and are particularly resistant to mitigation efforts. The continuing absence of a consensus point of view is reflected in the results from a 2011 Iowa Farm and Rural Life Poll, in which neither the scientific consensus about the anthropogenic origins of climate change nor the denialist position received support from a majority of Iowa farmers (Arbuckle, Morton, and Hobbs 2013). Prescriptions for dealing with the problem vary accordingly. Many farmers do not want government action, believing that businesses and individuals are best suited to solve the problem. Those who believe climate change is happening, but is naturally caused, may not take adaptive actions for a variety of reasons including a fatalism that it is beyond their control (Pidgeon and Fischhoff 2011; Donner 2011).

Rural residents and scientists often offer dramatically different perspectives on climate change. Rural residents base their views on memories of past weather and are preoccupied with current weather (such as flooding, drought, shifts in seasonality). Scientists track large-scale global patterns and model scenarios of climate change decades into the future. The diversity of viewpoints has frustrated not just lay people but also scientists (Pidgeon and Fischhoff 2011). The challenge is how to communicate about complex scientific findings in a context of shifting and volatile discourses, and about current climate conditions in ways that prepare and protect rural peoples, their livelihoods, and their quality of life.

Resilience and Adaptation in Rural America

The unprecedented numbers of extreme weather events in recent years have raised questions about the resilience of rural communities in the face of these

Box 9.2: Producers of corn, rice, soybeans, and wheat (which provide 75 percent of calories consumed by the world's population; the United States provides about 23 percent of calories) are likely to experience the following disruptive changes related to weather and make adaptations:

1. A longer growing season means producers can plant earlier and can use longer season hybrids.
2. Wetter springs leave a smaller window of time to plant and increase the need for larger machinery.
3. More summer precipitation in the north central United States will support higher plant densities for higher yields and change management practices.
4. Wetter springs and summers are likely to lead to closer spacing of subsurface tile drainage and tiling of sloped surfaces.
5. Increased precipitation variability (flooding and drought) may alter management practices and increase the need for conservation structures and different crop varieties and breeds.
6. Increased changes in seasonal temperatures are likely to increase demand for new crop varieties and breeds, improved IPM practices, and pest-suppression technologies.
7. Higher humidity and more pathogens will lead to more problems with fall dry-down, a need for wider bean heads for faster harvest, and a shorter harvest period during daytime (e.g., because of dew period).
8. Drier autumns could result in delayed harvests to take advantage of natural dry downs condition and reduce fuel costs.

disturbances. Communities of interest as well as communities of place have begun to respond to climate change in ways that should enable them to survive disturbances. In other instances where communities may not have the internal resources to cope with the changes, outside interventions have become more important to their survival.

Agribusinesses, farmers, land grant university experiment stations, and the United States Department of Agriculture (USDA) have all initiated lines of research intended to respond to anticipated and actual changes in temperature, precipitation, and atmospheric CO_2 concentration (Hatfield et al. 2011). In 2011, the USDA Agriculture and Food Research Initiative (2011) invested more than $113 million in research and extension programming related to climate change, agriculture, and forestry with foci on reducing greenhouse gas emissions (GHG), increasing carbon sequestration in agricultural and forest production systems, and preparing the nation's agriculture and forests to adapt to changing climates.

The range of adaptive strategies pursued by agricultural communities includes marketing as well as field management practices (see Box 9.2). For example, some farmers and foresters are particularly interested in carbon trading as it relates to climate mitigation and the sequestration of carbon to reduce atmospheric CO_2. This has led to increased interest in developing global carbon budgets and has accelerated evaluations of forest and land management impacts on vegetation and soil carbon dynamics and storage (Pan et al. 2011).

Other rural communities, in particular those that have few resources like the Inuit or that face large scale floods and fires, cannot possibly cope with these disturbances by themselves because they do not have the scale of services necessary to bring the floods and fires under control. Similarly, larger fires have led to more property damage, made restoration efforts increasingly expensive, and placed a large fiscal burden on governments. These events increase the magnitude of government transfer payments to rural regions and communities, both to counter the destructive climatic events and to restore productive activities in the burnt-over districts. In the words of one report, the "economic damage from severe weather has increased dramatically, due largely to increased value of the infrastructure at risk. Annual costs to North America have now reached tens of billions of dollars in damaged property and economic productivity" (Field et al. 2007, 619).

In this context, extreme weather events have elicited historically unprecedented relief efforts. In some instances, professions and NGOs have organized to deal with these contingencies—e.g., among fire fighters and relief groups. Higher-level authorities have also intervened. State level mobilizations and federal assistance programs (such as the Federal Emergency Management Agency and the USDA Risk Management Agency) have grown in scale. Disaster capitalist firms, some of them unscrupulous, have also sprung up (Klein 2007). Incremental social changes associated with migration and agricultural commodity price fluctuations now occur in a context increasingly marked by abrupt and disruptive changes following disasters that test the adaptive capacities of governing institutions at all scales. While outside interventions are crucial to efforts to restore basic services and sometimes the social fabric, such interventions inevitably exact a toll on the local autonomy of rural communities.

Conclusions

Rural America is a repository of American wealth. It covers 80 percent of the land area and contains a significant portion of the nation's natural resource assets. For this reason rural places and peoples will shoulder the brunt of the direct impacts from climate change. Because the productivity of natural resources varies with changes in precipitation, heat, humidity, and seasonality, climate change has begun to disrupt well-established routines for utilizing natural resources. This dynamic makes rural communities more vulnerable than their urban counterparts to climate-change-related disruptions. Rural populations are vulnerable because they depend on natural resources for their livelihoods and because they have fewer social and economic resources to employ in recovering from weather related disasters.

A variety of local, state, and national initiatives, such as the United States Global Change Research Program (2012), promise to assist rural America in addressing the impacts of climate change. It is important that rural citizens not only be engaged with their local leadership in identifying issues and pro-actively seeking adaptive strategies, but also that public and private resources and partnerships outside rural communities be available. The ad hoc and fragmented field of responder organizations limits both timely and effective responses. Sunk costs and the expense of small-scale reconstruction make it difficult to repair and restore services; extractive industries with their boom-bust cycles preoccupy rural workers, and the growing prevalence of absentee ownership cripples the capacity of local governments to mobilize and respond to climate change (Majumdar and Bailey 2011). Only a comprehensive response, engaging all sectors and scales of society, would seem sufficient to meet these challenges.

How can rural sociologists contribute to this effort? First, adaptation to climate change will require multidisciplinary teams of researchers to formulate and then evaluate adaptations that appropriately and effectively address farmers' agricultural production practices, inland and coastal land use and water management, and rural communities' weather emergency action plans. Rural sociologists, trained to speak the languages of other scientific disciplines, could play pivotal roles in these team efforts. Second, the mitigation of GHG poses particularly acute challenges for rural residents because they have lower incomes than other Americans, so strategies that entail the purchase of expensive clean energy devices seem less affordable for rural populations. With their detailed knowledge of rural cultures and social structures, rural social scientists could make major contributions to these mitigation efforts. Third, climate change threatens Americans with far-reaching social transformations, and sociologists with their knowledge about these processes seem well positioned to aid communities in turning these moments of change into opportunities. Lastly, sociologists can facilitate public dialogue and help bridge the knowledge divide between the accepted science of changing climate conditions and the realities of adapting to and even affecting the course of climate change.

Notes

1 This research was supported in part by the USDA-NIFA, Award No. 2011-68002-30190 "Cropping Systems Coordinated Agricultural Project (CAP): Climate Change, Mitigation, and Adaptation in Corn-Based Cropping Systems" and Iowa State University College of Agriculture and Life Sciences.

References

Alaska Native Science Commission. 2010. "Impact of Climate Change on Alaska Native Communities." Accessed 15 February 2012. http://www.nativescience.org/pubs/afn%202005%20impact%20of%20climate%20change%20on%20alaska%20native%20communities.pdf.

Arbuckle, J.G., L.W. Morton, and J. Hobbs. 2013. "Farmer Beliefs and Concerns about Climate Change and Attitudes toward Adaptation and Mitigation: Evidence from Iowa." *Climatic Change* 118 (3–4): 551–63. http://dx.doi.org/10.1007/s10584-013-0700-0.

Associated Press. 2012. "Gulf to Great Lakes, Storms Leave Carnage." *Des Moines Register*, 3 March, front page.

Bourdieu, P. 1977. *Outline of a Theory of Practice.* Cambridge, UK: Cambridge University Press. http://dx.doi.org/10.1017/CBO9780511812507.

Boykoff, M. 2011. *Who Speaks for the Climate? Making Sense of Media Reporting about Climate Change.* Cambridge, UK: Cambridge University Press. http://dx.doi.org/10.1017/CBO9780511978586.

Camillo, C.A. 2012. *Divine Providence: The 2011 Flood in the Mississippi River and Tributaries Project.* Vicksburg, MS: Mississippi River Commission.

Clayton, C. 2012. "Getting to the Heartland of the Climate Debate." *Progressive Farmer*, 17 February.

Collins, S.L., S.R. Carpenter, S.M. Swinton, D.E. Orenstein, D.L. Childers, T.L. Gragson, N.B. Grimm, J.M. Grove, S.L. Harlan, J.P. Kaye, et al. 2011. "An Integrated Conceptual Framework for Long-Term Social-Ecological Research." *Frontiers in Ecology and the Environment* 9 (6): 351–7. http://dx.doi.org/10.1890/100068.

Coumou, D., and S. Rahmstorf. 2012. "A Decade of Weather Extremes." *Nature Climate Change* 2: 491–6.

Desmond, M. 2007. *On the Fireline: Living and Dying with Wildland Firefighters.* Chicago, IL: University of Chicago Press. http://dx.doi.org/10.7208/chicago/9780226144078.001.0001.

Diffenbaugh, N.S., T.W. Hertel, M. Scherer, and M. Verma. 1 July 2012. "Response of Corn Markets to Climate Volatility under Alternative Energy Futures." *Nature Climate Change* 2: 514–18. Medline:23243468.

Donner, S.D. 2011. "Making the Climate a Part of the Human World." *Bulletin of the American Meteorological Society* 92 (10): 1297–302. http://dx.doi.org/10.1175/2011BAMS3219.1.

Field, C.B., L.D. Mortsch, M. Braklacich, D.L. Forbes, P. Kovacs, J.A. Patz, S.W. Running, and M.J. Scott. 2007. "Climate Change 2007: Impacts, Adaptation and Vulnerability." In *Contribution of Working Group II to the Fourth Assessment Report of the Intergovernmental*

Panel on Climate Change, ed. M.L. Parry, O.F. Canziani, J.P. Palutikof, P.J. van der Linden, and C.E. Hanson, 617–52. Cambridge, UK: Cambridge University Press.

Ford, James D., and M. Beaumier. 2011. "Feeding the Family during Times of Stress: Experience and Determinants of Food Insecurity in an Inuit Ccommunity." *Geographical Journal* 177 (1): 44–61. http://dx.doi.org/10.1111/j.1475-4959.2010.00374.x. Medline:21560272.

Gellman, E.S., and J. Roll. 2011. *The Gospel of the Working Class*. Urbana-Champaign: University of Illinois Press.

Gleick, P. 2012. "Climate Change, Disbelief, and the Collision between Human and Geologic Time." *Forbes*, 16 January. http://www.forbes.com/sites/petergleick/2012/01/16/climate-change-disbelief-and-the-collision-between-human-and-geologic-time/.

Hamilton, L.C., B.C. Brown, and B.D. Keim. 2007. "Ski Areas, Weather and Climate: Time Series Models for New England Case Studies." *International Journal of Climatology* 27 (15): 2113–24. http://dx.doi.org/10.1002/joc.1502.

Hansen, J., M. Sato, and R. Ruedy. 2012. "Perception of Climate Change." Proceedings of the National Academy of Sciences, early edition. http://www.pnas.org/content/109/37/E2415.

Hatfield, J.L., K.J. Boote, B.A. Kimball, L.H. Zisha, R.C. Izaurralde, D. Ort, A.M. Thomson, and D. Wolfe. 2011. "Climate Impacts on Agriculture: Implications for Crop Production." *Agronomy Journal* 103 (2): 351–70.

Howden, S.M., J.F. Soussana, F.N. Tubiello, N. Chhetri, M. Dunlop, and H. Meinke. 11 December 2007. "Adapting Agriculture to Climate Change." *Proceedings of the National Academy of Sciences of the United States of America* 104 (50): 19691–6. http://dx.doi.org/10.1073/pnas.0701890104. Medline:18077402.

IPCC. 2001. *Climate Change 2001: Synthesis Report. A Contribution of Working Groups I, II, and III to the Third Assessment Report of the Intergovernmental panel on Climate Change*. Cambridge, UK: Cambridge University Press.

IPCC. 2007. *Climate Change 2007: Synthesis Report. Contribution of Working Groups I, II, and III to the Fourth Assessment Report of the Intergovernmental Panel on Climate Change*. Cambridge, UK: Cambridge University Press.

Jackson, L., M. van Noordwijk, J. Bengtsson, W. Foster, L. Lipper, M. Pulleman, M. Said, J. Snaddon, and R. Vodouhe. 2010. "Biodiversity and Agricultural Sustainability: From Assessment to Adaptive Management." *Current Opinion in Environmental Sustainability* 2 (1–2): 80–87. http://dx.doi.org/10.1016/j.cosust.2010.02.007.

Klein, N. 2007. *The Shock Doctrine: The Rise of Disaster Capitalism*. New York: Henry Holt.

Koppel, N. 2012. "Texas Rice Farmers Lose their Water." *Wall Street Journal*, 3–4 March, A3.

Lal, P., J.R. Alavalapati, and E.D. Mercer. 2011. "Socio-economic Impacts of Climate Change on Rural United States." *Mitigation and Adaptation Strategies for Global Change* 16 (7): 819–44. http://dx.doi.org/10.1007/s11027-011-9295-9.

Leiserowitz, A., E. Maibach, C. Roser-Renouf, and N. Smith. 2011. "Global Warming's Six Americas." May. Yale University and George Mason University. New Haven, CT: Yale Project on Climate Change and Communication.

Majumdar, M., and C. Bailey. 2011. "Relationship between Absentee Landownership and Quality of Life in Alabama." Paper presented at the annual meeting of the Rural Sociological Society, Boise, ID, July 2011.

McCright, A.M., and R.E. Dunlap. 2011. "The Politicization of Climate Change and Polarization in the American Public's Views of Global Warming 2001–2010." *Sociological Quarterly* 52 (2): 155–94. http://dx.doi.org/10.1111/j.1533-8525.2011.01198.x.

Morello, L. 2011. "NOAA Makes it Official: 2011 among Most Extreme Weather Years in History." *Scientific American*, June 17. http://www.scientificamerican.com/article.cfm?id=noaa-makes-2011-most-extreme-weather-year.

Morton, L.W., and K.R. Olson. 2013. "Birds Point-New Madrid Floodway: Redesign, Reconstruction, and Restoration." *Journal of Soil and Water Conservation* 68 (2): 35A–40A. http://dx.doi.org/10.2489/jswc.68.2.35A.

Olson, K.R., and L.W. Morton. 2013. "Soil and Crop Damages as a Result of Levee Breaches on Ohio and Mississippi Rivers." *Journal of Earth Science and Engineering* 3 (3): 1–20.

Pan, Y., R.A. Birdsey, J. Fang, R. Houghton, P.E. Kauppi, W.A. Kurz, O.L. Phillips, A. Shvidenko, S.L. Lewis, J.G. Canadell, et al. 19 August 2011. "A Large and Persistent Carbon Sink in the World's Forests." *Science* 333 (6,045): 988–93. http://dx.doi.org/10.1126/science.1201609. Medline:21764754

Pidgeon, N., and B. Fischhoff. 2011. "The Role of Social and Decision Sciences in Communicating Uncertain Climate Risks." *Nature Climate Change* 1 (1): 35–41. http://dx.doi.org/10.1038/nclimate1080.

Riley, K. 2009. "Measuring Trends in Wildfire Severity and Magnitude." Presentation at the 4th International Fire Ecology Conference, Savannah, GA.

Slovic, P. 2009. *The Perception of Risk.* Sterling, VA: Earthscan Publications Ltd.

United States Global Change Research Program. 2012. Accessed 13 March 2012. http://www.globalchange.gov/.

United States Global Change Research Program. 2012. *Our Changing Planet.* Annual Report to Congress. Washington, DC.

USDA Agriculture and Food Research Initiative. 2011. "NIFA Announces Grant to Study the Effects of Climate Change on Agricultural and Forest Production." 18 February. http://www.nifa.usda.gov/newsroom/news/2011news/02181_climate_change_cap.html.

USDA Climate and Man Yearbook. 1941. "House document No. 27, 77th Congress, 1st Session." United States Department of Agriculture, Washington, DC, US Government Printing Office.

Walthall, C., J. Hatfield, P. Backlund, L. Lengnick, E. Marshall, M. Walsh, S. Adkins, M. Aillery, E.A. Ainsworth, C. Ammann, et al. 2012. *Climate Change and Agriculture in the United States: Effects and Adaptation.* USDA Technical Bulletin 1935, Washington, DC.

Weber, E.U., and P.C. Stern. May–June 2011. "Public Understanding of Climate Change in the United States." *American Psychologist* 66 (4): 315–28. http://dx.doi.org/10.1037/a0023253. Medline:21553956.

Westerling, A.L., H.G. Hidalgo, D.R. Cayan, and T.W. Swetnam. 18 August 2006. "Warming and Earlier Spring Increase Western U.S. Forest Wildfire Activity." *Science* 313 (5,789): 940–43. http://dx.doi.org/10.1126/science.1128834. Medline:16825536.

Willox, A. Cunsolo, S.L. Harper, J.D. Ford, K. Landman, K. Houle, and V.L. Edge, and the Rigolet Inuit Community Government. August 2012. "'From This Place and of This Place:' Climate Change, Sense of Place, and Health in Nunatsiavut, Canada." *Social Science & Medicine* 75 (3): 538–47. http://dx.doi.org/10.1016/j.socscimed.2012.03.043. Medline:22595069.

Winter, A. 2010. "Farm Bureau Fires Back against Climate Bill's 'Power Grab.'" *New York Times*, January 11. http://www.nytimes.com/cwire/2010/01/11/11climatewire-farm-bureau-fires-back-against-climate-bills-93758.html.

Yoder, F. January 2012. "Agriculture and Forestry in a Changing Climate: The Road Ahead." A product of the 25x'25 Adaptation Initiative.

CHAPTER 10

Contemporary Water Issues in Rural North America

Courtney G. Flint and Naomi Krogman

Introduction

In the social life of rural North America, water captures the inseparability between society and nature (Swyngedouw 1999, 446). Water shapes landscapes and gives life to socio-ecological systems and human experience. Water is a necessary prerequisite for rural and natural resource developments and a primary component of the cumulative effects of land use decisions. The food base and daily needs of the population are linked to the quality and quantity of water. Given the *relational* qualities of what we consider to be *rural* (Woods 2011), water provides the material and symbolic substance for relationships among rural residents, places, ecosystems, and urban counterparts. These core qualities of water—combined with global, regional, and local shifts in resource use and environmental conditions, including climate change—require careful inquiry, planning, and engagement. Rural sociologists are well poised for continued contributions in this arena.

In this chapter, we highlight interrelated themes regarding water in rural North America and relationships to urban areas and global change. First, we discuss the changing paradigms of human-nature relationships affecting hydraulic technology and the role of water infrastructure in rural development and landscape change. Inequities and injustices from long-standing and emerging power dynamics as well as the commodification and privatization of water in the twenty-first century permeate these paradigm shifts. Second, we highlight lingering and emerging water risks inherent in rural development, which are the focus of ongoing rural sociological research. Finally, we explore collective watershed management actions in response to uncertainty, risk, and opportunity in rural North America. Throughout, we emphasize the important role of rural sociologists in water research and engagement.

Exploring water in rural life reveals people and places as simultaneously *haves* and *have-nots*. Even in headwaters where water may be abundant, in rural spaces and places, water control is often in the hands of powerful forces elsewhere. As such, Samuel Taylor Coleridge's line from "The Rime of the Ancient Mariner," "Water, water, every where, Nor any drop to drink" (Coleridge 1956, 394) rings true for those experiencing poor water quality or at the losing end of water transfers or changing water rights regimes, whether they are upstream or downstream. The distributional impacts of water delivery systems are among the key areas of rural sociological water-issue inquiry (Mollinga 2008; Freeman 2000). In this vein, Nowak, Bowen, and Cabot's (2006) work on disproportionality contributes to rural sociological approaches by incorporating the interactive and multiplicative effects between social and biophysical systems to show how the haves and the have-nots (or perhaps the *dos* and *do-nots* in terms of conservation practice) rely on the buffering capacities of different biophysical settings in space, time, and other context-specific factors.

No topic lends itself to more interdisciplinary inquiry than water, given its universal essentiality. Rural sociology plays a key role in interdisciplinary and transdisciplinary interactions and investigations to address problems and opportunities in complex socio-ecological systems. We agree with Fortmann (in this volume) in asserting an imperative need for sociologists to work with other social and biophysical scientists, engineers, and planners, as well as with citizens and governmental and organizational representatives. Given their translational skills and ability to ground theoretical understanding in empirical, contextual inquiry, rural sociologists are essential bridge builders. Rural sociologists can be key interpreters of the social, ecological, economic, and political history of water in a region, and share insight about future critical distributional issues.

Rural sociology has much in common with human geography, anthropology, and other social sciences when it comes to understanding contextual relationships between water and rural society. Yet rural people, places, and spaces are sometimes cast aside and misrepresented by those who focus attention on urban water issues. The work of Swyngedouw (2004, 1) exemplifies this dismissal of the complexity of rural water issues: "Contrary to the rural realm where—at least under non-arid conditions—water of a reasonable quality is easily and often readily available, urban water supply and access relies on the perpetual transformation, mastering and harnessing of 'natural water.'"

"Natural water" almost always has some connection to rural spaces, and as shortages loom, rural areas are pressured to address their allocation of water, particularly in regards to groundwater use and irrigated agriculture. Sharp and Smith (2003, 914) contend, "Because of growth and development, the issue in some parts of rural America is not how to maintain local population in the face of agricultural consolidation, but how to maintain local agriculture while accommodating substantial nonfarm population growth and development." While water is often fundamental to rural identity and culture, it is by no means always of "reasonable" quality. And, even where abundant, rural water is subject to manipulation by powerful interests, the circulation of capital, and exclusionary practices leading to the same forms of "deprivation, disempowerment, and repressive social mechanisms" that Swyngedouw (2004, 1) claims are hallmarks of urban water systems. Most rural water systems in Canada and the United States were altered for large-scale agricultural and energy uses. New water management regimes that limit water use, increase or shift costs, change the way water is distributed, or introduce new stewardship models will represent challenges for institutions that use and manage rural water resources (Morton 2011).

Albrecht and Murdock (1986, 381) note "that the natural resource base of a society establishes the limits or constraints within which a society must operate." However, both historic and current experience with large-scale water development suggests power relationships around rural resource decisions present more profound limits or constraints on rural society than the presence or absence of the resource base itself. Rural people and processes are situated in a complex relational web of connections and governance spanning multiple scales. Thus, the abundance of water resources can have little to do with the availability of those resources for equitable local use. Abilities of rural communities to advocate for their long-term water interests are often "heavily constrained by their particular locations in social and economic structures" (Strang 2009, 281). This is especially the case for many parts of the United States, where water rights were given "first in time, first in right" and where allocation rights and the placement of dams were determined with little regard to environmental limits (Getches 2004). While by no means new to rural people and communities, environmental injustices regarding water resources deserve further attention by rural sociologists. We now turn to discuss how the infrastructure of early twentieth century created a path dependency in rural America that created today's water challenges.

Infrastructural Complexities: Shifting Paradigms of Water Development and Management

Water was harnessed for power early in US and Canadian history as a key part of settlement, expansion, and the industrialization of landscapes. Settlers from 1600 on brought mill technology from Europe, and gristmills, sawmills, and later textile mills were located where water, labor, and raw materials conveniently came together (Walter and Merritts 2008; Carlson 1981). Water mills dotted the Eastern rural landscape and contributed to large-scale deforestation, agricultural development, and socioeconomic change (Nye 1999; Cronon 1983). Water flowed into the hands of powerful mill owners and landowners, and was part of tumultuous labor equity struggles shaping rural social and economic realities (Bernstein 2010; Carlson 1981).

Waterwheels were eventually surpassed by other sources of power, but water continued to be critical to the complex energy infrastructure of North America (Nye 1999). By early in the twentieth century, a hydraulic paradigm emerged driven by engineers and politicians bent on controlling nature and harnessing the "wild" and "wasted" power of water. Construction of large-scale dams and water conveyance infrastructure was crucial to modern industrialization. In 1901, construction began on the Canadian Niagara Falls Power Plant. In 1902, the US Reclamation Act led to dam and canal construction ushering in a century of "hydraulic industrialization" (Howitt 2001, 301). The full force of industrial and government capital fueled dramatic landscape changes and the resettlement and subordination of rural communities. Rural water, and its captured power, was channeled toward urban centers of growth and power.

Large-scale dams and ship transportation channels required significant capital, generally supplied by the federal government to support the expansion of a particular industry, such as irrigated farming or increased energy supply for extractive resource development. The United States has one of the largest flood control infrastructures in the world (O'Neil 2006), and much of this development was prompted by local and regional elites (Hyde 2010). Freudenburg et al. (2009) document the influence of power and profit motives in shaping water infrastructure in their book, *Catastrophe in the Making: The Engineering of Katrina and the Disasters of Tomorrow.* They explain that local business and political leaders in New Orleans acquired federal funding to develop a seaport for their narrow economic interests. The promised economic benefits did not materialize, at a great cost to tax payers, but especially to rural residents who suffered devastating consequences from salt-water intrusion and erosion of the band of freshwater wetlands and cypress forests protecting rural communities from flooding.

The implications of these dramatic twentieth century changes for rural landscapes and communities, in North America and around the world, gave rise to powerful examples of injustice and deprivation. In Canada, the dislocation and disruption of First Nations communities for the creation of vast reservoirs and hydrologic power infrastructure has been well documented (Desbiens 2004; Howitt 2001; Ettenger 1998; Waldram 1988). The vulnerability of constructed levees along the Mississippi left nearly one million people inundated by floods in 1927, and in particular decimated black communities throughout the Delta region (Barry 1997). Hurricane Betsy in 1965 also involved levee failure and cries about injustices to rural communities (Henkel, Dovidio, and Gaertner 2006). The tragic repetition of water infrastructural vulnerability in Hurricanes Katrina and Rita highlights the complexity and interaction of engineering, socio-ecological conditions, and justice.

By the 1980s, global acknowledgment of the irreversible ecological and social impacts of large-scale water engineering and development was well understood (Scudder 2006; McCully 2001) and pointed to the need for transformations (Richter et al. 2010). The dominant paradigm of "controlling nature" with large-scale water development has to some extent given way to a more multifaceted appreciation for the benefits or services provided by ecosystems of which water is an essential element. Whereas the twentieth century was one of thinking and building "big" in terms of water engineering, Roy (1999) suggests the twenty-first might be the "Century of the Small," in which "small-scale decentralized systems and reducing wastefulness and overconsumption is the only viable approach to meeting current and future water and energy needs in a sustainable and equitable way" (McCully 2001, xl).

The recent ecosystem services paradigm emphasizes a shift in orientation toward the notion of increasing flows of benefits from natural "stock" found in ecosystems for human well-being (Norgaard 2010). This focus on balancing human needs with ecological capabilities has led to decommissioning of dams across North America (Gleick 2000) where it has in some cases been found to be cheaper to remove dams than maintain them (McCully 2001). Facilitating fish passage in the Western United States and Canada and recognizing the dynamics of flood disturbance ecology have gained influential dominance in water management science and planning (McCully 2001). Smaller-scale approaches to water management are said to be "more cost effective and less disruptive to local communities" (Gleick 2000, 136). However, looking back as far as the eighteenth and nineteenth century millponds, contemporary research shows that even small-scale, though abundant, impoundments altered stream hydrology and sediment and nutrient transport (Walter and Merritts 2008). Thus, continued monitoring of the cumulative effects of water management across scales is critically important.

Despite the decline of large dam construction and even decommissioning of dams, large-scale water transfer systems continue to be considered and constructed, and there is an increasingly dominant emphasis on market-based water trading and privatization of water rights. One such proposed large-scale water transfer would bring water to Las Vegas from rural ground and surface water sources in northern Nevada (Malewitz 2012). Transfers of water from rural to urban areas, driven by changes in sectoral water demand (Meinzen-Dick and Ringler 2008) and powerful urban and industrial interests, are contentious (Malewitz 2012) and lead to claims of injustice by rural communities and agricultural interests (Keenan, Krannich, and Walker 1999). Water transfers are noted to also have serious third-party consequences for particular social or user groups (e.g., rural poor, women, fisheries, and recreation) and it is often difficult to measure or compensate for their social or cultural losses (Meinzen-Dick and Ringler 2008).

Contemporary water infrastructure needs have prompted new debates around water engineering for delivery and waste systems as old infrastructure fails (Gasteyer 2011). The current challenge is how to address water infrastructure needs when the paradigm of controlling nature, which mobilized huge efforts and expenditures, may have largely passed. Where will the impetus and funding for rural infrastructural attention come from in the twenty-first century? For example, vast improvements are needed in rural plumbing facilities for reliable potable water supply and proper sanitation, particularly in Alaska Native and American Indian or First Nations communities (Gasteyer 2011). It is a challenge for rural communities to finance these needed improvements and navigate regulatory and planning requirements. Requirements for environmental impact statements and engineering plans are not easily met in small towns where expertise is limited and expensive. In addition, many rural American communities face solid-waste management challenges, where landfills are full and the costs to transport garbage elsewhere are high and expected to increase. Heightened concern about groundwater pollution issues associated with landfills makes the prospect of additional rural development initiatives more complicated, given the need to move away from various conventional infrastructure development around waste management.

Water resource access and use in rural North America is increasingly controlled by corporate interests, replacing what Wittfogel (1957) historically perceived as "hydraulic despotism" by autocratic governments with a twenty-first-century corporate despotism. Fears of water privatization of public water services, use of private property rights in relation to water, and water as a consumer commodity are linked to a rising trend of global opposition to corporate exploitation of water for profit (Arnold 2009). In particular, there are increasing international concerns that neoliberalism manifests itself in the expansion of market-based systems that provide avenues for corporate actors to purchase water rights (Petrova 2005), as occurred in the Chiapas area of Mexico

(Nash 2007). Bakker (2003) documents trends of water privatization in several medium-developed countries, highlighting populist protests and organized opposition about free or inexpensive water allocations for basic needs, such as drinking water, household use, and the maintenance of basic ecosystem goods and services (e.g., groundwater recharge). Many market-based systems benefit those who are in a position to pay for greater water rights and influence the institutional rules that govern that water use.

In the United States and Canada, privatization ranges from the private provision of services and supplies, such as laboratory analyses of water quality, to the outsourcing of operations and maintenance from a public utility to a private firm. Particularly since the 1990s, community concerns have been raised around the loss of control over a vital public service, the protection of water resources for watershed protection, reliable and affordable water service delivery, and the delegation of authority to monitor and enforce the contract terms and environmental regulations associated with private water use. Rural residents are also often wary of how competitive bidding of water resources may favor certain clientele, and concerned with the transparency of utility practices and policies (Jacobs and Howe 2005).

There are also a plethora of new market-based instruments being used to try to balance development with ecosystem integrity. Recognizing ecosystems' good and services to people and exchanging losses in one ecosystem for development gains elsewhere is seen as positive by some (Daily 1997). Others see this as problematic, where an ecosystem services paradigm is associated with an increasing commodification of water resources that allows for "literal and metaphorical abstraction of materials, detaching them from their ecological and social context and reframing them as property" (Strang 2009, 277). Norgaard (2010) suggests that the term ecosystem services artificially dissects the human benefits of various ecosystems so that they can be commodified and then more easily traded and paid for through various market mechanisms. In fact, the water, wetlands, watersheds, and plant and animal life are hydrologically connected, and by trading bits and parts, such connections can be forever altered without consideration to potential cascade effects. Wetland policy evaluation studies highlight regulatory weakness in protecting in situ wetlands, weak success of in-lieu fee payments or wetland restoration or enhancement efforts, and problems with substitution of suburban storm water ponds for wetlands elsewhere (Clare et al. 2011). Thus, many market-based systems relying on trade of "like for like" ecosystem goods and services are not replaced in a practical sense. As water and wetland quality problems and water quantity issues appear in rural areas, heightened debates may occur over the uneven success of market-based systems used to improve water management (McKenney and Kiesecker 2010; Walker et al. 2009; Gibbons and Lindenmayer 2007). Rural sociologists can play an important role in evaluating these programs, which are currently very popular in the United States and Canada, and document their effect on rural areas, their wetlands, watersheds, and water quality and quantity.

Even in places not dominated by agriculture or industry, such as natural amenity communities in rural areas, there are challenges related to water provisioning and quality (Krannich, Luloff, and Field 2011). Infrastructural developments are needed in fast-growing amenity areas to address water demand and run-off issues associated with changing land cover to more impervious surfaces. Recent modeling of rural groundwater risks reveals consequences from septic systems in close proximity to private wells due to rapid residential development in rural subdivisions (Wilcox et al. 2010). Uneven zoning and regulatory oversight in rapidly changing amenity communities creates challenges for water resources planning and management. The changing cultural contexts in these communities due to the mixing of newcomer and long-standing residents with diverse values challenge the success of participatory water resource planning (Schewe et al. 2012; Krannich, Luloff, and Field 2011; Keenan and Krannich 1997).

Responding to Water Risks in Contemporary Rural Development and Environmental Change

Large-scale agriculture, mining, and energy developments have long impacted rural North America, and related risks are emerging rapidly, particularly from shale oil and gas development (Brasier et al. 2011). Legacy water quality risks such as nutrient and pesticide use in conventional agricultural practices continue to be documented by rural sociologists (Jackson-Smith et al. 2010; Arbuckle et al. 2009; Constance, Rikoon, and Ma 1996; Nowak and Korsching 1988). Yet agricultural risks are by no means isolated to water quality. The irreplaceable depletion of groundwater resources, such as those of the Ogallala Aquifer, threatens rural communities and their urban counterparts. Food and fiber security in the North American breadbasket depends largely on irrigation from rapidly depleted groundwater sources (Little 2009).

The groundwater depletion and water quality problems are also combined in the dynamic context of oil and natural gas extraction using new, unconventional means, leading to rural conflicts and struggles to pursue economic development and protect the environment (Theodori 2009). Risks of water contamination appear to be high with hydraulic fracturing for natural gas development

(Osborn et al. 2011). The rapid expansion of natural gas drilling in the Marcellus Shale region is a priority concern of local residents (Brasier et al. 2011). Grassroots coalitions formed by rural landowners around natural gas development issues are proving to be important for negotiating compensation for environmental impacts (Jacquet and Stedman 2011; see also Kinchy et al. in this volume).

Rural vulnerabilities related to water are compounded by the uncertainties and anticipated fluctuations in precipitation, temperature, and severe weather that result from climate change (Morton and Rudel in this volume). Droughts, floods, and storms wreak havoc on rural communities, and particularly on marginalized groups within rural communities such as the elderly, impoverished, and those dependent for employment supported by impacted resources. While climate change related policies might offer economic opportunities for rural communities, such as alternative energy development, there may be unanticipated consequences for water supply. For example, water impacts from biofuels energy development are likely to be crop-specific and locally or regionally variable depending on whether water for biofuel crops is rain-fed or irrigated from surface or groundwater, and if it competes with other agricultural crops (de Fraiture, Giordano, and Liao 2008; Selfa and Bain in this volume).

Rural sociologists often look back in time in order to look forward in terms of natural resource and risk management. O'Neil's (2006) history of flood control in the United States highlights the contemporary conundrum of reducing ecological vulnerability when, historically, rivers were engineered for human-centered risk reduction and development goals. The ecosystem services approach may provide a compromise framework whereby restoring ecological functions can be framed as ultimately about human benefits and risk mitigation via multiple services including natural flood control, water quality, and aesthetics from natural amenities and biodiversity. Rural sociologists should play key roles in assessing rural impacts from social, political, and environmental changes as we discuss in the next section.

Watershed Organization and Action: Catalyzing the Role of Rural Sociologists

Water infrastructure needs are evolving and policy and technological tools that can be tailored to specific situations or contexts are required (Meinzen-Dick and Ringler 2008). Along with the paradigmatic change toward ecosystem and scale-specific responses, resource managers need to "develop the knowledge, skill and sensitivities to deal with the moral, ethical and political domains of resource management as well as the technical domain" (Howitt 2001, 6). Professional literacy to address socio-ecological complexities will increase as more focus is placed on "seeing" complex consequences, "thinking" about contextual complexities, and finding new ways of "doing" resource management (Howitt 2001, 8). Rural sociologists are uniquely trained and positioned to help with this process. Using participatory research and engagement methods, our skills help bring stakeholders beyond science and technical water management into the policy-making process.

The paradigm shift away from the more technocratic, hydraulic engineering approach to water management in recent decades has focused more attention on inclusive processes beyond science and engineering for governance solutions and "for participation from rural communities, indigenous and tribal peoples, women and other vulnerable groups" (McCully 2001, lxix). Yet shifting paradigms have also emphasized privatization and commodification of water resources that often stifle the less tangible, non-market values of water and their role in rural life, including attachment to place, aesthetic values, spirituality, and recreation. While local organization around water is to some extent "at the mercy of global political and economic relationships and market forces" (Strang 2009, 55), local watershed organizations emerged recently as an approach to protect valued interests and mitigate risks (Sabatier et al. 2005). Typically focused on environmental strategies and management, local-scale watershed organizations often have implications for community well-being even if such broader goals are not explicit in their organizational missions (Stedman et al. 2009; Strang 2009).

Despite literature claiming anthropogenic environmental risk situations invariably lead to social corrosion (Picou and Gill 2000; Freudenburg and Jones 1991), in their study of local response to farm chemical contamination of local waters Salamon, Farnsworth, and Rendziak (1998) show the possibility that trust and perceived economic interdependence among what might otherwise be divergent interests can support local-level cooperation. While sociologists are not always represented in interdisciplinary water resource research, Freeman (2000) highlights their contributions using common property approaches to understanding the relationship between individual users and state and federal entities, particularly in regards to water user associations, mutual companies, irrigation districts, *acequias* (community-operated waterways), and conservancy districts.

More recently, governance issues, especially those around rural local involvement in water-related decision-making, are gaining attention among rural sociologists. Rural sociologists have studied different forms of collaboratively managed water bodies and watersheds to understand the genesis and functional attributes of such cooperative organizations, as well as the role of public involvement, rules, systems of support and accountability in the function of watershed management (Barham 2010; Morton and Padgitt 2005). Webler and Tuler (2001), in a Q-Sort study, described the various frames the public accepts for involvement in decision making around watershed management. For some, the focus is on the popular acceptance of outcomes; for others, a good process is one that produces technically competent outcomes; for others, the process must be seen as fair, and finally still others appreciate attention to educating regional residents and promoting constructive dialogue. Other studies examine governance, power, and privilege, especially the way the state devolves power to local or regional decision makers favoring particular interest groups (Lane 2003).

Connections between culture, water management arrangements, and resilience are also important. For example, *acequias* in New Mexico and Colorado represent unique contemporary water management arrangements with deep cultural roots and evidence of the importance of water in "social cohesion" (Strang 2004, 246). *Acequias* refer to ditches in the southwest as well as to the local governing institutions regarding their use and maintenance (Hicks 2010). The "complex social fabric" woven by this community-based water management practice is seen in the "collective power of a ditch crew of twenty or thirty men . . . evolved out of hundreds of years of managing *acequias*" (Crawford 1988, 223). It can be challenging to maintain this type of communal water governance and management given the "prevailing legal and administrative order prioritizes water's commodity value" (Hicks 2010, 223).

Legal regimes are only one kind of barrier to local community engagement in watershed management. Other challenges include lack of leadership, insufficient resources and technical support, blockage by powerful interests, or deferring decisions to government and technical professionals (Morton 2011, 28). Despite obstacles, Morton, Selfa, and Becerra (2011, 29) note the increasing potential for collective water-related problem solving and mobilization of "people traditionally left out of decision-making processes." The inclusion of social indicators for watershed management and planning to reduce risks from poor water quality may help rural communities and regions reduce vulnerabilities (Brehm, Pasko, and Eisenhauer 2013; Genskow and Prokopy 2009).

The trend of state and federal governments devolving responsibility for watershed management to more regional and local actors (Andersson and Ostrom 2008) means that watershed groups are expected to pursue voluntary cooperation; self-generate their funding; develop cross-sectoral agreements; and engage place-based stakeholders, environmental nongovernmental organizations, and local governments in watershed management decision making (Sabatier et al. 2005). Pfeffer and Wagenet (2011, 111) provide recent evidence that many watershed management "communities of interest" provide a "powerful basis for successful negotiation of diverse interests into acceptable watershed management plans." Forty towns and villages in upstate New York were able to develop this community of interest, they found, by adopting common terms of reference, agreeing on physical and legal boundaries, and establishing standards of equity. Within this nexus, there is fertile ground for rural sociologists to study the evolution, success, and failures of these collaborative efforts.

Conclusions

Rural interests have often been marginalized when confronted by the circulation of urban-centered capital and manipulation by powerful urban interests, and nowhere is this clearer than in the case of water. Water continues to play a vital role in the identity of rural people and flows through cultural landscapes as part of social and governance arrangements, beliefs, practices, and economic and ecological conditions (Strang 2004, 5). Rural landscapes and communities are part of complex and interrelated socio-ecological systems, and understanding and adapting to twenty-first century challenges will increasingly require the insights and skills of rural sociologists to help bring diverse forms of knowledge and practical experiences together.

Rural sociologists study how rural areas develop, adapt, and transform in light of changing natural resource bases, policies, population shifts, land tenure arrangements, and environmental conditions and problems. They are in good positions to see linkages between the health of water systems and of agriculturalists, recreationists, property owners, town residents, and other community and landscape actors. We expect rural sociologists to play a critical role in examining the leverage of power and privilege in future water management decisions, especially as competition for water intensifies between rural and urban areas, upstream and downstream users, and across jurisdictional boundaries where inter-basin water transfers and new water infrastructure may be proposed.

Rural sociologists are often situated in interdisciplinary departments and engaged with those from other disciplines interested in rural social and biophysical processes. These connections place rural sociologists in positions to contribute to studies of intersections across climate change, water stress, and social justice. While work in these linked areas has recently focused on conditions in developing countries, rural sociologists will increasingly find social justice and water issues converging in the North American West, which is likely to face extreme aridity in the coming years (DuBuys 2011). Climate change (see

Morton and Rudel in this volume) intensifies many human-ecosystem dynamics of long-standing interest to rural sociologists, such as how farmers and others rural residents cope with drought, floods, invasive species, water shortages, threats to water quality, wetland and related biodiversity losses, and governmental struggles to delegate authority and responsibility for building better water-related infrastructure, regulatory systems, and watershed management organizations. We hope rural sociologists will interrogate the quality of implementation and outcomes of market-based policies designed to simultaneously manage water resources and promote or maintain economic growth, as these instruments dominate international rhetoric for water resource protection. Finally, we expect rural sociologists to contribute significantly by illuminating opportunities for water-related organizations to work together to create more socially just and ecologically sound water management systems.

References

Albrecht, D.E., and S.H. Murdock. 1986. "Natural Resource Availability and Social Change." *Sociological Inquiry* 56 (3): 381–95. http://dx.doi.org/10.1111/j.1475-682X.1986.tb00094.x.

Andersson, K.P., and E. Ostrom. 2008. "Analyzing Decentralized Resource Regimes from a Polycentric Perspective." *Policy Sciences* 41 (1): 71–93. http://dx.doi.org/10.1007/s11077-007-9055-6.

Arbuckle, J.G., Jr., C. Valdivia, A. Raedeke, J. Green, and J.S. Rikoon. 2009. "Non-operator Landowner Interest in Agroforestry Practices in Two Missouri Watersheds." *Agroforestry Systems* 75 (1): 73–82. http://dx.doi.org/10.1007/s10457-008-9131-8.

Arnold, C. 2009. "Water Privatization Trends in the United States: Human Rights, National Security, and Public Stewardship." *William and Mary Environmental Law and Policy Review* 33 (3): article 4. http://scholarship.law.wm.edu/wmelpr/vol33/iss3/4.

Bakker, K. 2003. "A Political Ecology of Water Privatization." *Studies in Political Economy* 70: 35–70.

Barham, E. 2010. "Ecological Boundaries as Community Boundaries: The Politics of Watersheds." *Society & Natural Resources* 14: 181–91.

Barry, J.M. 1997. *Rising Tide: The Great Mississippi Flood of 1927 and How it Changed America.* New York: Touchstone.

Bernstein, I. 2010. *The Lean Years: A History of the American Worker, 1920–1933.* Chicago: Haymarket Books.

Brasier, K., B. Lee, R. Stedman, and J. Weigle. 2011. "Local Champions Speak Out: Pennsylvania's Community Watershed Organizations." In *Pathways for Getting to Better Water Quality: The Citizen Effect*, ed. L.W. Morton and S.S. Brown, 133–44. New York: Springer. http://dx.doi.org/10.1007/978-1-4419-7282-8_11.

Brehm, J.M., D.K. Pasko, and B.W. Eisenhauer. July 2013. "Identifying Key Factors in Homeowner's Adoption of Water Quality Best Management Practices." *Environmental*

Management 52 (1): 113–22. http://dx.doi.org/10.1007/s00267-013-0056-2. Medline: 23609309.

Carlson, L.A. 1981. "Labor Supply, the Acquisition of Skills, and the Location of Southern Textile Mills, 1880–1900." *Journal of Economic History* 41 (1): 65–71. http://dx.doi.org/10.1017/S0022050700042777.

Clare, S., N. Krogman, L. Foote, and N. Lemphers. 2011. "Where is the Avoidance in the Implementation of Wetland Law and Policy?" *Wetlands Ecology and Management* 19 (2): 165–82. http://dx.doi.org/10.1007/s11273-011-9209-3.

Coleridge, S.T. 1956. "The Rime of the Ancient Mariner." In *English Romantic Poetry and Prose*, ed. R. Noyes, 392–401. New York: Oxford University Press.

Constance, D.H., J.S. Rikoon, and J.C. Ma. 1996. "Landlord Involvement in Environmental Decision-Making on Rented Missouri Cropland: Pesticide Use and Water Quality Issues." *Rural Sociology* 61 (4): 577–605. http://dx.doi.org/10.1111/j.1549-0831.1996.tb00635.x.

Crawford, S. 1988. *Mayordomo: Chronicle of an Acequia in Northern New Mexico.* Albuquerque: University of New Mexico Press.

Cronon, W. 1983. *Changes in the Land: Indians, Colonists, and the Ecology of New England.* New York: Hill and Wang.

Daily, G.C. 1997. *Nature's Services: Societal Dependence on Natural Ecosystems.* Washington, DC: Island Press.

de Fraiture, C., M. Giordano, and Y. Liao. 2008. "Biofuels and Implications for Agricultural Water Use: Blue Impacts of Green Energy." *Water Policy* 10 (S1): 67–81. http://dx.doi.org/10.2166/wp.2008.054.

Desbiens, C. 2004. "Producing North and South: A Political Geography of Hydro Development in Quebec." *Canadian Geographer* 48 (2): 101–18. http://dx.doi.org/10.1111/j.0008-3658.2004.00050.x.

DuBuys, W.E. 2011. *A Great Aridness: Climate Change and the Future of the American Southwest.* New York: Oxford University Press.

Ettenger, K. 1998. "A River That Was Once so Strong and Deep: Local Reflections on the East Main Diversion, James Bay Hydroelectric Project." In *Water, Culture, and Power: Local Struggles in a Global Context*, ed. J.M. Donahue and B.R. Johnston, 47–72. Washington, DC: Island Press.

Freeman, D.M. 2000. "Wicked Water Problems: Sociology and Local Water Organizations Addressing Water Resources Policy." *Journal of the American Water Resources Association* 36 (3): 483–91. http://dx.doi.org/10.1111/j.1752-1688.2000.tb04280.x.

Freudenburg, W.R., R. Gramling, S. Laska, and K.T. Erikson. 2009. *Catastrophe in the Making: The Engineering of Katrina and the Disasters of Tomorrow.* Washington, DC: Island Press.

Freudenburg, W.R., and T.R. Jones. 1991. "Attitudes and Stress in the Presence of Technological Risk: A Test of the Supreme Court Hypothesis." *Social Forces* 69: 1143–68.

Gasteyer, S. 2011. *Lessons for Rural Water Supply: Assessing Progress toward Sustainable Service Delivery.* The Hague: IRC International Water and Sanitation Centre.

Genskow, K., and L. Prokopy. 2009. "Lessons Learned in Developing Social Indicators for Regional Water Quality Management." *Society & Natural Resources* 23 (1): 83–91. http://dx.doi.org/10.1080/08941920802388961.

Getches, D. 2004. "Water Wrongs: Why Can't We Get It Right the First Time." *Environmental Law* (Northwestern School of Law) 34: 1–19.

Gibbons, P., and D.B. Lindenmayer. 2007. "Offsets for Land Clearing: No Net Loss of the Tail Wagging the Dog?" *Ecological Management & Restoration* 8 (1): 26–31. http://dx.doi.org/10.1111/j.1442-8903.2007.00328.x.

Gleick, P. 2000. "The Changing Water Paradigm: A Look at Twenty-First Century Water Resources Development." *Water International* 25 (1): 127–38. http://dx.doi.org/10.1080/02508060008686804.

Henkel, K.E., J.F. Dovidio, and S.L. Gaertner. 2006. "Institutional Discrimination, Individual Racism and Hurricane Katrina." *Analyses of Social Issues and Public Policy (ASAP)* 6 (1): 99–124. http://dx.doi.org/10.1111/j.1530-2415.2006.00106.x.

Hicks, G.A. 2010. "Acequias of the South-Western US in Tension with State Water Laws." In *Out of the Mainstream: Water Rights, Politics and Identity*, ed. R. Boelens, D. Getches, and A. Guevara-Gil, 223–34. London: Earthscan.

Howitt, R. 2001. *Rethinking Resource Management: Justice, Sustainability and Indigenous Peoples.* London: Routledge. http://dx.doi.org/10.4324/9780203221020.

Hyde, J. 2010. "Flood Control and the Growth Machine in Des Moines." *Cities in the 21st Century* 2 (1): article 5. http://digitalcommons.macalester.edu/cities/vol2/iss1/5.

Jacobs, J., and C.W. Howe. 2005. "Key Issues and Experience in U.S. Water Services Privatization." *International Journal of Water Resources Development* 21 (1): 89–98. http://dx.doi.org/10.1080/0790062042000316820.

Jackson-Smith, D., E. de la Hoz, M. Halling, J. McEvoy, and J. Horsburgh. 2010. "Measuring Conservation Program Best Management Practice Implementation and Maintenance at the Watershed Scale." *Journal of Soil and Water Conservation* 65 (6): 413–23. http://dx.doi.org/10.2489/jswc.65.6.413.

Jacquet, J., and R.C. Stedman. 2011. "Natural Gas Landowner Coalitions in New York State: Emerging Benefits of Collective Natural Resource Management." *Journal of Rural Social Sciences* 26: 62–91.

Keenan, S.P., and R.S. Krannich. 1997. "The Social Context of Perceived Drought Vulnerability." *Rural Sociology* 62 (1): 69–88. http://dx.doi.org/10.1111/j.1549-0831.1997.tb00645.x.

Keenan, S.P., R.S. Krannich, and M.S. Walker. 1999. "Public Perceptions of Water Transfers and Markets: Describing Differences in Water Use Communities." *Society & Natural Resources* 12 (4): 279–92. http://dx.doi.org/10.1080/089419299279605.

Krannich, R., A.E. Luloff, and D.R. Field. 2011. *People, Places and Landscapes: Social Change in High Amenity Rural Areas.* New York: Springer.

Lane, M.B. 2003. "Participation, Decentralization, and Civil Society: Indigenous Rights and Democracy in Environmental Planning." *Journal of Planning Education and Research* 22 (4): 360–73. http://dx.doi.org/10.1177/0739456X03022004003.

Little, J.B. 2009. "The Ogallala Aquifer: Saving a Vital US Water Source." *Scientific American*, 30 March. http://www.scientificamerican.com/article.cfm?id=the-ogallala-aquifer.

McKenney, B.A., and J.M. Kiesecker. January 2010. "Policy Development for Biodiversity Offsets: A Review of Offset Frameworks." *Environmental Management* 45 (1): 165–76. http://dx.doi.org/10.1007/s00267-009-9396-3. Medline:19924472.

Malewitz, J. 2012. "More Water for Las Vegas Means More Resentment in Rural Areas." *Stateline*, 4 January. http://www.governing.com/blogs/politics/more-water-for-las-vegas-means-more-resentment-in-rural-areas.html.

McCully, P. 2001. *Silenced Rivers: The Ecology and Politics of Large Dams.* London: Zed Books.

Meinzen-Dick, R., and C. Ringler. 2008. "Water Reallocation: Drivers, Challenges, Threats, and Solutions for the Poor." *Journal of Human Development* 9 (1): 47–64. http://dx.doi.org/10.1080/14649880701811393.

Mollinga, P. 2008. "Water, Politics and Development: Framing a Political Sociology of Water Resources Management." *Water Alternatives* 1: 7–23.

Morton, L.W. 2011. "Citizen Involvement." In *Pathways for Getting to Better Water Quality: The Citizen Effect*, ed. L.W. Morton and S.S. Brown, 15–28. New York: Springer. http://dx.doi.org/10.1007/978-1-4419-7282-8_2.

Morton, L.W., and S. Padgitt. April 2005. "Selecting Socio-economic Metrics for Watershed Management." *Environmental Monitoring and Assessment* 103 (1–3): 83–98. http://dx.doi.org/10.1007/s10661-005-6855-z. Medline:15861988.

Morton, L.W., T. Selfa, and T.A. Becerra. 2011. "Shared Leadership for Watershed Management." In *Pathways for Getting to Better Water Quality: The Citizen Effect*, ed. L.W. Morton and S.S. Brown, 29–39. New York: Springer. http://dx.doi.org/10.1007/978-1-4419-7282-8_3.

Nash, J. 2007. "Consuming Interests: Water, Rum, and Coca-Cola from Ritual Propitiation to Corporate Expropriation in Highland Chiapas." *Cultural Anthropology* 22 (4): 621–39. http://dx.doi.org/10.1525/can.2007.22.4.621.

Norgaard, R.B. 2010. "Ecosystem Services: From Eye-Opening Metaphor to Complexity Blinder." *Ecological Economics* 69 (6): 1219–27. http://dx.doi.org/10.1016/j.ecolecon.2009.11.009.

Nowak, P., S. Bowen, and P.E. Cabot. 2006. "Disproportionality as a Framework for Linking Social and Biophysical Systems." *Society & Natural Resources* 19 (2): 153–73. http://dx.doi.org/10.1080/08941920500394816.

Nowak, P., and P. Korsching. 1988. "The Human Dimension of Soil and Water Conservation: Historical and Methodological Perspective." In *Advances in Soil and Water Conservation*, ed. F.J. Pierce and W.W. Frye, 159–84. Chelsea, MI: Ann Arbor Press.

Nye, D.E. 1999. *Consuming Power: A Social History of American Energies.* Cambridge, MA: MIT Press. http://dx.doi.org/10.1109/TPC.1999.768169.

O'Neil, K.M. 2006. *Rivers by Design: State Power and the Origin of U.S. Flood Control.* Durham, NC: Duke University Press. http://dx.doi.org/10.1215/9780822387862.

Osborn, S.G., A. Vengosh, N.R. Warner, and R.B. Jackson. 17 May 2011. "Methane Contamination of Drinking Water Accompanying Gas-Well Drilling and Hydraulic Fracturing." *Proceedings of the National Academy of Sciences of the United States of America* 108 (20): 8172–76. http://dx.doi.org/10.1073/pnas.1100682108. Medline:21555547.

Petrova, V. 2005. "At the Frontiers of the Rush for Blue Gold: Water Privatization and the Human Right to Water." *Brooklyn Journal of International Law* 31: 535–76.

Pfeffer, M., and L. Wagenet. 2011. "Communities of Interest and the Negotiation of Watershed Management." In *Pathways to Getting Better Water Quality: The Citizen Effect*, ed.

L.W. Morton and S.S. Brown, 109–19. New York: Springer. http://dx.doi.org/10.1007/978-1-4419-7282-8_9.

Picou, J.S., and D. Gill. 2000. "The Exxon Valdez Disaster as Localized Environmental Catastrophe: Dissimilarities to Risk Society Theory." In *Risk in the Modern Age: Social Theory, Science and Environmental Decision-Making*, ed. M.J. Cohen, 143–70. New York: St. Martin's Press.

Richter, B.D., S. Postel, C. Revenga, T. Scudder, B. Lehner, A. Churchill, and M. Chow. 2010. "Lost in Development's Shadow: The Downstream Human Consequences of Dams." *Water Alternatives* 3: 14–42.

Roy, A. 1999. "The Greater Common Good." *Friends of the River Narmada*. Accessed 10 March 2012. http://www.narmada.org/gcg/gcg.html.

Sabatier, P.A., W. Focht, M. Lubell, Z. Trachtenberg, A. Vedlitz, and M. Matlock. 2005. *Swimming Upstream: Collaborative Approaches to Watershed Management*. Cambridge, MA: MIT Press.

Salamon, S., R.L. Farnsworth, and J.A. Rendziak. 1998. "Is Locally Led Conservation Planning Working? A Farm Town Case Study." *Rural Sociology* 63 (2): 214–34. http://dx.doi.org/10.1111/j.1549-0831.1998.tb00672.x.

Schewe, R.L., D.R. Field, D.J. Frosch, G. Clendenning, and D. Jensen. 2012. *Condos in the Woods: The Growth of Seasonal and Retirement Homes in Northern Wisconsin*. Madison: University of Wisconsin Press.

Scudder, T. 2006. *The Future of Large Dams: Dealing with Social, Environmental, Institutional and Political Costs*. Sterling: Earthscan.

Sharp, J.S., and M.B. Smith. 2003. "Social Capital and Farming and the Rural-Urban Interface: The Importance of Nonfarmer and Farmer Relations." *Agricultural Systems* 76 (3): 913–27. http://dx.doi.org/10.1016/S0883-2927(02)00083-5.

Stedman, R., B. Lee, K. Brasier, J.L. Weigle, and F. Higdon. 2009. "Cleaning up Water? Or Building Rural Community? Community Watershed Organizations in Pennsylvania." *Rural Sociology* 74 (2): 178–200. http://dx.doi.org/10.1111/j.1549-0831.2009.tb00388.x.

Strang, V. 2004. *The Meaning of Water*. Oxford: Berg.

Strang, V. 2009. *Gardening the World: Agency, Identity and the Ownership of Water*. New York: Berghahn Books.

Swyngedouw, E. 1999. "Modernity and Hybridity: Nature, Regeneracionismo, and the Production of the Spanish Waterscape, 1890–1930." *Annals of the Association of American Geographers* 89 (3): 443–65. http://dx.doi.org/10.1111/0004-5608.00157.

Swyngedouw, E. 2004. *Social Power and the Urbanization of Water: Flows of Power*. Oxford: Oxford University Press.

Theodori, G.L. 2009. "Paradoxical Perceptions of Problems Associated with Unconventional Natural Gas Development." *Southern Rural Sociology* 24: 97–117.

Waldram, J.B. 1988. *As Long as the Rivers Run: Hydroelectric Development and Native Communities in Western Canada*. Winnipeg: University of Manitoba Press.

Walker, S., A.L. Brower, R.T. Stephens, and W.G. Lee. 2009. "Why Bartering Biodiversity Fails." *Conservation Letters* 2 (4): 149–57. http://dx.doi.org/10.1111/j.1755-263X.2009.00061.x.

Walter, R.C., and D.J. Merritts. 18 January 2008. "Natural Streams and the Legacy of Water-Powered Mills." *Science* 319 (5,861): 299–304. http://dx.doi.org/10.1126/science.1151716. Medline:18202284.

Webler, T., and S. Tuler. 2001. "Public Participation in Watershed Management Planning: Views on Process from People in the Field." *Human Ecology Review* 8: 29–39.

Wilcox, J.D., M.B. Gotkowitz, K.R. Bradbury, and J.M. Bahr. 2010. "Using Groundwater Models to Evaluate Strategies for Drinking-Water Protection in Rural Subdivisions." *Journal of the American Planning Association. American Planning Association* 76 (3): 295–304. http://dx.doi.org/10.1080/01944361003742403.

Wittfogel, K. 1957. *Oriental Despotism: A Comparative Study of Total Power.* New Haven, CT: Yale University Press.

Woods, M. 2011. *Rural.* Abingdon, UK: Routledge.

CHAPTER 11

Resource Dependency in Rural America: Continuities and Change

Richard S. Krannich, Brian Gentry, A.E. Luloff, and Peter G. Robertson

Introduction

Over the past century, rural America has been confronted by broad-ranging economic, demographic, and social changes linked to natural resource conditions. Historically, relationships with resource-based industries have exerted considerable influence on social, cultural, and economic structures, and local as well as regional development conditions. However, technological changes affecting resource extraction, processing and utilization, shifting priorities regarding land and resource uses, restructuring of resource production and processing industries, and increased embeddedness of resource production and consumption in the global economy have altered these relationships. At the start of the twenty-first century there are important continuities and substantial changes in the nature and extent of "resource dependency" in rural America.

The Multifaceted Nature of Resource Dependency

For years, rural sociologists have focused on problems associated with reliance on economic activities tied to natural resource extraction and processing. Definitions and strategies for operationalizing the resource dependency concept have been highly variable. Most often, dependency is conceptualized as involving high levels of employment and/or income derived from resource extraction and processing industries. With respect to operationalization, localized areas (usually counties) are typically classified as resource dependent when at least 10 to 20 percent of income or employment is derived from such industries (Cook and Mizer 1994; Norton, Howze, and Robinson 2003; Stedman, Parkins, and Beckley 2005).

However, approaches focused solely on employment and income fail to capture other important linkages. Additional economic connections to resource conditions also merit consideration, including reliance by local governments on tax revenues or other fiscal inputs from resource industries, economic activity involving non-consumptive resource uses such as recreation and tourism, engagement by residents in subsistence activities, or the effects of natural amenities on economic growth and development (Haynes 2003; Stedman et al. 2007). In addition, some analysts argue for a focus on non-economic linkages, such as those involving place attachments, occupational identities, and community identities (Petrzelka, Krannich, and Brehm 2006; Stedman et al. 2007).

Regardless of whether the focus is on economic or socio-cultural factors, it is important to acknowledge that resource dependence conditions vary considerably across regions, resource types, and production sectors (Stedman, Parkins, and Beckley 2005). Moreover, conditions associated with dependency vary across more or less localized units of analysis, reflecting the "geographically-nested nature of dependence at different spatial scales" (Beckley 1998, 101). Put simply, resource dependency is a complex phenomenon that varies considerably across units of analysis, regions, specific commodity and non-commodity linkages, and time.

Consequences of Dependency

Sociological analyses of resource dependency have highlighted a number of vulnerabilities linked to reliance on resource-based industries. At least in the short term, high wages routinely paid to those working in mining, logging, and other extractive industries would seemingly represent important opportunities. The availability of employment linked to resource production can be especially appealing where good jobs are generally hard to come by. For example, an oil production boom now occurring across the northern Great Plains has created opportunities for jobs paying $100,000 a year or more in what was until recently a spatially isolated agricultural area with few employment opportunities and fewer chances to earn a livable wage. Nevertheless, the consequences associated with reliance on resource-based economies appear to be more accurately characterized by a range of threats that over the long term outweigh the benefits of employment growth and other economic opportunities. Analyses focusing on social and economic conditions in resource-dependent areas have repeatedly documented a variety of disruptions that result from sharp fluctuations and long-term declines in extraction-based employment, high rates of unemployment and underemployment, and disproportionately high levels of poverty

(Freudenburg 1992; Freudenburg and Gramling 1994; Stedman, Patriquin, and Parkins 2011).

Although sociologists have outlined several explanations for these patterns (Humphrey et al. 1993; Freudenburg 1992), the observation that "it is difficult to see much of a silver lining in the gathering gloom of the economic prospects of extractive industries" (Freudenburg and Gramling 1994, 19) has been widely supported. Pessimistic assessments of the consequences linked to resource-based economies are not the sole province of sociologists—economists addressing the "curse of natural resources" have also documented tendencies for resource dependence to be associated with slow economic growth and limited long-term economic opportunity, both cross-nationally and in rural America (Sachs and Warner 2001; James and Aadland 2011).

Central to the challenges confronting resource-dependent areas are cycles of growth and decline that destabilize economic and social structures and contribute to non-sustainable development patterns. Widespread job losses and episodes of rapid decline occur where commercially viable reserves of exhaustible resources, such as minerals or slow-to-renew resources like mature timber stands, are depleted. Major ecological events, such as the contemporary beetle infestation of forests throughout the Rocky Mountain region, can cause rapid declines in resource-based economies. Sudden destabilization can also result from corporate decisions to shut down in some areas and shift production to locations that promise greater profitability, a pattern reinforced by corporate consolidation and the dominance of many resource industries by a handful of large, often internationally active firms (Sinclair, Bailey, and Dubois 2003). Government restriction of resource extraction in some areas, often in response to concerns about environmental protection or ecological sustainability, can have similar destabilizing consequences, particularly where the resource base is managed as public rather than private property.

While sharp and unanticipated fluctuations are certainly an important facet of the instabilities associated with dependency, it is important to recognize that declines in resource-based economies also occur more gradually. Increased mechanization and the application of new extraction and processing technologies allow for expanded production even as the need for labor shrinks (Howze, Robinson, and Norton 2003). Long-term trends toward instability and decline also result from what Freudenburg (1992) describes as a "cost-price squeeze." As easily accessed resources are used, the costs of extracting increasingly hard-to-access deposits and reserves inevitably increase. Meanwhile, competition from suppliers operating in an increasingly globalized system of extraction and production limits commodity price increases as production shifts to lower-cost settings. As a result, many areas that once experienced a resource-based boom descend into stagnation and decline.

Conversely, new exploration and extraction technologies can foster renewed resource production in locations that previously boomed, then declined as deposits accessed via earlier technologies were exhausted. For example, over the past twenty years gold mining has surged in parts of Nevada that have a long boom-bust history, because chemical leaching processes now allow extraction of microscopic gold particles from low-grade ore that previously had no value. Such technologies can spur a revival of resource extraction in areas once assumed to be played out, or stimulate production in locations where lower-grade or harder-to-access resource deposits had remained undiscovered or untapped. This is precisely the issue affecting a number of areas across the United States today, with an explosion of shale-based oil and natural gas extraction emerging as rural America's newest "buffalo hunt" for employment and economic development opportunities (see Kinchy et al. in this volume).

Instability also results from shifting patterns of use involving particular resources across time. As public consumption preferences, industrial use patterns, and/or regulatory requirements change, demand for some resources can surge while demand for others wanes. For example, during the first half of the twentieth century the virtual disappearance of coal-fueled home heating contributed to demand shifts that deepened levels of economic and social despair throughout Appalachia. More recent shifts in the range of commonly used building materials, along with a changing regulatory environment that reduced timber harvests from many national forest lands, have contributed to stagnation and decline across portions of the Pacific Northwest and northern Rocky Mountain regions long characterized by dependency on logging and milling operations (Sherman 2009). Meanwhile, demand for wood products has been met by a shift of timber production and processing activities to other locales in the United States—most notably the Southeast region—and offshore locations (Howze, Robinson, and Norton 2003; Norton, Howze, and Robinson 2003).

The instabilities that result when any one or a combination of these forces are present lead to a broad range of what are generally adverse consequences affecting the well-being of resource-dependent areas and the people who live and work in them. Despite the prospect of widely available employment opportunities and high wages during up-cycle periods, the unpredictability and insecurity of resource-based economic opportunities contribute over the longer term to lower overall wage levels, fewer benefits, and higher unemployment and underemployment. Such problems are exacerbated by tendencies for people and communities to over-adapt to the readily available employment opportunities, higher wages, tax revenues, and economic growth opportunities present when extraction and processing activities are running full tilt (Freudenburg 1992). An example of individual level over-adaptation occurs when, confronted by the chance to earn high wages in resource-based jobs requiring little educational or occupational training, young adults forego further education to take advantage of such opportunities. At the collective level, communities often over-adapt by failing to plan for the almost-inevitable downturns in resource-based economic activity, or by forgoing opportunities to pursue development options that might help establish more diversified and sustainable local economies. By pursuing what may in the immediate term seem to be adaptive strategies that hinge on continued resource production, those making such choices decrease the likelihood they will be prepared to pursue alternative paths when a resource-based boom ends, jobs disappear, revenues decline, and an all-but-inevitable bust ensues. Such outcomes help to account for the well-documented spatial coincidence of long-term conditions of resource dependency and the concentration of rural poverty (Bliss and Bailey 2005). Perhaps the best exemplar of this in the United States is Appalachia, exploited initially for its timber resources and subsequently one of America's most valuable and, at the same time, most heavily scarred coal-mining regions. After over a century of essentially uninterrupted resource dependency, Appalachia remains one of America's most clearly defined areas of persistent rural poverty (Duncan 1992).

When faced with such circumstances, rural people and communities appear vulnerable to a variety of maladaptive responses. At the individual level, feelings of hopelessness, resignation, and fatalism serve as barriers to the motivation and action needed to pursue education, job training, relocation, or other changes that can improve life chances. At the community level, the persistence of stagnation and decline contribute to an erosion of financial, built, human, and social capital. Such conditions create substantial barriers to collective actions that might help communities pursue efforts to confront the problems of underdevelopment (Luloff and Krannich 2002). At the same time, resource-dependent areas faced with decline typically support almost any development opportunity, including those that might be bad deals. Examples include the siting of hazardous and noxious facilities, projects that threaten ecological or socioeconomic sustainability, and various dependency substitution strategies that may reinforce instability and vulnerability even as new forms of resource-based development unfold (Krannich and Luloff 1991).

A substantial body of research indicates that resource dependency represents a threat to multiple facets of social well-being. In cases involving large-scale resource extraction, such as major mining operations or oil and gas field developments, rapid population expansion associated with a spike in labor demand during exploration, extraction, and construction periods often creates boom growth effects. This is particularly true when development occurs in remote locations with small populations and little or no access to a regional workforce. In the short term at least, growth resulting from rapid expansion of resource-based developments can overwhelm the capacities of public and private sector organizations to provide the expanded infrastructure and services—housing, utilities, public safety, emergency response, medical care, retail outlets, and many other local services and facilities—that are desperately needed in locales where populations may double or triple within just a few years.

There is considerable evidence that an array of social disruptions accompany such growth. Studies have documented boom-induced declines in social integration, interaction with neighbors, levels of social participation, and community satisfaction (Brown, Dorius, and Krannich 2005). Freudenburg (1986) describes a reduction in the local "density of acquaintanceship" in boomtown settings, with associated deterioration of interpersonal trust, reduced "helping" behavior, and decreased effectiveness of informal social control. Although evidence regarding increases in crime, delinquency, and other forms of social deviance has been mixed, there is strong evidence that fear of crime increases substantially in areas affected by boom growth (Freudenburg and Jones 1991; Smith, Krannich, and Hunter 2001). Overall, both comparative and longitudinal analyses make it clear there is a significant deterioration in various dimensions of social well-being when boom growth occurs. However, there is also evidence of recovery over the longer term, as residents and organizations adapt to altered conditions and as rapid growth gives way to periods of relative stability or even decline (Brown, Dorius, and Krannich 2005; Smith, Krannich, and Hunter 2001).

Although much of the literature linking resource dependency to a deterioration of economic and social well-being has focused on areas affected by mining and energy extraction, there is also a long tradition of research addressing connections between well-being and forest dependence. While logging, milling, and processing of wood products are generally not associated with the boom growth effects accompanying some extractive industries, areas reliant on forest-based industries encounter substantial instabilities associated with market fluctuations, resource depletion, adoption of labor-saving technologies, shifting regulatory and resource management priorities, corporate restructuring, and regional as well as global shifts in the locations of timber supplies and processing activities. In particular, reliance on forest-based industries has been shown to have negative consequences with respect to income levels, unemployment, and poverty rates.

While there is general support for the notion that forest dependence contributes to adverse well-being outcomes, such effects vary considerably across specific sectors of the forest products industry, regions, time, and well-being dimensions. For example, Overdest and Green (1995) find that while dependence on "core" forest industries involving highly capitalized pulp and paper firms was positively associated with per capita income in rural Georgia, dependence on smaller, labor-intensive periphery forest industries had insignificant or negative income effects. Similarly, Stedman, Parkins, and Beckley (2005) report that while the pulp production sector in Canada was positively related to income levels, dependence on other forest industry sectors was associated with lower income, lower educational attainment, higher poverty, and higher unemployment. They also report substantial variation across provinces in the nature and strength of relationships between sector-specific dimensions of dependence and various well-being indicators, a finding consistent with observations about regional differences across timber-dependent regions in the United States (Norton, Howze, and Robinson 2003). The nature of timber dependence and its socioeconomic consequences have also been shown to vary across time, revealing additional complexities in how these relationships evolve in conjunction with changing industry structures, local and regional socioeconomic conditions, and broader patterns of social and economic change (Howze, Robinson, and Norton 2003; Sinclair, Bailey, and Dubois 2003).

Resource Dependency in the Twenty-First Century: Continuities and Changes

Now that we have entered the second decade of the twenty-first century, it seems important to reassess how, where, and why resource-based activities may be affecting social change and well-being across rural America. To a considerable extent, the literature addressing challenges accompanying resource dependency evolved from research conducted over the last several decades of the twentieth century. Without question there are important continuities with respect to how rural areas are affected by reliance on resource-based economies. However, there is also evidence of pattern shifts that have considerable potential to alter those relationships into the foreseeable future.

In some ways, resource dependency is less evident across contemporary rural America than was the case only a few decades ago. Expansions and relocations of high-tech, manufacturing, and service-sector industries previously concentrated in urban areas have contributed to economic diversification in many rural areas (McGranahan 2003). Such diversification has reduced reliance on resource-based economic activities in some settings, even when resource production remains important to the local economy. At the same time, many areas still rely heavily on resource extraction and processing industries. In some situations, the dominance of resource-based economies has emerged recently, while elsewhere such patterns have been evident for many years. In both cases the conditions and consequences of resource dependency at the start of the twenty-first century appear similar to those rural sociologists have previously documented.

Pockets of resource dependency remain evident across all regions of the United States. Using 15 percent or more of average annual earnings derived from mining (including minerals and oil and gas extraction) during 1998 to 2000 as their classification criterion, the USDA Economic Research Service (ERS) identified 113 nonmetropolitan counties (5.5 percent of nonmetro counties in the nation) as mining dependent (Economic Research Service 2012). Among these are numerous counties in Appalachia, where reliance on the coal industry and associated patterns of unemployment, underemployment, and poverty have been firmly entrenched for decades. Also included are a number of counties in east Texas, where oil production has been widespread since the start of the twentieth century. Other examples include portions of Nevada characterized by long-term reliance on precious minerals mining; the Powder River Basin of southeastern Montana and northern Wyoming, which since the 1970s have been heavily reliant on large-scale strip mining of coal; and portions of southwestern Wyoming, northeastern Utah, and northwestern Colorado, where extensive oil and natural gas development during the 1970s and early 1980s has been followed by a surge in exploration and extraction over the past decade.

The ERS typology does not include a classification of counties dependent on the timber industry, and our literature search has not revealed a national-level classification of timber-dependent areas for periods that encompass or extend beyond 2000. Certainly the extent of timber dependence has declined in the United States in recent decades, as has occurred in Canada (Stedman, Patriquin, and Parkins 2011). Yet it is also certain that as the end of the twentieth century arrived, some parts of rural America were substantially dependent on timber production and processing. Research comparing timber dependence in 1990 across states in the Northwest (Idaho, Oregon, and Washington) and the Southeast (Alabama, Georgia, and Mississippi) identified only seventeen counties in the Northwest states, but forty-six counties in the Southeast, where 20 percent or more of employment was in forest-based industries (Norton, Howze, and Robinson 2003). By the turn of the century the regional concentration of timber dependence had clearly shifted, with the Southeast emerging as the center of America's pulp and paper production industries (Sinclair, Bailey, and Dubois

2003, 73). Meanwhile, across much of the Pacific Northwest a century of regional and local reliance on the forest products industry left many areas ill-prepared to deal with major downturns in timber harvest and processing (Robbins 1985).

Since the start of the twenty-first century, the United States has witnessed a major surge in domestic energy development, driven largely by exploration for and extraction of oil and natural gas. This can be traced to some familiar forces and themes—including the effects of rising commodity prices linked to global demand along with the irrepressible corporate drive to expand production and market share that lies at the foundation of what sociologists refer to as the treadmill of production (Gould, Pellow, and Schnaiberg 2008). Much as occurred during the 1970s, the push for increased domestic energy production is legitimized and facilitated by a political mantra focused on reducing America's dependence on sometimes-unfriendly nations as suppliers of energy and other natural resources (Graetz 2012).

Although there are important distinctions between current energy development patterns and those experienced during the 1970s and 1980s, there also are important similarities. In particular, there are continuities involving the disruptive consequences of large-scale resource development, especially in locales impacted by boom growth. Sparsely populated and often spatially remote areas continue to be prime targets for resource extraction, and continue to experience social and economic ills linked to the effects of dependency. In the oft-quoted words of New York Yankees catcher Yogi Berra, reports of growth-induced problems accompanying the current surge in US energy development suggest that "it's déjà vu all over again" regarding the effects of this contemporary energy boom. Media reports focusing on areas now experiencing rapid expansion of oil and natural gas extraction highlight unmanageable population growth accompanying workforce in-migration, along with a wide-ranging list of social and economic problems. Concerns about inadequacies of infrastructure and services include a shortage of housing and inflated housing costs, deterioration of roads impacted by truck traffic, schools stretched beyond physical and fiscal capacity, and shortfalls in public safety and health care services. There are widespread reports of increased crime, with high-profile crimes like the 2012 kidnapping and murder of an eastern Montana school teacher fueling public fears about boom town crime and violence. In every respect, such reports mirror the substance as well as the levels of alarm evident in earlier accounts of social disruption that became a focus of sociological and policy attention during the western energy boom of the 1970s and early 1980s.

Forces of Change Affecting Resource Dependency in Contemporary Rural America

At least three major forces appear to be altering the conditions of resource dependency in rural America: (1) the effects of new technologies on the nature and locations of resource production activities; (2) shifting societal and political priorities that fuel demand for "clean" or "green" resource uses, particularly those involving energy production; and (3) the expanding influence of globalization on levels and patterns of resource production and consumption.

New Extractive Technologies

As we discussed above, technological changes have dramatically reduced labor demand in most resource-based industries, while creating new capacities to profitably extract or harvest resources that were previously inaccessible or not commercially viable. At the start of the twenty-first century, the effects of technological change in resource production are nowhere more evident than in the arena of oil and natural gas production (see Kinchy et al. in this volume). Among the most important of these innovations are directional and horizontal drilling methods that allow greater precision in accessing deep geologic strata containing oil and gas deposits. Directional drilling is often combined with hydraulic fracturing, or "fracking"—a process of pumping large quantities of water, sand, and chemicals under high pressure to fracture underlying geologic formations, allowing oil and gas to flow to the wellbore for collection.

Directional drilling and fracking have provided access to previously unrecoverable resources from oil and gas-holding shale, coal bed methane, and tight sand formations across much of the United States, and in the process altered the spatial distribution of resource-based development. Many areas affected by the current surge in oil and gas extraction have not previously experienced any type of resource-based boom, and others have not witnessed significant resource development for many years. Areas where unconventional oil and gas resources are now undergoing especially active development include the Marcellus shale region in Pennsylvania, New York, Ohio, Maryland, and West Virginia, the Barnett and Eagle Ford shales in Texas, the Bakken shales in western North Dakota and eastern Montana, and the Uinta-Piceance shales in Colorado and Utah.

To date relatively few social science analyses have focused on these new patterns of energy development, but available research highlights an array of negative impacts consistent with media reports and earlier studies of resource dependency and boom growth. Concerns about social effects tend to focus on changes in the quality of life for residents whose communities are impacted by an influx of temporary workers and rapid population growth (Jacquet 2012). Because much development is occurring in areas with primarily private land ownership, concerns are also evident regarding divisions and conflicts among neighbors when some receive financial gains through leasing or selling land and mineral rights while others experience negative effects accompanying production processes and rapid growth (Braiser et al. 2011). There are also substantial apprehensions about deterioration of environmental quality, overburdened public infrastructure and services, housing shortages, and changes in land use (Theodori 2009; Schafft, Borlu, and Glenna 2013). Environmental and health concerns include possible contamination of underground and surface water from the fracking process; depletion of water resources; reduced air quality from trucks, drill rigs, and compressor stations; disturbance effects on habitat and wildlife; discontent over changes in land use and the visual landscape; the brightness of nighttime lighting and flaring gas; and noise associated with drilling and production activities (Braiser et al. 2011; Jacquet 2012; Theodori 2009).

Environmentalization and the Push for Renewable Energy

Twenty years ago, a renowned rural sociologist wrote of the effects of environmentalization on rural America. According to Buttel (1992), largely urban-based public interests, priorities, and policies—particularly those associated with the pursuit of more environmentally friendly resource utilization practices—are exerting substantial and growing influence on rural-area land and resource use and development practices. The effects of this environmentalization process can be linked to a number of shifts in US resource use and development patterns, including in particular the virtual elimination of timber harvests from federal lands across much of the Pacific Northwest and northern Rockies regions, along with restrictions on or closure of mining operations in some environmentally sensitive or high-amenity locales.

Currently the effects of environmentalization on US resource use policies and trends are perhaps most clearly seen in the arena of electric power production. Growing concerns about emissions from coal-fired power plants and their effects on air quality and climate change have spurred new regulatory requirements to reduce emission levels. Those changes have led to the closure or planned closure of many older electric generating stations and a nationwide surge toward development of utility-scale renewable energy (primarily wind power) facilities. The closure of coal-fired power plants built decades ago in rural areas, most often to serve the needs of distant urban areas, will likely create considerable hardship in places that became economically dependent on those installations when jobs disappear and taxes paid to local governments evaporate. Meanwhile, rapid expansion of renewable energy developments poses both opportunities and threats to other rural areas.

As with the recent expansion of natural gas production, development of renewable energy systems has been spurred in part by technological changes, in part by calls for energy independence, and perhaps most importantly by concerns over the effects of fossil fuel emissions on air quality and climate change. Utility-scale wind power facilities are now scattered over much of the nation, with the largest concentrations located across a swath of the Great Plains stretching from North Dakota to Texas, portions of New England and the upper Midwest, much of the Intermountain West, and California. Utility-scale solar energy projects are also expanding rapidly but remain few in number, with most located or proposed for development in Arizona, Nevada, and California (Energy Information Administration 2012a). Growth in non-hydro power generation, primarily involving wind systems, has occurred very quickly. From 2005 to 2009, wind-based generating capacity in the United States increased by an average of 40 percent annually, and grew an additional 27 percent from 2010 to 2011. From 2006 through 2011, 36 percent of electric power capacity additions involved wind systems, and forecasts suggest wind generation levels will at least double by 2035 (Energy Information Administration 2012a; 2012b).

Expansion of such installations across rural America seems unlikely to generate many of the economic and social vulnerabilities associated with resource dependency, for several reasons. Short-term boom effects and related strains on local communities may accompany the arrival of a construction-phase workforce when installation of wind turbines or solar arrays and transmission facilities is underway. However, such boom (and subsequent bust) consequences are limited and short lived, since even large wind and solar installations can be built in a year or less. Furthermore, because these facilities create few operation-phase jobs (often fewer than twenty even at large installations), they will not create high levels of local-area employment that can contribute to dependency and economic vulnerability.

While employment linked to alternative energy systems falls well below levels typically associated with resource dependency, other economic effects may be of greater consequence. Where facilities are built on private lands, lease payments can become a key source of income for some landowners. In settings characterized by small populations, limited other income sources, and development of renewable facilities on parcels held by multiple owners, lease-based income could comprise a substantial portion of total income at a localized level. In addition, large renewable energy installations have in some contexts been a major boon with respect to local tax revenues. Research by two of this chapter's authors reveals that for one rural Utah county taxes generated by a wind power facility comprised one-third of total county revenue in the first full year of operation (Robertson and Krannich 2013). Such fiscal effects reinforce what are often positive expectations regarding the development benefits of renewable facilities, and can represent a financial windfall for rural areas where tax revenues are often severely limited. At that same time, they can contribute to a different form of economic dependency for local governments. In particular, such fiscal "opportunities" may create longer-term vulnerabilities or threats if cash-strapped rural counties and communities come to rely heavily on revenues from these facilities, since the flow of funds is likely to decline or disappear altogether as facilities age, the taxable value of capital equipment declines, and new technologies make some installations obsolete (Slattery et al. 2012).

Overall, results from attitudinal studies reveal broad-based public support for renewable energy development (Ansolabehere and Konisky 2012). Nevertheless, such facilities are not entirely benign. Major issues of concern associated with wind farm installations include effects on visual aesthetics, noise effects, disturbance of migratory patterns of birds and other wildlife, wildlife losses from turbine strikes and habitat fragmentation, the permanence of landscape alterations, potential displacement of or conflicts with current or future land uses, and the inconsistency of such changes with place identities and heritage values (Pasqualetti 2011; Robertson and Krannich 2013; Slattery et al. 2012). Where concerns about these and other threats become widespread, it is likely that controversy and community conflict will emerge, with adverse consequences for both individual and social well-being.

The Expanding Influence of Globalization

Finally, it is important to consider how the forces of globalization influence resource-based development and resource dependency. The increasingly international integration of commodity production, processing, and distribution systems; the ever-expanding influence of multinational corporations and vertically integrated production systems in the spatial distribution of resource development; the effects of international trade policies enacted by national governments; the transnational competition for market share, employment, and economic development opportunities; and growing global demand for raw materials and processed goods all combine to alter the occurrence and persistence of resource dependency and its consequences (see McMichael 1996).

The embedded nature of natural resource industries in the global economy has important implications for resource-dependent areas across rural America. Control over resource production by extra-local corporations has long been a source of instability and vulnerability in resource dependent areas, and the increasingly global reach of the world's largest resource production companies has exacerbated those vulnerabilities. Engagement of multinational corporations in resource production activities worldwide has contributed to the closure of US mines and processing facilities as production shifts toward international settings where labor and other costs are often considerably lower. For example, in recent years China has dominated the world market in tungsten production, contributing to the closure of all tungsten mining operations in the United States. Similarly, potash production has shifted to primarily international sources, with 80 percent of potash-based fertilizer products used in US agriculture now imported (Huang 2004). Such shifts toward global sourcing of resource commodities do, in some instances, contribute to lower costs for consumers. However, they also leave rural areas previously reliant on the extraction and processing of such materials in difficult circumstances when production levels drop or evaporate, and as lower international labor costs suppress wage rates in places where domestic production still occurs.

At the same time, forces of globalization are also contributing to new and expanded resource development in some areas of the United States. For example, BHP Billiton, headquartered in Australia and the world's largest mining company, recently became one of the fifteen largest natural gas producers in the United States following acquisition of shale gas fields in Arkansas, Louisiana, and Texas (Helman 2012). In addition, shifts in international development trends and consumption patterns are spurring increased demand for some resource-based products, potentially contributing to rising production levels and a surge in resource-based economic activity in some parts of rural America. Consider, for instance, how rapid industrial expansions occurring in China and other Asian nations are contributing to increased demand for US coal. While tightening air quality regulations will cause the closure of many coal-fired power plants and reduce domestic demand for coal over the next ten to twenty years, demand increases from European and Asian nations and a growing export market will almost certainly contribute to expanded production in some areas, preventing for the foreseeable future the broad-based downturn and associated bust effects that might otherwise occur in many of America's coal mining regions (see also Tallichet in this volume).

Conclusions

Resource dependency is a complex and multifaceted phenomenon in contemporary rural America, characterized by both continuities and changes. As rural economies have diversified, areas once highly reliant on resource production have become less dependent on it. In many areas the effects of technology on resource extraction and processing have reduced the labor inputs required for production, leading inexorably to a shift away from formerly high levels of dependence on resource-based employment. In addition, as some resource deposits are exhausted and attention shifts increasingly toward global sources, certain areas long dependent on resource production have either withered, or of necessity pursued alternative development strategies as resource-based economic activity waned. In many areas the conditions associated with resource dependency, at least as measured by high percentages of employment or income derived from resource-based industries, are no longer clearly in evidence. Of course, the legacies of resource dependency, particularly those associated with long-term economic stagnation and concentrated poverty, may last far beyond the time when resource-based employment began to erode.

At the same time, there are parts of rural America where resource dependency is alive and well, including both locations with long histories of resource-based development and also areas where resource extraction has emerged as a new and different form of local economic activity. New extractive technologies, shifting patterns of demand at the global scale, and changing societal preferences and priorities regarding the use of some resources combine to drive the development of new resource options, supplies, and production processes—at times in entirely new locations. In those settings, the changes associated with resource development exhibit important continuities with respect to the tensions between opportunities and threats that accompany rapid growth, unstable economic conditions, and development patterns that are typically unsustainable. Despite the welcoming response in many rural areas where residents and local officials are desperate for almost any form of economic development, dependency on resource-based activities continues to involve a Pandora's box of liabilities and problems.

Looking to the future, there are several important areas of opportunity for new and expanded research pertaining to resource dependency. There is clearly a need for more longitudinal studies to document and explain shifting social and economic well-being where resource dependency patterns change across time. Also needed are studies that examine the implications of changes in resource development processes and technologies—for example, dramatic declines in workforce requirements for drilling rigs could alter the nature of boom growth effects long associated with major energy developments. There is also much to be learned regarding the social implications of "new" resource use patterns—including those linked to major renewable energy developments, those associated with "unconventional" processes for extracting and processing oil and gas or other resources, and those involving contextual differences between areas with prior resource development experience and those for which such development is unprecedented.

References

Ansolabehere, S., and D.M. Konisky. 2012. "The American Public's Energy Choice." *Daedalus* 141 (2): 61–71. http://dx.doi.org/10.1162/DAED_a_00146.

Beckley, T.M. 1998. "The Nestedness of Forest Dependence: A Conceptual Framework and Empirical Exploration." *Society & Natural Resources* 11 (2): 101–20. http://dx.doi.org/10.1080/08941929809381066.

Bliss, J.C., and C. Bailey. 2005. "Pulp, Paper and Poverty: Forest-Based Rural Development in Alabama, 1950–2000." In *Communities and Forests: Where People Meet the Land*, ed. R.G. Lee and D.R. Field, 138–58. Corvallis: Oregon State University Press.

Braiser, K.J., M.R. Filteau, D.K. McLaughlin, J. Jacquet, R.S. Stedman, T.W. Kelsey, and S. Goetz. 2011. "Residents' Perceptions of Community and Environmental Impacts from Development of Natural Gas in the Marcellus Shale: A Comparison of Pennsylvania and New York Cases." *Journal of Rural Social Sciences* 26: 32–61.

Brown, R.B., S.F. Dorius, and R.S. Krannich. 2005. "The Boom-Bust-Recovery Cycle: Dynamics of Change in Community Satisfaction and Social Integration in Delta, Utah." *Rural Sociology* 70 (1): 28–49. http://dx.doi.org/10.1526/0036011053294673.

Buttel, F.H. 1992. "Environmentalization: Origins, Processes, and Implications for Rural Social Change." *Rural Sociology* 57 (1): 1–27. http://dx.doi.org/10.1111/j.1549-0831.1992.tb00454.x.

Cook, P.J., and K.L. Mizer. 1994. *The Revised ERS County Typology: An Overview*. Washington, DC: US Department of Agriculture, Economic Research Service, Report No. RDRR-89.

Duncan, C.M. 1992. "Persistent Poverty in Appalachia: Scarce Work and Regional Stratification." In *Rural Poverty in America*, ed. C.M. Duncan, 111–23. Westport, CT: Auburn House.

Economic Research Service. 2012. "County Typology Codes." Accessed 1 November 2012. http://www.ers.usda.gov/data-products/county-typology-codes/descriptions-and-maps.aspx.

Energy Information Administration. 2012a. *Annual Energy Review 2011*. Washington, DC: US Energy Information Administration, Office of Energy Statistics, US Department of Energy.

Energy Information Administration. 2012b. *Electric Power Monthly, March 2012*. Washington, DC: US Energy Information Administration, Office of Electricity, Renewables & Uranium Statistics, US Department of Energy.

Freudenburg, W.R. 1986. "The Density of Acquaintanceship: An Overlooked Variable in Community Research." *American Journal of Sociology* 92 (1): 27–63. http://dx.doi.org/10.1086/228462.

Freudenburg, W.R. 1992. "Addictive Economies: Extractive Industries and Vulnerable Localities in a Changing World Economy." *Rural Sociology* 57 (3): 305–32. http://dx.doi.org/10.1111/j.1549-0831.1992.tb00467.x.

Freudenburg, W.R., and R. Gramling. 1994. "Natural Resources and Rural Poverty: A Closer Look." *Society & Natural Resources* 7 (1): 5–22. http://dx.doi.org/10.1080/08941929409380841.

Freudenburg, W.R., and R.E. Jones. 1991. "Criminal Behavior and Rapid Community Growth: Examining the Evidence." *Rural Sociology* 56 (4): 619–45. http://dx.doi.org/10.1111/j.1549-0831.1991.tb00449.x.

Gould, K.A., D.N. Pellow, and A. Schnaiberg. 2008. *The Treadmill of Production: Injustice and Unsustainability in the Global Economy.* Boulder, CO: Paradigm.

Graetz, M.J. 2012. "Energy Policy: Past or Prologue?" *Daedalus* 141 (2): 31–44. http://dx.doi.org/10.1162/DAED_a_00144.

Haynes, R.W. 2003. *Assessing the Viability and Adaptability of Forest-Dependent Communities in the United States.* General Technical Report PNW-GTR-567. Portland, OR: USDA Forest Service, Pacific Northwest Research Station.

Helman, C. 2012. "Shale Game." *Forbes*, 27 February, 40–2.

Howze, G.R., L.J. Robinson, and J.F. Norton. 2003. "Historical Analysis of Timber Dependency in Alabama." *Southern Rural Sociology* 19 (2): 1–39.

Huang, W. 2004. "U.S. Increasingly Imports Nitrogen and Potash Fertilizer." *Amber Waves*, February. Washington, DC: US Department of Agriculture, Economic Research Service.

Humphrey, C.R., G. Berardi, M.S. Carroll, S. Fairfax, L. Fortmann, C. Geisler, T.G. Johnson, J. Kusel, R.G. Lee, S. Macinko, et al. 1993. "Theories in the Study of Natural Resource-Dependent Communities and Persistent Rural Poverty in the United States." In *Persistent Poverty in Rural America*, ed. Rural Sociological Task Force on Persistent Rural Poverty, 136–72. Boulder, CO: Westview.

Jacquet, J. 2012. "Landowner Attitudes toward Natural Gas and Wind Farm Development in Northern Pennsylvania." *Energy Policy* 50: 677–88. http://dx.doi.org/10.1016/j.enpol.2012.08.011.

James, A., and D. Aadland. 2011. "The Curse of Natural Resources: An Empirical Investigation of U.S. Counties." *Resource and Energy Economics* 33 (2): 440–53. http://dx.doi.org/10.1016/j.reseneeco.2010.05.006.

Krannich, R.S., and A.E. Luloff. 1991. "Problems of Resource Dependency in US Rural Communities." *Progress in Rural Policy and Planning* 1: 5–18.

Luloff, A.E., and R.S. Krannich. 2002. *Persistence and Change in Rural Communities: A Fifty-Year Follow-up to Six Classic Studies.* Okon, UK: CABI Publishing.

McGranahan, D.A. 2003. "How People Make a Living in Rural America." In *Challenges for Rural America in the Twenty-First Century*, ed. D.L. Brown and L.E. Swanson, 135–51. University Park: Penn State University Press.

McMichael, P. 1996. *Development and Social Change: A Global Perspective.* Thousand Oaks, CA: Pine Forge Press.

Norton, J.F., G.R. Howze, and L.J. Robinson. 2003. "Regional Comparisons of Timber Dependency: The Northwest and the Southeast." *Southern Rural Sociology* 19 (2): 40–59.

Overdest, C., and G.P. Green. 1995. "Forest Dependence and Community Well-Being: A Segmented Market Approach." *Society & Natural Resources* 8 (2): 111–31. http://dx.doi.org/10.1080/08941929509380906.

Pasqualetti, M.J. 2011. "Opposing Wind Energy Landscapes: A Search for Common Cause." *Annals of the Association of American Geographers* 101 (4): 907–17. http://dx.doi.org/10.1080/00045608.2011.568879.

Petrzelka, P., R.S. Krannich, and J. Brehm. 2006. "Identification with Resource-Based Occupations and Desire for Tourism: Are the Two Necessarily Inconsistent?" *Society & Natural Resources* 19 (8): 693–707. http://dx.doi.org/10.1080/08941920600801108.

Robbins, W.G. 1985. "The Social Context of Forestry: The Pacific Northwest in the Twentieth Century." *Western Historical Quarterly* 16 (4): 413–27. http://dx.doi.org/10.2307/968606.

Robertson, P.G., and R.S. Krannich. 2013. "Renewable Energy: Implications for Rural Development and Rural Policy in the Intermountain West." *Rural Connections* 7 (2): 19–22.

Sachs, J.D., and A.M. Warner. 2001. "The Curse of Natural Resources." *European Economic Review* 45 (4–6): 827–38. http://dx.doi.org/10.1016/S0014-2921(01)00125-8.

Schafft, K.A., Y. Borlu, and L. Glenna. 2013. "The Relationship between Marcellus Shale Gas Development in Pennsylvania and Local Perceptions of Risk and Opportunity." *Rural Sociology* 78 (2): 143–66. http://dx.doi.org/10.1111/ruso.12004.

Sherman, J. 2009. *Those Who Work and Those Who Don't: Poverty, Morality, and Family in Rural America.* Minneapolis: University of Minnesota Press.

Sinclair, P.R., C. Bailey, and M. Dubois. 2003. "One Engineer and a Dog: Technological Change and Social Restructuring in Alabama's Pulp and Paper Industry." *Southern Rural Sociology* 19 (2): 70–93.

Slattery, M.C., B.L. Johnson, J.A. Swofford, and M.J. Pasqualetti. 2012. "The Predominance of Economic Development in the Support for Large-Scale Wind Farms in the U.S. Great Plains." *Renewable & Sustainable Energy Reviews* 16 (6): 3690–701. http://dx.doi.org/10.1016/j.rser.2012.03.016.

Smith, M.D., R.S. Krannich, and L.M. Hunter. 2001. "Growth, Decline, Stability and Disruption: A Longitudinal Analysis of Social Well-Being in Four Western Rural Communities." *Rural Sociology* 66 (3): 425–50. http://dx.doi.org/10.1111/j.1549-0831.2001.tb00075.x.

Stedman, R.C., J.R. Parkins, and T.M. Beckley. 2005. "Forest Dependence and Community Well-Being in Rural Canada: Variation by Forest Sector and Region." *Canadian Journal of Forest Research* 35 (1): 215–20. http://dx.doi.org/10.1139/x04-140.

Stedman, R.C., M.N. Patriquin, and J.R. Parkins. 2011. "Forest Dependence and Community Well-Being in Rural Canada: A Longitudinal Analysis." *Forestry* 84 (4): 375–84. http://dx.doi.org/10.1093/forestry/cpr024.

Stedman, R., W. White, M. Patriquin, and D. Watson. 2007. "Measuring Community-Forest Sector Dependence: Does Method Matter?" *Society & Natural Resources* 20 (7): 629–46. http://dx.doi.org/10.1080/08941920701329660.

Theodori, G.L. 2009. "Paradoxical Perceptions of Problems Associated with Unconventional Natural Gas Development." *Southern Rural Sociology* 24: 97–117.

CHAPTER 12

The Gulf: America's Third Coast

Robert Gramling and Shirley Laska

Introduction

The coastline of the Gulf of Mexico is usually a gentle one, united by its primary source of water and divided by its subtle geomorphology and subsequent human settlement and use patterns. Setting aside rain and river discharge, most water that enters the Gulf comes from the Yucatán Current; out of the Caribbean Sea through the Yucatán Straits and into the Gulf of Mexico. A portion of the current turns east through the Florida Straits, between peninsular Florida and Cuba, initiating the Gulf Stream that flows up the Eastern Seaboard and on toward northern Europe. The remainder of the current flows across the Gulf, periodically reaching as far north as the bird-foot delta of the Mississippi River. Here the current splits setting up a counterclockwise circulation in the western Gulf—westerly and southwesterly along Louisiana and Texas—and a clockwise circulation in the eastern Gulf—easterly and southeasterly along Mississippi, Alabama, and Florida. Because these Caribbean waters come from near the equator they introduce a pool of warmer water into the central Gulf, which during the late summer and early fall can fuel the circulating heat engines that we call hurricanes when atmospheric conditions steer them across it. Hurricanes Katrina and Rita, which occurred in the mid-2000s, are cases in point.

Human use patterns of this low, marine terrain vary across accessibility, harvestable ecosystems, gulf/river navigation needs, water clarity, and soil types. Padre Island stretches along the lower Texas coast between Brownsville and Corpus Christi. The southern portion of the island is accessible from Brownsville, and an economy based on coastal beach tourism has emerged since World War II. The Mansfield channel bisects the island, and north of the channel the island becomes the Padre Island National Seashore with the hyper-saline Laguna Madre behind it. The effect of this geography has been to isolate much of near

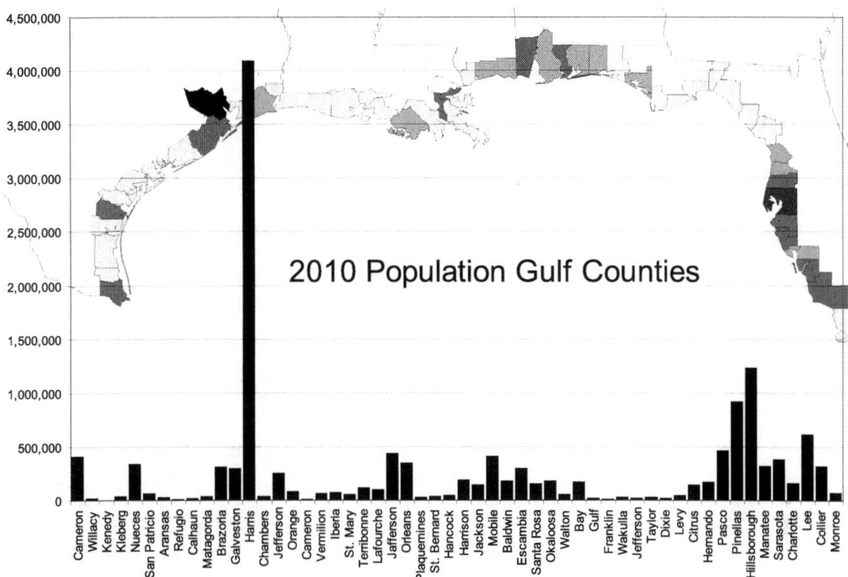

Figure 12.1. Diversity in size of Gulf coastal county populations, 2010. Source: U.S. Department of Commerce: Bureau of the Census, 2012.

coastal southeastern Texas between Brownsville and Corpus Christi from the Gulf of Mexico. The Texas counties along this stretch of the coast have the lowest population densities along the Gulf, remaining very rural and offering rural sociologists a potential control group for the study of rapid change that is coming to other rural coastal communities Gulf and world wide (see Figure 12.1). The northern Texas coast is dominated by Galveston Island, a traditional tourist destination, and by the industrial and population center surrounding Houston, which is one of the fastest growing areas in the country.

The Louisiana coastline is unique in North America. A low watery plain that extends twenty to forty miles inland, it is characterized by extensive open marsh, bays, and shallow estuaries, most of which are not accessible by road. The land was created by sediments carried downstream by the various configurations of the Mississippi River over thousands of years. Alluvial plains such as this are the constant battleground between the land-creating forces of deposition and the land-destroying forces of erosion from tidal processes, storm surges, and subsidence as the new land sinks under its own recent weight and the decay of the organic matter within it. Human intervention in the distribution of those sediments has meant that the land-destroying forces currently are in ascendency and coastal Louisiana is losing about twenty-five square miles of land every year. New Orleans is embedded in this liquid landscape, a major port, cultural center, and a city under siege from a decaying deltaic plain.

The Mississippi coast is sheltered behind a barrier island chain—Cat, Ship, Horn, and Petit Bois Islands—and by the Biloxi Marsh and the Chandeleur Islands, which are south of the Mississippi coast but are a part of Louisiana. None of the Mississippi barrier islands are connected by road, and thus development of the coast has occurred in this sheltered environment that does not evidence the clear waters and white sand beaches further east.

The barrier island complex that starts in Mississippi extends east into Alabama and to the largest island of that chain, Dauphin Island, which emerged as a community of individual, often vacation, homes, a pattern that has largely continued to the present. From Mobile Bay the Gulf coastline has clear waters and sandy beaches that stretch eastward. Following World War II, when changes in women's fashion allowed the display of more of the body and the emergence of the suntan as an appearance status (Steele 1985), these stretches have become centers for the rise of beach-oriented tourism. From Mobile Bay, the "sugar" sand beaches flow in an almost unbroken sweep eastward to Mexico Beach, Florida. Wherever there is easy access, beach tourism centers and then towns have emerged.

East of Pensacola and inland from the coast remains very rural, with low population densities and only occasional connections north to major highways. This rural swathe continues south of Tallahassee, around the "Big Bend," and down the west coast of Florida as far as Levy County. This approximately 500-mile swathe, with its pine and palmetto flora, is very different from the Florida that visitors to coastal environs see. Here, as with Texas behind Padre Island, there are stark contrasts between coastal and inland communities. Rural sociologists have largely ignored coastal communities, but at least in the United States these represent opportunities to examine some of the most rapid examples of transition away from the rural, an increasingly global phenomenon.

Continuing south along the Florida coast, beaches again become the dominant coastal landscape along with a development strategy that would be almost impossible to obtain a use permit for today. Developers dredged up narrow peninsulas, sometimes parallel to one another and jutting into the wetlands or bays, and sold waterfront lots on both side of the peninsula with a street down the middle. This technique for filling wetlands has been attributed to a 1920s developer on the east coast of Florida and quickly spread to the Florida west coast (Pittman and Waite 2009).

Beaches on the coast continue past the Tampa/St. Petersburg complex, a major urban center, although both Tampa/St. Petersburg and Sarasota to the south sport neighborhoods with small homes exhibiting post-World War II architecture. Holmes Beach and Longboat Key off Bradenton, Sarasota, Venice, Boca-Grande, Sanibel Island, Fort Myers Beach, and Naples are all centers for beach tourism. Moving down the coast the climate transitions from subtropical to true tropical. By Naples, the rubber plant that survives in pots in sunrooms throughout the nation has escaped into yards and grown to forty feet tall. South of Naples, the landscape becomes the 10,000 Islands area, where the Everglades taper into Florida Bay and beyond to become the Florida Keys.

Trends in the Gulf

In recent decades, five trends have emerged that characterize human-landscape interactions. These are: (1) the impact of increasingly powerful technologies to harvest seafood; (2) the transition to coastal beach tourism and recreation supplemented and sometimes replacing commercial renewable resource harvest; (3) the extraction of oil and gas, which has had profound social and ecological impacts; (4) the growth in importance of Gulf ports; and (5) the struggle of rural communities to maintain their boundaries and relevance, as they are increasingly dominated and/or surrounded by urban and beach tourism centers and invaded by the forces of gentrification.

Renewable Harvests from the Gulf

The harvest of renewable natural resources has long been a tradition in the coastal Gulf of Mexico, with seafood the principal resource harvested and Louisiana, with its unique estuarine environment, the primary player. The four primary species in terms of value are shrimp, oysters, blue crabs, and menhaden. The total dockside value of these four species in 2009 was $346 million, with $243 million of that in Louisiana (NMFS 2012).

Louisiana has long dominated Gulf shrimp production, but the annual harvests show considerable fluctuation and the industry today is characterized by overcapitalization and increased global competition from shrimp imports (Louisiana Department of Wildlife and Fisheries 2000). In 1975, 91,380 metric tons of shrimp were imported into the United States (Louisiana Department of Wildlife and Fisheries 2000). By 2009, imports had grown to 547,039 metric tons (NMFS 2012), a 500 percent increase. The primary exporting countries to the United States are in Asia, and most of this supply comes from ponds. Wild Gulf shrimp simply cannot compete with the price of foreign aquaculture. Well over three quarters of the shrimp consumed in the United States are imported. By 2010, with rising fuel costs and falling prices for wild shrimp, this overcapitalized, renewable resource extraction sector in the Gulf was in trouble and had been for a number of years. The effects of the British Petroleum (BP) spill, both in harvest amount and consumer willingness to eat the harvest from the area, are contributing to continued decline.

Oysters also show complex harvest patterns. Chesapeake Bay oysters were famous throughout US history, but starting in the 1980s harvests began to plummet, primarily due to over exploitation. Oysters thrive best in brackish water, and so Louisiana with its extensive bays and estuaries has always dominated Gulf oyster harvest. Today, a customer sitting at a restaurant overlooking Chesapeake Bay with a plate of raw oysters is probably eating a Louisiana product. Sharp declines in 2010 for Louisiana shrimp and oysters reflect the effect of the BP oil spill. Western Florida, primarily around Apalachicola, is also traditionally an area of oyster harvest, but competing interests (primarily from the city of Atlanta) for the water in the tributaries of the Apalachicola River threaten the delicate salinity balance and the oysters.

Coastal Tourism

While beach tourism was certainly not confined to the Gulf, the longer season in the Gulf compared to many parts of the country made it an ideal location for this type of activity. Changes in place use seldom have a sudden onset and indeed often emerge in a process that bears a certain resemblance to ecological succession (Freudenburg 1985) as one activity gradually takes over from another. This has happened for most of the Gulf coast.

Harvesters of natural resources (fish, oysters, shrimp, etc.) were the first to exploit and live on the coastlines. These are not high-paying occupations and fishermen's homes and rural communities were quite modest. As the recreational attractions to the beach expanded, property values rose and a form of gentrification emerged as wealthier populations bought up property and built recreational dwellings. Eventually single unit structures were replaced by multiple occupancy structures (condos, hotels) in a number of places, and the almost urban nature of the coastal strip now extends to the water. This evolution can be seen especially along the beaches of Baldwin County in Alabama, east of Mobile Bay.

While south Florida started out with deliberate exploitation of beaches and climate by powerful development interests (Gramling and Freudenburg 2013), this process was more gradual in other Gulf coastal areas. By the end of the twentieth century the clientele for warm beaches was truly global, particularly with "snow birds" from Europe and Canada in the winter joining their US counterparts. However, it is not necessary to have white sands and broad beaches for the areas near the Gulf to be attractive. In Louisiana there is only one

Table 12.1
Top twenty-five US ports by tonnage and value, 2011

Rank	Port	Million Tons	Rank	Port	Million Dollars
1	South Louisiana*	213	1	Los Angeles, CA	135,079
2	Houston, TX	211	2	New York, NY	130,838
3	New York, NY and NJ	145	3	Long Beach, CA	125,171
4	Long Beach, CA	73	4	Houston, TX	86,444
5	Corpus Christi, TX	68	5	Charleston, SC	52,483
6	New Orleans, LA*	68	6	Hampton Roads	44,658
7	Beaumont, TX	68	7	Baltimore, MD	35,637
8	Hunting Tristate	59	8	Seattle, WA	35,301
9	Los Angeles, CA	58	9	Tacoma, WA	33,788
10	Texas City, TX	53	10	Savannah, GA	33,424
11	Lake Charles, LA	52	11	Oakland, CA	32,885
12	Mobile, AL	52	12	New Orleans, LA	20,944
13	Baton Rouge, LA*	52	13	Miami, FL	19,899
14	Plaquemines, LA*	51	14	Philadelphia, PA	19,251
15	Norfolk Harbor, VA	40	15	Beaumont, TX	17,059
16	Pascagoula, MS	37	16	Jacksonville, FL	16,494
17	Tampa, FL	35	17	South Louisiana	15,630
18	Valdez, AK	34	18	Corpus Christie, TX	15,532
19	Port Arthur, TX	34	19	Port Everglades, FL	15,298
20	Pittsburgh, PA	33	20	Portland, OR	11,519
21	Savannah, GA	32	21	Texas City, TX	10,814
22	Philadelphia, PA	32	22	Freeport, TX	9,516
23	St. Louis, MO and IL	31	23	Christiansted, VI	9,151
24	Paulsboro, NJ	30	24	Baton Rouge, LA	8,753
25	Duluth-Superior, MN	30	25	Lake Charles, LA	8,386

Note: Mississippi River Complex ports (*) totaled 383 million tons. Source: American Association of Port Authorities (2012).

inhabited barrier island and a second small coastal beach near the Louisiana/ Texas border, and neither have white sands and clear water. Here, the competition for access to the water is increasingly found in areas where the population of commercial resource harvesters lived in rural inland communities along bayous with water access to the coast. When such takeovers occur, the earlier residents' presence and land use are generally invisible to those who imagine new uses and see the landscape from a blank slate perspective. The locale is seen as truly "empty" and thus available for whatever the in migrant/weekend residents wish to do with it.

This frequently results in barriers to the earlier uses of the land adjacent to the water, which disrupts the earlier social network patterns and starts a reinforcing feedback loop that supports the transition of land use. Add to such gentrification dynamics the damage experienced from hurricanes and the result is a dramatic decline in the permanent populations of coastal communities (Bailey, Laska, and Gramling 2012). The recreational homes remain after the original residents leave because they are newer, more expensive, and built to be more storm resistant. Thus, coastal gentrification of former resource harvest communities is occurring across the Gulf coast as new use patterns spread beyond the pristine beaches where they first emerged.

Ports

Table 12.1 shows the ranking of the top twenty-five ports in the United States by tonnage (volume) and value. Over half of the top twenty-five ports by tonnage are in the Gulf, with the ports of Houston and South Louisiana clearly dominant. The Port of South Louisiana lies between Baton Rouge and New Orleans and is part of an unbroken port complex that starts at Baton Rouge and ends well south of New Orleans. This port complex is the export point for the Mississippi River drainage basin that includes all or parts of thirty-one states between the Appalachian and Rocky Mountains, and is *the* export and import facility for bulk products in the entire central United States. Grains, soybeans, and coal are the primary products that come down the River for export. In addition, both the Mississippi River complex and Houston have major petrochemical plants and import oil to fuel them. The US Army Corps of Engineers is responsible for maintaining ports and navigable waters, and is highly responsive not only to navigation interests but also to the interests of exporters and importers who rely on the lower river and coastal ports. These interests may trump other waterway and coastal interests and responsibilities, including coastal management and restoration.

Offshore Oil and Gas

Offshore petroleum exploitation was invented in the Gulf in the 1940s and 1950s, and overwhelmingly offshore production on US outer continental shelf happens in the Gulf today (Gramling 1996). Because the United States has always required a lower royalty rate on federal lands than virtually all other nations (US Government Accountability Office 2007); because Congress cut royalties even further in the deep water to encourage exploitation of these "frontier" areas (US Energy Information Administration 2009); because federal leasing policy favors large multinational oil companies (Gramling and Freudenburg 2012); and because deep water reservoirs are some of the largest to be discovered in the Gulf and the pressures encountered at these depths meant that oil flowed out of wells and into pipelines at much higher rates, the deep water Gulf has experienced a boom in offshore development over the last decade (Freudenburg and Gramling 2011).

Some of the most profitable endeavors that major multinationals can engage in worldwide lie in the deep waters of the Gulf, and policies set at the highest levels of the US government encourage them in this direction. Over the last decade, movement into the deeper waters of the Gulf has increased outer continental shelf production. Because total US production has declined drastically since the 1970s, outer continental shelf production is now over 25 percent of total US crude oil production. Politically, much has been made of the rising price of gasoline and consequently the need to open up the US offshore. However, there is little connection here between the two factors. Oil is sold on a world market and at the same price whether it comes from Russia or the United States. Since the United States produces less than 9 percent of the world's oil, even if this could be increased by a few percentage points, it would still be far too little to affect world price by increasing total world supply.

Industrial development can proceed at a pace that outstrips the ability of those engaged in it to control unanticipated consequences, a situation that some authors have called a "Technological Peter Principle" (Erikson 1976; see also Freudenburg et al. 2009; Freudenburg and Gramling 2011). With deep-water drilling, specifically, this means that we are teetering on the very edge of our ability to control the forces at play and predict how the various elements will interact. The almost predictable result was the Deepwater Horizon blowout in the Gulf in 2010, which we discuss below.

Disruptions:

The 2005 and 2008 Hurricanes

In August 2005, Hurricane Katrina struck Louisiana and Mississippi. New Orleans and its surroundings were dramatically damaged by the most financially catastrophic tropical cyclone to ever strike the United States. Over 1,600 deaths were directly attributed to the storm and many others occurred due to the stress of the event, the lengthy evacuation, and the attempts to rebuild.

The elderly were especially hard hit. Officials and residents were uncertain that the region would ever return to a semblance of what it was before the event. At the time of this writing over nine years later, the region has demonstrated an amazing recovery albeit one flawed by the inability of many residents who wanted to return to do so. Some 100,000 fewer residents live in New Orleans than before the storm.

Communities in lower Plaquemines Parish—basically, the bird-foot delta of the Mississippi River—were literally destroyed. Houses and businesses were wiped down to the concrete slabs they were built on and sixty-foot shrimping vessels sat on the road and in former yards, the lucky ones right-side up. The disaster drew the attention of the world, but media coverage is easier in urban as opposed to rural areas and the paucity of rural media coverage reduced the visibility of the rural damage. Frequent comments about this difference in reporting are still heard from residents and leaders of the rural communities who feel they have been ignored in their time of trauma and recovery.

In Mississippi, as Hurricane Katrina approached, some casinos on barges were moved to the Back Bay and avoided the storm, but others became huge projectiles, driven inland by the thirty-foot storm surge and crushing homes and businesses. A few months later the Mississippi Legislature, recognizing both the economic importance of the casinos and the danger of having huge floating structures on the coast, amended regulations to allow the casinos to rebuild across the highway from the Gulf. Mississippi also lost some of the larger docks for shrimp boats to Katrina, affecting that industry (Nuwer 2012).

A month after Katrina struck eastern Louisiana and Mississippi, Hurricane Rita struck western Louisiana and threatened the east Texas coast. The rural coastal communities in western Louisiana were, like their counterparts in Plaquemines Parish, destroyed, and Texas experienced one of the greatest evacuation debacles in history. Although there were problems noted with the evacuation of New Orleans ahead of Katrina, the city had a plan, at least for those with automobiles. The interstates were turned to contra-flow—all lanes moving out—early, and all-in-all Katrina led to the most successful evacuation of a major city in human history. What was not planned was the evacuation of those without automobiles, estimated at 125,000, and the poor who could not afford to leave (Laska 2004). Their fate was represented worldwide in media accounts of suffering unheard of, before Katrina, in a disaster in a developed economy.

The early projected path of Rita was the Galveston/Houston vicinity, and as Rita approached over a million tried to evacuate. They did not have a plan. Interstates ground to a halt, vehicles ran out of gas in one-hundred-degree temperatures, and individuals were trapped for days in the ensuing snarl. Rita went ashore near the Louisiana/Texas border and Texas, being on the "back side" (west side) of the storm, was spared the onshore winds that destroyed rural communities in western Louisiana. Past experience led almost all Louisiana residents in the storm's path to evacuate early and almost all of the deaths associated with Rita were due to the Texas "evacuation," not the storm.

In 2008, two large hurricanes made landfall on the north Gulf coast: Gustav and Ike. Gustav threatened New Orleans, generating again a massive evacuation, this time more successful for all residents. Less than a week later Ike followed Rita's 2005 path, but veered slightly to the west going ashore around the east end of Galveston Island. The Bolivar Peninsula across the pass from Galveston took the full brunt of the storm and the rapidly growing suburban communities on it were almost completely destroyed.

Macondo

On 20 April 2010, fifty miles southeast of the Mississippi bird-foot delta, where indications are that safeguards and redundancies had been bypassed to save money and time, control of a deep-water oil well named Macondo was lost. Gas under thousands of pounds per square inch of pressure blew back up the riser, into the *Deepwater Horizon*, a drilling rig owned by TransOcean and under lease to BP. The explosion killed eleven crew members. Two days later the *Deepwater Horizon* sank, venting Macondo oil to the open Gulf. An estimated 200,000,000 gallons of crude oil poured out before the well was finally capped in September. Macondo was being drilled in water a mile deep and extended two and a half miles further below the ocean bottom into the underlying rock.

There is no polite way to describe the "containment" and "clean-up" efforts that followed. It started with BP's "Oil Spill Response Plan," a 582-page document that was a spectacular example of what Clarke (1999) calls "fantasy documents" and that was almost totally at variance with any reality on the ground. The plan ranged from claims about containment and clean-up abilities, which could not be met, to obvious inattention to the actual environment at risk. The plan listed walruses and seals under "sensitive biological resources," even though they have not lived in the Gulf for thousands of years. In actuality, very little can be done once oil is in the water and most of BP's frantic skimming, burning, and booming during the summer of 2010 was performed for media, not the environment (Freudenburg and Gramling 2011). Other questions arose concerning inspection schedules that were not met and a certain lack of vigilance in the overall regulatory environment in the Gulf (Freudenburg and Gramling 2011).

Oil fouled beaches from Grand Isle, Louisiana to Mexico Beach, Florida, and, most damaging, washed from west of Grand Isle east to the state line into the

Louisiana estuaries where there were no beaches and only remnants of barrier islands to block it. The commercial and recreational fisheries closed in both state and federal waters and the beach tourist season came to an abrupt end in the northern Gulf. Three years after the spill it is too soon to assess the ultimate effects, although numerous deformed marine species such as eyeless shrimp, crabs without claws, fish whose hearts do not fully form, unexplained lesions on all of these, and dolphins suffering from lung and liver disease are reported along the northern Gulf. In addition, coastal residents continue to complain of illnesses they believe have been induced by contaminant exposure living on the coast, working the clean up, or eating the seafood. As occurred with the Exxon Valdez spill, residents believe that government officials put more emphasis on denying such links than on investigating them. Those in the small towns at the edge of the Gulf are those most exposed to these risks and comment frequently on the "layering" of the oil spill impact with those of hurricane destruction and fisheries struggling with international competition (Laska et al. 2013).

Rural Communities

Rural communities, wherever their locations, evidence networks of interpersonal exchange (social capital), local knowledge about how to obtain the products of that exchange (cultural capital), and skill sets honed to harvest those products (human capital) (Flora and Flora 2013). When these communities are embedded in the incredible biological diversity of coastlines (natural capital), this results in a way of life in which human and environmental elements are almost "conjointly constituted" (Freudenburg, Frickel, and Gramling 1995).

Rural Gulf Coast communities face common dynamics and challenges with other rural areas. Residents find their fates influenced not only by their own goals and efforts but the economic linkages they have with their adjacent smaller cities, the more distant regional urban hubs, and the numerous places worldwide with which they compete in the globalization of the products for which the Gulf is known: petroleum, seafood, and tourism (Coreil 1993). They are also similar to rural areas that are located within other ecosystems defined as beautiful and/or desirable for recreational activities. The "original" rural economic activities are challenged in the local market by goods and services desired by those who want to use the community for recreational purposes (Brehm 2007; Bailey, Laska, and Gramling 2012).

Some small coastal communities have almost completely disappeared, replaced by high-rise hotel and condominium development and the accompanying outlet malls and beach amenities. They are in effect no longer rural, even though their off-season population is small. Due to the continuing challenge that rural residents have to achieve an adequate income as these changes happen, residents often embrace the gentrification even though it might dramatically affect their lifestyle.

Gulf coast communities do share some risks that other rural areas do not experience, especially those inland or on the West Coast. Hurricanes have been the way of life for the Gulf since the area was inhabited, and storms have been a continuous actor in the decline/improvement of coastal communities. This latest hurricane "barrage" in the Gulf was followed by a number of policy decisions at the state and national level that encouraged community residents to take buyouts of their damaged property, while at the same time the new, storm-resistant vacation homes of the recreational users sustained minimal damage and thus have survived to increasingly define the coastal area. Such changes in location—away from the ecosystems that support their harvest cultures—have robbed the Native American and Cajun communities in Louisiana of their cultural identities, practices, and lifestyles. Only five years after Katrina, the BP spill added more threat to the Gulf harvesting communities' economic base.

When the spill occurred foreign shrimp importers pushed to reduce or end the import tariffs, citing the reduced capacity to produce local seafood, brought on by the spill, as a reason to permit more foreign imports. The tariffs were not altered but the pressures to do so continue. While all areas of the Gulf are now open to harvesting, Louisiana oyster beds were extensively damaged by the spill, either by the oil itself or the fresh water that was forced across the beds from existing Mississippi River diversions in a failed attempt to prevent oil from entering estuaries. Texas oysters have gained a larger share of the market since these events occurred. It is not yet known if the beds will fully recover from the spill. Similarly, the southeastern Louisiana shrimpers are concentrating their efforts west of the usual delta locations because the harvest is better there. This puts pressure on the western shrimpers to share the harvest and thus the profits.

Major regional/national tourism events have played a role in reinvigorating seafood consumption in the Gulf coast. In New Orleans itself, Mardi Gras 2006 was held despite major odds against it happening. In the ensuing years, national events such as collegiate football and basketball championships and the reestablishment of the large music and food festivals have contributed to recovery of the restaurant industry. Much of BP's contribution to date to the recovery for the Gulf coast has gone into advertising for such activities as well as for beach tourism. The state seafood boards assure the public and tourists that the seafood is being appropriately tested for contamination and none has been found, although local residents do not trust the testing. The farther away the event gets in time, the more likely it is that consumers will accept or not even seek such assurances. An August 2012 report from the Harrison County, Mississippi, tourism director reported a flat year for tourism to date in that county despite the large amount of tourism advertising supported by BP (Phillips 2012).

Anthropogenic Impacts on the Gulf Coast

In addition to the channelization of the Mississippi River, which has largely blocked the flow of sediment needed to rebuild the Louisiana coastal wetlands, human intervention in coastal geomorphology—primarily supporting petroleum extraction and water transportation (navigation)—has been extensive. In the 1930s, mobile barge-mounted drilling rigs and barge-mounted draglines were introduced into Louisiana's coastal wetlands. Since it was easy to dig canals across the marsh or through shallow estuaries, float the drilling rig to the site, and supply the operation via vessels through the newly cut canals, this new technology moved ahead with little regulation (Gramling 1996). As a result, an extensive networks of canals associated with oil development along the northern Gulf Coast (primarily in Louisiana) was initiated. The eventual extent of the destructiveness of this practice has yet to be completely assessed. A network of pipeline corridors through the same wetlands only exacerbated the problem. There is little doubt that this channelization process, accompanied by erosion, alteration of the hydrologic regimes, and salt-water intrusion, has contributed greatly to the current annual loss of wetlands in the state.

The most noteworthy transportation related project was the Mississippi River Gulf Outlet (MRGO). MRGO (pronounced locally as Mister Go) was a ship channel constructed in the 1960s from the Industrial Canal in the heart of New Orleans to the Gulf, east of and bypassing the lower 125 miles of the Mississippi River. Supposedly, this shorter route to the Gulf would initiate a boom in Gulf shipping, but because of its limiting depth MRGO was an almost complete economic failure that allowed salt-water intrusion into the wetlands south and east of New Orleans. It has been argued that the loss of protective wetlands due to salt-water intrusion from MRGO was a major factor in the flooding of New Orleans by Hurricane Katrina (Freudenburg et al. 2009). In retrospect, even the Corps has implicitly admitted that MRGO was a mistake by constructing a multi-billion dollar sea wall east of New Orleans in an attempt to provide storm surge protection that was lost with the destruction of the wetlands. Because of its lack of economic merit and ecological destruction, MRGO has been sealed, which will at least slow future salt-water intrusion, but because over 200,000,000 cubic yards of dirt (more than for the Panama Canal) was removed for this mammoth project, filling in MRGO is not considered possible (Freudenburg et al. 2009).

What the Future Holds

The global trends shaping the Gulf coast—the importation of competing seafood to American consumers nationwide, the role of the Gulf ports in world shipping, the search for energy resources in the Gulf, the continued importance of beach tourism, and the gentrification of rural communities—will probably not significantly change in the next decade, and certainly risks associated with hurricanes and potential oil spills will not go away. Past experience tells us that usually whatever the development trajectory before the disaster events, that trajectory will be enhanced, even after catastrophic ones. If there is a demand for economic uses of the area, storms act as abrupt disruptions in existing uses, and recovery construction can shift land use forcefully in the new direction.

When the storm is catastrophic, two different competing dynamics come into play. A total annihilation of an area will impede its recovery because the "roots" (social and economic as well as physical infrastructure) of the recovery are not even there. Under these conditions the recovery may be very lengthy and may never fully occur. The western end of the Mississippi coast is an example. Bay St. Louis, Waveland, and Pass Christian are three communities still struggling in their recovery following Katrina.

However, the other factor that suggests what the future holds is contrary to this dynamic. The infusion of massive government resources for the rebuilding of infrastructure also affects recovery. Employment levels, housing values, and even municipal bond ratings remained high when the contrary might have been expected. Communities, from those in western Mississippi to St. Bernard, Plaquemines, and Orleans Parishes, appear new and functional. Infrastructure decrepit from aging before the storm has been replaced with new streets, roads, schools, and government buildings, which sometimes appear "supersized" given the communities' reduced populations, in effect likely prompting a fuller recovery to population sizes that existed before the storm.

Unfortunately, most of the severely damaged areas—which will be the ones most vulnerable to the next large hurricane—have not addressed recovery in a manner and at a scale adequate to protect themselves against future storms. Neither the social psychological inclination of members of American society—focused on immediate gratification and expectations of a privileged life—nor government policies and structures support such a risk-reducing recovery (Laska 2012). The devastation of any part of the Gulf coast that is now showing strong recovery—where risk reduction could have been practiced much more forcefully as the communities were rebuilding—could write the next decadal chapter of the region.

We have learned, or should have learned, several important things over the last decade in the Gulf that have implications for other coastal areas and their rural components:

> Coastal tourism is important; it is sometimes the dominating factor in local and regional economies, but it is quite vulnerable to natural and technological disasters and to national and international economic downturns.
>
> Offshore petroleum development is not as safe as we once thought, particularly in "frontier" areas. What we learned in Alaska with the *Exxon Valdez* spill, we relearned in the Gulf; we do not—and probably never will— have the technology to contain and clean up major oil spills in the marine environment. Given this, as our increasing thirst for oil will inevitably open other coastal areas to offshore petroleum development, our resources should probably be spent on prevention rather than on tweaking impotent clean-up technology.
>
> The rural coastal community, at least in the Gulf, is becoming a thing of the past, an "endangered species," and, except in a limited number of communities or parts thereof, that earlier way of life is also ending. At the same time, this rapid transition of coastal communities with nearby, inland, culturally similar, "control" communities, offer rural sociologists a laboratory to study this increasingly global transitional process.
>
> The human influenced geophysical/hydrologic processes of the coastal margins continue to play a role in the nature and success of human communities that inhabit it, as they have done since the stabilization of the sea level that made coasts the productive location of human settlements. (Day et al. 2012)

References

American Association of Port Authorities. 2012. Accessed 18 June 2012. http://www.aapa-ports.org/index.cfm.

Bailey, Conner, Shirley Laska, and Robert Gramling. 2012. "Restoration and Communities." In *Answering 10 Fundamental Questions about the Mississippi River Delta. A Report by the Mississippi River Delta Science and Engineering Special Team*, ed. John Day, 24–7. Accessed 19 July 2013. http://www.mississippiriverdelta.org/files/2012/04/MississippiRiverDeltaReport.pdf.

Brehm, Joan M. 2007. "Community Attachment: The Complexity and Consequences of the Natural Environment Facet." *Human Ecology* 35 (4): 477–88. http://dx.doi.org/10.1007/s10745-006-9104-3.

Clarke, Lee. 1999. *Mission Improbable: Using Fantasy Documents to Tame Disaster.* Chicago: University of Chicago Press.

Coreil, Paul. 1993. "The Diversification of a Louisiana Coastal Community." In *Coastlines of the Gulf of Mexico*, ed. Shirley Laska and Andrew Puffer, 96–102. New York: American Society of Civil Engineers.

Day, John W., Jr., Joel D. Gunn, William J. Folan, Alejandro Yáñez-Arancibia, and Benjamin P. Horton. 2012. "The Influence of Enhanced Post-Glacial Coastal Margin Productivity on the Emergence of Complex Societies." *Journal of Island & Coastal Archaeology* 7 (1): 23–52. http://dx.doi.org/10.1080/15564894.2011.650346.

Erikson, Kai T. 1976. *Everything in Its Path: The Destruction of Community in the Buffalo Creek Flood.* New York: Simon and Schuster.

Flora, Cornelia Butler, and Jan L. Flora. 2013. *Rural Communities: Legacy and Change.* 4th ed. Boulder: Westview Press.

Freudenburg, William R. 1985. "Succession and Success: A New Look at an Old Concept." *Sociological Spectrum* 5 (3): 269–89. http://dx.doi.org/10.1080/02732173.1985.9981757.

Freudenburg, William R., Scott Frickel, and Robert Gramling. 1995. "Beyond the Nature/Society Divide: Learning to Think about a Mountain." *Sociological Forum* 10 (3): 361–92. http://dx.doi.org/10.1007/BF02095827.

Freudenburg, William R., and Robert Gramling. 2011. *Blowout in the Gulf: The BP Oil Spill Disaster and the Future of Energy in America.* Cambridge, MA: MIT Press.

Freudenburg, William R., Robert Gramling, Shirley Laska, and Kai T. Erikson. 2009. *Catastrophe in the Making: The Engineering of Katrina and the Disasters of Tomorrow.* Washington, DC: Island Press.

Gramling, Robert. 1996. *Oil on the Edge: Offshore Development, Conflict, Gridlock.* Albany: SUNY Press.

Gramling, Robert, and William R. Freudenburg. 2012. "A Century of Macondo: United States Energy Policy and the BP Blowout Catastrophe." *American Behavioral Scientist* 56 (1): 48–75. http://dx.doi.org/10.1177/0002764211413115.

Gramling, Robert, and William R. Freudenburg. 2013. "The Growth Machine and the Everglades: Expanding a Useful Theoretical Perspective." *Society & Natural Resources* 26 (6): 642–54. http://dx.doi.org/10.1080/08941920.2013.779205.

Laska, Shirley. 2004. "What if Hurricane Ivan Had Not Missed New Orleans?" *Natural Hazards Observer*, 29 November, 5–6. http://www.colorado.edu/hazards/o/archives/2004/nov04/nov04c.html.

Laska, Shirley. 2012. "Dimensions of Resiliency: Essential Resiliency, Exceptional Recovery and Scale." *International Journal of Critical Infrastructures* 8 (1): 47–62. http://dx.doi.org/10.1504/IJCIS.2012.046552.

Laska, Shirley, Kristina Peterson, Crystlyn Rodrigue, Tia Cosse', Rosina Philippe, Olivia Burchett, and Richard Krajeski. 2013. "'Layering' of Natural and Human-Caused Disasters in the Context of Anticipated Climate Change Disasters: The Coastal Louisiana Experience."

Paper presented at the annual meeting of the American Sociological Society, 13 August, New York City.

Louisiana Department of Wildlife and Fisheries. 2000. *The Louisiana Shrimp Industry: A Preliminary Analysis of the Industry's Sectors. SRD Publication #6.* Baton Rouge, LA: Louisiana Department of Wildlife and Fisheries.

NMFS. 2012. "Annual Commercial Landing Statistics." National Oceans and Atmospheric Administration, National Marine Fisheries Service, Office of Science and Technology. Accessed 17 April 2012. http://www.st.nmfs.noaa.gov/st1/commercial.

Nuwer, Deanne S. 2012. Personal communication, telephone conversation with Laska and Gramling. 17 April.

Phillips, Steve. 2012. "Tourism Business Flat Despite Increased Spending. *WLOX*, Gulfport, MS, 20 August. http://www.wlox.com/story/19264490/guice-tourism-promotion-attracting-mobile-web-users.

Pittman, Craig, and Matthew Waite. 2009. *Paving Paradise: Florida's Vanishing Wetlands and the Failure of No Net Loss.* Gainesville: University Press of Florida.

Steele, Valerie. 1985. *Fashion and Eroticism: Ideals of Feminine Beauty From the Victorian Era to the Jazz Age.* New York: Oxford University Press.

US Energy Information Administration. 2009. *Outer Continental Shelf Deep Water Royalty Relief Act of 1995.* Accessed 22 April 2012. http://www.eia.gov/oil_gas/natural_gas/analysis_publications/ngmajorleg/continental.html.

US Government Accountability Office. 2007. *Oil and Gas Royalties: A Comparison of the Share of Revenue Received from Oil and Gas Production by the Federal Government and Other Resource Owners.* GAO-07-676R Oil and Gas Royalties.

CHAPTER 13

Biofuels and Rural Communities: Promises, Pitfalls, and Uneven Social and Environmental Impacts

Theresa Selfa and Carmen Bain

Introduction

In the mid-2000s, governments around the globe promoted biofuels projects, championing their triple benefits: rural economic development, climate change mitigation, and an alternative to fossil fuels in the time of "peak oil" (Worldwatch Institute 2006; FAO 2006). Development of the biofuels industry was seen as a lifeline for rural communities in many countries, and as an opportunity for employment and reversing out-migration. These overwhelmingly positive discourses about the benefits of biofuels for rural communities were prevalent in international institution policy papers, government policies, and nongovernmental organization (NGO) materials in Europe, the United States, and the global South (European Commission 2004; Kleinschmidt and Muller 2005; Hazell 2006).

High food prices and counter claims from the scientific community questioning the climate benefits of bioenergy (Searchinger et al. 2008; Fargione et al. 2008), especially the "food versus fuels" debates in 2008, muted the win-win biofuels narratives. Global land grabs brought even more critical attention to biofuels projects' potential to displace basic food production in the global South (GRAIN 2008; Oxfam International 2008; McMichael 2009). Climate and energy benefits from biofuels have been framed globally, but the socioeconomic and environmental impacts of these projects are experienced locally and have not been explored adequately (Bain and Selfa 2013; Selfa 2010; Munday, Bristow, and Cowell 2011). In this chapter, we compare rural development and environmental benefits claims from biofuels projects to the empirical evidence derived from case study research conducted in communities with biofuels plants in the Midwestern United States. In our analysis, we highlight inequalities in how the environmental and socioeconomic benefits and burdens of biofuels projects are distributed.

In this chapter, we review the primary theoretical frameworks that are emerging to conceptualize the biofuels industry; examine international, national, and state policies that stimulated the growth of that industry; and introduce case study materials from Kansas and Iowa to illustrate how the current grain-based biofuels industry is playing out in particular rural communities in the United States. In the final section, we discuss emerging private governance systems for biofuels, specifically sustainability certification systems; examine the challenges these systems face; and offer conclusions based on our analysis.

Framing Global Biofuels Development in a Neoliberal Era

Most of the social science literature that examines the biofuels industry has investigated the emergence of, and politics related to, global networks of agriculture and energy crop production. Arthur Mol (2007) draws from the sociology of networks and flows literature to conceptualize the emergence of a globally integrated biofuels network. In a later contribution, drawing on Sassen's (2006) work on global assemblages, Mol (2010) highlights tensions between the purported global environmental benefits and local environmental and food security concerns presented by biofuels, and how private market authorities (i.e., standards and certification systems) outside of traditional state regulatory authorities are increasingly mediating such contentious issues.

Other recent social science attention has focused on the social dynamics of developing country production of agrofuels crops, highlighting land grabs and food-security tensions, as an extension of earlier food regime analysis (McMichael 2010; Borras et al. 2011). Here biofuels are understood as an extension of the neoliberal agenda because they facilitate new enclosures—by the dispossession of small-scale farmers from their land and by impeding efforts from communities to control their own energy production—in favor of consolidating and expanding multinational corporate control over resources (Borras, McMichael, and Scoones 2010). In work focusing on the US biofuels industry, political ecology frameworks are used to examine the political dynamics of the growth of both the sugar cane and corn ethanol biofuels chains (Hollander 2010; Gillon 2010). In his analysis of the ethanol industry in Iowa, Gillon (2010) foregrounds the privileging of urban cosmopolitan environmental interests in carbon accounting over local social and ecological impacts related to the growth of the bioeconomy. Other work has also examined how environmental issues and impacts related to biofuels production at the local scale are both discredited and naturalized through "diversionary reframing" of the issues (Freudenburg and Gramling 1994; Bain and Selfa 2013).

With the expansion of the global biofuels complex, attention is turning more to understanding the role of governance, whereby decision making and conduct are not simply determined through government regulations but are increasingly shaped by non-state actors (Ponte, Gibbon, and Vestergaard 2011). Together, the liberalization of international trade, expansion of global value chains, intensification of neoliberal economic reforms, and prevalence of neoliberal ideology have constrained the state's ability to regulate the economic, social, and environmental spheres. Instead, we are witnessing the proliferation of private standards and audit procedures established by the private sector to govern the conduct of individuals and institutions (Busch 2011; Ponte, Gibbon, and Vestergaard 2011). Building on these literatures, we examine the promises, pitfalls, and uneven social and environmental impacts of biofuels development at the local level, and the prospects and limitations of governance systems.

Policy Frameworks and the Governance of Biofuels

Despite the prevalence of neoliberal ideology and practice, government policies have played a major role in the global expansion of the biofuels industry over the last decade. Many governments have instituted mandates for the production and use of biofuels, but far fewer have set standards for greenhouse gas (GHG) emissions reduction or socioeconomic criteria for biofuel use (German and Schoneveld 2011). As of 2009, biofuel mandates were in place in twenty-four nations spanning advanced-industrialized (the United States, Canada, Germany), middle-income (Chile and China), and developing-country (Peru, Colombia, and the Dominican Republic) contexts (Bailis and Baka 2011). In general, government mandates have privileged corporate ownership and control of energy resources over local biofuels development that could enhance local "energy sovereignty" (Borras, McMichael, and Scoones 2010, 578).

US National and State Policies and Their Impacts

In the early and mid-2000s, strong political support for renewable energy in the United States led to a suite of government policies, which in turn fueled the dramatic expansion in biofuel production (Lehrer 2010; Wallender, Claasen, and Nickerson 2011). Of particular significance was the 2005 Renewable Fuel Standard (RFS1), which established a guaranteed market for ethanol by requiring the blending of at least 4.7 billion gallons per year (bgy) of corn ethanol with petroleum. This mandate was expanded with the 2007 Energy Independence and Security Act (EISA) that required consumption of thirty-six bgy of biofuels (thirty-five of ethanol and one of biodiesel) by 2022 (National Research Council 2011, 20).

These incentives created an explosion in private investment in renewable energy. Between 1999 and early 2013, the number of ethanol plants in the United States increased from fifty to 211, production increased nearly from 1.7 bgy to 13.5 bgy, and the number of states with ethanol plants increased from seventeen to twenty-nine (RFA 2013). To help meet the demand for feedstocks, US corn production increased 32 percent, from 9.9 billion to 13.1 billion bushels, between 2000 and 2009 (Wallender, Claasen, and Nickerson 2011).

Since 2008, broad political and public support for biofuels has declined and as a result public incentives for biofuels have begun to shift (Lehrer 2010). In particular, biofuels' climate benefits were questioned and concerns emerged that diverting corn for ethanol was driving up food prices. In 2011, the federal government allowed the blenders' tax to expire, and pressure on the US government to end its favorable policies toward the ethanol industry intensified in mid-2012 as corn and soybean crops were hit hard by the worst drought the country had faced in half a century. As corn prices soared and concerns intensified over higher global food prices, critics of biofuels, including environmental organizations and food retailers, together with a number of major global bureaucracies, including the World Trade Organization (WTO), the United Nations' Food and Agricultural Organisation (FAO), and World Bank, called on the US government to end its mandate for biofuels production (*Wall Street Journal* 2012).

Governing the Sustainability of Biofuels

In response to concerns from scientists, NGOs, and other governments about the biofuels industry triggering the destruction of carbon rich ecosystems, the US government has developed some modest mandates for GHG emission reductions for corn ethanol relative to petroleum. For example, the 2009 Renewable Fuels Standard (RFS2) mandates a 20 percent reduction of GHG emissions for conventional biofuel and a 50 to 60 percent reduction for advanced or cellulosic biofuels. There are no socioeconomic sustainability criteria included in the RFS2.

In 2009, the European Union established the EU Renewable Energy Directive (RED), which mandates that 20 percent of transportation fuels will come from renewable sources by 2020 and requires that an initial 35 percent GHG reduction will increase to 50 percent by 2017. There are additional environmental sustainability criteria in the RED (German and Schoneveld 2011; Bailis and Baka

2011). These government mandates have driven the expansion of voluntary standards and certification schemes designed to ensure that biofuels exported to the European Union meet the RED sustainability rules. By 2013, member states approved fourteen such schemes for biofuels as meeting the RED regulations for reducing GHG emissions, including the Roundtable on Responsible Soy (RTRS), the Roundtable on Sustainable Bioenergy (RSB), Bonsucro, and several industry schemes, such as Greenergy (EU 2013). Most of these schemes are being developed and implemented by private-sector actors or multi-stakeholder initiatives that bring together NGOs and corporations (German and Schoneveld 2011). In addition, within several of these approved schemes, criteria for ensuring social sustainability are non-existent.

In sum, governments have intervened in the agricultural and energy sectors, providing numerous incentives to develop biofuels. As state policies are inevitably biased (Harvey 2005), in the case of biofuels, large-scale, globally oriented agribusiness and energy interests have benefited at the expense of small-scale, locally driven initiatives. However, in the context of neoliberalism and the expansion of global biofuels networks, governments have been reluctant to regulate the negative social and environmental impacts of biofuels. Instead, the governance of biofuels has increasingly shifted to the private sector.

Rural Community Impacts: Case Studies from Kansas and Iowa

Although proponents argue that biofuel industry will reinvigorate declining rural economies and communities, there has been very little empirical research on community impacts. To help illustrate some of the uneven local impacts of biofuel development, we present findings from our case study research investigating the benefits and burdens of the growth of the ethanol industry in six communities in Iowa and Kansas (reported on in more detail elsewhere: see Selfa et al. 2011; Bain and Selfa 2013; Bain et al. 2012). Our findings demonstrate that rural communities bear a disproportionate share of the economic and environmental risks, while the distribution of benefits is less equitable than proponents acknowledge.

Since the 1950s, many rural communities across the Midwest have struggled with long-term economic and population decline as employment opportunities within agriculture have declined (Johnson and Rathge 2006; Carr and Kefalas 2009). At both national and local levels, governments and local economic boosters widely promoted the ethanol industry as central to revitalizing these communities, especially through the creation of "green jobs" (Selfa 2012).

Our study participants reported the optimism and pride they felt because *their* community had been chosen as the site for a new plant. In a community focus group, one participant explained the effect of the plant on the community: "There's an attitude change too [because] you know, we have a new plant ... We don't get a lot of new industry out here, and so it was a big deal when they started building it." Yet, there was some surprise and disappointment among participants that more jobs had not been created. After the initial construction phase, which brought hundreds of mostly temporary jobs into the communities, the number of permanent jobs averaged around forty per plant in our study communities.

While they believed that their town would have been worse off without the plant, many study participants were disappointed that it had not generated greater economic multiplier effects within the community. They reported that the small number of employment opportunities meant that the plant was not sufficient to attract newcomers into the community, which could have boosted house sales and helped reverse declining school populations. City leaders reported seeing few new businesses. In open-ended comments in the community survey, residents' opinions about local benefits were quite diverse:

> "Most people don't have any idea about who runs the plant and who benefits from it locally."
>
> "... a disappointment in the addition of jobs that are not available to the local residents."
>
> "We need this ethanol plant for our local economy as we don't have much else to employ or keep people here."

Many study participants believed that the major beneficiaries of the ethanol industry were farmers. Yet, our interviews and focus groups with farmers revealed that this view was an oversimplification. Ethanol did add a new market for corn farmers, but many livestock producers felt that the ethanol industry had driven up their input costs. Caught in the middle, one farmer said: "It's kind of a two-edged sword for the livestock industry ... I love it when I sell grain but when I buy cattle feed, it's killing me." Many farmers and local officials expressed frustration that ethanol plants were not selling their dried distillers grains (DDGs), a by-product of ethanol production that is used as an animal feed, to local buyers as they had initially promised.

Assessing the overall economic risks and benefits of ethanol plants is complicated by the extent of local public investment that ethanol plants have received. In the midst of the "speculation mentality" that existed among rural communities in the mid-2000s, many local governments across the Midwest offered an array of economic incentives in the hope of attracting an ethanol plant to their communities (Bain 2011). Responses from our case study communities suggested that this strategy was broadly popular, since 70 percent of respondents in the community survey agreed that public funds should be used to attract new businesses to the area. Yet, it was not clear to residents that tax incentives and public investments, such as the provision or maintenance of new infrastructure to support the plant, could add up to millions of dollars in lost revenue or additional costs for the community. In addition, many residents were unaware that local governments were providing generous incentive packages to ethanol plants, some of which would have been built in their community irrespective of the incentives.

Ethanol plants can also strain local infrastructure, imposing costs that rural counties are not necessarily well positioned to assume. The ethanol industry has significantly boosted the number of heavy trucks on the road, which has increased the deterioration of the rural transportation infrastructure and added to maintenance costs. Rural counties feel this burden most acutely, since they are responsible for maintaining most of this infrastructure and are already overburdened (Gkritza et al. 2011). Yet, our interviews revealed that assessments of a plant's impact on local infrastructure were rarely conducted and that future costs to municipalities, such as road maintenance or water and sewer systems, were seldom calculated. In open-ended comments on the community survey, residents from every community expressed concerns about the tax burden brought about by the plant:

> "It may soon close and we will be burdened with the tax load, as we already are and had no say about it; no election! We done this, now you taxpayers eat it."

> "The only problems I have with the ethanol plant is why should our county go into debt to build a paved road to the plant to make the investors money?"

Our community-level research revealed that biofuel development may generate localized environmental risks to specific rural communities. In our survey, 25 percent of respondents were concerned about water resources used by the ethanol plant. Yet, among participants from drought-prone Russell, Kansas, 57 percent of respondents were concerned about water resources, and 67 percent of respondents said this was the most critical issue related to the plant. The semi-arid region of western Kansas relies primarily on the Ogallala aquifer for its water supply, and the long-term viability of the aquifer is threatened due to overuse from feedlots, irrigated agriculture, and residential and industrial uses (Sophocleous 2010). These tensions over ethanol plants' water use were amplified when the region suffered a long-term drought from 2001 to 2006 and residents in some communities were given water restrictions (Selfa et al. 2011). Respondents expressed related concerns in open-ended comments in the survey. One respondent wrote: “Not good. There is not that much water and in a few years there is the possibility that our water sources will be gone. The people for the ethanol plant will leave with their money and we will be stuck without water.” Another wrote: “Very negative. Our water rates have gone up, while we are under severe water restrictions. The ethanol plant gets the water, the citizens get the bill. People in this community can’t enjoy their own back yards.”

Community residents also face health and safety risks from exposure to ethanol plants’ air and water pollution. Selfa (2010) examines environmental violations by ethanol plants in Iowa and Kansas and finds that several plants had been cited for violating environmental standards for air and water quality. In fact, twenty-one of the twenty-six plants in Iowa had at least one citation for air quality violations and several plants had as many as seven. Citations for violations were given to local and absentee owned plants, challenging the view that locally owned plants are more community and environmentally conscious (Selfa 2010).

However, we also found that many residents were largely unaware of the impacts that the local plant might have on their community because of a lack of information and engagement between city leaders and residents (Selfa et al. 2011). As we outline above, many community leaders responded enthusiastically to the hype around ethanol and competed to have a plant built in their locale. Community impact assessments were rarely conducted and were superficial at best. Some survey respondents expressed their frustration at the lack of public information about the plant’s effects—“many didn’t really know the amount of water used or that the price of corn would go up”—and the lack of public engagement on the matter. In Liberal, Kansas, residents’ concerns about the impacts that the new ethanol plant would have on traffic and water usage and the landscape, as well as the exclusion of residents from the approval process, spilled out into the local newspapers.

In sum, our case study research highlighted several important local impacts experienced by rural communities involved in ethanol production. Yet, despite concerns about the distribution of economic benefits, quality of life issues, and the effect of ethanol plants on the local environment, it is important to acknowledge that the majority of study participants responded positively to the development of ethanol plants, espousing the discourse about positive economic benefits while ignoring or minimizing their negative social or environmental impacts. Many respondents assumed that the local plant brought economic benefits to their community, although they did not have any direct experience or evidence to support such assumptions. Similarly, in interviews, most informants assumed that there were no environmental problems or discounted their importance (Bain and Selfa 2013). Many interviewees minimized the environmental risks because of the perceived economic benefits the plant bought to the community. One participant explained: "There are environmental issues on just about everything you can have now. But . . . like I said, the smell and that is minor for what it does for the area." In our media content analysis, we also documented the overwhelmingly positive reporting on the plants by the local press, while any coverage that was at all critical of the biofuels industry was drawn from reprints from national news, mirroring the bandwagon effect documented elsewhere (Wright and Reid 2011).

The unqualified belief in local benefits from the biofuels industry is perhaps unsurprising since the economic alternatives for many of these communities have been industries considered far less environmentally benign than ethanol plants, including hog confinement lots, beef feedlots, oil refineries, asphalt manufacturing, and meat packing plants. Within a context of declining job opportunities and population loss, many rural communities feel they have few choices in terms of economic development, and the perceived need for any kind of economic growth acts to curtail criticism of an industry's negative impacts (Selfa 2010). However, residents who experienced direct negative impacts, such as the restrictions on residential water in some Kansas communities, were more critical of biofuels industry and circumspect about its benefits.

Ownership of Biofuels Plants and Rural Community Benefits

We also sought to understand the role that plant ownership might play in improving how a community might economically and environmentally benefit from the ethanol industry (Bain, Prokos, and Liu 2012; Bain 2011; Selfa et al. 2011). A wealth of social science research demonstrates that communities predominately made up of small, locally owned firms are associated with higher levels of social, economic, and political well-being than comparable communities dominated by large absentee-owned firms (Blanchard and Matthews 2006; Lobao and Stofferahn 2008). Yet, our community survey found that respondents were actually less likely to show high support for locally owned plants than for those with an absentee owner, and more likely to show low support (Bain, Prokos, and Liu 2012). Qualitative data from our interviews help to explain what may appear to be an anomaly.

Interviews with community leaders suggest that local ownership can directly benefit those locals who have the resources to invest in the plant (if the plant is profitable), but overall ownership is irrelevant in terms of the benefits that an ethanol plant may or may not bring to broader sections of the community (Bain 2011). For example, regardless of ownership, local residents do not benefit from lower gas prices, nor was there any evidence that farmers received better prices from local- versus absentee-owned plants. One of the major constraints on locally owned plants providing additional benefits to the community is the nature of the ethanol industry. Since ethanol must be blended with petroleum, it cannot be sold locally but rather is integrated into national and increasingly international supply chains where it can be sent to refineries that blend these energy sources. In addition, plant owners' overriding responsibility is to their investors, whether local or absentee. As one manager of a locally owned plant put it:

> The real winners out of the ethanol industry are not local communities but it's the corn farmers. The industry hasn't been developed or is being promoted because of concern with small communities but because of concern about farmers. And for farmers, local ownership is irrelevant.

When a number of ethanol companies began to go bankrupt in 2008, some community leaders felt that absentee-owned plants were actually preferable because they presented fewer local economic risks. A representative of a locally owned plant in western Kansas explained the fear that the plant management felt at potentially losing millions of dollars of local money that would be impossible to get back:

> This facility had an unbelievable loss. So much so that our member base was panicking because they thought, "oh, we've lost so much money" . . . If ethanol really heads south and heads south hard, you've got a lot of local people involved with it. There's probably fifty to sixty million dollars of [the local county's] money tied up in these things, you know. It's really important to not screw it up because that money . . . you can't go out and get that again.

Similarly, a community leader from Greene County, Iowa, argued that because of the "deep pockets" of the corporate-owned Louis Dreyfus plant, there would be less risk and more security for the community than with a locally owned plant, especially during a period of industry instability:

> [Louis Dreyfus] are in it for the long haul and the good thing about them is that they have deep pockets so that they can ride out the downturn in the market. The county is fortunate that we didn't end up with some local co-op building an undercapitalized forty to sixty million gallon per year plant and trying to make it. If anyone is going to be around in the future it will be [Louis Dreyfus].

In sum, our research suggests that local ownership within the US ethanol industry offers little potential for mitigating the negative economic and environmental effects of biofuels on rural communities. The profitability of ethanol plants is largely determined by government policies as well as the price of oil and corn, over which they have little control.

Prospects and Opportunities for Governing Biofuels and Sustainable Rural Development

The biofuels sector represents an interesting hybrid between state and market actors in the current neoliberal era. While the state has played a central role in promoting and developing the biofuels industry, it has been reluctant to advocate for any parallel social and environmental protections. Instead, we see a growing trend whereby sustainability issues and safeguards for public goods, such as water quality, are increasingly governed by private sector actors, especially through private standards and third-party certification.

Biofuels are anticipated to be increasingly traded in global markets to meet northern consumer countries' renewable energy demands. In response to concerns over environmental degradation and negative socioeconomic impacts occurring as a result of energy crop expansion, especially in the global South, stakeholders in many countries are developing systems for measuring and certifying the sustainability of biofuels production (Elgert 2012; Bailis and Baka 2011). Certification systems are one effort to insert the values of social and environmental sustainability into biofuels value chains and global markets (National Research Council 2010; Zarrilli 2008). Currently, most biofuels certification systems being developed are voluntary (German and Schoneveld 2011). Other systems have regulatory implications, such as EU RED which, as we discuss above, requires that an increasing percentage of EU transportation fuels be comprised of renewable fuels that are produced in sustainable systems, based on both environmental and social criteria (European Commission 2009). Most of the sustainability metrics for biofuels systems focus on environmental impacts, but measures for social sustainability are being developed as well.

Research into the efficacy of sustainability metrics and certification systems for biofuels has begun, and preliminary findings suggest caution about the likelihood that these non-state, private market-driven systems can ensure that environmental and social sustainability are embedded in biofuels production and trade. Past case study research literature on agricultural and forest certification illustrates some of the challenges and shortcomings of these systems and helps inform the analysis of biofuels governance (Friedmann and McNair 2008; Klooster 2006; Konefal and Hatanaka 2011).

In their examination of the social fuels certificate (SFC) program for the Brazilian national biodiesel program, Wilkinson and Herrera (2010) highlight some of the challenges to implementing certification systems. Initiated in response to long standing criticisms of poor working conditions, environmental externalities from manually cutting and burning sugarcane, and the dominance of large farmers in the sugar-based ethanol system, the Brazilian biodiesel program was launched to promote inclusion of smaller farmers growing preferred feedstocks in different regions of the country (Wilkinson and Herrera 2010). Mandatory blending of biodiesel was imposed, and targets for percentages of family farm participants were established by region. While initially the SFC was restricted to biodiesel produced by small farmers of castor and palm oil, over time it proved challenging to obtain sufficient quantity due to structural problems related to access to land, lack of resources and technical assistance, and labor out-migration. Therefore, larger, more consolidated soy farms producing biodiesel have become dominant and have been able to take advantage of the SFC, while smaller castor and palm oil farms have not. If these trends continue, larger farmers and agribusiness interests will dominate the SFC program, undermining its underlying social and environmental objectives.

A comprehensive analysis of EU-approved social sustainability schemes related to biofuels has recently been completed. Because most of these schemes are incipient and therefore difficult to evaluate on the basis of long-term impacts, German and Schoneveld (2011) focus more on analyzing their scope and substantive content. They identify several problematic issues with the way that "social sustainability" is defined and operationalized in the certification schemes: (1) some key social sustainability components are not included; (2) some sustainability certification schemes are devoid of any social criteria and; (3) the lack of procedural rules governing applicability of these criteria, i.e., a clear statement of who must comply with which metric. They emphasize the important role of consumer policies in the European Union and United States to demand and enforce these voluntary sustainability schemes, which in turn can be strengthened through greater access to information about the socioeconomic and ecological impacts of these schemes in producer countries.

Conclusions

We have shown that despite promises of bringing rural economic, environmental, and energy security benefits, biofuels have a mixed track record. The contribution of corn-based biofuels toward addressing climate change has certainly been contested, and its tendency toward locking in paths of unsustainable agricultural systems also undermines its benefits. The critical role of governance of biofuels systems in both industrialized and developing countries emerges from our case study research and from recent literature discussing the emergence and limits of biofuels certification systems. We have argued that while national and state governments have incentivized the rise of biofuels production in many countries, less policy attention has been given to managing the impacts of production on communities and environments. Corporate environmentalism in the form of voluntary certification for biofuels sustainability has limitations in terms of mitigating localized social and environmental impacts (Levidow 2013; Dauvergne and Lister 2010). While certification systems are clearly imperfect mechanisms for governance, they are a growing trend in the current neoliberal era of public private partnerships for global sustainable development (Glasbergen, Biermann, and Mol 2007; Silva-Casteneda 2012).

In addition to the social and environmental limitations of first generation biofuels, it is clear that corn ethanol cannot resolve the problems of growing US and global demand for energy. Within this context, public policy efforts also need to focus on expanding the range of more socially and environmentally sustainable energy solutions. These include efforts to expand other renewable energy sources, and to bring to commercial viability second-generation biofuels systems that use feedstocks that do not compete with food crops, produce fewer greenhouse gases, and are less environmentally damaging to produce. In addition, the production and distribution systems of second-generation feedstocks are more decentralized and have been shown to provide important rural development benefits, at least on a small scale (Bailey et al. 2011). However, in considering such alternatives, it is important to keep in mind that energy conservation would have the most significant, immediate impact on reducing our dependence on fossil fuels and minimizing our impact on the environment (Union of Concerned Scientists 2007). Thus, it is imperative that we continue to pursue policies that seek to reduce our overall energy consumption. Regardless of which paths we pursue, it is clear that rural people and places will continue to be at the center of efforts to site alternative energy sources in the United States and around the globe. As rural sociologists, our job will be to understand the promises, pitfalls, and impacts, and how they are distributed.

While public policy enthusiasm for corn ethanol appears to have waned, biofuel derived from plant materials remains one of the most rapidly growing renewable energy technologies. The inherent link between these technologies and natural resources, agriculture, and rural communities mean it is critical that analyzing such systems remains at the forefront of rural sociological work. As part of any future research agenda, sociologists should prioritize understanding the socioeconomic forces and political context that facilitates the development—or failure—of certain techno-scientific trajectories and not others. Here it is necessary to understand how the benefits and risks of particular technologies are framed, and by whom, and how these framings are then translated into certain policies. Finally, as current renewable energy technologies expand and new ones are instituted, sociologists should be at the forefront in assessing their social, environmental, and economic impacts and distributional effects at various scales. Such research on biorenewables is increasingly important today to help ensure that such technologies are designed to enhance the well-being of rural communities and the sustainability of agricultural and natural resource systems in rural places.

References

Bailey, C., J. Dyer, and L. Teeter. 2011. "Assessing the Rural Development Potential of Lignocellulosic Biofuels in Alabama." *Biomass and Bioenergy* 35 (4): 1408–17. http://dx.doi.org/10.1016/j.biombioe.2010.11.033.

Bailis, R., and J. Baka. 2011. "Constructing Sustainable Biofuels: Governance of the Emerging Biofuel Economy." *Annals of the Association of American Geographers* 101 (4): 827–38. http://dx.doi.org/10.1080/00045608.2011.568867.

Bain, C. 2011. "Local Ownership of Ethanol Plants: What are the Effects on Communities?" *Biomass and Bioenergy* 35 (4): 1400–7. http://dx.doi.org/10.1016/j.biombioe.2010.07.031.

Bain, C., A. Prokos, and H. Liu. 2012. "Community Support of Ethanol Plants: Does Local Ownership Matter?" *Rural Sociology* 77 (2): 143–70. http://dx.doi.org/10.1111/j.1549-0831.2012.00072.x.

Bain, C., and T. Selfa. 2013. "Framing and Reframing the Environmental Risks and Economic Benefits of Ethanol Production in Iowa." *Agriculture and Human Values* 30 (3): 351–64. http://dx.doi.org/10.1007/s10460-012-9401-y.

Blanchard, T., and T. Matthews. 2006. "The Configuration of Local Economic Power and Civic Participation in the Global Economy." *Social Forces* 84 (4): 2241–57. http://dx.doi.org/10.1353/sof.2006.0080.

Borras, S.M., Jr., R. Hall, I. Scoones, B. White, and W. Wolford. 2011. "Towards a Better Understanding of Global Land Grabbing: An Editorial Introduction." *Journal of Peasant Studies* 38 (2): 209–16. http://dx.doi.org/10.1080/03066150.2011.559005.

Borras, S.M., Jr., P. McMichael, and I. Scoones. 2010. "The Politics of Biofuels, Land and Agrarian Change: Editors' Introduction." *Journal of Peasant Studies* 37 (4): 575–92. http://dx.doi.org/10.1080/03066150.2010.512448. Medline:20873025.

Busch, L. 2011. *Standards: Recipes for Reality*. Cambridge, MA: MIT Press.

Carr, P., and M. Kefalas. 2009. *Hollowing out the Middle: The Rural Brain Drain and What it Means for America*. Boston, MA: Beacon Press.

Dauvergne, P., and J. Lister. 2010. "The Prospects and Limits of Eco-consumerism: Shopping Our Way to Less Deforestation?" *Organization & Environment* 23 (2): 132–54. http://dx.doi.org/10.1177/1086026610368370.

Elgert, L. 2012. "Certified Discourse: The Politics of Developing Soy Certification Standards." *Geoforum* 43 (2): 295–304. http://dx.doi.org/10.1016/j.geoforum.2011.08.008.

European Commission. 2004. "Promoting Biofuels in Europe: Securing a Cleaner Future for Transport." Accessed 12 September 2011. http://ec.europa.eu/energy/res/publications/doc/2004_brochure_biofuels_en.pdf.

European Commission. 2009. "Directive 2009/28/EC of the European Parliament and of the Council of 23 April 2009 on the Promotion of the Use of Energy from Renewable Sources and Amending and Subsequently Repealing Directives 2001/77/EC and 2003/30/EC." Accessed 10 September 2012. http://eur-lex.europa.eu/johtml.do?uri=oj:l:2009:140:som:en:html.

European Union (EU). 2013. "Renewable Energy Recognized Voluntary Schemes." Accessed 19 June 2013. http://ec.europa.eu/energy/renewables/biofuels/sustainability_schemes_en.htm.

FAO (Food and Agriculture Organization of the United Nations). 2006. "Introducing the International Bioenergy Platform." Rome: FAO. Accessed 12 September 2011. ftp://ftp.fao.org/docrep/fao/009/a0469e/a0469e00.pdf.

Fargione, J., J. Hill, D. Tilman, S. Polasky, and P. Hawthorne. 29 February 2008. "Land Clearing and the Biofuel Carbon Debt." *Science* 319 (5,867): 1235–38. http://dx.doi.org/10.1126/science.1152747. Medline:18258862.

Freudenburg, W., and R. Gramling. 1994. "Mid-range Theory and Cutting Edge Sociology: A Call for Cumulation." *Environment, Technology and Society* 76 (1): 3–6.

Friedmann, H., and A. McNair. 2008. "Whose Rules Rule? Contested Projects to Certify 'Local Production for Distant Consumers." *Journal of Agrarian Change* 8 (2–3): 408–34. http://dx.doi.org/10.1111/j.1471-0366.2008.00175.x.

German, L., and G. Schoneveld. 2011. "Social Sustainability of EU-Approved Voluntary Schemes for Biofuels: Implications for Rural Livelihoods." Bogor, Indonesia: Center for International Forestry Research Working Paper 75.

Gillon, S. 2010. "Fields of Dreams: Negotiating an Ethanol Agenda in the Midwest United States." *Journal of Peasant Studies* 37 (4): 723–48. http://dx.doi.org/10.1080/03066150.2010.512456. Medline:20873029.

Gkritza, K., I. Nlenanya, W. Jiang, R. Sperry, and D. Smith. 2011. "Infrastructure Impacts of Iowa's Renewable Energy." *Transportation Research Record: Journal of the Transportation Research Board* 2,205 (1): 238–46. http://dx.doi.org/10.3141/2205-30.

Glasbergen, P., F. Biermann and A. Mol, eds. 2007. *Partnerships, Governance and Sustainable Development. Reflections on Theory and Practice.* Cheltenham: Edward Elgar. http://dx.doi.org/10.4337/9781847208668.

GRAIN. 2008. "Seized! The 2008 Land Grab for Food and Financial Security." Accessed 28 July 2011. http://www.grain.org/article/entries/93-seized-the-2008-landgrab-for-food-and-financial-security.

Harvey, D. 2005. *A Brief History of Neoliberalism.* Oxford: Oxford University Press.

Hazell, P. 2006. *Developing Bioenergy: A Win-Win Approach that Can Serve the Poor and the Environment.* Washington, DC: International Food Policy Institute. http://dx.doi.org/10.2499/Focus14CH12.

Hollander, G. 2010. "Power is Sweet: Sugarcane in the Global Ethanol Assemblage." *Journal of Peasant Studies* 37 (4): 699–721. http://dx.doi.org/10.1080/03066150.2010.512455. Medline:20873028.

Johnson, K., and R. Rathge. 2006. "Agricultural Dependence and Changing Population in the Great Plains." In *Population Change and Rural Society*, ed. W. Kandell and D. Brown, 197–217. Dordrecht, Netherlands: Springer. http://dx.doi.org/10.1007/1-4020-3902-6_9.

Kleinschmidt, K., and M. Muller. 2005. *Cultivating a New Rural Economy.* Minneapolis: Institute for Agriculture and Trade Policy.

Klooster, D. 2006. "Environmental Certification of Forests in Mexico: The Political Ecology of a Nongovernmental Market Intervention." *Annals of the Association of American Geographers* 96 (3): 541–65. http://dx.doi.org/10.1111/j.1467-8306.2006.00705.x.

Konefal, J., and M. Hatanaka. 2011. "Enacting Third-Party Certification: A Case Study of Science and Politics in Organic Shrimp Certification." *Journal of Rural Studies* 27 (2): 125–33. http://dx.doi.org/10.1016/j.jrurstud.2010.12.001.

Lehrer, N. 2010. "(Bio)fueling Farm Policy: The Biofuels Boom and the 2008 Farm Bill." *Agriculture and Human Values* 27 (4): 427–44. http://dx.doi.org/10.1007/s10460-009-9247-0.

Levidow, L. 2013. "EU Criteria for Sustainable Biofuels: Accounting for Carbon, Depolicising Plunder." *Geoforum* 44: 211–23. http://dx.doi.org/10.1016/j.geoforum.2012.09.005.

Lobao, L., and C.W. Stofferahn. 2008. "The Community Effects of Industrialized Farming: Social Science Research and Challenges to Corporate Farming Laws." *Agriculture and Human Values* 25 (2): 219–40. http://dx.doi.org/10.1007/s10460-007-9107-8.

McMichael, P. 2009. "The Agrofuels Project at Large." *Critical Sociology* 35 (6): 825–39. http://dx.doi.org/10.1177/0896920509343071.

McMichael, P. 2010. "Agrofuels in the Food Regime." *Journal of Peasant Studies* 37 (4): 609–29. http://dx.doi.org/10.1080/03066150.2010.512450.

Mol, A. 2007. "Boundless Biofuels? Between Vulnerability and Environmental Sustainability." *Sociologia Ruralis* 47 (4): 297–315. http://dx.doi.org/10.1111/j.1467-9523.2007.00446.x.

Mol, A. 2010. "Environmental Authorities and Biofuels Controversies." *Environmental Politics* 19 (1): 61–79. http://dx.doi.org/10.1080/09644010903396085.

Munday, M., G. Bristow, and R. Cowell. 2011. "Wind Farms in Rural Areas: How Far Do Community Benefits from Wind Farms Represent a Local Economic Development Opportunity?" *Journal of Rural Studies* 27 (1): 1–12. http://dx.doi.org/10.1016/j.jrurstud.2010.08.003.

National Research Council. 2010. *Committee on Certification of Sustainable Products and Services. Certifiably Sustainable?: The Role of Third-Party Certification Systems: Report of a Workshop.* Washington, DC: National Research Council.

National Research Council. 2011. *Renewable Fuel Standard: Potential Economic and Environmental Effects of U.S. Biofuels Policy.* Washington, DC: National Academies Press.

Oxfam International. 2008. "Another Inconvenient Truth: How Biofuels Policies are Deepening Poverty and Accelerating Climate Change." Accessed 15 September 2011. http://www.oxfam.org/en/grow/policy/another-inconvenient-truth.

Ponte, S., P. Gibbon, and J. Vestergaard. 2011. "Governing through Standards: An Introduction." In *Governing through Standards: Origins, Drivers and Limitations*, ed. S. Ponte, P. Gibbon, and J. Vestergaard, 1–24. London: Palgrave Macmillan.

RFA (Renewable Fuels Association). 2013. Accessed 14 August 2013. http://www.ethanolrfa.org/pages/statistics.

Sassen, S. 2006. *Territory-Authority-Rights: From Medieval to Global Assemblages.* Princeton, NJ: Princeton University Press.

Searchinger, T., R. Heimlich, R.A. Houghton, F. Dong, A. Elobeid, J. Fabiosa, S. Tokgoz, D. Hayes, and T.H. Yu. 29 February 2008. "Use of U.S. Croplands for Biofuels Increases Greenhouse Gases through Emissions from Land-Use Change." *Science* 319 (5,867): 1238–40. http://dx.doi.org/10.1126/science.1151861. Medline:18258860.

Selfa, T. 2010. "Global Benefits, Local Burdens? The Paradox of Governing Biofuels Production in Kansas and Iowa." *Renewable Agriculture and Food Systems* 25 (2): 129–42. http://dx.doi.org/10.1017/S1742170510000153.

Selfa, T. 2012. "Depopulation and Energy Production—The Dynamics of Conflicting Landscape Visions: An American Perspective." In *The Political Ecology of Depopulation: Inequality, Landscape and People*, ed. A. Panaiagua, R. Bryant, and T. Kizos, 273–98. Spain: Rolde Foundation, CEDDAR.

Selfa, T., L. Kulcsár, C. Bain, R. Goe, and G. Middendorf. 2011. "Biofuels Bonanza? Exploring Community Perceptions of the Promises and Perils of Biofuels Production." *Biomass and Bioenergy* 35 (4): 1379–89. http://dx.doi.org/10.1016/j.biombioe.2010.09.008.

Silva-Casteneda, L. 2012. "A Forest of Evidence: Third Party Certification and Multiple Forms of Proof—Case Study of Oil Palm Plantations in Indonesia." *Agriculture and Human Values* 29: 361–70.

Sophocleous, M. 2010. "Review: Groundwater Management Practices, Challenges, and Innovations in the High Plains Aquifer, USA—Lessons and Recommended Actions." *Hydrogeology Journal* 18 (3): 559–75. http://dx.doi.org/10.1007/s10040-009-0540-1.

Union of Concerned Scientists. 2007. "Principles for Bioenergy Development." Accessed 30 March 2012. http://www.ucsusa.org/assets/documents/clean_energy/ucs-bioenergy-principles.pdf.

Wall Street Journal. 2012. "Ethanol vs. the World." 11 August, A16.

Wallender, S., R. Claasen, and C. Nickerson. 2011. "The Ethanol Decade: An Expansion of US Corn Production, 2000–09." EIB-79, August. Washington, DC: Economic Research Service, US Department of Agriculture.

Wilkinson, John, and Selena Herrera. 2010. "Biofuels in Brazil: Debates and Impacts." *Journal of Peasant Studies* 37 (4): 749–68. http://dx.doi.org/10.1080/03066150.2010.512457.

Worldwatch Institute. 2006. "Biofuels for Transportation: Global Potential and Implications for Sustainable Agriculture and Energy in the 21st Century." Prepared by Worldwatch Institute for the German Federal Ministry of Food, Agriculture and Consumer Protection, in cooperation with the Agency for Technical Cooperation and the Agency of Renewable Resources.

Wright, Wynne, and Taylor Reid. 2011. "Green Dreams or Pipe Dreams? Media Framing of the U.S. Biofuels Movement." *Biomass and Bioenergy* 35 (4): 1390–99. http://dx.doi.org/10.1016/j.biombioe.2010.07.020.

Zarrilli, S. 2008. *Making Certification Work for Sustainable Development: The Case of Biofuels.* Geneva, NY: United Nations.

CHAPTER 14

New Natural Gas Development and Rural Communities: Key Issues and Research Priorities

Abby Kinchy, Simona Perry, Danielle Rhubart, Richard Stedman, Kathryn Brasier, and Jeffrey Jacquet

Introduction

Natural gas provided approximately 25 percent of the total energy used in the United States in 2010 (EIA 2011a). This percentage is expected to grow: production of natural gas has burgeoned in the past decade due to technological advances that have made the development of "unconventional" natural gas sources economically feasible. Unconventional gas resources are found in low-permeability rock, which previously made extraction technically difficult and economically undesirable. Today, however, drilling operations use a combination of techniques, including drilling horizontally through the gas-bearing formation and using perforation and slickwater hydraulic fracturing techniques (commonly called "fracking") to stimulate the gas well. Hydraulic fracturing uses a mixture of water, sand, and chemicals under very high pressure to fracture the formation and release gas. These techniques have vastly increased the potential for producing natural gas, spurring a rapid build-up of gas industry activity in many parts of the United States and Canada. As of 2011, three unconventional shale gas resources (shale gas, tight gas sands, and coal bed methane) make up 57 percent of the proven technically recoverable natural gas produced in the United States (EIA 2011a; Figure 4.1; Table 4.1). In the United States, natural gas is expected to be recoverable from a total of nineteen shale formations in the lower forty-eight states (EIA 2011b), with seven formations the main focus of activity (US DOE 2009).

This new wave of energy extraction directs researchers to explore the implications of development for places experiencing rapid growth. During the 1970s, social scientists and community planners reported on rapid population growth and change from development of energy sources in the intermountain West of the United States, giving rise to the "boomtown" or "social disruption" model of energy-based development (Cortese and Jones 1977). Much of this literature is relevant to the new natural gas boom. Re-engaging this literature enhances the applicability of sociological research to local and regional impact analysis. Moreover, we must assess these dynamics within the context of international and national social, political, and economic structures. Doing so raises critical sociological questions about the dynamics of conflicts over the use of rural space and the implications of energy policies and development for rural people, particularly the generation or reproduction of economic and environmental inequalities.

In this chapter, we review the state of knowledge and suggest a research agenda that addresses these critical issues and reasserts the role of rural sociology and other social sciences in energy development debates. In the next section, we provide background on the drivers of the new natural gas rush and summarize its potential implications for rural communities. We then use this summary to highlight critical tensions and areas needing additional research.

Lessons from Boomtown Research

Local community leaders, journalists, and other observers have begun to raise hard questions about the social impacts of unconventional gas development. Many of these concerns echo rural sociological research on boomtowns. Such work, initiated in the 1970s and 1980s and continued in the on-shore and off-shore energy development context, provides one critical foundation for identifying potential social impacts of the current wave of energy development. The boomtown model describes a generalized process in which natural resource extraction leads to rapid escalation of economic activity and related population growth and infrastructure development. When the activity decreases, the community experiences economic decline and related out-migration. These boom-bust cycles are driven by a number of factors external to the local community, including demand, prices, changes in technology, organization of the extraction process, and local and global political forces (Cortese and Jones 1977).

Boomtown research offers several key insights with respect to new gas developments. Studies indicate that positive economic impacts occur during the boom stages, but these impacts are often below expectations during the initial stages of development and then decline as development proceeds (Thompson and Blevins 1983). Such findings challenge the assumption that unconventional natural gas development creates prosperity in areas facing economic decline. A widely criticized 2009 report by researchers in the Department of Energy and Mineral Engineering at the Pennsylvania State University estimates that Marcellus Shale development in Pennsylvania will generate tens of thousands of jobs and billions of dollars of revenue (Considine et al. 2009; cf. MSETC 2011; 2012). In contrast, Kinnaman (2011) finds that many of the non-peer-reviewed studies that address economic impacts overstate the fiscal gains of unconventional gas development. Businesses that provide goods and services to the extractive industry and the burgeoning population do provide economic growth and employment in the retail, service, and construction sectors, through a ripple effect (Marchand 2012). The service sector, in particular, sees increased retail activity for businesses that serve the new residents (Longbrake and Geyler 1979). However, the opportunity for spillover effects of employment opportunities into other sectors of the economy is constrained by multiple factors and may be small relative to the overall impact of energy development (Black et al. 2005). The magnitude of economic activity likely varies according to a community's size, degree of isolation, and preexisting infrastructure and economic activity (Brown et al. 2011).

Research also suggests that economic change associated with resource extraction can foster inequality (for a review, see Freudenburg and Wilson 2002). The combination of increased demand for goods and services and new labor force participants with elevated spending power can result in rapidly escalating prices, particularly in housing markets. This effect is particularly acute in more isolated rural areas with limited housing stock prior to natural gas development. In the case of Marcellus Shale development, the cost of housing (including hotels, rentals, and sales) has increased due to growing demand and energy workers' greater purchasing power. As a result, families on the economic margin (e.g., working poor, disabled, seniors) are pushed out of the housing market and services that provide emergency housing and subsidies are strained. In Pennsylvania, homelessness in rural counties experiencing rapid unconventional gas development has risen, and some residents have migrated outside of the region to find affordable housing (Williamson and Kolb 2011). Recent research suggests that new housing development in rural areas can allow communities to adapt (Farren et al. 2013).

Public services are often strained by rapid energy development. For example, water and sewer systems may be overwhelmed as they attempt to accommodate a growing population (Cortese and Jones 1977). Social services, such as the criminal justice system and health services, may also be strained, although studies of these impacts have mixed or inconclusive findings (Freudenburg and Jones

1991; Kowalski and Zajac 2012). Tax revenues levied on the industry may bring about the potential for additional public resources (Theodori 2009), but the magnitude of these resources and their distribution differ by state. Further, such new funding streams may be significantly delayed relative to the rapid growth or dwarfed by the need for expanded infrastructure and public services. Complaints about roads, traffic, and public safety are among the greatest concerns of residents in the new boomtowns (Brasier et al. 2011; Jacquet and Stedman 2013a; Theodori 2009; Perry 2012a). Local government capacity to address these problems is challenged by jurisdictional unevenness, insufficient control over land use, volatile production patterns, lack of information about development patterns, and lags in funding (Jacquet 2009). In many cases, long-time residents may resent changes in the role of local government, and officials must make decisions in a context of conflict, opposition, and uncertainty.

Residents of energy boomtowns perceive changes to their communities in a way that is often manifested in decreased senses of security, changes in community identity and well-being, and residual impacts on social relationships (Freudenburg 1982; Jobes 1987). Individuals' experiences of change can be affected by their connection to the industry, socioeconomic standing, and social position (Jacquet 2012a), and these differences can generate conflict. In cases where landowners contract privately with gas companies and receive lease and royalty payments, as in the development of the Marcellus Shale, schisms may emerge between landowners and non-landowners, and between those landowners who leased early for smaller amounts and those who leased later for larger payments (Brasier et al. 2011).

Beyond the Boomtown Model

The new unconventional natural gas boomtowns may experience many of the changes seen in other energy boomtowns, documented in the literature summarized above and elsewhere in this volume. However, the evidence and logic of boomtown analyses have been debated (e.g., Krannich and Greider 1990). Brown et al. (2005) suggest that "boom-bust-recovery" more accurately portrays the stages, as they find that community members adapt by creating new interpretations and relationships to their community over time. Most research has tended to rely on case studies and cross-sectional data collection. Consequently, much of this research has suffered from criticisms related to the inability to establish causal relationships between social changes and the extractive activity and gathering timely, high-quality data (Freudenburg 1982; Brookshire and D'arge 1980). Further, the impacts of energy extraction, and perceptions of it, vary across regions, communities, and individuals (Freudenburg and Gramling 1993; Stedman et al., 2013).

Better understanding the variables and causal relationships that create impacts can help a community prepare for and harness the effects of extractive industries, especially in the context of multiple demands on rural space. We see several research paths that would lead to a more refined boomtown model. First, careful longitudinal and comparative analyses are needed to effectively understand the impacts of boomtown development in the current context of energy development (Brown et al. 2005). Research should comprehensively examine the fit of the boomtown model to the areas experiencing development, especially given their varied histories with extraction and social and ecological contexts. It can be challenging to discriminate between the effects of energy development and other local, regional, or national trends. New boomtown research needs to consider simultaneous and interrelated effects of multiple—and potentially contrasting—forms of rural development (Brown et al. 2011).

The current controversy surrounding unconventional natural gas development points to new research questions not previously addressed by the boomtown model. Researchers studying the new boomtowns will have to consider the changing institutional context, particularly the increasingly global reach of the industry and new approaches to environmental governance. Boomtown research of the 1970s took place during the high point of public support for federal government action to protect the environment, just as many new federal environmental protection laws were going into effect. However, the environmental impacts of energy development were, for the most part, peripheral concerns to those social scientists studying the social disruptions associated with boomtowns. Today, in contrast, it would be insufficient to study new natural gas development without attention to its environmental and public health effects. Social and environmental disruptions associated with gas development are deeply intertwined, and fracking is a public controversy in a way that the technologies of the prior wave of energy boomtowns were not. Therefore, boomtown literature needs to be integrated with other theoretical orientations to address critical questions faced by communities planning for the impacts of development.

In particular, new research on gas development must be attentive to the uncertainty and growing conflict surrounding its environmental and public health impacts. Extracting gas from unconventional reserves differs in several respects from past forms of energy development in North America: the extraction techniques are novel, and the full range of their impacts on the air, soil, and water is still relatively unknown. The horizontal and hydraulic fracturing techniques currently being used to develop unconventional natural gas resources can mean less surface disturbance at well sites than traditional vertical drilling techniques. However, the liquid and solid waste that unconventional gas development operations produce can pose significant environmental and public health risks if not handled securely (Entrekin et al. 2011; Colborn et al. 2011), and spills and other violations have been cited (Staaf 2012). In addition, numerous incidents of private well water contamination (particularly from methane migration) linked to drilling activities are now the subject of a variety of investigations (e.g., Jackson et al. 2013). The use, and potential contamination, of millions of gallons of fresh water for hydraulic fracturing operations is a major social and environmental concern (Soeder and Kappel 2009). Other concerns include the impact of drilling, building pipelines, and other infrastructure on forests and wildlife, public health, air quality, soil contamination, large-scale land use change, truck traffic, and the risk of chemical spills at drilling sites and along trucking routes, as well as a more general concern about protecting the rural landscape and quality of life (Perry 2012a; 2013; Brasier et al. 2011). In addition, the disposal of waste water in deep storage wells has been linked to seismic activity (Ellsworth 2013).

In this context, four areas of research seem particularly important. One deals with questions about the public policy and regulatory environment for unconventional natural gas development. Another key area for research concerns environmental inequality. A third research domain addresses changes in land use. Finally, there is great potential for studying gas development through a focus on community members' sense of place. We will now discuss each of these.

Public Policy and Regulation

Understanding the rush toward unconventional natural gas development requires study of the ways that oil and gas firms, states, and civil society organizations have contributed to the construction of favorable governance arrangements in support of these new activities. This is an area where historically minded and policy-oriented scholars can make an important contribution. There is a need for additional examination of the history of research, technology development, industry strategizing, and policymaking behind the current natural gas rush. How have diverse actors framed and generated hype for unconventional gas? For example, the claim that natural gas serves as a "bridge fuel" has mobilized both environmentalists and policymakers in support of gas exploration (Stephenson et al. 2012), and echoes an almost identical push for coal development in the 1970s (e.g., Wilson 1980). Academic reports have also lent support to domestic natural gas development. A multidisciplinary report published by MIT in 2011 indicates that natural gas could be a carbon-reducing substitute for coal in many applications and that it would help support wind power generation (MIT Energy Initiative 2011). Howarth et al. (2011) present a dissenting view of the carbon impacts of natural gas. Government and industrial research spending that led to development of high-volume hydraulic fracturing is a researchable topic. As President Barack Obama indicated in the 2012 State of the Union Address: "it was public research dollars, over the course of thirty years, that helped develop the technologies to extract all this natural gas out of shale rock—reminding us that government support is critical in helping businesses get new energy ideas off the ground" (Obama 2012; see also EIA 2011b).

Emerging governance arrangements and institutional changes should also be studied in more detail. In particular, struggles over the scale of governance—from individual landowners and municipalities up to federal and potentially transnational institutions—would be particularly fruitful areas of investigation. New natural gas developments come at a time when, generally speaking, neoliberal projects have rolled back state functions designed to curb the environmentally destructive effects of capitalism (McCarthy and Prudham 2004; Malin 2013). Such restructuring of environmental governance has occurred through market-based privatization, state budget cuts, rescaling of levels of environmental governance resulting in weakened environmental protections, and a shift to voluntary rather than mandatory environmental standards. Many argue that "the regulation of oil and gas field activities is managed best at the state level where regional and local conditions are understood and where regulations can be tailored to fit the needs of the local environment" (Ground Water Protection Council 2009, 6). Consistent with this argument, the oil and gas industry has long been exempt from many federal regulations, such as the Emergency Planning and Community Right-to-Know Act of 1984, which requires manufacturers to inform the public about toxic chemicals they use or release. Federal oversight of the environmental impacts of the industry was further reduced with the Energy Policy Act of 2005, which amended the Safe Drinking Water Act to exclude hydraulic fracturing from federal regulations intended to protect underground sources of drinking water from the long-term underground storage of hazardous wastes. States, rather than the EPA, have the majority of the responsibility for regulating the impacts of hydraulic fracturing on drinking water. Conflicts over the appropriate scale of governance have thus become a central feature of new natural gas developments, consistent with a great deal of research on neoliberalism and the politics of scale (Finewood and Stroup 2012; Kinchy 2014).

There have been efforts to govern gas development at the local or municipal level, even though private ownership of mineral rights can limit collective decision making. In New York, some communities are forming landowner cooperatives, which enable them to bargain with gas companies for higher payments, greater environmental protections, and other concessions (Jacquet and Stedman 2011). In addition, in New York and Pennsylvania, some municipalities have attempted to ban or limit gas development activity through zoning and community charters that prohibit certain kinds of industrial activity (Kennedy 2011). The law in some states discourages local control; for example, Pennsylvania recently passed a law (Act 13) that replaces local zoning with uniform state zoning regulations. Nevertheless, a growing anti-fracking movement has begun to forge local-global and rural-urban solidarities against the policies and regulations that currently govern unconventional oil and gas development in North America and elsewhere (Perry 2011; Pearson 2013; Control Risks 2012; de Rijke 2013a). These political struggles are important topics for research, with implications well beyond the specific case of natural gas development.

Environmental Inequality

Economic benefits and environmental health consequences of unconventional natural gas development are not distributed equitably. As in many other sites of fossil fuel production (e.g., coal mining regions or communities located near oil refineries), some areas become "sacrifice zones" to meet the broader national and global demand for fuel (Kuletz 1998; Fox 1999). There is an urgent need for research on the historical and political processes by which these environmental inequalities are generated. How does the history of coal mining in Appalachia, which created an "internal colony" of the United States (Gaventa 1978, 53), compare to the processes by which oil and gas companies are securing economic dominance and social consent in the new gas development regions (Hudgins 2013)?

We could also compare unconventional gas development in rural areas to the typically urban development dynamics through which the "poisons of the rich [are] offered as short-term economic remedies for poverty" (Bullard and Johnson 2000, 574). In particular, the case of Marcellus Shale development indicates that a variety of stakeholders—from the gas industry to university scientists to local municipal leaders—have promoted gas drilling as a solution to the economic problems of communities where agriculture is in decline and rural poverty is widespread. Importantly, as Pellow (2002) cautions, we should not view this as a simple story of perpetrators versus victims. Frequently, leaders and members of politically and culturally marginalized communities "are deeply implicated in creating" environmental inequality as they pursue pro-growth policies that displace other social goals such as securing healthy environments or sustaining an agrarian way of life (Pellow 2002, 3, 16). Understanding how and why this is the case should be a research priority.

In addition to the distribution of economic benefits and environmental burdens, an emerging topic of research on environmental inequality concerns the production of knowledge gaps and the failure of public agencies to produce risk information that is relevant to vulnerable communities. Recently, social scientists have advanced the concept of undone science, which refers to "areas of research that are left unfunded, incomplete, or generally ignored but that social movements or civil society organizations often identify as worthy of more research" (Frickel et al. 2010). This is clearly relevant to the case of fracking (Kinchy and Perry 2012). Scientific and regulatory communities have struggled to fully document and analyze the widely dispersed impacts of unconventional natural gas development. Academic researchers have voiced concerns, citing an overall lack of independent scientific assessments to understand the possible short- and long-term environmental risks and costs to society (Entrekin et al. 2011; Phillips 2011; Perry 2012b). Scientific ignorance about the impacts of shale gas development may contribute to the creation of environmental inequality by allowing development to proceed without full consideration of its environmental and human health consequences.

Land Uses in Conflict

Another research area that deserves greater attention examines changes in land use and associated social impacts. Researchers and communities alike have questions about how unconventional gas development may impact existing agricultural and forestry practices, tourism and recreation, and community character. Rural sociology as a discipline has witnessed and analyzed the supposed steady movement away from rural economies based on traditional resource dependence toward more diversified forms of rural development (e.g., Stedman et al. 2012). As such, transitions back to resource development represent a major analytic challenge to the field.

A primary question for many rural communities is how gas development will affect farming and other major land uses. Farmers and forest owners may stand to benefit most directly from natural gas development, as the majority of leasing and royalty payments should flow to these larger landowners (Jacquet and Stedman 2011). It is not yet clear whether such payments will encourage or discourage farming and forestry practices. In Pennsylvania, for example, some supporters of gas development have favorably characterized it as an opportunity for struggling farms to pay off debts. However, areas in Pennsylvania with significant gas development are also seeing decreases in dairy production at higher rates than in other counties (Adams and Kelsey 2012; see also Finkel et al. 2013). The exact cause of the higher rate of decline is unclear, indicating the need for additional research on the intersection of unconventional natural gas development with long-term trends in dairy farming in these regions. In addition, environmental advocates, including some organic food processors, point out that the industry poses risks to safe food production by impacting water, air, and soil resources in the long term (e.g., Miller 2012). Pennsylvania Certified Organic outlines specific requirements that it will expect of certified organic farms where natural gas exploration and drilling is taking place, and states that "all land disturbed by industry may have to be removed from certification for at least three years" (Pennsylvania Certified Organic 2012).

Some lessons may be drawn from the unconventional gas and oil fields in Alberta, Canada. In that case, the speculative value of land for non-agricultural purposes (including housing and other infrastructure development related to the energy industry) forced competition between agricultural and nonagricultural land uses (Ag Summit and Agrivantage Strategic Initiatives Committee 2005, 19). In addition, farmers reported that natural gas developments de-valued the productivity and rural quality of life provided by well-managed agricultural lands (Worbets and Berdahl 2003). While these findings suggest that economic necessity and environmental resource constraints may force farmers to choose between gas-related land development and agricultural production, more research is needed to fully understand how gas development affects farming and food systems (de Rijke 2013b).

Community and Sense of Place

Another important area of research where rural sociology is poised to make an impact involves the sense of place—the meanings and attachments that people hold for their local landscape—in areas affected by gas development. Attachment is seen as a generally positive bond between people and setting (Low and Altman 1992). Symbolic meanings give life to questions about what kind of place the setting represents (Stedman 2008; Davenport and Anderson 2005). Important place meanings (e.g., "a close knit place" or "an idyllic rural setting") that underpin attachment can be challenged by the social and ecological changes associated with the boomtown phenomena of rapid resource development. Regardless of whether qualitative, phenomenological, or more quantitative hypothesis-testing modes of inquiry are used (for a review, see Trentelman 2009), such work can provide valuable insights and illuminate the experiences, cultures, and perspectives of rural people whose lives are changing as a consequence of energy policies and industrial developments at a local, national, and global scale. In particular, it is necessary to better understand how rural residents' sense of place shapes their individual and collective experience, as well as subsequent responses to the natural gas industry and conflicts.

Natural gas development can involve the transformation of rural landscapes, potentially threatening land uses that are symbolically and personally meaningful to local residents. For example, important meanings may emphasize the quality of the natural environment (Stedman 2003), and as such, may be challenged by discrete events (i.e., spills) occurring at other stages of the energy extraction process. It is also important to recognize that power is important to the creation of local place meanings (e.g., Stokowski 2008), and that energy companies themselves play a role in trying to promulgate associated community identity (Bell and York 2010).

Research on the relationship between sense of place and energy is in relative infancy. Devine-Wright and Howes (2010) apply this framework to examine opposition to an offshore wind farm in North Wales, and, in a study of Marcellus Shale development, Brasier et al. (2011) concludes that differences related to the meanings of place were at the heart of some conflicts between long-term and seasonal residents (see also Jacquet 2012b; Jacquet and Stedman 2013b; Perry 2012a). Previous research shows that place meanings and attachment may affect how certain people engage in, opt out of, or ignore conflicts and rapid changes involving the future of a place (Davenport and Anderson 2005). For example, Vorkinn and Riese (2001) find that residents' sense of place and attachments to places that were affected by hydropower development were a better predictor of attitudes toward that development than their socio-demographic characteristics. Sense of place may also shape perceptions of risk and opportunity (Brasier et al. 2013; Schafft et al. 2013). Thus, understanding how unconventional natural gas developments may be perceived as a threat or an opportunity related to a community's sense of place may help social scientists understand the relationship between the values, beliefs, perceptions, and behaviors of those local communities and provide important context for understanding short- and long-term sociological responses to changes brought about by energy developments.

Conclusions

We have outlined several priorities for social scientific study of unconventional natural gas development in North America. There are many unknowns about the interrelated social and environmental impacts of unconventional natural gas development at this scale, and studying and documenting its effects requires a proportionately large outlay of investment and effort.

In addition to the research agenda described here, we see a need for greater interdisciplinarity in research on natural gas development, drawing together anthropological, economic, humanistic, political, ecological, health, and engineering knowledge. There are many opportunities for scholars who have not typically studied energy or extractive industries to address the questions raised in this chapter. For example, there is a great need for agrifood scholars to examine how agricultural production is changing in relation to gas development. We see an important opportunity for environmental sociologists, political ecologists, geographers, cultural anthropologists, and others attuned to nature-society interactions to bring perspectives to bear on the ways that rural peoples' sense of place and cultural attachment to the land encounter global processes of energy development. Environmental justice scholars can document patterns of inequality reproduced or newly emerging in the development of unconventional energy resources. Finally, natural scientists and engineers are crucial sources of knowledge about the effects of unconventional natural gas development. Given the deep interconnections between social and environmental disruptions, there are many points of potential collaboration and interchange.

Beyond interdisciplinary collaboration, "transacademic" (Fortmann in this volume) research may be a promising way to address the kinds of questions and problems that matter to rural communities affected by gas development. Collaborations between academic researchers and nonacademic community members could facilitate community-driven research agendas. There are many successful models of "citizen science" aimed at documenting changes to the natural world, including the impacts of fracking (Jalbert et al. 2013), yet many social scientists have been slow to engage in such work. We envision programs that would offer local training in social science research or participatory action research, promoted in a way that gives rural communities their own tools and capacity to adapt or even thrive in the face of rapid change. Such efforts would not only support rural communities, but also prompt academic researchers to critically examine our own relationships and obligations to rural communities, the energy industry, and dominant systems of governance. Perhaps an unintended consequence of the natural gas rush will be a deeper discussion among rural sociologists about the nature of our work and our ties to the communities we study.

References

Adams, Riley, and Timothy W. Kelsey. 2012. "Pennsylvania Dairy Farms and Marcellus Shale, 2007–2010." Accessed 12 September 2012. http://pubs.cas.psu.edu/freepubs/pdfs/ee0020.pdf.

Ag Summit and Agrivantage Strategic Initiatives Committee. 2005. "Land Use Policy and the Agri-food Industry in Alberta. Alberta, Canada: Agriculture and Food Council." Accessed 10 September 2012. http://www4.agr.gc.ca/resources/prod/doc/pol/consult/miss/pdf/c06.pdf.

Bell, Shannon Elizabeth, and Richard York. 2010. "Community Economic Identity: The Coal Industry and Ideology Construction in West Virginia." *Rural Sociology* 75 (1): 111–43. http://dx.doi.org/10.1111/j.1549-0831.2009.00004.x.

Black, Dan, Terra McKinnish, and Seth Sanders. 2005. "The Economic Impact of the Coal Boom and Bust." *Economic Journal* 115 (503): 449–76. http://dx.doi.org/10.1111/j.1468-0297.2005.00996.x.

Brasier, Kathryn J., Matthew R. Filteau, Diane K. McLaughlin, Jeffrey Jacquet, Richard C. Stedman, Timothy W. Kelsey, and Stephan J. Goetz. 2011. "Residents' Perceptions of Community and Environmental Impacts from Development of Natural Gas in the Marcellus Shale: A Comparison of Pennsylvania and New York Case Studies." *Journal of Rural Social Sciences* 26 (1): 32–61.

Brasier, Kathryn J., Diane K. McLaughlin, Danielle Rhubart, Richard Stedman, Matthew Filteau, and Jeffrey Jacquet. 2013. "Risk Perceptions of Natural Gas Development in the Marcellus Shale." *Environmental Practice* 15 (2): 108–22. http://dx.doi.org/10.1017/S1466046613000021.

Brookshire, David S., and Ralph C. D'arge. 1980. "Adjustment Issues of Impacted Communities or, Are Boomtowns Bad?" *Natural Resources Journal* 20: 523–46.

Brown, Ralph B., Shawn F. Dorius, and Richard S. Krannich. 2005. "The Boom-Bust-Recovery Cycle: Dynamics of Change in Community Satisfaction and Social Integration in Delta, Utah." *Rural Sociology* 70 (1): 28–49. http://dx.doi.org/10.1526/0036011053294673.

Brown, Timothy C., William B. Bankston, Craig J. Forsyth, and Emily R. Berthelot. 2011. "Qualifying the Boom-Bust Paradigm: An Examination of the off-Shore Oil and Gas Industry." *Sociology Mind* 1 (3): 96–104. http://dx.doi.org/10.4236/sm.2011.13012.

Bullard, Robert D., and Glenn S. Johnson. 2000. "Environmentalism and Public Policy: Environmental Justice: Grassroots Activism and Its Impact on Public Policy Decision Making." *Journal of Social Issues* 56 (3): 555–78. http://dx.doi.org/10.1111/0022-4537.00184.

Colborn, Theo, Carol Kwiatkowski, Kim Schultz, and Mary Bachran. 2011. "Natural Gas Operations from a Public Health Perspective." *Human and Ecological Risk Assessment* 17 (5): 1039–56. http://dx.doi.org/10.1080/10807039.2011.605662.

Considine, Timothy, Robert Watson, Rebecca Entler, and Jeffrey Sparks. 2009. *An Emerging Giant: Prospects and Economic Impacts of Developing the Marcellus Shale Natural Gas Play.* The Pennsylvania State University College of Earth and Mineral Sciences, Department of Energy and Mineral Engineering. Accessed 12 September 2012. http://s3.amazonaws.com/propublica/assets/monongahela/EconomicImpactsMarcellus.pdf.

Control Risks. 2012. *The Global Anti-fracking Movement: What It Wants, How It Operates and What's Next.* London: Control Risks. Accessed 18 December 2013. http://www.controlrisks.com/Oversized%20assets/shale_gas_whitepaper.pdf.

Cortese, Charles F., and Bernie Jones. 1977. "The Sociological Analysis of Boomtowns." *Western Sociological Review* 8 (1): 75–90.

Davenport, Mae, and Dorothy Anderson. 2005. "Getting from Sense of Place to Place-Based Management: An Interpretive Investigation of Place Meanings and Perceptions of Landscape Change." *Society & Natural Resources* 18 (7): 625–41. http://dx.doi.org/10.1080/08941920590959613.

Devine-Wright, Patrick, and Yuko Howes. 2010. "Disruption to Place Attachment and the Protection of Restorative Environments: A Wind Energy Case Study." *Journal of Environmental Psychology* 30 (3): 271–80. http://dx.doi.org/10.1016/j.jenvp.2010.01.008.

EIA (US Energy Information Administration). 2011a. Annual Energy Review 2010. Washington, DC: Department of Energy. Accessed 10 September 2012. http://www.eia.gov/totalenergy/data/annual/pdf/aer.pdf.

EIA (US Energy Information Administration). 2011b. *Review of Emerging Resources: U.S. Shale Gas and Shale Oil Plays*. Washington, DC: Department of Energy.

Ellsworth, W.L. 12 July 2013. "Injection-Induced Earthquakes." *Science* 341 (6,142): 1225942. http://dx.doi.org/10.1126/science.1225942. Medline:23846903.

Entrekin, Sally, Michelle Evans-White, Brent Johnson, and Elisabeth Hagenbuch. 2011. "Rapid Expansion of Natural Gas Development Poses a Threat to Surface Waters." *Frontiers in Ecology and the Environment* 9 (9): 503–11. http://dx.doi.org/10.1890/110053.

Farren, M., A. Weinstein, M. Partridge, and M. Betz. 2013. "Too Many Heads and Not Enough Beds: Will Shale Development Cause a Housing Shortage?" *Ohio State University Extension*. http://aede.osu.edu/sites/aede/files/publication_files/Shale%20Housing%20June%202013.pdf.

Finewood, Michael H., and Laura J. Stroup. 2012. "Fracking and Neoliberalization of the Hydro-Social Cycle in Pennsylvania's Marcellus Shale." *Journal of Contemporary Water Research & Education* 147 (1): 72–9. http://dx.doi.org/10.1111/j.1936-704X.2012.03104.x.

Finkel, Madelon L., Jane Selegean, Jake Hays, and Nitin Kondamudi. 2013. "Marcellus Shale Drilling's Impact on the Dairy Industry in Pennsylvania: A Descriptive Report." *New Solutions* 23 (1): 189–201. http://dx.doi.org/10.2190/NS.23.1.k. Medline:23552654.

Fox, Julia. 1999. "Mountaintop Removal in West Virginia: An Environmental Sacrifice Zone." *Organization & Environment* 12 (2): 163–83. http://dx.doi.org/10.1177/1086026699122002.

Freudenburg, William R. 1982. "The Impacts of Growth on the Social and Personal Well-Being of Local Community Residents." In *Coping with Rapid Growth in Rural Communities*, ed. Bruce A. Weber and Robert E. Howell, 137–70. Boulder: Westview Press.

Freudenburg, William R., and Robert Gramling. 1993. "Socioenvironmental Factors and Development Policy: Understanding Opposition and Support for Offshore Oil." *Sociological Forum* 8 (3): 341–64. http://dx.doi.org/10.1007/BF01115049.

Freudenburg, William R., and Robert Emmett Jones. 1991. "Criminal Behavior and Rapid Community Growth: Examining the Evidence." *Rural Sociology* 56 (4): 619–45. http://dx.doi.org/10.1111/j.1549-0831.1991.tb00449.x.

Freudenburg, William R., and Lisa J. Wilson. 2002. "Mining the Data: Analyzing the Economic Implications of Mining for Nonmetropolitan Regions." *Sociological Inquiry* 72 (4): 549–75. http://dx.doi.org/10.1111/1475-682X.00034.

Frickel, Scott, Sahra Gibbon, Jeff Howard, Joanna Kempner, Gwen Ottinger, and David Hess. 2010. "Undone Science: Charting Social Movement and Civil Society Challenges to Research Agenda Setting." *Science, Technology & Human Values* 35 (4): 444–73. http://dx.doi.org/10.1177/0162243909345836.

Gaventa, John. 1978. *Power and Powerlessness: Quiescence and Rebellion in an Appalachian Valley.* Champaign: University of Illinois Press.

Ground Water Protection Council. 2009. "State Oil and Natural Gas Regulations Designed to Protect Water Resources." Accessed 10 September 2012. http://www.gwpc.org/sites/default/files/state_oil_and_gas_regulations_designed_to_protect_water_resources_0.pdf.

Howarth, R.W., R. Santoro, and A. Ingraffea. 2011. "Methane and the Greenhouse Gas Footprint of Natural Gas from Shale Formations." *Climatic Change* 106 (4): 679–90. http://dx.doi.org/10.1007/s10584-011-0061-5.

Hudgins, Anastasia. 2013. "Fracking's Future in a Coal Mining Past: Subjectivity Undermined." *Culture, Agriculture, Food and Environment* 35 (1): 54–9. http://dx.doi.org/10.1111/cuag.12005.

Jackson, R.B., A. Vengosh, T.H. Darrah, N.R. Warner, A. Down, R.J. Poreda, S.G. Osborn, K. Zhao, and J.D. Karr. 9 July 2013. "Increased Stray Gas Abundance in a Subset of Drinking Water Wells near Marcellus Shale Gas Extraction." *Proceedings of the National Academy of Sciences of the United States of America* 110 (28): 11250–55. http://dx.doi.org/10.1073/pnas.1221635110. Medline:23798404.

Jacquet, Jeffrey. 2009. *Energy Boomtowns & Natural Gas: Implications for Marcellus Shale Local Governments & Rural Communities. NERCRD Rural Development Paper 43.* University Park: Northeast Regional Center for Rural Development.

Jacquet, Jeffrey B. 2012a. "Landowner Attitudes toward Natural Gas and Wind Farm Development in Northern Pennsylvania." *Energy Policy* 50: 677–88. http://dx.doi.org/10.1016/j.enpol.2012.08.011.

Jacquet, Jeffrey B. 2012b. *Landowner Attitudes and Perceptions of Impact from Wind and Natural Gas Development in Northern Pennsylvania: Implications for Energy Landscapes in Rural America.* PhD dissertation. Ithaca, NY: Cornell University.

Jacquet, Jeffrey, and Richard C. Stedman. 2011. "Natural Gas Landowner Coalitions in New York State: Emerging Benefits of Collective Natural Resource Management." *Journal of Rural Social Sciences* 26 (1): 62–91.

Jacquet, Jeffrey B. and Richard C. Stedman. 2013a. "Perceived Impacts from Wind Farm and Natural Gas Development in Northern Pennsylvania." *Rural Sociology* 78 (4): 450–72. http://dx.doi.org/10.1111%2Fruso.12022

Jacquet, Jeffrey B. and Richard C. Stedman. 2013b. "The Risk of Social-Psychological Disruption as an Impact of Energy Development and Environmental Change." *Journal of Environmental Planning and Management* (ahead of print). http://dx.doi.org/10.1080%2F09640568.2013.820174

Jalbert, Kirk, Abby J. Kinchy, and Simona L. Perry. 2013. "Civil Society Research and Marcellus Shale Natural Gas Development: Results of a Survey of Volunteer Water Monitoring Organizations." *Journal of Environmental Studies and Sciences* (ahead of print). http://dx.doi.org/10.1007%2Fs13412-013-0155-7.

Jobes, Patrick C. 1987. "The Disintegration of Gemeinschaft Social Structure from Energy Development: Observations from Ranch Communities in the Western United States." *Journal of Social Research* 3 (3): 219–29.

Kennedy, Michelle L. 2011. "The Exercise of Local Control over Gas Extraction." *Fordham Environmental Law Review* 22: 375.

Kinchy, Abby. 2014. "Political Scale and Conflicts over Knowledge Production: The Case of Unconventional Natural Gas Development." in *Routledge Handbook of Science, Technology, and Society*, ed. Daniel L. Kleinman and Kelly Moore. New York: Routledge.

Kinchy, Abby J., and Simona L. Perry. 2012. "Can Volunteers Pick up the Slack? Efforts to Fill Knowledge Gaps about the Watershed Effects of Marcellus Shale Gas Development." *Duke Environmental Law and Policy Forum* 22: 303–39.

Kinnaman, Thomas C. 2011. "The Economic Impact of Shale Gas Extraction: A Review of Existing Studies." *Ecological Economics* 70 (7): 1243–9. http://dx.doi.org/10.1016/j.ecolecon.2011.02.005.

Kowalski, Lindsay, and Gary Zajac. 2012. "A Preliminary Examination of Marcellus Shale Drilling Activity and Crime Trends in Pennsylvania." Penn State Justice Center for Research. Accessed 10 September 2012. http://justicecenter.psu.edu/documents/marcellusfinalreport.pdf/view.

Krannich, Richard S., and Thomas R. Greider. 1990. "Rapid Growth Effects on Rural Community Relations." In *American Rural Communities*, ed. A.E. Luloff and Louis E. Swanson, 61–73. Boulder: Westview.

Kuletz, Valerie L. 1998. *The Tainted Desert: Environmental Ruin in the American West.* New York: Routledge.

Longbrake, D., and J.F. Geyler. 1979. "Commercial Development in Small, Isolated Energy Impacted Communities." *Social Science Journal* 16: 51–62.

Low, Setha M., and Irwin Altman. 1992. "Place Attachment: A Conceptual Inquiry." In *Place Attachment*, ed. Setha M. Low and Irwin Altman, 1–12. New York: Plenum Press. http://dx.doi.org/10.1007/978-1-4684-8753-4_1.

Malin, Stephanie. 2013. "There's No Real Choice but to Sign: Neoliberalization and Normalization of Hydraulic Fracturing on Pennsylvania Farmland." *Journal of Environmental Studies and Sciences.* http://dx.doi.org/10.1007/s13412-013-0115-2 http://link.springer.com/article/10.1007%2Fs13412-013-0115-2#.

Marcellus Shale Training and Education Center (MSETC). 2011. "Economic Impacts of Marcellus Shale in Pennsylvania: Employment and Income in 2009." Williamsport, PA: Marcellus Shale Education and Training Center, Pennsylvania College of Technology. Accessed 10 September 2012. http://www.shaletec.org/docs/EconomicImpactFINALAugust28.pdf.

Marcellus Shale Education and Training Center (MSETC). 2012. "Economic Impacts of Marcellus Shale Development in Bradford County: Employment and Income in 2010." Williamsport, PA: Shale Training and Education Center, Pennsylvania College of Technology. Accessed 10 September 2012. http://extension.psu.edu/natural-resources/natural-gas/publications/economic-impact-study-in-5-counties/economic-impacts-of-marcellus-shale-in-bradford-county-employment-and-income-in-2010/view.

Marchand, Joseph. 2012. "Local Labor Market Impacts of Energy Boom-Bust-Boom in Western Canada." *Journal of Urban Economics* 71 (1): 165–74. http://dx.doi.org/10.1016/j.jue.2011.06.001.

McCarthy, James, and Scott Prudham. 2004. "Neoliberal Nature and the Nature of Neoliberalism." *Geoforum* 35 (3): 275–83. http://dx.doi.org/10.1016/j.geoforum.2003.07.003.

Miller, Jeff. 2012. "'Fracking' a Big Concern for Growing Nunda Organic Foods Company."

Evening Tribune, January 29. http://www.eveningtribune.com/x430730443/-Fracking-a-big-concern-for-growing-Nunda-organic-foods-company.

MIT Energy Initiative. 2011. *The Future of Natural Gas: An Interdisciplinary MIT Study*. Cambridge: Massachusetts Institute of Technology. Accessed 12 September 2012. http://mitei.mit.edu/publications/reports-studies/future-natural-gas.

Obama, Barack H. 2012. "Remarks of President Barack Obama—As Prepared for Delivery." January 24. Transcript provided by C-SPAN. http://www.c-span.org/SOTU/.

Pearson, Thomas. 2013. "Frac-sand Mining in Wisconsin: Understanding Emerging Conflicts and Community Organizing." *Culture, Agriculture, Food, and Environment* 35 (1): 30–40. http://dx.doi.org/10.1111/cuag.12003.

Pellow, David Naguib. 2002. *Garbage Wars: The Struggle for Environmental Justice in Chicago*. Cambridge: MIT Press.

Pennsylvania Certified Organic. 2012. "Guidance for Natural Gas Exploration and Drilling on Certified Organic Farms." Accessed 13 March 2012. http://www.paorganic.org/wp-content/plugins/download-monitor/download.php?id=80.

Perry, Simona L. 2011. "Energy Consequences and Conflicts across the Global Countryside: North American Agricultural Perspectives." Forum on Public Policy. Accessed 1 September 2012. http://forumonpublicpolicy.com/vol2011.no2/environment2011vol2.html.

Perry, Simona L. 2012a. "Development, Land Use and Collective Trauma: The Marcellus Shale Gas Boom in Rural Pennsylvania." *Culture, Agriculture, Food, and Environment* 34 (1): 81–92. http://dx.doi.org/10.1111/j.2153-9561.2012.01066.x.

Perry, S.L. 2012b. "Addressing the Societal Costs of Unconventional Oil and Gas Exploration and Production: A Framework for Evaluating Short-Term, Future, and Cumulative Risks and Uncertainties of Hydrofracking." *Environmental Practice* 14 (4): 352–65. http://dx.doi.org/10.1017/S1466046612000336.

Perry, Simona L. 2013. "Using Ethnography to Monitor the Community Health Implications of Onshore Unconventional Oil and Gas Developments: Examples from Pennsylvania's Marcellus Shale." *New Solutions* 23 (1): 33–53. http://dx.doi.org/10.2190/NS.23.1.d. Medline:23552647.

Phillips, Susan. 2011. "Research on Marcellus Drilling Hampered by Lack of Data, Lack of Funding, and Concerns of Bias." *StateImpact*, 24 October. http://stateimpact.npr.org/pennsylvania/2011/10/24/research-on-marcellus-drilling-hampered-by-lack-of-data-lack-of-funding-and-concerns-of-bias/.

de Rijke, Kim. 2013a. "Coal Seam Gas and Social Impact Assessment: An Anthropological Contribution to Current Debates and Practices." *Journal of Economic and Social Policy* 15 (3): Article 3. Accessed 18 December 2013. http://epubs.scu.edu.au/jesp/vol15/iss3/3.

de Rijke, Kim. 2013b. "The Agri-gas Fields of Australia: Black Soil, Food, and Unconventional Gas." *Culture, Agriculture, Food, and Environment* 35 (1): 41–53. http://dx.doi.org/10.1111/cuag.12004.

Schafft, Kai A., Yetkin Borlu, and Leland Glenna. 2013. "The Relationship between Marcellus Shale Gas Development in Pennsylvania and Local Perceptions of Risk and Opportunity." *Rural Sociology* 78 (2): 143–66. http://dx.doi.org/10.1111/ruso.12004.

Soeder, Daniel J., and William M. Kappel. 2009. "Water Resources and Natural Gas Production from the Marcellus Shale." US Geological Survey, US Department of the

Interior, Fact Sheet 2009-3032. May 2009. http://pubs.usgs.gov/fs/2009/3032/pdf/FS2009-3032.pdf.

Staaf, Erika. 2012. "Risky Business: An Analysis of Marcellus Shale Gas Drilling Violations in Pennsylvania 2008–2011." Penn Environment Research and Policy Center. Accessed 11 September 2012. http://pennenvironmentcenter.org/sites/environment/files/reports/Risky%20Business%20Violations%20Report_0.pdf.

Stedman, Richard C. 2003. "Is it Really Just a Social Construction? The Contribution of the Physical Environment to Sense of Place." *Society & Natural Resources* 16 (8): 671–85. http://dx.doi.org/10.1080/08941920309189.

Stedman, Richard C. 2008. "What do We 'Mean' by Place Meanings? Implications of Place Meanings for Managers and Practitioners." In *Understanding Concepts of Place in Recreation Research and Management*, ed. Linda E. Kruger, Troy E. Hall, and Maria C. Stiefel, 71–82. Portland, OR: US Department of Agriculture, Forest Service, Pacific Northwest Research Station.

Stedman, Richard C., J.B. Jacquet, M.R. Filteau, F.K. Willits, K.J. Brasier, and D.K. McLaughlin. 2012. "Marcellus Shale Gas Development and New Boomtown Research: Views of New York and Pennsylvania Residents." *Environmental Practice* 14 (4): 382–93. http://dx.doi.org/10.1017%2FS1466046612000403.

Stedman, Richard C., Mike N. Patriquin, and John R. Parkins. 2012. "Dependence, Diversity, and the Well-Being of Rural Community: Building on the Freudenburg Legacy." *Journal of Environmental Studies and Sciences* 2 (1): 28–38. http://dx.doi.org/10.1007/s13412-011-0055-7.

Stephenson, E., A. Doukas, and K. Shaw. 2012. "Greenwashing Gas: Might a 'Transition Fuel' Label Legitimize Carbon-Intensive Natural Gas Development?" *Energy Policy* 46: 452–9. http://dx.doi.org/10.1016/j.enpol.2012.04.010.

Stokowski, Patricia A. 2008. "Creating Social Senses of Place: New Directions for Sense of Place Research in Natural Resources Management." In *Understanding Concepts of Place in Recreation Research and Management*, ed. Linda E. Kruger, Troy E. Hall, and Maria C. Stiefel, 31–60. Portland, OR: US Department of Agriculture, Forest Service, Pacific Northwest Research Station.

Theodori, Gene L. 2009. "Paradoxical Perceptions of Problems Associated with Unconventional Natural Gas Development." *Southern Rural Sociology* 24 (5): 97–117.

Thompson, James G., and Audie L. Blevins. 1983. "Attitudes toward Energy Development in the Northern Great Plains." *Rural Sociology* 48: 148–58.

Trentelman, Carla Koons. 2009. "Place Attachment and Community Attachment: A Primer Grounded in the Lived Experience of a Community Sociologist." *Society & Natural Resources* 22 (3): 191–210. http://dx.doi.org/10.1080/08941920802191712.

US DOE (Department of Energy). 2009. *Modern Shale Gas Development in the United States: A Primer*. US Department of Energy, Office of Fossil Energy, National Energy Technology Laboratory.

Vorkinn, Marit, and Hanne Riese. 2001. "Environmental Concern in a Local Context: The Significance of Place Attachment." *Environment and Behavior* 33 (2): 249–63. http://dx.doi.org/10.1177/00139160121972972.

Williamson, Jonathan, and Benita Kolb. 2011. *Marcellus Natural Gas Development's Effect on Housing in Pennsylvania*. Center for the Study of Community and the Economy, Lycoming

College. Accessed 11 September 2012. http://www.phfa.org/forms/housing_study/2011/marcellus_report.pdf.

Wilson, C.L. 1980. *Coal—Bridge to the Future: A Report of the World Coal Study, WOCOL.* Ballinger Publishing Company.

Worbets, Barry, and Loleen Berdahl. 2003. "Western Canada's Natural Capital: Towards a New Policy Framework." Canada West Foundation. Accessed 11 September 2012. http://cwf.ca/pdf-docs/publications/August2003-Western-Canada%E2%80%99s-Natural-Capital-Toward-a-New-Public-Policy-Framework.pdf.

CHAPTER 15

Got Coal? The High Cost of Coal on Mining-Dependent Communities in Appalachia and the West

Suzanne E. Tallichet

Introduction

Call it what you will, black gold or the dirty rock, coal has literally fueled the rise of nations while contributing to more than its fair share of global warming and climate change. During the past century, the "dirt that burns" has supplied steel mills and power plants and created jobs wherever it has been mined. However, it has also always fueled controversy. Throughout history, coal has been a symbol of disappointment (Freese 2003). As early as 1306, King Edward tried to have coal banned because of its smoky and smelly emissions. The use of coal inspired Marx and Engels' writing of the *Communist Manifesto.* More recently, a popular country song aptly refers to coal as "hope in a hopeless place" because in rural communities exploitation and poverty have gone along with coal mining. Although coal has been credited with building economies, it has also been subjected to their forces. The demand for coal-based energy at home and abroad has led to shifts from underground to surface mining favoring the West over Appalachia. Politically, neoliberalism, with its emphasis on market fundamentalism, has accelerated market trends and related threats to the health and well-being of coal-impacted communities. Ecologically, due to the shift toward surface mining, parts of Appalachia and the West have begun to resemble moonscapes rather than mountainous landscapes.

Today, a host of factors, such as competition between lower cost surface-mined western coal and coal mined in central Appalachia, the depletion of economically recoverable Appalachian coal, and competition from natural gas, along with deregulation, are contributing to significant changes in the

US coal industry (Bonskowski 1999; Bonskowski and Watson 2006). Neoliberalism in the form of deregulation and lax enforcement is affecting these domestic trends in the coal industry and in turn is having significant impacts on coal-dependent communities in Appalachia and the West regarding pollution and residents' poverty, poor health, and well-being. Meanwhile, grassroots citizen groups are challenging federal and state officials to take more action to enforce environmental regulations while developing the means for the economic transition of their post-extractive communities. Understanding the impact these trends are having on the land and people of both regions is very important to the mission of rural sociologists, academics in related fields, and citizen activists.

Coal Production and Employment Trends

Driven by an ever-increasing demand for electric power, coal production in the United States has risen dramatically, almost doubling since 1950 (Bonskowski and Watson 2006). The way producers meet this demand has changed dramatically during the past thirty years, with the greatest technological and regional changes occurring during the 1990s. Coal is mined today in three regions of the United States: Appalachia, the Interior Basin, and the West (Bonskowski and Watson 2006). The most common type of coal is bituminous. Ranked according to its use, lower grades of bituminous coal, called "steam coal" or "thermal coal," are burned at power plants for generating electricity, while higher grades, called "metallurgic coal" or "coking coal," are usually used for making steel. Since most coal mined domestically now comes from western surface mines followed by surface and underground mines in central Appalachia, the present discussion will be confined to these major coal-producing regions.

Underground mining, also known as deep mining, involves tunneling horizontally or vertically below the earth's surface. Coal is extracted from the seam using augers, continuous mining machines, or long-wall systems that use conveyor belts and shuttle cars to carry the coal outside. In contrast, surface mining, also known as strip mining, employs large-scale earth-moving equipment for extracting coal from outcroppings or by removing the overlying soil and rock or overburden. Some surface techniques, such as contour and high-wall surface mining, extract coal vertically from the hillside. The most radical and controversial type of surface mining, known as mountaintop removal mining (MTR), removes massive amounts of overburden horizontally across sometimes hundreds of acres. All the trees and topsoil are removed first, followed by the broad layers of rock, which eventually reduces the elevation of a ridge by 250 to 600 feet. These strata as well as the coal seam are blasted and extracted by large draglines that dump the overburden in an adjacent valley known as a "valley fill" (Bonskowski and Watson 2006). Generally, surface mining operations are more cost efficient than underground mining, which is more labor intensive (EIA 2006).

Historically, the Appalachian states of West Virginia, Kentucky, and Pennsylvania produced the most coal, most of which came from underground mines. Out West, coal has been mined underground in Utah and Colorado and surface-mined in Wyoming and Montana. During the 1970s, underground and surface mines produced equal amounts of the nation's coal, but over the next thirty years surface mine production dramatically outpaced underground production. Regionally, surface mining increased rapidly in the West, particularly in the Powder River Basin, and to a lesser extent in central Appalachian states, such as West Virginia and Kentucky, so that by 2007 surface-mined coal production from MTR mines exceeded deep-mined coal production in central Appalachia for the first time (McIlmoil and Hansen 2009).

Eventually, regional topography and the more efficient extraction of coal using surface mining techniques, along with regulations meant to reduce emissions by burning lower sulfur coal and the deployment of long-distance rail haulage, have all favored the ever-increasing production of surface-mined western coal (Bonskowski 1999; Bonskowski and Watson 2006; MACED 2009; McIlmoil and Hansen 2009). As a result, during the late 1990s, western coal production surpassed Appalachian coal for the first time ever (Bonskowski 1999; EIA 2006). In 2010, Wyoming produced 41 percent of the nation's coal compared with the second largest producer, West Virginia, which produced only 12 percent (EIA 2011).

These shifts in the application of mining technology and regional production have also been accompanied by significant changes in prices and coal mining employment (Bonskowski and Watson 2006; MACED 2009; McIlmoil and Hansen 2009). As with any extractive industry, coal companies are in constant competition with each other and other energy-producing industries, such as natural gas. According to coal industry analysts, keen price competition was the driving force behind increased surface mining employment in both regions and reducing underground coal mining employment in the United States, particularly in central Appalachia (Bonskowski and Watson 2006; McIlmoil and Hansen 2009). Mining employment in the United States has declined sharply since the early 1970s (EIA 2006). In 1973 there were over 111,000 underground miners nationwide, but thirty years later that figure had dropped by half (Bonskowski and Watson 2006). During this same period, Appalachia lost two thirds of its underground mining jobs compared to no losses out West, where surface jobs increased threefold. In central Appalachia, the closing of underground mines and smaller surface mines, and the increasing number of larger MTR surface operations, resulted in employment declines, especially among unionized underground coal miners.

Future International and Regional Coal Trends

During the past decade, coal's share of domestic energy generation has been declining from roughly half in 2009 to about 39 percent in 2012 (EIA 2012b). Coal industry analysts predict a general decline in the demand for coal as a sizable number of coal-fired electric generation plants are being retired due to pressure from environmental groups and as competition from natural gas and potentially from renewable energy sources, such as wind and solar, increase (EIA 2012a; McIlmoil and Hansen 2009). Given these current and projected economic trends, mining companies in the United States have begun to sell more of their coal on the international market (Wellstead 2012). During 2010, only 7 percent of domestically mined coal was shipped overseas, but as domestic demand declines, companies are looking more and more at Asian markets (EIA 2011; EIA 2012a; Wellstead 2012). Companies making steel in India and China purchased almost three-quarters of domestically mined metallurgic coal in 2011 (Elmquist 2012; McGarvey 2006). In particular, central Appalachian coal producers who have been struggling to remain competitive with western surface mine producers have found a new market for their metallurgic coal overseas. At the same time, even the West's low sulfur coal, which is in great demand domestically, is finding markets overseas (Thompson 2011). Moreover, while coal corporations in the United States own and operate mines overseas, foreign ownership and control of coal mining operations in Appalachia and the West by corporations based in China, India, and former Soviet-bloc countries are increasing (Thompson 2011; Zeller 2008).

Coal is an important global commodity, the market for which increasingly is unpredictable (McGarvey 2006). Price volatility is typical of today's coal market due to volatility of international demand (Elmquist 2012; Jaffe 2012). Coal companies in the United States have sought to reduce risk and market uncertainty and to maintain or enhance profits through expanding exports and corporate consolidation (Bonskowski 1999; McGarvey 2006; Wellstead 2012).

Regionally, production at western surface mines accounts for most of the projected domestic increases from its current 47 to 56 percent by 2035, while Appalachia's share will decline from 39 to 29 percent (EIA 2012a). After peaking during the mid-1990s, the decline in Appalachian coal production is expected to continue (McIlmoil and Hansen 2009). Appalachia's mines hold economically recoverable coal reserves, but these seams have become less accessible and more difficult to mine since the mid-1990s (MACED 2009; McIlmoil and Hansen 2009). Production from both underground and surface mines in central Appalachia is expected to decline due not only to depletion of the most accessible reserves, but also because of increasing competition from western mines and the challenge of environmental regulations (Luppens et al. 2009; McIlmoil and Hansen 2009). The most significant changes in the coal industry affecting coal-dependent communities in Appalachia and the West are the direct result of regional intra-industry competition, trends that deregulation and the lax enforcement of existing regulations have facilitated.

Neoliberalism and the Coal Industry

In the broader context of globalization, the neoliberalism of the past thirty years has emphasized "free trade," deregulation, and lax enforcement of regulations meant to protect workers and the environment. Generally speaking, the industry's productivity rates are inversely related to the effects of these regulations (Bonskowski and Watson 2006). Thus, political and economic trends that support greater productivity for the coal industry have led to decreased mining employment, particularly of unionized labor, while increasing the externalized costs of coal by degrading local environments and severely threatening the health and well-being of coal- dependent community residents in central Appalachia and the West.

There are several examples of how deregulation accompanied by lax enforcement has promoted the coal industry's goals. During the 1990s, deregulation of electric utilities pressured power producers to look for lower-cost coal supplies (Bonskowski 1999). Meanwhile, the deregulation of fiscal policies permitted new financing options supported by investors seeking equity and high-yield capital markets that led to acquisitions, mergers, and expansion of coal companies (Bonskowski 1999). The coal industry enjoyed record production supported by a smaller number of larger mines as mine ownership and operations have become more concentrated. Railroad deregulation, beginning in the late 1980s, facilitated the transportation of western coal beyond the region's typical domestic distribution points, which exacerbated inter-regional competition at the expense of central Appalachian mines and miners (Bonskowski 1999; MACED 2009).

Other forms of regulation that dampened productivity were meant to address miners' safety, such as the Mine Safety and Health Act of 1977 and the

Mine Improvement and New Emergency Response Act of 2006, and to minimize pollution and ecological destruction, such as the Surface Mine and Reclamation Act of 1977 (SMCRA), the Clean Air Act of 1970 (CAA), and Clean Water Act of 1972 (CWA), along with their subsequent amendments (Bonskowski and Watson 2006; MACED 2009). Despite miner safety regulations, lax enforcement contributed to underground mine disasters, such as West Virginia's Upper Big Branch mine explosion in 2010 and the roof collapse at Utah's Crandall Canyon mine in 2007. Recently, the Centers for Disease Control and Prevention reported a rise in the rates of black lung among both underground and surface miners (Ungar 2012). In part, industry analysts attribute avoidable disasters and increased rates of occupation-related disease to a reduced number of union miners, noting that most companies try to avoid unions because they are disruptive to the production process (Bonskowski 1999). However imperfectly enforced, underground safety regulations increase the cost of production, which has led some central Appalachian operators to increase their use of surface mining (MACED 2009).

Just over a decade ago, during the Bush administration, Deputy Secretary for the federal Department of the Interior Steven Griles changed language in SMCRA that promoted the use of MTR in central Appalachia (Goodell 2006). According to SMCRA, the overburden or debris from the MTR process was classified as mining "waste." In a political maneuver meant to undercut environmentalists' legal challenges to MTR, Griles, a former coal industry lobbyist, reclassified MTR overburden as "fill," making it legally less objectionable even though this debris—which is deposited into adjacent valleys—is known to leach large quantities of heavy metals into streams. Around the same time, states began to liberalize their rules regarding MTR. For example, in 1998, West Virginia legislators passed a controversial bill relaxing rules that restricted this type of surface mining (Bonskowski 1999).

States are delegated the responsibility, however imperfectly, for enforcing federal regulations, and do so according to the state agencies' interpretations. Too often state agencies charged with monitoring pollution from coal mines are overwhelmed and lack the necessary resources to thoroughly police pollution in their state, and may also be politically compromised (Duhigg 2009; Palmer et al. 2010). As a result, citizen environmental groups have had to take the lead in bringing CWA violations by coal companies operating in or near their communities to the attention of state regulators and filing lawsuits against the violating companies in state courts (MACED 2009).

Coal industry representatives have argued that declines in mining employment are due solely to increasing regulation, using the common refrain that "coal means jobs." However, increased use of surface techniques such as MTR makes a small contribution to mining employment in Appalachian communities where that practice is widespread (Woods and Gordon 2011). Recent regulatory and litigation decisions meant to curtail MTR have actually resulted in a slight although temporary increase in underground coal mining employment even during a recession (Wasson 2011). In the long run, despite the coal industry's attempts to re-legitimize its importance to coal-based communities in the region, coal companies are not creating jobs but actually taking them away (Bell and York 2010).

Coping with the Regional Consequences of Coal Mining

Historically, communities in central Appalachia and the West have experienced "land (mineral) grabs" facilitated through control of local institutions by absentee elites whose singular purpose has been transformation of natural capital (coal reserves) into financial capital while employing exploited local labor living in relatively remote rural areas (England and Brown 2003; Humphrey et al. 1993). Such resource-dependent communities generally become absentee-owned mono-economies or even highly specialized "addictive economies" where resource extraction has reduced the use value of other environmental resources, such as land and water, and created poverty amidst plenty (Freudenburg 1992). Although it has been heralded as a cheap and abundant fuel that keeps the lights on, the costs of coal during every phase of its life cycle (extraction, processing, transportation, and combustion) exact a terribly burdensome if not sorrowful variety of externalities involving pollution, poor health and well-being, and unemployment and poverty among residents of coal-dependent communities (Epstein et al. 2011).

Resident activists living in both Appalachia and the West have remarked that their regions have become national sacrifice zones for domestic and more recently international energy demand (Eller 2008; Thompson 2011). In the West, the effects of surface mining are often hidden from view and occur in less densely populated places, but reports have also emerged attesting to the pollution of air and both surface and ground water (Tyer 2011). In Appalachia, surface mining, particularly MTR, is done much closer to where people live, resulting in damage to homes from flying debris and increased flooding, reduced air quality from dust, and the toxic tainting of well water and municipal water supplies (Palmer et al. 2010). Both the Environmental Protection Agency (EPA 2011) and the Government Accounting Office (GAO 2010) have released reports that document the ecological damage resulting from MTR, such as the loss of headwater streams and the toxic impact on local waterways threatening birds, fish, and other aquatic life. The GAO report also finds that most MTR sites are not properly reclaimed as required by federal SMCRA regulations. Central Appalachian coal states do not require adequate financial assurances from coal companies for this purpose.

In coal mining communities of Appalachia and the West, thousands of miners have died or been maimed in accidents at both underground and surface mines. Both underground and surface miners also face the threat of pneumoconiosis, or "black lung." Residents in Appalachian coal communities face an additional threat when impoundment ponds filled with either toxic waste water, or "sludge," or coal ash break or leak. In order to meet environmental regulations or steel-making requirements, Appalachian coal must be washed more often than western coal before being burned at a power plant or in a blast furnace (Bonskowski and Watson 2006). The sludge is then stored in large impoundment ponds that can hold between tens of millions to billions of gallons and are often located near residences, schools, and towns. The threat of a spill is ever present, and sometimes these impoundments do fail. For example, in 1972 a sludge spill roared through Buffalo Creek, West Virginia, killing 125 residents and virtually flattening the town. In 2000, a 300-million-gallon sludge spill in Martin County, Kentucky, engulfed the town of Inez, permanently polluting the soil and waterways including the Big Sandy River (Eller 2008). Similar to sludge ponds, after coal is burned at power plants the ash is mixed with water and held in huge ponds. In 2008, a failed coal ash pond near Kingston, Tennessee, spewed one billion gallons of toxic waste covering three hundred acres that included residences, creeks, and rivers. Near Colstrip, Montana, a coal ash pond has been leaking toxic chemicals into local reservoirs for the past thirty years (McRae 2012).

In recent years, community health and social researchers have documented the harmful and even deadly effects MTR has on human health and well-being. Scientists with the US Geological Survey found that residents of southern West Virginia live in a more toxic environment than residents in the rest of the state, asserting that mining is at least partly to blame for residents' elevated health problems (Su 2012). In a comparative study of West Virginia counties, community health researchers found that rates of mortality, cancer, and birth defects are significantly higher in MTR counties than in counties without mining (Ahern et al. 2011; Hendryx and Ahern 2009). A 2011 Gallup-Healthways Well-Being Index of residents in all of the nation's 436 congressional districts revealed that those districts in southern West Virginia and southeastern Kentucky where MTR predominates ranked near last and last, respectively, in residents' reported physical and emotional health, life expectancy, and overall well-being (Gallup-Healthways 2011). Moreover, sociologist Bell (2009) found a decline of social capital (trust, network connections, and shared norms) among residents living in coal mining communities in southern West Virginia, which she attributed to depopulation and the loss of union status at a nearby coal mine.

Coal mining dependent communities have commonly been associated with high rates of unemployment and rural poverty (England and Brown 2003; Humphrey et al. 1993). Deregulation and lax regulatory enforcement have hastened use of technologies that enhance productivity, but in the process have reduced both economically recoverable coal reserves and mining employment. The rates of decline in these coal reserves in Appalachia and the West are similar, but central Appalachia has fewer remaining reserves (Bonskowski 1999). It would be understandable if poverty followed resource depletion, but Freudenburg (1992) asserts that more commonly economic hardship occurs long before resources have run out due to the cost-price squeeze experienced by extractive resource firms and the communities' level of dependency on those firms.

During the 1980s, Nord and Luloff (1993) found that coal mining affected residents' well-being more negatively in the coal-dependent communities of the South, including central Appalachian states, than in the western coal states. They explained that western operations consisted of open pit surface mines that employed newer capital-intensive technologies associated with a different occupational structure, including a greater proportion of skilled and professional jobs, than those mines found in the South. Today, central Appalachian coal-producing counties have some of the highest poverty and unemployment rates in a region already plagued with some of the nation's highest unemployment rates and persistent poverty (MACED 2009; McIlmoil and Hansen 2009). While there may be numerous reasons for poverty, the higher rates in these counties were directly associated with coal mining employment, particularly where MTR mining predominates (Hendryx 2011). In the future, the coal industry may play a short-term role by providing jobs, but its long-term economic role is likely to diminish (MACED 2009). As mining employment declines in central Appalachia, coal-dependent communities will need other sources of employment to offset job losses and retain younger educated workers for continued economic development.

Production efficiency and market demand favor the West over central Appalachia, but recent reports reveal that western coal seams are becoming less accessible and more difficult to mine, that production costs have more than doubled, and that more stringent regulation of coal-fired power plant emissions and enactment of new climate change laws could dampen western coal production and employment (Bonskowski and Watson 2006; Jaffe 2012; MACED 2009). The economic future of western coal could also depend on firms' abilities to export coal overseas, where they can sell it for six times the cost of its production (Eilperin 2012). Out West, having large surface coal mining operations has promoted economic development rather than conferring economic disadvantage to residents in coal mining communities, and residents may be less dependent on coal mining due to the presence of other forms of resource extraction, such as those related to petroleum and other mineral-based resources (Nord and Luloff 1993). In this regard, most western communities' relatively greater economic diversification and opportunities for entrepreneurship will no doubt soften the blows to their socioeconomic well-being (England and Brown 2003; Nord and Luloff 1993; Thompson 2011).

Most coal-impacted communities in Appalachia have entered their post-extraction period and, as the demand for coal declines, some coal communities in the West may begin to show economic and population declines along with related ecological and social issues (England and Brown 2003; Plumer 2011). These are communities where mining operations have either shut down or slowed production. At that point, communities that lose working-age adults also experience an eroding tax base needed to remediate pollution of soil and water supplies and deal with the waste generated from mining operations.

For over a century, absentee owners have drained coal-mining communities of their natural and financial resources without paying their fair share of taxes. In Appalachia, citizens struggled for decades to finally institute a coal severance tax during the 1970s that would support county-based service institutions almost a century after the coal industry's arrival in the region (Eller 2008). Even so, studies in Kentucky and West Virginia show that the relative differences between coal-related revenues and expenditures in the state result in heavy taxpayer subsidies to the coal industry (Konty and Bailey 2009; McIlmoil et al. 2010). Out West, politicians in states such as Wyoming began taxing coal mining and other extractive companies during the 1970s boom periods, resulting in relatively greater revenues for residents' benefit (Goodell 2006).

The domination of communities by coal mining firms also has a significant effect on households' economic structure (Humphrey et al. 1993). Social problems commonly associated with poverty, such as domestic violence and substance abuse, can overwhelm local social service agencies and residents who are also attempting to cope with the decline of social capital in their communities. When men's jobs are lost in logging, mining, or other extractive industries, women often become their family's sole or primary breadwinners (Maggard 1994; Miewald and McCann 2004). Beginning in the early 1990s, the

Appalachian economy began restructuring that favored service sector employment over dwindling jobs in or associated with coal mining. In Appalachian families, this has led to tremendous strains between former coal mining husbands and service sector working wives suddenly thrust into the breadwinner role. For these families, earnings fell and health insurance evaporated, leading to the greater impoverishment of adults and children while incidents of domestic violence spiked. Unemployment and underemployment in central Appalachian communities have been accompanied by the legitimate and illegitimate influx of prescription pain pills into the region, which has resulted in overdoses and an addiction epidemic (Eller 2008). Appalachians once dependent on and controlled by transnational corporations are in danger of becoming dependent on state and federal agencies to help them deal with the consequences of economic restructuring (England and Brown 2003).

Citizens' Challenges, Communities' Transitions, and Future Research

Citizens intent on achieving a successful transition beyond coal for their communities will need to overcome the heavy influence mining corporations have over state agencies charged with protecting the natural capital of their areas and to gain more general control over the political and economic affairs of their communities (England and Brown 2003; Humphrey et al. 1993). Over the past decade, numerous grassroots and citizen-based movements in Appalachia have challenged the coal industry's violating environmental regulations due to state agencies' lack of regulatory enforcement. Similar to the logging industry, the coal industry has attempted to avoid taking political responsibility for worker layoffs by blaming citizen activists and government regulators rather than their own practices (Freudenburg 1992). In Appalachia, environmental activists are working hard to expose the false contradiction between the coal industry's "jobs versus the environment" rhetoric (Bell and York 2010). Out West, activists are protesting the expansion of western coal production via the leasing of federal lands for coal mining and the expansion of rail terminals for increased exports (Eilperin 2012). Using a combination of lobbying and litigation, organized groups of local and regional activists are continuing to pressure federal and state agencies to act on their behalf rather than supporting the politically powerful coal industry. These same activists are reaching out and forming coalitions well beyond their regional and national borders in pursuit of human rights and economic justice.

For generations, coal-mining families have lived with death, dismemberment, and disease while collectively coping with economic and environmental decline.

Achieving sustainable communities may be more challenging in central Appalachia because their ability to diversify may be much more compromised than among western coal mining communities (Freudenburg 1992). However, it is also entirely possible that, similar to the logging communities in the Northwest, as dependency on mining decreases in central Appalachia in particular, residents' well-being could increase if they are successful in promoting economic diversification (National Research Council 2000). The economic redevelopment of former timber-dependent communities in the Northwest was accompanied by a redefining of the relationship between communities and forests (Maleki 2008).

A recent study has shown that residents of regions plagued with chronic unemployment and poverty, such as central Appalachia, favor conserving those resources upon which future job creation and economic development depend (Hamilton, Colocousis, and Duncan 2010). Already, some Appalachian communities have turned to tourism that showcases their past extractive histories, such as exhibition mines, and forms of recreation that use the remaining local natural resources. In addition, researchers have suggested that politicians take steps to improve the quality of life and reinvigorate local economies in the coal-impacted communities of central Appalachia by developing jobs in renewable energy, such as solar and wind energy, and in sustainable timber, small-scale agriculture, and ecosystem restoration using coal severance tax revenues to fund education and job training programs (Epstein et al., 2011; Hendryx and Ahern 2009; Palmer et al. 2010). Recovery is also contingent on maintaining the social capital necessary to support these efforts. In one western mining community, Brown, Dorius, and Krannich (2005) found that residents who had adopted a "through thick and thin" orientation toward their community demonstrated the most resilience during the post extractive period. Similarly, Appalachian residents historically have demonstrated a profound and persistent attachment to place (Eller 2008). In short, for decades they have known that the welfare of their families and communities is up to them as reflected in the popular slogan: "It has to come from the people." Nonetheless, such transitioning will also require collaboration among diverse members of local communities and beyond, to people such as state agency officials, politicians, and researchers.

Future Research

Rural sociologists can and should continue to deepen our understanding of rural people's problems in order to improve their lives. Communities whose prosperity once depended on coal mining are now facing futures of economic downturns, unemployment, and increasing poverty. However, this apparently bleak situation portends both real and potential opportunities for communities to begin transitional economic diversification and to realize increased democratization. There is a need for longitudinal studies across regions and communities that have already begun successful transitions away from being coal-dependent. The role of grassroots movements in resisting corporate economic, political, and ideological control, and in promoting appropriate solutions to economic and social issues for their communities, is another important area of study. Moreover, studies about communities' transition must also consider micro-scale issues in light of larger economic forces of change such that the attempts toward economic development must be defined by those directly involved with these day-to-day struggles.

Researchers will need to apply theoretical perspectives that allow for power analyses and the deconstruction of dominant ideologies affecting residents of coal-impacted communities. These perspectives would include feminist, postmodernist, post-structuralist, and postcolonial theories because they focus on power relationships and question the role of the other by legitimating marginalized voices and hidden lives (Harris 2001). Furthermore, these perspectives support methodological approaches that allow for the collaborative efforts between citizens and researchers, such as participatory action research, that allow citizens to engage in research that empowers them and propels them to act for themselves. We need to know what citizens know about their communities and what they want for themselves and for future generations.

This may require researchers to relinquish some of their discipline-based and academic authority. Due to the complex interconnections of economic, social, cultural, and ecological issues, rural sociologists will need to step up our efforts to work with anthropologists, historians, economists, and community health and environmental researchers. Their work supports and contextualizes our own, begging for interdisciplinary collaborative efforts. Moreover, while researchers need not become activists, we will eventually have to come to terms with our potential role as advocates for citizens. Already different academic organizations, such as the Appalachian Studies Association and the Society for the Study of Social Problems, have weighed in on issues such as MTR. Recall that in 2005 Michael Burawory, then-president of the American Sociological Association, along with past presidents of the Rural Sociological Society, such as Carolyn Sachs (2007) and Conner Bailey (2013), have challenged social scientists to bring about positive social change by engaging in "public sociology." Some exemplary academics have been actively collaborating with community activists in substantive and meaningful ways that work toward lasting solutions to communities' social, economic and environmental challenges (McSpirit, Faltraco, and Bailey 2012). The seriousness and multi-faceted nature of the problems the residents of coal-impacted communities in Appalachia and the West now face compel us to do even more during the coming decade and beyond.

References

Ahern, Melissa M., Michael Hendryx, Jamison Conley, Evan Fedorko, Alan Ducatman, and Keith J. Zullig. August 2011. "The Association between Mountaintop Mining and Birth Defects among Live Births in Central Appalachia, 1996–2003." *Environmental Research* 111 (6): 838–46. http://dx.doi.org/10.1016/j.envres.2011.05.019. Medline:21689813.

Bailey, Conner. 2013. "Local Solutions to Inequality: Steps towards Fostering a Progressive Social Movement." *Rural Sociology* 78 (4): 411–28. http://dx.doi.org/10.1111/ruso.12032.

Bell, Shannon. 2009. "'There Ain't No Bond in Town like There Used to Be': The Destruction of Social Capital in the West Virginia Coalfields." *Sociological Forum* 24 (3): 631–57. http://dx.doi.org/10.1111/j.1573-7861.2009.01123.x.

Bell, Shannon, and Richard York. 2010. "Community Economic Identity: The Coal Industry and Ideology Construction in West Virginia." *Rural Sociology* 75 (1): 111–43. http://dx.doi.org/10.1111/j.1549-0831.2009.00004.x.

Bonskowski, Richard. 1999. *The U.S. Coal Industry in the 1990s: Low Prices and Record Production.* Washington, DC: Energy Information Administration.

Bonskowski, Richard, and William D. Watson. 2006. *Coal Production in the United States: An Historical Overview.* Washington, DC: Energy Information Administration.

Brown, Ralph, Shawn F. Dorius, and Richard S. Krannich. 2005. "The Boom-Bust Recovery Cycle: Dynamics of Change in Community Satisfaction and Social Integration in Delta, Utah." *Rural Sociology* 70 (1): 28–49. http://dx.doi.org/10.1526/0036011053294673.

Duhigg, Charles. 2009. "Clean Water Laws Are Neglected, at a Cost in Suffering." *New York Times*, 12 September. http://www.nytimes.com/2009/09/13/us/13water.html?pagewanted=all.

Eilperin, Janet. 2012. "Powder River Basin Coal Leasing Prompts IG, GAO Reviews." *Washington Post*, 24 June. http://articles.washingtonpost.com/2012-06-24/national/35459046_1_lease-rights-coal-companies-coal-leases.

Eller, Ronald D. 2008. *Uneven Ground: Appalachia since 1945.* Lexington, KY: University of Kentucky Press.

Elmquist, Sonja. 2012. "Appalachian Coal Fights for Survival on Shale Boom: Commodities." *Bloomberg*, 21 March. http://www.bloomberg.com/news/2012-03-21/appalachian-coal-fights-for-survival-on-shale-boom-commodities.html.

Energy Information Administration (EIA). 2006. "Annual Energy Outlook with Projections to 2030." February. http://www.scag.ca.gov/rcp/pdf/publications/1_2006AnnualEnergyOutlook.pdf.

Energy Information Administration (EIA). 2011. "What is the Role of Coal in the U.S.?" 27 May. http://www.eia.gov/energy_in_brief/article/role_coal_us.cfm.

Energy Information Administration (EIA). 2012a. "Annual Energy Outlook (AEO) 2012 Early Release Overview." 23 January. http://www.eia.gov/forecasts/aeo/er/early_production.cfm.

Energy Information Administration (EIA). 2012b. "Coal's Share of Electricity Generation in December Fell Below 40 Percent for the First Time since 1978." 9 March. http://205.254.135.7/todayinenergy/detail.cfm?id=5331.

England, Lynn, and Ralph Brown. 2003. "Community Resource Extraction in Rural America." In *Challenges for Rural America in the Twenty-First Century*, ed. David L. Brown and Louis Swanson, 317–28. University Park: Penn State University Press.

Environmental Protection Agency (EPA). 2011. "The Effects of Mountaintop Mines and Valley Fills on Aquatic Ecosystems of the Central Appalachian Coalfields." Washington, DC: Office of Research and Development, National Center for Environmental Assessment. EPA/600/R-09/138F.

Epstein, Paul R., Jonathan J. Buonocore, Kevin Eckerle, Michael Hendryx, Benjamin M. Stout, III, Richard Heinberg, Richard W. Clapp, Beverly May, Nancy L. Reinhart, Melissa M. Ahern, et al. 2011. "Full Cost Accounting for the Life Cycle of Coal." *Annals of the New York Academy of Sciences* 1219: 73–98. http://dx.doi.org/10.1111/j.1749-6632.2010.05890.x.

Freese, Barbara. 2003. *Coal: A Human History*. Cambridge, MA: Perseus Publishing.

Freudenburg, William R. 1992. "Addictive Economies: Extractive Industries and Vulnerable Localities in a Changing World Economy." *Rural Sociology* 57 (3): 305–32. http://dx.doi.org/10.1111/j.1549-0831.1992.tb00467.x.

Gallup-Healthways. 2011. "Gallup-Healthways Well-Being Index, 2011: City, State and Congressional District Well-being Reports." Accessed 24 March 2012. http://www.healthways.com/solution/default.aspx?id=1125.

Goodell, Jeff. 2006. *Big Coal: The Dirty Secret behind America's Energy Future*. New York: Houghton Mifflin Company.

Government Accounting Office (GAO). 2010. "Surface Mining Coal: Financial Assurances for and Long Term Oversight of Mines with Valley Fills in Four Appalachian States." GAO-10-206. Washington, DC: United States Government Printing Office.

Hamilton, Lawrence C., Chris R. Colocousis, and Cynthia M. Duncan. 2010. "Place Effects on Environmental Views." *Rural Sociology* 75 (2): 326–47. http://dx.doi.org/10.1111/j.1549-0831.2010.00013.x.

Harris, Rosalind. 2001. "Hidden Voices: Linking Research, Practice and Policy to the Everyday Realities of Rural People." *Southern Rural Sociology* 17: 1–11.

Hendryx, M. 2011. "Poverty and Mortality Disparities in Central Appalachia: Mountaintop Mining and Environmental Justice." *Journal of Health Disparities Research and Practice* 4 (3): 44–53.

Hendryx, Michael, and Melissa M. Ahern. July–August 2009. "Mortality in Appalachian Coal Mining Regions: The Value of Statistical Life Lost." *Public Health Reports* 124 (4): 541–50. Medline:19618791.

Humphrey, Craig, Gigi Berardi, Matthew S. Carroll, Sally Fairfax, Louise Fortmann, Charles Geisler, Thomas G. Johnson, Jonathan Kusel, Robert G. Lee, Seth Macinko, et al. 1993. "Theories in the Study of Natural Resource-Dependent Communities and Persistent Rural

Poverty in the United States." In *Persistent Poverty in Rural America*, ed. Rural Sociological Society Task Force on Persistent Rural Poverty, 136–72. Boulder, CO: Westview Press.

Jaffe, Mark. 2012. "Rising Coal Costs Will Be Felt in Electric Bills." *Denver Post*, 24 October. http://www.denverpost.com/business/ci_16412425.

Konty, Melissa Fry, and Jason Bailey. 2009. "The Impact of Coal on the Kentucky State Budget." 25 June. Berea, KY: Mountain Association for Community Economic Development.

Luppens, J.A., T.J. Rohrbacher, L.M. Osmonson, and M.D. Carter. 2009. "Coal Resource Availability, Recoverability, and Economic Evaluations in the United States—A Summary." In *The National Coal Resource Assessment Overview*, ed. B.S. Pierce and K.O. Dennen, 1–17. Professional Paper 1625-F, Chapter D. Reston, VA: United States Geological Survey.

Maggard, Sally Ward. 1994. "From Farm to Coal Camp to Back Office and McDonald's: Living in the Midst of Appalachia's Latest Transformation." *Journal of Appalachian Studies Association* 6: 14–38.

Maleki, Sussane. 2008. "Understanding the Social and Economic Transitions of Forest Communities." Science Update 18: 1–12. Portland, OR: United States Forest Service, Pacific Northwest Research Station.

McGarvey, Robert. 2006. "Globalization and the Future of the Coal Industry." Strategic Performance. Accessed 23 February 2012. http://www.beckettadvisors.com/pdfs/globalization_11_06.pdf.

McIlmoil, Rory, and Evan Hansen. 2009. "The Decline of Central Appalachia Coal and the Need for Economic Diversification." 19 January. Morgantown, WV: Downstream Strategies.

McIlmoil, Rory, Evan Hansen, Ted Boettner, and Paul Miller. 2010. "Coal and Renewables in Central Appalachia: The Impact of Coal on the West Virginia State Budget." 22 June. Morgantown, WV: Downstream Strategies.

McRae, Clint. 2012. "Rancher Says Coal Ash Regulation is Overdue." *High Country News*. 19 June. http://www.hcn.org/wotr/rancher-says-coal-ash-regulation-is-overdue.

McSpirit, Stephanie, Lynne Faltraco, and Conner Bailey. 2012. *Confronting Ecological and Community Crisis in Appalachia: University and Community Partnerships*. Lexington: University of Kentucky Press.

Miewald, Cristiana E., and Eugene J. McCann. 2004. "Gender Struggle, Scale, and the Production of Place in the Appalachian Coalfields." *Environment & Planning* 36 (6): 1045–64. http://dx.doi.org/10.1068/a35230.

Mountain Association for Community and Economic Development (MACED). 2009. *The Economics of Kentucky Coal: Current Impacts and Future Prospects*. Berea, KY: Mountain Association for Community Economic Development.

National Research Council. 2000. "Forest Management and Rural Communities in the Pacific Northwest." In *Environmental Issues in Pacific Northwest Forest Management*, ed. National Academy of Sciences, 160–70. Washington, DC: National Academy Press.

Nord, Mark, and A.E. Luloff. 1993. "Socioeconomic Heterogeneity of Mining-Dependent Counties." *Rural Sociology* 58 (3): 492–500. http://dx.doi.org/10.1111/j.1549-0831.1993.tb00507.x.

Palmer, M.A., E.S. Bernhardt, W.H. Schlesinger, K.N. Eshleman, E. Foufoula-Georgiou, M.S. Hendryx, A.D. Lemly, G.E. Likens, O.L. Loucks, M.E. Power, et al. 8 January 2010. "Science and Regulation. Mountaintop Mining Consequences." *Science* 327 (5,962): 148–49. http://dx.doi.org/10.1126/science.1180543. Medline:20056876.

Plumer, Brad. 2011. "Can Appalachia Survive When the Coal Runs Out?" *Washington Post*, 29 September. http://www.washingtonpost.com/blogs/wonkblog/post/can-appalachia-survive-when-the-coal-runs-out/2011/09/29/gIQAM0Dr7K_blog.html.

Sachs, Carolyn. 2007. "Going Public: Networking Globally and Locally." *Rural Sociology* 72 (1): 2–24. http://dx.doi.org/10.1526/003601107781147400.

Su, Alice. 2012. "Study Finds Toxins from Mountaintop Coal Mining Sites." Center for Public Integrity (Environment) website. Accessed 24 July 2012. http://www.publicintegrity.org/2012/07/20/9947/study-finds-toxins-mountaintop-coal-mining-sites.

Thompson, Jonathan. 2011. "The Global West." *High Country News*, 25 July.

Tyer, Brad. 2011. "Lost Opportunity: The Hidden Costs of a Historic Mine Cleanup." *High Country News*, 19 September.

Ungar, Laura. 2012. "Kentucky Surface Miners Hit Hard by Black Lung, Study Finds—Central Appalachia, Notably KY Hit Worst." *Louisville Courier Journal*, 16 June. http://www.courier-journal.com/article/20120617/business/306170039/?nclick_check=1.

Wasson, Matt. 2011. "Fact Checking CNN's New Documentary about Mountaintop Removal: The 'Jobs versus Environment' Frame is Dead Wrong Once Again." *Appalachian Voices*, 3 August. http://appvoices.org/2011/08.

Wellstead, James. 2012. "Coal Hits a Wall." *Resource Investigating News*, 27 February. http://resourceinvestingnews.com/32249-coal-hits-a-wall-in-us-market.html.

Woods, Brad R., and Jason S. Gordon. 2011. "Mountaintop Removal and Job Creation: Exploring the Relationship Using Spatial Regression." *Annals of the Association of American Geographers* 101 (4): 806–15. http://dx.doi.org/10.1080/00045608.2011.567947.

Zeller, Tom, Jr. 2008. "India Shopping for Coal Mines in Appalachia." *New York Times*, 23 October. http://www.green.blogs.nytimes.com/2008/10/23/india-shopping-for-coal-mines-in-appalachia/.

PART III

Population Change in Rural North America

Rural Population Change in Social Context

David L. Brown

Population change does not occur in a vacuum. Rather, population dynamics, social organization, and social change are inextricably and mutually interrelated. Regardless of whether one focuses on fertility, mortality, migration, or immigration, population changes respond to transformations in other aspects of economy and society, while at the same time affecting these institutional domains. The Great Recession's impact on migration, for example, illustrates this observation. The volume of immigration to the United States slowed appreciably during the recession and its aftermath, from about 1.3 million legal immigrants in 2006 to about 1.07 million per year in 2008 to 2010 (Migration Policy Institute 2012).[1] Internal migration is also at an historic low in the United States as households struggle with declining housing values, the credit crunch, and a lack of available jobs in alternate locations (Frey 2009). In turn, the slowdown in population mobility has affected the demand for housing, school enrollment, the market for goods and services in a wide range of locations, as well as other demographic processes such as fertility, mortality, and population aging.[2]

Change, not stability, characterizes rural America, and that goes for rural population dynamics as well. Overall, three demographic trends have been most notable during recent times: (1) fluctuations in the relative rates of population growth between rural and urban areas and, hence, the direction of urban-rural population redistribution, (2) population aging, and (3) increasing race-ethnic diversity of the rural population.[3] In addition, rather than being independent phenomena, these three demographic trends affect and are affected by each other. For example, immigration tends to lower the average age of populations, contributes to higher fertility, and can sometimes transmit diseases that affect morbidity and mortality rates. Since family and individual life are embedded in social institutions, having babies, succumbing to death, and moving are all affected by social structure and social change.

Transformations Affecting Rural Population Dynamics

The social and economic organization of rural life in America has been thoroughly transformed during recent decades. Since it is not possible to discuss all of the changes that have characterized rural America recently, I will briefly describe three changes that have fundamentally altered rural communities and rural opportunity structures in ways that affect individual and household decisions about moving or staying, and forming families and having children. The fundamental changes I review include industrial restructuring, the devolution of governmental responsibilities, and an intensification of global-local linkages.

Industrial Restructuring

The industrial composition of rural economies has experienced two major transformations since the middle of the twentieth century that continue to affect opportunity structures for rural employment and economic security. First, beginning in the mid-twentieth century, dependence on agriculture and other extractive activities declined as manufacturing and other transformative activities became the main rural employers. Then, during the late 1960s and 1970s, manufacturing's dominance began to give way and services, especially private services, became dominant employers. In 2012, agriculture and mining employed less than 5 percent of rural workers, manufacturing employed about one in five rural workers, and most workers, rural and urban alike, were employed in services. However, while the rate of growth in services has been similar across rural and urban areas, the growth of higher paying producer services has been very modest in rural economies. Hence, the majority of jobs available to rural workers tend to be low-wage and low-skill with limited career advancement opportunities and sparse benefits. The industrial profile of rural labor markets results in a lack of economic security and out-migration, especially among better-educated young adults. In contrast, some rural areas with reasonable access to urban labor markets have been able to retain their residential function, but workers are forced to commute long distances to obtain well-paying jobs.

One accompaniment of this industrial restructuring is that rural economies—with their heavy dependence on personal services, including tourism and recreation—tend to experience high *under*employment. As Jensen et al. (1999) show, the chief component of underemployment in rural areas is working part time or/and holding temporary or seasonal jobs. Hence, a disproportionate share of rural workers, regardless of their work effort or intensions to work, are unable to earn sufficient income to provide a reasonable level of economic security for themselves and their families. They tend to be what is characterized as the "working poor."

Devolution

Beginning in the 1980s, public policies have favored the decentralization of governing responsibility from higher to lower levels of government. This reversed a trend that began in the Great Depression in which the national (and state) government played a growing role in the financing and production of local services (Lobao and Kraybill 2005). This reversal reflects an ideological belief that decision making should reside as close as possible to those it is intended to affect. Devolution has gone hand in hand with privatizing services that previously were publically administered (Warner 2009). As Warner (2009, 113) observes, "both privatization and decentralization represent an ascendance of market-based approaches to governmental service delivery."

These shifts in governmental roles that increase reliance on markets to produce public services cannot be assumed to automatically result in equal access by under-resourced people and communities. This is particularly salient in rural areas where lower population density and more dispersed settlement tends to increase the per person cost of service delivery, especially if areas have weak, undiversified economies. As Warner and Pratt (2005) show, rural areas, especially those with weak economic performance, tend to have a limited tax base, reduced public investment, and economic decline. As a result, their ability to provide essential services through either the private or public sector is limited. This lack of high-quality and affordable services further diminishes a place's chances for economic development, since services are a fundamental attribute for attracting and retaining both employers and workers. In other words, places with low fiscal capacity and limited service sectors face a vicious cycle where the lack of services undermines their development chances and thus their ability to produce services (Warner 2003).

Global-Local Linkages

Rural areas, while somewhat geographically separate, are not now, nor were they ever, truly separate from the rest of American society. Even during the colonial and revolutionary eras, rural areas were affected by regional, national, and international forces such as laws and regulations, treaties, tariffs, and the urban and international demand for raw materials and commodities produced there. While global-local linkages have always affected rural people's opportunities and demographic behavior, their nature has changed and become more intense and asymmetric. Of course, in discussing devolution, I have already indicated one of the ways in which local/non-local relationships have been transformed. Here I focus on the further incorporation of rural areas into the national and global economy.

The "protection of distance" experienced by rural communities was diminished by advances in transportation and communication during the late nineteenth and twentieth centuries as rural areas became increasingly incorporated within the national polity and economy. However, the degree of incorporation accelerated with the development of information technologies, financial and other forms of deregulation, the ascendency of transnational corporations, and the establishment and empowerment of transnational organizations such as the IMF, WTO, and World Bank. The resulting globalized system involves a unified world economy that replaced the international federation of states created after World War II, the so-called Breton Woods system (McMichael 2012). As Brown and Schafft (2011, 157) observe, globalization is a vision of the world as a "globally organized and managed free trade, free enterprise economy pursued by largely unaccountable political and economic elites."

Many critics contend that globalization reduces the sustainability of local economies by making them more vulnerable to external control and influence.[4] Globalization's most profound negative impact on rural economic activity is permanent job loss and displacement through "offshoring," automation, and other processes. Since offshoring reflects changes in corporate strategy, not fluctuations in the business cycle, it entails permanent job loss, not short-term unemployment. This benefits firms, but undermines the economic opportunities and security available in local labor markets. This is particularly critical for rural labor markets with low-wage, low-skill non-durable manufacturing—exactly the kind of firms most likely to seek cheaper labor elsewhere. As Glasmeier and Salant (2006) show, once rural jobs are lost to international competitors, they are seldom replaced.

How have restructuring, devolution, and globalization interacted with rural population dynamics? In the next section, I address this question by focusing on three demographic trends characteristic of rural populations.[5] To foreshadow, I argue that these relationships are causally complex and, taken together, turn the logic of demographic determinism on its head. I will return to this in the conclusion.

Rural Population Dynamics

Urban-Rural[6] Population Redistribution

After a long history of uninterrupted urbanization, the United States has experienced four major reversals in the relative rate of rural-urban population change since 1970. In that year, and to the surprise of most social scientists, America experienced an unprecedented "counter-urbanization" with rural areas growing at a faster rate than urban areas. The 1980s were characterized as the decade of rural population reversal as the long-term trend of urbanization reemerged. The 1990s appeared to be another decade of counter-urbanization, but this was only true from 1990 to 1995. As a consequence, urban areas outgrew rural areas over the ten-year period as a whole. Since 2000 the urban growth advantage has accelerated, with urban areas growing by over 10 percent compared to about 3 percent in rural areas. At present, urban areas are growing by 0.9 percent per year while rural areas have dipped into decline for the first time (USDA 2014).

Most of these reversals were powered by changes in the direction of net internal migration that favored rural areas in the 1970s, urban areas in the 1980s, rural areas in the early 1990s, and urban areas in the remainder of the decade. In contrast, the role of natural increase has reasserted itself since 2000. As Johnson and Lichter (2012, 32) observe, "natural increase has re-emerged as a prominent demographic force in the growth of rural America in the first decade of the 21st century." Ironically, natural increase reasserted itself as a positive contributor to rural population growth at the same time that over one-third of US counties experienced natural decrease, an all-time high for the nation, and a significant increase over the previous decade (Johnson 2013). As I will discuss below, the re-emergence of natural increase as a positive component of rural population change is associated with the recent in-migration of Hispanics to rural America.

How do these trends and changes in population redistribution relate to the structural transformations discussed earlier? Fluctuation in the direction of rural-urban population redistribution is mainly associated with the declining fortunes of rural economies. As noted above, the availability of well-paying, secure rural jobs has declined in recent decades because of deindustrialization, global offshoring, and weak public sectors that result from devolution and diminished tax bases. In other words, rural economies' ability to provide well-paying jobs that attract and retain workers is highly contingent on the global economic context, and the national policy environments, in which rural areas are embedded. The strength and agency of local community remains an important determinant of social and economic sustainability, but the interaction of local and global trumps the strictly local.

With the exception of the 1970s, when manufacturing firms moved from large metropolises in the Northeast and Midwest to both urban and rural destinations in the South and Southwest, rural manufacturing jobs have declined and have been replaced by low-paying, insecure jobs in private services, tourism, and recreation (Vias and Nelson 2006). As a result, rural areas have experienced a net loss of working age persons and their families in every decade since 1950

(Johnson and Cromartie 2006). Moreover, rural populations would have fallen even farther behind urban areas had it not been for immigration that brought Hispanic workers and their families to many rural locations in the Midwest, Southeast, and other regions (Johnson and Lichter 2012). The rising and falling tide of immigration, of course, is associated with the global flow of capital as workers follow jobs internationally. The present low rate of immigration reflects the international recession and the associated slowdown of capital mobility. Hispanic immigration has a second-order effect on rural population growth since fertility among immigrants is relatively high, thereby contributing to natural increase, which is a growing component of rural population growth (Johnson and Lichter 2012).

Rural Population Aging

The population of the United States is aging, and the extent of aging is especially high in rural areas. Data from the American Community Survey show that the median age of the US rural population exceeded that of the urban population by more than four years in 2009 (39.7 versus 35.6).[7] Moreover, median age is even higher in lower density and more isolated locations, where almost one in six persons is age sixty-five or older, compared with one in eight in the nation as a whole (Berry 2012).[8] That 17.3 percent of older Americans lived in rural areas compared with 16.4 percent of all persons indicates that older people are disproportionately concentrated in rural areas. Population aging results from lower fertility and increased longevity, but migration also contributes to the disproportionate concentration of older people in rural areas of the United States. Chronic out-migration of young adults from rural to urban areas to obtain better educational and job opportunities, as well as net in-migration of older people to attractive, or amenity-rich, rural destinations, have withdrawn younger persons and added older persons resulting over time in rural population aging.

Population aging is particularly notable in two somewhat different contexts—rural retirement destinations and areas experiencing natural population decrease (Glasgow and Brown 2012). In the first case, older persons tend to concentrate in amenity-rich locales where recreation and tourism developed in earlier times (Brown et al. 2011). These areas attract relatively prosperous older persons at or around retirement age. In contrast, natural decrease results when several generations of younger persons move from rural areas, taking their children and childbearing potential with them. Destinations of older migration are typically framed as a development success, while natural decrease is seen as a symptom of economic malaise and stagnation. However, while these two types of areas may seem diametrically different, because older in-migration is often unaccompanied by in-migration of youth, almost one half of rural retirement destinations in the United States today also have natural decrease (Glasgow and Brown 2012).[9]

How does population aging[10] *relate to the structural transformations discussed earlier in this chapter?* Populations grow older because one or more of the following demographic processes is occurring: low fertility, net out-migration of young adults, net in-migration at the oldest ages, or/and aging in place of persons in late middle age. Increased immigration, a fundamental aspect of globalization, provides the most direct link between changes in social and economic structure and population aging. Immigrants are younger than the destination populations they join, and immigrants are increasingly accompanied by children or have children soon after arriving in rural destinations.

Internal migration also affects age composition because it is selective of the working and family formation ages. Places that attract and retain well-paying jobs also attract and retain younger workers and their families. Hence, deskilling of rural manufacturing and offshoring of many of the remaining non-durable firms displaces workers from rural labor markets.

Natural population decrease reflects a long history of net out-migration of young adults. This phenomenon is geographically concentrated in the nation's midsection, where decades of agricultural transformation have resulted in a highly concentrated farm structure featuring a small number of large producers. This structural transformation displaces farmers, farm workers, and persons who supplied farmers and farm households with supplies and services. With few non-agricultural jobs to absorb the farm labor surplus, workers have no choice but to move away (Carr and Kefalas 2009).

Extreme aging as reflected by natural population decrease is also characteristic of certain rural areas with natural amenities that attract older migrants. Where communities have commodified amenities as recreation and tourism, visitors sometimes become in-migrants later in their lives. Hence older migration, if not accompanied by migration at the working ages, will produce extremely old populations and natural decrease (Brown et al. 2011; Glasgow and Brown 2012).

The Rural Population's Changing Race-Ethnic Composition

Rural areas have generally been thought of as more racially homogeneous than their urban counterparts. As Michael Woods (2005, 282) observes, rural space has been positioned as a "White space." He contends that this tends to reinforce the social exclusion of racial and ethnic minorities in rural areas. However, as Brown and Schafft (2011, 122) observe, rural America is "far more ethnically and racially diverse than the popular imagination would presume." Racial and ethnic minorities have constituted significant proportions of the rural population for a long time, but they have tended to concentrate in particular regions. Rural African Americans live mostly in the South, American Indians west of the Mississippi River, and until recently rural Hispanics have been concentrated in the Southwest. Between 1990 and 2006 to 2008, the number of Hispanics living in rural areas increased from about 2 million to 3.4 million, and their geographic location dispersed from the Southwest toward the Midwest and Southeast (Johnson 2012; Kandel and Parrado 2006). At the same time, US Census Bureau data indicate that the rural African American population declined by 11.6 percent from 4.8 million to 4.2 million, while the American Indian and Asian populations living in rural areas remained stable at around 1 million and .5 million respectively (Brown and Schafft 2011).

New streams of immigration originating in Mexico and Central America into rural regions that have heretofore had relatively small Hispanic populations largely accounts for the dispersion of rural Hispanics to the Midwest and Southeast (Sáenz 2012). These immigration streams are largely motivated by the demand for low-wage labor in the food processing, construction, and personal services industries. However, as Johnson and Lichter (2012) demonstrate, natural increase replaced immigration as the main source of rural (and urban) population growth after 2005. In fact, almost six out of ten new Hispanic persons living in rural America were added through natural increase. The impact of Hispanic increase on overall population growth in rural America is large and generally unappreciated. Hispanics comprised 5.4 percent of the rural population in 2000, but accounted for 44 percent of rural population growth from 2000 to 2006 (Johnson and Lichter 2012). Hence, in addition to its positive effect on rural population size, Hispanic growth has contributed to diversifying the rural population.

How does the increased race-ethnic diversity of rural populations relate to the structural transformations discussed earlier in this chapter? The changing race-ethnic composition of the rural population was initially accounted for by Hispanic immigration but is more affected now by fertility and natural increase. Immigration, the root cause of Hispanic population growth even if fertility is the proximate cause in recent years, results from strategic decisions made by food processers, and especially meat packers, to move production facilities closer to supply and to attract immigrant workers to communities with little previous migration experience. Hence, once again, we see the result of globalization and industrial restructuring on rural population change. It should be noted that Hispanic population growth in rural areas is often accompanied by the absolute declines in non-Hispanic whites (Johnson and Lichter 2012). While little research has been conducted on the determinants of these divergent trends for whites and Hispanics, it would appear that the very jobs that attract Hispanics repel non-Hispanic whites. In addition, some analysts believe that the concentrated in-movement of immigrant populations may deflect longer-term residents, at least in the suburbs of metropolitan areas (Frey and Liaw 1996; Light 2006). However, research on social relations between immigrants and longer-term residents in rural contexts casts doubt on this conclusion. Immigrants and longer-time residents seem to live in separate societies with little or no interaction (deLima, Parra, and Pfeffer 2012).

To observe that immigration is a highly contentious issue is an understatement. This is especially true today because the devolution and states' rights agendas discussed earlier are helping to shape the debate. Many states and localities are proposing to regulate immigration at the state and local levels. Laws passed in Arizona and Alabama seem destined for the Supreme Court, and immigration remains a contentious issue in President Obama's second term. If the states' rights agenda prevails, localities, including rural localities, will gain the authority to regulate immigration and will thereby affect future changes in their population compositions.

Conclusions

In this chapter, I have contended that population change is influenced by broader social and economic structures and changes therein. I have focused on the ways in which societal transformations such as industrial restructuring, governmental devolution, and globalization have resulted in fluctuating directions of internal migration and rural-urban population redistribution, extreme population aging, and increased rural population diversity. But my focus could have just as easily have been the opposite—how population changes influence institutions from the economy to education to health care to local governance. In fact, positing population change as the "independent variable" and examining its social and economic consequences is the more typical approach. From the Population Bomb of the 1960s (Ehrlich 1968) to the hyperbole surrounding reaching a world population of seven billion in 2011, many persons assume that population change results in social problems, whether environmental degradation, food shortages, budget deficits related to expensive social programs, or crime and delinquency. In many cases, population change does contribute to adverse outcomes, but it is seldom the main or exclusive cause of social problems. My goal in this chapter has been to demonstrate that population change and institutional change are mutually dependent, and that the impacts of population change are contingent on the social and economic structures in which people live and work. For example, the same rate of population decline in two rural communities of similar size and location does not necessarily have the same results. In one community a decline in the school age population may result in school closure or consolidation, while in another similar place it might result in inter-local cooperation, outsourcing of administrative functions, or simply deciding to spend more per student in order to maintain the status quo. In other words, the local impacts of population change depend on political will, and the economic feasibility, and social acceptability of proposed actions. Demography is not destiny.

Notes

1 This is true of other more developed nations as well.

2 While the recession had a slight negative affect on the US total fertility rate, declining to 1.9 in 2010 and 2011, it rebounded to 2.06 by 2012. Relative stability in the TFR during the recession and its aftermath largely results from immigration which while slowed remains at a relatively high level. Since immigrants are younger than the native population and tend to come from countries with higher fertility rates than the United States, they tend to push the TFR higher (World Bank 2011).

3 While nationwide trends and patterns can be identified, it is important to acknowledge regional and situational variations in demographic patterns and changes.

4 However, a more balanced perspective acknowledges that while globalization diminishes local autonomy, it also opens up access to external resources and opportunities (Stiglitz 2002).

5 Of course, the social and economic changes discussed in this section are not the only reasons for these demographic trends—in fact, some of the causes are demographic themselves—but they play important roles. Moreover, as indicated earlier, the direction of causation between structural change and demographic change runs in both directions. In other words, while population change may be a determinant of social and economic change, structural transformations can also be a determinant of changes in demographic behavior.

6 For ease of exposition, I use *urban-rural* and *metropolitan-nonmetropolitan* interchangeably in this chapter even though most data I refer to utilize the metropolitan-nonmetropolitan distinction.

7 Similarly, the percent of the population age sixty-five or older is almost a year higher in rural America (13.3 versus 12.4).

8 For example, the median age of micropolitan populations was 38.5 in 2009 compared with 41.0 in non-core areas. Micropolitan counties are nonmetropolitan and include a place that has a population of at least 10,000. Noncore counties lack even one place of 10,000 people.

9 This is because older in-migration, if not accompanied by in-migration at younger ages, will eventually lead to natural decrease. In other words, older in-migration, ageing in place of both migrants and longer-term residents, and a lack of younger in-migration produces an age structure that results in fewer births than deaths regardless of the fertility rate of persons in their childbearing years.

10 Population aging should be differentiated from individual aging, which concerns increased longevity rather than the redistribution of persons among a population's age groups.

References

Berry, E. 2012. "Rural Aging in International Context." In *The Handbook of Rural Demography*, ed. Laszlo J. Kulcsar and Katherine Curtis, 67–79. Dordrecht: Springer. http://dx.doi.org/10.1007/978-94-007-1842-5_6.

Brown, David L., Benjamin C. Bolender, Laszlo J. Kulcsar, Nina Glasgow, and Scott Sanders. 2011. "Intercounty Variability of Net Migration at Older Ages as a Path-Dependent Process." *Rural Sociology* 76 (1): 44–73. http://dx.doi.org/10.1111/j.1549-0831.2010.00034.x.

Brown, David L., and Kai Schafft. 2011. *Rural People and Communities in the 21st Century: Resilience and Transformation.* Cambridge: Polity Press.

Carr, Patrick J., and Maria J. Kefalas. 2009. *Hollowing out the Middle: The Rural Brain Drain and What It Means for America.* Boston, MA: Beacon.

deLima, Philomena, Pilar Parra, and Max Pfeffer. 2012. "Conceptualizing Contemporary Immigrant Incorporation in the Rural United States and United Kingdom." In *Rural Transformations and Rural Policies in the UK and US*, ed. Mark Shucksmith, David L. Brown, Sally Shortall, Jo Vergunst, and Mildred E. Warner, 79–99. New York, Oxford: Routledge.

Ehrlich, Paul. 1968. *The Population Bomb.* New York: Ballentine Books.

Frey, William. 2009. "The Great American Migration Slowdown." Washington, DC: Brookings Institution. Accessed 14 January 2012. http://www.brookings.edu/~/media/research/files/opinions/2011/1/12%20migration%20frey/1209_migration_frey.pdf.

Frey, William, and K. Liaw. 1996. "The Impact of Recent Immigration on Population Redistribution within the United States." Working Paper 96–376. Ann Arbor: Population Studies Center of the University of Michigan.

Glasgow, Nina, and David L. Brown. 2012. "Rural Ageing in the United States: Trends and Contexts." *Journal of Rural Studies* 28 (4): 422–31. http://dx.doi.org/10.1016/j.jrurstud.2012.01.002.

Glasmeier, Amy, and Priscilla Salant. 2006. "Low Skill Workers in Rural America Face Permanent Job Loss." Policy Brief No. 2. Durham, NH: Carsey Institute.

Jensen, Leif, Jill L. Findeis, Wan-Ling Hsu, and Jason P. Schachter. 1999. "Slipping into and out of Underemployment: Another Disadvantage for Nonmetropolitan Workers." *Rural Sociology* 64 (3): 417–38. http://dx.doi.org/10.1111/j.1549-0831.1999.tb00360.x.

Johnson, Kenneth M. 2012. "Rural Demographic Change in the New Century Slower Growth, Increased Diversity." Issue Brief No. 44. Carsey Institute. Accessed 14 March 2013. http://www.carseyinstitute.unh.edu/publications/IB-Johnson-Rural-Demographic-Trends.pdf.

Johnson, Kenneth M. 2013. "Deaths Exceed Births in Record Number of U.S. Counties." Fact Sheet No. 25. Carsey Institute. Accessed 14 March 2013. http://www.carseyinstitute.unh.edu/sites/carseyinstitute.unh.edu/files/publications/fs-johnson-natural-decrease-us-counties-web.pdf.

Johnson, Kenneth M., and John Cromartie. 2006. "The Rural Rebound and its Aftermath." In *Population Change in Rural Society*, ed. William Kandel and David L. Brown, 25–49. Dordrecht: Springer. http://dx.doi.org/10.1007/1-4020-3902-6_2.

Johnson, Kenneth M., and Daniel T. Lichter. 2012. "Rural Natural Increase in the New Century: America's Third Demographic Transition." In *The Handbook of Rural Demography*, ed. Laszlo J. Kulcsar and Katherine J. Curtis, 17–34. Dordrecht: Springer. http://dx.doi.org/10.1007/978-94-007-1842-5_3.

Kandel, W., and E. Parrado. 2006. "Rural Hispanic Population Growth: Public Policy Impacts in Nonmetro Counties." In *Population Change in Rural Society*, ed. William Kandel and David L. Brown, 155–75. Dordrecht: Springer. http://dx.doi.org/10.1007/1-4020-3902-6_7.

Light, Ivan. 2006. *Deflecting Immigration*. New York: Russell Sage.

Lobao, Linda, and David Kraybill. 2005. "The Emerging Roles of County Governments in Metropolitan and Nonmetropolitan Areas: Findings from a National Survey." *Economic Development Quarterly* 19 (3): 245–59. http://dx.doi.org/10.1177/0891242405276514.

McMichael, Phillip. 2012. *Development and Social Change: A Global Perspective*. Thousand Oaks, CA: Sage.

Migration Policy Institute. 2012. "MPI Data Hub." Accessed 14 January 2012. http://www.migrationinformation.org/datahub/charts/historic1.cfm.

Sáenz, Rogelio. 2012. "Rural Race and Ethnicity." In *The Handbook of Rural Demography*, ed. Laszlo J. Kulcsar and Katherine J. Curtis, 207–23. Dordrecht: Springer. http://dx.doi.org/10.1007/978-94-007-1842-5_15.

Stiglitz, Joseph E. 2002. *Globalization and Its Discontents*. New York: Norton.

USDA (U.S. Department of Agriculture). 2014. Population and Migration. 3 April 2014. Washington, DC: USDA Economic Research Service. Available at http://www.ers.usda.gov/topics/rural-economy-population/population-migration.aspx. Accessed on 1 June 2014.

Vias, Alexander C., and Peter Nelson. 2006. "Changing Livelihoods in Rural America." In *Population Change in Rural Society*, ed. William Kandel and David L. Brown, 75–102. Dordrecht: Springer. http://dx.doi.org/10.1007/1-4020-3902-6_4.

Warner, Mildred E. 2009. "Civic Government or Market-Based Governance? The Limits of Privatization for Rural Local Governments." *Agriculture and Human Values* 26 (1–2): 133–43. http://dx.doi.org/10.1007/s10460-008-9181-6.

Warner, Mildred E., and James E. Pratt. 2005. "Spatial Diversity in Local Government Revenue Effort under Decentralization: A Neural Network Approach." *Environment and Planning. C, Government & Policy* 23 (5): 657–77. http://dx.doi.org/10.1068/c16r.

Warner, Mildred M. 2003. "Competition, Cooperation and Local Governance." In *Challenges for Rural America in the 21st Century*, ed. David L. Brown and Louis E. Swanson, 252–61. University Park: Penn State Press.

Woods, Michael. 2005. *Rural Geography*. London: Sage.

World Bank. 2011. "World Bank Development Indicators." Accessed 14 January 2012. http://data.worldbank.org/data-catalog/world-development-indicators/wdi-2011.

CHAPTER 16

Demographic Trends in Nonmetropolitan America: 2000 to 2010[1]

Kenneth M. Johnson

Introduction

In his introductory chapter to this section, David L. Brown identifies three critical demographic trends with significant implications for rural areas: population change, population aging, and growing racial-ethnic diversity. Analysis of longitudinal demographic change in rural America illustrates the complex interplay between migration, natural increase, aging, and diversity that produced the population redistribution trends evident today (Johnson and Cromartie 2006). In this chapter, I examine the influence of these demographic forces on nonmetropolitan population redistribution trends in the United States in the first decade of the twenty-first century.

The United States has experienced a selective de-concentration of its population over the past several decades (Long and Nucci 1998; Frey and Johnson 1998; Johnson and Cromartie 2006; Vining and Strauss 1977). This produced a spatially uneven pattern of population redistribution in rural America that favored some areas at the expense of others. Rural America is a big place, encompassing nearly 75 percent of the nation's land area and fifty-one million people. Population redistribution in this vast area is far from monolithic. Some rural regions have experienced decades of sustained growth, while large segments of the agricultural heartland continued to lose people and institutions. Findings from other developed nations indicate de-concentration (or "counter-urbanization") is underway there as well (Boyle and Halfacree 1998; Champion 1998; Champion and Sheppard 2006).

Population growth in rural America has always reflected a balance between natural increase (births minus deaths) and net migration (in-migration minus out-migration). Early in the nation's history, net in-migration fueled most rural growth as vast new frontiers of the country were opened to homesteading and commercial development (e.g., forestry and mining) (Fuguitt, Brown, and Beale 1989; Fischer and Hout 2006). Soon after settlement, natural increase began to contribute heavily to population growth, due to high rural fertility and low mortality rates among the growing young rural population. By the 1920s, however, people were leaving rural America, both attracted by the economic and social opportunities in the nation's booming big cities, and pushed from rural areas by the mechanization and consolidation of agricultural production (Greenwood 1975; Easterlin 1976). The magnitude of rural net out-migration varied from decade to decade and from place to place, but the general pattern was unchanging: more people moved away from rural areas than to them (Figure 16.1). Of course, there were exceptions to this trend in some industrializing regions, such as the Northeast, and at the urban fringe. Still, more than half of the nation's rural counties lost population between 1920 and 1970 (Johnson 1985; Johnson 2006).

By the mid-twentieth century, rural net out-migration losses were so great that the modest rural population gains were fueled entirely by natural increase (Johnson 2006). High rural fertility—helped along by the post–World War II baby boom—brought a surplus of births over deaths that offset the substantial migration losses to urban areas. With the waning of the baby boom in the late 1960s, the natural increase that sustained modest nonmetro population growth diminished. The relentless out-migration of young adults, along with aging in place, produced an older rural age structure that resulted in fewer births and more deaths (Johnson 2011; Johnson et al. 2005; Lichter et al. 1981). Rural-urban fertility also converged with modernization and rural development (Fuguitt, Beale, and Reibel 1991), so net migration came to play a more prominent role in rural population change.

The diminishing population gains that characterized rural America for the first two-thirds of the century ended abruptly with the onset of the remarkable demographic turnaround of the 1970s. For the first time in at least 150 years, population gains in nonmetro areas exceeded those in metro areas; indeed, nonmetro areas grew at the expense of metro areas, as more people left urban areas than arrived in them (Fuguitt 1985). Widespread net migration gains in rural counties were fueled by rural restructuring—job growth associated with rural retirement migration, natural resources (e.g., coal and gas), and recreational development—as well as by urban sprawl and changing residential preferences (Brown and Wardwell 1981; Fuguitt 1985). The rural-urban turnaround was short-lived. Rural population growth slowed in the 1980s with the return of widespread net out-migration from rural areas. But just as

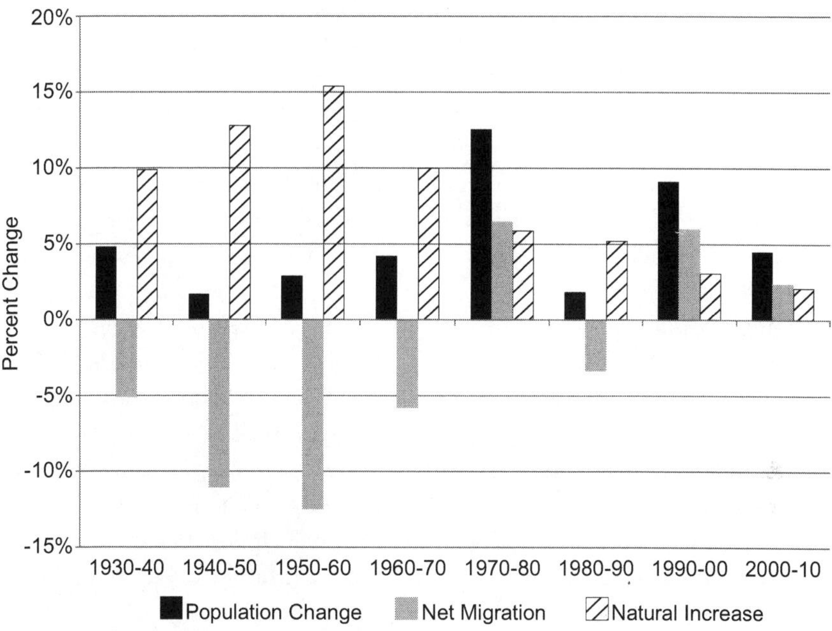

Figure 16.1. Nonmetropolitan demographic change, 1930 to 2010. Source: U.S. Census 1930-2010 and FSCPE.

unexpectedly, rural population growth rebounded in the 1990s as migration to rural areas accelerated (Johnson and Beale 1994). However, as the 1990s came to an end, there was again evidence that nonmetro population gains were slowing (Cromartie 2001; Beale 2000; Johnson and Cromartie 2006). Thus, at the dawn of the twenty-first century the demographic implications of natural increase and net migration for the future of rural America are once again in question.

Data and Methods

Counties are the unit of analysis. They have historically stable boundaries and are a basic unit for reporting fertility, mortality, and census data. Counties are designated as metro or nonmetro using criteria developed by the US Office of Management and Budget (county-equivalents are used for New England). A constant 2004 metro-nonmetro classification is used here because it removes the effect of reclassification from the calculation of longitudinal population change. Metro areas include counties containing an urban core of 50,000 or more population (or central city), along with adjacent counties that are highly integrated with the core county as measured by commuting patterns. There are 1,090 metro counties. The remaining 2,051 counties are nonmetro.

Counties are also classified using a typology developed by the Economic Research Service of the US Department of Agriculture, which classifies nonmetro counties along economic and policy dimensions (Economic Research Service 2004). The county classification developed by Johnson and Beale (2002) was also used to identify nonmetro counties where recreation is a major factor in the local economy.

County population data come from the decennial Census of Population for 1990, 2000, and 2010. They are supplemented with data from the Federal-State Cooperative Population Estimates program (FSCPE), which provides data on the number of births and deaths in each county for April 1990 to July 2009 (US Census Bureau 2010).[2] Births and deaths from July 2009 to the census in April 2010 were estimated at .75 of the amount from July 2008 to July 2009. The estimates of net migration used here were derived by the residual method, whereby net migration is what is left when natural increase is subtracted from total population change.

Data for racial and Hispanic origin of the population are from the 2000 and 2010 Census and include five racial/Hispanic origin groups: (1) Hispanics of any race, (2) non-Hispanic whites, (3) non-Hispanic blacks, (4) non-Hispanic Asians, and (5) all other non-Hispanics, including those who reported two or more races. To examine the uneven spatial distribution of different racial and ethnic populations, I estimate the number and percentage of *majority-minority counties*—those with at least half their population from minority groups in 2010—and *near majority-minority* counties—those with between 40 and 50 percent minority populations.

Analysis

Recent Demographic Change in Nonmetro and Metro Areas

Rural population gains between 2000 and 2010 were greatest in the West and Southeast, as well as on the periphery of large urban areas in the Midwest and Northeast (Figure 16.2). Scattered population gains also were evident in recreational areas of the upper Great Lakes, the Ozarks, and Northern New England. Population losses were common in the Great Plains and Corn Belt, in the Mississippi Delta, in parts of the Northern Appalachians, and in the industrial and mining belts of New York and Pennsylvania.

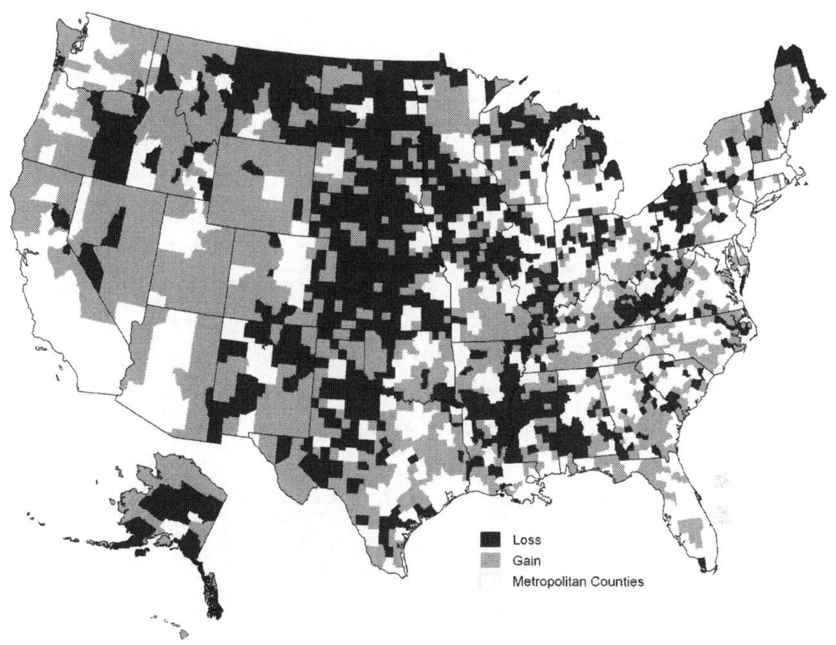

Figure 16.2. Nonmetropolitan population change, 2000 to 2010. Source: U.S. Census Bureau, Census 2000 and 2010.

Nonmetro population growth slowed precipitously after 2000. Between 2000 and 2010, rural counties gained 2.2 million residents (4.5 percent) to reach a population of fifty-one million in April 2010. This growth rate was roughly half that during the 1990s, when the rural population grew by 4.1 million. This slowdown was evident in rural counties both proximate to and remote from urban areas. Gains were greater in nonmetro counties adjacent to metro areas, just as they were from 1990 to 2000. In these adjacent counties, the population gain was 5.5 percent between 2000 and 2010—only 57 percent of what it had been during the 1990s. In all, 63.4 percent of the adjacent counties gained population between 2000 and 2010. Among more remote nonmetro counties, the gain was considerably smaller (2.7 percent). This was significantly less than the 6.4 percent gain such counties experienced during the 1990s. Only 44 percent of the nonadjacent counties gained population between 2000 and 2010. Metro population gains also diminished (from 14.0 to 10.8 percent), but the reduction was much more modest. A key question becomes, how did the demographic components of change combine to produce the smaller nonmetro population gains during the post-2000 period?

How Did Natural Increase and Net Migration Contribute to Rural Demographic Change?

During the 1990s, migration accounted for nearly two-thirds of the nonmetro population gain of 4.1 million, but after 2000, less than half (46 percent) of the smaller population gain of 2.2 million came from migration. Nonmetro counties gained 2.7 million residents from migration during the 1990s, but only about one million between 2000 and 2010.[3] Migration gains also occurred in fewer rural counties during the last decade. Only 46 percent of the rural counties experienced a net migration gain between 2000 and 2010, compared to 65 percent between 1990 and 2000. Because natural increase in rural areas remained relatively stable over the two decades, the absence of significant migration gains after 2000 was the primary cause of the sharply diminished rural population growth.

In rural counties remote from metro areas, there was a minimal net migration gain estimated at 46,000 (.3 percent) between 2000 and 2010. Just 35 percent of these nonadjacent counties gained migrants. In contrast, such counties had a migration increase of 544,000 during the 1990s. Migration gains were greater (980,000) in counties that were adjacent to metro areas. This represents a 3 percent gain from migration. Overall, 53 percent of the adjacent counties gained migrants between 2000 and 2010. Nonetheless, this recent migration gain was considerably smaller than that during the 1990s, when adjacent counties gained 2.4 million migrants (7.4 percent).

With migration gains diminishing, natural increase produced most of the nonmetro population growth between 2000 and 2010, accounting for 1.2 million of the gain of 2.2 million rural residents (54 percent). In fact, in nonadjacent nonmetro counties, the natural increase of 418,000 (2.5 percent) accounted for 90 percent of the population gain. In adjacent nonmetro counties, the natural increase was 760,000 (2.4 percent). Here the contributions of natural increase and net migration were more balanced, with natural increase accounting for 44 percent of the population increase of 1.7 million. Though natural increase provided the majority of the rural population gain between 2000 and 2010, the absolute gain from natural increase in nonmetro counties was smaller than during the 1990s. Rural natural increase was already slowing in the 1990s when it supplied 1.4 million new residents. By the first decade of the new century, it produced just 1.2 million new residents.

Further evidence of the diminishing excess of births over deaths in nonmetro areas is reflected in a sharp increase in the incidence of natural *decrease* there. Natural decrease, an excess of deaths over births, has been unusual in the

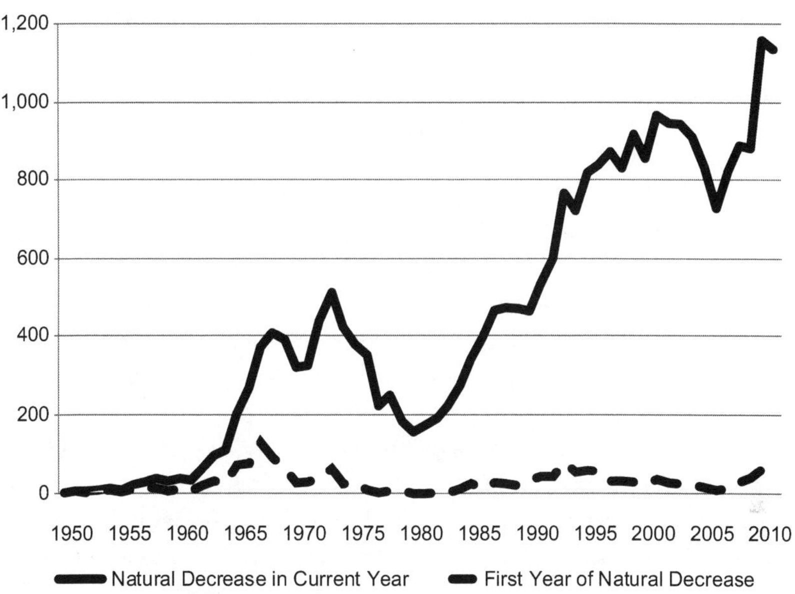

Figure 16.3. Natural decrease in US counties, 1950 to 2012. Source: CDC-NCHS, Census Bureau FSCPE.

American experience. Near the end of the Great Depression, natural decrease occurred in a few counties (Dorn 1939), but it was short-lived. As Figure 16.3 suggests, natural decrease remained rare during the high fertility era of the baby boom but became more common near the end of the 1960s as fertility levels waned (Beale 1964; 1969; Johnson and Purdy 1980). The incidence of natural decrease rose sharply in the early 1970s, diminished through 1982, and then began a period of sustained growth (Fuguitt et al. 1989; Johnson 1993; Johnson and Beale 2002). Natural decrease reached a peak of 985 counties in 2002 before subsiding. However, recent Census Bureau estimates of births and deaths through July 2012 suggest that natural decrease is now at the highest level in US history (Johnson 2011; 2013).

In parts of rural America, deaths have exceeded births for decades, and more than 90 percent of US counties with episodes of natural decrease are nonmetro (Johnson 2011). Between 2000 and 2009, nearly 750 nonmetro counties (36 percent) experienced an overall natural decrease. This number is up from approximately 29 percent in the 1990s and represents the highest level of sustained natural decrease in US history. Within rural areas, the incidence of natural decrease is influenced by proximity to metro areas. Nearly 43 percent of nonadjacent counties had natural decrease between 2000 and 2009, compared to 30 percent of the adjacent counties.

Natural decrease is geographically widespread, but tends to cluster spatially. Once natural decrease occurs in a county, the probability that it will reoccur is extremely high (Johnson 2011). Natural decrease occurred first in agricultural areas of the Great Plains, Western and Southern Corn Belt, East and Central Texas; in the Ozark-Ouachita Uplands; in some mining- and timber-dependent rural counties of the Upper Great Lakes; and in some Florida counties that were among the first to receive retirement migrants. In the 1990s, natural decrease spread to rural areas of the South, New York and Pennsylvania, the Upper Great Lakes, and parts of the West; more recently, it has spread to Indiana and Ohio (Johnson 2011).

Natural decrease is the ultimate demographic consequence of the dwindling number of young adults and the growing older population in rural America. It is caused by two interrelated demographic factors. The more influential is a local age structure that has few young adults of child-bearing age and a large surplus of older adults at high risk of mortality. Beale (1969) argues that such population aging is caused by protracted age-specific migration, a finding a substantial body of research supports (Adamchak 1981; Chang 1974; Johnson 2011; 1993; Johnson and Beale 1992; Johnson and Purdy 1980). For decades, migration drained young adults from rural areas (Fuguitt and Heaton 1995; Johnson et al. 2005; Johnson and Fuguitt 2000). As a result, natural decrease counties have significantly fewer twenty- to thirty-nine-year-olds than other areas. In 2000, for example, counties with sustained natural decrease averaged 27 percent fewer residents in their twenties than the United States as a whole (Johnson 2011).[4] The demographic impact of this young adult out-migration is magnified by the aging in place of older generation and by an influx of older migrants to retirement areas. For example, in 2000, counties with sustained natural decrease had 59 percent more people over the age of seventy than the country as a whole. Thus, for several generations the older population has grown in natural decrease areas, while the young population has dwindled.

The second factor increasing the likelihood of natural decrease is diminishing fertility (Dorn 1939). Women in natural decrease counties do not have fewer children than women elsewhere, but longitudinal declines in US fertility rates coupled with the diminishing numbers of young women in natural decrease counties eventually results in births insufficient to offset the rising number of deaths among older cohorts (Beale 1969; Johnson 2011; 1993; Johnson and Beale 1992). So, both temporal variations and normative changes in fertility have contributed to the rising incidence of natural decrease in rural America.

How Does Demographic Change Vary across Rural America?

Rural America is a diverse place. With nearly 75 percent of the nation's land area and fifty-one million residents, it is not surprising that there is significant variation in the patterns of demographic change across this vast region. Demographic processes at work in nonmetro counties that represent the old and new elements of the rural economy illustrate this.

Farming and mining no longer monopolize the rural economy, but they remain important. Farming still dominates the local economy of some 403 rural counties. Mining (which includes oil and gas extraction) is a major force in another 113 counties. Between 2000 and 2010, the population of farming-dependent counties grew by just .3 percent, and only 29 percent of them gained population. This minimal population gain was entirely due to a natural increase gain of 3.0 percent, which was large enough to offset a migration loss. In contrast, farm counties grew by 5 percent during the 1990s because of the contribution of natural increase and migration. Mining counties were also entirely dependent on natural increase for their modest population gain of 2.7 percent. In all, just 56 percent of the mining counties gained population between 2000 and 2010.

Small population gains or outright decline in farming and mining counties are well known, but manufacturing counties have traditionally been a bright spot of rural demographic change. In fact, rural development strategies traditionally focused on expanding the manufacturing base. Manufacturing is important to the rural economy because it employs a larger proportion of the rural labor force than it does in urban areas (Johnson 2006). In all, there are 584 rural manufacturing counties (including those that specialize in meat and poultry processing), and their population grew 8.1 percent during the 1990s, due mostly to migration. However, growth slowed dramatically to just 3.1 percent between 2000 and 2010, though most manufacturing counties (57 percent) continued to grow. A natural increase of 430,000 accounted for 75 percent of this population gain. In contrast, migration contributed only modestly to the increase, with only 47 percent of the manufacturing counties gaining migrants. Globalization coupled with the recent economic downturn adversely impacted the rural manufacturing sector, which includes many low-technology, low-wage jobs that are increasingly shifting offshore or disappearing as technology replaces labor (Johnson and Cromartie 2006; Johnson 2006).

The demographic story was quite different in rural counties that focused on natural amenities, recreational opportunities, or quality of life advantages rather than on traditional rural activities. Major concentrations of these counties exist in the mountain and coastal regions of the West, in the upper Great Lakes, in coastal and scenic areas of New England and upstate New York, in the foothills of the Appalachians and Ozarks, and in coastal regions from Virginia to Florida (Johnson and Beale 2002; McGranahan 1999; Economic Research Service 2004). Such high-amenity counties have consistently been the fastest growing in rural America. The 277 rural counties that are destinations for retirement migrants exemplify this trend. In each of the past several decades, they have grown faster than any other rural county type. For example, their population gain was 13.4 percent between 2000 and 2010. The 299 nonmetro recreational counties were close behind at 10.7 percent. Overall, 84 percent of the retirement destination counties and 69 percent of the recreational counties gained population during the decade. Migration fueled almost all this growth, accounting for 89 percent of the population gain in retirement counties and 81 percent in recreational counties. These migration streams include both the amenity migrants themselves and other migrants attracted by the economic opportunities generated by such rapid growth. However, recent population gains were considerably smaller than those during the 1990s, when retirement counties grew by 26 percent and recreational counties by 20 percent.

How Have Minority Populations Contributed to Rural Demographic Change?

Any analysis of recent demographic trends in rural America must be cognizant of the growing demographic impact that minority populations are having on rural population change. Between 2000 and 2010, the minority population accounted for 83 percent of the overall nonmetro population gain, though it represented just 21 percent of the rural population. Overall, the nonmetro minority population grew by 1.8 million (21.3 percent) compared to a gain of just 382,000 (.95 percent) among the much larger non-Hispanic white population between 2000 and 2010. Thus, while nonmetro America remains less diverse than urban America (which is 36 percent minority), minority growth now accounts for most rural population increase, just as it does in urban areas.

There is considerable geographic variation in the levels of diversity in rural America. Large concentrations of African Americans remain in the rural Southeast, despite the migration of millions of blacks from the South during the first two-thirds of the twentieth century. This outflow of blacks from the South has ended and the region is now seeing an influx of black migrants, though most are going to metro areas (Frey 2009). Hispanic population concentrations of long-standing in the Southwest remind us that there have been Hispanic rural residents in the region for centuries. Recent research documents the spread of

Hispanics from these historical areas into rural areas of the Southeast and Midwest (Kandel and Cromartie 2004; Johnson and Lichter 2008). Though small in overall numbers, native peoples also represent an important element of many rural communities in the Great Plains as well as in parts of the West. There are scattered areas in the Southwest where native peoples and Hispanics are found in the same counties, as well as growing areas in the Southeast and East Texas where blacks and Hispanics reside in the same county. But in general, though rural America is becoming more diverse, it is on a modest scale with one or at most two racial groups residing in the same rural county. Large areas of nonmetro America remain overwhelmingly non-Hispanic white.

The driving force behind this substantial minority population gain in nonmetro areas is the sustained growth of the Hispanic population. Hispanics remain spatially concentrated in urban areas. However, Hispanics—both native and foreign-born—are rapidly diffusing spatially, especially into smaller metro cities (Singer 2004), small towns, and rural areas in the South and Midwest (Lichter and Johnson 2006). Hispanics account for a rapidly accelerating share of rural population growth over the past two decades. During the 1990s, Hispanics accounted for 25 percent of the entire rural population gain though they represented only 3.5 percent of the rural population in 1990. Between 2000 and 2010, Hispanics accounted for 54 percent of the rural gain, though they represented only 5.4 percent of the population in 2000. By 2010, the Hispanic population of rural America stood at 3.8 million—a gain of 45 percent from 2000.

Hispanic migrants have large secondary demographic effects on fertility and natural increase in rural areas (Johnson and Lichter 2008; 2010). Between 2000 and 2005, more than 58 percent of the nonmetro Hispanic increase and 55 percent of the metro Hispanic population increase was due to the excess of births over deaths (Johnson and Lichter 2008). Hispanics are rapidly dispersing geographically, with about one-half of the nonmetro Hispanic population now residing outside of traditional Hispanic settlements in the rural Southwest (Johnson and Lichter 2008). Rural Hispanic resettlement patterns and natural increase have been instrumental in offsetting non-Hispanic white population declines, especially in the Great Plains (Johnson and Lichter 2008).

Children are in the vanguard of this growing diversity in rural America. Nearly 28 percent of the nonmetro population under the age of eighteen in 2010 belongs to a minority, compared to 18 percent of the adult population. Hispanics represent the largest share of this minority nonmetro youth population, and more than 12 percent of all rural children are Hispanic (Johnson and Lichter 2010). The conventional wisdom is that growing child diversity is largely a big-city phenomenon. However, minority child gains were particularly important in rural areas, where the child population actually declined by nearly 900,000 (a 10 percent loss) between 2000 and 2010. This decline occurred because there were 940,000 (a 10 percent loss) fewer non-Hispanic white children in rural areas and the black child population also declined (11.6 percent). This demonstrates that the overall loss of children was cushioned somewhat because the rural Hispanic child population grew by 434,000 (45.1 percent). The significant loss of white children coupled with a growing Hispanic child population accelerated the diversification of the rural child population (Johnson and Lichter 2008).

The geographic implications of this growing child diversity is reflected in the fact that 591 counties now have a majority of minority young people (i.e., majority-minority counties) and another 300 are "near" majority-minority, with between 40 and 50 percent minority youth populations (Figure 16.4). Of these, 356 majority-minority youth counties are nonmetro, as are 178 of the near majority-minority counties. These patterns among young people are clearly a harbinger of future racial change and diversity in rural America, especially as minority births disproportionately replace deaths among the aging white population.

What Impact Has the Great Recession Had on Nonmetro Demographic Trends?

Occurring late in the first decade of the twenty-first century, the Great Recession's impact on migration has reverberated through the entire nonmetro hierarchy. In nonmetro America as a whole, growth slowed late in the decade because the in-migration to such areas has slowed dramatically.[5] To examine this, the decade is divided into three periods to reflect the pre-boom (April 2000 to July 2004), the boom period (July 2004 to July 2007), and the recession period (July 2007 to July 2010). In rural America as a whole, population growth slowed in the recessionary period. The annual population gain between 2004 and 2007 was 304,000, but this slowed to 178,000 between 2007 and 2010. Natural increase remained stable during both periods. So, the population slowdown was the result of a sharp reduction in net migration from 180,000 during the mid-decade boom to just 56,000 during the recessionary period.

The impact of the recession on migration was spatially uneven. It was greater in adjacent nonmetro areas, where the booming economy fueled peripheral growth and spatial sprawl from nearby urban areas during the peak years. Here the downturn sharply diminished net migration gains from an average annual gain of 155,000 during the boom years to just 40,000 per year during the

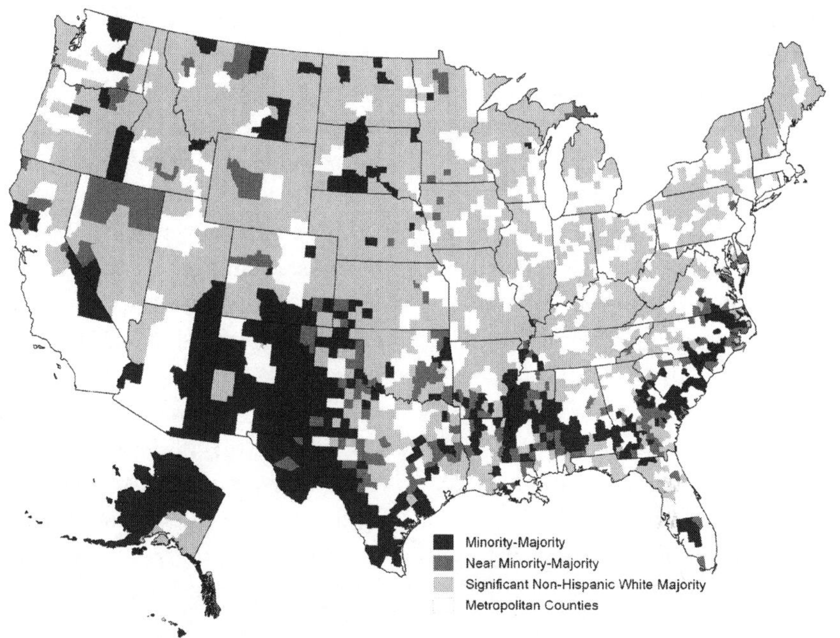

Figure 16.4. Nonmetropolitan minority child population concentration, 2010. Source: U.S. Census Bureau, Census 2010.

recession—a reduction of 74 percent. These smaller net migration gains reduced the population gain in these formerly fast-growing areas.

Paradoxically, in remote rural areas, which have historically experienced slow growth or population decline, the impact of the recession on migration has not been as great. Remote rural counties experienced migration losses early in the decade, gains during the mid-decade boom, and then diminished gains during the recession. However, the reduction in net migration during the recession was far more modest in these remote rural counties. Migration declined by 32 percent in the remote counties compared to 74 percent in adjacent counties. As a result, the population gain in adjacent counties, which was nearly ten times that in nonadjacent counties during the early part of the decade, was just 1.8 times the nonadjacent gain during the recession.

Migration stream data illustrate how net migration was influenced by the recession. Internal Revenue Service county-to-county migration data (Internal Revenue Service 2013), which measures the movement of domestic migrants only, suggest that the migration slowdown in adjacent nonmetro counties occurred because fewer people moved there during the recessionary period.

During the mid-decade boom, adjacent counties had an inflow of 4.57 million domestic migrants compared to 4.29 million out-migrants; producing a net migration gain of 280,000. During the recession, in-migration dropped to 4.34 million, while out-migration remained steady at 4.29 million. The result was a net of 229,000 fewer migrants. The advantages that adjacent counties derive from urban proximity—access to the urban labor market and spillover migration—clearly eroded during the recession as potential migrants from proximate metro areas were now "frozen in place" because of houses that were difficult to sell, badly depleted retirement accounts, and fewer job prospects. This migration slowdown in adjacent rural counties echoes the dramatic reduction in migration to the metro periphery due to the recession (Frey 2009).

The situation in nonadjacent nonmetro counties was strikingly different. Here there was little change in net migration because the inflow and outflow of migrants remained stable during the recessionary period. Thus, the overall change in net migration to nonadjacent counties was just 8,000 compared to a net slowdown of 229,000 in adjacent counties. In essence, the freezing in place of the population occasioned by the recession dramatically slowed the inflow of migrants to adjacent counties, while hardly impacting the flows to more remote counties. As a result, the population gain in adjacent areas during the recessionary period declined sharply, while it remained stable in nonadjacent counties.

Domestic migration is not the only demographic component affected by recent economic dislocations. Data from the Pew Hispanic Center show that the net flow of new immigrants into the United States also slowed during the recessionary period (Passell 2011). Immigrants are an important source of new growth in nonmetro areas, so any recessionary slowdown in immigration is likely to influence rural areas (Lichter and Johnson 2006). In addition, new data from the National Center for Health Statistics show a fertility decline of nearly 7.3 percent in the last three years (Hamilton, Martin, and Ventura 2011). Given the importance of natural increase and immigration to nonmetro growth, fertility declines and reduced immigration have significant implications for future rural demographic trends.

Conclusions

In the first decade of the twenty-first century, rural population gains were considerably smaller than they had been during the rural rebound of the 1990s. Nonmetro areas grew by just 2.2 million people between 2000 and 2010—a gain barely half as great as the 4.1 million person gain of the 1990s. Migration contributed far less to the growth of rural America in the first decade of the twenty-first century than it had in the last decade of the twentieth. It did continue to account for the majority of the population gain in rural counties adjacent to metro areas as well as in fast growing recreational and retirement counties. But, even here, population gains were considerably smaller than they had been during the 1990s because migration gains diminished. In counties situated proximate to urban areas, net migration gains were particularly hard hit by the recession because fewer people moved to them. Natural increase accounted for more than half of the rural population gain between 2000 and 2010—far more than it did in the 1990s. It was especially important in remote rural areas, including those dependent on farming, where natural increase accounted for most of the population growth. In contrast, migration contributed little to the growth of nonadjacent counties, though the recession impacted migration streams to more remote rural areas less adversely. In many rural areas, natural decrease is now on the rise. Natural decrease is the eventual demographic consequence of the protracted out-migration of generations of young adults from rural areas. The spatial clustering of rural natural decrease exacerbates its adverse consequences for rural economic development efforts.

The first decade of the twenty-first century also saw the growing importance of minorities to the demographic future of rural America. The minority population represents just 21 percent of the rural population, but minorities produced nearly 83 percent of the rural population increase between 2000 and 2010. Hispanics, in particular, represent a new source of demographic vigor in many parts of rural America. They accounted for more than half of the entire rural population gain between 2000 and 2010. The rapid growth of the Hispanic population—fueled increasingly by natural increase rather than in-migration—also underscores the changing racial and ethnic mix of rural America's young people. Young people are in the vanguard of rural America's new diversity because the minority child population is growing and because there was an absolute decline in the non-Hispanic white youth population.

These demographic changes have important policy implications. First, as rural America becomes more racially and ethnically diverse, rural institutions that serve young people, such as those related to education and health care, will be the first to feel the impact. Such institutions are among the most expensive for local governments. Nor are financial problems the only challenges rural communities face in dealing with diversity. Minorities are transforming the social fabric of many small towns, raising important policy questions (e.g., related to schooling, political participation, racial tensions, etc.) about their successful incorporation into American society (Massey 2008). Second, population growth is slowing overall in rural America, but there is considerable variation in the patterns of population change. For fast-growing rural counties, programs and expertise are needed to address the complex issues of managing growth and development. Elsewhere, the population slowdown has been profound. Here, rural policy must ameliorate the adverse impacts of a diminishing population on the provision of critical services and support programs as well as provide access to the resources (Internet, capital, and expertise) needed to expand the local infrastructure and enhance future development opportunities. In all cases, policymakers must understand the varied patterns of demographic change in rural communities, and design policies that are comprehensive enough to address the multifaceted challenges these communities face.

In conclusion, this research contributes new information delineating the rapidity and geographic scale at which demographic change is occurring in rural America. Rural areas both here and abroad are being buffeted by economic, social, and governmental transformations from far beyond their borders. As David Brown suggests in his opening essay to this section, and as I have demonstrated in this chapter, these structural transformations are reflected in the demographic trends playing out across the vast rural landscape in the first decade of the twenty-first century. This underscores the ongoing need for timely analysis of contemporary demographic data. Demography may not be destiny, but rural scholars and policy makers ignore it at their peril.

Notes

1 This research has been supported by grants from the Northern Research Station of the USDA Forest Service and the New Hampshire Agricultural Experiment Station through Hatch Multi-State Projects W-2001 and W-3001, and by grants to the Carsey Institute from the Annie E. Casey Foundation, the W.K. Kellogg Foundation, and an anonymous donor. Research support provided by Luke Rogers and Barb Cook of the Carsey Institute.

2 The late Calvin Beale, senior demographer at the Economic Research Service of the USDA, provided data on the incidence of natural decrease from 1950 through 1966. See Johnson (2011) for details on other sources for data on natural decrease.

3 Immigration contributed more to rural migration gains between 2000 and 2010 than it did during the 1990s. No definitive immigration data are currently available for the period, but estimates from 2000 to 2009 suggest a substantial inflow of immigrants to both adjacent and nonadjacent counties. However, even with immigration on the rise, overall migration gains were significantly smaller in rural areas during the first decade of the twenty-first century.

4 Sustained natural decrease is natural decrease that occurred continuously from 1990 to 2000.

5 I have adjusted these estimates to reflect the influence of recently released intercensal population estimates that incorporate data from the 2010 US Census.

References

Adamchak, D.J. 1981. "Population Decrease and Change in Nonmetropolitan Kansas." *Transactions of the Kansas Academy of Science* 84 (1): 15–31. http://dx.doi.org/10.2307/3628222.

Beale, C.L. 1964. "Rural Depopulation in the United States: Some Demographic Consequences of Agricultural Adjustments." *Demography* 1: 264–72.

Beale, C.L. 1969. "Natural Decrease of Population: The Current and Prospective Status of an Emergent American Phenomenon." *Demography* 6 (2): 91–99. http://dx.doi.org/10.2307/2060383.

Beale, C.L. 2000. "Nonmetro Population Growth Recedes in a Time of Unprecedented National Prosperity." *Rural Conditions and Trends* 11: 27–31.

Boyle, P., and K. Halfacree. 1998. *Migration in to Rural Areas.* Chichester, UK: Wiley.

Brown, D.L., and J.M. Wardwell. 1981. *New Directions in Urban/Rural Migration: Population Turnaround in Rural America.* New York: Academic Press.

Champion, T. 1998. "Studying Counterurbanization and the Rural Population Turnaround." In *Migration into Rural Areas: Theories and Issues*, ed. P.J. Boyle and K.H. Halfacree, 21–40. London: Wiley.

Champion, T., and J. Sheppard. 2006. "Demographic Change in Rural England." In *The Ageing Countryside: The Growing Older Population of Rural England*, ed. P. Lowe and L. Speakman, 21–40. London: Age Concern England.

Chang, H.C. November 1974. "Natural Population Decrease in Iowa Counties." *Demography* 11 (4): 657–72. http://dx.doi.org/10.2307/2060476 Medline:21279751.

Cromartie, J.B. 2001. "Nonmetro Outmigration Exceeds Inmigration for the First Time in a Decade." *Rural America* 16: 35–37.

Dorn, H.E. 1939. "The Natural Decrease of Population in Certain American Counties." *Journal of the American Statistical Association* 34 (205): 106–9. http://dx.doi.org/10.1080/01621459.1939.10502371.

Easterlin, R. 1976. "Population Change and Farm Settlement in the Northern United States." *Journal of Economic History* 36 (1): 45–75. http://dx.doi.org/10.1017/S002205070009450X.

Economic Research Service. 2004. "Measuring Rurality: 2004 County Typology Codes Methods, Data Sources, and Documentation." Accessed 15 July 2011. http://www.ers.usda.gov/briefing/rurality/typology/methods.

Fischer, Claude S., and Michael Hout. 2006. *Century of Difference: How America Changed in the Last One Hundred Years.* New York: Russell Sage Foundation.

Frey, W.H. 2009. *The Great Migration Slowdown: Regional and Metropolitan Dimensions.* Washington, DC: Brookings Institution.

Frey, W.H., and K.M. Johnson. 1998. "Concentrated Immigration, Restructuring, and the Selective Deconcentration of the U.S. Population." In *Migration into Rural Areas: Theories and Issues*, ed. P.J. Boyle and K.H. Halfacree, 79–105. London: Wiley.

Fuguitt, G.V. 1985. "The Nonmetropolitan Population Turnaround." *Annual Review of Sociology* 11 (1): 259–80. http://dx.doi.org/10.1146/annurev.so.11.080185.001355 Medline:12313950.

Fuguitt, G.V., C.L. Beale, and M. Reibel. 1991. "Recent Trends in Metropolitan-Nonmetropolitan Fertility." *Rural Sociology* 56 (3): 475–86. http://dx.doi.org/10.1111/j.1549-0831.1991.tb00444.x.

Fuguitt, G.V., D.L. Brown, and C.L. Beale. 1989. *Rural and Small Town America.* New York: Russell Sage Foundation.

Fuguitt, G.V., and T.B. Heaton. 1995. "The Impact of Migration on the Nonmetropolitan Population Age Structure, 1960–1990." *Population Research and Policy Review* 14 (2): 215–32. http://dx.doi.org/10.1007/BF01074459.

Greenwood, Michael J. 1975. "Research on Internal Migration in the United States: A Survey." *Journal of Economic Literature* 13: 397–433.

Hamilton, B.E., J.A. Martin, and S.J. Ventura. 2011. "Births Preliminary Data for 2010." *National Vital Statistics Reports* 60 (2): 1–26.

Internal Revenue Service. 2013. "U.S. Population Migration Data: Strengths and Limitations." Accessed 20 December 2013. http://www.irs.gov/uac/SOI-Tax-Stats-Migration-Data-Users-Guide.

Johnson, Kenneth M. 1985. *The Impact of Population Change on Business Activity in Rural America.* Boulder, CO: Westview Press.

Johnson, Kenneth M. 1993. "When Deaths Exceed Births: Natural Decrease in the United States." *International Regional Science Review* 15 (2): 179–98. Medline:12286502.

Johnson, Kenneth M. 2006. "Demographic Trends in Rural and Small Town America." *Carsey Institute Reports on America* 1: 1–35. Durham: Carsey Institute, University of New Hampshire.

Johnson, Kenneth M. 2011. "The Continuing Incidence of Natural Decrease in American Counties." *Rural Sociology* 76 (1): 74–100. http://dx.doi.org/10.1111/j.1549-0831.2010.00036.x.

Johnson, Kenneth M. 2013. "Deaths Exceed Births in Record Number of U.S. Counties." Fact Sheet. Durham, NH: Carsey Institute.

Johnson, Kenneth M., and Calvin L. Beale. 1992. "Natural Population Decrease in the United States." *Rural Development Perspectives* 8: 8–15.

Johnson, Kenneth M., and Calvin L. Beale. 1994. "The Recent Revival of Widespread Population Growth in Nonmetropolitan Areas of the United States." *Rural Sociology* 59 (4): 655–67. http://dx.doi.org/10.1111/j.1549-0831.1994.tb00553.x.

Johnson, Kenneth M., and Calvin L. Beale. 2002. "Nonmetro Recreation Counties: Their Identification and Rapid Growth." *Rural America* 17: 12–9.

Johnson, Kenneth M., and John B. Cromartie. 2006. "The Rural Rebound and its Aftermath: Changing Demographic Dynamics and Regional Contrasts." In *Population Change and Rural Society*, ed. William Kandel and David L. Brown, 25–49. Dordrect, Netherlands: Springer. http://dx.doi.org/10.1007/1-4020-3902-6_2.

Johnson, Kenneth M., and Glenn V. Fuguitt. 2000. "Continuity and Change in Rural Migration Patterns, 1950–1995." *Rural Sociology* 65 (1): 27–49. http://dx.doi.org/10.1111/j.1549-0831.2000.tb00341.x.

Johnson, Kenneth M., and Daniel T. Lichter. 2008. "Natural Increase: A New Source of Population Growth in Emerging Hispanic Destinations in the United States." *Population and*

Development Review 34 (2): 327–46. http://dx.doi.org/10.1111/j.1728-4457.2008.00222.x.

Johnson, Kenneth M., and Daniel T. Lichter. 2010. "Growing Diversity among America's Children and Youth: Spatial and Temporal Dimensions." *Population and Development Review* 36 (1): 151–76. http://dx.doi.org/10.1111/j.1728-4457.2010.00322.x.

Johnson, Kenneth M., and R.L. Purdy. February 1980. "Recent Nonmetropolitan Population Change in Fifty-Year Perspective." *Demography* 17 (1): 57–70. http://dx.doi.org/10.2307/2060963 Medline:7353708.

Johnson, Kenneth M., Paul R. Voss, Roger B. Hammer, Glenn V. Fuguitt, and Scott McNiven. November 2005. "Temporal and Spatial Variation in Age-Specific Net Migration in the United States." *Demography* 42 (4): 791–812. http://dx.doi.org/10.1353/dem.2005.0033 Medline:16463922.

Kandel, William, and John Cromartie. 2004. *New Patterns of Hispanic Settlement in Rural America. Rural Development Research Report 99.* Washington, DC: Economic Research Service, USDA.

Lichter, Daniel T., Glenn V. Fuguitt, Tim B. Heaton, and William B. Clifford. July 1981. "Components of Change in the Residential Concentration of the Elderly Population: 1950–1975." *Journal of Gerontology* 36 (4): 480–9. http://dx.doi.org/10.1093/geronj/36.4.480 Medline:7252082.

Lichter, Daniel T., and Kenneth M. Johnson. 2006. "Emerging Rural Settlement Patterns and the Geographic Redistribution of America's New Immigrants." *Rural Sociology* 71 (1): 109–31. http://dx.doi.org/10.1526/003601106777789828.

Long, L., and A. Nucci. 1998. "Accounting for Two Population Turnarounds in Nonmetropolitan America." *Research in Rural Sociology and Development* 7: 47–70. Medline:12294800.

Massey, Douglas S. 2008. *New Faces in New Places: The Changing Geography of American Immigration.* New York: Russell Sage Foundation.

McGranahan, David A. 1999. *Natural Amenities Drive Population Change.* Agricultural Economics Report No. 718. Washington, DC: Economic Research Service, US Department of Agriculture.

Passell, J. 2011. "Comings and Goings: Unauthorized Immigrants and the Great Recession." Cornell Population Program Seminar Series, 4 March 2011.

Singer, Audrey. 2004. *The Rise of New Immigrant Gateways. The Living Cities Census Series.* Washington, DC: Brookings Institution.

US Census Bureau. 2010. "Annual County Resident Population Estimates by Age, Sex, Race, and Hispanic Origin: April 1, 2000 to July 1, 2009." Accessed 20 December 2013. http://www.census.gov/popest/data/counties/asrh/2009/CC-EST2009-agesex.html.

Vining, D.R., Jr., and A. Strauss. 1977. "A Demonstration that the Current Deconcentration of Population in the United States is a Clean Break with the Past." *Environment & Planning A* 9 (7): 751–8. http://dx.doi.org/10.1068/a090751 Medline:12310795.

CHAPTER 17

Population Shifts across US Nonmetropolitan Regions

John B. Cromartie and Timothy S. Parker

Introduction

A severe housing-market disruption and the worst recession in eighty years combined with long-term demographic trends and other factors to cause a slowdown in population growth throughout rural and small-town America during the past decade. In this chapter, we take a regional perspective to summarize recent demographic trends for the total US nonmetropolitan population and for selected race-ethnic and age groups. We highlight spatial diversity by comparing demographic trends across nine regions. We explore two time frames. First, we describe the downward shift in nonmetro population growth rates between the 1990s and the 2000s, with a primary focus on its regional diversity. Second, to better understand connections between rural population shifts and global economic-financial disruptions occurring in the middle of the decade, we use the same regional framework to trace year-to-year shifts in total population change during the 2000s. Taken together, these analyses help identify nonmetro areas that are exhibiting continued population gains or losses, or that are experiencing new demographic trajectories. We also report associated changes in regional demographic composition, for instance, identifying where older populations are concentrating or where Hispanic in-migration is adding to ethnic diversity.

Geography is an intrinsic dimension of rural studies and regional analyses such as this one have always been a central component of rural demography (Baker 1936; Voss 2007). Our findings are meant, in part, to encourage a geographically informed perspective on policymaking and program implementation, because most US demographic trends that are strong enough to affect rural policy decisions display considerable spatial variation. For example, the effects of population loss persist in some regions and are largely absent from others. Population retrenchment often cuts into economic prospects in rural labor markets by creating a circular causation dynamic between job loss and out-migration. It challenges fiscal viability and quality of life in many rural communities. Within high out-migration areas, factors affecting population loss vary across space and over time. One set of policy-relevant questions that we begin to address in this chapter centers on the contribution of short-lived economic and housing-market shocks versus longer-term economic and demographic restructuring to the current rural population slowdown. Were low net migration levels during the 2000s primarily a function of the former, in which case the potential for demographic recovery is higher? Or were they tied to built-in demographic momentum (such as fertility decline and aging), economic restructuring, or permanent changes in the comparative economic advantage of rural areas, as many argue regarding globalization effects? As with any issue affecting the well-being of people and places, answers depend on where you are in rural America.

Though primarily descriptive in scope and purpose, we include causal or correlative interpretations of the recent nonmetro downturn meant to guide subsequent research. Regional disaggregation allows us to make preliminary judgments on factors driving nonmetro population growth, such as recreation, retirement, immigration, energy extraction, urban agglomeration, or metro proximity. Such conclusions are based on well-established empirical generalizations regarding factors driving rural population change, as well as knowledge of the characteristics of the regions being compared. For instance, a nonmetro population downturn in highly urbanized regions suggests the need to analytically focus on diminished metropolitan expansion as an explanatory factor. Similarly, as David Brown notes in his introduction to this section, population declines in rural labor markets with high shares of low-wage manufacturing jobs point to the impact of offshoring on rural communities and the need to focus on the effects of industrial restructuring and globalization processes. While not directly answering the questions posed above regarding the potential for demographic recovery, our analysis takes a helpful first step in sorting out the relative importance of short- and long-term demographic influences, with special emphasis on how these connections might play out differently across regions of the United States.

Data and Methods

We analyze geographic and temporal shifts in rural and small-town demographic trends by comparing rates of population change among nine uniform regions across two decades (1990s and 2000s) and year-to-year changes in rates during the 2000s. For the two-decade comparison, we use short-form (100 percent count) data from the 1990, 2000, and 2010 decennial censuses to track population change for the total population and for race-ethnicity and age groups. The Census Bureau's Population Estimates Program provides data for the year-to-year analysis from July 2000 to July 2010.

Nonmetropolitan counties define our study area and we use a constant (2003) nonmetro delineation to compare trends during the 1990s and 2000s. Complementary insights can be gained by employing floating metro-nonmetro definitions (Artz and Orazem 2006). For instance, 1990s nonmetro population growth rates would be higher for 1993 nonmetro counties, because fast-growing counties were reclassified as metro in 2003. A floating nonmetro definition would accentuate the contrast between decades but would complicate interpretation of results across regions, requiring decomposition between metropolitanization effects and other factors contributing to the 2000 to 2010 nonmetro population downturn. Beyond a two-decade comparison, constant definitions become problematic, and thus we use a floating nonmetro delineation in our brief examination of historical population shifts.

We capture regional dimensions of the nonmetro population downturn using a nine-level, county classification system designed to group nonmetro areas with reasonably similar climatic, physiographic, economic, historic, socio-cultural, and/or urban-rural characteristics (Figure 17.1). These regions are mostly aggregations from a twenty-six-level delineation used to study post-1970 rural population trends (Morrison 1977; Fuguitt and Beale 1996). These twenty-six regions, in turn, were combinations of over 500 State Economic Areas (Bogue and Beale 1961). The only major modification was to shift the boundary between the Rio Grande-Southwest and West to better demarcate a widely recognized, historical-cultural heartland for rural Hispanics (Hudson 2002; Kandel et al. 2011). In addition, five counties were shifted to combine the southern Appalachians, Ozark-Ouachitas, and other interior highlands into one undivided region. Otherwise, boundaries follow combinations of the initial set of twenty-six uniform regions (see Fuguitt and Beale 1978 for a detailed discussion).

We analyze overall population growth here rather than its components—net migration and natural increase, to streamline the discussion and for other reasons. County net migration estimates by age and race were not available for 2000 to 2010 at the time of writing. Also, annual population estimates by age and race (another data analysis option) are constructed in a way that may mask emerging age-specific nonmetro or regional trends. Our geographic-temporal findings

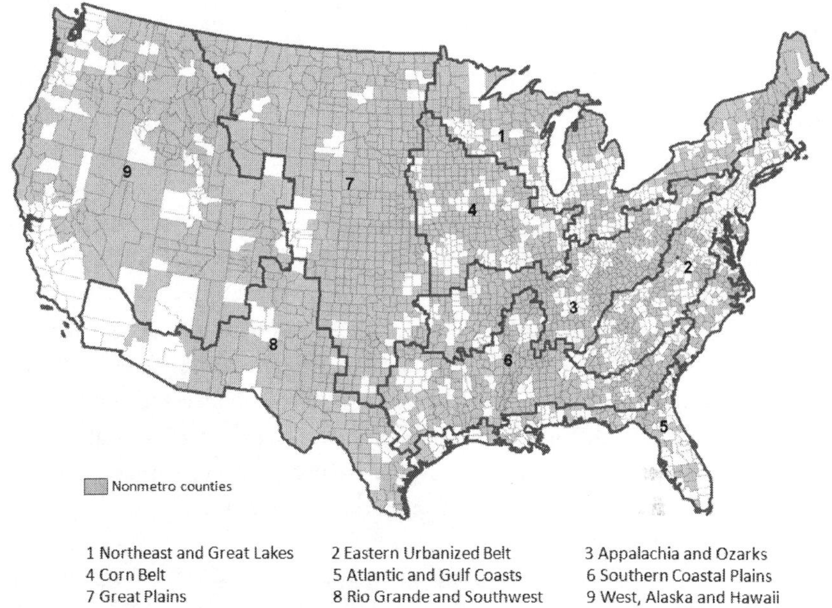

Figure 17.1. US regions based on state economic areas. Note: Regions shown here are aggregations of twenty-six subregions delineated by Calvin Beale (Fuguitt and Beale 1978), which, in turn, were drawn from over 500 State Economic Areas (Bogue and Beale 1961). Changes were made here to identify a Rio Grande and Southwest region (8) and to connect eastern upland subregions into a single unit (3).

for population change are almost exclusively driven by migration changes, because natural change contributes very little to the short-term shifts described here, either across decades (the 1990s and 2000s) or year to year through the 2000s. Except for newly emerging regional impacts of natural change associated with Hispanic in-migration (Johnson and Lichter 2012), nonmetro population growth from natural increase continued to bottom out at historic lows with no significant regional fluctuations. However, both natural change and net migration contribute to the relative position of regions in terms of population growth. For instance, during 2000 to 2005, the Rio Grande-Southwest had lower net migration rates compared with all other regions, but showed higher overall population growth rates than the Great Plains, Corn Belt, and two other regions due to higher fertility rates and a younger population. Thus, even though findings here are primarily migration driven, statistics on total population change are preferred for comparisons across regions.

Results

Between 2000 and 2010, the nonmetro population grew by 2.2 million people compared with an additional 5.3 million people added during the "rural rebound" of the 1990s. Overall, the nonmetro population growth rate fell from 10 percent in the 1990s to 4 percent during the 2000s. Nonmetro areas are currently growing at half the metro rate, and the overall percentage of the US population living in nonmetro areas has fallen from over 20 percent in the 1990s to 16 percent today. This most recent downward shift was not as severe as the population reversal twenty years earlier, when the nonmetro growth rate shifted from 13.5 percent in the 1970s to 2.6 percent in the 1980s (Johnson and Cromartie 2006, 32). However, the downward shift between the 1990s and 2000s was similarly pervasive across diverse regions (Figure 17.2). One in five nonmetro counties did grow at a higher rate during the 2000s, but in the aggregate, significantly slower growth occurred in all nine regions analyzed in this study, as it did during the 1980s.

Regional stability despite temporal fluctuations describes historic population trends in nonmetro areas, especially since 1970 (Figure 17.2). Nonmetro population change was somewhat more geographically volatile during the 1950s and 1960s as farm depopulation and rural-to-urban migration reached historic highs and America went through a baby boom. For instance, nonmetro population rates slowed in most regions between the 1950s and 1960s, but in three eastern and southern regions (the Eastern Urbanized Belt, Appalachia-Ozarks, and the Southern Coastal Plains), renewed growth during the 1960s foreshadowed the population turnaround that became pervasive after 1970.

Since 1970, nonmetro areas in the West and in the Atlantic-Gulf Coast regions have consistently grown faster than elsewhere. The Great Plains and Corn Belt have been the slowest-growing nonmetro regions and the only two to experience overall population loss for an entire decade (during the 1980s and 2000s). Geographic stability suggests that temporal shifts in migration patterns are largely influenced by national-level factors, either macroeconomic business-cycle period effects, or demographic lifecycle cohort effects (Johnson and Cromartie 2006; McHugh and Gober 1992; Plane 1992). There is some evidence of nonmetro convergence during 2000 to 2010—that is, the range of population growth rates separating the slowest- and fastest-growing regions was smaller than in previous decades. However, for the decade as a whole at least, regionally entrenched geographic differences remained.

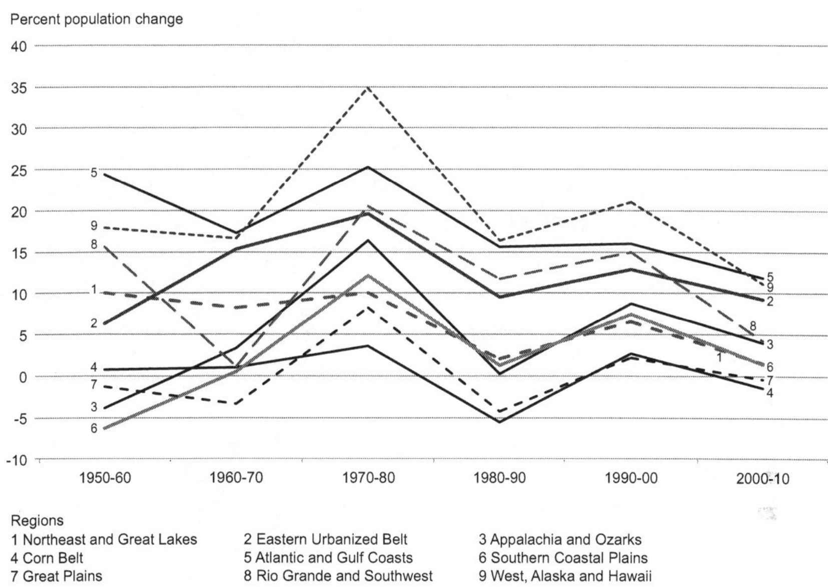

Figure 17.2. Nonmetro population change, decade by region, 1950 to 2010. Note: Statistics are based on nonmetro areas defined as of the beginning of each decade, except for 1950 to 1960, for which nonmetro areas as of the 1960 decennial census were used. Historical metro county lists are available from the US Census Bureau (2013). Source: ERS-USDA using data from the US Census Bureau.

Regional Differences in Factors Associated with Nonmetro Population Growth

These regional differences are strongly influenced by factors long recognized as primary determinants of nonmetro migration destination choices: urban population size, metro proximity, attractive scenery, and recreation potential. Compared with other "non-core" nonmetro counties, faster growth in micropolitan counties (centered around urban areas containing 10,000 to 49,999 people) reflects basic, long-standing urban agglomeration advantages (Mulligan 1984). Persistently higher net migration into counties proximate to metro areas is a result of two factors: suburban "spillover" effects and a marked preference among nonmetro-destined migrants for locations with high urban access (Brown et al. 1997). In addition to urban influence, the major driver of nonmetro population growth over the past forty years has been amenity-based migration and a steadily booming recreation-tourism-retirement economic sector in regions with mountains, lakes, moderate climates, and/or other attractive natural amenities (McGranahan 1999; McGranahan, Wojan, and Lambert 2010).

Two of the three fastest-growing regions, the Eastern Urbanized Belt and the Atlantic-Gulf Coasts, had the highest proportion of populations living in counties adjacent to metro areas with 93 and 87 percent respectively. The percent of population living in high-amenity counties was three times the national average in the West, the other rapid-growth region, and its micropolitan population was higher in proportion than all but one other region. Two regions that lost population during the 2000s, the Corn Belt and Great Plains, had less than 10 percent of their populations living in high-amenity counties, compared with a 25 percent nonmetro average. Both also were well below average in terms of urban size and metro proximity.

Population density is positively correlated with population growth, but the association is weaker than sometimes assumed by urban-growth theories stressing agglomeration advantages. Many remote, low-density areas, in the West especially, developed as recreation and retirement destinations. Even when numerically small, newcomers to such areas can generate large population changes on a percentage basis. The expected relationship (lower density, lower population growth) holds in other remote settings more commonly found in the Great Plains, where the much smaller number of in-migrants cannot match the persistent loss of young adults in the years after high school. The Rio Grande-Southwest, the third region with very low population densities among nonmetro counties, contains a more balanced mix of high-amenity and low-amenity remote areas compared with the West or the Great Plains, which may, in part, explain its intermediate rate of population growth during the 2000s.

Changing Race-Ethnicity Composition

Rapid growth and geographic dispersion among nonmetro Hispanics, coupled with lower birth rates and continued out-migration among non-Hispanic whites and blacks, fueled regionally diverse compositional changes throughout rural and small-town America during the 1990s and 2000s. Continuing a twenty-year trend, population growth among nonmetro Hispanics outpaced other race-ethnicity groups by wide margins, 45 percent during 2000 to 2010 compared with less than 5 percent growth among whites and blacks. The number of Hispanics added to the nonmetro population increased marginally between the 1990s and 2000s from roughly 1.0 to 1.2 million, not enough to avoid a significant decrease in population rates (64 to 45 percent). The same pattern occurred for the US Hispanic population as a whole (metro and nonmetro areas combined); the rate growth declined from 58 percent in the 1990s to 43 percent in the 2000s despite a slight numerical increase in population change (from thirteen to fifteen million). These relatively similar levels of numeric growth between the 1990s and 2000s mask historic changes in the sources of Hispanic population growth during this period. In both metro and nonmetro areas, lower immigration levels from Mexico and Central America, especially since 2006, are being offset by higher birth rates (Johnson and Lichter 2012; Pew Hispanic Center 2011). Significant changes in the age structure, sex ratio, and household composition of the nonmetro population accompany these types of long-term shifts in the underlying causes of population growth.

Regional population change statistics for nonmetro Hispanics provide evidence for a continued trend of geographic redistribution out of long-established Hispanic settlement areas. To a great extent during the 1990s, regional differences reflected newly emerging population growth in regions with quite small Hispanic populations, a trend that resulted in very large, attention-grabbing percentage changes. For instance, the nonmetro Hispanic population in the Corn Belt grew by 143 percent during the 1990s, generating media and research attention even though numeric growth (64,000) was less than half that found in the two most populous Hispanic regions (Rio Grande-Southwest and West). Evaluated on the basis of percentage changes, geographic realignment of nonmetro Hispanics was not as dramatic during the 2000s, because it was no longer a new trend and the base populations in regions outside the Southwest had increased so much. The Corn Belt added more Hispanics during the 2000s compared with the 1990s, but the rate of population change dropped by half. However, evaluated on the basis of numeric changes, it can be claimed that geographic dispersion of nonmetro Hispanics intensified during the 2000s. All but two regions (the Northeast-Great Lakes and the Corn Belt) experienced higher numeric growth among nonmetro Hispanics compared with the Rio Grande-Southwest during the 2000s. Researchers have already documented the particularly striking numeric increases in the Appalachia-Ozarks and the Eastern Urbanized Belt, which includes eastern edges of Appalachia (Barcus 2007; Farmer, Moon, and Miller 2008).

The Rio Grande-Southwest was the only region that showed a significant drop in the number of Hispanics added to the nonmetro population between these two decades (from 146,000 to 111,000). Hispanics have made up a majority of the nonmetro population in the Rio-Grande-Southwest since before the region's annexation by the United States, and will continue to do so despite this slowdown in growth. The number of Hispanics added to the nonmetro population also showed a drop, though a much smaller one, in the Great Plains region, which also contains areas with long-established Hispanic communities (e.g., the Texas Panhandle, southwestern Kansas). These trends do not diminish Hispanics' demographic importance in these regions, because rates of population growth among non-Hispanics are still lower. But they do signal a continuing increase of Hispanics' relative demographic importance in other nonmetro areas throughout all other regions of the United States.

The 2000 to 2010 population downturn was strongly evident among non-Hispanic blacks, the nation's largest nonmetro minority. For the whole United States (metro and nonmetro areas combined), black population growth was roughly half the rate during the 2000s compared with the 1990s, largely reflecting lower levels of natural change rather than any significant decrease in immigration. For the nonmetro United States, a dramatic shift to population loss among blacks occurred in the Southern Coastal Plains, where blacks make up nearly 30 percent of the population. Here, both net domestic migration declines and lower birth rates contributed to the shift between decades. In contrast, the Atlantic-Gulf Coast region continued to attract non-Hispanic blacks and add to its already substantial population base, showing the largest numeric gains among regions during the 2000s. Lower poverty levels, better employment opportunities, and increasing retirement-based migration along the coasts are among factors that likely explain the stark demographic contrast between these two southern regions (Beale and Fuguitt 2011; Fuguitt, Fulton, and Beale 2001).

Population growth rates are somewhat higher among nonmetro blacks outside the South, indicating a continuation from the 1990s of a very limited form of population de-concentration. In contrast to the Hispanic population, however, rates are not high enough to significantly shift the relative regional distribution of non-Hispanic blacks, which remains largely concentrated in the South. Even at low redistribution levels, however, notable contrasts exist between regions in which the population downturn among nonmetro blacks was clearly evident (the Eastern Urbanized Belt and the Rio Grande-Southwest) and neighboring regions where the downturn was notably absent (the Appalachia-Ozarks and the West).

Changing Nonmetro Age Structure

Large and geographically diverse shifts in the age structure of nonmetro communities occurred in the context of the 2000 to 2010 nonmetro population downturn, particularly among younger and older segments of the population. Growth rates increased among seniors in both metro and nonmetro areas between the 1990s and 2000s, as larger birth cohorts (those born in the late 1930s and early

1940s) turned sixty-five. Rates of growth are poised to jump dramatically and remain high for the next twenty years, and a key question facing researchers is how much retirement-based migration among baby boomers will contribute to nonmetro population growth in the coming years (Cromartie and Nelson 2009; Nelson in this volume). Between the 1990s and the 2000s, nonmetro population growth among seniors increased from 8 to 12 percent, fueled by increased rates in regions such as the Atlantic-Gulf Coasts and the West that have been attracting retirees for decades.

Rapid growth among seniors in the Eastern Urbanized Belt (which increased from 16 to 22 percent between decades) is typical of nonmetro areas where aging is partly a function of in-migration of newcomers to retirement destinations. High in-migration to nonmetro areas in this region—southern New Hampshire, the Catskills, or the eastern edges of the southern Appalachians—suggests continuation of long-held preferences for scenic but urban-proximate locations (Brown et al. 1997; Johnson et al. 2005). A very different dynamic shows up in the Corn Belt and Great Plains, where population decline among seniors reflects some small levels of out-migration among this age group, but mostly represents an aging-in-place process little affected by retiree in-migration. In contrast to regions with high elderly percentages and major retirement destinations (such as the Atlantic and Gulf coasts), the high elderly percentage of the Corn Belt can be traced to decades of persistent out-migration heavily concentrated among younger age groups (Brown et al. 2011). These two aging scenarios lead to very different socioeconomic profiles for elderly populations in nonmetro regions. For example, aging populations in out-migration regions tend to have lower incomes and less access to medical services.

The US population under eighteen years of age grew substantially—by 24 percent for the total population—during the 1990s. This high growth came about as a result of a steady rise in births beginning in the mid-1970s, which in the 1990s created a substantial gap between the large cohort of infants being added to the under-eighteen population and the much smaller cohort of seventeen year olds aging out of the group every year. This gap largely disappeared during the 2000s, because births had leveled off in the previous decade, and thus child population growth between the 1990s and 2000s slowed from 14 to 3 percent.

Compared with metro areas, growth rates were dramatically lower in nonmetro areas for the under-eighteen age group (see Nelson and Shoff in this volume). Not only was the rate of population growth significantly lower in nonmetro areas during the 1990s (3 percent compared with a 14 percent national rate) but population began to decline among this age group during 2000 to 2010.

This dramatic age structure shift in the nonmetro population occurred despite new evidence of increasing birth rates among nonmetro Hispanics (Johnson and Lichter 2012). Nonmetro population gain in the 1990s turned to population loss for this age group in the nonmetro West, a surprising turnaround given that the under-eighteen age group had been growing at a rate near the national rate in this part of the nonmetro US during the 1990s. Only two nonmetro regions, the Eastern Urbanized Belt and the Atlantic-Gulf Coasts, gained population among children during the last decade. This is likely due, in part, to high levels of suburbanization beyond metro borders into adjacent nonmetro counties occurring in these regions, a population trend normally containing a very high proportion of families with children.

The share of population under eighteen years old, a critical determinant of future population growth, was only slightly higher in the total US population in 2010 (24 percent) compared with nonmetro areas (23 percent). Also, under-eighteen shares exhibited little regional variation among nonmetro areas, from 22 percent in the Eastern Urbanized Belt to 26 percent in the Rio Grande-Southwest. However, age structure gaps will begin to emerge if the current pattern of child population growth continues. Under such a scenario, metro areas will become younger as will a few select nonmetro regions, compared with nonmetro regions currently exhibiting population declines for this important age group.

Regional Population Shifts since 2006

Annual population estimates for nonmetro counties as a group, and for three of the nine regions analyzed here, show sharp, migration-fueled rises in population growth until 2006, followed by equally sudden declines thereafter (Figure 17.3). The three regions setting this pattern (the Eastern Urbanized Belt, the Atlantic-Gulf Coasts, and the West) were also the fastest-growing regions by a substantial margin during the 2000s. All three grew twice as fast as any other region and together they accounted for over 70 percent of the 2.2 million people added to the nonmetro population.

Two other regions, the Appalachia-Ozarks and the Southern Coastal Plains, experienced a similar but much more moderate up-and-down pattern. Clearly, the nonmetro population downturn in the 2000s was closely linked to the home mortgage crisis starting in late 2006 and the global recession that commenced a year later. In particular, these nonmetro regions were strongly affected by the significant reduction in both domestic migration and immigration that emerged following these period "shocks" (Frey 2009; Johnson 2009; Singer and Wilson 2010). If nonmetro net migration had continued its upward

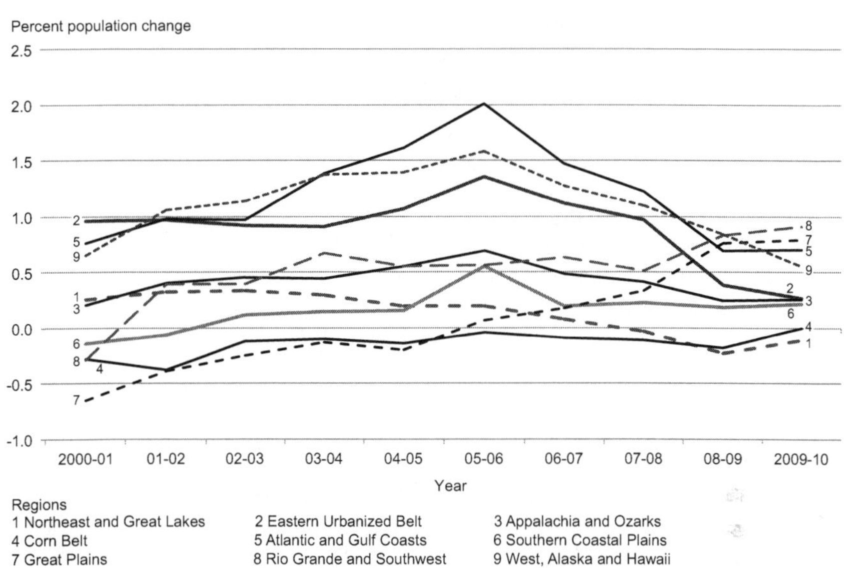

Figure 17.3. Nonmetro population change, annual by region, 2000 to 2010. Note: Statistics are for nonmetro areas defined in 2003, based on the 2000 decennial census (US Census Bureau 2013). Source: ERS-USDA using data from the US Census Bureau.

trajectory past 2006, as some anticipated (Cromartie and Nelson 2009), population growth for the decade would have likely equaled or exceeded the 1990s "rural rebound" rates.

Regional differences in annual population growth rates point to other, possibly long-term, demographic and economic influences as well. The Corn Belt lost population each year and exhibited no major shift in rates of population change, while the Northeast-Great Lakes showed steadily declining annual rates and was losing nonmetro population by the end of the decade. Both regions have an aging population, both continue to lose young-adult populations through out-migration to Sun Belt destinations, and both depend heavily on a rapidly declining manufacturing sector. High job losses in manufacturing in the early 2000s likely played a role in the failure of these regions to follow the upward trend in nonmetro population growth seen elsewhere during 2000 to 2006.

Most surprisingly, by the end of the decade, the highest rates of nonmetro population growth had shifted to the Great Plains and the Rio Grande-Southwest. This represents such a surprising turnaround because these two regions began the decade with population declines (between July 2000 and July 2001) and shared the bottom three positions among nonmetro regions with the Corn Belt (Figure 17.3). The Great Plains and the Rio Grande-Southwest did not experience the dominant up-and-down trajectory common to the decade for nonmetro areas, and instead showed steady increases in population rates from slowest- to fastest-growing regions. In fact, the Great Plains lost population until 2006. These trends point to the extensive revitalization of the energy sector that took place in major sections throughout the region, such as in North Dakota's Williston Basin and in parts of Kansas, Colorado, Oklahoma, and Texas. However, an analysis of county-level population change maps (not shown here) indicates renewed growth in areas not directly affected by the energy boom. Further analysis is required to identify other factors responsible for this regional-demographic realignment, including recession-influenced declines in out-migration and increases in natural change rates. Combined with the population downturn in fast-growing regions, population gains in these two regions have led to a dramatic narrowing of regional differences in growth rates.

Conclusions

In this chapter, we use a comparative, regional-demographic methodology to describe significant spatial differences in population trends associated with the most recent downturn in nonmetro population growth rates, from over 10 percent in the 1990s to below 5 percent during 2000 to 2010. Two time frames, one focused on a broad comparison of regional shifts across the last two decades and the other focused on year-to-year changes before and after major financial-economic dislocations, provide complementary findings that confirm the geographic complexity of demographic trends and the factors that influence migration-driven redistribution. Regional comparative frameworks have been a cornerstone of population studies focused on rural and small-town America for decades. They are designed in large part to inform rural policy-making and program implementation. Here we identify in some detail sections of the country that are exhibiting continued population gains or losses, as well as those that experienced unforeseen demographic shifts. Associated changes in regional racial-ethnic make-up and age structure point to opportunities to better fit rural policies and programs to different demographic conditions.

Three major findings highlight the research value and policy relevance of geographically informed, descriptive analysis. First, as with other demographic shifts in recent decades, the most recent population downturn was felt across all nine nonmetro regions studied here and, for most of the decade at least, at roughly similar levels. Up through 2008, historically fast-growing regions in the South and West continued to attract more migrants while slower growth was evident in persistent out-migration sections of the Northeast, Midwest, and Great Plains. Such patterns of regional entrenchment point to the continued dominance of urban size, metro proximity, and natural amenities that have driven population redistribution for decades. Efforts to generate jobs and revitalize slumping rural economies in many regions must contend with built-in locational disadvantages that make it difficult to retain natives or attract newcomers.

Second, the demographic make-up of rural communities is undergoing significant transformations due primarily to rapid growth and redistribution of Hispanic and older populations. Despite a dramatic, post-recession drop in immigration from Mexico and in domestic migration, the nonmetro Hispanic population increased by a higher number (1.2 million) during the 2000s compared with the 1990s. As in the 1990s, redistribution was widespread and the highest rates of growth were in eastern and midwestern regions, far from established Hispanic settlement areas in the Southwest. Growth among populations age sixty-five and older is much more variable and highly concentrated in regions with established retirement destinations. The Northeast-Great Lakes region is typical of several with senior populations growing much faster than other age groups and younger populations declining; in this region, the total nonmetro population grew by 1.5 percent, the under-eighteen population declined by 9 percent, and the sixty-five-and-over population increased by 11 percent. Other strongly aging regions following this pattern that are similarly poised to undergo a rapid acceleration in aging over the next two decades include the Appalachia-Ozarks, the Southern Coastal Plains, the Rio Grande-Southwest, and the West. Rural communities and policy experts are very much attuned to the economic contributions of both of these groups, but also to the social challenges and the rapidly changing demands in services that accompany these types of compositional shifts.

Third, regional population shifts since 2006 represent the strongest convergence trend among nonmetro regions in fifty years. Only one percentage point now separates the slowest-growing region (the Northeast-Great Lakes, down 0.2 percent) from the fastest (the Rio Grande-Southwest, up 0.9 percent). Regional patterns point to significant shifts in migration flows in response to economic restructuring, specifically the decline in manufacturing and renewed growth in the energy sector, but further research is needed to distinguish these effects from other possible explanations. Regional convergence could be a sign of long-term demographic equilibrium conditions predicted by regional economic theory (Sjaastad 1962). However, it is more likely a consequence of the nationwide lowering of migration propensities—a decrease in the percentage of Americans that change residences every year. If fewer people move long distances, and the decline is spatially uniform, then out-migration regions will lose fewer people and in-migration areas will add fewer. Recent migration trends described here suggest a possibly pivotal role for these short-term, recession-related, and housing-market period effects. This conclusion, in turn, bodes well for a return to higher nonmetro population growth as unemployment declines and housing markets recover, and a resumption of strong regional effects reflecting geographic differences in urban size, metro proximity, and recreation-retirement potential.

References

Artz, Georgeanne M., and Peter F. Orazem. 2006. "Reexamining Rural Decline: How Changing Rural Classifications Affect Perceived Growth." *Review of Regional Studies* 36: 163–91.

Baker, O.E. 1936. "Rural and Urban Distribution of the Population in the United States." *Annals of the American Academy of Political and Social Science* 188 (1): 264–79. http://dx.doi.org/10.1177/000271623618800126.

Barcus, Holly R. 2007. "The Emergence of New Hispanic Settlement Patterns in Appalachia." *Professional Geographer* 59 (3): 298–315. http://dx.doi.org/10.1111/j.1467-9272.2007.00614.x.

Beale, Calvin L., and Glenn V. Fuguitt. 2011. "Migration of Retirement-Age Blacks to Nonmetropolitan Areas in the 1990s." *Rural Sociology* 76 (1): 31–43. http://dx.doi.org/10.1111/j.1549-0831.2010.00037.x.

Bogue, Donald J., and Calvin L. Beale. 1961. *Economic Areas of the United States.* New York: The Free Press of Glencoe, Inc.

Brown, David L., Benjamin C. Bolender, Laszlo J. Kulcsar, Nina Glasgow, and Scott Sanders. 2011. "Intercounty Variability of Net Migration at Older Ages Path-Dependent Process." *Rural Sociology* 76 (1): 44–73. http://dx.doi.org/10.1111/j.1549-0831.2010.00034.x.

Brown, David L., Glenn V. Fuguitt, T.B. Heaton, and S. Waseem. 1997. "Continuities in Size of Place Preferences in the United States, 1972–1992." *Rural Sociology* 62 (4): 408–28. http://dx.doi.org/10.1111/j.1549-0831.1997.tb00657.x.

Cromartie, John, and Peter B. Nelson. 2009. *Baby Boom Migration and Its Impact on Rural America. Economic Research Report No. (ERR-79).* Washington, DC: Economic Research Service, USDA.

Farmer, Frank L., Zola K. Moon, and Wayne P. Miller. 2008. *Growth and Change in Arkansas' Hispanic Population.* Fayetteville, AR: University of Arkansas, Cooperative Extension Service.

Frey, William H. 2009. *The Great American Migration Slowdown: Regional and Metropolitan Dimensions.* Washington, DC: Brookings Institution.

Fuguitt, Glenn V., and Calvin L. Beale. November 1978. "Population Trends of Nonmetropolitan Cities and Villages in Subregions of the United States." *Demography* 15 (4): 605–20. http://dx.doi.org/10.2307/2061210 Medline:738484.

Fuguitt, Glenn V., and Calven L. Beale. Spring 1996. "Recent Trends in Nonmetropolitan Migration: Toward a New Turnaround?" *Growth and Change* 27 (2): 156–74. http://dx.doi.org/10.1111/j.1468-2257.1996.tb00901.x Medline:12320416.

Fuguitt, Glenn V., John A. Fulton, and Calvin L. Beale. 2001. *The Shifting Pattern of Black Migration from and into the Nonmetropolitan South, 1965–95.* Washington, DC: Economic Research Service, US Department of Agriculture.

Hudson, John C. 2002. *Across This Land: A Regional Geography of the United States and Canada.* Baltimore: John Hopkins University Press.

Johnson, Kenneth M. 2009. "With Less Migration, Natural Increase is Now More Important to State Growth." Fact Sheet. Durham, NH: Carsey Institute.

Johnson, Kenneth M., and John B. Cromartie. 2006. "The Rural Rebound and its Aftermath: Changing Demographic Dynamics and Regional Contrasts." In *Population Change and Rural Society*, ed. William A. Kandel and David L. Brown, 25–49. The Netherlands: Springer. http://dx.doi.org/10.1007/1-4020-3902-6_2.

Johnson, Kenneth M., and Daniel T. Lichter. 2012. "Rural Natural Increase in the New Century: America's Third Demographic Transition." In *The Handbook of Rural Demography*, ed. Laszlo J. Kulcsar and Katherine Curtis, 17–34. Dordrecht: Springer. http://dx.doi.org/10.1007/978-94-007-1842-5_3.

Johnson, Kenneth M., Paul R. Voss, Roger B. Hammer, Glenn V. Fuguitt, and Scott McNiven. November 2005. "Temporal and Spatial Variation in Age-Specific Net Migration in the United States." *Demography* 42 (4): 791–812. http://dx.doi.org/10.1353/dem.2005.0033 Medline:16463922.

Kandel, William, Jamila Henderson, Heather Koball, and Randy Capps. 2011. "Moving up in Rural America: Economic Attainment of Nonmetro Latino Immigrants." *Rural Sociology* 76 (1): 101–28. http://dx.doi.org/10.1111/j.1549-0831.2011.00047.x.

McGranahan, David A. 1999. "Natural Amenities Drive Rural Population Change." Agricultural Economics Report, Number 718. Washington, DC: US Department of Agriculture, Economic Research Service.

McGranahan, David A., Timothy R. Wojan and Dayton M. Lambert. 2010. "The Rural Growth Trifecta: Outdoor Amenities, Creative Class and Entrepreneurial Context." *Journal of Economic Geography*, Advance Access (May). http://dx.doi.org/10.1093/jeg/lbq007.

McHugh, Kevin E., and Patrica Gober. Fall 1992. "Short-Term Dynamics of the U.S. Interstate Migration System, 1980–1988." *Growth and Change* 23 (4): 428–45. http://dx.doi.org/10.1111/j.1468-2257.1992.tb00943.x Medline:12285786.

Morrison, Peter A. 1977. *Current Demographic Change in Regions of the United States.* Santa Monica, CA: Rand Corp.

Mulligan, Gordon F. 1984. "Agglomeration and Central Place Theory: A Review of the Literature." *International Regional Science Review* 9 (1): 1–42. http://dx.doi.org/10.1177/016001768400900101.

Pew Hispanic Center. 2011. *The Mexican-American Boom: Births Overtake Immigration.* Washington, DC: Pew Hispanic Center.

Plane, David A. 1992. "Age-Composition Change and the Geographical Dynamics of Interregional Migration in the U.S." *Annals of the Association of American Geographers* 82 (1): 64–85. http://dx.doi.org/10.1111/j.1467-8306.1992.tb01898.x.

Singer, Audrey, and Jill H. Wilson. 2010. "The Impact of the Great Recession on Metropolitan Immigration Trends." In *State of Metropolitan America*. Washington, DC: Brookings Institution.

Sjaastad, Larry A. 1962. "The Costs and Returns of Human Migration." *Journal of Political Economy* 70 (S5): 80–93. http://dx.doi.org/10.1086/258726.

US Census Bureau. 2013. "Historical Statistical Area Delineations." Last revised 6 May 2013. http://www.census.gov/population/metro/data/pastmetro.html.

Voss, Paul R. 2007. "Demography as a Spatial Social Science." *Population Research and Policy Review* 26 (5–6): 457–76. http://dx.doi.org/10.1007/s11113-007-9047-4.

CHAPTER 18

Rural Families and Households and the Decline of Traditional Structure

Jessica A. Carson and Marybeth J. Mattingly

Introduction

Traditional images of rural America center on communities in idealized agrarian landscapes, bound by shared ethics and strong kinship ties (MacTavish and Salamon 2003; Tarmann 2003). Traditional family structure is also part of this image, and for decades rural families were indeed larger, more stable, and less diverse than their urban counterparts (e.g., Johnson 2006; Snyder 2011). However, toward the end of the twentieth century, in the face of dramatic economic and social changes, the characteristics of rural and urban families started to become more similar, a convergence that continued into the 2000s.

This confluence is due in part to major changes in the composition of families nationwide. For example, over the past several decades, there have been steep rises in cohabitation and non-marital births (Bumpass and Lu 2000), increasing age at first marriage, and high rates of martial dissolution (Smock and Greenland 2010). In more recent years, research shows an increase in "doubled up" households, particularly since the onset of the Great Recession (Seltzer, Lau, and Bianchi 2012). In an age of residential mobility, technology-aided communication, and changing family culture, contemporary rural families are less isolated than their historical counterparts, and are more similar to families residing in suburban and urban places.

We explore how some of these social and demographic changes have played out for rural families over the first decade of the millennium. We measure these effects by focusing on three particular areas of rural households and families: (1) household composition, (2) household and family size, and (3) household demographics. Within each of these three areas, we first provide a portrait of rural families in 2010 that can be used as a benchmark as we proceed toward 2020. We then document the changes in rural households and families between 2000 and 2010, and compare these shifts with those occurring in suburban and urban places.[1] In considering new rural household and family patterns, we situate rural life within the landscape of increasingly complex household formations, influenced by declining rates of marriage, increases in cohabitation, and increases in living alone.

Aside from the necessity of documenting family trends to provide demographers and policy makers with a current portrait of rural families, growing family heterogeneity can be accompanied by challenges to families and communities. With increased diversity may come increased inequality between households, particularly in families with a single earner (McLanahan and Casper 1995). In addition, household instability may impede families' ability to meet long-term needs, such as raising children and caring for the elderly (MacTavish and Salamon 2003). Increasingly diverse families can translate to communities that are progressive and inclusive, promoting the well-being of all residents. While authors in subsequent chapters in this volume focus more explicitly on rural inequality, children and youth, and the elderly, here we provide a thorough examination of family and household structure as a backdrop for considering those specific issues. Throughout this chapter, we rely upon nationally representative data collected through the 2000 Decennial Census and the 2005–2010 American Community Survey.[2]

Household Composition

We begin with a snapshot of rural household composition at the end of the decade, provide an assessment of how rural households have changed between 2000 and 2010, and compare patterns and trends among rural households to those in urban and suburban areas. To clarify, throughout this section, we use the terms *family household* and *nonfamily household* as used by the US Census Bureau. The census considers a family household to contain at least one person related to the householder by birth, marriage, or adoption (Simmons and O'Neill 2000), while a nonfamily household is precisely the opposite—a household in which no person is related to the householder (e.g., college students living as roommates or a person living alone).

Rural Households in 2010

Family Households

In 2010, 68 percent of households in rural America were family households. Of these, the most prevalent type were households headed by a married couple,

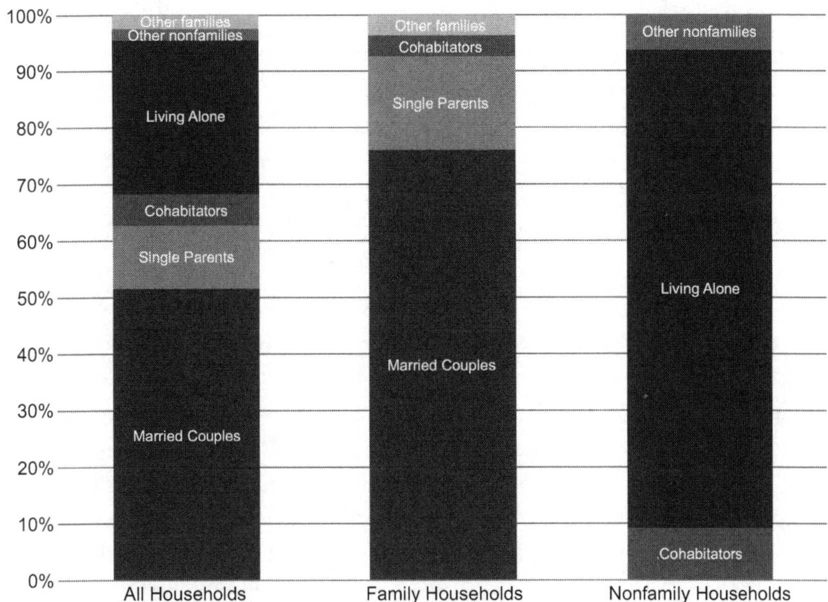

Figure 18.1. Rural household composition, 2010. Source: American Community Survey 2010

accounting for three quarters (76 percent) of family households (see Figure 18.1) and more than half (52 percent) of all rural households. Comprising a much smaller proportion of family households were those headed by single parents (nearly 17 percent), of which 80 percent were headed by single mothers. The next group of family households is those where one or more "other" family members, for example, a sibling, parent, aunt, or grandparent, lived with the head. These households accounted for just 4 percent of all rural family households in 2010.

Cohabiting Households

Somewhere between family and nonfamily households are households headed by cohabiters, or "unmarried partners." These households are increasingly common nationwide (e.g., Fry and Cohn 2011; Kreider 2010), yet are only considered a family household if the home contains someone who is related to the householder by blood or marriage. Thus, a woman who lives with her child and her partner in his home are not considered a family, as neither she nor her child are technically related to the householder. Because of these murky classifications, throughout this chapter, we discuss cohabiters separately from family and nonfamily households.

In 2010, 6 percent of rural households contained a cohabiting couple. Of these households, 44 percent reported having at least one child in the house, related to either the householder or the cohabiting partner.

Included among cohabiters are same-sex couples. Although gay male couples and, to a somewhat lesser extent, lesbian couples disproportionately reside in urban places (Gates and Ost 2004), research suggests that 15 percent of same-sex unmarried partners reside in nonmetropolitan counties (Poston and Kincannon 2008; Smith and Gates 2001), and that 99 percent of US counties and 97 percent of census tracts are home to same-sex couples (Gates and Ost 2004). Here, we consider same-sex couples' households to be those containing an unmarried partner whose sex is the same as the householder. In 2010, same-sex couples accounted for 6 percent of all rural cohabiting households and less than 1 percent of all rural households. However, data estimating the prevalence of same-sex couples are still somewhat unclear. Gates and Steinberger (2010) suggest that up to 25 percent of "same-sex couples" in the American Community Survey may actually be miscoded opposite-sex couples. This is due to the Census Bureau's practice of editing these items such that a married couple reporting both partners of the same sex is recoded to become a same-sex unmarried partner couple. However, this practice does not account for opposite-sex married couples who simply misreport one partner's sex, leading to potential overestimation of same-sex couples (Gates and Steinberger 2010). On the other hand, the American Community Survey cannot account for same-sex couples who report their relationship as something other than spouses or unmarried partners (e.g., housemates), which could artificially deflate these estimates.

Nonfamily Households

At the end of the decade, nonfamily households comprised about one third of all rural households. The vast majority (85 percent) of nonfamily households were householders living alone, part of a much larger trend toward living alone, discussed below.

Rural Change throughout the Decade

Married Couple Households

Over the decade, rural America realized a slight decline in family households, from 70 percent in 2000 to 68 percent in 2010. This drop appears to be largely driven by the fastest shrinking rural household type—households headed by married couples. Since 2000, married couple households declined by three percentage points, comprising 52 percent of rural households by 2010. The drop in family households has been accompanied by slight increases in those living alone and in cohabiting households, each up by more than one percentage point since 2000.

With declining shares of married couple households, it is useful to consider which groups are becoming less likely to marry. Research shows that there are education-based differences in national marriage trends—college graduates are more likely to marry than their less-educated counterparts (Pew Research Center 2010)—a trend that is also evident in rural America. College graduates are the most likely to live in married couple households (62 percent), followed by householders who completed some college (52 percent)—shares that remained stable across the decade. Conversely, rural residents who never attended college became less likely to live in married couple households over time, and by 2010, just 50 percent of high school graduates and 40 percent of nongraduates lived in these households. In short, the uneven distribution of these declines actually served to widen the gap in married couple households between the least and the most educated over time.

Research also shows that marriage rates are strongly linked to race and ethnicity, with black and Hispanic householders being less likely to be married than their white counterparts (Pew Research Center 2010). In rural places, we indeed find that married couple households vary by race, with white householders most likely to live in these households (54 percent), closely followed by Hispanics (52 percent), and then black householders (29 percent).[3] However, unlike with education, in rural places, racial gaps in marriage are not necessarily widening over time. Both black and white householders were less likely to live in married couple households at the end of the decade, while Hispanic householders' proportion remained stable.

Other Household Types

In addition to declines in married couple households, the new millennium brought changes in the prevalence of other household types. For example, households containing cohabiters increased by more than one percentage point across the decade, to comprise about 6 percent of all rural households by 2010. Unlike changes in marriage, this shift did not differ by education, as everyone from high school dropouts to college graduates was more likely to live in a cohabiting household by 2010. Increases in cohabitation may be attributed to broader-scale influences in ideational culture, set in motion decades before the turn of the century. Smock, Casper, and Wyse (2008, 6) propose some of the cultural changes that may have contributed to rising cohabitation, including "increasingly egalitarian attitudes about gender roles; the sexual revolution of the 1960s, diminishing much of the earlier stigma associated with living together outside of marriage; the rise in independent living in young adulthood, bringing with it reductions in family surveillance; and a decline in the perceived authority of religions institutions." It is reasonable to expect that rural America would not have been immune to these social changes, an expectation that our data support.

Over the decade, rural America also witnessed an increase in householders living alone, part of a longer-term, national trend toward single-person households. Nationally, nine percent of households were comprised of one person in 1950, compared with more than 26 percent in 2010 (Klinenberg 2012). Klinenberg (2012) cites several reasons behind this increase, including the rising status of women (particularly increased employment, education, and access to contraceptives) and the widespread use of communications technology, which allows dispersed families to stay in touch. As with the cultural trends impacting cohabitation, these factors are likely as important for shaping rural families as for families in other places.

An additional important change throughout the decade was the rise in multigenerational households. We define multigenerational households as those containing more than two generations. While still accounting for only a very small proportion of all rural households (3 percent in 2010), multigenerational households saw a large proportional increase in the latter half of the decade, rising by 22 percent between 2005 and 2010. Indeed, since the recession began in December 2007 (National Bureau of Economic Research 2010), public discourse has emerged about households that are doubled up, or "sharing a housing unit, often temporarily, and usually because of economic difficulties" (Elliott, Young, and Dye 2011, 3). Again, the influence of national sociocultural trends bears on rural America, and it is possible that economic responses may have played a role in rising rural multigenerational homes since 2005.

Finally, the share of rural households headed by single parents remained stable over time. Indeed, this too is part of a larger trend spanning several decades (Mather 2010; O'Hare et al. 2009), wherein rates of single parenthood rose rapidly throughout the 1980s and 1990s, and then began to stabilize closer to the turn of the century. Although rural rates remained steady overall, Hispanics and those with less than a high school diploma did experience increases in single parent homes by the end of the decade.

Comparisons across Place Type

Above we identified several major changes in the household composition of rural families including a decline in the proportion of married couple families, a steady proportion of single parents, an increase in cohabiting households, and a rise in living alone. Perhaps one indication of the modernizing rural landscape

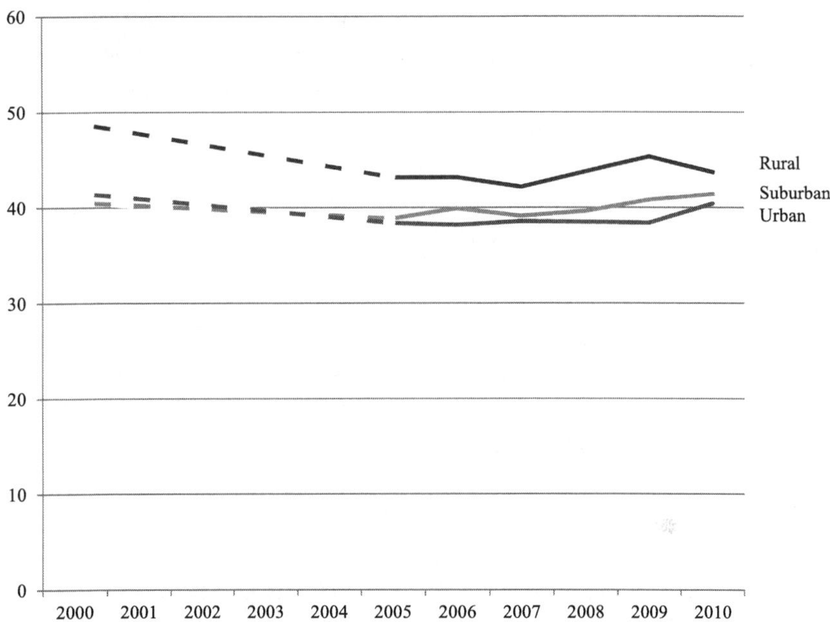

Figure 18.2. Percent of cohabiting households containing children, by place type, 2000 to 2010. Sources: United States Census 2000 and American Community Survey 2005–2010.

is how closely these changes mirror the trends that occurred in suburban and urban places across the decade. Of course, rural households still have some substantial differences from their urban counterparts; for example, single parent households were more common in urban places in 2010, at 16 percent, versus 11 and 12 percent in rural and suburban places, respectively.

Despite these place-based differences in the occurrence of particular household types, the direction and pace of household change in rural, suburban, and urban areas is remarkably similar. Consider the declining rates of households headed by married couples. In 2000, 55 percent of rural households, 57 percent of suburban households, and 37 percent of urban households were of this type. By 2010, all three place types had undergone a similar pattern of change, with the proportion of households headed by married couples dropping by 5 to 6 percent in each place type.

Beyond similarities in the pattern and pace of change, the makeup of rural, suburban, and urban households is also becoming more similar. Despite initial differences in the prevalence of cohabiting couples with children, their share of all households is converging between place types (see Figure 18.2). At the start of the decade, the rural-urban gap in the percent of cohabiting couples with children was seven percentage points; by 2010, the gap was less than half that, at three percentage points. Though there are still small differences in the rates of cohabiting couples with children, this convergence is further evidence of shrinking differences between rural and nonrural places.

Household and Family Size

In this section, we examine household and family size over time. As in the previous section, we begin with a description of rural households in 2010, and then provide an overview of how these households have changed since 2000. We conclude by comparing patterns of changes in rural households to those that occurred in suburban and urban places since the turn of the millennium.

Rural Household and Family Size in 2010 and Change Since 2000

By 2010, the average rural household contained 2.4 people, and the average family size was 2.3 people. While these households and families may seem small, it should be noted that this average includes the 27 percent of rural households that were comprised of a householder living alone. Among households containing more than one person, the average household included 3 people, and the average family contained 2.8 people. Household size varies significantly by race and ethnicity. White-headed households contained an average of 2.4 people in 2010, while households headed by black householders and those of "other" races averaged 2.6 people. Larger still were households headed by Hispanic householders—containing an average of 3.3 people—which accords with Johnson and Lichter's (2012) finding that Hispanics have higher fertility than their white counterparts.

At the end of the decade, 37 percent of all rural households and 55 percent of rural family households included at least one child. Among those with at least one child, the average home contained 1.8 children in 2010; 80 percent had two or fewer, 94 percent three or fewer, and 98 percent had four or fewer. The prevalence of small families contradicts historical stereotypes of large, rural families, and continues a trend in motion since the 1980s (MacTavish and Salamon 2003). Average rural household and family size declined modestly (each by approximately one-tenth of a person) across the decade. Contributing to this was the four percentage point decline in the proportion of rural households containing children and a smaller mean number of children among rural households with kids since 2000. Again, these trends are part of a national pattern of declining household size, often attributed to increasing "wealth, individuality, and mobility" (Besharov 2001, 5; see also Mather 2010) that facilitates family members moving out, moving away, and/or living alone.

Comparisons across Place Type

Between 2000 and 2010, household and family size also declined modestly in suburban and urban places. However, despite the similar pacing of these changes, there are still some place-based differences in household and family size, with suburban places averaging the largest households (2.6 people) compared with rural and urban averages of 2.4 people.

Relatedly, the proportion of households containing children declined across place types, albeit at a faster pace in rural places than in urban or suburban locales (four and two percentage points, respectively). Finally, though the number of children in family households declined in all place types, rural households still had fewer children on average in 2010 than households in suburban or urban places. These trends accord with research suggesting that while rural households were historically larger than urban ones, the average size of rural and nonrural households converged around 1980 (MacTavish and Salamon 2003). Further, rural households are shrinking faster than their urban counterparts, a decline that the research suggests "likely reflects the aging population in rural places as much as it does rural parents having fewer children" (MacTavish and Salamon 2003, 76).

Family Demographics

The final section of this chapter details the characteristics of rural households by summarizing the demographic characteristics of various household types. We begin with an overview of rural households and families in 2010, followed by a description of how these characteristics changed since 2000, and then explore differences between households in rural and nonrural places.

Rural Demographics in 2010

Despite increasing diversity in rural places, the vast majority of rural householders (84 percent) were white, with much smaller proportions of householders who were black (7 percent), Hispanic (5 percent) or of "other" races (3 percent). Altogether, rural householders reported an average age of 53 years, though the changing racial and ethnic composition of rural America is altering its age structure. For example, in 2010, white rural householders reported an average age of 53.7, compared to 44.5 for Hispanics, illustrating one effect of rural Hispanic migration and fertility patterns. Regarding rural socioeconomic status, more than two in five rural householders had attended or graduated college and about 57 percent were employed in 2010. Finally, the median income for a rural household was $40,305, and 17 percent of rural householders were poor.[4]

Demographic characteristics vary by household type. Rural householders in married couple homes reported an average age of 52, were most often white (88 percent), and nearly half had attended or graduated college (47 percent). Just 7 percent were poor, 62 percent were employed, and their median income stood at $58,442 in 2010. In many ways, rural married couple households are better off than those in other household types. For example, though cohabiting couple households reported the next highest income, they still trailed married couples by more than $17,000 annually. Of course married couple households are not necessarily better off *because* they are married, and indeed it is possible that wealthier and more educated rural residents are simply more likely to marry, also known as the "selection effect" (Amato et al. 2007).

However, cohabiting couple households also differed from married couple households beyond income disparities, as their householders were substantially younger, at an average age of thirty-nine, and slightly less likely to be white (81 percent compared with 88 percent of married householders). Cohabiting householders were also considerably less likely to have graduated college (13 percent, versus 23 percent of married householders), and despite more often being employed than their married counterparts, one-third of cohabiting couple households were poor in 2010.

It is somewhat difficult to draw conclusions about "other families" and "other non-families," because both of these household types encompass a broad array of living arrangements. For example, other non-families could include college students living as roommates or a long-term boarder living with a senior citizen. Other families are just as varied, and could include, for example, a grandparent raising children, an adult caring for an aging parent, or adult siblings living together. Despite these diverse circumstances, we find that generally, these households have lower earnings and educational attainment than married couple households.

Householders who lived alone had some of the most challenging household characteristics. These householders were older than householders of other types, at an average of sixty years old, and more than half (53 percent) were out of the labor force. These characteristics perhaps explain why nearly a quarter of these householders were poor and their incomes were lower than any other household type, at $20,152 in 2010.

Characteristics of Householders

Across the decade, there were substantial shifts in the characteristics of rural householders in all household types. For example, the average age of a rural householder increased from fifty-one to fifty-three between 2000 and 2010, Hispanic householders became more prevalent, and the share of black householders receded. These changing demographics are particularly evident amidst some rural household types. For example, by 2010, the share of single parent homes headed by a black householder had declined by seven percentage points, while the proportion headed by a Hispanic householder increased by three percentage points.

Across the decade, rural householders became increasingly more educated, as the 21 percent with no high school diploma in 2000 plummeted to 14 percent in 2010. This shift was most dramatic among householders living alone—the more than one-quarter who had no diploma in 2000 fell to just 17 percent by 2010. With the exception of those heading other families and other non-families, all householders were more likely to have a college degree in 2010 than in 2000. This population of increasingly educated householders is good news for rural populations long concerned with the issue of the rural "brain drain," (Carr and Kefalas 2009), the migration of the youngest and brightest rural residents to more populated areas to seek work and educational opportunities.

Despite rising educational attainment, rural places were not immune to the issues plaguing the rest of the country over the decade, including the onset of recession in late 2007. For married couples, the percent of householders employed fell by nearly seven percentage points, while cohabiting householders saw a decline of four percentage points between 2000 and 2010. However, responses to this shift were not uniform, as married couple householders increasingly left the labor force and cohabiting householders became unemployed (i.e., were looking for work).

In addition to changes in the rural workforce, the decade also saw shifts in income, though the percent of rural families who were poor hovered around 16 percent. Across households, median household income fell by $322 (in 2010 dollars),[5] though married couple households, those living alone, and those in other non-families actually saw an increase in income across the decade (see Table 18.1).

Young Adults and Children

By examining the household and family situations of rural children and young adults (aged eighteen to thirty), we are better equipped to understand the directions in which rural families and households are moving. Nationally,

Table 18.1
Demographic characteristics of rural householders, by household type, 2010

	Family Households							
	All Households	Change 2000–2010	Married Couples	Change 2000–2010	Single Parents	Change 2000–2010	Other Families	Change 2000–2010
Mean Age	52.8	2.0 ***	52.5	2.6 ***	46.7	1.5 ***	52.2	0.5
Median Household Income	$40,305	-$322 *	$58,442	$1,500 ***	$27,004	-$80 ***	$33,352	-$181
Race/Ethnicity:								
White, Non-Hispanic	84.0	0.4	87.8	-0.1	69.1	3.7 ***	67.9	6.8 ***
Black, Non-Hispanic	7.5	-2.4 ***	4.2	-1.8 ***	18.3	-7.2 ***	18.3	-8.7 ***
Hispanic	5.2	1.4 ***	5.3	1.4 ***	7.9	3.0 ***	8.5	1.2
Other/Multiracial, Non-Hispanic	3.3	0.6 ***	2.8	0.5 ***	4.7	0.5	5.3	0.7
Percent Poor	16.6	0.3	6.8	0.0	33.1	1.6	20.2	-2.6
Employment:								
Employed	56.7	-4.0 ***	62.3	-6.7 ***	60.3	−0.9	49.0	0.4
Unemployed	4.9	2.2 ***	3.9	1.7 ***	7.9	3.1 ***	6.5	1.9 *
Not in Labor Force	38.4	1.9 ***	33.8	5.0 ***	31.8	−2.1 **	44.6	-2.3
Education:								
Less than High School	14.0	-6.9 ***	10.9	-6.7 ***	18.1	-5.5 ***	23.1	-7.4 ***
High School	42.8	-1.3 ***	41.9	-2.8 ***	43.6	-2.9 ***	43.4	2.0
Some College	24.0	4.6 ***	24.2	4.7 ***	26.7	6.0 ***	21.7	5.9 ***
College Graduate or Higher	19.2	3.6 ***	23.0	4.7 ***	11.6	2.4 ***	11.8	-0.5

			Nonfamily Households			
	Cohabiters	Change 2000–2010	Living Alone	Change 2000–2010	Other Non-families	Change 2000–2010
Mean Age	39.4	2.6 ***	59.8	1.0 ***	40.2	4.6 ***
Median Household Income	$41,111	-$1,566	$20,152	$806 ***	$34,259	$2,532
Race/Ethnicity:						
White, Non-Hispanic	80.8	4.3 ***	85.2	0.1	81.5	-1.5
Black, Non-Hispanic	7.0	-5.3 ***	8.4	−1.4 ***	6.3	-0.9

Table 18.1 continued

	Nonfamily Households					
	Cohab-iters	Change 2000–2010	Living Alone	Change 2000–2010	Other Non-families	Change 2000–2010
Hispanic	7.3	0.8	3.2	0.7 **	7.4	0.8
Other/Multi-racial, Non-Hispanic	4.9	0.3	3.2	0.7 ***	4.9	1.5
Percent Poor	33.0	3.2 *	23.2	-1.8 ***	37.9	-5.5 ***
Employment:						
Employed	69.6	-3.5 **	42.4	0.4	62.3	-1.2
Unemployed	10.1	4.5 ***	4.3	2.0 ***	6.9	2.8 **
Not in Labor Force	20.3	-0.9	53.3	-2.4 ***	30.8	-1.6
Education:						
Less than High School	14.9	-5.9 ***	17.2	-9.2 ***	13.0	-1.3 *
High School	46.5	-5.2 ***	44.0	2.0 ***	33.2	1.9
Some College	26.2	6.8 ***	21.4	4.2 ***	35.8	-3.6
College Graduate or Higher	12.5	4.3 ***	17.4	3.0 ***	18.0	3.0

Sources: US Census 2000 and American Community Survey 2010.

two-thirds of children live with married parents (not necessarily both biological), an additional one-quarter live with a single parent, 3 percent live with their unmarried parents, and 4 percent live with someone other than a parent (Kreider 2004). We find that children's living situations are similar in rural places, and shifted in tandem with national trends across the decade. In 2000, 70 percent of rural children lived in a married couple household, which was true of 66 percent of children by 2010. In 2010, one-third of children lived with an unmarried householder, compared with 28 percent in 2000. Again, these shifting family arrangements reflect the changes in both rural places and America more broadly.

In addition to rural children's changing living situations in the new millennium, we see substantial changes in household composition among young rural adults (aged eighteen to thirty). In many cases, the shifts in household composition among young adults mirror those of the larger rural population, albeit at an exaggerated pace. For example, while married couple households shrank by three percentage points in rural places, this decline was seven percentage points among rural young adults, consistent with research indicating marriage is occurring later and less often (Smock and Greenland 2010). Cohabiting couple households increased at a rapid rate among this group, up six percentage points to 17 percent in 2010, compared with the 1.4 percentage point increase among all rural householders. Finally, like the larger rural population, these young householders experienced unchanging rates of single parenthood over the decade. Other changes among young adults diverged from those seen in the broader rural population. Young adults were no more likely to live alone at the end of the decade than at the beginning, and young adults saw an increase in other nonfamily households, while householders in general did not. Taken together, the exaggerated pace of some changes among these younger adults lead us to suspect that the decadal trends evident among rural households are bound to continue, perhaps at an increasing pace, into the future.

Comparisons across Place Type

Comparing demographic characteristics across place types again demonstrates that, while rural, suburban, and urban differences still exist, the trend is convergence. For example, while rural householders are still older than those in urban and suburban places, the average householder's age increased between 2000 and 2010 in all places. And while rural householders are still more often white than those in other places, rural, suburban, and urban householders were all more likely to be Hispanic in 2010 than in 2000. Further similarities between places include increasingly educated householders, and similarly paced increases in unemployment (two to three percentage points).

However, not all demographic change in the new millennium has been shared across place types. For example, rural and suburban householders saw declines in employment across the decade, while urban places saw a *rise* in the proportion of householders who were employed. While urban places saw a decline in the proportion of householders who were not in the labor force, rural places saw an increase. And, while poverty rates shifted upward for householders in both urban and suburban places, the percent poor remained stable in rural places from 2000 to 2010.

Conclusions

Recent family scholarship documents the decline of marriage and traditional family forms (for a summary of this literature, see Amato et al. 2007). Scholars of this framework, sometimes referred to as the "marriage decline" approach, view the types of demographic changes described throughout this chapter (e.g., rising cohabitation, delays in first marriage) as supportive of growing autonomy, rising independence, and "a corresponding deinstitutionalization of marriage" (Amato et al. 2007, 15). Some suggest this deinstitutionalization leads to poor results not only for the adults involved in such marriages, but also for their children and society at large (Amato et al. 2007).

Rural places have historically been seen as the last bastion of conventional family forms—the last stronghold where marriage and family can prevail over modern norms (Imig 1983; Miller and Crader 1979). However, our findings in this chapter beg a different conclusion by illuminating the remarkable similarity between trends experienced on the national level and those playing out in rural places. Indeed, rural places are no longer "safe" from the spread of large-scale social trends, and instead are keeping pace with their suburban and urban counterparts.

Though rural demographics increasingly resembled the rest of the nation, the rural family is not necessarily in decline. For example, in rural America, more than half of all households are headed by married couples, and the majority of these couples have children. Nearly seven in ten rural households are still "family households," with people who are sharing space and making ends meet together, just as families always have. What has changed, however, are the ways in which we understand what it means to be a family. Today, in rural, as well as non-rural areas, we see increasing diversity in the constitution of families, as marriage and childrearing become disconnected, and new family forms, including those headed by cohabiters, single householders, or same-sex couples, prosper. We suggest that our findings are more closely aligned with the marital resilience framework, which proposes that multiple family forms—beyond just married heterosexual couples with children—are inevitable, and can be healthy for families and communities (Amato et al. 2007). Especially considering the heightened pace of family change among young adults, it is critical to consider new notions of rural families that are inclusive and grounded in modern realities. Indeed, shifting family forms do not necessarily have negative consequences for children and society at large, but rather may be part of a natural diversification of the family form over time.

Perhaps most importantly, the rural family is not in danger of becoming obsolete or extinct, even into the new millennium. Rather, rural families are keeping pace with modernity, experiencing the flux and growth that is common to families nationwide.

Notes

1 For the purposes of this chapter, we delineate between three types of households: (1) nonmetropolitan households (rural households); (2) metropolitan households that lie within a

central city (urban households); and (3) households that lie within metropolitan places but outside of the central city (suburban households).

2 We chose to rely upon the American Community Survey data (Ruggles et al. 2010) for this chapter for several reasons. First, the sample size of the survey (approximately 3.5 million addresses per year) allows us to examine trends in the less-dense geographies of nonmetropolitan places. Second, these data provide a consistent definition of "metropolitan" over the course of the decade, a benefit not found in alternative data sources (e.g., the Current Population Survey). Throughout this chapter, we describe characteristics of the rural "householder," who is "the person, or one of the people, in whose name the home is owned, being bought or rented and who is listed on line one of the survey questionnaire" (US Census Bureau 2011, 73).

3 Note that throughout this chapter, we rely on four categories of race/ethnicity: "white" refers to respondents who are white, but not Hispanic; "black" refers to those who identify as black, but not Hispanic; "Hispanic" refers to respondents who are of Mexican, Puerto Rican, Cuban, or other Hispanic origin, and may be of any race; and "other" refers to respondents who are American Indian, Alaska Native, Chinese, Japanese, other Asian or Pacific Islander, other race or multiracial, and also non-Hispanic.

4 It should be noted that the analyses in this chapter are largely presented at the household level, while poverty is measured at the family level. In all cases here, the household is assigned the poverty status of the family of which the householder is a part.

5 Note that not only have these income estimates been adjusted for inflation, they have also been adjusted with the Census Bureau's "adjustment factor." Because the American Community Survey is administered year-round, and the income questions refer to the twelve months prior, respondents have different reference periods for each year's survey. To account for this, the Census Bureau averages each month-specific adjustment into a single adjustment factor that can then be applied for each case (month-specific adjustment factors could ease the identification of particular cases, so the Census Bureau forgoes this option). For more detail, see IPUMS 2012.

References

Amato, Paul R, Alan Booth, David R. Johnson, and Stacy J. Rogers. 2007. *Alone Together: How Marriage in America is Changing*. Boston, MA: Harvard University Press.

Besharov, Douglas. 2001. "Reflections on Family: A Conversation with Douglas Besharov." *U.S. Society and Values* 6: 5–7.

Bumpass, Larry, and Hsien-Hen Lu. 2000. "Trends in Cohabitation and Implications for Children's Family Contexts in the United States." *Population Studies* 54 (1): 29–41. http://dx.doi.org/10.1080/713779060.

Carr, Patrick, and Maria J. Kefalas. 2009. *Hollowing out the Middle: The Rural Brain Drain and What It Means for America*. Boston, MA: Beacon Press.

Elliott, Diana B., Rebekah Young, and Jane Lawler Dye. 2011. "Variation in the Formation of Complex Family Households during the Recession." Paper presented at National Council on Family Relations 73rd Annual Conference, Orlando, FL, 16–19 November.

Fry, Richard and D'Vera Cohn. 2011. *Living Together: The Economics of Cohabitation*. Washington, DC: Pew Research Center.

Gates, Gary J., and Jason Ost. 2004. *The Gay and Lesbian Atlas*. Washington, DC: Urban Institute Press.

Gates, Gary J., and Michael D. Steinberger. 2010. "Same-Sex Unmarried Partner Couples in the American Community Survey: The Role of Misreporting, Miscoding and Misallocation." Unpublished manuscript.

Imig, David R. 1983. "Urban and Rural Families: A Comparative Study of the Impact of Stress on Family Interaction." *Rural Educator* 1: 43–6.

IPUMS. 2012. *Note on the Standardization of ACS/PRCS Income Variables and Other Dollar Amount Variables.* Minneapolis, MN: Minnesota Population Center.

Johnson, Kenneth M. 2006. *Demographic Trends in Rural and Small Town America.* Durham, NH: Carsey Institute.

Johnson, Kenneth M., and Daniel T. Lichter. 2012. "Rural Natural Increase in the New Century: America's Third Demographic Transition." In *International Handbook of Rural Demography*, ed. L.J. Kulcsár and K.J. Curtis, 17–34. New York: Springer. http://dx.doi.org/10.1007/978-94-007-1842-5_3.

Klinenberg, Eric. 2012. *Going Solo: The Extraordinary Rise and Surprising Appeal of Living Alone.* New York: Penguin Press.

Kreider, Rose M. 2004. *Living 2008. Arrangements of Children.* Washington, DC: US Census Bureau.

Kreider, Rose M. 2010. *Increase in Opposite-Sex Cohabiting Couples from 2009 to 2010 in the Annual Social and Economic Supplement (ASEC) to the Current Population Survey (CPS).* Washington, DC: US Census Bureau.

MacTavish, Kate, and Sonya Salamon. 2003. "What Do Rural Families Look Like Today?" In *Challenges for Rural America in the Twenty-First Century*, ed. David L. Brown and Louis E. Swanson, 73–85. University Park: Pennsylvania State University Press.

Mather, Mark. 2010. *U.S. Children in Single-Mother Families.* Washington DC: Population Reference Bureau. http://www.prb.org/pdf10/single-motherfamilies.pdf.

McLanahan, Sara, and Lynne Casper. 1995. "Growing Diversity and Inequality in the American Family." In *State of the Union: America in the 1990s*, ed. Reynolds Farley, 1–45. New York: Russell Sage.

Miller, Michael K., and Kelly W. Crader. 1979. "Rural-Urban Differences in Two Dimensions of Community Satisfaction." *Rural Sociology* 44: 489–504.

National Bureau of Economic Research. 2010. *U.S. Business Cycle Expansions and Contractions. Memo.* Washington, DC: Public Information Office.

O'Hare, William, Wendy Manning, Meredith Porter, and Heidi Lyons. 2009. *Rural Children Are More Likely to Live in Cohabiting-Couple Households.* Durham, NH: Carsey Institute.

Pew Research Center. 2010. *The Decline of Marriage and Rise of New Families.* Washington, DC: Pew Research Center.

Poston, Dudley L., Jr., and Heather Terrell Kincannon. 2008. "Patterns of Homosexuality in the Nonmetropolitan United States in 2000." Presented at the Annual Meeting of the Population Association of America, New Orleans, LA, April.

Ruggles, Steven J., Trent Alexander, Katie Genadek, Ronald Goeken, Matthew B. Schroeder, and Matthew Sobek. 2010. "Integrated Public Use Microdata Series: Version 5.0." Minneapolis: University of Minnesota.

Seltzer, Judith A., Charles Q. Lau, and Suzanne M. Bianchi. September 2012. "Doubling up When Times are Tough: A Study of Obligations to Share a Home in Response to

Economic Hardship." *Social Science Research* 41 (5): 1307–19. http://dx.doi.org/10.1016/j.ssresearch.2012.05.008. Medline:23017934.

Simmons, Tavia, and Grace O'Neill. 2000. *Households and Families: 2000. Census 2000 Brief.* Washington, DC: US Census Bureau.

Smith, David M., and Gary J. Gates. 2001. *Gay and Lesbian Families in the United States: Same-Sex Unmarried Partner Households. A Human Rights Campaign Report.* Washington, DC: Human Rights Campaign.

Smock, Pamela J., Lynne M. Casper, and Jessica Wyse. 2008. *Nonmarital Cohabitation: Current Knowledge and Future Directions for Research.* Ann Arbor: University of Michigan Population Studies Center.

Smock, Pamela J., and F.R. Greenland. 2010. "Diversity in Pathways to Parenthood: Patterns, Implications and Emerging Research Directions." *Journal of Marriage and the Family* 72 (3): 576–93. http://dx.doi.org/10.1111/j.1741-3737.2010.00719.x.

Snyder, Anastasia. 2011. "Patterns of Family Formation and Dissolution in Rural America and Implications for Well-Being." In *Economic Restructuring and Family Well Being in Rural America*, ed. Kristin E. Smith and Ann R. Tickamyer, 124–35. University Park: Pennsylvania State University Press.

Tarmann, Allison. 2003. *Is America Settling Down?* Washington, DC: Population Reference Bureau Reports. http://www.prb.org/publications/articles/2003/isamericasettlingdown.aspx.

US Census Bureau. 2011. "2010 American Community Survey Subject Definitions." Washington, DC: US Census Bureau. http://www.census.gov/acs/www/downloads/data_documentation/subjectdefinitions/2010_acssubjectdefinitions.pdf.

CHAPTER 19

Children and Youth in Rural America

Diane K. McLaughlin and Carla Shoff

Introduction

Every family, community, and nation depends on its youth to grow, thrive, and take leadership to ensure a successful future. A successful future includes having a workforce with the education, resources, and skills necessary to support its own families and ensure a similar or better quality of life for its children. Rural America is no different from other places in this regard, though it differs by the challenges and opportunities people face as they look toward the middle of the twenty-first century. In this chapter, we examine the change in poverty of children, the education and labor force activity of youth, and youth retention in nonmetropolitan America from 2000 to 2010. Diversity across nonmetro America is captured using the Rural Urban Continuum Codes (ERS USDA 2012) to examine how urban population size and adjacency to metropolitan areas are associated with the well-being of children and youth in rural America.

Rural America is diverse. Some areas of rural America are facing declining populations (Johnson and Rathge 2006; McGranahan, Cromartie, and Wojan 2010), while others are experiencing population growth (Brown and Glasgow 2008; Elliott and Perry 1996; Krannich and Petrzelka 2003). Poverty rates are high or increasing where economies are weak or declining, making it more difficult for families to support their children (Crowley, Lichter, and Qian 2006; Snyder, McLaughlin, and Findeis 2006). Higher poverty, in particular, places members of the next generation at risk for fewer opportunities and lower well-being than their parents (O'Hare 2009). The racial and ethnic composition of some areas is changing rapidly, while other areas see little change (Jensen 2006; Johnson and Lichter 2010; Lichter 2012). Because the increasing racial-ethnic diversity of children in rural America has been carefully documented in prior recent research, we do not address it in this chapter.

The US population grew overall by 9.7 percent between 2000 and 2010, much faster than the 2.6 percent increase in the number of children under age eighteen. The most rural areas of the United States have the largest decline in the share of the population under age eighteen, even though the population overall increased. Despite growth in numbers of children, children under age eighteen declined as a percentage of the US population overall and in nonmetro areas. The smaller and declining percentages of children in nonmetro areas suggest continued aging of the nonmetro population and a more rapid decline in the share of children in nonmetro than metro areas.

Changing population composition and poverty can cause uncertainty and reduce families' ability to raise children who are prepared to be successful in a constantly changing world. These changes may affect how the United States, and nonmetro areas in particular, plans for the future. In areas where poverty and out-migration are high, these challenges will be even greater (Johnson and Rathge 2006). Increasing numbers of rural children in female-headed families and high poverty among rural youth were identified as important issues in 2000 (Lichter, Roscigno, and Condron 2003). These situations have changed little since, and in some cases they have worsened amidst the Great Recession.

Lichter, Roscigno, and Condron (2003) also identify high school dropouts and educational attainment as important issues facing rural areas. The completion of high school and the transition from school to work is particularly important for adult success (Arnett 2004; Snyder, McLaughlin, and Coleman-Jensen 2009). Yet, rural areas differ from urban areas and from each other in their ability to provide youth with educational and job opportunities (Partridge and Rickman 2006; McGrath et al. 2001). Limited opportunities may result in youth dropping out of high school, which reduces their chances of finding a job that supports a family. Youth who leave for opportunities elsewhere are likely to be those who seek higher education and occupations not available or who see no future in rural communities (Carr and Kefalas 2009; Demi, McLaughlin, and Snyder 2009).

In this chapter, we examine change in poverty of families with children and describe the education and work experiences of youth as they transition to adulthood. Most comparisons of children and youth focus on rural-urban or metropolitan-nonmetropolitan differences. To capture the diversity that exists within and across rural places, we use the Rural-Urban Continuum Codes (RUCC) to examine how characteristics of children and families with children differ with rurality (ERS USDA 2012). These codes classify counties by their adjacency to metropolitan counties and the size of their urban population.

Poverty among Families with Children

One of the distinctive characteristics of children in nonmetropolitan areas has been their relatively high poverty (Lichter and Johnson 2007; Lichter and McLaughlin 1995; O'Hare 2009; Snyder, McLaughlin, and Findeis 2006), which rivals or exceeds that of children in central cities (Lichter, Roscigno, and Condron 2003; McLaughlin and Sachs 1988; Rogers 2001). Family structure is one of the most critical factors placing children at risk of being poor (Snyder, McLaughlin, and Findeis 2006; Swanson and Dacquel 1996). Bean and Mattingly (in this volume) suggest greater prevalence of specific family types (e.g., single parent families) is associated with higher poverty rates of children. We document these relationships in this chapter.

The characteristics of the places in which children live also affect their likelihood of being poor (Cotter, Hermsen, and Vanneman 2007; Lichter and McLaughlin 1995; Lyson and Falk 1993; Partridge and Rickman 2006; Rogers 2001; Voss et al. 2006). Poverty rates tend to be high in the most rural places and in areas with long histories of persistent poverty (Mattingly, Johnson, and Schaefer 2011). A lack of employment opportunities and limited access to services also increase the likelihood of poverty. Children in poor families face increased risks of poor health, slower cognitive development, poorer performance in school, and lower educational attainment (O'Hare 2009). They also may have fewer work or job training opportunities as adults (Iceland 2006), and experience higher risks of becoming parents as teenagers.

Tables 19.1 and 19.2 show the percentage of families with children in poverty by family structure, age of children, and type of nonmetro county for 2000 and for 2006 to 2010. Family poverty rates for 2000 are based on annual income from 1999 reported in the 2000 Census of Population and Housing; for 2006 to 2010, poverty rates are shown for the 2006 to 2010 five-year estimates from the American Community Survey (ACS). Three years of the ACS income data precede the Great Recession and two years are during or immediately following.

In the United States, the percentage of families with children under age eighteen in poverty grew from 13.6 to 15.7 percent from 2000 to 2006 to 2010. The percentage of families with children in poverty in 2000 was higher in nonmetro than metro counties. This was especially the case in the most rural counties (RUCC 9), where 19.2 percent of all families with children were poor and just over one-quarter of families with children both under age five and ages five to seventeen were poor. Unlike urban areas, by 2006 to 2010, the highest poverty rates for nonmetro families with children were lower than or similar to those in

Table 19.1

Percentage of families with children under eighteen in poverty by family type, age of children, and RUCC code, 2000

	US Total	Non-metro	RUCC 4	RUCC 5	RUCC 6	RUCC 7	RUCC 8	RUCC 9
All families with children under 18								
Children under 5 only	14.1	19.0	17.6	19.5	19.0	20.8	18.3	21.0
Children 5 to 17 only	11.3	14.0	12.1	13.5	14.4	15.1	15.7	16.9
Children both under 5 and 5 to 17	19.7	22.7	21.1	22.8	23.0	24.0	23.1	25.6
Children under 18	13.6	16.6	14.9	16.5	16.9	17.8	17.5	19.2
Married couple families with children under 18								
Children under 5 only	6.3	8.9	7.4	8.6	9.1	10.1	9.7	12.0
Children 5 to 17	5.2	7.1	5.7	6.2	7.3	8.2	8.7	10.4
Children both under 5 and 5 to 17	10.6	13.2	11.5	12.4	13.6	14.3	14.8	16.7
Children under 18	6.6	8.7	7.2	7.9	8.9	9.7	10.1	11.9
Female-headed families with children under 18								
Children under 5 only	41.0	52.2	50.2	51.9	52.1	55.8	51.1	55.1
Children 5 to 17	27.7	34.9	31.5	34.2	35.9	37.2	38.5	40.0
Children both under 5 and 5 to 17	51.3	58.3	56.0	59.0	58.6	60.2	58.3	62.9
Children under 18	34.3	42.1	39.2	41.9	42.7	44.6	43.8	46.4
Male-headed families with children under 18								
Children under 5 only	19.4	22.9	20.9	24.3	22.8	24.7	24.3	26.6
Children 5 to 17	15.0	19.0	16.0	18.7	19.5	20.7	22.6	24.0
Children both under 5 and 5 to 17	26.5	30.4	29.6	29.2	29.1	32.5	29.3	38.9
Children under 18	17.7	21.4	19.0	21.5	21.5	23.1	23.8	26.5

RUCC 4: Nonmetro county with urban population of 20,000 or more, adjacent to a metropolitan area.
RUCC 5: Nonmetro county with urban population of 20,000 or more, not adjacent to a metropolitan area.
RUCC 6: Nonmetro county with urban population of 2,500 to 19,999, adjacent to a metropolitan area.
RUCC 7: Nonmetro county with urban population of 2,500 to 19,999, not adjacent to a metropolitan area.
RUCC 8: Nonmetro county completely rural or less than 2,500 urban population, adjacent to a metropolitan area.
RUCC 9: Nonmetro county completely rural or less than 2,500 urban population, not adjacent to a metropolitan area.
Source: US Census of Population and Housing, 2000.

Table 19.2

Percentage of families with children under eighteen in poverty by family type and age of children and RUCC code, 2006 to 2010

	US Total	Non-metro	RUCC 4	RUCC 5	RUCC 6	RUCC 7	RUCC 8	RUCC 9
All families with children under 18								
Children under 5 only	17.1	18.2	17.4	18.4	18.5	19.3	18.0	17.5
Children 5 to 17 only	12.8	13.3	12.7	11.3	14.0	14.2	12.5	11.9
Children both under 5 and 5 to 17	23.5	24.3	23.9	21.1	25.3	25.4	23.2	22.5
Children under 18	15.7	16.4	15.8	14.6	17.1	17.4	15.6	15.1
Married couple families with children under 18								
Children under 5 only	6.4	7.0	6.7	6.8	7.2	7.5	6.9	6.6
Children 5 to 17	5.3	5.5	5.3	4.9	5.9	5.8	5.3	5.0
Children both under 5 and 5 to 17	12.2	12.7	12.7	11.7	13.3	13.5	11.7	11.1
Children under 18	7.0	7.3	7.1	6.7	7.7	7.8	6.9	6.6
Female-headed families with children under 18								
Children under 5 only	45.8	47.9	45.8	53.5	47.3	49.2	48.6	49.4
Children 5 to 17	30.0	31.1	29.9	30.7	31.6	33.0	30.2	29.6
Children both under 5 and 5 to 17	55.5	57.3	56.5	55.0	57.1	57.9	58.4	57.8
Children under 18	37.4	38.9	37.4	39.6	39.0	40.5	38.6	38.5
Male-headed families with children under 18								
Children under 5 only	22.3	23.6	22.1	23.3	23.3	25.3	24.4	24.0
Children 5 to 17	16.1	16.8	15.7	14.1	17.5	17.7	16.4	16.2
Children both under 5 and 5 to 17	29.6	31.0	28.3	31.8	33.3	30.9	31.6	29.1
Children under 18	19.6	20.4	19.1	18.4	21.1	21.5	20.4	19.7

RUCC 4: Nonmetro county with urban population of 20,000 or more, adjacent to a metropolitan area.
RUCC 5: Nonmetro county with urban population of 20,000 or more, not adjacent to a metropolitan area.
RUCC 6: Nonmetro county with urban population of 2,500 to 19,999, adjacent to a metropolitan area.
RUCC 7: Nonmetro county with urban population of 2,500 to 19,999, not adjacent to a metropolitan area.
RUCC 8: Nonmetro county completely rural or less than 2,500 urban population, adjacent to a metropolitan area.
RUCC 9: Nonmetro county completely rural or less than 2,500 urban population, not adjacent to a metropolitan area.
Source: Table B17010 in 2006–2010 American Community Survey.

2000. An increase in poverty of families with children was not observed in most nonmetro areas. This is consistent with the less severe recession in 2007 to 2009 in nonmetro than metro areas (USDA ERS 2012).

The most striking differences in child poverty occur across family structure. During both time periods and across county types, the highest poverty rates occur in female-headed families with children. Married-couple families with children are the least likely to be poor. In 2000, 34.3 percent of all female-headed families with children under eighteen in the United States were poor; 42.1 percent of such families in nonmetro areas were poor. The highest poverty rates were in the most rural counties (RUCC 9) where 62.9 percent of female-headed families with all-age children were poor; more than half of these families were poor in each of the nonmetro categories. Between 2000 and 2006 to 2010, the poverty rate for female-headed families with children under eighteen in the United States increased by 3.1 percentage points to 37.4 percent. Across most nonmetro RUCC categories, poverty rates among female-headed families with children declined from 2000 to 2006 to 2010.

Poverty among male-headed (no spouse present) families with children was substantially lower than that of female-headed families, but more than double that for married-couple families with children. The highest poverty rates for married-couple families with children and male-headed families with children occur in the most rural counties. As with female-headed families, poverty rates for most male-headed and married-couple families with children declined from 2000 to 2006 to 2010 in nonmetro counties.

There was variation in the change in poverty across RUCC codes and family types. In the most urban nonmetro counties (RUCC 4), almost half of the family types experienced increases in family poverty from 2000 to 2006 to 2010. In the most rural areas (RUCC 9), poverty rates in 2006 to 2010 were lower than those in 2000 across family types and children's ages, suggesting that counties *not* adjacent to metropolitan areas experienced more stability in income during the Great Recession.

Youth Transitions from School to Work

Successful transitions to adulthood include completing high school, completing vocational training or a college education, and entering the workforce (Arnett 2004; Hamilton and Hamilton 2006). Idle youth are those who are not in school or working (Snyder, McLaughlin, and Coleman-Jensen 2009). The higher poverty rates among many nonmetro families with children suggest nonmetro youth likely have more difficulty with successful transitions from school to

Table 19.3

Percentage of youth ages sixteen to nineteen in school, in the labor force, or idle by RUCC code, 2000

Youth Ages 16 to 19	US Total	Non-metro	RUCC 4	RUCC 5	RUCC 6	RUCC 7	RUCC 8	RUCC 9
Total enrolled in school	80.2	79.3	79.4	81.7	78.1	79.4	78.5	80.7
Employed	37.4	37.2	38.6	38.3	36.3	37.8	33.8	33.3
Unemployed	8.1	7.9	8.6	9.5	7.5	7.6	5.6	5.9
Not in the labor force	54.5	54.9	52.8	52.2	56.2	54.6	60.6	60.8
Not enrolled in school	19.8	20.7	20.6	18.3	21.9	20.6	21.5	19.3
High school graduate	50.1	51.2	50.9	53.8	50.1	51.3	54.0	51.2
Employed	65.3	65.3	67.0	65.6	64.7	64.6	62.4	63.5
Unemployed	12.4	13.0	12.8	13.5	12.8	12.9	14.1	13.0
Not in labor force	22.4	21.8	20.3	21.0	22.5	22.4	23.6	23.4
Not high school graduate (dropouts)	49.9	48.8	49.1	46.2	49.9	48.7	46.0	48.8
Employed	43.8	41.0	42.9	40.7	40.8	40.3	39.0	36.1
Unemployed	16.3	16.8	16.5	18.3	16.5	16.4	16.8	17.9
Not in the labor force	39.9	42.3	40.6	41.1	42.7	43.4	44.2	45.9
Percentage Idle	6.2	6.6	6.2	5.5	7.1	6.7	7.1	6.6

RUCC 4: Nonmetro county with urban population of 20,000 or more, adjacent to a metro area.
RUCC 5: Nonmetro county with urban population of 20,000 or more, not adjacent to a metro area.
RUCC 6: Nonmetro county with urban population of 2,500 to 19,999, adjacent to a metro area.
RUCC 7: Nonmetro county with urban population of 2,500 to 19,999, not adjacent to a metro area.
RUCC 8: Nonmetro county completely rural or less than 2,500 urban population, adjacent to metro area.
RUCC 9: Nonmetro county completely rural or less than 2,500 urban population, not adjacent to metro area
Source: Table P038, Summary File 3, US Census of Population and Housing, 2000 Sample data (data on Armed Forces not used).

work. Rural youth have fewer opportunities to obtain college education or vocational training in their home communities, and local job opportunities may not include careers to which they aspire (Carr and Kefalas 2009; Hecktner 1995; Huang et al. 1997; Sherman and Sage 2011). Fewer options may encourage youth to leave rural areas in search of opportunities elsewhere (Johnson 2003). To examine youth education to work transitions, we look at youth ages sixteen to nineteen using data from the 2000 Census and the 2006 to 2010 ACS.

Tables 19.3 and 19.4 show the percentage of youth ages sixteen to nineteen by school enrollment and labor force activity in 2000 and 2006 to 2010, distinguished by whether or not they graduated from high school. Within each of these groups, the percentages currently employed, unemployed, and not in the labor force, and the percentage of all youth idle (neither in school, working, nor looking for work) are reported.

Roughly four-fifths of youth ages sixteen to nineteen were enrolled in school across the United States in both time periods. In 2006 to 2010 across nonmetro counties, between 80.6 and 84.0 percent of youth ages sixteen to nineteen were enrolled in school, an increase of roughly four percentage points since 2000. Among those enrolled, between 52.2 and 60.8 percent were *not* in the labor force in 2000. The percentage of those in school and not in the labor force increased in all but the most rural counties by the 2006 to 2010 period. This lower labor force participation of more urban youth is consistent with stronger effects of the Great Recession in metro areas and more urban nonmetro counties.

Among those not enrolled in school, the percentage that had completed high school increased. In 2000, roughly half of those not enrolled in school were high school graduates, with the highest percentage, 54 percent, in more rural counties (RUCC 8). By 2006 to 2010, the percentage not enrolled in school who were high school graduates had increased by roughly ten percentage points, and varied little across types of nonmetro counties. This is an impressive gain in high school completion in just ten years.

Among high school graduates not enrolled in school, the percentage employed overall in nonmetro areas dropped to 58.5 percent (compared to 65.3 percent in 2000), and the unemployment rate rose from 13 percent in 2000 to 16.9 percent. Nonmetro high school dropouts also lost ground, with a 6.9 percentage point decline in employment rate by 2006 to 2010 and a 1.5 percentage point increase in unemployment to 18.3 percent. Across nonmetro counties, regardless of school or graduation status, the percentage of sixteen to nineteen year olds employed decreased and the percentages unemployed and not in the labor force increased from 2000 to the 2006 to 2010 period. This suggests poorer job prospects among the newest entrants to the labor force. The percentage of sixteen to nineteen year olds who were idle—neither in school, working or looking for work, declined from 2000 to the 2006 to 2010 period. The declining economy may have forced some of these youth to stay in high school, rather than leaving high school for work.

In the time frame just before and during the beginning of the Great Recession, living in counties adjacent to a metro area was associated with poorer employment prospects for sixteen- to nineteen-year-old youth. Living in nonmetro counties with a larger urban center and not adjacent to metro areas offered somewhat better opportunities for youth, although they still were poorer than

Table 19.4
Percentage of youth ages sixteen to nineteen in school, working, or idle by RUCC code, 2006 to 2010

Youth Ages 16 to 19	US Total	Non-metro	RUCC 4	RUCC 5	RUCC 6	RUCC 7	RUCC 8	RUCC 9
Total enrolled in school	84.0	83.2	80.6	84.0	83.8	83.9	83.8	83.4
Employed	29.0	28.3	18.1	34.2	28.8	31.0	30.9	33.6
Unemployed	8.5	8.7	9.4	7.9	8.5	9.3	8.3	8.1
Not in the labor force	62.5	63.0	72.5	57.9	62.7	59.6	60.8	58.2
Not enrolled in school	16.0	16.8	19.4	16.0	16.2	16.1	16.2	16.6
High school graduate	61.0	60.4	60.4	63.1	59.8	59.4	61.5	61.8
Employed	58.1	58.5	59.5	62.4	55.9	58.0	59.5	61.7
Unemployed	17.0	16.9	16.0	15.5	17.1	18.5	17.7	15.3
Not in labor force	24.9	24.7	24.6	22.1	27.0	23.5	22.8	23.0
Not high school graduate (dropouts)	39.0	39.6	39.6	36.9	40.2	40.6	38.5	38.2
Employed	34.1	34.1	35.5	37.4	31.8	34.4	36.1	34.7
Unemployed	18.5	18.3	17.5	16.9	18.9	19.3	16.4	18.2
Not in labor force	47.5	47.7	47.1	45.7	49.3	46.3	47.5	47.1
Percentage Idle	5.4	5.7	6.5	4.9	5.8	5.3	5.3	5.3

RUCC 4: Nonmetro county with urban population of 20,000 or more, adjacent to a metro area.
RUCC 5: Nonmetro county with urban population of 20,000 or more, not adjacent to a metro area.
RUCC 6: Nonmetro county with urban population of 2,500 to 19,999, adjacent to a metro area.
RUCC 7: Nonmetro county with urban population of 2,500 to 19,999, not adjacent to a metro area.
RUCC 8: Nonmetro county completely rural or less than 2,500 urban population, adjacent to metro area.
RUCC 9: Nonmetro county completely rural or less than 2,500 urban population, not adjacent to metro area.
Source: 2006–2010 American Community Survey, Table 14005.

those available in 2000. Overall, the most positive indicator is the substantial increase in sixteen to nineteen year olds enrolled in school and who had graduated from high school between 2000 and the 2006 to 2010 period. These youth have a much better chance of success in life because they stayed in or completed high school.

Loss (or Gain) of Children and Youth in Rural Areas

Out-migration of youth and young adults from nonmetropolitan areas is a significant and intractable problem, especially in areas that are more geographically isolated or poor (Johnson and Rathge 2006; Lichter, McLaughlin, and Cornwell 1995). Limited opportunities for higher education and jobs are the explanations most often provided for the out-migration of youth and young adults (Carr and Kefalas 2009; Demi, McLaughlin, and Snyder 2009; Hecktner 1995; Sherman and Sage 2011). Out-migration of youth and young adults results in fewer new families with children and fewer workers, volunteers and citizens who will invest in the future of the community (Carr and Kefalas 2009; Johnson and Rathge 2006). The loss of youth and young adults is especially problematic if it is not offset by young adults moving into the community.

Nonmetro areas close to rapidly growing metropolitan areas are increasing in population (Elliott and Perry 1996) and may see increases in numbers of children and young adults. Newcomers in search of jobs, educational opportunities in college towns, or amenities may bolster the young-adult population in nonmetro counties. Population change pyramids from the 2000 to 2010 US censuses (US Census Bureau 2000; 2010), based on single years of age, reveal the extent to which the numbers of youth and young adults in selected nonmetro areas changed from 2000 to 2010.

Figure 19.1 shows a population change pyramid for the most urban nonmetro counties (RUCC 4) and the most rural nonmetro counties (RUCC 9). On the left side of the pyramid is the number of people by single years of age for those ages five to nineteen in 2000. Youth these ages were most likely to move away from (or move to) a particular area over the ten years from 2000 to 2010. On the right-hand side are the 2010 population counts for individuals who were ages fifteen to twenty-nine in 2010. These individuals would have been ages five to nineteen ten years earlier in 2000; for example, those who were age five in 2000 would be age fifteen in 2010.

Births, deaths, in-migration, immigration, and out-migration affect population change. Births do not affect population change in Figure 19.1 because the population in 2000 begins at age five. Children born after 1996 are not included. Deaths do occur in these age groups, but the age-specific mortality rates are relatively low (12.2, 15.7, and 53.5 per 100,000 for ages five to nine, ten to fourteen, and fifteen to nineteen, respectively) (Kochanek et al. 2011) and would affect all counties. The majority of population change in these age groups occurs due to in- and out-migration, so that an increase in the population ten years later for those children age five in 2000 would be the result of net in-migration (in-migration plus immigration minus out-migration). A decline in the number of youth in an age cohort ten years later, for example those nine years old in 2000 to nineteen years old in 2010, largely reflects net out-migration. Younger children would leave the area with their families, while older youth and young adults

RUCC 4: Metro Adjacent, 20,000 or More Urban Population

223,884 Age 19 | Age 29 182,131
217,780 Age 18 | Age 28 180,263
216,024 Age 17 | Age 27 182,116
212,414 Age 16 | Age 26 177,604
213,883 Age 15 | Age 25 183,293
214,614 Age 14 | Age 24 186,753
209,472 Age 13 | Age 23 189,149
209,050 Age 12 | Age 22 202,776
209,419 Age 11 | Age 21 216,515
215,807 Age 10 | Age 20 230,325
212,677 Age 9 | Age 19 239,421
206,543 Age 8 | Age 18 227,862
200,990 Age 7 | Age 17 216,692
194,646 Age 6 | Age 16 211,405
189,658 Age 5 | Age 15 206,067

300,000 200,000 100,000 0 100,000 200,000 300,000

2000 RUCC 4 Population
2010 RUCC 4 Population

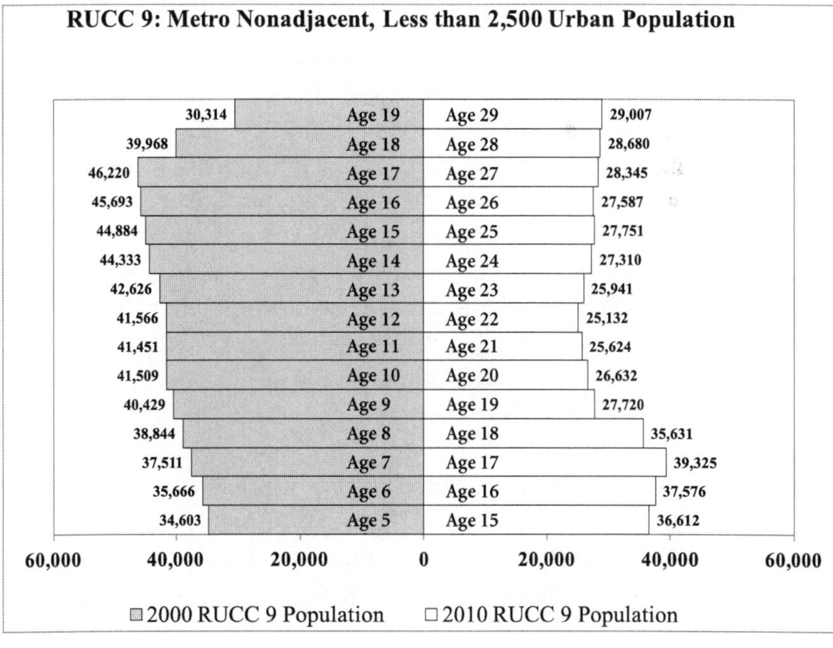

Figure 19.1. Population Change by Age, 2000 to 2010, RUCC 4 and RUCC 9.

likely leave on their own to pursue education or employment opportunities, experience new places, or start a family elsewhere.

The population change pyramids for the nonmetro county RUCC classifications look quite different across RUCC classifications. The most urban nonmetro counties (RUCC 4) show an increase in each age category from 2000 to 2010 for ages five to eleven in 2000 (age fifteen to twenty-one in 2010). The large influx of young adults ages eighteen to twenty by 2010 suggests the presence of colleges, military bases, or job opportunities in counties in this RUCC code. Among those ages twelve and higher in 2000, by 2010 when the youth were ages twenty-two and higher, their numbers had declined, suggesting some had moved elsewhere. Overall, the most urban nonmetro counties experienced an influx of people who were ages five to eleven in 2000, especially among those ages nine and ten, and a loss of those ages twenty-two to twenty-nine in 2010. There was a net loss of 18.6 percent (from 223,884 to 182,131) of those who were age nineteen in 2000 by 2010. Overall, the numbers of those ages five to nineteen in 2000 had declined by 3.6 percent by 2010.

The most rural counties (RUCC 9) have a pronounced loss of both youth and young adults from 2000 to 2010. By 2010, there were modest increases in the number of individuals who would have been ages five, six, and seven in 2000. The numbers of those ages nine to seventeen in 2000 declined between 24.8 percent and 33.4 percent by 2010. While we do not know the specific age at which these youth left their 2000 county of residence, substantial numbers did leave. By 2010, the most rural county group (RUCC 9) lost 25.9 percent of those ages five to nineteen in 2000. The smaller numbers among those ages eighteen and nineteen in 2000 suggest that loss of youth from these counties begins once youth complete high school. Numbers of youth ages nine and over in 2000 (those most likely to leave for school or job opportunities elsewhere by 2010) had declined between 30 and 40 percent, depending on age. By 2010, every nonmetro RUCC category experienced a loss of those ages fifteen to nineteen in 2000 (not shown).

This analysis reflects an estimate of net migration from 2000 to 2010. The overall pattern shows the loss of substantial numbers of those who normally would have aged into young adulthood across nonmetro counties and provides indirect evidence of substantial out-migration of youth and young adults, especially from the most rural areas of the United States. Without question there are many rural counties that are growing and that may be experiencing in-migration of youth and young adults. However, the aggregated data using RUCC codes suggests these are the exception rather than the rule for nonmetropolitan America. Less is known about whether the youth who leave in search of education or new experiences return to rural areas to raise their families.

Conclusions

Change is a constant for rural America. Some changes present opportunities, others pose challenges, and some changes are both opportunity and challenge. High poverty in families with children remains a challenge, as does out-migration of children and youth. But these challenges are not spread evenly across nonmetro America. Variations occur with adjacency to metropolitan areas and the size of urban populations in nonmetro counties. Policy responses to these opportunities and challenges vary as well. Given limited federal or state assistance, local leaders and residents will need to find innovative solutions to challenges and identify strategies and policies to enhance opportunities that reduce poverty and encourage youth to stay or attract young adults to nonmetro areas.

Poverty of families with children is still a challenge, especially in families with one parent present. By the 2006 to 2009 period, nonmetro counties had not been as hard hit by the Great Recession as metro areas. It is uncertain whether the effects of the Great Recession will hit nonmetro areas later than metro areas or if the effects will be limited. Regardless of the Great Recession, poverty rates for families with children remain high. Youth out-migration is highest in the most rural counties, where poverty in families with children tends to be high and youth who had not completed high school had difficulty finding jobs. Such areas face particular challenges for improving conditions and sustaining the community.

The patterns of population change, poverty, and work among children and youth suggest what has been documented in prior decades—the most rural places in the United States still struggle, while those with larger urban populations seem more stable or experience modest population growth. Youth out-migration and family poverty arise from the same challenges—lack of educational and economic opportunities to sustain families and keep youth in some nonmetro areas, and difficulty in preparing all youth for a successful future.

Possible policies and strategies specific to the challenges of child poverty, out-migration, and creating work opportunities for youth and young adults would draw upon a combination of local and state or federal resources and more innovative partnerships. Slowing youth out-migration is a major concern for communities, yet teachers and parents often encourage their children to seek opportunities elsewhere (Carr and Kefalas 2009). Success means going away to college and getting a good job in the city. Rural youth are more likely to want to leave communities in which they do not feel welcome (Pretty 2002). Including youth in conversations about community decisions and seriously considering their suggestions may make them feel more welcome, like part of the community, and inclined to find ways to stay. Participatory approaches can also increase awareness of the types of careers and jobs available locally.

In many rural areas, lack of appropriate jobs is an issue, but youth who do not or are not encouraged to see a viable future in the community are less likely to stay or return. Job shadowing and job training programs for youth during high school could make them aware of local jobs, including local jobs that require a college education. These programs may be especially important for youth who do not plan to attend college, have dropped out of high school, or whose parents have limited knowledge of educational or work options in the area. Programs where schools work with businesses and families, especially low-income families, to provide mentors from the community, opportunities for families to come together to share strategies and successes, and tutoring for parents and children can improve children's success in school and the workforce (Fischer 2003).

The most difficult challenge facing rural communities is creating jobs that pay a living wage. Attracting large firms requires resources beyond those available locally, and recruitment of a large business has been argued to often cost more than they bring to the community. This leaves the option of starting new local businesses and retaining those already in the area. Recent community case studies suggest that small businesses are stronger in small towns where local business owners work with each other and with local government to improve business opportunities (Fortunato 2011), and where residents support local businesses. The markets for the products of these businesses may be local, regional, or national, but the jobs provided are local.

Much recent policy has tended to emphasize local efforts and communities taking the lead in improving local conditions. Federal budget crises suggest investments in local development efforts will continue to be limited or may decline further. However, this emphasis on local efforts to lead change ignores the variation in local resources available to foster change to strengthen local schools and job prospects for parents, teens, and young adults. Programs that rely totally on local initiative will favor those communities that already have established local leadership and the resources to pursue federal or state funding. These are not likely to be communities or regions with high poverty, but rather communities already doing well.

The Stronger Economies Together (SET) program, sponsored by USDA Rural Development and the Regional Rural Development Centers, provides an example of a region-based strategy to identify local resources in areas seeking assistance in encouraging local people to come together to identify and develop strategies to meet local needs and solve local problems. The focus is on using local resources, but in doing so to build relationships among and capacity of people and institutions to address local problems, meet local needs, or achieve local goals. This program is designed to build human and institutional capacity in a region (defined by local people). This capacity provides people in the region with knowledge, skills, and relationships to continue to improve the region after the formal SET program has ended. SET also helps to link local efforts to resources from outside the region. Programs like SET should focus on those areas that are the most challenged by poverty and out-migration and so likely the most in need of local capacity building. The intent is to increase access to resources to support these regions in achieving their own goals while building capacity to continue to act in the future.

Throughout, it is important to acknowledge and accept the knowledge, skills, and resources that individuals, organizations, and businesses already in the community or region could contribute to achieving community goals. Failure of leaders and residents to recognize the interdependent futures and potential contributions of all of those in the community results in missed opportunities to use existing assets to strengthen the community and look toward the future.

References

American Community Survey (ACS). 2010. "American Community Survey 5-Year Estimates." http://www.socialexplorer.com.

Arnett, Jeffrey Jensen. 2004. *Emerging Adulthood: The Winding Road from the Late Teens through the Twenties.* New York: Oxford University Press.

Brown, David L., and Nina Glasgow. 2008. "Who Moves to Rural Retirement Communities, and Why Do They Move There?" In *Rural Retirement Migration*, ed. David L. Brown, Nina Glasgow, Laszlo J. Kulcsar, B.C. Bolender, and M.J. Arguillas, 91–115. Dordrecht: Springer. http://dx.doi.org/10.1007/978-1-4020-6895-9_4.

Carr, Patrick J., and Maria J. Kefalas. 2009. *Hollowing out the Middle: The Rural Brain Drain and What It Means for America.* Boston, MA: Beacon Press.

Cotter, David A., Joan M. Hermsen, and Reeve Vanneman. 2007. "Placing Family Poverty in Area Contexts: The Use of Multilevel Models in Spatial Research." In *The Sociology of Spatial Inequality*, ed. Linda M. Lobao, Gregory Hooks, and Ann R. Tickamyer, 163–88. Albany, NY: SUNY Press.

Crowley, Martha, Daniel T. Lichter, and Zenchao Qian. 2006. "Beyond Gateway Cities: Economic Restructuring and Poverty among Mexican Immigrant Families and Children." *Family Relations* 55 (3): 345–60. http://dx.doi.org/10.1111/j.1741-3729.2006.00407.x.

Demi, Mary Ann, Diane K. McLaughlin, and Anastasia R. Snyder. 2009. "Rural Youth Residential Preferences: Understanding the Youth Development-Community Development Nexus." *Community Development: Journal of the Community Development Society* 40 (4): 311–30. http://dx.doi.org/10.1080/15575330903279606.

Economic Research Service (ERS). USDA. 2012. "Rural-Urban Continuum Codes. 2003 Codes." Updated 5 July. http://www.ers.usda.gov/data-products/rural-urban-continuum-codes/documentation.aspx.

Elliott, James R., and Marc J. Perry. 1996. "Metropolitanizing Nonmetro Space: Population Redistributions and Emergent Metropolitan Areas, 1965–90." *Rural Sociology* 61 (3): 497–512. http://dx.doi.org/10.1111/j.1549-0831.1996.tb00631.x.

Fischer, Deborah. 2003. *Assets in Action: A Handbook for Making Communities Better Places to Grow Up*. Minneapolis: Search Institute.

Fortunato, Michael W.-P. 2011. "The Individual-Institutional-Opportunity Nexus: Examining Interaction, Purpose and Opportunity in Rural Entrepreneurship Development." PhD dissertation, rural sociology. University Park: Pennsylvania State University.

Hamilton, Stephen F., and Mary Agnes Hamilton. 2006. "School, Work and Emerging Adulthood." In *Emerging Adults in America: Coming of Age in the 21st Century*, ed. Jeffrey J. Arnett and Jennifer L. Tanner, 257–77. Washington, DC: American Psychological Association. http://dx.doi.org/10.1037/11381-011.

Hecktner, Joel M. 1995. "When Moving up Implies Moving Out: Rural Adolescent Conflict in the Transition to Adulthood." *Journal of Research in Rural Education* 11: 3–14.

Huang, Gary G., Stanley Weng, Fan Zhang, and Michael P. Cohen. 1997. "Out-Migration among Rural High School Graduates: The Effect of Academic and Vocational Programs." *Educational Valuation and Policy Analysis* 19: 360–72.

Iceland, John. 2006. *Poverty in America: A Handbook*. Berkeley: University of California Press.

Jensen, Leif. 2006. *New Immigrant Settlements in Rural America: Problems, Prospects, and Policies. Report on Rural America 1(3)*. Durham, NH: Carsey Institute.

Johnson, Kenneth M. 2003. "Unpredictable Directions of Rural Population Growth and Migration." In *Challenges for Rural America in the Twenty-First Century*, ed. David L. Brown and Louis E. Swanson, 19–31. University Park: Penn State University Press.

Johnson, Kenneth M., and Daniel T. Lichter. 2010. "Growing Diversity among America's Children and Youth: Spatial and Temporal Dimensions." *Population and Development Review* 36 (1): 151–76. http://dx.doi.org/10.1111/j.1728-4457.2010.00322.x.

Johnson, Kenneth M., and Richard W. Rathge. 2006. "Agricultural Dependence and Changing Population in the Great Plains." In *Population Change and Rural Society*, ed. William A. Kandel and David L. Brown, 197–217. The Netherlands: Springer. http://dx.doi.org/10.1007/1-4020-3902-6_9.

Kochanek, Kenneth D., Jiaquan Xu, Sherry L. Murphy, Arialdi M. Minino, and Hsiang-Ching Kung. 2011. "Deaths: Final Data for 2009." *National Vital Statistics Reports* 60 (3).

Krannich, Richard S., and Peggy Petrzelka. 2003. "Tourism and Natural Amenity Development: Real Opportunities?" In *Challenges for Rural America in the Twenty-First Century*, ed. David L. Brown and Louis E. Swanson, 190–99. University Park: Penn State University Press.

Lichter, Daniel T. 2012. "Immigration and the New Racial Diversity in Rural America." *Rural Sociology* 77 (1): 3–35. http://dx.doi.org/10.1111/j.1549-0831.2012.00070.x.

Lichter, Daniel T., and Kenneth M. Johnson. 2007. "The Changing Spatial Concentrations of America's Rural Poor Population." *Rural Sociology* 72 (3): 331–58. http://dx.doi.org/10.1526/003601107781799290.

Lichter, Daniel T., and Diane K. McLaughlin. 1995. "Changing Economic Opportunities, Family Structure, and Poverty in Rural Areas." *Rural Sociology* 60 (4): 688–706. http://dx.doi.org/10.1111/j.1549-0831.1995.tb00601.x.

Lichter, Daniel T., Diane K. McLaughlin, and Gretchen T. Cornwell. 1995. "Migration and the Depletion of Human Resources in Rural America." In *Investing in People: The Human Capital Needs of Rural America*, ed. Lionel J. Beaulieu and David Mulkey, 235–56. Boulder, CO: Westview Press.

Lichter, Daniel T., Vincent J. Roscigno, and Dennis J. Condron. 2003. "Rural Children and Youth at Risk." In *Challenges for Rural America in the Twenty-First Century*, ed. David L. Brown and Louis E. Swanson, 97–108. University Park: Penn State University Press.

Lyson, Thomas A., and William W. Falk. 1993. *Forgotten Places: Uneven Development in Rural America.* Lawrence, KS: University of Kansas Press.

Mattingly, Marybeth J., Kenneth M. Johnson, and Andrew Schaefer. 2011. "More Poor Kids in More Poor Places: Children Increasingly Live Where Poverty Persists." Issue Brief No. 38. Durham, NH: Carsey Institute.

McGranahan, David, John Cromartie, and Timothy Wojan. 2010. *Nonmetropolitan Outmigration Counties: Some Are Poor, Many Are Prosperous.* US Department of Agriculture, Economic Research Service. Economic Research Report 107. http://dx.doi.org/10.2139/ssrn.1711309.

McGrath, Daniel J., Raymond R. Swisher, Glen H. Elder, Jr., and Rand D. Conger. 2001. "Breaking New Ground: Diverse Routes to College in Rural America." *Rural Sociology* 66 (2): 244–67. http://dx.doi.org/10.1111/j.1549-0831.2001.tb00066.x.

McLaughlin, Diane K., and Carolyn Sachs. 1988. "Poverty in Female-Headed Households: Residential Differences." *Rural Sociology* 53: 287–306.

O'Hare, William. 2009. *The Forgotten Fifth: Child Poverty in Rural America.* Carsey Report No. 10. University of New Hampshire, Carsey Institute.

Partridge, Mark D., and Dan S. Rickman. 2006. *The Geography of American Poverty: Is There a Need for Place-Based Policies?* Kalamazoo, MI: W.E. Upjohn Institute for Employment Research.

Pretty, Grace M.H. 2002. "Young People's Development of the Community-Minded Self." In *Psychological Sense of Community: Research, Applications and Implications*, ed. Adrian T. Fisher, Christopher C. Sonn, and Brian J. Bishop, 183–203. New York: Klewer Academic/Plenum. http://dx.doi.org/10.1007/978-1-4615-0719-2_10.

Rogers, Carolyn C. 2001. "Factors Affecting High Child Poverty in the Rural South." *Rural America* 15: 50–8.

Sherman, Jennifer, and Rayna Sage. 2011. "Sending off All Your Good Treasures: Rural Schools, Brain Drain, and Community Survival in the Wake of Economic Collapse." *Journal of Research in Rural Education* 26: 1–14.

Snyder, Anastasia R., Diane K. McLaughlin, and Alisha Coleman-Jensen. 2009. *The New, Longer Road to Adulthood: Schooling, Work and Idleness among Rural Youth.* Report No. 9. University of New Hampshire, Carsey Institute.

Snyder, Anastasia R., Diane K. McLaughlin, and Jill L. Findeis. 2006. "Household Composition and Poverty among Female-Headed Households with Children: Differences by Race and Residence." *Rural Sociology* 71 (4): 597–624. http://dx.doi.org/10.1526/003601106781262007.

Swanson, Linda L., and Laarni T. Dacquel. 1996. "Rural Child Poverty and the Role of Family Structure." In *Racial/Ethnic Minorities in Rural Areas: Progress and Stagnation, 1980–90*, ed. Linda L. Swanson, 33–41. Washington, DC: Rural Economy Division, Economic Research Service, US Department of Agriculture.

US Census Bureau. 2010. "Census 2010 Summary File 1 and 3, Detailed Tables." http://www.socialexplorer.com.

US Census Bureau. 2000. "Census 2000 Summary File 1 and 3, Detailed Tables." http://www.socialexplorer.com.

USDA, Economic Research Service. 2012. "Rural America at a Glance: 2012 Edition." Economic Brief Number 21. Washington, DC: Economic Research Service, US Department of Agriculture.

Voss, Paul R., David D. Long, Roger B. Hammer, and Samantha Friedman. 2006. "County Child Poverty Rates in the US: A Spatial Regression Approach." *Population Research and Policy Review* 25 (4): 369–91. http://dx.doi.org/10.1007/s11113-006-9007-4.

CHAPTER 20

Concentrations of the Elderly in Rural America: Patterns, Processes, and Outcomes in a Neoliberal World

Peter B. Nelson

Introduction

Median age in the United States has risen to over thirty-seven years—increasing by approximately five years in the last two decades alone (Howden and Meyer 2011)—a trend reflecting the aging of the baby boom and increased life expectancies. While population aging has been steady, its geography is more uneven. Rural areas tend to have higher elderly concentrations, making aging a particularly acute issue for rural communities. Different demographic forces (elderly in-migration, youth out-migration, and aging in place) contribute to these concentrations and lay the groundwork for current or future periods of natural decrease at the county level (Johnson 2011). Moreover, concentrations of elderly present distinct implications for rural communities ranging from healthcare to economic development, and the far-reaching effects of neoliberal ideologies and globalization reshape the impact of population aging on rural America in unique ways.

The rural elderly have attracted considerable attention from geographers, sociologists, economists, and demographers, and this body of research informs policy discussions at local, regional, and national scales (Glasgow and Berry 2013). In this chapter, I combine a statistical description of the elderly in rural America based on the 2010 Decennial Census with a theoretically informed discussion of the impact of aging on various dimensions of rural communities.

Locating Concentrations of Elderly Populations in Rural America

The US 2010 Census reveals that while 13 percent of the US population was sixty-five or older, nonmetropolitan areas were considerably older than metropolitan areas, with 16.2 and 12.4 percent of their respective populations being in that age group. At a regional scale, throughout much of the twentieth century, processes of youth out-migration have resulted in the population of the Great Plains being relatively older while that in the Rockies is somewhat younger (Fuguitt and Heaton 1995). Figure 20.1 uses location quotients (benchmarked to the United States) to display relative concentrations of population sixty-five and older by county and illustrates that these regional tendencies have continued through the 2010 census.[1] Large swathes of the Great Plains have location quotients greater than 1.5, indicating that more than 20 percent of the resident population is sixty-five or older. At the same time, many metropolitan counties fall in the lowest range of location quotients, with less than 11 percent of their populations sixty-five or older. The difference between metropolitan and nonmetropolitan age structure is most noticeable in areas around Minneapolis-St. Paul where the metropolitan counties fall almost entirely in the lowest range of location quotients while the surrounding nonmetropolitan counties lie at the high end of the distribution. Across much of the country, there are metropolitan islands of youth surrounded by a much older countryside, and such patterns result from extended periods of youth out-migration as younger community residents are drawn to urban centers in search of more promising economic opportunities (Johnson 2011; Erickson, Call, and Brown 2012).

Table 20.1 summarizes the location quotients of those sixty-five and older by census division and reveals considerable regional variation. While the metropolitan core is consistently youngest in the South and West, portions of the rural South and West are quite old. The nonmetropolitan South Atlantic and Pacific divisions have two of the three highest concentrations of elderly of any division, demonstrating high variability between the urban and rural parts within these divisions. In other words, the differences between the cities and the countryside are most pronounced in these areas, especially in the Pacific division. The northern Great Plains (West North Central Census Division) also shows dramatic differences between relatively young metropolitan counties and quite old nonmetropolitan counties, and this gap has been widening for several decades (Wilson 2009).

While Table 20.1 does show metropolitan regions to be relatively young in the aggregate, this is largely the result of the influence of the largest metropolitan

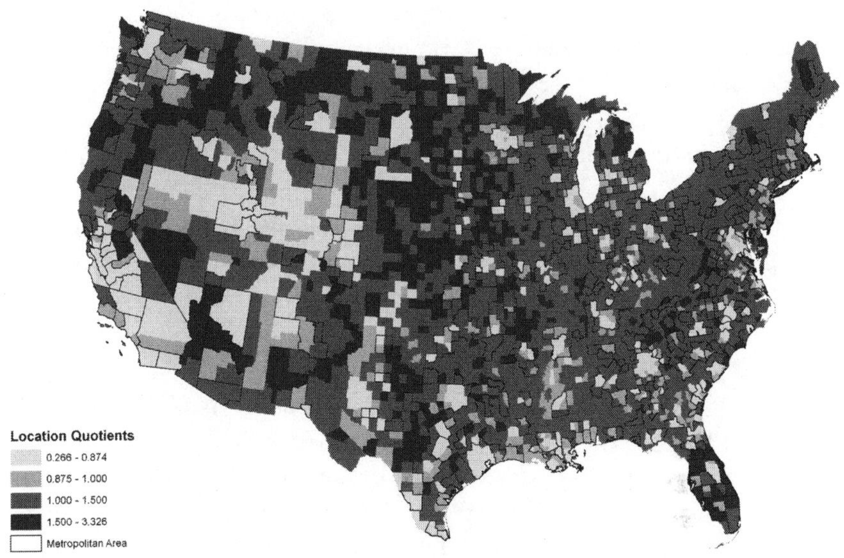

Figure 20.1. Location quotients for the population over age sixty-five by county. Source: United States Census 2010.

Table 20.1
Location quotients and percent of population over age sixty-five by census division, 2010

	Nonmetro		Metro	
Census Division	% 65 and Older	Location Quotient	% 65 and Older	Location Quotient
New England	16.23	1.24	13.84	1.06
Mid-Atlantic	16.28	1.25	13.89	1.06
East-North Central	16.14	1.24	12.74	0.98
West-North Central	17.02	1.30	12.02	0.92
South Atlantic	16.76	1.28	13.42	1.03
East-South Central	15.18	1.16	12.43	0.95
West-South Central	15.70	1.20	10.23	0.78
Mountain	14.71	1.13	11.60	0.89
Pacific	17.48	1.34	11.41	0.87
Total	16.15	1.24	12.44	0.95

Source: United States Census 2010.

regions. In fact, only metropolitan areas with populations over one million have location quotients under 1.00 (results available from the author on request). All other counties have above-average concentrations of elderly, even the smaller metropolitan counties. Metropolitan and micropolitan counties alike have the lowest location quotients, whereas noncore counties have the highest. Moreover, counties with the highest location quotients are those noncore counties without any urbanized area over 2,500 people. Thus, the most rural counties in the United States have the highest concentrations of populations aged sixty-five or older—nearly 20 percent of their populations.

In addition to variations across regions and urban influence, concentrations of elderly differ by certain socioeconomic characteristics. The highest concentrations of elderly are found in farm-dependent and population-loss counties as well as recreation and retirement destinations (results available from the author on request). The high location quotients reflect consistent concentrations of elderly in these types of places, yet they mask different underlying demographic processes. Farm-dependent and population-loss counties have higher concentrations of elderly that are likely the result of high rates of out-migration of younger residents (Rathge and Johnson 2005) whereas recreation and retirement counties tend to be destinations of in-migrating retirees (Brown et al. 2011). Thus, the similarly high concentrations of elderly in these types of counties are produced by dramatically different migration processes.

What Processes Account for the High Concentrations of Elderly in Rural America?

Migration is a selective process shaping the distribution of elderly across rural America in distinct and complex ways. On the one hand, many rural areas, especially in the Corn Belt and Great Plains, have suffered youth out-migration for several decades. Youth out-migration leaves behind a more concentrated older population that ages in place (Morrill 1995) and fewer residents of childbearing age (Fuguitt and Heaton 1995; Johnson et al. 2005). On the other hand, certain types of rural areas have long been attractive destinations for older in-migrants because of their environmentally pleasing qualities. In such places, positive net migration can result in higher concentrations of elderly residents, and this situation is common in places like the Ozarks, Southern Appalachia, and the Pacific Coast.

The impacts of these two different processes that lead to elderly concentration in rural areas are equally distinct. As Rogers and Woodward (1988, 451) argue, "an elderly population that grows due to migration may have very different socioeconomic and demographic characteristics than an elderly population that has primarily aged in place." In-migrating retirees tend to be healthier and wealthier, bringing with them significant financial resources (Nelson 2005). Therefore, areas attracting a higher than expected share of retirees can see their arrival as a possible growth sector (Reeder 1998), as retiree expenditures can stimulate expansion in construction, personal services, and healthcare (Deller 1995; Sastry 1992; Serow and Haas 1992; Serow 2003). In contrast, youth out-migration and aging in place can present challenges to communities trying to maintain critical services such as healthcare (Rowles and Watkins 1993; Keating and Phillips 2008). Out-migration can further compromise social networks important in assisting aging populations in formal and informal ways (Erickson, Call, and Brown 2012). In addition, places characterized by youth out-migration are likely to have depressed real estate markets, presenting potential challenges for the elderly who may need to draw on home equity in retirement.

Given the varied impacts of these different forces contributing to an aging countryside, it is important to identify which factors drive aging in different places. Age-specific estimates of net migration by county are not yet available for 2010 at the time of writing, so this section of the analysis employs a simple estimation technique to differentiate areas with high out-migration of the non-elderly from areas with high elderly in-migration.[2] These techniques identify change in any particular age cohort exceeding that which is expected given overall changes in age composition. The expected changes were calculated using Equation 1:

$$CS_{a,i} = \Delta P_{a,i,2000-2010} - \left(\dot{P}_{a,US,2000-2010}\right) P_{a,i,2000}$$

The cohort shift (CS) for any age cohort (a) in county (i) is derived by taking the difference between the actual change in the size of the cohort (ΔP) and that predicted by applying the national rate of change ($\dot{P}$) of that cohort to the population at the start of the decade (Plane 1992). Counties with positive cohort shifts are either gaining residents in that age cohort at higher than expected rates, or losing them at slower rates. While life expectancy varies across space due to a combination of factors—such as race, per capita income, and geography—that could influence the distribution of elderly in rural areas, life expectancies have risen only slightly over the past two decades (Murray et al. 2006). Thus, migration is a more powerful factor influencing changing concentrations of elderly across space. The discussion below focuses on the most extreme cohort shifts: the top decile for the cohort born prior to 1945 (labeled as elderly), and the bottom decile for those born between 1945 and 1985 (labeled as non-elderly). By focusing the discussion on the top and bottom deciles, the analysis is better able to identify areas where differential migration is the likely driver of higher concentrations of elderly. As of 2010, the elderly cohort was sixty-five years old or older, and the non-elderly cohort was twenty-five through sixty-four years of age.

Table 20.2 summarizes these two groups of counties by census division and reveals distinct geographic variation in demographic processes resulting in higher concentrations of elderly in specific places. The variations across divisions are quite striking. These two groups are based on the two extreme deciles, so all other things being equal one would expect roughly 10 percent of each division to fall in these categories. More than 20 percent of counties in the South Atlantic, Mountain, and Pacific fall in the top decile for the elderly cohort shifts, and not surprisingly, these divisions host popular retirement destinations such as the Oregon Coast, Southern Appalachians, and the Desert Southwest. In contrast, the East South Central, West South Central, and West North Central all have disproportionate shares of counties in the bottom decile of cohort shifts for the non-elderly, and these divisions are home to the Great Plains, Corn Belt, and the Mississippi Delta region, which have long struggled to retain their younger populations.

The geographic distribution presented above clearly indicates certain regions are more apt to benefit from the positive aspects associated with in-migration of elderly while other regions are likely to struggle with the consequences of out-migration of the non-elderly. Areas with higher levels of urban influence (those with micropolitan centers or adjacent to metropolitan regions) tend to have strong positive cohort shifts for the elderly, and relatively few of these counties fall in the bottom decile for the non-elderly (results available from the author on request). Combined, these two patterns indicate that counties more closely connected to urban centers are gaining elderly due to in-migration while simultaneously retaining larger shares of their non-elderly. In contrast, the most rural counties (non-core not adjacent) have more than their expected share of counties in the bottom decile for the non-elderly and many fewer counties in the top decile for elderly. In other words, these remote areas have an elderly population that is aging in place, and a non-elderly population that is declining faster than expected, likely through out-migration.These dynamics vary considerably by county type. Farm-dependent, persistent-poverty, and population-loss counties have higher concentrations of elderly due to more rapid decreases in their non-elderly populations. This is most pronounced in persistent-poverty and population-loss counties, more than 15 percent of which have a non-elderly

Table 20.2
Percent of nonmetro counties by census division falling in top and bottom decile

Division	Bottom Decile Non-elderly (%)	Top Decile Elderly (%)
New England	0.00	9.09
Mid-Atlantic	9.84	3.28
East North Central	6.87	2.29
West North Central	10.83	2.56
South Atlantic	4.30	21.85
East South Central	13.41	3.25
West South Central	15.29	6.73
Mountain	9.55	30.00
Pacific	1.47	27.94

Source: United States Census 2010

population declining at higher than expected rates. In contrast, 30 percent or more of recreation and retirement counties appear to be gaining older populations at higher than expected rates, and it is quite uncommon (fewer than 5 percent) for these types of counties to experience decreasing younger populations. This reflects the economic opportunities created by the arrival of retirees identified in earlier work (Deller 1995; Rogers and Woodward 1988; Rowles and Watkins 1993; Sastry 1992).

Implications of Population Aging and Elderly Concentration for Rural Communities

The aging of the baby boomers promises increasing numbers of rural elders. Moreover, as populations age, they show an increased propensity to move from urban to rural locations (Fuguitt, Beale, and Tordella 2002; Fuguitt and Heaton 1995; Wilson 1988), and estimates suggest nonmetropolitan counties could gain upwards of three million baby boomer migrants in the coming years (Nelson and Cromartie 2009). In the final section I discuss the implications of these trends and situates them in the context of neoliberalism and globalization. I take neoliberalism to be an economic and political philosophy that emphasizes the role of free markets, deregulation, privatization, and minimal state intervention beyond that which is necessary to ensure the unhindered operations of the market (Harvey 2005). In the discussion below I connect the impacts of population aging with different factors driving rural aging identified above, and emphasize implications for local economies and social landscapes.

Aging and Its Impacts on Local Economies

An aging population has the potential to generate growth in local economies because older people draw on retirement savings and contribute to the local economic base. Yet, it can also stress certain sectors such as healthcare, and elderly populations leaving the labor force present unique challenges for important rural industries, namely agriculture. In both cases, decreased state intervention in markets and increased individual responsibilities implicit under neoliberalism suggest rural economies will face a greater degree of economic uncertainty, more volatility, and potentially dramatic transformations as their populations age.

Rural and other communities with a greater prevalence of elders become increasingly dependent upon nonearnings income (social security, pensions, etc.). Individuals in their twenties derive over 90 percent of their income from wages and salaries; whereas seventy to seventy-four year olds derive over 80 percent from nonearnings sources (Nelson 2005). In 2009, 43 percent of personal income in nonmetropolitan America came from nonearnings sources compared with 34 percent for metropolitan counties. For 375 nonmetropolitan counties, the majority of personal income is from nonearnings sources (BEA 2012). Places with high dependence on nonearnings income vary geographically, from farm-dependent counties such as McPherson, Nebraska, and Prairie, Montana on the Plains, to amenity destinations like San Juan, Washington, and Teton, Wyoming. Furthermore, nonearnings income can contribute to a community's economic base in substantial ways (Nelson and Beyers 1998). Just as income derived by selling locally produced products to external markets brings income into a county economy, nonearnings income is typically derived from non-local sources. Pensions and dividends, interest, and rental income come from investments made in national and international stock markets, making these sources truly global in origin.

Given the ways retirement income can contribute to the local economic base, attracting retirees has been touted as a rural development strategy (Reeder 1998). Indeed, input-output analysis shows how a growing retirement population can lead to job creation, with estimates indicating that the spending of each retiree generates between one-third and one-half of a new job (Sastry 1992; Serow and Haas 1992; Serow 2003). Areas with high concentrations of elderly can enjoy heightened prosperity during a robust economy, as nonearnings payments increase during stock market expansion. Nowhere was this more evident than in the rural Mountain west during the 1990s, where counties with the highest dependence upon nonearnings income showed robust growth in terms of population and employment (Nelson and Beyers 1998; Shumway and Otterstrom 2010). Not surprisingly, many of these counties also have relatively high concentrations of elderly and are classified as retirement counties.

Recent market volatility has destabilized many of these formerly prosperous areas. As rural populations continue to age, rural communities will become increasingly vulnerable to stock market volatility. For example, Teton, Wyoming, where over 63 percent of personal income comes from dividends interest and rent, enjoyed incredible growth during the 1990s when the Dow Jones Industrial Average increased approximately fourfold. Yet, more recently, the DJIA has suffered dramatic losses as the global economy struggles to pull itself out of the Great Recession. Not surprisingly, the most recent estimates suggest the Teton, Wyoming area has experienced net out-migration over the last several years indicative of the volatility associated with rising dependence on nonearnings sources. As the elderly become increasingly concentrated in rural areas and, in turn, rural areas become more dependent on nonearnings income, economic volatility will increasingly impact these counties.

Social security, in its current form, has the potential to offer economic stability in areas with concentrations of elderly because it provides a defined benefit over time regardless of market conditions. However, neoliberal approaches to the challenges facing social security may render rural people and places even *more* prone to economic volatility. Many Republicans advocate privatizing at least a portion of social security, and the rise of groups like the Tea Party emphasizing smaller government and reduced spending embrace privatization schemes. Under such plans, individuals would be allowed to invest portions of their social security contributions in private investment accounts, and this shift from state support to personal responsibilities is a hallmark of neoliberalism. Under such privatization plans, rural people and places could be exposed to greater economic risk and volatility from global market conditions because of their increased concentrations of elderly and dependence on nonearnings income.

Population aging also presents challenges in key rural industries such as agriculture. While the overall level of employment in farming declined steadily throughout the twentieth century, agriculture remains dominant in terms of rural land-use (Leonard, Deane, and Gutmann 2011). More importantly, rural aging and the future of agricultural lands are intricately linked. Since the 1970s, there has been a dramatic increase in the proportion of older farmers to the point where in 2007, 30 percent of farm operators were over the age of sixty-five. Roughly another third were over fifty-five, and combined this represents the largest proportion of older farm operators in United States history (Ahearn 2011). As these farmers continue to age, the future of their operations and farming in general become complicated in several ways.

The composition of assets differs considerably between farm and non-farm households in the United States, and so the ways farm households plan for retirement also differ. The average US household's single largest economic asset is its principal residence (29 percent) followed by stocks, mutual funds, and other financial vehicles (21 percent). Business equity comprises a relatively small portion (17 percent) of the average household's portfolio, yet it is the largest asset for farm households—it represents 54 percent of the average farm household's portfolio, more than triple that of the average household (Mishra 2005). In contrast, only 7 percent of farm households' portfolios are in stocks, mutual funds, and other financial assets. These variations in asset composition have implications for how aging farmers plan for retirement, a somewhat ambiguous concept to farmers in and of itself (Leonard and Gutmann 2006).

Over a typical working career, non-farmers contribute to social security and other retirement savings vehicles (e.g., IRAs), and then draw upon these assets to support themselves in old age. While most farmers do contribute in some way to retirement savings, most of their wealth is tied up in the equity of the farm enterprise. Therefore, their options when facing retirement are somewhat different (Leonard and Gutmann 2006). They may continue operating their farm as always, or perhaps continue farming less intensively (i.e., shifting from crop production to ranching, or enrolling land in the Conservation Reserve Program). Alternatively, they may gradually transfer farm assets to a younger generation, provided the farm operation is sufficiently large to support both the younger family and the older household in retirement. A final possibility is to sell or lease farm holdings to other farm operators or real estate developers. Since the pace of exit from farming greatly exceeds its rate of entry (Gale 2003), this final possibility results in increasing farm size as agricultural lands become controlled by fewer farm operators. This trend has been evident for decades (Lyson 2004; Vias and Nelson 2006) but is likely to accelerate as farm operators age.

When surveyed, most farm operators indicate a preference for transferring the farm operations to younger family members (Leonard and Gutmann 2006), but past demographic shifts and current tax policies challenge this. First, intergenerational transfers require a willing and able younger generation to carry on, but decades of youth out-migration from rural areas (Johnson et al. 2005) have reduced this pool. Moreover, those willing to continue farming must have the financial resources to compensate siblings or other heirs for their share of the business assets. These complications increase the likelihood that, when facing retirement, older farm operators will sell or lease their land to existing operations in the area leading to further consolidation of farmland into fewer farms. Second, intergenerational transfers of farm assets face the prospect of paying capital gains taxes (albeit at somewhat reduced rates) on the appreciation of farmland values. These capital gains create barriers to transferring farm assets from one generation to the next, complicating future farmland management: "Among farm operators who plan to retire in the next five years, about a fifth reported that they plan to rent out the farm, and another fifth plan to sell the farm. The remaining operators plan to turn over operations to others or convert their land to other uses" (Mishra 2005, 18).

Rising neoliberalism and its influence on policy are likely to further impact the intersections between aging and its influence on agricultural lands in a variety of ways. First, the geography of farm consolidation is uneven with greater degrees of farm consolidation in regions with more persistent population loss (Leonard and Gutmann 2006; Vias and Nelson 2006). In particular, the Great Plains demonstrates some of the most dramatic farm consolidation, and this has been linked to heavy dependence on federal programs (Goetz and Debertin 1996). Moreover, as shown, the Great Plains has some of the highest concentrations of elderly due to high youth out-migration. With increased uncertainty of the future of federal farm subsidies under neoliberal regimes emphasizing reduced government interventions in markets, the pace of exit from farming and farm consolidation may both accelerate, especially in places like the Great Plains that are heavily reliant on these government transfers. At the same time, neoliberal thinking could result in an overall reduction in taxes on intergenerational transfers of farm assets, which has the potential to enable younger generations to continue farming as their elderly parents retire.

Aging and Its Impacts on Rural Social Landscapes

Aging in rural America has distinct implications on social dimensions of rural communities. Scholars have examined the strength of social ties for rural elderly populations, and social integration has been linked to elderly residents' well-being. At the same time, aging may in fact be linked to other forms of demographic heterogeneity in rural America, including drawing immigrants to rural destinations and reshaping family structures. Once more, this heterogeneity can be linked to broader forces of globalization and neoliberal restructuring as Brown outlines in the introduction to this section.

Elderly integration into the social fabric of communities has long interested sociologists and gerontologists (see, for example, Liu and Besser 2003). This is especially true for rural scholars because of a perception that rural residents, and the elderly in particular, rely more heavily than their urban counterparts on strong informal ties embedded within the community. Such ties can be quite beneficial to rural elders because there are demonstrated connections between informal social ties within a community and distinct health outcomes. Rural residents with higher instances of face-to-face visits with friends, relatives, and neighbors reported higher levels of subjective well-being when compared with urban and suburban residents (Mair and Thivierge-Rikard 2010). Moreover, the outcomes extend beyond the subjective, as places with higher indications of social capital have lower age-adjusted mortality rates (Yang, Jensen, and Haran 2011). Therefore, social integration can literally enhance community vitality. Stronger social ties among rural elders may become an increasingly important community asset within the context of neoliberalism and its policy influence. As government social services such as Medicare come under fire from neoliberal reformers emphasizing individual responsibilities, informal support systems provided by family and friends will likely become more important in maintaining healthy communities. At the same time, migration dynamics and economic restructuring are reshaping family structures and the informal social ties they enable. Census 2000 revealed a growing share of the United States population over age thirty residing with grandparents, with the highest concentrations in rural South and pockets of the Plains (Simmons and Dye 2003). There is a need for new research on differences between urban and rural areas in the rise of these intergenerational households and the implications they have for social relations.

The complex forces of rural aging have consequences for social integration in rural communities that are likely to vary across space. In their 2006 study, Glasgow and Brown survey elderly residents in rural retirement destinations and find very minor differences between elderly in-migrants and longer-term residents with respect to social integration. On some measures (attending cultural events, exercise classes, and participation in sports), recent migrants participate at higher rates. Places that are aging as a result of elderly in-migration may benefit from relatively high levels of social integration and the positive outcomes associated with it. Yet, when out-migration of youth drives rural population aging, social integration, informal ties, and population stability may be compromised. Population stability plays a critical role in shaping the positive health outcomes associated with strong social capital. As Yang et al. (2011, 369) argue, "when a place has a low turnover rate and safe living environment, residents have more opportunities to know each other, devote themselves to community development, organize voluntary activities, and cultivate common interests. Accordingly, the degree of mutual trust and reciprocity in a place will rise and be conducive to high civic engagement, and a strong collective conscience. In turn, these may be related to more tangible resource support, better mental health, stronger immune systems, and other proximate determinants of physical health and mortality." As globalization and neoliberalism continue to shape the geographic structure of the rural economy, farm consolidation and restructuring in the manufacturing sectors (Parker, Kusmin, and Marre 2010) are likely to accelerate further, drawing employment opportunities for younger generations away from the countryside. Such processes will amplify the effects of out-migration and its impacts on social connectedness in rural communities.

Apart from age-specific internal migration, there are considerably more ways in which rural aging influences social landscapes. Over the last thirty years, rural populations have become increasingly diverse (Jones, Kandel, and Parker 2007), and aging populations are linked to this heterogeneity. The concentration of elderly in any particular place can stimulate employment growth in specific sectors, attracting additional migration streams. Not surprisingly, immigrants (particularly Latinos) have been attracted to many of these emerging labor market opportunities created by the growing retirement population (Nelson and Nelson 2011; Nelson, Lee, and Nelson 2009), and some have argued that immigration policy can be intentionally used as a mechanism to respond to rising labor demand in sectors such as healthcare (Lowell, Martin, and Stone 2010). As globalization creates an increasingly integrated transnational workforce, the connections between aging rural populations and immigrant labor will only strengthen.

Conclusions

For decades and today, rural areas have been home to larger shares of elderly than urban areas. Yet, the distribution of elderly populations across the rural United States is quite uneven, varying by region, urban influence, and type of place. Rural portions of the northern Great Plains, South Atlantic, and Pacific divisions tend to have higher concentrations of elderly when compared to other regions, especially the Rocky Mountains. Moreover, the concentration of elderly differs by degree of urban influence, with the most rural regions having the highest concentrations of those sixty-five and over. These remote rural areas far from any large city have nearly 50 percent greater concentrations of elderly when compared with the entire United States.

The demographic processes producing high concentrations of elderly are quite distinct across space. Regions such as the Southeast and Southwest, traditional retirement destinations, tend to have concentrations of elderly resulting from higher than expected growth of their older cohorts. In contrast, farm-dependent regions and those characterized by chronic population loss, such as the Great Plains, have concentrations of elderly largely resulting from higher than expected declines in the non-elderly. Such a situation is also more common at the most rural end of the urban influence spectrum.

Finally, there are distinct implications of a concentrated elderly population on rural communities, ranging widely from the social to the economic. Farming, long considered the economic backbone of rural America, is facing a critical crossroads as farm operators age rapidly. Decades of out-migration from farm-dependent regions have decreased the pool of younger farmers, raising questions about the inter-generational transfer of farm operations. This intersection of demographics and economics has distinct implications for rural farm-dependent communities as many of these aging farm operators consider their options for retirement. At the same time, other areas have turned to attracting retirees as a development strategy, as retirement income can contribute to a community's economic base. Areas with concentrations of elderly resulting from more rapid growth of older populations than expected may see improved economic conditions. Layered on top of these economic impacts of rural aging is a complex web of social implications. Scholarship to date suggests that elders' social integration appears to be somewhat higher in rural communities, and this may have beneficial impacts on health outcomes for the rural elderly. However, persistent out-migration of the non-elderly may undermine inter-generational social networks in rural communities compromising their ability to draw on valuable social capital for support. More recently, immigrants from abroad are arriving in certain rural destinations at previously unthinkable rates, and, in part, these immigrants are responding to opportunities created by an aging population. Immigrants have arrived to fill jobs in agriculture, construction, healthcare, and household services created by either retirement spending or vacated by out-migrating younger workers. Thus, the rural elderly are but one demographic group in an increasingly diverse rural population.

Aging within the "global countryside" (Woods 2007) presents several critical questions within the context of globalization and neoliberal restructuring for future scholars. I close with a few questions directly connected to themes raised above. First, how might social security reform impact rural regions, as elderly populations become increasingly dependent on this source of income, and what new forms of economic volatility are rural regions susceptible to as individual retirement plans based on investments in global stock markets become more common vehicles for retirement saving? Second, how might a downsized USDA and reduced income support for farmers reshape agriculture and farm transfer from older to younger generations? Third, as off-farm economic opportunities such as manufacturing in rural areas face increasing pressure to move offshore in search of lower production costs (Vias and Nelson 2006), what strategies do aging farm households employ to supplement farm income, and how do family structures adapt to these new economic realities? Fourth, given labor mobility as a hallmark of globalization (Castells and Miller 1998; Harvey 1989), how do rural areas maintain social cohesion while simultaneously facing increasing flows of people (retirees, youth, and immigrants) both into and out of their communities? Finally, I have treated "the elderly" as a singular group, yet there are certainly variations within elderly populations, most notably between the "young-old" and the "old-old" (Litwak and Longino 1987). Future work should consider this distinction and compare the concentrations of young-old and old-old populations. Given that the old-old will likely draw more frequently on medical services and social networks as they age, it will be crucial to have a geographical understanding of these different segments of the elderly population. Clearly, the aging countryside is a reality with distinct social and economic implications that require targeted research to better understand.

Notes

1 A location quotient is a measure of relative concentration comparing an individual county with the overall benchmark region, in this case the United States. The location quotient for the population over age sixty-five in any particular county (i) is computed as:

$$Q_i = \frac{\%Over65_i}{\%Over65_{UnitedState}}$$

Values greater than 1.00 indicate the population over age sixty-five is more concentrated in that county than in the United States as a whole.

2 In fact, the higher concentration of elderly in most nonmetropolitan counties results from a combination of forces including aging in place, but given the dominance of aging in place and its consistency across space, I focus on the differences between in- and out-migration streams because these factors show the most geographic variability.

References

Ahearn, Mary. 2011. "Farm Household Economics and Well-Being: Beginning Farmers, Demographics, and Labor Allocations." US Department of Agriculture, Economic Research Service. http://www.ers.usda.gov/topics/farm-economy/farm-household-well-being.aspx.

BEA. 2012. "Regional Economic Accounts." Department of Commerce, Bureau of Economic Analysis. Accessed 29 March 2012. http://www.bea.gov/regional/index.htm.

Brown, David L., Benjamin C. Bolender, Laszlo J. Kulcsar, Nina Glasgow, and Scott Sanders. 2011. "Intercounty Variability of Net Migration at Older Ages as a Path-Dependent Process." *Rural Sociology* 76 (1): 44–73. http://dx.doi.org/10.1111/j.1549-0831.2010.00034.x.

Castells, Stephen, and Mark J. Miller. 1998. "The next Waves: The Globalisation of International Migration." In *The Age of Migration: International Population Movements in the Modern World*, ed. Stephen Castells and Mark J. Miller, 104–40. New York: Guildford.

Deller, S.C. 1995. "Economic-Impact of Retirement Migration." *Economic Development Quarterly* 9 (1): 25–38. http://dx.doi.org/10.1177/089124249500900103.

Erickson, Lance D., Vaughn R. A. Call, and Ralph B. Brown. 2012. "SOS—Satisfied or Stuck, Why Older Rural Residents Stay Put: Aging in Place or Stuck in Place in Rural Utah." *Rural Sociology* 77 (3): 408–34. http://dx.doi.org/10.1111/j.1549-0831.2012.00084.x.

Fuguitt, Glenn, Calvin Beale, and Stephen Tordella. 2002. "Recent Trends in Older Population Change and Migration for Nonmetro Areas, 1970–2000." *Rural America* 17: 11–9.

Fuguitt, Glenn V., and Timothy B. Heaton. 1995. "The Impact of Migration on the Nonmetropolitan Population Age Structure, 1960–1990." *Population Research and Policy Review* 14 (2): 215–32. http://dx.doi.org/10.1007/BF01074459.

Gale, H. Frederick. 2003. "Age-Specific Patterns of Exit and Entry in U.S. Farming, 1978–1997." *Review of Agricultural Economics* 25 (1): 168–86. http://dx.doi.org/10.1111/1467-9353.00052.

Glasgow, Nina, and Edna Berry, eds. 2013. *Rural Aging in the 21st Century*. Dordrecht, Netherlands: Springer. http://dx.doi.org/10.1007/978-94-007-5567-3.

Glasgow, Nina, and David Brown. 2006. "Social Integration among Older in-migrants in Nonmetropolitan Retirement Destination Counties: Establishing New Ties." In *Population Change and Rural Society*, ed. William Kandel and David Brown, 177–96. Dordrecht, Netherlands: Springer. http://dx.doi.org/10.1007/1-4020-3902-6_8.

Goetz, Stephen J., and David L. Debertin. 1996. "Rural Population Decline in the 1980s: Impacts of Farm Structure and Federal Farm Programs." *American Journal of Agricultural Economics* 78 (3): 517–29. http://dx.doi.org/10.2307/1243270.

Harvey, David. 1989. *The Condition of Postmodernity*. Cambridge: Basil Blackwell.

Harvey, David. 2005. *A Brief History of Neoliberalism*. New York: Oxford University Press.

Howden, Lindsay, and Julie Meyer. 2011. *2010 Census Briefs: Age and Sex Composition: 2010*. United States Census Bureau. Report Number C2010BR-03. http://www.census.gov/prod/cen2010/briefs/c2010br-03.pdf.

Johnson, Kenneth M. 2011. "The Continuing Incidence of Natural Decrease in American Counties." *Rural Sociology* 76 (1): 74–100. http://dx.doi.org/10.1111/j.1549-0831.2010.00036.x.

Johnson, Kenneth M., Paul R. Voss, Roger B. Hammer, Glenn V. Fuguitt, and Scott McNiven. November 2005. "Temporal and Spatial Variation in Age-Specific Net Migration in the United States." *Demography* 42 (4): 791–812. http://dx.doi.org/10.1353/dem.2005.0033. Medline:16463922.

Jones, Carol A., William Kandel, and Timothy Parker. 2007. "Population Dynamics Are Changing the Profile of Rural Areas." *Amber Waves* 5: 30–5.

Keating, Norah, and Judith Phillips. 2008. "A Critical Human Ecology Perspective on Rural Ageing." In *Rural Ageing: A Good Place to Grow Old?* ed. Norah Keating, xii–10. London: Policy Press. http://dx.doi.org/10.1332/policypress/9781861349019.003.0001.

Leonard, Susan, Glenn Deane, and Myron Gutmann. 1 June 2011. "Household and Farm Transitions in Environmental Context." *Population and Environment* 32 (4): 287–317. http://dx.doi.org/10.1007/s11111-010-0118-9. Medline:21643468.

Leonard, Susan, and Myron Gutmann. 2006. "Land Use and Transfer Plans in the U.S. Great Plains." *Great Plains Research* 16: 181–94.

Litwak, Eugene, and Charles Longino Jr. June 1987. "Migration Patterns among the Elderly: A Developmental Perspective." *Gerontologist* 27 (3): 266–72. http://dx.doi.org/10.1093/geront/27.3.266. Medline:3609792.

Liu, Amy, and Terry Besser. 2003. "Social Capital and Participation in Community Improvement Activities by Elderly Residents in Small Towns and Rural Communities." *Rural Sociology* 68 (3): 343–65. http://dx.doi.org/10.1111/j.1549-0831.2003.tb00141.x.

Lowell, B. Lindsay, Susan Martin, and Robyn Stone. 2010. "Ageing and Care Giving in the United States: Policy Contexts and the Immigrant Workforce." *Journal of Population Ageing* 3 (1–2): 59–82. http://dx.doi.org/10.1007/s12062-010-9029-x.

Lyson, Thomas. 2004. *Civic Agriculture: Reconnecting Farm, Food, and Community.* Medford, MA: Tufts University. http://dx.doi.org/10.1526/0036011041730464.

Mair, Christine, and R.V. Thivierge-Rikard. 2010. "The Strength of Strong Ties for Older Rural Adults: Regional Distinctions in the Relationship between Social Interaction and Subjective Well-Being." *International Journal of Aging & Human Development* 70 (2): 119–43. http://dx.doi.org/10.2190/AG.70.2.b. Medline:20405586.

Mishra, Ashok. 2005. "How Do US Farmers Plan for Retirement?" *Amber Waves* 3: 13–8.

Morrill, Richard L. 1995. "Aging in Place, Age Specific Migration and Natural Decrease." *Annals of Regional Science* 29 (1): 41–66. http://dx.doi.org/10.1007/BF01580362. Medline:12319442.

Murray, Christopher J.L., Sandeep C. Kulkarni, Catherine Michaud, Niels Tomijima, Maria T. Bulzacchelli, Terrell J. Iandiorio, and Majid Ezzati. September 2006. "Eight Americas: Investigating Mortality Disparities across Races, Counties, and Race-Counties in the United States." *PLoS Medicine* 3 (9): e260. http://dx.doi.org/10.1371/journal.pmed.0030260. Medline:16968116.

Nelson, Lise, and Peter B. Nelson. 2011. "The Global Rural: Gentrification and Linked Migration in the Rural USA." *Progress in Human Geography* 35 (4): 441–59. http://dx.doi.org/10.1177/0309132510380487.

Nelson, Peter B. 2005. "Migration and the Regional Redistribution of Nonearnings Income in the United States: Metropolitan and Nonmetropolitan Perspectives from 1975 to 2000." *Environment & Planning A* 37 (9): 1613–36. http://dx.doi.org/10.1068/a37170.

Nelson, Peter B., and William B. Beyers. 1998. "Using Economic Base Models to Explain New Trends in Rural Income." *Growth and Change* 29 (3): 295–318. http://dx.doi.org/10.1111/0017-4815.00089.

Nelson, Peter B., and John B. Cromartie. 2009. *Baby Boom Migration and Its Impact on Rural America.* Economic Research Service, US Department of Agriculture. Report Number 79. www.ers.usda.gov/publications/err79/err79.pdf.

Nelson, Peter B., Ahn Wei Lee, and Lise Nelson. 2009. "Linking Baby Boomer and Hispanic Migration Streams into Rural America—A Multi-scaled Approach." *Population Space and Place* 15 (3): 277–93. http://dx.doi.org/10.1002/psp.520.

Parker, Timothy, Lorin Kusmin, and Alexander Marre. 2010. "Economic Recovery: Lessons Learned from Previous Recessions." *Amber Waves* 8: 42–47.

Plane, David. 1992. "Age-Composition Change and the Geographical Dynamics of Interregional Migration in the U.S." *Annals of the Association of American Geographers* 82 (1): 64–85. http://dx.doi.org/10.1111/j.1467-8306.1992.tb01898.x.

Rathge, Richard, and Kenneth Johnson. 2005. *Policy Brief: Does Rural Great Plains Depopulation Reflect Failed Public Policy.* North Dakota State University. Report Number 2005–01. http://www.ndsu.edu/sdc/publications/reports/GPPolicyBrief_1_03_06.pdf.

Reeder, Richard. 1998. *Retiree Attraction Policies for Rural America.* US Department of Agriculture, Economic Research Service. Report Number AIB#741. http://www.ers.usda.gov/publications/aib741/AIB741a.PDF.

Rogers, Andrei, and Jennifer Woodward. 1988. "The Sources of Regional Elderly Population Growth: Migration and Aging-in-Place." *Professional Geographer* 40 (4): 450–9. http://dx.doi.org/10.1111/j.0033-0124.1988.00450.x.

Rowles, Graham, and John Watkins. Fall 1993. "Elderly Migration and Development in Small Communities." *Growth and Change* 24 (4): 509–38. http://dx.doi.org/10.1111/j.1468-2257.1993.tb00136.x. Medline:12287091.

Sastry, M. Lakshminarayan. Winter 1992. "Estimating the Economic Impacts of Elderly Migration: An Input-Output Analysis." *Growth and Change* 23 (1): 54–79. http://dx.doi.org/10.1111/j.1468-2257.1992.tb00572.x. Medline:12284915.

Serow, William J. December 2003. "Economic Consequences of Retiree Concentrations: A Review of North American Studies." *Gerontologist* 43 (6): 897–903. http://dx.doi.org/10.1093/geront/43.6.897. Medline:14704389.

Serow, William J., and William H. Haas. 1992. "Measuring the Economic Impact of Retirement Migration: The Case of Western North Carolina." *Journal of Applied Gerontology* 11 (2): 200–15. http://dx.doi.org/10.1177/073346489201100206.

Shumway, J. Matthew, and Samuel Otterstrom. 2010. "US Regional Income Change and Migration: 1995–2004." *Population Space and Place* 16: 483–97.

Simmons, Tavia, and Jane Dye. 2003. *Grandparents Living with Grandchildren: 2000.* United States Census Bureau. Report Number C2KBR-31. http://www.census.gov/prod/2003pubs/c2kbr-31.pdf.

Vias, Alex, and Peter Nelson. 2006. "Changing Rural Livelihoods." In *The Population of Rural America: Demographic Research for a New Century*, ed. William Kandel and David Brown, 75–102. New York: Kluwer. http://dx.doi.org/10.1007/1-4020-3902-6_4.

Wilson, Franklin D. February 1988. "Components of Change in Migration and Destination-Propensity Rates for Metropolitan and Nonmetropolitan Areas: 1935–1980." *Demography* 25 (1): 129–39. http://dx.doi.org/10.2307/2061482. Medline:3169314.

Wilson, Steven. 2009. *Population Dynamics of the Great Plains: 1950–2007.* Report Number P25-1137. http://www.census.gov/prod/2009pubs/p25-1137.pdf.

Woods, Michael. 2007. "Engaging the Global Countryside: Globalization, Hybridity and the Reconstitution of Rural Place." *Progress in Human Geography* 31 (4): 485–507. http://dx.doi.org/10.1177/0309132507079503.

Yang, Tse-Chuan, Leif Jensen, and Murali Haran. 2011. "Social Capital and Human Mortality: Explaining the Rural Paradox with County-Level Mortality Data." *Rural Sociology* 76 (3): 347–74. http://dx.doi.org/10.1111/j.1549-0831.2011.00055.x.

CHAPTER 21

New Rural Immigrant Destinations: Research for the 2010s

Martha Crowley and Kim Ebert

Introduction

For more than a century, immigrants entering the United States have tended to join their co-nationals in urban gateways such as New York, Los Angeles, and Chicago. The past few decades, however, have witnessed growing numbers of immigrants flowing to alternative destinations, including rural parts of the Midwest and Southeast, with Latinos and especially Mexicans leading the way (Hirschman and Massey 2008; Kandel and Cromartie 2004). This geographic diversification of Latinos has transformed the demographic landscape of rural America. Just 3.5 percent of the nonmetropolitan population in 1990, Latinos were responsible for 26 percent of rural growth during the 1990s and 46 percent of growth occurring between 2000 and 2006, when their population share reached 6.3 percent (Johnson and Lichter 2012; Saenz 2008). Furthermore, Latino population growth is gaining momentum in new rural destinations as evidenced by population gains attributable to natural increase (a surplus of births versus deaths) relative to in-migration (Johnson and Lichter 2012).

In many places, these shifts have reversed or ameliorated rural population declines due to youth out-migration, aging, and deaths of long-time residents (Donato et al. 2007; Johnson and Lichter 2012). Yet receiving communities have often struggled to accommodate newcomers' educational, health, and social service needs, owing largely to language barriers and cultural differences (Griffith 2008; Stull and Broadway 2001; Kandel and Parrado 2005). Their presence, moreover, has challenged historical black-white racial dynamics, as most new rural immigrant destinations lack recent immigration histories and exposure to residents outside the bounds of their traditional race/ethnic categories (Lichter 2012; Marrow 2011; Winders and Smith 2010).

In this chapter, we review research pertaining to the causes and consequences of this demographic shift. We begin with a discussion of global political, economic, and industrial changes contributing to the formation of new rural immigrant destinations and how the economic recession has impacted migration to and from these areas. We then review research on the implications of demographic change for receiving communities, particularly with regard to institutional strains, economic impacts, intergroup relations, and political activity. We conclude with recommendations for policy conducive to long-term community well-being and avenues for future research.

New Destination Formation

Formation of new rural immigrant destinations reflects numerous interrelated political, economic, and social shifts occurring at global, regional, and local levels that, together, have reshaped the nature and balance of incentives associated with crossing the border for work and settlement in particular locales (Massey and Capoferro 2008; McConnell 2008). The 1986 Immigration Reform and Control Act (IRCA), which granted amnesty and thus geographic mobility to three million people, including 2.3 million Mexicans, is perhaps the most oft-cited factor contributing to the rise of new rural immigrant destinations. This legislation not only facilitated immigrant movement away from traditional enclaves, but also promoted exit from immigrant-saturated urban labor markets by indirectly contributing to deterioration of wages—a function of increased supply of legal labor and employers' increased reliance on subcontractors to avoid new sanctions for hiring undocumented workers (Durand, Massey, and Charvet 2000; Massey and Capoferro 2008; McConnell 2008).

Just as important, however, were economic, political, and social shifts propelling individuals out of Mexico, away from traditional US destinations, and toward new settlement areas. Around the time the legislation was passed, "push" factors were emerging in both Mexico and in California, where immigrants from Mexico often settled. By the mid-1980s, the Mexican government's liberalization of the economy had increased flexibility for corporations in hiring, firing, and setting wages, and promoted low-cost (low-wage) *maquiladora* export production, which in turn contributed to job insecurity, wage stagnation, and underemployment among workers (Canales 2003; Smith 2000). Economic recession associated with the Mexican government's 1994 devaluation of the peso further eroded wages and employment opportunity—prompting individuals in places and population segments outside traditional migration circuits (including middle-class workers without previous migration experience) to seek employment in the United States (Canales 2003; Durand, Massey, and Charvet 2000). At the same time, conditions for immigrants were worsening in California, where approximately half of Mexican immigrants had settled in previous years (Durand, Massey, and Charvet 2000). Anti-immigrant sentiment rooted in economic recession following end-of-Cold War cutbacks in defense spending—and fueled by Governor Pete Wilson's efforts to revive a flagging 1994 reelection campaign—culminated in the 1994 passage of Proposition 187, a ballot initiative that sought to deny social services to undocumented immigrants (Massey and Capoferro 2008). Although most of its provisions were later ruled unconstitutional, the law conveyed that undocumented immigrants in particular were unwelcome.

These changes coincided with dramatic increases in demand for workers in low-wage, low-skill jobs outside traditional settlement areas—especially in the meat industry, where consumer demand was increasing but industrial restructuring and wage reductions rooted in a competitive global market had driven away native-born workers (Kandel and Parrado 2005). Firms specialized (slaughtering and processing a single species, for example), and larger ones used economies of scale to produce great quantities of product at lower prices. Smaller firms were driven out of business, and larger ones devised productivity-enhancing methods that routinized work, deskilled tasks, increased pace of production, and reduced wages. Resulting labor shortages were exacerbated by firms' tendency to relocate to less populous rural areas, which offered an escape from unionized labor and savings on land, taxes, and transportation, but lacked the needed supply of workers willing to work in demoralizing, hazardous conditions for such low pay (Kandel and Parrado 2005).

Rural communities with no recent history of immigration saw immigrant numbers soar as Latinos relocated to fill these labor vacuums. Latinos, especially Mexican nationals, moved to the rural Midwest for jobs in meat and poultry processing; to the rural Southeast for employment in poultry, meat, and fish processing; and to rural Arkansas and east Texas for poultry processing jobs (Artz, Jackson, and Orazem 2010; Gozdziak and Martin 2005; Kandel and Parrado 2005; Zúñiga and Hernández-León 2005)—some capitalizing on networks and skills developed in their native Mexico (Sanderson and Painter 2011; see also Farmer and Moon 2009; McConnell 2008). Opportunities in other non-durable manufacturing industries (e.g., oil, timber, furniture, carpeting, and textiles in the Southeast) and servicing the amenity-driven economies of the Mountain West and West encouraged relocation to new rural destinations, as well (Donato et al. 2008; Jensen 2006). These changes coincided with a 1993 to 1994 tightening of border controls around San Diego and El Paso, which encouraged undocumented immigrants to enter the United States further to the east and to stay longer and send for families rather than incur additional expense and risk of repeated border crossing (Hirschman and Massey 2008; Massey and Capoferro 2008). Once sufficient numbers of immigrants arrived, natural growth and processes of "cumulative causation"—wherein incorporation of family and friends extends the base of migration to such a degree that the original push and pull factors fade in importance—took hold (Johnson and Lichter 2012; Leach and Bean 2008).

Expanding social networks and positive assessments of quality of life (see Garcia 2009; Marrow 2011) may help to explain why new rural immigrant destinations continue to attract newcomers, despite what appear to be diminishing economic incentives. Controlling for metro/nonmetro status, residence outside the Southwest reduced odds of poverty among Mexicans in 2000, and in 2005/2006 rural Latino immigrants in new destination states had higher rates of full-time employment and lower poverty, despite lower levels of education and US experience, compared to those living in traditional destinations such as California and Texas (Crowley, Lichter, and Qian 2006; Koball et al. 2008a). Poverty rates are converging, however, having declined more slowly in new than in traditional rural destinations (Koball et al. 2008b). Indeed, after controlling for individual characteristics, new immigrant destinations are associated with *lower* economic well-being compared to other place types, with a widening gap favoring urban over rural settlement on most dimensions (Kandel et al. 2011).

Some have wondered whether economic recession might encourage immigrants to return to their countries of origin. Because immigrants living in new rural destinations comprise a mostly marginalized and vulnerable workforce, they are disproportionately subject to the whims of global economic change and industrial restructuring (Brown and Schafft 2011; Lichter 2012). Because they are mobile, they could conceivably have fled new destinations as economic conditions deteriorated. Immigrants indeed experienced sharp increases in unemployment following the 2008 recession—a change that seems to have slowed immigration into the United States without prompting mass departures among those who arrived prior to the downturn (Papademetriou and Terrazas 2009). In the two years following the first signs of economic trouble ahead (2006 to 2008), however, Latino immigrants became more likely to migrate from new destinations to more traditional destinations, suggesting a need to reassess demographic trends and their impacts further into the economic recovery (Parrado and Kandel 2011b).

Community Impacts: Variations, Intergroup Relations, and Politics

Of course, economic incentives are not the only reasons that immigrants have moved into new destinations. Safer neighborhoods and a quiet, rural way of life are some of the non-economic factors immigrants use to explain their decisions to move (Garcia 2009). Coincidentally, immigrants' impacts on these aspects of community life have been among long-time residents' chief concerns. In many communities, the initial response was marked by fear that that poorly educated Latinos migrating for low-wage jobs would increase local levels of poverty, welfare dependence, and crime. Compared to rural whites and African Americans, rural Latinos indeed have less education, are younger, have higher birth rates, and are often poor despite low levels of unemployment (Saenz 2008). Yet, concerns about local economic upheaval and rising crime have not materialized, at least at the aggregate level. Rural counties with high rates of Latino growth had lower rates of poverty and public assistance both before and after Latino influxes and larger declines in crime during the 1990s than did those without significant Latino increases (Crowley and Lichter 2009). To the degree that Latino population growth is associated with poverty or inequality in new rural destinations, it is more a matter of local employment structure than the presence of Latinos—expansion of low-wage jobs having attracted low-skill workers, not vice versa (Broadway 2007; Parrado and Kandel 2010). Latino consumers have revitalized rural economies by spending dollars locally and opening mom and pop stores that cater to newcomers (Kasarda and Johnson 2006). State-level investigations have documented a net positive impact of Latino presence, which has enabled expansion of the economic sectors where they are concentrated (Capps et al. 2007; Waslin 2008).

Aggregate data can mask variations across or within communities, however. Although local economies have benefitted from large influxes of Latino immigrants, strains are apparent in other institutional contexts, especially education and health care. Sharp increases in proportions of school-age children with limited English proficiency represent a key strain on rural schools, which were markedly ill equipped to address language barriers when newcomers began to arrive (Artz, Jackson, and Orazem 2010; Broadway 2007; Crowley and Lichter 2009; Wainer 2006). Some states have come forward with additional funding to cover these expenses, but declining test scores attributable to the presence of newcomers can lead to withdrawal of needed funds in the era of No Child Left Behind (Broadway 2007; Griffith 2008; Kandel and Parrado 2006). Whether long-time residents will continue to invest in education as the proportion Latino in the school-age population grows is unknown (Burton et al. 2013).

Strains are also particularly evident with respect to health and health care. Poverty, especially child poverty, is high among rural Latinos (Burton et al. 2013). Although immigrants are generally healthier than native populations owing to selection bias, adults often suffer from conditions associated with harsh working conditions and economic hardship, such as respiratory problems, chronic stress, sleep deprivation, and poor nutrition (Broadway 2007; Dalla, Cramer, and Stanek 2002; Jensen 2006). Latino children, too, face health challenges rooted in intersecting domains of disadvantage (poverty, minority racial/ethnic status, rurality), including food insecurity, poor nutrition, infectious diseases, exposure to environmental hazards, and familial stress (Burton et al. 2013). Lower rates of health insurance, social isolation, lack of transportation to clinics, and undocumented immigrants' fear of discovery and deportation discourage newcomers from taking advantage of available services, leading many to forego prenatal care, immunizations, and other preventative care in rural areas (Cristancho et al. 2008; Erwin 2003; Harari, Davis, and Heisler 2008; Jensen 2006). Providers are able to meet newcomers' needs in some rural places partially as a result of federal funding for urgent and primary care for uninsured people (Casey, Blewett, and Call 2004). Yet, they often have difficulty providing adequate translation services, which is a further impediment to health care and a potential violation of immigrants' civil rights (Casey, Blewett, and Call 2004; Cristancho et al. 2008; Griffith 2008; Perez 2003).

Communities have been varied in their responses to immigrant influxes and associated strains. Some have responded with anti-immigrant sentiment and have engaged in outright hostility toward immigrant newcomers (Fennelly and Federico 2008; Millard, Chapa, and McConnell 2004). Hazelton, Pennsylvania's Illegal Immigration Relief Act, for example, targeted unauthorized immigrants in their homes and workplaces by requiring all tenants of rental properties to obtain a license, and all employees to have their legal status verified by the town. More commonly, communities have avoided overt antagonism, responding instead with ambivalence (Culver 2004; Jensen 2006; Shultz 2008; Sizemore 2004). Some communities have endeavored to embrace newcomers. While these sometimes can result in superficial celebrations of stereotypical Mexican culture (Shutika 2011), they have, on occasion, involved in-depth explorations of newcomers' background, motivations, and needs, with local leaders taking great care to promote mutual understanding between residents. Such was the case in Marshalltown, Iowa, where leaders ventured to Villachuato, Mexico, to learn more about the backgrounds of those recently arrived. Finding few jobs, harsh living conditions, and limited educational opportunities for children, they gained an understanding of why migrants sought better opportunities and improved living conditions elsewhere, and they used this knowledge to bridge social divides at home (Grey and Woodrick 2005).

Variations are apparent not only across communities, but also within them, as individual residents greet newcomers with animosity, tolerance, understanding or apathy, with responses often varying along lines of class, age, and race. More educated individuals and members of the middle- and upper-classes tend to be more receptive to growing immigrant communities, while the working class tends to express more anti-immigrant prejudice and stereotypes (Vogt et al. 2006)—perhaps because they perceive themselves to be in more direct competition with newcomers, while higher-status individuals (employers and small business owners) stand to make financial gains (Crowley and Lichter 2009; Kasarda and Johnson 2006; Waslin 2008).

The arrival of Latino immigrants also can generate racial tensions between the newcomers and existing African American communities. Even when controlling for class, African Americans perceived Latino immigrants as economic threats, and those who held more negative stereotypes of Latino newcomers regarded immigration as decreasing African Americans' economic opportunities (McClain et al. 2007). Scholars debate the impacts of immigrant influxes on wages and migration among the native-born. Some argue that immigrant population growth has a small but negative impact on wages that can drive away unskilled native-born workers, while others note that immigrants have little impact on wages and do not generate outmigration of the native-born (Borjas 1999; Card 2001; Hamermesh and Bean 1998). Still others find that migration decisions of unskilled immigrant and native-born workers are *positively correlated*, as immigrant Latinos, native-born Latinos, native-born whites, and native-born African Americans move to similar areas of employment growth (Parrado and Kandel 2011a). Immigrant inflows could conceivably have a larger impact on labor markets in new rural destinations, where smaller population size heightens sensitivity to demographic shifts. Yet, immigrants relocating to new destinations have tended to be absorbed by an expanding job base, and changes in the aggregate well-being of African Americans and whites in rural Latino boomtowns between 1990 and the mid-to-late 2000s paralleled those of same-race populations in comparable rural counties without Latino influxes (Crowley, Lichter, and Turner 2013; Martin and Midgley 2006).

Intergroup relations may hinge on perceived competition for jobs, and so actions taken by employers can have important consequences for ethno-racial relations. They can exacerbate intergroup tensions, as was the case in a rural

Central Mississippi poultry plant where employer preference for immigrant workers fueled animosity between Latino and African American employees (Gordon and Lenhardt 2007). Alternatively, employers can foster positive relations. For example, managerial enforcement of anti-discrimination policies seems to have improved relations between Latino immigrant and African American workers in a rural eastern North Carolina poultry plant, since intergroup relations inside the plant were smoother than in the community at large (Marrow 2011).

Contact can be pivotal for breaking down barriers fueling intergroup prejudice; for example, contact with Latino youths in schools and residential areas fostered more welcoming attitudes among working-class white adolescents (Gimpel and Lay 2008). However, opportunities for same-status intergroup contact are limited in new destinations. Immigrants and the native-born often work in different industrial and occupational sectors (Martin and Midgley 2006), and while racial/ethnic residential segregation is declining in the Southwest and in metropolitan areas, it is higher in new destinations compared to established ones, especially in rural places, and is highest in new destinations with sizable African American populations (Lichter et al. 2010). Patterns of residential segregation reflect other factors as well, including place-specific history pertaining to race—sometimes with unexpected results. For example, racial homogeneity in a former "sundown town" (a reference to African Americans having been historically unwelcome within city limits after dark) meant an absence of discriminatory land-use and zoning ordinances that might otherwise have restricted newcomers' access to white neighborhoods (McConnell and Miraftab 2009).

Immigration and racial histories of new destination communities also influence more symbolic divides associated with ethno-racial hierarchies (i.e., the "color line") (Frank, Akresh, and Lu 2010; Lee and Bean 2010). Most new rural immigrant destinations lack recent immigration histories and exposure to residents who are neither white nor African American. In at least some of those communities, the color line appears to be transitioning from a white-black racial hierarchy toward one based on a black-nonblack distinction, owing in part to Latinos' perception that boundaries between themselves and whites are more permeable (Marrow 2011), and anti-black prejudice among Latinos and other immigrant groups (Morales 2012). Strengthening of the black-nonblack color line—evident in growth of black-nonblack segregation in rural areas, small towns, small cities, and suburbs—supports Gans' (2007) notion of "African American exceptionalism" (Parisi, Lichter, and Taquino 2011).

Perceived disruption of the established racial order may have contributed to expansion of hate groups in some rural areas. Extremist hate groups have increased nationally from 602 in 2000 to 1,007 in 2012. Since 2010, however, the number of anti-immigrant hate groups has declined from 319 in 2010 to thirty-eight in 2012, perhaps owing to the appropriation of extremist ideology by mainstream politics, as evidenced by anti-immigrant laws passed by state and local governments (Potok 2013). Municipalities across the United States passed more than 180 exclusionary ordinances from 2005 to 2009 (the total for the previous five years was fewer than ten) (O'Neil 2010). At the state level, legislators enacted approximately seventy-five restrictive laws from 2000 to 2004; three times that many were passed during the next five years (Ebert, Estrada, and Lore 2012).

In some cases, restrictive legislation is intended to make living conditions so harsh for immigrants that they opt to move elsewhere (Robertson and Preston 2012). This so-called self-deportation approach is most common in nonmetropolitan communities, smaller cities, and states with a strong rural population (Fennelly and Federico 2008). Arizona's S.B. 1070, Alabama's H.B. 56, Georgia's H.B. 87, Hazleton, Pennsylvania's Illegal Immigration Relief Act, and the like create a hostile environment for not only immigrants, but also native-born citizens mistaken for immigrants (García and Keyes 2012; Massey and Sánchez 2010; O'Neil 2010). Research suggests that these policies have no discernible impact on immigrants' internal (state-to-state) migration (Ebert, Leach, and Estrada 2013). Instead, those at risk tend to reduce public interaction, alter their appearance, and rely on documented relatives and friends to perform routine tasks (García and Keyes 2012). Such policies interfere with successful incorporation of immigrants and reduce their willingness to cooperate with authorities (Bean et al. 2013; Carr, Lichter, and Kefalas 2012; Kirk et al. 2012). They may also diminish responsiveness among public bureaucrats (e.g., from social services, health care agencies, and educational systems) who have generally led the way in understanding and meeting newcomers' needs in rural areas (Marrow 2011). This may already have begun to occur as rural and nonrural communities alike have adopted the ICE 287(g) program, which transfers immigration enforcement powers from federal to local authorities (Nguyen and Gill 2010).

The self-deportation approach to immigration policymaking became a part of the national conversation in 2012 when the Republican Party endorsed it on its official platform (Preston 2012). This approach may have backfired, as immigrant groups and their supporters overwhelmingly backed the Democratic Party in that year's presidential election. The policies themselves may also backfire, in that they tend to strengthen social cohesion in immigrant communities and encourage immigrants to fight back in the form of protest (Benjamin-Alvarado, DeSipio, and Montoya 2008; Okamoto and Ebert 2010). Interestingly, restrictive policies can lead to increased citizenship acquisition among immigrant groups as individuals seek resources to protect themselves (Cort 2012).

Policy Recommendations

Exclusionary policies run counter to public health, social integration, and educational gains needed for long-term community success. We recommend policymakers take a more inclusive approach, placing priority on interventions with the most potential for long-term gains. What can policymakers do to ease transitions and establish foundations for long-term success in America's new rural destinations? First, they must prioritize health care and social service outreach to address needs of isolated immigrant communities, focusing particular attention on preventative care and treatment of conditions with cascading impacts, such as domestic violence and child abuse.

Second, easing the path to citizenship and English-language acquisition would go a long way toward facilitating self-sufficiency, ameliorating poverty among immigrants, and improving the second generation's cognitive and educational outcomes (Bean et al. 2013; Glick, Walker, and Luz 2013). Citizenship does not guarantee that immigrants will escape poverty, however. Many authorized immigrants are paid less than minimum wage, due in part to lax enforcement of labor laws (Medina 2013; Bernhardt et al. 2009). Enforcement of existing laws would help to address such inequalities and may increase tax revenues by reducing the proportion of workers paid under the table.

Third, policymakers should focus their efforts on strengthening immigrants' and the children of immigrants' attachment to school. Unfortunately, immigrants are more likely to drop out of school in comparison to natives, and those residing in new destinations are particularly at risk, especially where there are rapid increases in the foreign-born population (Fischer 2010). Educational advancement is particularly important for today's second-generation children, who will enter adulthood in far less advantageous economic circumstances relative to their twentieth-century counterparts, and for second-generation children residing in nonmetropolitan areas, where they are less likely to experience the "second generation advantage" enjoyed by those residing in metropolitan areas (where children of immigrants can select traits from their parents and native-born peers that facilitate upward mobility in school, the workplace, and sometimes politics) (Kasinitz et al. 2008).

An exclusionary, self-deportation approach to policymaking not only foregoes these potential benefits, it also risks alienating immigrant communities and a potentially powerful voting bloc of immigrants and their native-born children, many of whom will be intimately acquainted with the damaging impacts of exclusionary policies. Immigrants and those with whom they are connected often watch politics closely. Political party identification within families is strong and, once established, can last generations (Niemi and Jennings 1991). It is in any political party's best interest to consider how current platforms and legislation will shape the political behavior of Latinos, whose population shares continue to increase.

Conclusions

What are the consequences of the global economic recession and economic recovery for new rural immigrant destinations and their residents? How will intergroup relations evolve as children of long-term and immigrant residents age together, and in the context of broader shifts in perspectives on race in America? What does the future hold for these children and the communities they inhabit? Research addressing these questions, and others posed throughout this chapter, would help to advance our understanding of new rural immigrant destinations. Further into the economic recovery, an analysis of demographic patterns and the well-being of long-term residents, immigrant newcomers, the second generation and communities overall will help to determine whether and how the economic recession and recovery have disrupted growth and/or progress in new rural immigrant destinations, and whether the impact of immigrants on indicators of well-being vary with economic context.

More research is needed to understand how social service needs changed as new rural immigrant destinations matured; how local governments, service providers, and community members (including immigrant communities) fared with respect to meeting these needs; and how their capacities were impacted by broader economic context and changing demographic trends. With respect to intergroup relations, research should more closely examine the impact of political polarization on immigrants and communities and identify more ways of breaking down the boundaries between newcomers and long-time residents in rural destinations. As part of this effort, scholars may want to investigate how relationships are impacted by contact in different institutional settings, including work and politics.

Finally, we hope scholars will continue to investigate factors that encourage upward mobility among the second generation. As the children of immigrants age, scholars may want to examine not only family, school, and community factors promoting educational achievement, but also how Latino youths' educational decisions and mobility choices are impacted by familial ties and labor markets in new immigrant destinations. Much is riding on how these youth fare, what they want, and whether they remain. If we can gain an understanding of these issues, we might see into the future of these communities.

References

Artz, Georgeanne, Rebecca Jackson, and Peter F. Orazem. 2010. "Is It a Jungle put There? Meat Packing, Immigrants, and Rural Communities." *Journal of Agricultural and Resource Economics* 35 (2): 299–315.

Bean, Frank D., Susan K. Brown, Mark A. Leach, James D. Bachmeier, and Jennifer Van Hook. 2013. *Unauthorized Mexican Migration and the Socioeconomic Integration of Mexican Americans.* New York: Russell Sage Foundation.

Benjamin-Alvarado, Jonathan, Louis DeSipio, and Celeste Montoya. 2008. "Latino Mobilization in New Immigrant Destinations: The Anti-HR 4437 Protest in Nebraska's Cities." *Urban Affairs Review* 44 (5): 718–35. http://dx.doi.org/10.1177/1078087408323380.

Bernhardt, Annette, Ruth Milkman, Nik Theodore, Douglas Heckathorn, Mirabai Auer, James DeFilippis, Ana Luz González, Victor Narro, Jason Perelshteyn, and Diana Polson. 2009. *Broken Laws, Unprotected Workers.* New York: National Employment Law Project.

Borjas, George J. 1999. *Heaven's Door: Immigration Policy and the American Economy.* Princeton, NJ: Princeton University Press.

Broadway, Michael. 2007. "Meatpacking and the Transformation of Rural Communities: A Comparison of Brooks, Alberta and Garden City, Kansas." *Rural Sociology* 72 (4): 560–82. http://dx.doi.org/10.1526/003601107782638701.

Brown, David L., and Kai A. Schafft. 2011. *Rural People and Communities in the 21st Century: Resilience and Transformation.* Malden, MA: Polity Press.

Burton, Linda M., Daniel T. Lichter, Regina S. Baker, and John M. Eason. 2013. "Inequality, Family Processes, and Health in the 'New' Rural America." *American Behavioral Scientist* 57 (8): 1128–51. http://dx.doi.org/10.1177/0002764213487348.

Canales, Alejandro I. 2003. "Mexican Labour Migration to the United States in the Age of Globalisation." *Journal of Ethnic and Migration Studies* 29 (4): 741–61. http://dx.doi.org/10.1080/1369183032000123486.

Capps, Randolph, Everett Henderson, John Kasarda, James H. Johnson, Stephen Appold, Derrek Croney, Donald Hernandez, and Michael E. Fix. 2007. *A Profile of Immigrants in Arkansas.* Washington, DC: Urban Institute.

Card, David. 2001. "Immigrant Inflows, Native Outflows and the Local Labor Market Impacts of Higher Immigration." *Journal of Labor Economics* 19 (1): 22–64. http://dx.doi.org/10.1086/209979.

Carr, Patrick J., Daniel T. Lichter, and Maria J. Kefalas. 2012. "Can Immigration Save Small-Town America? Hispanic Boomtowns and the Uneasy Path to Renewal." *Annals of the American Academy of Political and Social Science* 641 (1): 38–57. http://dx.doi.org/10.1177/0002716211433445.

Casey, Michelle M., Lynn A. Blewett, and Kathleen T. Call. October 2004. "Providing Health Care to Latino Immigrants: Community-Based Efforts in the Rural Midwest." *American*

Journal of Public Health 94 (10): 1709–11. http://dx.doi.org/10.2105/AJPH.94.10.1709. Medline:15451737.

Cort, David A. 2012. "Spurred to Action or Retreat? The Effects of Reception Contexts on Naturalization Decisions in Los Angeles." *International Migration Review* 46 (2): 483–516. http://dx.doi.org/10.1111/j.1747-7379.2012.00894.x.

Cristancho, Sergio, D. Marcela Garces, Karen E. Peters, and Benjamin C. Mueller. May 2008. "Listening to Rural Hispanic Immigrants in the Midwest: A Community-Based Participatory Assessment of Major Barriers to Health Care Access and Use." *Qualitative Health Research* 18 (5): 633–46. http://dx.doi.org/10.1177/1049732308316669. Medline:18420537.

Crowley, Martha, and Daniel T. Lichter. 2009. "Social Disorganization in New Latino Destinations?" *Rural Sociology* 74 (4): 573–604. http://dx.doi.org/10.1526/003601109789864026.

Crowley, Martha, Daniel T. Lichter, and Zhenchao Qian. 2006. "Beyond Gateway Cities: Economic Restructuring and Poverty among Mexican Immigrant Families and Children." *Family Relations* 55 (3): 345–60. http://dx.doi.org/10.1111/j.1741-3729.2006.00407.x.

Crowley, Martha, Daniel T. Lichter, and Richard N. Turner. 2013. "Diverging Fortunes: Economic Well-Being of African Americans and Whites in New Rural Destinations." Paper presented at the annual meeting for the Rural Sociological Society, New York, 6–9 August.

Culver, Leigh. 2004. "The Impact of New Immigration Patterns on the Provision of Police Services in Midwestern Communities." *Journal of Criminal Justice* 32 (4): 329–44. http://dx.doi.org/10.1016/j.jcrimjus.2004.04.004.

Dalla, Rochelle L., Sheran Cramer, and Kaye Stanek. 2002. "Economic Strain and Community Concerns in Three Meatpacking Communities." *Rural America* 17 (1): 20–25.

Donato, Katharine M., Charles Tolbert, II, Alfred Nucci, and Yukio Kawano. 2007. "Recent Immigrant Settlement in the Nonmetropolitan United States: Evidence from Internal Census Data." *Rural Sociology* 72 (4): 537–59. http://dx.doi.org/10.1526/003601107782638666.

Donato, Katharine M., Charles Tolbert, Alfred Nucci, and Yukio Kawano. 2008. "Changing Faces, Changing Places: The Emergence of New Nonmetropolitan Immigrant Gateways." In *New Faces in New Places: The Changing Geography of American Immigration*, ed. Douglas S. Massey, 75–98. New York: Russell Sage Foundation.

Durand, Jorge, Douglas S. Massey, and Fernando Charvet. 2000. "The Changing Geography of Mexican Immigration to the United States: 1910–1996." *Social Science Quarterly* 81: 1–15.

Ebert, Kim, Emily Estrada, and Michelle Lore. 2012. "When Organizations Matter: Threatening Demographics, Supportive Politics, and Lawmaking." Paper presented at the annual meeting for the Southern Sociological Society, New Orleans, 21–4 March.

Ebert, Kim, Brandi Leach, and Emily Estrada. 2013. "To 'Self-Deport' or Stay the Course?" Paper presented at the annual meeting for the Southern Sociological Society, Atlanta, 24–7 April.

Erwin, Deborah O. 2003. "An Ethnographic Description of Latino Immigration in Rural Arkansas: Intergroup Relations and Utilization of Healthcare Services." *Rural Sociology* 19: 46–72.

Farmer, Frank L., and Zola K. Moon. 2009. "An Empirical Examination of Characteristics of Mexican Migrants to Metropolitan and Nonmetropolitan Areas of the United States." *Rural Sociology* 74 (2): 220–40. http://dx.doi.org/10.1111/j.1549-0831.2009.tb00390.x.

Fennelly, K., and C. Federico. 2008. "Rural Residence as a Determinant of Attitudes toward US Immigration Policy." *International Migration* (Geneva, Switzerland) 46 (1): 151–90. http://dx.doi.org/10.1111/j.1468-2435.2008.00440.x.

Fischer, Mary J. 2010. "Immigrant Educational Outcomes in New Destinations: An Exploration of High School Attrition." *Social Science Research* 39 (4): 627–41. http://dx.doi.org/10.1016/j.ssresearch.2010.01.004.

Frank, Reanne, Ilana Redstone Akresh, and Bo Lu. 2010. "Latino Immigrants and the US Racial Order: How and Where Do They Fit In?" *American Sociological Review* 75 (3): 378–401. http://dx.doi.org/10.1177/0003122410372216.

Gans, Hebert J. 2007. "The Possibility of a New Racial Hierarchy in the Twenty-First-Century United States." In *The Inequality Reader: Contemporary and Foundational Readings in Race, Class, and Gender*, ed. David Grusky and Szonja Szelényi, 266–75. Boulder, CO: Westview Press.

García, Angela S., and David G. Keyes. 2012. *Life as an Undocumented Immigrant: How Restrictive Local Immigration Policies Affect Daily Life.* Washington, DC: Center for American Progress.

Garcia, Carlos. 2009. "The Role of Quality of Life in the Rural Resettlement of Mexican Immigrants." *Hispanic Journal of Behavioral Sciences* 31 (4): 446–67. http://dx.doi.org/10.1177/0739986309345994.

Gimpel, James G., and Celeste J. Lay. 2008. "Political Socialization and Reactions to Immigration-Related Diversity in Rural America." *Rural Sociology* 73 (2): 180–204. http://dx.doi.org/10.1526/003601108784514561.

Glick, Jennifer E., Laquitta Walker, and Luciana Luz. January 2013. "Linguistic Isolation in the Home and Community: Protection or Risk for Young Children?" *Social Science Research* 42 (1): 140–54. http://dx.doi.org/10.1016/j.ssresearch.2012.08.003. Medline:23146603.

Gordon, Jennifer, and R.A. Lenhardt. 2007. *Conflict and Solidarity between African American and Latino Immigrant Workers. The Chief Justice Earl Warren Institute on Race, Ethnicity, and Diversity.* Berkeley: University of California.

Gozdziak, Elzbieta M., and Susan Forbes Martin. 2005. *Beyond the Gateway: Immigrants in a Changing America.* Lanham, MD: Lexington Books.

Grey, Mark A., and Anne C. Woodrick. 2005. "Latinos Have Revitalized Our Community: Mexican Migration and Anglo Responses in Marshalltown, Iowa." In *New Destinations: Mexican Immigration in the United States*, ed. Victor Zúñiga and Ruben Hernández-León, 133–54. New York: Russell Sage Foundation.

Griffith, David. 2008. "New Midwesterners, New Southerners: Immigration Experiences in Four Rural American Settings." In *New Faces in New Places: The Changing Geography of American Immigration*, ed. Douglas S. Massey, 179–210. New York: Russell Sage Foundation.

Hamermesh, Daniel S., and Frank D. Bean, eds. 1998. *Help or Hindrance? The Economic Implications of Immigration for African Americans.* New York: Russell Sage Foundation.

Harari, Nurit, Matthew Davis, and Michele Heisler. November 2008. "Strangers in a Strange Land: Health Care Experiences for Recent Latino Immigrants in Midwest Communities." *Journal of Health Care for the Poor and Underserved* 19 (4): 1350–67. http://dx.doi.org/10.1353/hpu.0.0086. Medline:19029757.

Hirschman, Charles, and Douglas S. Massey. 2008. "Places and Peoples: The New American Mosaic." In *New Faces in New Places: The Changing Geography of American Immigration*, ed. Douglas S. Massey, 1–21. New York: Russell Sage Foundation.

Jensen, Leif. 2006. *New Immigrant Settlements in Rural America: Problems, Prospects, and Policies*. Durham, NH: Carsey Institute.

Johnson, Kenneth M., and Daniel T. Lichter. 2012. "Rural Natural Increase in the New Century: America's Third Demographic Transition." In *International Handbook of Rural Demography*, ed. László J. Kulcsár and Katherine J. Curtis, 17–34. New York: Springer. http://dx.doi.org/10.1007/978-94-007-1842-5_3.

Kandel, William, and John Cromartie. 2004. New Patterns of Hispanic Settlement in Rural America. Report Number 99. US Department of Agriculture, Economic Research Service, Rural Development.

Kandel, William, Jamila Henderson, Heather Koball, and Randy Capps. 2011. "Moving up in Rural America: Economic Attainment of Nonmetro Latino Immigrants." *Rural Sociology* 76 (1): 101–28. http://dx.doi.org/10.1111/j.1549-0831.2011.00047.x.

Kandel, William, and Emilio Parrado. 2005. "Restructuring of the US Meat Processing Industry and New Hispanic Migrant Destinations." *Population and Development Review* 31 (3): 447–71. http://dx.doi.org/10.1111/j.1728-4457.2005.00079.x.

Kandel, William, and Emilio Parrado. 2006. "Hispanic Population Growth and Public School Response in Two New South Immigrant Destinations." In *Latinos in the New South: Transformations of Place*, ed. Heather A. Smith and Owen J. Furuseth, 111–34. Burlington: Ashgate Publishing Company.

Kasarda, John D., and James H. Johnson. 2006. *The Economic Impact of the Hispanic Population on the State of North Carolina*. Chapel Hill, NC: Frank Hawkins Kenan Institute of Private Enterprise.

Kasinitz, Philip, John H. Mollenkopf, Mary C. Waters, and Jennifer Holdway. 2008. *Inheriting the City: The Children of Immigrants Come of Age*. New York: Russell Sage Foundation.

Kirk, David S., Andrew V. Papachristos, Jeffrey Fagan, and Tom R. Tyler. 2012. "The Paradox of Law Enforcement in Immigrant Communities: Does Tough Immigration Enforcement Undermine Public Safety?" *Annals of the American Academy of Political and Social Science* 641 (1): 79–98. http://dx.doi.org/10.1177/0002716211431818.

Koball, Heather, Randy Capps, William Kandel, Jamila Henderson, and Everett Henderson. 2008a. "Integrating Latino Immigrants in New Rural Destinations." *Mathmatica Policy Research*, November, Issue Brief Number 1.

Koball, Heather, Randy Capps, William Kandel, Jamila Henderson, and Everett Henderson. 2008b. "Social and Economic Integration of Latino Immigrants in New Rural Destinations." *Mathematica Policy Research*, November, Issue Brief Number 2.

Leach, Mark A., and Frank D. Bean. 2008. "The Structure and Dynamics of Mexican Migration to New Destinations in the United States." In *New Faces in New Places: The Changing Geography of American Immigration*, ed. Douglas S. Massey, 51–74. New York: Russell Sage Foundation.

Lee, Jennifer, and Frank Dawson Bean. 2010. *The Diversity Paradox: Immigration and the Color Line in Twenty-First Century America*. New York: Russell Sage Foundation.

Lichter, Daniel T. 2012. "Immigration and the New Racial Diversity in Rural America." *Rural Sociology* 77 (1): 3–35. http://dx.doi.org/10.1111/j.1549-0831.2012.00070.x.

Lichter, Daniel T., Domenico Parisi, Michael C. Taquino, and Steven Michael Grice. 2010. "Residential Segregation in New Hispanic Destinations: Cities, Suburbs, and Rural Communities Compared." *Social Science Research* 39 (2): 215–30. http://dx.doi.org/10.1016/j.ssresearch.2009.08.006.

Marrow, Helen. 2011. *New Destination Dreaming: Immigration, Race, and Legal Status in the Rural American South.* Stanford, CA: Stanford University Press.

Martin, Philip, and Elizabeth Midgley. 2006. "Immigration: Shaping and Reshaping America." *Population Bulletin* 61 (4): 1–28.

Massey, Douglas S., and Chiara Capoferro. 2008. "The Geographic Diversification of American Immigration." In *New Faces in New Places: The Changing Geography of American Immigration*, ed. Douglas S. Massey, 25–50. New York: Russell Sage Foundation.

Massey, Douglas S., and Magaly Sánchez. 2010. *Brokered Boundaries: Creating Immigrant Identity in Anti-Immigrant Times.* New York: Russell Sage Foundation.

McClain, Paula D., Monique L. Lyle, Niambi M. Carter, Victoria M. DeFrancesco Soto, Gerald F. Lackey, Kendra Davenport Cotton, Shayla C. Nunnally, Thomas J. Scotto, Jeffrey D. Grynaviski, and J. Alan Kendrick. 2007. "Black Americans and Latino Immigrants in a Southern City." *Du Bois Review* 4 (1): 97–117. http://dx.doi.org/10.1017/S1742058X07070063.

McConnell, Eileen Diaz. 2008. "The U.S. Destinations of Contemporary Mexican Immigrants." *International Migration Review* 42 (4): 767–802. http://dx.doi.org/10.1111/j.1747-7379.2008.00147.x.

McConnell, Eileen Diaz, and Faranak Miraftab. 2009. "Sundown Town to 'Little Mexico': Old-Timers and Newcomers in an American Small Town." *Rural Sociology* 74 (4): 605–29. http://dx.doi.org/10.1526/003601109789864044.

Medina, Jennifer. 2013. "Being Legal Doesn't End Poverty." *New York Times*, 20 July.

Millard, Ann V., Jorge Chapa, and Eileen Diaz McConnell. 2004. "Not Racist Like Our Parents': Anti-Latino Prejudice and Institutional Discrimination." In *Apple Pie and Enchiladas: Latino Newcomers in the Rural Midwest*, ed. Ann V. Millard and Jorge Chapa, 102–24. Austin: University of Texas Press.

Morales, Erica. 2012. "Parental Messages Concerning Latino/Black Interracial Dating: An Exploratory Study Among Latina/o Young Adults." *Latino Studies* 10 (3): 314–33. http://dx.doi.org/10.1057/lst.2012.24.

Nguyen, Mai Thi, and Hannah Elizabeth Gill. 2010. *The 287 (g) Program: The Costs and Consequences of Local Immigration Enforcement in North Carolina Communities.* Chapel Hill, NC: Latino Migration Project, The Institute for the Study of the Americas and the Center for Global Initiatives.

Niemi, Richard G., and M. Kent Jennings. 1991. "Issues and Inheritance in the Formation of Party Identification." *American Journal of Political Science* 35 (4): 970–88. http://dx.doi.org/10.2307/2111502.

O'Neil, Kevin. 2010. "Hazleton and Beyond: Why Communities Try to Restrict Immigration." Migration Policy Institute, Migration Information Source, November.

Okamoto, Dina G., and Kim Ebert. 2010. "Beyond the Ballot: Immigrant Collective Action in Gateways and New Destinations in the United States." *Social Problems* 57 (4): 529–58. http://dx.doi.org/10.1525/sp.2010.57.4.529.

Papademetriou, Demetrios G., and Aaron Terrazas. 2009. "Immigrants in the United States and the Current Economic Crisis." Migration Policy Institute, Migration Information Source, April.

Parisi, Domenico, Daniel T. Lichter, and Michael C. Taquino. 2011. "Multi-scale Residential Segregation: Black Exceptionalism and America's Changing Color Line." *Social Forces* 89 (3): 829–52. http://dx.doi.org/10.1353/sof.2011.0013.

Parrado, Emilio, and William Kandel. 2010. "Hispanic Population Growth and Rural Income Inequality." *Social Forces* 88 (3): 1421–50. http://dx.doi.org/10.1353/sof.0.0291.

Parrado, Emilio, and William Kandel. 2011a. "Industrial Change, Hispanic Immigration, and the Internal Migration of Low-Skilled Native Male Workers in the United States, 1995–2000." *Social Science Research* 40 (2): 626–40. http://dx.doi.org/10.1016/j.ssresearch.2010.11.001.

Parrado, Emilio, and William Kandel. 2011b. "Economic Recession, Anti-immigrant Climate, and Hispanic Immigrant Mobility in New and Established Destinations." Paper presented at the annual meetings of the Population Association of America, 31 March to 2 April.

Perez, Thomas E. 2003. "The Civil Rights Dimension of Racial and Ethnic Disparities in Health Status." In *Unequal Treatment: Confronting Racial and Ethnic Disparities in Health Care*, ed. Brian D. Smedley, Adrienne Y. Stith, and Alan R. Nelson, 626–63. Washington, DC: National Academes Press.

Potok, Mark. 2013. *The Year in Hate and Extremism*. Issue Number 149. Southern Poverty Law Center Intelligence Report.

Preston, Julia. 2012. "Republican Immigration Platform Backs 'Self-Deportation.'" *New York Times*, 23 August.

Robertson, Campbell, and Julia Preston. 2012. "Appeals Court Limits Alabama's Immigration Law." *New York Times*, 21 August.

Saenz, Rogelio. 2008. *A Profile of Latinos in Rural America*. Carsey Institute, Fact Sheet Number 10.

Sanderson, Matthew, and Matthew Painter, II. 2011. "Occupational Channels for Mexican Migration: New Destination Formation in a Binational Context." *Rural Sociology* 76 (4): 461–80. http://dx.doi.org/10.1111/j.1549-0831.2011.00061.x.

Shultz, Benjamin J., and the Benjamin J. Shultz. 2008. "Inside the Gilded Cage: The Lives of Latino Immigrant Males in Rural Central Kentucky." *Southeastern Geographer* 48 (2): 201–18. http://dx.doi.org/10.1353/sgo.0.0024.

Shutika, Debra Lattanzi. 2011. *Beyond the Borderlands: Migration and Belonging in the United States and Mexico*. Berkeley: University of California Press. http://dx.doi.org/10.1525/california/9780520269583.001.0001.

Sizemore, David S. 2004. "Ethnic Inclusion and Exclusion: Managing the Language of Hispanic Integration in a Rural Community." *Journal of Contemporary Ethnography* 33 (5): 534–70. http://dx.doi.org/10.1177/0891241604266987.

Smith, Clint E. 2000. *Inevitable Partnership: Understanding Mexico-US Relations.* Boulder, CO: Lynne Rienner Publishers.

Stull, Donald D., and Michael J. Broadway. 2001. "'We Come to the Garden'...Again: Garden City, Kansas, 1990–2000." *Urban Anthropology* 30 (4): 269–99.

Vogt, Rebecca J., Randolph L. Cantrell, Miguel A. Carranza, Bruce B. Johnson, and Alan J. Tomkins. 2006. Perceptions of Latin American Immigration among Rural Nebraskans. Center Research Report 06–5. University of Nebraska Center for Applied Rural Innovation.

Wainer, Andrew. 2006. "The New Latino South and the Challenge to American Public Education." *International Migration (Geneva, Switzerland)* 44 (5): 129–65. http://dx.doi.org/10.1111/j.1468-2435.2006.00389.x.

Waslin, Michele. 2008. *Assessing the Economic Impact of Immigration at the State and Local Level.* Washington, DC: American Immigration Law Foundation, Immigration Policy Center.

Winders, Jamie, and Barbara Ellen Smith. 2010. "New Pasts: Historicizing Immigration, Race, and Place in the South." *Southern Spaces*, 4 November.

Zúñiga, Victor, and Ruben Hernández-León, eds. 2005. *New Destinations: Mexican Immigration in the United States.* New York: Russell Sage Foundation.

PART IV

Diversity in Rural America

Gender, Race, Ethnicity, Class, and Sexuality in Rural America

Carolyn Sachs

The media and popular stereotypes portray rural places in the United States as white, patriarchal, working class, and heterosexual havens where racism, sexism, homophobia, and ethnocentrism abound. The issues of gender, race, ethnicity, and class infuse all aspects of life and work in rural America. While a number of rural sociologists address these structures and identities in detail, a deeper understanding of these issues and the complex relations between them has not permeated the broader study of rural places.

Looking toward globalization proves useful. Global changes including heightened global restructuring, neoliberalism, and the pull back from state welfare impact gender, race, ethnicity, sexuality, and class issues in rural America. In addition, global efforts by the United Nations (UN) and a number of nongovernmental organizations to push for human rights, especially women's rights, rights of indigenous people, rights for gays, lesbians, and transgender people, and rights of minorities impact the lives of rural people in the United States.

I begin by offering several critiques of our understandings of rural people in the United States. First, much of the scholarship on gender, race, ethnicity, and class in rural America stops short of interrogating global issues and intersections of these issues. Second, despite decades of work on issues of gender, race, ethnicity, and class, much of this scholarship remains at the margins of academic understanding of rural places and rural life. Our understandings of gender, race, ethnicity, and class have not been adequately integrated into the broader understanding of rural life. Third, scholarship has not effectively investigated the intersections of these different identities and structures. Black feminist scholars and critical race scholars have called for attention to intersectionality— the complex relationships among between gender, race, ethnicity, sexuality, and class—in efforts to understand social life. With a few exceptions, studies of intersectionality in rural spaces remain elusive.

In this chapter, I first look at gender through focusing on global drivers of shifts in women's and men's employment in rural areas, women's movement into agriculture, a focus on reproductive labor, and theoretical shifts toward intersectionality. Second, I discuss race and ethnicity in two sections on crossing borders, focusing on Latinos in the United States and staying behind which focuses primarily on blacks in the South. Third, in the section on moving past heteronormativity, I argue for greater attention to sexuality. Next, I discuss how class issues in rural areas have often been studied through demographic and spatial analysis of pockets of poverty, but less attention has focused on the way differences across rural spaces impacts gender, race, ethnicity, and class issues. Then, I briefly mention two other global drivers impacting these issues: climate change and global human rights initiatives. Finally, I provide suggestions for future work.

Enter the Global Feminization of Work: From Bad Jobs to Worse

Restructuring of employment opportunities in the rural United States involves the precipitous decline in manufacturing employment, natural resource related jobs in forestry and fisheries, the demise of agricultural employment, and the increase in service-related jobs. As these shifts alter the gender, racial, and ethnic composition of the rural workforce, rural places and families also change.

Perhaps most striking is the change in work patterns of men and women in rural areas. With the shift to service-sector employment, rural women have been both pushed and pulled into the work force (Smith 2011). The decline in jobs for rural men in manufacturing and natural resources pushed women into the workforce in order to increase income in their households (Falk and Lobao 2003). In fact, as Jensen and Jensen (2011) show in their detailed analyses of data from the Current Population Survey, rural men have been more disadvantaged from structural shifts in the economy than either urban men or rural women. Rural men's situations in the labor market have worsened over time in contrast to rural women, whose employment situations have improved markedly. The trend toward the feminization of employment in the United States is mirrored in many regions of the world as a key component of neoliberal globalization. The feminization of employment involves both the increasing proportion of women in the workforce and the deterioration of labor conditions for both men and women (Peterson 2005). Women's formal employment has increased worldwide, while men's employment is declining—this does not necessarily translate into empowerment for women, but rather deteriorating working conditions for men. As Peterson (2005, 509) writes: "In short, as more jobs become casual, irregular, flexible and precarious, more women—and feminised men—are doing them."

Even though rural women's employment has increased, they often work in unfavorable circumstances of low pay, unpredictable hours, and temporary employment. Women's employment in the rural United States is best understood in the broader context of globalization and neoliberalism. As Patricia Fernández-Kelly (2007) suggests in comparing women workers in factories in the United States with those in other parts of the world, most women's search for jobs is driven by their concern to maintain living standards for themselves and their families rather than to achieve emancipation. As she states, "despite their comparative prosperity—U.S. women bear a striking resemblance to their counterparts in China, Nicaragua, and Mexico. Despite such commonalities, national background and race continue to fragment gender and class consciousness" (Fernández-Kelly 2007, 520).

Into the Fields: Shifting Gender Relations in Agriculture

Shifts in the global restructuring in agriculture, natural resource extraction, and manufacturing have differential impacts by gender, race, ethnicity, and class. Much of the scholarship on rural women in the United States has focused on women in agriculture, especially women farmers. Recently scholars have focused on the increase in women farmers, especially on sustainable and organic farms (Trauger et al. 2009; Hall and Mogyorody 2007), but with limited analysis of the impact of global agricultural restructuring on gender issues in farming in the United States. Global and regional trade agreements that cut subsidies and supports for traditional commodities often result in shifts in gender relations on farms. Global and national policies that favor large-scale corporate agriculture have led to the decline in the number of medium-sized farms and the heavy reliance of small- and medium-sized farms on off-farm employment. In some instances, men leave farms or seek employment off the farm, opening up space for women to move into farming or in some places resulting in the feminization of agriculture. Studies in Europe have emphasized how policies that have shifted to support multifunctional agriculture, such as tourism, have shifted gender relations on farms, undermined patriarchal power, and created more equitable and empowering opportunities for women (Brandth and Haugen 2010). At the same time, these shifts have resulted in redefinitions of masculinity on farms. Limited attention has been directed at how these global shifts impact gender relations or women on farms in North America. Shifts in the global agrifood system created by various trade agreements, loan repayment policies, and corporate agriculture have impacted women in agriculture in multiple ways (Sachs and Alston 2010). The global South has responded through production and processing of non-traditional crops such as vegetables, fruits, and flowers, which rely heavily on women's labor. Women are valued laborers because they can be paid less and are willing to work in more-flexible and less-stable work arrangements. The global and the local are highly linked in terms of women's employment opportunities; "the comparative advantage of agrifood industries in global markets rests on the comparative disadvantage of rural women in national labor markets" (Preibisch and Grez 2010, 291). While women are often the preferred workers in corporate agricultural production in developing countries, single migrant male workers who are most often from Mexico are often the preferred hired agricultural laborers in the United States and Canada (Preibisch and Grez 2010.) Rural sociologists have rarely studied the complex intersections of gender, race, and ethnicity in corporate agriculture in North America.

Beyond the Market: What about Reproduction?

While neoliberal globalization clearly alters the employment landscape in rural areas, the impact of these shifts extends beyond formal employment. As Peterson (2005, 27) notes, these shifts "reduce the emotional, cultural and material resources necessary for the wellbeing of most women and families." Women in most regions of the globe, and especially those who lack resources, are spending increasing amounts of time on reproductive labor, including feeding their families, providing health care, taking care of children and the elderly, and providing emotional support. The legacy of structural adjustment programs that have reduced government services have left the provision of many of these services to the unpaid work of women. While there is some evidence that rural men are taking up reproductive work, few studies have compared shifting gender divisions of labor in households between rural and urban areas. Also, the decline and lack in government services also means declining employment for women in rural areas, especially in so-called good jobs such as social work and teaching.

Shifts in women's and men's work patterns result in changes in household relationships as well. In her ethnographic study of a sawmill closure in a small logging and mill town in rural California, Sherman (2011) reveals the multiple ways that gender roles shift in response to men's job loss. Some men respond by adhering to rigid masculine identities and struggle to maintain traditional gender roles. This struggle often has devastating consequences including substance abuse and domestic violence. However, she also found a surprising amount of resilience and adoption of flexible masculine roles that emphasized more active fathering roles.

In many rural communities, reliance on government programs and services is often low due to limited availability of services or lack of adequate transportation. With the neoliberal push for the decline of government services and social supports, rural programs are often the first to go. For example, fewer programs exist to support rural women who are victims of sexual assaults. In addition, women are often reluctant to report sexual assaults due to lack of anonymity, physical isolation, and distrust of public agencies. People with HIV/AIDS in rural areas are also less likely to seek and obtain adequate treatment due to lack of appropriate health care providers, stigma attached to the disease, and transportation issues (Preston and D'Augelli 2012; Heckman et al. 1998).

Clearly, global shifts in employment opportunities have altered gender relations. In some cases, a re-inscription of traditional gender roles results in problematic family and household dynamics. In other cases, what Brandth and Haugen (2010) refer to as the detraditionalization of gender roles in rural areas offers possibilities for new and more equitable relations between rural men and women. Exactly when, where, and how these different dynamics play out deserves further study.

Moving beyond Western Feminism to Intersectionality

Critiques of feminist scholarship from third world women and US women of color have moved scholarship from focusing on women to the intersections of gender, race, ethnicity, citizenship, and sexual identity to studying intersectionality. Crenshaw (1991) coins the concept of intersectionality to describe how black women's experiences are shaped by both racism and sexism and cannot be understood by looking at race or gender experiences separately. Mohanty's (1988) classic critique of Western feminist writings about women in developing countries reveals that through portraying women in developing countries as unilaterally poor, uneducated, and disempowered, women in developed countries then seem to be agentic, empowered, and positioned to save the women in developing countries. This move of describing the "other" as universally disempowered and undifferentiated must be avoided in rural scholarship on gender, sexuality, race, and class. These theoretical pushes to move beyond simple analysis of gender, nation, class, ethnicity, and race can provide direction for future work in rural sociology.

Crossing Borders: Latinos in the Rural United States

Another major shift in rural areas is the increased employment of Latino/as, especially Mexicans, in the rural United States. More than ten years after the implementation of NAFTA, economic prosperity in Mexico continues to plummet and Mexicans have responded by crossing the border in pursuit of livelihoods (Patel 2009). As NAFTA policies support agribusinesses and larger scale industries on both sides of the border, Mexicans have lost out and are migrating when possible (Pechlaner and Otero 2010) Recently, immigrants from Mexico have begun to move outside of their traditional destinations in California and the Southwest to new destination rural communities (Nelson, Oberg, and Nelson 2010). Migrants to rural areas differ compared to migrants to urban areas, and one study found that the characteristics of migrants coming to rural areas after the passage of NAFTA shifted. These more recent migrants are more likely to be single, less educated, less fluent in English, have less work experience, and are more likely to come from small towns and rural places in Mexico (Farmer and Moon 2009).

aThese new destination rural communities often have meat-processing plants, other agricultural processing facilities, or tourist- and service-related jobs. An increasing number of largely Latino/a farmworkers are settling in rural communities. This influx of Latino immigrants to rural communities in the United States has raised concerns about the impact of new immigrants on rural populations (Jensen 2006; Kandel and Cromartie 2004; Lichter and Johnson 2007). The most recent studies show that the influx of large numbers of Latino/as have surprisingly little impact on the economic well-being of local populations (Crowley and Lichter 2009). Most studies focus on local communities and longer-term populations rather than on the immigrants' well-being. One exception is Pfeffer and Parra's (2009) study of rural immigrants in New York, where they find that new immigrants' networks and social ties are instrumental in helping them find jobs. In another study, Schmalzbauer (2011) looked at the well-being of immigrants and the gender dynamics in households. She found that immigrant women who transgressed their traditional gender roles and assumed jobs in the formal economy tried to protect men's masculinity by performing a particular gender script. The rise of anti-immigration movements in states and local communities has made life exceedingly difficult for immigrants, especially those without documentation.

Staying Behind: Racism Reigns

The long history of disfranchisement, discrimination, and violence against rural blacks in the United States is clearly tied to global trade in commodities and people from the time of the Atlantic slave trade. While some changes have occurred, the political economy of the plantation South has left a legacy of black rural poverty steeped in racism (Tickamyer and Duncan 1990). In discussing the persistent problems in the Black Belt region, R. Wimberly (2010, 178) notes that despite civil rights, technological shifts and globalization "race, region, and rurality still combine to restrict both children and adults from enjoying the many social advantages and opportunities held by U.S. residents of other regions." With globalization, blacks in rural America have provided free and cheap labor to fuel global trade for centuries.

Black land ownership continues to decline (Gilbert, Sharp, and Felin 2002). For blacks in the rural South, land represents more than economic security, but also a level of independence and personal security. Rural blacks have deep emotional attachments to the land (Falk 2004; Dyer and Bailey 2008). However, they continue to lose access to this land.

Native Americans continue to live in dire economic circumstances. Nearly 60 percent of Native Americans who live outside of metropolitan areas live in poor counties. Those who live on reservations experience extreme poverty and unemployment. Economic development largely eluded them until the 1987 legislation that legalized gaming operations on tribal land (Gonzales 2003). Controversy exists surrounding the impact of gaming on tribal land, but certainly many tribes experience increased income, better infrastructure, and improved social services. However, more research is needed in terms of the short- and long-term impact of gaming on social and cultural issues on reservations.

Possible benefits of globalization seem to have passed by many of these communities, but some places are more deeply impacted. For example, climate change as the result of the incessant use of fossil fuel will likely have major impacts on indigenous people in the Arctic region (Cuomo, Eisner, and Hinkel 2008). There is now unsubstantiated evidence that further changes associated with global warming will have a profound impact on and generate additional risks for Arctic communities.

While class and race intersect with rural poverty in the Deep South, some other pockets of rural poverty remain predominantly white. Persistent poverty and class inequality in Appalachia has long been understood through the political economic structures of the region and referred to as internal colonialism. Clearly, Appalachian poverty and class inequality reflects the dominance and control of outside corporate interests. The abundance of coal that is primarily owned and controlled by outside interests has brought anything but prosperity to the region. Shifts from deep mining to shift mining to mountaintop removal have brought about increasing degradation of the landscape and water systems in Appalachia in conjunction with the decline in the number of jobs available in the coalfields. Recent discoveries of natural gas in Marcellus Shale in the mid-Appalachian region and the availability of hydraulic fracturing technologies have resulted in local people selling mineral rights. Although these new natural gas developments promise jobs and employment possibilities, they are also characterized by outside ownership of mineral rights and severe environmental threats to water systems.

Moving past Heteronormativity

Much of the literature on rural places assumes a heteronormativity in terms of identities, households, and communities. In the mid- to late-1990s, some scholars began to interrogate rural sexualities with a focus on gay and lesbian identities in rural places. The early scholarships on rural gays and lesbians emphasized their marginality in rural places. In fact, in her article, "Get Thee to a Big City," Kath Weston (1995) neatly sums up early academic thinking on rural gays and lesbians. Rural places were viewed as overwhelming heterosexual, homophobic, and downright dangerous for rural gays and lesbians. Even more recent work argues that rural communities constitute spaces of highly conventional sexualities (Little and Leyshon 2003). Life for rural gay men in particular is extremely difficult as they face social stigma related to homosexuality and the lack of anonymity in rural places (Preston and D'Augelli 2012). But there is emerging scholarship on rural sexuality that challenges the assumption that rural places are unilaterally inhospitable to gays and lesbians. Gray (2009) argues that the urban LGBT emphasis on visibility and coming out occludes the presence of queer people in rural areas. She argues that rural queer practices are invisible to those observing through an urban or academic lens. Exactly how life is for rural gay men clearly varies by location.

Across Different Spaces: Pockets of Poverty and More

All rural places in the United States are not the same (Falk and Lobao 2003). How gender, race, ethnicity, and class impact rural people's lives in these various types of rural spaces deserves further attention. Feminist scholars insist on the importance of situated knowledges—of taking care not to universalize about views from nowhere. Cindy Katz (2001) creatively weaves together how to understand globalization works in particular locations without romanticizing the local. Her motivation is to find new political responses that "transcend both place and identity and foster a more effective cultural politics to counter the empirical, patriarchal, and racist integument of globalization" (Katz 2001, 1,216).

In looking at class issues in rural spaces, many scholars have studied the concentration of poverty in particular rural countries, especially in the South, the Appalachian region, and the Texas borderland. Shortage of jobs and limited upward mobility for workers is nothing new for rural people, especially in certain locations (Tickamyer and Duncan 1990). Licthter et al.'s (2012) recent analysis found that rural pockets of poverty might be drying up with the exception of high levels of concentrated poverty among minorities. In fact, approximately one-half of rural blacks and one-third of rural Hispanics live in poor counties, and the concentration of rural minority children is more extreme, with over 80 percent living in poor counties.

Impoverishment, lack of access to land, high unemployment, and inequality between and within places does not bode well for rural blacks living in the Black Belt south. From R. Wimberly's (2010) perspective, changing the course of poverty in the Black Belt region is the major challenge facing rural sociologists. D. Wimberly (2010, 116) argues that government cutbacks promoted by neoliberal globalizations have replaced possible solutions for the Black Belt, including "minimum wages, unemployment compensation, labor rights protection, Social Security disability benefits, antidiscrimination enforcement; progressive taxation, adequately-paid government jobs (often replaces with privatized services): government-supported medical care; and government-provided income, food, and housing support for the poor."

Considering Other Global Drivers: Climate Change and Human Rights

Two other trends related to globalization with differential impacts by gender, race, ethnicity, and class are worth mentioning. First, climate change and the resultant warming, increases in drought and desertification, and more violent and unpredictable storms and weather will have different impacts. Indigenous people, people living in substandard housing, and poor women have been and will continue to be more affected by climate change. The recent movement for climate justice often focused on inequalities at the nation-state level, but women and indigenous people are increasingly pushing for attention to their rights.

At the global level, the UN and other organizations have been pushing for human rights for women, lesbian, gay, and transgender people; minorities; and indigenous people. Emphases on social and political rights have resulted in major shifts in social and cultural arenas but have been less successful in providing economic justice. How these international movements impact changing gender, race, ethnicity, and sexuality issues in rural places remains a question to be explored.

For the Future

While much research has been conducted on gender, race, ethnicity, sexuality, and class in rural America, many issues call for further investigation. Here, I suggest five areas of research that will enhance our understanding and possibilities for change in rural places.

1. As globalization continues to impact rural America, a deeper infusion of scholarship inclusive of questions of gender, race, ethnicity, and sexuality will enrich our understanding of rural life in the United States. Despite strong scholarship in these areas, some of these concerns remain marginal and not fully integrated into the broader scholarship of rural America. More scholarship focusing on these groups is particularly absent in certain areas such as community and natural resource sociology. While several excellent detailed community and ethnographic studies have tackled issues of gender, race, or ethnicity, much more work is called for in different types of communities. More quantitative studies can also contribute to our understandings of how gender, race, and ethnicity relate to community concerns across a wider range of rural places.

2. Rural scholars can address the issues discussed above through a deeper engagement with feminist scholarship and critical race theory in their calls for intersectional analysis. Many studies focus on race, gender, or ethnicity in rural places, but only a few studies seriously interrogate how these multiple identities impact the livelihoods and well-being of rural people. Efforts to understand these complicated identities open up a vast realm of new scholarship.

3. As global attention increasingly turns to issues of climate change, a growing number of groups are insisting on climate justices. As in the environmental justice movement, people of color in the United States have often been most affected by environmental problems. People of color, indigenous people, and poor women are often most impacted by natural disasters, as witnessed in the events related to Hurricane Katrina. African Americans, women, and the elderly experienced the most loss and had fewer resources to adapt to the devastation from the flooding. People who live in marginal

environments will be most impacted by climate change and many of these are people of color.

4. Very limited scholarship exists on rural sexualities especially focused on lesbians, gays, bisexuals, and transgender people's lives in rural communities. Heteronormativity prevails in our understanding of rural places and metronormativity prevails in our understanding of the LGBT community. New scholarship on rural sexualities raises difficult questions. Some studies suggest that gays and lesbians experience extreme prejudice, stigma, and violence in rural places, while others suggest that urban biases misrepresent the difficulties encountered by rural sexual minorities. Clearly, these issues vary in different types of rural places, but the door is wide open for more research.

5. Gender, race, ethnic, class, and sexuality injustices are always being challenged. Many of these movements now cross national borders and have now gone global through efforts to resist impacts of globalization by women, people of color, and sexual minorities. The Occupy Wall Street movement that protests against social and economic inequality is largely an urban social movement. But global protests are not limited to urban people. Most notably, a growing worldwide movement led by *La via Campesina* is mobilizing indigenous people, small farmers, and women to push for social and economic justice related to climate justice, sustainability, and biodiversity. Studies of agency and resistance, as well as collaborations of rural sociologists with practitioners and community organizers, will help lead the way to social justice in rural America.

References

Brandth, Berit, and Marit Haugen. 2010. "Doing Farm Tourism: The Intertwining Practices of Gender and Work." *Signs (Chicago, Ill.)* 35 (2): 425–46. http://dx.doi.org/10.1086/605480.

Chakroborti, Neil, and John Garland. 2012. *Rural Racism*. London: Routledge.

Crenshaw, Kimberly. 1991. "Mapping the Margins: Intersectionality, Identity Politics, and Violence against Women of Color." *Stanford Law Review* 43 (6): 1241–99. http://dx.doi.org/10.2307/1229039.

Crowley, Martha, and Daniel T. Lichter. 2009. "Social Disorganization in New Latino Destinations." *Rural Sociology* 74 (4): 573–604. http://dx.doi.org/10.1526/003601109789864026.

Cuomo, Chris, Wendy Eisner, and Kenneth Hinkel. 2008. "Indigenous Knowledge, Environmental Change, and Subsistence on Alaska's North Slope." *S&F Online* 8 (1). http://sfonline.barnard.edu/ice/cuomo_eisner_hinkel_01.htm.

Dyer, Janice, and Conner Bailey. 2008. "A Place to Call Home: Cultural Understandings of Heir Property among Rural African Americans." *Rural Sociology* 73 (3): 317–38. http://dx.doi.org/10.1526/003601108785766598.

Falk, William. 2004. *Rooted in Place: Family and Belonging in a Southern Black Community.* New Brunswick, NJ: Rutgers University Press.

Falk, William, and Linda Lobao. 2003. "Who Benefits from Economic Restructuring? Lessons from the Past, Challenges for the Future." In *Challenges for Rural America in the Twenty-First Century*, ed. David Brown and Louis Swanson, 152–65. University Park: Penn State University Press.

Farmer, Frank, and Zola Moon. 2009. "An Empirical Examination of Characteristics of Mexican Migrants to Metropolitan and Nonmetropolitan Areas of the United States." *Rural Sociology* 74 (2): 220–40. http://dx.doi.org/10.1111/j.1549-0831.2009.tb00390.x.

Fernández-Kelly, Patricia. 2007. "The Global Assembly Line in the New Millennium: A Review Essay." *Signs (Chicago, Ill.)* 32 (2): 509–21. http://dx.doi.org/10.1086/508226.

Gilbert, J., G. Sharp, and M.S. Felin. 2002. "The Loss and Persistence of Black-Owned Farms and Farmland: A Review of the Research Literature and Its Implications." *Southern Rural Sociology* 18: 1–30.

Gonzales, Angela. 2003. "Gaming and Displacement: Winners and Losers in American Indian Casino Development." *International Social Science Journal* 55 (175): 123–33. http://dx.doi.org/10.1111/1468-2451.5501012.

Gray, Mary L. 2009. *Out in the Country: Youth, Media, and Queer Visibility in Rural America.* New York: New York University Press.

Hall, Alan, and Veronika Mogyorody. 2007. "Organic Farming, Gender, and the Labor Process." *Rural Sociology* 72 (2): 289–316. http://dx.doi.org/10.1526/003601107781170035.

Heckman, T.G., A.M. Somlai, J. Peters, J. Walker, L. Otto-Salaj, C.A. Galdabini, and J.A. Kelly. June 1998. "Barriers to Care among Persons Living with HIV/AIDS in Urban and Rural Areas." *AIDS Care* 10 (3): 365–75. http://dx.doi.org/10.1080/713612410. Medline:9828979.

Jensen, Leif. 2006. "New Immigrant Settlements in Rural America: Problems, Prospects and Policies." Carsey Institute Report 1(3). Durham: University of New Hampshire.

Jensen, Leif, and Eric Jensen. 2011. "Employment Hardship among Rural Men." In *Economic Restructuring and Family Well-Being in Rural America*, ed. Kristin Smith and Ann Tickamyer, 40–59. University Park: Penn State University Press.

Kandel, W., and J. Cromartie. 2004. *New Patterns of Hispanic Settlement in Rural America.* Rural Development Research Report 99. Washington, DC: Economic Research Service, USDA.

Katz, Cindy. 2001. "On the Grounds of Globalization: A Topography for Feminist Political Engagement." *Signs* (Chicago, Ill.) 26 (4): 1213–34. http://dx.doi.org/10.1086/495653. Medline:17615660.

Lichter, Daniel, and Kenneth Johnson. 2007. "The Changing Spatial Concentration of America's Rural Poor Population." *Rural Sociology* 72 (3): 331–58. http://dx.doi.org/10.1526/003601107781799290.

Lichter, Daniel, Domenico Parisi, and Michael C. Taquino. 2012. "The Geography of Exclusion: Race, Segregation, and Concentrated Poverty." *Social Problems* 59: 364–88.

Little, Jo, and Michael Leyshon. 2003. "Embodied Rural Geographies: Developing Research Agendas." *Progress in Human Geography* 27 (3): 257–72. http://dx.doi.org/10.1191/0309132503ph427oa.

Mohanty, Chandra. 1988. "Under Western Eyes: Feminist Scholarship and Colonial Discourses." *Feminist Review* 30 (Autumn): 61–88.

Nelson, Peter B., Alexander Oberg, and Lise Nelson. 2010. "Rural Gentrification and Linked Migration in the United States." *Journal of Rural Studies* 26 (4): 343–52. http://dx.doi.org/10.1016/j.jrurstud.2010.06.003.

Patel, Raj. 2009. *Stuffed and Starved: Markets, Power and the Hidden Battle for the World's Food System.* London: Portobello.

Pechlaner, G., and G. Otero. 2010. "The Neoliberal Food Regime: Neoregulation and the New Division of Labor in North America." *Rural Sociology* 75 (2): 179–208. http://dx.doi.org/10.1111/j.1549-0831.2009.00006.x.

Peterson, V. Spike. 2005. "How (the Meaning of) Gender Matters in Political Economy." *New Political Economy* 10 (4): 499–521. http://dx.doi.org/10.1080/13563460500344468.

Pfeffer, Max J., and Pliar A. Parra. 2009. "Strong Ties, Weak Ties, and Human Capital: Latino Immigrant Employment outside the Enclave." *Rural Sociology* 74 (2): 241–69. http://dx.doi.org/10.1111/j.1549-0831.2009.tb00391.x.

Preibisch, Kerry, and Evelyn Encalada Grez. 2010. "The Other Side of el Otro Lado: Mexican Migrant Women and Labor Flexibility in Canadian Agriculture." *Signs (Chicago, Ill.)* 35 (2): 289–316. http://dx.doi.org/10.1086/605483.

Preston, Deborah, and Anthony D'Augelli. 2012. *The Challenges of Being a Rural Gay Man: Coping with Stigma.* New York: Routledge.

Sachs, Carolyn, and Margaret Alston. 2010. "Global Shifts, Sedimentations, and Imaginaries: An Introduction to the Special Issue on Women and Agriculture." *Signs* (Chicago, Ill.) 35 (2): 277–87. http://dx.doi.org/10.1086/605618.

Schmalzbauer, Leah. 2011. "'Doing Gender,' Ensuring Survival: Mexican Migration and Economic Crisis in the Rural Mountain West." *Rural Sociology* 76 (4): 441–60. http://dx.doi.org/10.1111/j.1549-0831.2011.00058.x.

Sherman, Jennifer. 2011. "Men Without Sawmills: Job Loss and Gender Identity in Rural America." In *Economic Restructuring and Family Well-Being in Rural America*, ed. Kristin Smith and Ann Tickamyer, 82–102. University Park: Penn State University Press.

Smith, Kristin. 2011. "Changing Roles: Women and Work in Rural America." In *Economic Restructuring and Family Well-Being in Rural America*, ed. Kristin Smith and Ann Tickamyer, 60–81. University Park: Penn State University Press.

Tickamyer, Ann, and Cynthia Duncan. 1990. "Poverty and Opportunity Structure in Rural America." *Annual Review of Sociology* 16 (1): 67–86. http://dx.doi.org/10.1146/annurev.so.16.080190.000435.

Trauger, A., C. Sachs, M. Barbercheck, K. Brasier, and N.E. Kiernan. 2009. "'Our Market is Our Community': Women Farmers and Civic Agriculture in Pennsylvania, USA." *Agriculture, Food and Human Values* 26 (1): 43–55.

Weston, Kath. 1995. "Get Thee to a Big City: Sexual Imaginary and the Great Gay Migration." *GLQ: A Journal of Lesbian and Gay Studies* 2 (3): 253–77.

Wimberly, Dale. 2010. "Quality of Life Trends in the Southern Black Belt, 1980–2005: A Research Note." *Journal of Rural Social Sciences* 25 (1): 103–18.

Wimberly, Ronald. 2010. "It's Our Most Rural Region; It's the Poorest, It's the Black Belt South, and It Needs Our Attention." *Journal of Rural Social Sciences* 25 (2): 175–82.

CHAPTER 22

The Status of African Americans in the Rural United States

John J. Green

Introduction

In this chapter, I explore the status of African Americans in the rural United States. Using the livelihoods theoretical framework from development studies, I explore literature and data regarding the regional location and spatial concentration of rural African Americans and their socioeconomic position relative to whites. Findings demonstrate that the presence of African Americans in rural areas continues to be a largely southern phenomenon rooted in the history of slavery and its aftermath. Although extant research shows some improvements in quality of life among African American rural residents, disparities remain relative to their counterparts in metropolitan places and to whites in both metropolitan and nonmetropolitan/rural areas. These patterns are demonstrated by my analysis of contemporary data from the American Community Survey as well. I explore the implications of these findings and their importance to the pursuit of greater equality during this time in our global era.

A common understanding of race and ethnicity among sociologists is that each racial and ethnic category carries with it an ascribed status and socioeconomic location for its members. Although people identify themselves with these groups (and often with combinations of multiple groups), it is the broader society that structures inequality according to the status of the group rather than the merit of its members. This is beneficial to some groups and problematic for others. Of the minority racial groups most studied in the United States, the trajectory of African Americans uncovers a great deal about American society, both historically and in contemporary times. It is also instructive for exploring the position, opportunities, and barriers traditionally marginalized groups face in the global age and what this means for attempts to achieve a more equitable and socially just society. As a leading work on the lives of African Americans in the era following the Civil War—*The Souls of Black Folk* (Du Bois 2008, originally published in 1903)—argued more than a century ago, the study of racial inequality sheds light on the state of our society. In this chapter, I build on notable attempts to assess the status of African Americans living in rural areas over the past two decades (Harris and Worthen 2003; Stewart and Allen Smith 1995).

Theoretical Framework

In discussing the status of African Americans living in the rural United States, it is necessary to go beyond basic description to explore the factors associated with influences on this social group's position and status in broader society. Much of the literature concerning African Americans in rural areas published in recent decades has focused on national patterns of migration, segregation, inequality, and poverty, with race often included as one among many variables. These are informative empirical studies, yet their theoretical propositions tend not to explicitly address race. This is a continuation of the gaps in research regarding African Americans noted by Harris and Worthen (2003) a decade ago and earlier by Snipp (1996).

Still, there are social theories concerning race that are informative. Of particular note are critical race studies (Delgado and Stefancic 2011) and intersectionality theory (Collins 2000). Critical race studies is a field of scholarship providing direct attention to the ways in which racial identities, power, and inequality are instituted in the structure and processes of society. Intersectionality theory, largely articulated within feminist scholarship, seeks to investigate the connections and interplay between multiple and complex identities, including gender, race, and class, and the inequalities tied to them. Studying the position of African Americans in terms of racial and spatial inequality is well warranted (Green and Mitra 2013), but as Sachs (in this volume) notes, the rural dimensions to such intersections have been understudied.

Although considerable attention has been directed toward documenting, analyzing, and even explaining racial inequalities and how they intersect with other socioeconomic factors, much of this work has not been deeply integrated within broader development conversations or frameworks. To build on the existing knowledge base and help translate it for discussions to inform action and development, the livelihoods framework is illuminating. Based in international human, social, and economic development literature (Bebbington 1999; de Haan and Zoomers 2005), the livelihoods framework focuses attention on the material and experiential resources and strategies that individuals, households, and communities have access to and utilize in their everyday lives. It also gives attention to the inequalities that shape what development pathways some groups have access to while others find these pathways blocked. Pathways are shaped at multiple levels of society, including global processes of economic restructuring, as has been seen in the agrifood system (Green and Kleiner 2009a). Global economic restructuring may result in further shocks and stresses to people's livelihood systems.

Within livelihoods studies, various forms of resources and assets/capital are assessed, an approach that is compatible with the community capitals framework found in rural sociology and community development (Green and Haines 2008; Flora and Flora 2007). Gutierrez-Montes, Emery, and Fernandez-Baca (2009) note that the community capitals framework expands on the livelihoods approach by including a more comprehensive list of capitals (e.g., human, social, cultural, political, natural, financial, and built) and moving analysis to entail the broader community level.

Investigated through the livelihoods framework, it is apparent that pathways being blocked by racism, discrimination, and segregation have shaped the position of African Americans in rural society, leaving them vulnerable to shocks and stresses to their livelihood systems. These are coupled with the broader political and economic forces resulting in underdevelopment and uneven development in the spaces where African Americans in rural areas have traditionally resided, such as the South. However, numerous opportunity pathways have been opened over the course of time in the realms of civil rights, educational attainment, and economic resources, contributing to both human and political capital development. Much of this has been the result of long-term social movements and protracted efforts to change policy, laws, and the social structure. Even with these intense efforts, inequality between whites and African Americans continues. With global economic restructuring, dominance of the market regime, and disinvestments in social development, it is likely that these issues will become more complex and challenges exacerbated.

Historical Context

In the current era of globalization and scholarly explorations of global phenomena, it is important to note that the southern United States has long influenced and been influenced by international and global trends, especially at the intersection of race relations and agriculture. This profoundly influenced development trajectories through the construction and maintenance of the plantation political economy and culture evident in most aspects of social and economic life (Asch 2008; Beckford 1999), with emphasis on export industries. Without implying racial conflict as directly being a causal force, Woodward (1966) proposes analyzing the different phases of US southern history in terms of the relations between racial groups.

As a starting point, it is key to recognize that the large majority of people from African backgrounds originally came to North America as slaves, thereby establishing unequal power relationships between whites and people of color with legacies that persist to present times (Snipp 1996; Trotter 2001). Primarily, slaves were exploited for agricultural development and production in southern states and territories, but they were also used in domestic activities and industry (Beale 1966). Although slavery is often conceptualized as being outside of industrial capitalism's development trajectory, McMichael (1991) notes that slavery in the American South was part of the broader global system of industrial production, such as that found in cotton.

Following the end to legal slavery with emancipation and the conclusion of the Civil War (1865), there was a period of Reconstruction whereby African Americans enjoyed some political and economic freedoms unheard of before in the United States. However, this period was short-lived, and many of the promises to formers slaves were not kept, thus closing off potential pathways for development. Many areas of the South transitioned toward tenant and sharecropping systems whereby laborers continued to work the land for landowners and did so with limited power and under heavy burdens of debt. This was paralleled with political and legal formulations that kept African Americans in a lower social position and status, using mechanisms of discrimination and segregation codified into the so-called Jim Crow laws (Woodward 1966).

Despite these challenges, there was resistance among many African Americans in rural areas, and efforts were made toward self-determination and livelihood security through institutions such as the 1890 Land Grant Universities, other historically black colleges and universities, businesses, and community-based cooperatives. A self-help approach to education and development was constructed and refined. The institutional legacy of this work is still found in higher education and rural development today.

Even with these hard-won advances, rural African Americans, much like their more urban counterparts, continued to face discrimination, state-sanctioned segregation in education and public facilities, and too few economic opportunities. In addition, major political, economic, and environmental shifts made life in the rural South particularly harsh, such as the Great Depression, Boll Weevil attack on cotton, and later agricultural mechanization and reductions in farm jobs (Fite 1984). In this context, many African Americans began to move northward in search of jobs, especially in factories, and better living conditions. The Great Migration of African Americans moving northward, primarily to urban centers, started in the late 1800s and continued through the middle half of the 1900s, with a few periods of slow down. As Tolnay (2003, 210) points out, "The 'Great Migration' of African Americans out of southern states and into northern cities was one of the most significant demographic events to occur in the United States during the twentieth century."

There were African Americans who stayed involved in agriculture as hired laborers, tenants, sharecroppers, and independent farmers. The early quarter of the twentieth century showed the largest number of African American farmers and farm operations, followed by a rapid decline in numbers (Wood and Gilbert 1998). With the loss of African American farms, there was a parallel loss of African American-owned land. A wealth of research has been conducted to document and analyze the troubling position faced by African American farmers and landowners with particular focus on institutional discrimination (Civil Rights Action Team 1997; Daniel 2013; Gilbert, Sharp, and Felin 2002; Green, Green, and Kleiner 2011; Marable 1979). The history of discrimination against African American agricultural producers in more recent years—the early 1980s through the mid-1990s—received legal attention through a series of class action lawsuits and settlements, generally referred to under one of the suit names, *Pigford v. Glickman* (1999).

Beyond agricultural production, land ownership continues to be important for both wealth and identity, and loss of land due to complications over heir property without a clear title trajectory is viewed as particularly problematic (Gilbert, Sharp, and Felin 2002). Still, some research suggests that familial collective land ownership does provide emotional and material security (Dyer and Bailey 2008), a potential livelihood response to structural arrangements in the economy.

The post–World War II Civil Rights Movement is often spoken of as an urban phenomenon, with the best-known leaders and activities taking place in Montgomery and Birmingham (Alabama), Atlanta (Georgia), Jackson (Mississippi), and Memphis (Tennessee), to name just a few. Nonetheless, rural areas throughout the region involved people working on multiple sides of the struggle. It is worth noting that the death of young Emmett Till in Tallahatchie County, Mississippi, and the murder of three civil rights activists in Neshoba County, Mississippi, took place in rural areas around smaller towns. Furthermore, numerous movement leaders lived in rural areas, including Fannie Lou Hamer in Sunflower County, Mississippi (Asch 2008; Dittmer 1995). Prolonged community organizing took place to expand economic opportunities and protect African American land and businesses. This was often contextualized as being part of the unfinished business of the Civil Rights Movement to reduce rural poverty and open economic opportunities through New Poor People's Cooperatives (Marshall and Godwin 1971). Some of the work took place through the Federation of Southern Cooperatives/Land Assistance Fund, its grassroots member organizations across the South, and broader affiliated organizations at the national level such as the Rural Coalition (Green and Kleiner 2009b).

There was much made of the so-called New South where economic opportunities increased rapidly after legally mandated segregation phased out and race was to become less of a defining structure of society. Places like Atlanta are the most-often identified with this pattern of development, and to be sure such areas did experience economic booms. Of course, they have been shown to still have segregation and discrimination with the new often simply covering up the old institutions and arrangements that continue to define everyday life for African Americans in urban areas (Bullard 1989). The economic opportunities have not reached as far into rural places. Facing many of the challenges plaguing the nation, significant portions of the rural South have faced long-term poverty, with African Americans often positioned much worse than their white counterparts. As an example, Gyawali and colleagues (2008) note that even during a period of some income growth for rural areas in the Alabama Black Belt region (between 1980 and 2000), changes in income were strongly associated with racial composition. Majority black areas fared significantly worse than majority white spaces.

With this broad stroke of a historical backdrop, in the following section I direct attention toward the relative position of African Americans living in rural areas in contemporary times. I begin with a general analysis of regional concentration and migration flows of African Americans. Building on the work of Harris and Worthen (2003), in the following sections I also delve into patterns of inequality as a way of shining a light on the unfinished business of constructing a more equitable society.

Demographic and Socioeconomic Patterns

With one exception, all of the counties with 50 percent or more of the population identifying as African American/black (alone or in combination with other races) were located in the South in 2010 (Rastogi et al. 2011).[1] Importantly, a majority of African Americans living in rural areas were located in the South. This concentration is part of an historical trend dating back to the era of slavery that continued after emancipation to the late 1800s and through the

Table 22.1
Principal operators and farm operations by race, 2007

Characteristics	White	African American
Farms	2,114,325	30,599
Land in farms	863,819,828	3,182,313
Avg. farm size (acres)	409	104
Farms by size		
1 to 9 acres	9.9%	12.6%
10 to 49 acres	28.0%	38.3%
50 to 179 acres	30.1%	36.6%
180 to 499 acres	17.0%	10.0%
500 acres or more	15.0%	2.5%
Farms by economic class		
Less than $1,000	22.2%	31.9%
$1,000 to $2,499	12.2%	17.5%
$2,500 to $4,999	11.1%	15.1%
$5,000 to $9,999	11.5%	14.3%
$10,000 to $24,999	12.5%	11.5%
$25,000 to $49,999	7.5%	4.6%
$50,000 or more	23.0%	5.1%
Example farm production by NAICS*		
Oilseed and grain	15.8%	7.8%
Cotton	0.5%	0.6%
Vegetable and melon	1.6%	5.6%
Beef cattle	29.5%	46.1%
Farms receiving government payments		
CCC loans	2.4%	1.0%
Conservation programs	16.1%	8.4%
Other farm programs	31.8%	22.7%

Note: North American Industrial Classification System (NAICS) codes are used to reference farms with primary production in particular realm. Numbers here do not include all possible areas.
Table compiled by the University of Mississippi Center for Population Studies. Source: US Department of Agriculture, National Agricultural Statistics Service (2007). Data are for individuals reporting single racial group identities.

1900s (Beale 1966; Falk 2004). Analysis of 2010 US Decennial Census data by region and metropolitan/nonmetropolitan classification (using updated rural-urban continuum county designations based on US Department of Agriculture Economic Research Service classifications) demonstrates that the presence of

African Americans in rural areas is an overwhelmingly southern phenomenon.[2] As an indicator of spatial concentration, it is helpful to investigate the location of counties in the southern region where one-half of the population or more is identified as African American. Data from the 2010 US Decennial Census demonstrated that these spaces are located in the areas known as the Black Belt and the Delta regions of the country (US Census Bureau 2010b). Wimberley and Morris (1997; 2002) contribute to our understanding of these areas through regional demographic and socioeconomic analysis, thereby documenting the overlay of racial and spatial inequalities.

Agriculture

Major declines in the number of African American farmers occurred in the twentieth century, yet members of this racial group do continue to participate in agriculture. Beale (1966) and Wood and Gilbert (1998) document steep declines during the twentieth century. Contemporary analysis of US Census of Agriculture data from 2007 resulted in estimates of 30,599 African American principal farm operators in the United States (Table 22.1). Relative to white principal operators, African Americans were more likely to have smaller-scale enterprises (measured in acreage and economic class); more likely to produce fruits, vegetables, and livestock; and less likely to receive government program payments. The continuing presence of African Americans as agricultural producers is particularly notable when considering the history of past abuses, institutional neglect, and broader forces of consolidation and globalization.

Migration and Location

Around the 1970s, a stream of migration developed from other regions of the United States into the South, including the return of southern-born African Americans (Adelman, Morett, and Tolnay 2000). The push factors for this, as Adelman and colleagues (2000) theorize, were the worsening socioeconomic conditions of urban areas in the North, with the pull factors being improved living conditions in the South. These factors may be interpreted in relation to the livelihood pathways and associated strategies that are available to individuals and their families. Improvements did not necessarily occur evenly across the region but varied across the rural-urban continuum, and sometimes people return on the basis of wanting to help improve the place they call home. In all, as Stack (1996) notes, the factors involved are complex and multilayered.

According to analysis of contemporary trends, research demonstrates a pattern where African Americans—when compared with whites—have been increasingly less likely to move away from the South to other regions of the country, and more likely to move to the South from the North (Hunt, Hunt, and Falk 2008). Beale and Fuguitt (2011) find patterns showing African American migration to the South. Although some of this involved retirees moving to the same places favored by retirees from other races, a considerable portion of African American migration to the South was to nonmetropolitan counties.

Out-migration occurs in many rural areas, but is not consistent across racial/ethnic groups. Brooks and Redlin (2009) find that the complex intersections of identity (e.g., race and gender), social position, and occupational aspirations influence migration decisions.

It may be common for casual observers to assume that the African Americans living in rural areas were "left behind" or were "unable to leave" because of their socioeconomic position and blocked pathways for improvement. Indeed, there has been significant out-migration of whites and middle-class African Americans from rural places, especially in the Black Belt and Mississippi Delta regions, thereby leaving these places with fewer people and resources. Still, it is particularly important to recognize that people often identify with and are attached to their communities, and sometimes choose not to leave or strive to return (Falk 2004). Beyond Falk's (2004) research in the Carolinas, this sense of identity and attachment is clearly displayed in majority African American communities with long histories rooted in the hopes and dreams of emancipation from slavery, such as in Mound Bayou, Mississippi (Hermann 1999; Rosen 2011).

Despite legal and regulatory changes, racial and ethnic residential segregation is a continued social phenomenon in rural America. Lichter et al. (2007) note that segregation patterns in rural areas are similar to those in urban places. There were declines in the level of residential segregation in rural areas in the 1990s, but although there were improvements, African Americans in nonmetropolitan places continued to be the most highly segregated.

From the existing literature and patterns observed in secondary data, it is clear that the location of African Americans in rural areas is multifaceted. Migration flows have been both inward and outward, and a considerable number of African Americans live in rural spaces, especially in the South. There is evidence to suggest that these patterns relate to ongoing changes in the opportunities and barriers available in different areas outside of the rural South.

Socioeconomic Inequalities

Harris and Worthen (2003) review extant literature, noting inequalities in education, income, and poverty among African Americans relative to whites. The scholarly debate about inequality and race has come from two different opposing positions—the declining significance of race (Wilson 1978; 2011) versus the continued relevance of race and racism (Feagin 2010). What these positions tend to underappreciate in their class versus race explanations is the importance of the intersections between race, socioeconomic position, and spatial location. Considering the importance of intersectionality and using the livelihoods framework to interpret existing work on race and inequality, it may be argued that, as Duncan (1999, 96) notes, "the social class structure reflects racial stratification," partially as a result of the patterns and norms rooted in structures and processes developed more than a century ago. These legacies are apparent in the rural American South.

Upon investigating the connections between race and socioeconomic position, numerous inequalities can be identified. Although disparities between whites and African Americans have declined somewhat over time, the differences have been pronounced and continue to endure. For instance, major disparities in underemployment and hardship have been identified between whites and minority racial/ethnic groups, especially in nonmetropolitan areas (Slack and Jensen 2002). Even as pockets of concentrated poverty in rural areas shrink, concentration of poverty among rural minorities persists (Lichter and Johnson 2007). More recently, research from the Economic Research Service (2011)—based on analysis of the US Census Bureau's Current Population Survey—showed that African Americans had the highest rates of nonmetropolitan poverty (nearly 33 percent).

Analysis of five-year estimates (2006 to 2010) from the US Census Bureau's American Community Survey demonstrates marked socioeconomic inequalities at the intersections of spatial location and race. Compared to whites living in metropolitan and nonmetropolitan areas, African Americans living in nonmetropolitan areas were more likely to have lower levels of educational attainment. Furthermore, African Americans in nonmetropolitan areas were more likely to have household incomes less than $50,000, and were more likely than their white counterparts to be living below the poverty line.[3]

Exploring racial inequality specifically in nonmetropolitan areas, 18.8 percent of whites aged twenty-five and older were estimated to have a college degree or higher, whereas the figure was 8.6 percent for all African Americans, according to 2006 to 2010 estimates from the American Community Survey. In terms of household income, 56.5 percent of whites were below $50,000 compared with 78.6 percent of African Americans. Pointedly, while 9.1 percent of white individuals were at or below the poverty line, the poverty level was considerably higher for African Americans, at 23.2 percent. Disparities followed similar patterns in the nonmetropolitan southern counties, with poverty rates particularly high among African Americans (35.2 percent).

These socioeconomic inequalities are associated with health disparities. A larger body of research investigating numerous health outcomes demonstrates both socioeconomic and racial group differences. For instance, county-level ecological analysis showed an association between minority concentration, income inequality, and mortality (McLaughlin and Stokes 2002). Unfortunately, there have been a limited number of studies investigating the intersections of race and rurality in the health literature. Nonetheless, this is a growing area of investigation, with important calls being made for more attention to race and space (Probst et al. 2004). Albrecht, Clarke, and Miller (1998) assess factors associated with health outcomes in rural areas, with specific analysis for racial/ethnic groups. A study conducted in the Mississippi Delta region indicates that although there were some similarities between the socioeconomic factors associated with health status for whites and African Americans in this rural region, there was variation in these pathways between racial groups (Green, Kerstetter, and Nylander 2008).

A Case of Inequality: The Mississippi Delta

As previously noted, regional research by Wimberley and Morris (1997; 2002) shows the challenges faced by African American residents in the broad multistate Black Belt region in the southern United States. One of the subregions with particularly high representation of African Americans and socioeconomic inequality is the lower Mississippi River Delta, which encompasses parts of many states, including Arkansas, Louisiana, and Mississippi.

The Delta counties in Mississippi are illustrative of these inequalities. The eleven rural counties in the northwestern region of the state that fall in the floodplain of the Yazoo River and Mississippi River were originally settled for plantation style agricultural production (Saikku 2005), with much of the development occurring in the latter half of the 1800s and early 1900s. Historically, the numeric majority of the population has been African American. Relative to the state, the Delta region has lower levels of educational attainment, lower median household incomes, and higher poverty rates, with major disparities between whites and African Americans (Cosby et al. 1992; Duncan 1999; Kersen 2002).

Continuation of these patterns is demonstrated in data from the 2006–2010 American Community Survey, with pronounced socioeconomic inequality between whites and African Americans. For example, estimated poverty rates are high, but most alarmingly, the estimated percentage of African Americans below the poverty threshold in the core Delta region ranges from 30 percent to approximately 56 percent.

Future Research and Policy Concerns

> Rural sociologists have an opportunity to make a unique contribution to what is known about American racial and ethnic relations because their research takes them into areas and regions where the institutions of racial opposition were first established and consequently, the last to be dismantled. (Snipp 1996, 140)

Drawing from Hirschman and Snipp (1999), Slack and Jensen (2002) rightfully argue that attending to the socioeconomic position of minority groups helps to illuminate rigid social structures and the challenges of achieving social justice. In addition, such investigations provide the basis for better understanding patterns of uneven development and globalization. As illuminated through the livelihoods approach and demonstrated through the literature, although African Americans living in rural areas have seen gains in both opportunities and outcomes, inequality persists. Contemporary data provide a base against which future progress toward a more equitable society can be judged.

More research on the position of rural African Americans is warranted, and the livelihoods approach (Bebbington 1999; de Haan and Zoomers 2005; Green and Kleiner 2009a; Gutierrez-Montes, Emery, and Fernandez-Baca 2009) provides a framework for these investigations. In our ever-shifting global world, the livelihood pathways for this racial group might be blocked, stagnate, or change based on policy changes, program development, and grassroots collective action. Although the economy of southern states may not be developing as quickly as many analysts envisioned, the fallout of economic restructuring in the northern United States (especially in manufacturing) may be resulting in the perception of there being relatively better opportunities in the South in the context of familial and community networks. At the same time, the combined stresses of economic crisis and efforts to reduce state spending on educational and social welfare programs may block opportunities in these same spaces.

Continued national and regional statistical analysis of trends among African Americans should be a part of this research agenda. However, this work needs to go beyond treating race primarily as a control variable in explaining other social phenomena (social problems such as poverty), and shift more toward investigating the ways in which social structures, power, and historical legacies are used to maintain racial differences (Carter 2009) and the intersections of race with other categories, including rurality. This approach will provide greater insights into the maintenance and thus persistence of disparities between racial groups between and across geographic spaces.

Additional qualitative research and multi-method studies (quantitative and qualitative designs) are needed if we are to go beyond the current knowledge base and ask deeper questions about how and why particular development pathways are opened and closed for African Americans in rural areas, and how these shift over the course of time. For instance, Falk's (2004) study of African Americans and their connection to place and Stack's (1996) research on African Americans migrating to the South have been highly influential, yet studies of this kind are few and far between. Although Duncan's (1999) study of three regions in the United States incorporates analysis of racial dynamics, the research was primarily focused on understanding poverty rather than on inequality between racial groups or race relations directly. There is also a need for detailed analyses of how global forces are experienced by different racial groups in the rural context, as Sachs (in this volume) notes.

In addition to continuation of the major substantive areas of focus concerning migration, segregation, and socioeconomic characteristics, more research on health and the peculiarities of race/space combinations is needed. Augmenting efforts to differentiate between whether one racial group is more or less healthy than another and whether people living in one space are more or less healthy than their counterparts, attention should turn toward the ways in which race and space intersect and how this knowledge may help to deepen our understanding of inequality, poverty, and health to inform the actions that can be taken to increase development pathways and improve quality of life. The livelihoods framework provides an analytic tool for exploring these issues and informing initiatives aimed at increasing capabilities through asset development and reducing vulnerability in the face of shocks and stresses.

Regarding policy, much of the discussion concerning the challenges African Americans in rural areas face has focused on improving human capital through education and workforce development (Duncan 1999; Stewart and Allen Smith 1995). Such efforts are clearly necessary, especially given historic disparities at the intersections of race and space in regions such as the Black Belt and the Mississippi Delta. With fast-paced technological and economic change, it will be imperative for improved education and workforce development efforts to reach rural areas.

Although educational and workforce development policy agendas are necessary, they are not sufficient.[4] More rapid reductions in disparities between

African Americans and whites, while at the same time improving livelihood opportunities for all racial/ethnic groups, will require attention to the structural and institutional factors associated with inequality and poverty. Instead of individualizing the challenges and blaming individuals for disparities between groups, more work is needed on the policy reformulations that restructure business as usual. This should help to drive investments to increase access to and utilization of other assets for development. A notable move in this direction is found in reforms within the US Department of Agriculture including the Program for Technical Assistance to Socially Disadvantaged Farmers and Ranchers and creation of the position of the Undersecretary of Civil Rights (Green, Green, and Kleiner 2011). These efforts combine attention to human capital with access to natural, financial, and built capital.

Addressing the need for spatially oriented approaches to addressing persistent social concerns, regional initiatives have been developed in recent decades to address socioeconomic development and poverty. The Delta Regional Authority and versions of a Black Belt Regional Commission are two notable examples, both of which were influenced by the significantly older Appalachian Regional Commission. Research was used to inform these endeavors involving a long list of rural sociologists and other social scientists. Notably, Black Belt scholars have included Rosalind Harris, Ron Wimberley, Libby Morris, and Dreamal Worthen, among others. As these regional initiatives mature, it will be critical to monitor whether they serve to open up development pathways for African Americans and help to reduce inequality with whites at the same time as improving the social and economic position of people across racial groups.

Monitoring and assessing the impact of social change and development is of importance not only to African Americans and scholars of race and ethnicity. Instead, this type of analysis is critical to all people concerned about overcoming inequality and pursuing justice in our society. Scholars of rural society have a major role to play in this regard.

Notes

1 I used the US Census Bureau regional classification system for the analysis presented in this chapter. Accordingly, the South consists of the following states: Alabama, Arkansas, Delaware, Florida, Georgia, Kentucky, Louisiana, Maryland, Mississippi, North Carolina, Oklahoma, South Carolina, Tennessee, Texas, Virginia, West Virginia, and the District of Columbia.

2 Noting the presence of African Americans in rural areas as a more common characteristic in the southern United States is not intended to dismiss the fact that there are rural areas in other places throughout the country with African American residents.

3 American Community Survey estimates are based on samples and should be interpreted along with the corresponding margins of error. All of the estimates compared for this analysis included attention to the 90 percent confidence intervals. All of the disparities between white

and black groups were found to be statistically significant with differences beyond the margins of error. Additionally, similar analysis was conducted using 2007 to 2011 estimates and the patterns were the same.

4 This chapter was written amidst the recognition and celebration of the fifty-year anniversary of James Meredith's work to integrate the University of Mississippi in 1962. Although major educational advancements have been made, there is considerable room for improving the livelihood opportunities for African Americans.

References

Adelman, Robert M., Chris Morett, and Stewart E. Tolnay. 2000. "Homeward Bound: The Return Migration of Southern-Born Black Women, 1940 to 1990." *Sociological Spectrum* 20 (4): 433–63. http://dx.doi.org/10.1080/02732170050122639.

Albrecht, Stan L., Leslie L. Clarke, and Michael K. Miller. 1998. "Community, Family, and Race/Ethnic Differences in Health Status in Rural Areas." *Rural Sociology* 63 (2): 235–52. http://dx.doi.org/10.1111/j.1549-0831.1998.tb00673.x.

Asch, Chris Myers. 2008. *The Senator and the Sharecropper: The Freedom Struggles of James O. Eastland and Fannie Lou Hamer*. New York: The New Press.

Beale, Calvin L. 1966. "The Negro in American Agriculture." In *The American Negro Reference Book*, ed. John P. Davis, 161–204. Englewood Cliffs, NJ: Prentice Hall.

Beale, Calvin L., and Glenn V. Fuguitt. 2011. "Migration of Retirement-Age Blacks to Nonmetropolitan Areas in the 1990s." *Rural Sociology* 76 (1): 31–43. http://dx.doi.org/10.1111/j.1549-0831.2010.00037.x.

Bebbington, Anthony. 1999. "Capitals and Capabilities: A Framework for Analyzing Peasant Viability, Rural Livelihoods, and Poverty." *World Development* 27 (12): 2021–44. http://dx.doi.org/10.1016/S0305-750X(99)00104-7.

Beckford, George L. [1972] 1999. *Persistent Poverty: Underdevelopment in Plantation Economies of the Third World*. Barbados: University of the West Indies Press.

Brooks, W. Trevor, and Meredith Redlin. 2009. "Occupational Aspirations, Rural to Urban Migration, and Intersectionality: A Comparison of White, Black, and Hispanic Male and Female Group Chances for Leaving Rural Communities." *Southern Rural Sociology* 24 (1): 130–52.

Bullard, Robert D. 1989. *In Search of the New South: Black Urban Experience in the 1970s and 1980s*. Tuscaloosa: University of Alabama Press.

Carter, Perry L. 2009. "Geography, Race, and Quantification." *Professional Geographer* 61 (4): 465–80. http://dx.doi.org/10.1080/00330120903143466.

Civil Rights Action Team. 1997. *Civil Right at the United States Department of Agriculture*. Washington, DC: United States Department of Agriculture.

Collins, Patricia H. 2000. *Black Feminist Thought: Knowledge, Consciousness, and the Politics of Empowerment*. New York: Routledge.

Cosby, Arthur, Mitchell Brackin, T. David Mason, and Eunice McCulloch. 1992. *A Social and Economic Portrait of the Mississippi Delta*. Mississippi: Mississippi State University, Social Science Research Center.

Daniel, Pete. 2013. *Dispossession: Discrimination against African American Farmers in the Age of Civil Rights*. Chapel Hill, NC: University of North Carolina Press.

de Haan, Leo, and Annelies Zoomers. 2005. "Exploring the Frontier of Livelihoods Research." *Development and Change* 36 (1): 27–47. http://dx.doi.org/10.1111/j.0012-155X.2005.00401.x.

Delgado, Richard, and Jean Stefancic. 2011. *Critical Race Theory: An Introduction*. New York: New York University Press.

Dittmer, John. 1995. *Local People: The Struggle for Civil Rights in Mississippi*. Chicago: The University of Illinois Press.

Du Bois, W.E.B. [1903]. 2008. *The Souls of Black Folk*. Rockville, MD: ARC Manor.

Duncan, Cynthia M. 1999. *Worlds Apart: Why Poverty Persists in Rural America*. New Haven, CT: Yale University Press.

Dyer, Janice, and Conner Bailey. 2008. "A Place to Call Home: Cultural Understandings of Heir Property among Rural African Americans." *Rural Sociology* 73 (3): 317–38. http://dx.doi.org/10.1526/003601108785766598.

Economic Research Service. 2011. "Rural Income, Poverty, and Welfare: Poverty Demographics." US Department of Agriculture. Accessed 1 March 2012. http://www.ers.usda.gov/topics/rural-economy-population/rural-poverty-well-being.aspx.

Falk, William W. 2004. *Rooted in Place: Family and Belonging in a Southern Black Community*. Piscataway, NJ: Rutgers University Press.

Feagin, Joe R. 2010. *Racist America: Roots, Current Realities, and Future Reparations*, 2nd ed. New York: Routledge.

Fite, Gilbert C. 1984. *Cotton Fields No More: Southern Agriculture 1865–1980*. Lexington: The University Press of Kentucky.

Flora, Cornelius, and Jan Flora. 2007. *Rural Communities: Legacy and Change*, 3rd ed. Boulder, CO: Westview Press.

Gilbert, Jess, Gwen Sharp, and M. Sindy Felin. 2002. "The Loss and Persistence of Black-Owned Farms and Farmland: A Review of the Research Literature and Its Implications." *Southern Rural Sociology* 18 (2): 1–30.

Green, Gary P., and Anna Haines. 2008. *Asset Building and Community Development*, 2nd ed. Los Angeles: Sage.

Green, John J., Eleanor M. Green, and Anna M. Kleiner. 2011. "From the Past to the Present: Agricultural Development and Black Farmers in the American South." *Cultivating Food Justice: Race, Class and Sustainability*, ed. Alyson H. Alkon and Julian Agyeman, 47–64. Cambridge, MA: MIT.

Green, John J., Kathleen Kerstetter, and Albert B. Nylander, III. 2008. "Socioeconomic Resources and Self-Rated Health: A Study in the Mississippi Delta." *Sociological Spectrum* 28 (2): 194–212. http://dx.doi.org/10.1080/02732170701796551.

Green, John J., and Anna M. Kleiner. 2009a. "Exploring Global Agrifood Politics and the Position of Limited Resource Producers in the United States." In *Politics of Globalization*, ed. Samir Dasgupta and Jan Nederveen Pieterse, 313–33. Los Angeles: Sage. http://dx.doi.org/10.4135/9788132108283.n14.

Green, John J., and Anna M. Kleiner. 2009b. "Escaping the Bondage of the Dominant Agrifood System: Community-Based Cooperative Strategies." *Southern Rural Sociology* 24 (2): 149–68.

Green, John, and Debarashmi Mitra. 2013. "Intersections of Development, Poverty, Race, and Space in the Mississippi Delta in the Era of Globalization: Implications for Gender-Based Health Issues." In *Forthcoming in Poverty and Health in America*, ed. K. Fitzpatrick, 177–205. Westport, CT: Praeger Publishers.

Gutierrez-Montes, Isabel, Mary Emery, and Edith Fernandez-Baca. 2009. "The Sustainable Livelihoods Approach and the Community Capitals Framework: The Importance of System-Level Approaches to Community Change Efforts." *Community Development* 40 (2): 106–13. http://dx.doi.org/10.1080/15575330903011785.

Gyawali, Buddhi, Rory Fraser, James Bukenya, and John Schelhas. 2008. "Income Convergence in a Rural, Majority African-American Region." *Review of Regional Studies* 38 (1): 45–65.

Harris, Rosalind P., and Dreamal Worthen. 2003. "African Americans in Rural America." In *Challenges for Rural America in the Twenty-First Century*, ed. David L. Brown and Louis E. Swanson, 32–42. University Park: The Pennsylvania State University Press.

Hermann, Janet S. 1999. *Pursuit of a Dream*. Jackson, MS: University Press of Mississippi.

Hirschman, Charles, and C. Matthew Snipp. 1999. "The State of the American Dream: Race and Ethnic Socioeconomic Inequality in the United States, 1970–1990." In *A Nation Divided: Diversity, Inequality, and Community in American Society*, ed. Phyllis Moen, Donna Dempster-McClain, and Henry A. Walker, 89–107. Ithaca, NY: Cornell University Press.

Hunt, Larry L., Matthew O. Hunt, and William W. Falk. 2008. "Who is Headed South? U.S. Migration Trends in Black and White, 1970–2000." *Social Forces* 87 (1): 95–119. http://dx.doi.org/10.1353/sof.0.0099.

Kersen, Thomas M. 2002. *The Changing Delta, 1990–2002*. Mississippi State, MS: Social Science Research Center.

Lichter, Daniel T., and Kenneth M. Johnson. 2007. "The Changing Spatial Concentration of America's Rural Poor Population." *Rural Sociology* 72 (3): 331–58. http://dx.doi.org/10.1526/003601107781799290.

Lichter, Daniel T., Domenico Parisi, Steven Michael Grice, and Michael C. Taquino. 2007. "National Estimates of Racial Segregation in Rural and Small-Town America." *Demography* 44 (3): 563–81. http://dx.doi.org/10.1353/dem.2007.0030. Medline:17913011.

Marable, Manning. 1979. "The Land Question in Historical Perspective: The Economics of Poverty in the Blackbelt South, 1865–1920." In *The Black Rural Landowner-Endangered Species: Social, Political, and Economic Implications*, ed. Leo McGee and Robert Boone, 3–24. Westport, CT: Greenwood Press.

Marshall, Ray, and Lamond Godwin. 1971. *Cooperatives and Rural Poverty in the South*. Baltimore, MD: Johns Hopkins Press.

McLaughlin, Diane, and C.S. Stokes. January 2002. "Income Inequality and Mortality in US Counties: Does Minority Racial Concentration Matter?" *American Journal of Public Health* 92 (1): 99–104. http://dx.doi.org/10.2105/AJPH.92.1.99. Medline:11772770.

McMichael, Philip. 1991. "Slavery in Capitalism: The Rise and Demise of the U.S. Ante-Bellum Cotton Culture." *Theory and Society* 20 (3): 321–49. http://dx.doi.org/10.1007/BF00213550.

Pigford v. Glickman. 1999. 185 F.R.D. 82 (D.D.C.).

Probst, Janice C., Charity G. Moore, Saundra H. Glover, and Michael E. Samuels. October 2004. "Person and Place: The Compounding Effects of Race/Ethnicity and Rurality on

Health." *American Journal of Public Health* 94 (10): 1695–703. http://dx.doi.org/10.2105/AJPH.94.10.1695. Medline:15451735.

Rastogi, Sonya, Tallese D. Johnson, Elizabeth M. Hoeffel, and Malcolm P. Drewery, Jr. 2011. "The Black Population: 2010." *2010 Census Briefs.* US Census Bureau.

Rosen, Joel N. 2011. *From New Lanark to Mound Bayou: Owenism in the Mississippi Delta.* Durham, NC: Carolina Academic Press.

Saikku, Mikko. 2005. *This Delta, This Land: An Environmental History of the Yazoo-Mississippi Floodplain.* Athens: University of Georgia Press.

Slack, Tim, and Leif Jensen. 2002. "Race, Ethnicity, and Underemployment in Nonmetropolitan America: A 30-Year Profile." *Rural Sociology* 67 (2): 208–33. http://dx.doi.org/10.1111/j.1549-0831.2002.tb00101.x.

Snipp, C. Matthew. 1996. "Understanding Race and Ethnicity in Rural America." *Rural Sociology* 61 (1): 125–42. http://dx.doi.org/10.1111/j.1549-0831.1996.tb00613.x.

Stack, Carol. 1996. *Call to Home: African Americans Reclaim the Rural South.* New York: Basic Books.

Stewart, James B. and Joyce E. Allen Smith, eds. 1995. *Blacks in Rural America.* New Brunswick, NJ: Transaction Publishers.

Tolnay, Stuart E. 2003. "The African American 'Great Migration' and Beyond." *Annual Review of Sociology* 29 (1): 209–32. http://dx.doi.org/10.1146/annurev.soc.29.010202.100009.

Trotter, Joe William, Jr. 2001. *The African American Experience.* Boston, MA: Houghton Mifflin Company.

US Census Bureau. 2010a. "2010 American Community Survey Five-Year Estimates." *American Factfinder.* Accessed 1 August 2012. http://factfinder2.census.gov/faces/nav/jsf/pages/index.xhtml.

US Census Bureau. 2010b. "2010 Decennial Census." *American Factfinder.* Accessed 1 August 2012. http://factfinder2.census.gov/faces/nav/jsf/pages/index.xhtml.

US Department of Agriculture, National Agricultural Statistics Service. 2007. "2007 Census of Agriculture." Accessed 1 August 2012. http://www.agcensus.usda.gov/Publications/2007/Full_Report/.

Wilson, William J. 1978. "The Declining Significance of Race." *Society* 15 (2): 56–62. http://dx.doi.org/10.1007/BF03181003.

Wilson, William J. 2011. "The Declining Significance of Race: Revisited and Revised." *Daedalus* 140 (2): 55–69. http://dx.doi.org/10.1162/DAED_a_00077.

Wimberley, Ronald C., and Libby V. Morris. 1997. *The Southern Black Belt: A National Perspective.* Lexington, KY: TVA Rural Studies.

Wimberley, Ronald C., and Libby V. Morris. 2002. "The Regionalization of Poverty: Assistance for the Black Belt South?" *Southern Rural Sociology* 18 (1): 294–306.

Wood, Spencer D., and Jess Gilbert. 1998. "Re-entering African-American Farmers: Recent Trends and a Policy Rationale." *Land Tenure Center Working Paper, North America Series.* Madison: University of Wisconsin.

Woodward, C. Vann. 1966. *The Strange Career of Jim Crow,* 2nd ed. New York: Oxford University Press.

CHAPTER 23

Hispanic Immigration, Global Competition, and the Dairy Industry in Rural Communities

J.D. Wulfhorst, Priscilla Salant, Leigh A. Bernacchi, Stephanie L. Kane, Philip Watson, and Erinn Cruz

Introduction

Globalization has greatly affected Hispanics,[1] specifically through rapid and uncertain effects of socioeconomic policies and neoliberal market manipulations. Simultaneously, Hispanics affect international contexts such as geographies and economies through immigration and redistribution of the global labor force. Immigration across the US-Mexico border remains a dominant, recurring pattern and debate in US politics and media. Arguably, the tensions between state and federal governments and impacts to community institutions—especially education and health care—mask the substantive contribution of Hispanic labor to the US economy.

Focusing on rural America, in this chapter we describe some of the effects of globalization, immigration, and Hispanic foreign-born labor (FBL) within an agricultural context—notably the dairy industry. Based on relevant literature, we describe the current status of rural sociological research on the Hispanic condition. In the second half of the chapter, we use a case study from the dairy industry of Idaho, now ranked third nationally in overall dairy production, to give the reader an impetus for greater critical contextualization by rural sociologists of Hispanics in rural America.

Addressing social dimensions of Latin American issues confronts complexities due to the diversity of peoples and cultures they include. As such, we risk use of monolithic terminology as reductionist. Some researchers, through careful ethnographies, successfully situate immigrants' past and present homes spatially and culturally (Massey and Capoferro 2008, Massey, Durand, and Capoferro 2005, Flores-Yeffal and Aysa-Lastra 2011). Much of rural sociological scholarship related to Hispanics has focused on Mexican immigration, per se. Focusing on the sociological frame of "modes of incorporation" and "contexts of reception" as Marrow (2005, 783) addresses, we establish a conceptual framework for this chapter, provide more context on Hispanics' contemporary experiences in rural America, and apply these within the larger context of neoliberal globalization.

Sociological Framing of Hispanic Experience

As the largest Hispanic immigrant group, Mexicans assimilate into American culture and influence the cultural fabric of rural communities, including ethnic transformation (Allensworth and Rochín 1998). Stabilization for newcomers often comes from compatriots or *paisanos* in rural areas, while family members have traditionally more often relocated to urban areas (Flores-Yeffal and Aysa-Lastra 2011). Since the North American Free Trade Agreement (NAFTA), however, the overall pattern of immigration shifting toward small towns and rural areas (Farmer and Moon 2009; Flores-Yeffal and Aysa-Lastra 2011) has created more widespread change in new American landscapes that had previously experienced relatively few impacts or change from recent immigration (Hirschmann and Massey 2008).

Amidst this change, second generations, or the children of Mexican immigrants, strongly identify as Mexican, especially those with increased levels of education (Tovar and Feliciano 2009). As with identity shift, other social and cultural structures also continue to experience effects related to change in migration patterns. For example, rural Mexican migrant women entering the workforce since the economic crisis that began in 2008 affect gender role negotiation related to men's sense of masculinity within the family (Schmalzbauer 2011).

For communities impacted by immigration, racial and ethnic change depends on the region and histories. Despite trends of retaining ethnic identities noted above, Marrow (2009a) also documents how Hispanic immigrants generally assimilate more rapidly with non-Hispanic whites than blacks in the rural South, and how natives and institutions respond to the newcomers (Marrow 2009b). Mize (2006, 105) describes the Bracero program during the years of 1942 to 1964 as a "coercive factory regime [that] introduced mechanization and increased work hazards, and employed a dual wage structure to keep Mexican contract workers at a serious disadvantage to advance their own collective well-being." Between 1975 and 1980, California surpassed Texas and Illinois surpassed Arizona as immigration destinations; and, at that point, nine of ten Mexicans who crossed the border into the United States could be found in California, Texas, and Illinois (Massey and Capoferro 2008). Some migrant farm workers have stayed and made permanent residences in the United States, though Hispanics are less likely than other immigrants to naturalize (Marrow 2005). In 2011, California's persons of Hispanic or Latino origin (38.1 percent) compared closely with the white non-Hispanic population (39 percent) (US Census Bureau 2011).

Several longitudinal and mixed methodology studies have documented ethnic transformations and integrations in rural America. A Midwestern case study documented how white residents of former "sundown towns" integrate with Hispanics spatially and socially in rural communities throughout the United States (McConnell and Miraftab 2009, 605). In California, Mexicans and long-term white residents struggle to gain respect within community development and social organizations in an agrarian context (Chávez 2005). Allensworth and Rochín (1998) show how housing costs and year-round job availability explain Hispanic migrations, leading to ethnic and economic differentiation. In these contexts, debates over immigration policies have continued to escalate at local, state, and national levels (Downes 2012).

Human Capital Framing of Hispanic Experiences

Applying a human capital frame within a neoliberal utilitarian context, the US economy has depended upon Hispanic, primarily Mexican, FBL in every sector. Some foreign-born laborers are unauthorized but have identity documentation in order to get jobs and become employed (Mortensen 2009). The Pew Research Center estimates unauthorized immigrants constituted over 11.2 million laborers in the United States in 2010, with 58 percent from Mexico (Passel and Cohn 2011). The growth in FBL seen since 2000 leveled off in 2007 to 2008 (Passel and Cohn 2011), with a declining trend (in 2008 to 2012) for the first time in forty years (Dougherty and Jordan 2009). Mexico, described as an unskilled and labor abundant country (Esquivel and Rodríguez-López 2003), continues to supply labor despite its decline in birth rate and potential inability to fill its own labor needs. Higher wages in the United States (Hanson 2005) and the myth of the American dream perpetuate immigration, supplying the demand for labor, primarily in hospitality services, construction, landscaping, and agricultural sectors. Effects to commerce and communities, including "rural industrialization strateg[ies]" have attempted to secure FBL in certain sectors and regions (McConnell and Miraftab 2009, 609).

In particular, the agricultural sector has benefitted from immigrant labor. Farm production cycles lead to seasonal labor demand in harvest and packaging of certain goods (Ziebarth 2006). Some production systems, like livestock, poultry processing, and dairy, operate year round.

Arguably, NAFTA, narcotics trafficking, gang violence, and the familial detriment of the exodus of generations of young men have added to destabilized elements within Mexican culture (Hanson 2005; Molzahn, Viridiana, and Shirk 2012; Rendall, Brownell, and Kups 2011), as well as a decline in the Mexican birth rate (Eberstadt 2010). This trend follows the global "fertility implosion" and forecasts a future of decreased Hispanic immigration and US labor force participation (Brooks 2012; Eberstadt 2010; Jensen in this volume). Overall, immigration rates to the United States—authorized and unauthorized—have declined from historical trends, especially since 2007 (Myers 2012; Passel and Cohn 2011). Evidence of a skills shortage has begun to manifest in parts of North America (Hunter and Walton 2012), and has further complicated projected labor pools. In this context, immigration to the United States will become more important (Kotkin and Ozuna 2012) with respect to industry sectors and community structures now tied to the long-standing base of Hispanic immigrants. The US dairy industry, especially in the western United States, represents a prime example of both the globalization of labor as well as an agricultural economic base tied to a capital-driven neoliberal model for commodity production.

A report of state- and local-level analyses indicates immigrants' contributions to state and local economies exceed the social costs, taking into account impacts to health care and educational systems by unauthorized immigrants (Immigration Policy Center 2010). Given regional differences, however, the variable impacts to rural and metropolitan areas suggest a lack of uniform relationships between FBL and more localized economies (Farmer and Moon 2009). Policy analysis by Hanson (2009, 5) indicates "the U.S. economy could no doubt survive the departure of these laborers, but it would cause disruptions in labor-intensive industries and the regions in which they are concentrated."

Common misconceptions that FBL is replaceable and that its social costs outweigh its laborers' value emerge from poorly contextualized media. Related, regional and state social services remain sensitive to the size and distribution of immigrant populations; however, immigrants unequivocally contribute to federal taxes more than they cost social welfare systems (Marrow 2005). Yet few analyses have focused on the magnitude of economic impact FBL generates at state and local levels, with a notable recent exception (Watson et al. 2012).

Researchers have paid little attention until recently to the intersection of Hispanic immigration shifts, policy conflicts, and rural labor supply uncertainties that risk food production and harvest systems in the United States. While popular media have documented these effects (Bowers 2007), research remains limited on many aspects of unauthorized laborers' lives, their contributions to communities and economies, and the social impacts of escalated fear in communities.

New Destination Immigration and Hispanics

In the last decade, market demands and immigrant preferences on location have led to greater dispersion of the FBL population. Mexican immigrants in particular no longer concentrate solely in established gateway states, and have moved to rural areas that have been relatively uninhabited by immigrants in the past (Marrow 2005). Nelson and Nelson (2011) describe a previously undocumented connection between the movement of baby boomers and middle-to-upper-class Americans to rural areas and the migration of Hispanics to fulfill service industry demands (see also Nelson, Lee, and Nelson 2009). Other research (Jensen and Tienda 1989; Tienda and Jensen 1986) demonstrates that not all immigrants take advantage of social services systems to the same extent or to the extent perceived by media or the public. Moreover, not all new destinations are equal. Griffith's (2005, 50) ethnography delineates the differences among farm labor suppliers, such as more rigorous immigration inspections between North Carolina and Virginia, noting, "for many Mexican farm workers, even deep inside the U.S. a border remains a significant force in their lives."

The number of immigrants living in the Mountain West states (including Nevada, Arizona, New Mexico, Colorado, Utah, Idaho, Wyoming, and Montana) has more than tripled since 1990 (US Census Bureau 1990; 2010). The majority of these immigrants are Hispanic. Though Hispanics still comprise only a small share of the region's overall population, one-third of the Mountain West's Hispanics immigrated to the United States since 2000 despite the national downturn. While some states outside the Mountain West (including California, Texas, and Florida) have much larger overall Hispanic immigrant populations, the Mountain West was home to roughly 1.5 million foreign-born Hispanics in 2010.

Evidence from Idaho

The Idaho case study was designed to address the question of how the labor force in a globally competitive and highly concentrated industry impacts rural communities (see Salant et al. 2009 for a full report and elaboration of this section). How an industry's labor force impacts communities depends largely on who works in that industry. Thus, the first research question concerned worker characteristics and concerns about deportation. If workers reside in communities on a stable basis with their families, the impacts on schools, hospitals, and other parts of communities will be different than if they are single men moving in and out of the country. And, regardless of whether the workers are single or married with children, if they fear deportation because of document questionability or immigrant raids, they will become less involved in their community. Immigrants must feel safe to interact with their children's schools, get medical care, and conduct other activities that non-immigrants do not consider risky behaviors.

In response to concerns and public criticisms about the industry's use of immigrant workers, the Idaho Dairymen's Association (IDA) commissioned a study to investigate and document the variety of positive and negative community-based impacts stemming from rapid concentration and growth of the region's dairy industry. The research team designed the methodology, collected and analyzed the data, and reported findings without interference from the IDA. While the study was not confined to the intersection between the growth of a globally competitive industry and immigration, the correlation between the two trends catalyzed a major focus within the data collection and analysis.

Why Idaho?

Idaho offers a valuable case study of how development of global agricultural markets (in this instance, markets for dairy products) relate to both immigration and multidimensional change in rural communities. The case illustrates how globalization can have both positive and negative effects on services and institutions on which rural residents rely. Nationally, Idaho ranks above average in terms of the share of unauthorized immigrants among foreign-born residents (Passel and Cohn 2009). And, between 1990 and 2008, the estimated number of unauthorized immigrants in Idaho nearly quadrupled (Passel and Cohn 2011). Thus, amidst the notable recent decline in national level immigration, Idaho's numbers and share of unauthorized immigrants have both continued to increase (Migration Policy Institute 2009) dramatically during the last decade.

Coinciding with the increase in unauthorized immigration, Idaho's dairy industry changed structurally. From 1997 to 2007, the number of dairy cows in southern Idaho increased from 264,000 to 534,000 (US Department of Agriculture 2007). Between 1997 and 2008, Idaho's cash receipts from milk sales more than tripled, increasing from $634 million to $2.15 billion (Eborn et al. 2003; Eborn, Patterson, and Taylor 2008). Over this same period, the number of dairy farm employees in southern Idaho grew almost as rapidly, from 2,100 to 6,100 (Idaho Department of Labor 2009), suggesting direct connections between the availability of reliable labor and industry growth.

While the industry has been changing and demand for labor rising, exports have grown dramatically, reflecting increased globalization in the dairy sector. Although state-level export data are not available, national level data are consistent with anecdotal evidence from Idaho. Since 1997, US exports of all dairy products (measured in current dollar value and including processed products) have increased sixfold to $3.7 billion in 2011 (current data available from Livestock Marketing Information Center 2012). Within this trend, the number of dairy farms has declined but those that remain, on average, are larger. In 1997, the average number of cows on an Idaho dairy farm was 189. By 2007, the number more than tripled to 661, while the number of dairy farms declined from 1,404 to 811 (US Department of Agriculture 2007).

During this same period, the Hispanic population grew rapidly. From 1997 to 2010, the number of Hispanics in southern Idaho grew by 110 percent, compared to 32 percent for southern Idaho's population as a whole (US Census Bureau 1997–2008; 2010). This is in contrast to many farm-dependent, rural parts of the country that experienced out-migration or stagnation during the same period.

These two trends—concentration in the industry and a growing Hispanic population—are national and influenced by global markets for labor and agricultural commodities. The dairy industry is becoming more concentrated in certain regions of the country, specifically, California's Central Valley, Idaho's south central region, and the Texas panhandle (MacDonald et al. 2007). Similarly, the growth in Idaho's Hispanic population is also consistent with the national growth trend.

Methodology and Study Limitation

Using a two-part methodology, we examined how people who work on dairy farms impact local economies, schools, health care providers, justice systems, and other aspects of life in communities in southern Idaho. The methodology included public surveys, personal interviews,[2] and secondary data analysis to mirror the complexity of the community-level issues addressed. The outcome of using this mixed-methods approach is an aggregated analysis that yielded policy-relevant analysis and results.

We conducted sixty-three semi-structured interviews with key informants in face-to-face settings convenient to the interviewees (Miles and Huberman 1994) and across a spectrum of professional and thematic subject areas. Primary categories included: government; business and economic development; education; religious and community action; public assistance, health, and social services; the justice system; and dairy producers.

The key informant interviews yielded valuable data on perceptions of and opinions about dairy workers and the industry's community-level impacts. They provided context to examine emerging research expectations that were analyzed using data from multiple secondary sources, including federal, state, and county agencies and religious organization records. Language and lack of access prevented us from interviewing dairy workers themselves. Instead, the research team developed the description of dairy workers based on qualitative interviews with other key informants and on secondary data sources.

Characterizing Dairy Industry Labor Force

Based on interview data collected for the study, the vast majority of Idaho's dairy workers are Hispanic and foreign born. The large dairy farms that produce most of the state's milk and milk products require a workforce made up of "*very strong, agile young men*" who can handle the physical requirements of the job.[3] Work schedules and pay rates vary by farm, but milkers (about half of all dairy workers) work an average of ten to twelve hours a day, four to six days in a row, and are paid about $2,000 per month after taxes. Other types of workers earn less, while feeders, inseminators, and herdsman earn more.

Worker turnover is high—"*at least 30 percent per year*" according to one manager of a farm with over 5,000 cows. Another person familiar with the industry said: "*The typical worker keeps his job for a while, then goes back to Mexico when another guy from his network of cousins takes the job while he's away.*" And, "*It's a revolving door—one month here, the next month gone. Friends and relatives fill jobs vacated by each other.*" Not everyone who was interviewed agreed that turnover was high. One person familiar with the industry said that it takes a long time for dairy owners to train workers and thus the owners strive to prevent high turnover. We concluded that there is likely to be significant variation across dairy farms and among workers in terms of length of time on the job.

In this context, working on a dairy farm is not the kind of job that many young men aspire to keep for long, nor is it a job that a person with other opportunities would always continue to choose to do: "*The guys might work on dairies for three or four months, and then move on to another, better job.*" As one dairy farmer put it, "*I don't see a lot of guys laid off from Micron* [a high-tech company based in southern Idaho] *come around here looking for work.*" Another employer explained, "*The whole reason dairy jobs are held by immigrants is because white people won't take those jobs.*" And yet another said about the immigrants, "*We would have a labor shortage without those folks, so they are providing a service.*"

While there are sources of data on the proportion of foreign-born workers in the US labor force, there is no single source on the proportion of foreign-born workers who have legal work documents. Based on multiple interviews, we concluded that whether or not dairy workers have legal documents, the stricter enforcement of immigration laws that has taken place in recent years has had profound consequences for workers' lives. Simply because they are Hispanic, they are at risk. One interviewee noted, "*Now that pathways to residency are so hard and illegal immigration is so dangerous, Hispanics are coming [across the border] alone.*"

While the young men who work on dairy farms may have families in Mexico, interviewees' experiences in southern Idaho indicate many immigrants now cross the border by themselves, leaving wives and children behind. Once they get to the United States, many are afraid of deportation. One business owner noted workers are "*in lock up; they go to work, come home, go to work, come home.*"

The secondary data analysis supplemented what we learned from the interviews. Data on age and gender further support evidence that south central Idaho's Hispanic population is growing in parallel with, if not response to, the dairy industry's demand for labor. Data also show high numbers of youth, again indicating a correlation between dairies and other industries employing Hispanic workers with families and reflecting the longer-term pattern of immigration prior to the very recent shift toward "single males" described above.

Local Economic Impacts

The dairy industry has contributed to economic growth in south central Idaho, whether measured by job numbers, unemployment rates, per capita income, or other economic indicators. Nevertheless, some local residents face serious economic hardship. Child poverty rates are higher in the dairy region than in the state as a whole. So, too, are the proportions of children eligible for reduced price school meals. Based on the interviews, many people in the dairy region are "working poor" but no evidence collected during the study attributes this directly to the changing dairy industry.

Impacts on Crime

Law enforcement and justice system employees interviewed indicated that dairies do not serve as a catalyst for increasing crime. Instead, the main community-level impacts are related to increases in foreign-born individuals who may need additional or special assistance if and when they do enter the law or criminal justice systems. According to a judge, there is an increasing "*need for public defenders, translators, and Spanish-speaking attorneys, which can cause a strain on the justice system.*" Little or no evidence suggests that growth in the dairy industry has caused an increase in felonies.

Impacts on Schools

The changing dairy industry has contributed to two main educational impacts. First, many school districts in south central Idaho are coping with the increased ethnic diversity as well as with an increase in students from low-income families. Second, the increase in Hispanic students means some districts are growing when they would otherwise be shrinking. The increase in Hispanic students in these districts more than makes up for a loss in non-Hispanic students.

Growing diversity brings both challenges and opportunities. Districts must now find money and staff to work with growing numbers of English language learners and lower income students. However, Hispanic parents, as a rule, value education and want their children to do well. Furthermore, children in integrated schools learn how to get along in our increasingly multicultural and ethnically mixed society.

Impacts on Health Care

Interviews with health professionals indicated no disproportionate use of health care services by the Hispanic population in general or employees known to work in the dairy industry. The researchers attempted to learn whether dairy workers might be responsible for changes in the indigent health care costs (part of which county agencies must cover in Idaho). However, county-level data on indigent health care costs are not complete enough to indicate whether this is true or not. While these costs are increasing on a per capita basis in some southern Idaho counties, neither the interviews nor the county-level data indicate the increase can be attributed to dairy workers.

Other Community Impacts

In addition to the core community systems described above, the secondary data also highlighted a miscellaneous set of factors we describe generically as other impacts. In brief, most of the findings relate to two recurrent themes—culture and language—often described in the interviews as manifestations of how communities adapt and change. Although somewhat indirect, these impacts also have a relationship to the dairy industry's growth.

The intensity of the dairy workers' schedules often precludes full integration into local cultural activities, even if workers are willing to participate. One leader in the Hispanic community explained, "*They come here to work. It leaves them little time to be part of the community or socialize. They work lots of shifts with no days off.*" However, both the Catholic Church and the Church of Jesus Christ of Latter-Day Saints provide religious support and community engagement opportunities.

Key informants reported very little racial tension in south central Idaho. Interviewees referred to Hispanics as model community members who aim to contribute to the public good and integrate with the whole rather than maintain themselves in isolation. Other interviewees noted exceptions and that longer-term residents have had more trouble adjusting to the contemporary changes: "*It is very contentious here. People say amazing things in open meetings. There is a lot of hostility. Long-time residents feel like Little Tijuana is being forced on them and they have a sense that their hometown is being transformed.*"

With respect to language, a recent Pew Hispanic Center report (Passel and Cohn 2009) notes that although language barriers are becoming less of an issue for the children of immigrants than they continue to be for their parents, sometimes communication barriers still exist between the sub-groups within the communities. For instance, as noted above, the emerging demographic of many dairy workers as young single men reinforces the cultural isolation that can occur with the effect of missed opportunities and connections. A business owner observed, "*Look around and see who speaks English and who doesn't. Who learns it and who doesn't? If you just work in the dairy, you don't learn English.*"

A significant overlap exists with issues of language and the educational system impacts described above. A school district superintendent described how language is embedded in the struggle for many families and public systems in everyday life: "*It's a challenge for us, as the school, to meet our requirements with such a high proportion of non-English speakers. Many parents are illiterate, even in Spanish. Some choose not to have contact with the schools where their children attend because of their immigrant status, but yet they have a strong value placed on learning as a means for their children to do better than themselves.*"

Case Study Conclusions

This case study informed a dimension of the public debate about Idaho's dairy industry, specifically, how the industry impacts local communities. In the course of interviewing school teachers, elected officials, local leaders, health specialists, and others, the researchers realized that these community impacts revolve primarily around the dairy workers. In the end, how and to what extent the industry intersects with community systems is manifested substantively through the labor force. The impacts depend on who those workers are, and thus how much they are paid; where they spend their wages; and how they interact with schools, justice systems, and health care providers. Less direct community-level impacts related to the growth of the dairy industry have also occurred in the areas of culture, language, and identity.

The best estimate is that most dairy farm workers are young foreign-born adult men. Virtually all are Hispanic. Some are single and others have families, but there appears to be more single men. Especially with the economic downturn in 2008 and 2009, competition for their jobs has intensified. Even so, the labor force is mobile and some, if not many, workers do not stay in their jobs for long periods of time.

In his book, *Importing Poverty: Immigration and the Changing Face of Rural America*, economist Philip Martin (2009) writes about an immigration treadmill in rural America. With a particular focus on seasonal farm work, Martin describes harsh working conditions and low pay rates that discourage workers from holding onto their jobs for any length of time. As new immigrants with little education eventually manage to move up the occupational ladder and out of agriculture, others come to fill their places.

Martin (2009) focuses on seasonal work rather than full-time employment on dairy farms, but we found similarities between what Martin describes and conditions in south central Idaho. Although dairy farmers pay wages that provide a near middle-class lifestyle, the jobs are demanding and the hours long. Couple these conditions with constant fear of deportation, and the result is a labor force made up of people who may feel inhibited to actively participate in what makes up a community. As such, those individuals may feel more excluded than included by the very community systems to which they seek to contribute. As one farmer put it, "*A lot of progress on community integration will be stopped. We are creating a new population of single, lonely guys who are not part of the community. They will bring problems.*"

Clearly, the dairy industry has positive economic impacts on local communities. It has brought jobs and people to towns that otherwise would likely be in decline, as are many farm-dependent communities around the country. However, in the absence of an immigration policy that guarantees a stable and legal labor force, the industry also imposes some degree of costs, most notably on schools and somewhat less so on health care and justice systems. Moreover, community-level impacts, especially across a vast region like southern Idaho, are not equally distributed. Benefits may accrue disproportionately in some communities, while costs accrue disproportionately in others. These trends make sense by understanding a critical difference between society's private and public sectors. Parts of south central Idaho represent a microcosm of both.

Public agencies cannot always respond quickly to new demands associated with migrant populations. Before these entities can cope with changing demographics by hiring more bi-lingual teachers and court translators, or before they can establish more effective measures to mitigate gang-related activities, they must convince voters to pay higher taxes to cover the costs of economic growth. Benefits accrue to private sector businesses—including to dairy farmers when times are good—but the public sector pays a price. Overall, we found that communities are better off economically because of the dairy industry, but they struggle to adjust to the challenges of a changing and growing population.

Considering Globalization Effects

In Idaho, the dairy industry grew rapidly, which both enabled and relied on parallel growth in Hispanic immigrants seeking employment in the region. Growth in FBL, but especially Hispanics, has fueled discussion of immigration policy reform in Idaho at a less aggressive rate, but there are still debates similar to those in many other states (Downes 2012). Proactive steps on the part of the Idaho dairy commodity group as well as a coalition of business sector entities catalyzed two unique studies to document how these trends have affected southern Idaho communities and to project state-level economic impacts from a potential reduction in FBL.

Idaho's growth in Hispanic immigration remains robust compared to other major destination states such as New York, Florida, and Arizona—all of which have lost significant proportions of unauthorized immigrants since 2007. As migratory destinations shift, job availability and networks of support become critical decision criteria for potential migrants. In a recent analysis, Sanderson and Painter (2011) indicate occupational channeling occurs among migrants such that connections between agricultural, manufacturing, and service sectors cut across Mexico and the United States to foster economic mobility of migrants via family networks and continuity with previous employment. And, consistent with Pfeffer and Parra (2009), this community-level impacts study yielded evidence that Hispanic immigrants in rural communities rely on intra-ethnic networks for key community-based functions.

These trends relate to the reconfiguration of time and space within globalization and the neoliberal regime. While seeking fewer regulatory restrictions and greater adherence to market mechanisms in its shift to Idaho, the dairy industry has simultaneously experienced heightened environmental concern from non-governmental entities. Dairy consolidation and changes to achieve economies of scale for industry structure increases average dairy size as well as concentration and, thus, externalities such as regional air and water quality compromises in neighboring communities. In many of the same communities, due to the in-migration of families to fill positions that native-born labor rarely seeks, the dairies *as an industry* have played a major role to reverse educational instability plaguing many rural areas—especially within agricultural regions. In Idaho's dairies, starting positions constitute difficult physical work but offer a good comparative wage. Even as stepping-stone positions, the cultural work ethics and economic goals lead migrants from Latin America to the United States but depend on varying patterns of migration relating to rural versus urban origins and family support during migration (Flores-Yeffal and Aysa-Lastra 2011).

Within the agricultural sector, dairies present an interesting contrast in demand for labor compared to most other agricultural sectors. Due to the increase of dairy mechanization, milking floors operate around the clock to maximize production. Thus, the dairy industry disproportionately relies on an enduring labor force supply and, as such, becomes more vulnerable to policy shifts affecting supply. In contrast with globalization trends and neoliberal goals to reduce state intervention, the dairy industry finds itself in a position to support immigration reform because worker stability translates to operational stability. Yet, as dairies incentivize immigrant laborers with higher than minimum wages, commodity prices remain subject to external factors such as fuel and fertilizer input costs, food versus fuel trends for grains, and increasing costs of environmental regulations. In these contexts, Hispanic immigrants make decisions about whether to cross the borders; whether to do mundane things like go out into the community for groceries as foreign-born citizens (perceived or real); and whether to invest in real estate, businesses, or other services to form a local society (Wilkinson 1991).

The case-study analysis from Idaho connects to an amalgam of industry, labor, and political economic factors. While some aspects of globalization may have positive effects (e.g., industry mobility) for Hispanic immigrants, other effects (e.g., states' rights movement to devolve immigration policies) will continue to make these opportunities dynamic and vulnerable for some sectors of the migratory population. In the global context of international change in fertility in key regions, the competition for labor may lead to unprecedented food security stress despite benefits such as community diversification related to immigration.

Notes

1 We acknowledge the term *Hispanic(s)* may have more narrow and specific connotations than Latinos, but have elected to use the former term for this chapter as popular nomenclature while not ignoring the debate over terminologies and meanings. Where possible, we delineate when we refer to a specific nationality.

2 The University of Idaho Institutional Review Board approved this project for human subjects research assurances.

3 Quotations from interviewees in the study appear italicized and in quotation marks.

References

Allensworth, Elaine M., and Regugio I. Rochín. 1998. "Ethnic Transformation in Rural California: Looking beyond the Immigrant Farmworker." *Rural Sociology* 63 (1): 26–50. http://dx.doi.org/10.1111/j.1549-0831.1998.tb00663.x.

Bowers, Faye. 2007. "Along US-Mexico Border, Not Enough Hands for the Harvest." *Christian Science Monitor*, 22 February. http://www.csmonitor.com/2007/0222/p02s01-usec.html.

Brooks, David. 2012. "The Fertility Implosion." *New York Times*, 12 March. http://www.nytimes.com/2012/03/13/opinion/brooks-the-fertility-implosion.html.

Chávez, Sergio. 2005. "Community, Ethnicity, and Class in a Changing Rural California Town." *Rural Sociology* 70 (3): 314–35. http://dx.doi.org/10.1526/0036011054831224.

Dougherty, Conor, and Miriam Jordan. 2009. "Recession Hits Immigrants Hard." *Wall Street Journal*, 23 September. http://online.wsj.com/news/articles/SB125356996157829123.

Downes, Lawrence. 2012. "When States Put out the Unwelcome Mat." *New York Times*, 11 March. http://www.nytimes.com/2012/03/11/opinion/sunday/when-states-put-out-the-unwelcome-mat.html?_r=1.

Eberstadt, Nicholas. 2010. "The Demographic Future: What Population Growth—and Decline—Means for the Global Economy." *Foreign Policy* 89 (6): 54–64.

Eborn, Ben, C. Wilson Gray, Paul Patterson, and Garth Taylor. 2003. *The Financial Condition of Idaho Agriculture: 2003 Projections.* Moscow: University of Idaho Extension and University of Idaho, College of Agricultural and Life Sciences.

Eborn, Ben, Paul Patterson, and Garth Taylor. 2008. *The Financial Condition of Idaho Agriculture: 2008 Projections.* Moscow: University of Idaho Extension and University of Idaho, College of Agricultural and Life Sciences.

Esquivel, Gerardo, and Jose Antonio Rodríguez-López. 2003. "Technology, Trade, and Wage Inequality in Mexico Before and After NAFTA." *Journal of Development Economics* 72 (2): 543–65. http://dx.doi.org/10.1016/S0304-3878(03)00119-6.

Farmer, Frank L., and Zola K. Moon. 2009. "An Empirical Examination of Characteristics of Mexican Migrants to Metropolitan and Nonmetropolitan Areas of the United States." *Rural Sociology* 74 (2): 220–40. http://dx.doi.org/10.1111/j.1549-0831.2009.tb00390.x.

Flores-Yeffal, Nadia Y., and Maria Aysa-Lastra. 2011. "Place of Origin, Types of Ties, and Support Networks in Mexico-U.S. Migration." *Rural Sociology* 76 (4): 481–510. http://dx.doi.org/10.1111/j.1549-0831.2011.00060.x.

Griffith, David C. 2005. "Rural Industry and Mexican Immigration and Settlement in North Carolina." In *New Destinations: Mexican Immigration in the United States*, ed. Víctor Zúñiga and Rubén Hernández-León, 50–75. New York: Russell Sage Foundation.

Hanson, Gordon H. 2005. "Globalization, Labor Income, and Poverty in Mexico." In *Globalization, Labor Income, and Poverty in Mexico, National Bureau of Economic Research Working Paper Series No. 11027*, ed. Ann Harrison, 417–54. Chicago: University of Chicago Press. http://dx.doi.org/10.3386/w11027.

Hanson, Gordon H. 2009. "The Economics and Policy of Illegal Immigration in the United States." The Migration Policy Institute, Washington, DC. Accessed 10 August. http://www.migrationpolicy.org/pubs/Hanson-Dec09.pdf.

Hirschmann, Charles and Donald S. Massey. 2008. "People and Places: The New American Mosaic." In *New Faces and New Places: The Changing Geography of American Immigration*, ed. Douglas S. Massey, 1–22. New York: Russell Sage Foundation.

Hunter, Justine, and Dawn Walton. 2012. "Desperate for Workers, West Seeks Immigration Powers." *Globe and Mail*, March 11. http://www.theglobeandmail.com/news/politics/desperate-for-workers-west-seeks-immigration-powers/article553012.

Idaho Department of Labor. 2009. "Employer Quarterly Reports." Data obtained via e-mail from Jan Roeser, Regional Labor Economist, Idaho Department of Labor, 7 July.

Immigration Policy Center. 2010. "Assessing the Economic Impact of Immigration at the State and Local Level." Immigration Policy Center, Washington, DC. Accessed 25 August. http://www.immigrationpolicy.org/sites/default/files/docs/State_and_Local_Study_Survey_041310_1.pdf.

Jensen, Leif, and Marta Tienda. 1989. "Nonmetropolitan Minority Families in the United States: Trends in Racial and Ethnic Economic Stratification, 1959–1986." *Rural Sociology* 54 (4): 509–32.

Kotkin, Joel, and Erika Ozuna. 2012. "America's Demographic Future." *Cato Journal* 32: 55–69.

Livestock Marketing Information Center. 2012. "Livestock Marketing Information Center Website." Accessed 10 September. http://www.lmic.info.

MacDonald, James M., William D. McBride, Erik O'Donoghue, Richard F.F. Nehring, Carmen Sandretto, and Roberto Mosheim. 2007. "Profits, Costs, and the Changing Structure of Dairy Farming." Economic Research Report ERR-47. http://dx.doi.org/10.2139/ssrn.1084458.

Marrow, Helen B. 2005. "New Destinations and Immigrant Incorporation." *Perspectives on Politics* 3 (4): 781–99. http://dx.doi.org/10.1017/S1537592705050449.

Marrow, Helen B. 2009a. "New Immigrant Destinations and the American Colour Line." *Ethnic and Racial Studies* 32 (6): 1037–57. http://dx.doi.org/10.1080/01419870902853224.

Marrow, Helen B. 2009b. "Immigrant Bureaucratic Incorporation: The Dual Roles of Professional Missions and Government Policies." *American Sociological Review* 74 (5): 756–76. http://dx.doi.org/10.1177/000312240907400504.

Martin, Philip. 2009. *Importing Poverty: Immigration and the Changing Face of Rural America.* New Haven: Yale University Press.

Massey, Douglas S., and Chiara Capoferro. 2008. "The Geographic Diversification of American Immigration." In *New Faces in New Places: The Changing Geography of American Immigration*, ed. Douglas S. Massey, 25–50. New York: Russell Sage Foundation.

Massey, Douglas S., Jorge Durand, and Chiara Capoferro. 2005. "The New Geography of Mexican Immigration." In *New Destinations of Mexican Migration in the United States: Community Formation, Local Responses, and Inter-group Relations*, ed. Rubén Hernández León and Victor ZúÁiga, 1–20. New York: Russell Sage Foundation.

McConnell, Eileen Diaz, and Faranak Miraftab. 2009. "Sundown Town to 'Little Mexico': Old-Timers and Newcomers in an American Small Town." *Rural Sociology* 74 (4): 605–29. http://dx.doi.org/10.1526/003601109789864044.

Migration Policy Institute. 2009. "MPI Data Hub, Migration Facts, Stats, and Maps: Idaho Social and Demographic Characteristics, 2009." Accessed 28 January. http://www.migrationinformation.org/dataHub/state.cfm?ID=ID.

Miles, Matthew, and A. Michael Huberman. 1994. *Qualitative Data Analysis: An Expanded Sourcebook*. 2nd ed. Thousand Oaks, CA: Sage Publications.

Mize, Ronald L., Jr. 2006. "Mexican Contract Workers and the U.S. Capitalist Agricultural Labor Process: The Formative Era, 1942–1964." *Rural Sociology* 71 (1): 85–108. http://dx.doi.org/10.1526/003601106777789765.

Molzahn, Cory, Ríos Viridiana, and David A. Shirk. 2012. "Drug Violence in Mexico: Data Analysis through 2011." Trans-Border Institute, Joan B. Kroc School of Peach Studies. San Diego: University of San Diego. Accessed 25 May. http://justiceinmexico.files.wordpress.com/2012/03/2012-tbi-drugviolence.pdf.

Mortensen, Ronald W. 2009. "Illegal, but Not Undocumented: Identity Theft, Document Fraud, and Illegal Employment." Center for Immigration Studies, Washington, DC. Accessed 8 July. http://www.cis.org/IdentityTheft.

Myers, Dowell. 2012. "The Next Immigration Challenge." *New York Times*, 12 January. http://www.nytimes.com/2012/01/12/opinion/the-next-immigration-challenge.html.

Nelson, Lise, and Peter B. Nelson. 2011. "The Global Rural: Gentrification and Linked Migration in the Rural USA." *Progress in Human Geography* 35 (4): 441–59. http://dx.doi.org/10.1177/0309132510380487.

Nelson, Peter B., Ann W. Lee, and Lise Nelson. 2009. "Linking Baby Boomer and Hispanic Migration Streams into Rural America—A Multi-scaled Approach." *Population Space and Place* 15 (3): 277–93. http://dx.doi.org/10.1002/psp.520.

Passel, Jeffrey S. and D'Vera Cohn. 2009. "A Portrait of Unauthorized Immigrants in the United States." Washington, DC: Pew Hispanic Center.

Passel, Jeffrey S. and D'Vera Cohn. 2011. "Unauthorized Immigrant Population: National and State Trends, 2010." Washington, DC: Pew Hispanic Center.

Pfeffer, Max J., and Pilar A. Parra. 2009. "Strong Ties, Weak Ties, and Human Capital: Latino Immigrant Employment outside the Enclave." *Rural Sociology* 74 (2): 241–69. http://dx.doi.org/10.1111/j.1549-0831.2009.tb00391.x.

Rendall, Michael S., Peter Brownell, and Sarah Kups. August 2011. "Declining Return Migration from the United States to Mexico in the Late-2000s Recession: A Research Note." *Demography* 48 (3): 1049–58. http://dx.doi.org/10.1007/s13524-011-0049-9. Medline:21744184.

Salant, Priscilla, J.D. Wulfhorst, and Stephanie Kane, with Christine Dearien. 2009. "Community Level Impacts of Idaho's Changing Dairy Industry." Moscow: College of Agricultural and Life Sciences, University of Idaho.

Sanderson, Matthew, and Matthew Painter, II. 2011. "Occupational Channels for Mexican Migration: New Destination Formation in a Binational Context." *Rural Sociology* 76 (4): 461–80. http://dx.doi.org/10.1111/j.1549-0831.2011.00061.x.

Schmalzbauer, Leah. 2011. "'Doing Gender,' Ensuring Survival: Mexican Migration and Economic Crisis in the Rural Mountain West." *Rural Sociology* 76 (4): 441–60. http://dx.doi.org/10.1111/j.1549-0831.2011.00058.x.

Tienda, Marta, and Leif Jensen. 1986. “Immigration and Public Assistance Participation: Dispelling the Myth of Dependency.” *Social Science Research* 15 (4): 372–400. http://dx.doi.org/10.1016/0049-089X(86)90019-0.

Tovar, Jessica, and Cynthia Feliciano. 2009. “‘Not Mexican-American, but Mexican’: Shifting Ethnic Self-Identifications among Children of Mexican Immigrants.” *Latino Studies* 7 (2): 197–221. http://dx.doi.org/10.1057/lst.2009.18.

US Census Bureau. 1990. “Decennial Census.” Accessed 17 April 2011. http://factfinder2.census.gov.

US Census Bureau. 1991–1999. “Population Estimates Program, Historical Data.” Accessed 3 June 2011. http://www.census.gov/popest/data/historical/index.html.

US Census Bureau. 1997–2008. “Population Estimates Program, Historical Data.” Accessed 3 June 2011. http://www.census.gov/popest/data/historical/index.html.

US Census Bureau. 2000. “Decennial Census.” Accessed 17 April 2011. http://factfinder2.census.gov.

US Census Bureau. 2010. “American FactFinder.” Accessed 13 July 2012. http://factfinder2.census.gov.

US Census Bureau. 2011. “American Community Survey Single-Year and 3-Year Estimates, 2005–2007.” Accessed 3 June. http://factfinder2.census.gov.

US Department of Agriculture. 2007. “Census of Agriculture.” Accessed 3 April 2012. http://www.agcensus.usda.gov/.

Watson, Philip, Kim Castelin, Priscilla Salant, and J.D. Wulfhorst. 2012. “Estimating the Impacts of a Reduction in the Foreign-Born Labor Supply on a State Economy: A Nested CGE Analysis of the Idaho Economy.” *Review of Regional Studies* 42 (1): 51–74.

Wilkinson, Kenneth P. 1991. *The Community in Rural America*, 3rd ed. New York: Greenwood Press.

Ziebarth, Ann. 2006. “Housing Seasonal Workers for the Minnesota Processed Vegetable Industry.” *Rural Sociology* 71 (2): 335–57. http://dx.doi.org/10.1526/003601106777789693.

CHAPTER 24

Native Nations in a Changing Global Economy

Sarah Dewees

Introduction

Native nations in North America represent a complex mosaic of different tribal governmental entities, unique cultural histories, and modern social organizational structures. Over 565 distinct federally recognized tribal governments coexist with the United States. In addition to the federally recognized tribes in the lower forty-eight states, there is great diversity in the indigenous population of Alaska as well as in non-federally recognized tribal communities. Each of these Native nations faces a different set of economic challenges and opportunities, whether it be their historical treaty rights; the characteristics of the natural resources they own and control; or the size, location, and legal status of their land base. For example, some Native nations have no reservation land or reservations that measure less than one hundred acres, while the Navajo Nation has over seventeen million acres. A few Native nations, such as the Salt River Pima Maricopa Indian Community, are close to urban markets and are able to operate successful businesses such as gaming operations. Other tribes reside on lands that are located in remote rural areas far from urban markets. Tribes that possess land-based resources like coal, such as the Hopi Tribe, have generated significant revenue from tribal enterprises based on these natural resources. Yet many Native nations own land that has few natural resources, is of little agricultural value, and is remotely located, and these nations have not been as successful in developing profitable tribal industries. Despite the diversity found among Native nations and their citizens, there are some common themes that can help to explain the current economic and social conditions of Native American populations and the reservation communities within which some of them reside. In this chapter, I will explore these themes and discuss the opportunities and challenges presented by Native nations' unique legal, economic, and social organization in an increasingly neoliberal and globalizing economy.

Tribal Sovereignty

Indian tribal governments have a unique relationship with the federal government, one that is rooted in American history and federal Indian case law. Tribal nations have legal rights that allow them to form governments; determine tribal membership; and make, enforce, and prosecute violations of some laws on their reservations. Increasingly, tribes also exercise their sovereignty to direct economic activities on their tribal lands through the regulation of commerce and trade. Each Native nation in the United States has a distinct history, but because of their unique sovereign status, all federally recognized tribal governments interact with federal and state governments in a way that is unlike any other minority group in the United States.

The sovereign status of Native nations is a result of treaties signed with foreign nations during a period of time when European governments were starting colonies in the "New World" and negotiating with tribal leaders over control of land and natural resources. These treaties recognized Indian nations as military and political equals with powers of self-governance and independent control over internal and external legal affairs. Subsequent military conflicts and resultant treaties limited the land holdings of many tribes but continued to uphold their independent sovereign powers. These treaties, signed by different Native nations, and subsequent federal court decisions and legislation have led to a complex and often-confusing patchwork of federal Indian law that now guides the interaction between the federal government and tribes (Pevar 2002).

While the internal governing powers of Native nations have been recognized by the US federal government through countless treaty agreements, federal court cases, and acts of Congress (Wilkins 2002), their sovereignty has also been steadily curtailed by often the same federal cases and legislation. In 1831, US Supreme Court Chief Justice John Marshall wrote in *Cherokee Nation v. Georgia* that while the Cherokee Nation was a "distinct political society that was separated from others, capable of managing its own affairs, and governing itself," it had limited rights to deal with foreign powers, and that tribes could best be described as "domestic dependent nations" with a relationship to the federal government similar to "that of a ward to his guardian" (Pevar 2002, 34). Subsequent court cases have reaffirmed the powers of tribal governments to manage their own internal affairs and remain free from regulation or control by state governments. However, tribes' sovereignty is increasingly limited as federal litigation and legislation chips away each tribe's rights to negotiate with other foreign powers. Most importantly, legal interpretations of the Commerce Clause of the US Constitution have reaffirmed US Congress's ultimate power "to regulate Commerce with foreign Nations, and among the several States, and with the Indian Tribes" (I.8.3). Thus, Congress has ultimate power to pass legislation affecting tribal governments and their citizens, even if that legislation abrogates previously agreed upon treaty rights.

This legal framework shaping the rights and powers of tribal governments results in a complex bureaucratic relationship between tribes and the US federal government, one that has interacted with the economic and cultural vitality of Native nations over the past 300 years with differing results. From the Marshall ruling stems the current notion of the "trust responsibility" between the federal government and Native nations, which implies that the federal government or its agents are to act in the best interest of Native nations and "with the utmost integrity in its legal and political commitments to Indian peoples as outlined in treaties or governmental policies . . . in its self-assumed role as the Indians' 'protectors'" (Wilkins 2002, 108). This understanding of the trust responsibility has resulted in the US government providing some health care, education, and other services to citizens of tribal nations to this day. However, the concept of the trust responsibility also resulted in the creation of a large federal administrative structure that has intervened in the affairs of Native nations for many decades, with many arguing that federal Indian policy helped shape the historical patterns of American Indian economic inequality that still persist today (Fixico 1998; Pevar 2002). This paternalistic bureaucracy has been increasingly challenged by tribal leaders and since the passage of the Indian Self-Determination and Education Assistance Act of 1975 and its amendments, tribal governments are more actively exercising their self-governance powers and forging new paths toward economic and cultural self-determination in the twenty-first century.

The significant social services provided to tribal citizens as part of the federal government's trust responsibility and the growth of development programs focused on reservation economies has resulted in policies that run counter to neoliberal programs adopted elsewhere in the global economy. In contrast to the neoliberal push for a decline in government services and social supports, the concept of the federal trust responsibility preserves many aspects of the social welfare state for tribal citizens, and the provision of these services by both the federal government and also local tribal governments remains fairly robust. While the quality of the health, education, and welfare services the federal government provides to many tribal citizens is subpar and underfinanced, the assumption of the right to access these services has thus far easily survived any legal or administrative challenges, largely because of the precedent for upholding the trust responsibility. Increasingly, tribal governments, such as the Oneida Nation of Wisconsin, are developing their own tribally funded social welfare programs, such as an Elders retirement fund, and in general tribal citizens view tribal benefits as an important component of tribal citizenship.

Despite the popularity of the neoliberal emphasis on individualism and private sector dominance, Native nations and their citizens have yet to fully embrace this model. While more research is needed on the intersection of ethnicity, gender, and class in American Indian communities, it appears neoliberal policies have had an uneven application in reservation-based economies. Another unusual outcome of the history of externally imposed economic development policies has been the emphasis on tribal governments, or the tribal public sector, to take the lead as developers and owners of businesses, due to purported comparative advantages related to unique tribal legal rights. This has led to an unusual dynamic on some reservations that prioritizes the collective (tribal government) over the individual (tribal citizen), even to the point of hindering individual entrepreneurial activity. Ironically, this emphasis on tribal government business ownership was the product of a set of policies designed to wean tribal governments off financial investments by the United States, policies that have been protested as an abandonment of the federal government's trust responsibility and treaty obligations. These policies persist, however, and tribal governments have been encouraged to continue their tribally owned business development and to interact in global markets, both as the seekers of international capital (in the form of investments in tribal gaming enterprises, for example) and as the providers of cheap labor. This dynamic continues to develop in the new millennium and will prove to be an important area for future research.

Trends in Demographic and Socioeconomic Conditions

While there is great diversity in the cultural traditions and historical experiences of indigenous people in what is now the United States, there are some commonalities in the modern socioeconomic characteristics of this population. These can be difficult to identify, however, because American Indian identity has long been contested. Cultural definitions often differ from administrative and academic definitions, making it challenging to collect accurate data on these communities (see Chaat Smith 2009; Deloria 1998; Snipp 1996). Historically, indigenous populations in North America self-identified with their tribe of origin or ancestry and did not view themselves as a homogeneous racial grouping. Starting with the establishment of the US Bureau of Indian Affairs (BIA) and the later adoption of tribal constitutions in the early 1900s, several administrative definitions of distinct tribal membership were developed, often based on blood quantum or an assumed measure of genetic heritage (Thornton 2005). These administrative definitions became increasingly important as certain tribal benefits were made available only to tribal members. American Indians were first counted as a separate category in the 1860 decennial census, and Alaska Natives were enumerated separately starting in 1940, but only in Alaska. With increasing tribal self-determination and activism starting in the 1970s, the Census refined its categories and in subsequent censuses used more detailed categories to collect information about American Indian and Alaska Native populations, including information about their distinct tribal affiliations. The American Indian civil rights movement helped shape a common American Indian identity in the United States and ushered in the use of the term *Native American*, although it was not without controversy and remains disputed to this day (Tucker et al. 1995).[1]

Data from the US Census Bureau remains our best source of information on American Indian populations in the United States, although the data suffer from some limitations. First, since 1960, the census has relied on self-reported racial data (Thornton 2005), and as a result census data often differ from administrative data collected by tribal governments, with a larger number of individuals claiming American Indian heritage than appear on tribal government rolls. Second, there is a distrust of census enumerators and the federal government in many Native American communities, which results in significant under-participation. Despite both under- and over-counting errors, census data provide some useful information to inform an aggregate picture of the American Indian population in the United States, and through an examination of this granular data an overall demographic portrait becomes clearer.

Beginning in 2000, respondents to the decennial census could claim more than one racial or ethnic affiliation, resulting in many who claim American Indian or Alaska Native identity in addition to one or more other race. According to the 2010 decennial census, over 5.2 million people, or 1.7 percent of the US population, self-identified as Native American (US Census Bureau 2012).[2] Although Native Americans comprise a small percentage of the US population, their population group is growing faster than the overall population—by 27 percent compared to 9.7 percent in the overall US population between 2000 and 2010 (US Census Bureau 2012).

Contrary to popular belief, the majority of Native American people do not live on rural reservations or tribal lands. In 2010, only 22 percent of Native Americans lived on reservation land. However, counties with high Native American population tend to be closer to reservations or Oklahoma tribal statistical areas (US Census Bureau 2012). Nonetheless, the majority of Native Americans in the United States live in urban areas. In 2010, New York City represented the largest concentrated population of American Indian or Alaska Native people, numbering around 112,000, with Los Angeles a close second (US Census Bureau 2012). Federal policies encouraging tribal citizens to leave their reservations and seek wage labor in cities lead to significant fluctuations in population over time, including periodic out-migration and often seasonal relocation. Even today, many Native Americans live and work in urban areas but move back and forth from reservation land, and this population group remains very dynamic. The states with the largest percentage of Native American people are Alaska, Oklahoma, New Mexico, Arizona, Montana, Oklahoma, North Dakota, and South Dakota (US Census Bureau 2012).

American Indians have some of the highest rates of poverty among any racial or minority group, and they suffer from low education levels and high levels of chronic diseases. American Indians have higher mortality rates than all other Americans (Snipp 1996). Nationally, American Indians and Alaska Natives are 2.3 times more likely to have diabetes than the general US population (O'Connell et al. 2010). Native American youth are more likely to be obese and more likely to suffer from mental health issues (CDC 2013). Official unemployment on Indian reservations is close to 22 percent annually, and on some reservations seasonal unemployment can be as high as 60 percent (Taylor and Kalt 2005, 28). Only 77 percent of Native Americans ages twenty-five and older have at least a high school diploma or GED, compared to 86 percent of the overall US population. The number is even lower among Native Americans living on reservations, where only 70 percent have a high school diploma. While poverty levels for American Indians are high overall, with 28 percent of the population in poverty, rates are often much higher for individuals residing on tribal reservation land. Over 38 percent of Native American families on reservations live below the poverty level, and in 2004 per capita income was $7,942 (US Census Bureau 2004).[3] In 2007, 39 percent of American Indian children age five and under were living in poverty, a rate nearly twice that of children five and under in the total US population, which was 21 percent (American Community Survey 2007). The American Indian population in the United States is comparatively very young, with a larger proportion of young people than most other population groups and therefore a higher dependency ratio. About 30 percent of American Indians and Alaska Natives are children under eighteen, compared with about 22 percent of non-Hispanic Whites (US Census Bureau 2004).

Economic Development Strategies in the New Millennium

Against the backdrop of poor socioeconomic indicators, leaders of Native nations are increasingly adopting proactive social and economic development strategies with the goal of restoring cultural and economic vibrancy to their communities. Starting in the 1960s and achieving momentum with the passage of the Indian Self-Determination and Education Assistance Act of 1975, tribal leaders are designing and managing their own social and economic development programs in ways that align with their cultural values and reflect self-governance. While many argue that the post-colonial landscape of economic dependency represents a nearly insurmountable challenge to economic development (Fixico 1998; Wilkins 2002), others point to a vibrant history of market exchange in many Native communities that is still reflected today (Miller 2012). Economic development strategies for Native nations are as controversial as their legal rights, with a strong contingent promoting traditional market-based development building on the comparative advantages presented by unique legal and natural resource attributes (HPAIED 2008), and another contingent promoting a more holistic model that focuses on intertwined social and economic efforts (see Salway Black 1994). Increasingly tribal leaders and others recognize the importance of growing the private sector on reservations and have developed programs for both the private non-profit sector and also individual entrepreneurial businesses. While historical economic development models externally imposed on tribal economies reflect neoliberal tenets, in the new millennium tribal leaders are increasingly developing complex, multifaceted, and innovative strategies that reflect the interconnectedness of social, cultural, and economic growth (HPAIED 2008).

As the leaders of Native nations consider economic development strategies, they are faced with a series of unique challenges and opportunities. Many reservation-based American Indian communities have severely underdeveloped financial, physical, social/cultural, and political/legal infrastructures (Dewees and Sarkozy-Banoczy 2007; 2008; HPAIED 2008) and require a multifaceted policy response to these challenges in order to support both private and public sector business development. As I discuss below, tribal leaders are increasingly pursuing strategies to develop these infrastructures.

Tribal Investments in the Financial Infrastructure of Reservation-Based Communities

Native nations face many barriers related to the financial infrastructure in their communities. Most critically, individuals and business owners lack access to credit, which often limits formal entrepreneurship (CDFI Fund 2001; Hillabrant et al. 2004; HPAIED 2008). There are few banks on reservations, and few banks give loans to tribal members who live on reservations. Many banks remain wary of conducting business on tribal lands due to a lack of clarity related to loan foreclosures and underdeveloped legal codes used to enforce contracts. Increasingly, Native communities, tribal governments, and Native non-profit organizations are working to provide access to credit and financial services through other means. Many successful models of Native community development financial institutions (CDFIs) provide access to "right sized" credit in the form of micro loans or starter loans (small loans that eventually lead to larger loans). In addition, Native CDFIs usually provide culturally appropriate technical assistance and training before ever offering a loan, and can provide ongoing technical assistance to an entrepreneur throughout the term of the loan. There are currently over seventy-four US Treasury–certified Native CDFIs located in Native communities across North America, and many more are in the development stage. Several tribes, such as the Standing Rock Sioux Tribe and the Menominee Indian Tribe of Wisconsin, provide a tribally sponsored loan fund to their citizens. Increasingly, tribal leaders are establishing credit unions. The Hopi Indian Reservation, a rural 1.5-million-acre reservation located in northeastern Arizona, is served by the Hopi Credit Association, which was established in 1952 to serve as a re-lending program to members of the Hopi Tribe. The Hopi Credit Association is also a certified Native CDFI. More recently, the Native CDFI Lakota Funds established the Lakota Federal Credit Union to serve residents of the Pine Ridge Indian Reservation.

Other tribes have been encouraging banks to provide basic financial services on their reservation. On the Pine Ridge Indian Reservation, a mobile banking unit provides access to tellers, cash machines, and other basic services on a daily basis. The mobile unit travels to different towns on the reservation, providing service across the 2.7-million-acre territory. As Native nations grow and develop their citizens as entrepreneurs, and as some of the tribes themselves become financially powerful, banks have recognized that economic partnerships with Native communities, tribes, and individuals can lead to new clients and so have developed products to meet the needs of this market.

Tribal Investments in the Physical Infrastructure of Reservation-Based Communities

Tribal nations face numerous challenges related to their physical infrastructure, including the lack of buildings to house businesses; lack of quality roads; and underdeveloped electric, water/sewer, and telecommunications infrastructure.

Tribally owned land is often interspersed, or *checker-boarded*, with privately owned land in a checker-board pattern of ownership that poses challenges for land use management and planning. Tribal leaders have adopted a range of proactive strategies to overcome these barriers. Many tribal governments recognize the challenges associated with finding a building to house a private enterprise. A common remedy is for a tribe to purchase or build a strip mall or other building to provide commercial space for businesses. On the Fort Belknap Indian Reservation, the tribe owns a strip mall that houses several tribal offices and a privately owned restaurant. On the Oneida Nation of Wisconsin's reservation, the tribe owns a strip mall that houses several retail stores. The Menominee Indian Tribe of Wisconsin supports the Menominee Business Center. The center offers technical assistance and functions as business incubator, providing start-ups with office space and a collective work area with Internet access, a copier, a conference table, and a fax machine for a small fee.

Tribal Investments in the Social/Cultural Infrastructure of Reservation-Based Communities

As tribes exercise their self-determination and work to recover from centuries of colonialism, tribal leaders support programs promoting educational attainment, wellness, language and cultural revitalization, and personal self-sufficiency. Tribal governments created tribal colleges in part as a response to the low educational success rate for many Native students and the negative experiences many Native students had at mainstream institutions (HPAIED 2008, 212). Higher educational attainment has long been a significant predictor of economic growth and development (Barro 1998; Barro and Lee 1993, 363–94). Investments in education are investments in the citizens of a nation to promote the growth of competencies necessary for citizens to participate effectively in the economy and government. The growth of tribal colleges over the past forty years represents a long-term investment in an economic development strategy that promotes educational attainment for tribal members, creates jobs for residents of reservations, and promotes an educated workforce for the tribal government.

To address the poor health conditions of many tribal members, tribal governments are increasingly building health and wellness centers that provide free gym facilities and classes on healthy living to tribal members. The Seneca Nation of New York recently built a state-of-the-art wellness facility with a pool, walking track, and exercise equipment. The Oneida Nation of Wisconsin offers monthly classes related to diabetes management and supports the Just Move It Oneida program, a series of monthly non-competitive walks/runs. The Three Affiliated

Tribes of the Fort Berthold Indian Reservation built a five-mile walking track to encourage exercise and physical activity.

Several Native nations also support cultural revitalization programs and language retention efforts. The Eastern Band of Cherokee Indians offers preschool care at a language immersion daycare center where Cherokee youth are exposed to their traditional language. Aaniiih Nakoda College, serving residents of the Fort Belknap Indian Reservation, hosts a language immersion camp every year. First Nations Development Institute, a national Native-led 501(c)(3) nonprofit corporation that promotes culturally appropriate economic development, has funded over 200 tribal programs through its Native Youth and Culture Fund, a grant program that promotes strategies for cultural revitalization and youth and elder interaction.

The social infrastructure in many Native communities has been identified as a factor affecting the type and pace of economic development (Hillabrant et al. 2004; HPAIED 2008; Jorgensen and Taylor 2000; Pickering 2004). The social infrastructure of a community refers to the collection of social norms, networks, and institutions that contribute to the mobilization of community resources for economic development (Flora and Flora 1993). While each Native community is unique and faces different challenges, some themes emerge (CDFI Fund 2001; Dewees and Sarkozy-Banoczy 2007). Most practitioners identify the dominance of the public sector economy, the lack of Native owned businesses, a post-colonial history of poverty and culture of dependence, and low levels of financial literacy as significant challenges to formal private entrepreneurship and economic development (CDFI Fund 2001). Decades of federal policies that promoted tribal governments owning and operating reservation businesses over individual entrepreneurship have also helped shape and reproduce social norms that suppress private business ownership on many reservations.

Native entrepreneurship is slowly increasing as new generations of tribal members start businesses, become comfortable with financial institutions, and benefit from changing tribal government policies that support individual ownership. There are many institutions in tribal communities that contribute to a slowly emerging business class, and together they support the development of a community-based entrepreneurship development system (Lichtenstein and Lyons 2001). These institutions, including nonprofits, Native CDFIs, and, in some cases, tribal governments, are working to change the social and policy supports for private business owners. Tribal colleges often contribute to the culture of entrepreneurship in a community by providing role models and resources, and by promoting personal financial education. Tribal colleges offer a range of resources through business education programs, business clubs such as American Indian Business Leaders (AIBL), and workshops. At Fort Peck Community College, College of Menominee Nation, and others, the tribal college business programs work closely with business centers and Native CDFIs to help students start small businesses, access financing, and receive ongoing technical assistance. Many Native CDFIs and other institutions have identified other ways to develop an environment on their reservations that is supportive of local business owners and entrepreneurs. On the Pine Ridge Indian Reservation, Lakota Funds, Inc., has helped create the Pine Ridge Chamber of Commerce, which provides networking opportunities and a voice for challenging tribal government policy to be supportive of individually owned businesses. Many other communities are experimenting with chambers of commerce, business associations, and other similar clubs.

Tribal Investments in the Political/Legal Infrastructure of Reservation-Based Communities

Jorgensen and Taylor (2000, 4) of the Harvard Project on American Indian Economic Development (HPAIED) provocatively argue, "poverty in Indian country is a political problem—not an economic one." The authors state:

> There has been a substantial supply of labor in Indian Country for decades, yet scores of economic development plans have been unable to tap that supply on a sustained basis and thereby improve the futures of Indian households. Likewise, tribes possessing natural or capital resources have not led the vanguard of development. While a lack of resources can hamper tribes, and certain systemic features of Indian Country confound investment (for example, the difficulty collateralizing trust lands), the Harvard Project finds that the real deficiency in Indian Country is a shortage of safe havens for capital. The ability to create these safe havens is largely a matter of tribal politics and institutional effectiveness.

While Jorgensen and Taylor's claims are controversial, the argument that uneven and unpredictable legal infrastructure on many reservations hampers investment is one that has resonance with many scholars of American Indian economic development. Increasingly, tribal governments and Native non-profit organizations are working to change the legal and political environments in reservation-based communities to make them more supportive of business development. Drawing upon research from HPAIED, many tribes are implementing effective governance practices and adopting a series of policies that appear to be correlated to successful economic growth: separating politics from business affairs, developing the legal infrastructure for business development by passing supportive legislation, and developing an independent judiciary and administrative institutions that can provide legal enforcement of tribal codes (HPAIED 2008, 123). A growing number of tribes, such as the Eastern Band of Cherokee Indians, the Navajo Nation, and the Winnebago Tribe, are passing Uniform Commercial Codes and other codes related to debt, foreclosure, and financial regulation.

The legal status of land held in trust on reservations and its fractionated heirship makes it difficult to use land for collateral or other economic activity, effectively rendering it "dead capital" (De Soto 2000). While the issues surrounding the limitations of trust land and the problems associated with fractionated land are too vast to cover in this chapter, it is worth noting that several tribes are buying back their ancestral homelands in order to consolidate their checkerboarded reservations. The Confederated Tribes of the Umatilla Indian Reservation developed a vision statement in 1990 that included buying back traditional lands and adding it to the reservation base held in trust for the tribes. With the aid of gaming revenue, the tribe has purchased 14,000 acres and now owns about 29 percent of the land on the reservation. The Oneida Nation of Wisconsin and many other tribes have also implemented a land buy-back program. Through innovative programs such as land consolidation, promoting effective governance strategies, strengthening the tribal judiciary, developing internal tribal laws, and advocating externally to protect their sovereignty, tribal governments are investing in the development of their legal and political infrastructure to promote sustainable economic development.

Indian Gaming

One of the most well-known and least-understood economic development strategies adopted by tribes over the past thirty years is gaming. Casino development has been a successful economic development strategy for many tribes, but many misconceptions exist about this strategy and the impact it has had on the economic status of tribes and their citizens. Indian gaming was actually encouraged by federal officials in the 1980s as a way for tribes to generate a new income stream, reduce their economic dependency on the federal government, and move toward economic self-sufficiency during an era of sharp reductions in federal aid to tribes (Snipp 1995). Because of their unique sovereign status, tribes can operate gaming facilities even in states where state law restricts them, and several tribes, especially those located near large urban markets, have opened successful gaming operations that generate significant revenue.

The economic impact of Indian gaming has been uneven. While there are more than 200 Native nations in twenty-eight states with gaming operations, most of these operations are small and not very profitable for the tribe. A minority of operations account for a majority of the income—only 5 percent of all of Indian gaming operations generate 40 percent of the total revenue according to the National Indian Gaming Commission. Tribes with larger, well-run facilities located near large urban markets are more likely to generate significant income. State and local governments also benefit from Indian gaming operations because they employ a large number of local residents who in turn pay state and local income tax. In this way, tribal gaming contributes to local government revenue and promotes economic development for many "off reservation" rural communities, a fact that popular media coverage often overlooks.

It is also important to note that tribes pay a portion of their gaming revenues to state governments and charitable organizations in local communities. The success of Indian gaming attracted the interest of state government officials who wanted to capture some of the revenue. In 1988 the federal government passed the Indian Gaming Regulatory Act, which created a structure for shared state-tribal policies to regulate Indian gaming operations. As a result, tribal nations must negotiate with state governments to determine whether they may open an operation, how they may use the revenues from the operation, and what percentage they must pay out to local and state governments and charitable programs. This legislation has not been well received by many Native leaders because they believed it diminishes their sovereign status and contradicts long-standing federal Indian law that suggests that interaction with Native nations is a federal, not state, government matter. Moreover, many Native leaders argue that the states looking to capitalize on the success of Indian gaming are continuing the history of oppressive policies that take resources from Native people and place them in the hands of non-Natives (Corntassel and Witmer 2008). Over the past thirty years, there have been many high-profile conflicts between tribal and state governments over the portion of Indian gaming revenues committed to state government programs.

Revenue from Indian gaming has helped many tribes build their financial, physical, social, and legal infrastructure. Using gaming revenues, tribes have funded educational scholarship funds, wellness centers, childcare centers, health clinics, and paid for other tribal government operations such as the judiciary, tribal police forces, and fire departments. In addition, gaming revenues are used to pay down debts associated with the enterprise and cover the operating expenses. A small number of tribes pay out dividends to their members that assist in increasing their income, and research suggest that these payments improve quality of life for Indian children and families (Costello et al. 2003). Unfortunately, there is a common misconception in America that Indian gaming operations have solved the problem of Indian poverty. This is simply not the case. The gap between the income levels of Indians on reservations and the larger US population still remains very large, even for residents of reservations with casinos (Taylor and Kalt 2005). Today, Indian gaming remains only one of many different strategies to spur economic development on Native lands and their surrounding rural communities. But Indian gaming continues to be a contentious issue, and states will continue to fight for increasing benefits from and control over Indian gaming revenues and operations. New challenges are already emerging as state governments open up state-owned gaming facilities and divert revenues from tribal enterprises. As more tribes open casinos (and compete for the same customers) and the global capital constriction has reduced demand for gaming products, tribes are increasingly looking for ways to diversify their revenue streams and the impact of gaming on Native and rural communities appears to be waning.

Natural Resource Extraction

Indian nations hold approximately 30 percent of the nation's coal resources, 10 percent of the natural gas resources, and 5 percent of the oil resources. Some estimates suggest that a total of 10 percent of the nation's energy resources lie within the boundaries of Native American reservations (Lui et al. 2005). Tribes earn only marginal returns on these natural resources in comparison to the returns produced by private industries, however. In reaction to evidence of mismanagement by the BIA, an increasing number of tribes have sought to take over the management of their natural resource-based industries, a strategy that has resulted in increased returns and economic growth on reservations. For example, the Southern Ute Indian Tribe is the only Native nation in the United States that has complete control of its energy resources (First Nations Development Institute 2009). In 1992, the tribe formed the Red Willow Production Company to buy back leases and upgrade the performance of the wells on its reservation. Since that time, the tribe has bought back 100 percent of its leases and has expanded its business of oil and gas production beyond reservation borders.

In addition to oil, coal, and natural gas, Indian governments own large quantities of land, the majority of which—approximately forty-seven million acres—is used for ranching and farmland (HPAIED 2008, 161). Unfortunately, much of the agricultural land is leased out to non-Native farmers and ranchers. Nevertheless, several Native nations, like the Oneida Nation of Wisconsin, operate successful tribally owned farms that create jobs and revenue for tribal citizens while producing healthy food for the local market. In addition to economic activity related to farming and ranching, approximately ten million acres of Indian land is used for commercial forest operations (HPAIED 2008, 162). Many tribes, including the Menominee Indian Tribe of Wisconsin, have taken control of their forest operations and now use sustainable forest management practices to responsibly harvest their forests to generate economic revenue. As Native nations build their managerial capacity, they are taking back control of their natural resource-related enterprises. By exerting control over the leasing process or initiating direct management of operations related to energy, agriculture, or timber, tribes are more successful in capturing the economic benefits from these resources and creating economic opportunities for tribal members.

Conclusions

The history of economic development policy on Indian reservations is one of externally imposed models that were often poorly designed, dismissive of local culture and leadership, and extractive of natural resources (Fixico 1998; Wilkins 2002, 160). Early economic development strategies focused on cultural assimilation, out-migration of tribal citizens to urban areas, or paternally managed natural resource extraction. Starting in the 1950s and 1960s, federal agencies began to promote industrial development on reservations and a new one-size-fits-all model of economic development came into vogue, although with a focus on government-owned enterprises. While this factory-based model, alongside the continuing natural resource-extraction model, did successfully create jobs and a revenue stream for both tribal governments and tribal citizens, it did not lead to sustained economic growth or increased diversification of tribal economies, partially because it failed to fully develop internal leadership capacity or address the underlying weaknesses in financial, physical, social/cultural, and political/legal infrastructure that were present on most reservations (HPAIED 2008). As they face the next century, tribal leaders are exercising their self-determination and developing proactive, multifaceted, and innovative strategies that reflect the interconnectedness of social, cultural, and economic growth for their communities. As Native nations and their citizens continue to grow their economic enterprises, nearby rural communities will increasingly find mutually beneficial arrangements to both support and prosper from this economic growth.

There is a need for more research on the myriad economic development models, philosophies, and strategies currently being adopted by tribal leadership across North America, and how these models are influenced by and interact with modern notions of tribal sovereignty, globalization, and neoliberalism. The historical vestiges and modern administrative structures that make up the current relationship between tribal governments and the federal government have resulted in surprising and counter-cyclical patterns unfolding in reservation economies. The dominance of the public sector, the importance of social services, and the emphasis on government-led economic development means that neoliberal tenants have not been adopted at the local level in the same way as other rural communities. However, from both federal policy makers and tribal leaders, there is an increasing emphasis on free-market economics, individual self-sufficiency, and private business development. These dynamics should continue to be analyzed, and represent a wealth of information for future research.

Notes

1 In this chapter, I use the terms *American Indian* and *Native American* interchangeably to describe individuals who are citizens of a tribal nation or have a heritage associated with peoples indigenous to North America.

2 Either alone or in combination with some other race.

3 The low participation by Native Americans in the decennial census and the American Community Survey may limit the accuracy of these data.

References

American Community Survey. 2007. "American FactFinder Table S0201." http://factfinder2.census.gov.

Barro, Robert J. 1998. *Determinants of Economic Growth: A Cross-Country Empirical Study.* Cambridge: MIT Press.

Barro, Robert J, and Jong-Wha Lee. 1993. "International Comparisons of Educational Attainment." *Journal of Monetary Economics* 32 (3): 363–94. http://dx.doi.org/10.1016/0304-3932(93)90023-9.

CDFI (Community Development Financial Institutions) Fund. 2001. *The Report of the Native American Lending Study.* Washington, DC: US Department of the Treasury.

Centers for Disease Control. 2013. *CDC Health Disparities and Inequalities Report—United States, 2013.* 62 (3): 22 November 2013. http://www.cdc.gov/mmwr/pdf/other/su6203.pdf.

Corntassel, Jeff, and Richard C. Witmer. 2008. *Forced Federalism: Contemporary Challenges to Indigenous Nationhood.* Norman: University of Oklahoma Press.

Costello, Jane, Scott N. Compton, Gordon Keeler, and Adrian Angold. 15 October 2003. "Relationships between Poverty and Psychopathology: A Natural Experiment." *Journal of the American Medical Association* 290 (15): 2023–29. http://dx.doi.org/10.1001/jama.290.15.2023. Medline:14559956.

De Soto, Hernando. 2000. *The Mystery of Capital: Why Capitalism Triumphs in the West and Fails Everywhere Else.* New York: Basic Books.

Deloria, P.J. 1998. *Playing Indian.* New Haven, CT: Yale University Press.

Dewees, Sarah, and Stewart Sarkozy-Banoczy. 2007. "Transforming Economies: Entrepreneurship in Native Communities." In *Integrated Asset-Building Strategies for Reservation-Based Communities*, ed. First Nations Development Institute, 155–88. Longmont: First Nations Development Institute.

Dewees, Sarah, and Stewart Sarkozy-Banoczy. 2008. *Investing in Native Community Change: Understanding the Role of Community Development Financial Institutions.* Washington, DC: CDFI Fund.

First Nations Development Institute. 2009. *Native American Asset Watch: Rethinking Asset-Building in Indian Country.* Longmont, CO: First Nations Development Institute.

Fixico, Donald L. 1998. *The Invasion of Indian Country in the Twentieth Century: American Capitalism and Tribal Natural Resources.* Niwot: University Press of Colorado.

Flora, Cornelia Butler, and Jan L. Flora. 1993. "Entrepreneurial Social Infrastructure: A Necessary Ingredient." *Annals of the American Academy of Political and Social Science* 529 (1): 48–58. http://dx.doi.org/10.1177/0002716293529001005.

Hillabrant, William, J. Earp, and Michael Rhoades. 2004. *Overcoming Challenges to Business and Economic Development in Indian Country.* Princeton, NJ: Mathematic Policy Research, Inc.

HPAIED (Harvard Project on American Indian Economic Development). 2008. *The State of Native Nations: Conditions under U.S. Policies of Self-Determination.* New York: Oxford University Press.

Jorgensen, Miriam, and John Taylor. 2000. *What Determines Indian Economic Success? Evidence from Tribal and Individual Indian Enterprises.* Cambridge, MA: Harvard University, John F. Kennedy School of Government.

Lichtenstein, Greg, and Timothy Lyons. 2001. "The Entrepreneurial Development System: Transforming Business Talent and Community Economies." *Economic Development Quarterly* 15 (1): 3–20. http://dx.doi.org/10.1177/089124240101500101.

Lui, Meizhu, Barbara Robles, Betsy Leondar-Wright, Rose Brewer, and Rebecca Adamson. 2005. *The Color of Wealth: The Story Behind the U.S. Racial Divide.* New York: The New Press.

Miller, Robert J. 2012. *Reservation "Capitalism."* Denver, CO: Praeger.

O'Connell, Joan, Rong Yi, Charlton Wilson, Spero Mason, and Kelly Acton. 2010. "Racial Disparities in Health Status: A Comparison of the Morbidity among American Indian and U.S. Adults with Diabetes." *Diabetes Care* 33 (7): 1463–70. http://dx.doi.org/10.2337/dc09-1652.

Pevar, Stephen. 2002. *The Rights of Indian and Tribes.* 3rd ed. Carbondale: Southern Illinois University Press.

Pickering, Kathleen. 2004. "Culture and Reservation Economies." In *A Companion to Anthropology of American Indians, Blackwell Companions to Anthropology*, ed. T. Biolsi, 112–29. Malden, MA: Blackwell Publishing. http://dx.doi.org/10.1002/9780470996270.ch7.

Salway Black, Sherry. 1994. *Redefining Success in Community Development: A New Approach for Determining and Measuring the Impact of Development.* Medford, MA: Lincoln Filene Center at Tufts University.

Smith, Chaat Paul. 2009. *Everything You Know about Indians is Wrong.* Minneapolis: University of Minnesota Press.

Snipp, Matthew. 1995. "American Indian Economic Development." In *The Changing American Countryside: Rural People and Places*, ed. Emery N. Castle, 303–37. Lawrence: University of Kansas Press.

Snipp, Matthew. 1996. "The Size and Distribution of the American Indian Population: Fertility, Mortality, Residence, and Migration." In *Changing Numbers, Changing Needs: American Indian Demography and Public Health*, ed. Gardy D. Sandefur, Ronald R. Rindfuss, and Barney Cohen, 17–52. Washington, DC: National Academy Press.

Taylor, Jonathan, and Joseph Kalt. 2005. *American Indians on Reservations: A Databook of Socioeconomic Change between the 1990 and 2000 Censuses.* Cambridge, MA: The Harvard Project on American Indian Economic Development.

Thornton, Russell. 2005. "Native American Demographic and Tribal Survival into the Twenty-First Century." *American Studies (Lawrence, Kan.)* 46 (3/4): 23–38.

Tucker, Clyde, Brian Kojetin, and Roderick Harrison. 1995. "A Statistical Analysis of the CPS Supplement on Race and Ethnic Origin." Bureau of Labor Statistics Bureau of the Census. Accessed 18 June 2012. http://www.census.gov/prod/2/gen/96arc/ivatuck.pdf.

US Census Bureau. 2004. "The American Community: American Indians and Alaska Natives." http://www.census.gov/prod/2007pubs/acs-07.pdf.

US Census Bureau. 2010. "Census Brief: Overview of Race and Hispanic Origin." http://www.census.gov/prod/cen2010/briefs/c2010br-02.pdf.

US Census Bureau. 2012. "The American Indian and Alaska Native Population, 2010." Accessed 18 June 2012. http://www.census.gov/prod/cen2010/briefs/c2010br-10.pdf.

Wilkins, David E. 2002. *American Indian Politics and the American Political System.* Lanham: Rowman & Littlefield.

CHAPTER 25

The Past is the Present: Gender and the Status of Rural Women

Cynthia B. Struthers

Introduction

Given that neoliberalism and market fundamentalist philosophy has dominated social, economic, and political discourse and policy for the last four decades, it is difficult to distinguish what is "new" in the study of gender and the status of women in the 2010s. In this chapter, I will first discuss major issues confronting rural women from the previous decennial volumes. I will then discuss contemporary issues. I will include social, economic, and political trends that have marked the period between 2000 and 2010 and that continue to shape the current decade. I will conclude with a discussion of policy and practices that impact the quality life of rural women and suggestions to improve the conditions of their lives.

A Review of the 1980s, 1990s, and 2000s

Haney (1982) illustrates how the focus on productive activity and agricultural production as "work" fails to acknowledge women's unpaid contributions to the farm and makes invisible their labor on behalf of the farm, home, and community. When rural women's efforts were acknowledged, their contributions were defined as "helping," which diminished their value. In her analysis of the existing literature, Haney concludes that the focus on paid work and the structure of agri-business reinforced traditional sex-role stereotypes and disadvantaged and discriminated against rural women. The secondary status of women on the farm and in society results in disadvantage in employment, legislation such as social security, tax policies, and inheritance and estate taxes.

Structural forces prior to the 1980s that shaped rural places and women's lives included the reorganization of agricultural production, the growth of labor-intensive industries in rural places, migration turnaround, and the expansion of extractive industries. At the same, time social services expanded in rural places, opening a new sector of the labor market to rural women. Changes in the rural economy meant that farm workers needed to seek off-farm employment, but evolving rural industries produced mostly low-skill and low-wage work. Rural women entered the formal labor market even though they had few occupational choices or job opportunities. Still, women's employment helped sustain their households' standard of living. Unfortunately, most jobs created in response to the reorganization of agriculture provide little to no promotional opportunities and are part-time rather than full-time. As a result, women experience greater employment vulnerability then rural men.

Changing economic and social trends in the 1970s and into the 1980s reshaped not only rural families but also households across the United States. These trends increased age at first marriage, higher divorce rates, and declining fertility, and have continued across the United States and in rural places. Haney (1982, 131–2) makes a number of research recommendations, which include the need to focus on:

> The contribution of various members of rural families to the household and family economy and relate these work and economic patterns to family decision making and authority relations; (the) connection between public policies and interpersonal relations within the family; (whether) existing patterns of authority restrict rural women's ability to organize effectively and represent their interest in the economic and political arena; the extent to which rural communities rely on the voluntary efforts of women for the delivery of many community services, the availability of services that are of particular importance to rural women, such as health and child care, welfare, and low-cost legal aid; and (the) need to consider the overall consequences of social processes and state policy for rural women.

In short, Haney calls for a research focus on rural women and their experience and the adoption of new approaches to understanding and improving rural women's lives. She does not include much discussion of rural non-farm women. Haney's analysis and recommendations were consistent with evolving feminist theory and practice in the 1970s and 1980s, and she makes a significant contribution to our understanding of rural women.

Given Haney's recommendations for more research to better understand rural women, it is interesting that Flora and Christenson (1991) do not include a chapter about rural women in their decennial volume. In four chapters, they highlight issues raised by Haney (1982), such as poverty, work, and jobs in rural places; family life; and aging. Though there is considerable overlap among the four chapters, a few key issues from each require mention as they pertain to women and gender in the 1990s. Deavers and Hoppe (1991) show that women head a significant proportion of rural families, and that these families are disproportionately poor. They discuss how female-headed households are eligible for various federal and state anti-poverty programs, such as Aid to Families with Dependent Children (AFDC) and Medicaid. But Deavers and Hoppe also show that rural areas have a significant proportion of working poor households composed of married couples and households headed by men whose incomes were at or below established poverty thresholds. Gender bias in existing social welfare policies prevented many rural households from benefiting from existing anti-poverty programs. One conclusion they make is that existing welfare programs make it impossible to alleviate rural poverty, a theme that Sherman (in this volume) repeats.

Deavers and Hoppe also discuss how existing poverty programs fail to consider specific rural circumstances. For example, eligibility for federal, state, or local public aid does not guarantee rural residents access to services. Sparsely populated areas make service delivery difficult and expensive. Based on their analysis, Deavers and Hoppe conclude there was little hope that programming for the rural poor would expand in the coming decade.

Rather than focusing on the degree of rural poverty and limits to existing anti-poverty programs, Tickamyer and Duncan (1991) examine aspects of the rural labor market that perpetuate poverty. Like Haney (1982), they identify the limited number of employment opportunities, lack of full-time jobs, and limited training and educational opportunities available to rural people as the causes of rural poverty. Research shows these problems are intensified for rural women and minorities, especially where labor markets are tight. In addition, they discuss how rural educational institutions were "underfunded, inadequate, and easily manipulated politically" in ways that disadvantaged rural workers and failed to prepare them for employment (1991, 106). Tickamyer and Duncan advocate for policies that would make rural jobs that provide a living wage, and emphasize the need for year-round employment opportunities for rural workers. Rural unemployment and underemployment perpetuates poverty and creates stress for rural individuals and families.

Bokemeier and Garkovich (1991, 117) focus on a number of chronic stressors that rural families' face, such as economic uncertainty, limited housing options, and "inadequate, inaccessible, and inappropriate support services." These problems affect rural low-income individuals and households and farm and non-farm families alike. They posit that the stressors afflicting rural people are chronic because there are insufficient rural health and social services to help individuals cope with their economic and social circumstances. They identify the structural barriers that perpetuate the stress faced by rural residents and prevent rural communities from increasing rural services. These include community instability due to limited tax bases and other rural conditions that interfere with expanding basic services.

Chronic stress interferes with individuals and households' ability to meet daily and unexpected financial pressures. Rural families that experience poorer health and are underemployed are unable to invest in their children's education, and as a result rural children fair more poorly in school. Holding multiple jobs increased time in paid employment, and leaves rural parents with less time at home and less time to devote to children and kin. The rural elderly had less family support, which further increased their vulnerability. Though both rural men and women face chronic stress, women remain responsible for the care of children, kin, and household in ways men do not (Bokemeier and Garkovich 1991).

Kaiser (1991) discusses the rural aged. His work shows that rural residents are older than their urban counterparts and most will age in place. Studies at the time show that older rural men tended to stay on the farm as they aged, while older women tended to move to town. Like Haney (1982), Kaiser discusses how limited rural employment opportunities shaped the incomes and resources available to the rural elderly in retirement. Research continues to find that rural workers had less access to jobs that provided pensions, and poor-paying jobs reduced the amount of social security the rural elderly receive. In addition, Kaiser finds that rural seniors disproportionately suffer from disabilities associated with their occupations, with farm men more likely to suffer a debilitating condition at a younger age than non-farm residents of both genders. Overall, disabilities and poorer health are more common among older rural residents than older persons living in other areas.

Kaiser (1991) challenges a number of myths that non-rural people have of the rural elderly. He shows that older rural residents have less family and kin to depend on but have more contact with friends and neighbors than urban residents. But he also finds rural seniors are not involved in many community organizations beyond their local church. Health care, social services, financial support, and transportation are all problematic for the rural elderly. He challenges the dominate view that rural aging was healthier or easier than aging elsewhere.

When taken together, authors in the 1991 volume show that rural people face a number of similar problems including poverty, limited job opportunities, and low wages. Additional research indicates that the social and economic conditions of rural places disadvantage rural women in particular ways. Women are disproportionately poor and have a difficult time securing employment, benefits, or social services that provide opportunities for a stable family life. Rural communities lack infrastructure that can support rural family life. In the absence of more and better paying jobs, the rural elderly and especially elderly women face economic hardship as they age. Though increased numbers of rural women entered the paid labor force during the 1970s and 1980s, there was little in the 1991 decennial volume that illustrates a vast improvement in their status or the material conditions of rural life.

What the first two decennial volumes share is a focus on an essentialized experience of rural women. Though distinctions begin to emerge between farm and non-farm women, there is no discussion in these chapters about the differential experiences of women of different racial or ethnic backgrounds, or of regional differences in rural places and people. There is little to indicate differences between communities based on agriculture and those that depend on fishing, forestry, or mining, or the proximity of rural communities to urban places.

The 2000s and Rural Women

In Brown and Swanson (2003), Tickamyer and Henderson show how an emphasis on gender issues has transformed how women and rural places are studied. They attribute this transformation to the influence of feminist theories and practice. What they find is that studies of rural women throughout the 2000s "show less change in women's actual work and activity than in how scholars have come to view these women" (Tickamyer and Henderson 2003, 109). They posit that what is different is the emphasis placed on spatial and cultural diversity, intersecting social locations such as race, class, gender, and place, and on the choices and constraints that rural women face.

When examining the literature with a lens of continuity and change, they illustrate that rural women continue to work hard in support of their families. Rural women have entered the labor force and now work in traditional and non-traditional occupations, such as coal mining (Tallichet 2006). When rural women work outside the home, they continue to work on behalf of home and community, resulting in a double day.

When summarizing the similarities and changes diverse rural women experience, Tickamyer and Henderson look to Appalachia, the Pacific Northwest, and the Midwest. In each region, rural women adopt different formal and informal economic strategies to maintain home and family as economic restructuring ravages rural places. Likewise, they consider the very different experiences of rural African American and Latino women in rural places by highlighting specific differences in cultural histories and circumstances in relation to the dominant culture. Tickamyer and Henderson provide evidence of rural women's resistance and activism in the face of continued economic uncertainty.

The decennial volumes illustrate that the work of rural women is shaped by neoliberal policies throughout the three periods, and that these policies perpetuate rural disadvantage broadly. Research on rural women after Haney (1982) reflects a women-centered agenda that called for and included women's contributions to farm, household, and community; the impacts of public policies on rural households, existing patterns of authority, and women's ability to organize; the importance of women's contributions to community life; and the need to examine the social processes and state policies that impact women's lives. Subsequent researchers adopt new strategies to answer these questions.

Social, political, and economic processes since the 1970s shape rural women's experiences today. Rural women continue to enter the labor market due to changes in production agriculture, manufacturing, and the proliferation of health and social service jobs. They remain in the labor market due to declines in wages and job opportunities for rural men and family structure continues to change in response to social and economic processes. Yet, for all that has changed in our research and practice to better understand rural women's lives, rural places have not changed for the better over time. In the next section, I examine many enduring problems and processes associated with contemporary rural life.

Forty Years of Neoliberalism: Current Women's Issues Persistent Rural Problems

Economic, social, and political forces have resulted in broad changes in US society, and rural women have responded. The concurrent and interwoven forces that are changing rural places and our understanding of them include the continued influence of feminist and gender theory, the rural labor market, changes in agricultural production and extractive industries, migration, the systematic dismantling of the social safety net, and more recently the Great Recession, the devolution of federal and state programs, the current state of the US economy, and the increased influence of national and international corporations on national governments.

The intersections of the growth in national and international corporations and chain stores and declines in the social safety net have had a significant influence on women's employment locally, nationally, and globally. Taken together, these forces have produced a race to the bottom in the low-wage labor market. Women have increased their labor force participation, but the jobs created in the 1980s, 1990s, and 2000s in services, retail, and hospitality do not pay enough to improve their standard of living (Collins and Mayer 2010). In a longitudinal study of women's wages, England, Allison, and Wu (2007) show that women's wages have remained low over time. Though a higher percentage of women in any given occupation is associated with lower wages and the casual relationship between gender composition and wages has a long history, the authors argue that low wages paid to women is a result of "institutional inertia" (England, Allison, and Wu 2007). The same could be said of rural disadvantage. The current conditions of rural life are not only a result of deliberate neoliberal policies, but also the unintended consequences of these policies on rural places and women lives.

Poverty is not evenly distributed across rural America or by race and ethnicity. White Americans continue to constitute much of the poverty population in Appalachia, just as poor Black Americans are more likely to live in the rural South, impoverished Native Americans on reservations in the Dakotas and Southwest, and Hispanics located in Southwest, although increasingly located throughout rural America (e.g., Oregon, Idaho). Racial and ethnic populations have become more disperse across rural places. The counties in which nonmetro Hispanics and African Americans live have higher concentrations of poverty, which coincides with these counties having fewer available jobs, lower educational attainment, fewer public services, and poorer infrastructure (Lichter and Johnson 2007). Poverty rates vary not only by race and residence, but also by marital status.

Though research has long shown that female-headed households are more likely to be poorer than married and/or two-parent households, variation can and does exist. Family types are more diverse than just married couples and single-parent households. Snyder, McLaughlin, and Findeis (2006) examine the differences among female-headed households by studying rural cohabiting and grandmother-headed households. Grandmother-headed households are most common among rural African American and Native American families. Rural female-headed households tend to rely on various forms of public assistance. The presence of another wage earner is significant in reducing poverty in female-headed households, and this holds true in both cohabiting arrangements and grandmother-headed households. Cohabiting is a strategy adopted to stabilize the economic position of the household, but tends to be a more unstable family form.

Recent studies by Mattingly and Bean (2010) and Mattingly, Johnson, and Schaefer (2011) show that childhood poverty is on the rise. Poverty is most common among children under the age six who live in rural areas, and is consistently higher among black, Native, and Hispanic children than among white children. Rural single mothers have a poverty rate that is close to five times higher than the rate of married couples living in the same areas (Mattingly and Bean 2010). About 81 percent of rural counties have persistently high child poverty. Poverty among children is greatest in Appalachia, the Ozarks, Mississippi Delta, the Texas-Mexico border, and Native America areas of the Great Plains and Oklahoma (Mattingly, Johnson, and Schaefer 2011). Chronically poor rural mothers tend to be women of color, have low educational attainment levels, have few job skills, and lack basic work supports like reliable transportation, day care, and health care. Poverty and economic hardship is a reality of rural life for many rural women, especially racial and ethnic women.

Current research on rural women reflects the contemporary economic, political, and social realities where the jobs that rural workers depend on have disappeared due to international competition and fundamental changes in industries. The shift from manufacturing to service work has been devastating to rural workers by increasing male unemployment and the further concentration of women in the service sector. Job loss has been especially hard on rural workers with only high school degrees or less (Glasmeier and Salant 2006). Women who made inroads in nontraditional fields in the 1990s and were able to increase their earnings relative to women in the service sector have since disproportionately lost such jobs. Fewer coal jobs has resulted in male unemployment and confined women to the service sector (Kelly 2007; Tallichet 2011). What has changed is that wages are currently so low that many rural women must work multiple low-paying jobs to provide for their family (Ames, Brosi, and Damiano-Teixeira 2006; Kelly 2007).

Given that women's wages have historically been lower than men's, the biggest shift in rural labor markets is the loss of male employment opportunities. Many rural households now depend on the wages paid to women. Though rural employment has often been cyclical, the absence of male employment is new. In her study of a Northern California rural logging community, Sherman (2009) finds that as economic uncertainty grows, rural identity is asserting itself in ways that allow residents to retain a sense of place and moral center. Sherman (2009) finds that rural men and women continue to idealize the traditional family type even in the absence of male employment by focusing on family stability. Rural men and women are judged and judge others by their ability to maintain a stable family, not by traditional gender roles.

Grigsby (2012) also finds reaffirmation of traditional gender roles among working-class families in the rural Midwest. In her study of "noodlers," rural working-class women seek recognition as "worthy" wives and mothers by assuming the roles of "helpmates, care takers, tom boys, or Daddy's girls." Noodling is primarily a male activity, but it is also a "family" activity that includes fishing, eating, and socializing. By adhering to traditional gender roles within the noodling subculture, conservative attitudes and patriarchy remain embedded in rural places. Through noodling rural blue-collar people differentiate themselves and their families from urban values and behaviors they abhor. Social class, family, and rural activities distinguish rural people from urban people in economically uncertain times.

Much contemporary scholarship on rural women refocuses attention on women's participation in agriculture. Agriculture and other extractive industries provide an enduring and gendered legacy of male privilege. Pilgeram (2007) finds that women both reinforce traditional views of masculinity in livestock farming as they challenge it at the auction house. Trauger et al. (2010) show that gender shapes women farmers' approach to agriculture and the farming practices they adopt. Much of the farming that women do is outside of the complex world of large-scale production agriculture. Women engage in a counter-agriculture where they are more intimately connected to their customers, environment, and communities. These are aspects of farming that female farmers find most rewarding.

One more recent trend that has increased rural women's visibility in agriculture is having more legal and legitimate claim to land and rural resources. In a recent study of landownership and decision making in the Great Lakes, Petrzelka and Marquart-Pyatt (2011) find that even though more women own land, they do not necessarily control decisions regarding planting or environmental practices, especially when they no longer reside on the farm. They find that older women acquiesce to male family members to keep peace within the family. Reducing and eliminating conflict is more important than asserting their authority over farming practices.

Current agricultural practices produce a rift between rural women. Machum (2011) finds that rural Canadian women use the adoption of new farm technology, farm size, hired labor, and legal status of farm operation as ways to distinguish class location. These things are important to "expanders" who adopt the bigger is better discourse of production agriculture. Expanders disparage "sustainers," or those who adopt policies of sustainability and practices they feel support "family farms." Social class is just one way that that divisions among rural residents are evolving.

Class distinctions and different orientations and understandings of rural create interesting tensions. Social class shapes perspectives about what one can and should do as rural residents. Middle class people who move to rural areas seek to "make" rural community based on an idealized vision of the rural. Rural working-class residents see no reason to actively engage in community life other than that related to the family, kin, and rural activities in which they have always engaged (Macgregor 2010). These divergent views impact rural community members' ability to work together. Social class and class difference has emerged as a central theme for understanding divisions in rural places, rural/urban difference, and differences between countries and regions of the world.

The impact of the globalization and neoliberalism is made manifest in the passage of North American Free Trade Agreement (NAFTA) and Central American Free Trade Agreement (CAFTA). These agreements impact rural people and women across North America. Outcomes of NAFTA have included the privatization of public services such as health care and education, the lowering of existing environmental and labor laws, the loss of small land holdings, and subsistence farming as production moves from filling local needs to export. NAFTA has resulted in the disproportionate displacement of poor and indigenous people, the loss of land, and increased food insecurity (Fosse 2003).

Displaced rural residents have found other employment, but in poor paying jobs with poor working conditions in non-unionized shops. Rural Mexican women have increasingly entered the formal labor market to support their families. But the loss of public support and services has resulted in additional informal work in an effort to support self and family. Mexican women are less likely to voluntarily opt out of the formal sector and their informal work is more pervasive and low paying than men's (Biles 2008).

NAFTA and CAFTA have had a number of differential impacts on rural women because they have led to cuts in education, training, and social services that could improve women's lives. Women are more likely to be caught up in labor smuggling, have no labor protections, face sexism on and off the job, endure low wages and poor working conditions, and face exploitation. The impact on their home countries is to increase class distinctions between those households with remittance income from those where no migration occurs and in the case of the migration of higher skill workers such as nurses, a brain drain results in sending countries. The intersectionality of race, class, and gender is seen in the jobs and occupations native and immigrant populations obtain (Duffy 2007)

The presence of female Mexican migrants in Canadian agriculture illustrates how agricultural production is both gendered and racialized. Preibisch and Grez (2011) show how women from the South are becoming a predominant force in commercial agriculture in Canada. They find that women migrants from Mexico and Central America are granted temporary work visas to engage in the most "dirty, difficult, and dangerous jobs" in commercial agriculture (Preibisch and Grez 2011, 101). Gender, race, and ethnicity are used to sort migrants into different jobs. Migrant women are rewarded for fulfilling their work obligations in gender appropriate ways and are sent home when they act out.

People may view migration from Mexico and Central America as a blessing and a curse. Much of the population growth occurring in rural places in the United States is a result of immigration, with the most growth occurring in counties that attract Mexican and Latino migrants. Though some of these households consist solely of adult migrants, increasingly they consist of families. Though rural communities have not rushed to embrace Latinos or other immigrants groups, immigrants are increasingly recognized as saving small rural towns from disappearing (Longworth 2008; Sulzberger 2011).

Issues for the Current Decade

Poverty, low wages, and cuts to social and public programs like health care and education continue to disproportionately impact rural women and households. Rural areas must confront the reality of long-term male unemployment. Concurrent social, economic, and political trends perpetuate not only divisions between rural and urban populations but also those between corporate interests in agriculture, mining, and energy in rural places, and between other rural residents. The 2010s look very much like the 1970s and 1980s. There are however some important additional concerns facing rural America.

Military Service

Rural areas are paying a high price for US military missions in Iraq and Afghanistan because the military is disproportionately composed of rural people (Heady 2007; Carr and Kefalas 2009). In the absence of other jobs with benefits, rural residents join the military and they tend to remain in the reserves or National Guard over time (Cebula, Menon, and Menon 2008). Returning veterans, both male and female, will require care and support that many rural communities are poorly equipped to provide (Weeks, Wallace, Wang, Lee, and Kazis 2006). The need for family and formal support for rural military veterans will continue well into the current decade. The burden of care will fall to family members.

Women's Health

Rural women disproportionately face limited health care options. Across the United States, rural residents encounter severe shortages in mental health services, primary care, and access to specialists, including in geriatrics and pediatrics.

Regional disparities exist in infant mortality rates, pregnancy outcomes, and prenatal and obstetrical care. Infant mortality rates overall are highest in the South and in nonmetropolitan areas of the South and West. Rural mothers face a number of adverse pregnancy outcomes including higher fetal death rates, lower birth weights, longer stays in the hospital, and higher costs. Rural women receive less prenatal care and delay seeking care, and rural women often seek obstetrical care outside their local community (Peck and Alexander 2003). Rural residents are more likely to be uninsured or underinsured, and are more dependent on Medicaid and Medicare for health care. Moreover, divorced women in rural areas experience poorer long-term health outcomes due, at least in part, to the loss of health insurance upon divorce (Lavelle, Lorenz, and Wickrama 2012). Low-income rural residents also have difficulty finding physicians and dentists who will accept Medicaid, and residents with health insurance face problems paying for rising co-payments (Struthers and Smith 2012). Though health care is difficult for many rural residents to access, women are primarily responsible for finding health care for their children and caring for sick relatives (AORN Journal 2003). Because states set their own rules and regulations for Medicaid, eligibility and reimbursements for services rendered tend to decline when state budgets are tight.

Aging

Aging in rural places has been well documented, as has changing migration patterns. A number of recent studies are looking at how changing family patterns will impact rural aging. Studies have already shown that rural residents have no more family or kin to rely on in rural locations (Goins and Krout 2006). Marital status, particularly divorced and never-married status, a decreased number of children, and out-migration result in fewer potential sources of support as the rural population ages (Tamborini 2007).

Housing

Though rural areas were not unscathed by the Great Recession, it has impacted rural places in different ways. Rural poverty grows when poorer persons move to rural places for cheaper housing. The lack of affordable housing in urban and suburban areas pushes urban dwellers to seek "cheaper" housing in rural places (Fitchen 1991). Other problems associated with rural housing include deteriorating housing stock, absentee landlords, and affordability. What is new is that a shortage of urban public housing is leading poor women to seek units and Section 8 vouchers far beyond the boundaries of metropolitan areas (Clark 2012). Welfare use, different expectations, and culture clashes impact relationships between long-time residents and newcomers to rural places.

Conclusions

Neoliberalism and globalization have wrought profound changes on rural places throughout North America. It has changed rural people's labor market opportunities and their ability to provide for their families. Welfare reform in the 1990s was successful at moving women into the labor market because the jobs created were consistent with the types of labor women were doing in their own households. The economy of the 2000s has not been so robust. There are fewer jobs and more unemployment. A continued decline in public services continues to disproportionately affect rural places and rural women. Rural women and rural places face a number of old and new challenges.

As the decade has progressed, the United States has experienced a financial crisis, housing crisis, and a soaring federal deficit perpetuated in part by military interventions in Iran and Afghanistan. The federal debt has grown exponentially and the federal budget faces severe deficits in expenses to income. State budgets are also in financial upheaval, resulting in significant cuts to major social and human service programs. Most states will suffer from the effects of the Great Recession well into the 2010s (McNichol, Oliff, and Johnson 2012). So, states' ability to provide needed public services like education, health care, and social services will likely remain severely limited. Cuts in these areas will disproportionately impact women and will further increase gaps in education, health care, and wages.

Reassertion of rural identity appears to be a way to legitimize rural living and family life in the face of economic uncertainty. Rural families are willing to endure economic and material disadvantage in order to stay in rural places. Small towns, rural people, and the values rural people hold separate them from places, people, and values they perceive to be different from their own. Neoliberalism in thought and practice reinforces the beliefs about working hard, providing for self and family, and independence that rural residents value.

Though birthrates have declined, having children remains important to rural women within and outside the confines of marriage. It is due to many women's continued commitment to family and child rearing that family values and the American dream are preserved (Sidel 2006). Recommendations for the future remain much the same as in the past. Rural women need access to education for themselves and their children. They need jobs that pay family wages and benefits. They need access to basic goods and services, including health care. Women with children need safe and reliable childcare that coincides with the hours they work.

Tallichet (2006) identifies ways that rural women challenge the conservative and patriarchal structure of rural places through increased activism. Trauger et al. (2010) show that rural women are able to carve out alternative spaces in which to work and participate in community life. Scrivener (2009) sees women and feminist opposition to NAFTA and CAFTA through the organization of Transnational Advocacy Networks. New communication technologies have facilitated these networks among women in Canada, the United States, Mexico, and Central America.

We know much more about rural places and rural women than we have in the past, but rural sociologists have not seriously considered how to use research to advocate for rural places and rural people. We know that place matters, but what is needed are policies, research, and advocacy in which rural people matter. Rural families and households must be the focus in the coming decade. We need to more aggressively look at the ways that change in federal and state policies impact rural places and the people who live there. For example, how do changes in Medicaid and Medicare impact the rural poor and the elderly? How does the lack of coherent national immigration policy differentially impact rural families? How do educational policies and current practices help or hurt the educational opportunities of rural women and their children? In what ways are rural women organized, how are rural issues reflected in national women's group's platforms, and what opportunities exist to organize around women's issues across countries? What rural organizations actively advocate for rural health care, social services, and housing, and how effective are these organizations in improving the lives of rural people and the conditions of rural life? How are rural places and rural women differentially affected by globalization and capitalist processes?

It is not a dearth of knowledge about rural places or rural women that is the problem—it is that rural areas are an afterthought to other pressing issues of the twenty-first century.

References

Ames, B.D., W.A. Brosi, and K.M. Damiano-Teixeira. 2006. "'I'm Just Glad My Three Jobs Could Be During the Day': Women and Work in a Rural Community." *Family Relations* 55 (1): 119–31. http://dx.doi.org/10.1111/j.1741-3729.2006.00361.x.

Biles, J. 2008. "Informal Work and Livelihoods in Mexico: Getting by or Getting Ahead?" *Professional Geographer* 60 (4): 541–55. http://dx.doi.org/10.1080/00330120802288743.

Bokemeier, J., and L. Garkovich. 1991. "Meeting Rural Family Needs." In *Rural Policies for the 1990s*, ed. C.B. Flora and J.A. Christenson, 114–27. Boulder, CO: Westview Press.

Brown, D.L., and L.E. Swanson, eds. 2003. *Challenges for Rural America in the Twenty-First Century*. University Park: Penn State University Press.

Carr, P.J., and M.J. Kefalas. 2009. *Hollowing out the Middle: The Rural Brain Drain and What it Means for America*. Boston: Beacon Press.

Cebula, R.J., S. Menon, and M. Menon. 2008. "Military Enlistment: A Panel Data Set Analysis, 2003–2005." *Review of Business Research: International Academy of Business and Economics* 8 (3): 9–16.

Clark, S. Lawson 2012. "In Search of Housing: Urban Families in Rural Contexts." *Rural Sociology* 77 (1): 110–34. http://dx.doi.org/10.1111/j.1549-0831.2011.00069.x.

Collins, J.L., and V. Mayer. 2010. *Both Hands Tied: Welfare Reform and the Race to the Bottom of the Low-Wage Labor Market.* Chicago: University of Chicago Press. http://dx.doi.org/10.7208/chicago/9780226114071.001.0001.

Deavers, K.L., and R.A. Hoppe. 1991. "The Rural Poor: The Past as Prologue." In *Rural Policies for the 1990s*, ed. C.B. Flora and J.A. Christenson, 85–101. Boulder, CO: Westview Press.

Duffy, M. 2007. "Doing the Dirty Work: Gender, Race, and Reproductive Labor in Historical Perspective." *Gender & Society* 21 (3): 313–36. http://dx.doi.org/10.1177/0891243207300764.

England, P., P. Allison, and Y. Wu. 2007. "Does Bad Pay Cause Occupations to Feminize, Does Feminization Reduce Pay, and How Can We Tell with Longitudinal Data?" *Social Science Research* 36 (3): 1237–56. http://dx.doi.org/10.1016/j.ssresearch.2006.08.003.

Fitchen, J. 1991. *Endangered Spaces, Enduring Places: Change, Identity, and Survival in Rural America.* Boulder, CO: Westview Press.

Flora, Cornelia B., and James A. Christenson, eds. 1991. *Rural Policies for the 1990s.* Boulder, CO: Westview Press.

Fosse, F. 2003. "Voices from Central America: Behind the Trade Agreements." *Center Focus* 1 (February/March): 1–3.

Glasmeier, A., and P. Salant. 2006. *Low-Skill Workers in Rural America Face Permanent Job Loss.* Policy Brief No. 2. Durham, NH: Carsey Institute.

Goins, R.T., and J.A. Krout. 2006. "Introduction: Aging in Rural America." In *Service Delivery to Rural Older Adults: Research, Policy, and Practice*, ed. R.T. Goins and J.A. Krout, 3–20. New York: Springer Publishing Company.

Grigsby, M. 2012. *Noodlers in Missouri: Fishing for Identity in a Rural Subculture.* Kirksville, MO: Truman State University Press.

Haney, W. 1982. "Women." In *Rural Society in the U.S.: Issues for the 1980s*, ed. D.A. Dillman and D.J. Hobbs, 124–35. Boulder, CO: Westview Press.

Heady, H.R. 2007. *Rural Veterans: A Special Concern for Rural Health Advocates.* National Rural Health Association Issue Paper.

AORN Journal. 2003. "Women Primarily Responsible for Family Health Needs." *AORN Journal* 1087 (June). http://www.highbeam.com/doc/1G1-103379505.html.

Kaiser, M.A. 1991. "The Aged in Rural America." In *Rural Policies for the 1990s*, ed. C.B. Flora and J.A. Christenson, 128–39. Boulder, CO: Westview Press.

Kelly, E. Brooke. 2007. "Leaving and Losing Jobs: The Plight of Rural Low-Income Mothers." *Perspectives* 4 (1): 4–7.

Lavelle, Bridget, Frederick O. Lorenz, and K.A.S. Wickrama. 1 December 2012. "What Explains Divorced Women's Poorer Health?: The Mediating Role of Health Insurance and Access to Health Care in a Rural Iowan Sample." *Rural Sociology* 77 (4): 601–25. http://dx.doi.org/10.1111/j.1549-0831.2012.00091.x. Medline:23457418.

Lichter, D.T., and K.M. Johnson. 2007. "The Changing Spatial Concentration of America's Rural Poor Population." *Rural Sociology* 72 (3): 331–58. http://dx.doi.org/10.1526/003601107781799290.

Longworth, R.C. 2008. *Caught in the Middle: America's Heartland in the Age of Globalism.* New York: Bloomsbury.

Macgregor, L.C. 2010. *Habits of the Heartland: Small Town Life in Modern America.* Ithaca, NY: Cornell University Press.

Machum, S. 2011. "Articulating Social Class: Farm Women's Competing Vision of the Family Farm." In *Reshaping Gender and Class in Rural Spaces*, ed. B. Pini and B. Leach, 53–72. Surrey, UK: Ashgate Publishing Limited.

Mattingly, M.J., and J.A. Bean. 2010. "The Unequal Distribution of Child Poverty: High Rates among Young Blacks and Children of Single Mothers in Rural America." Issue Brief No. 38. Durham, NH: Carsey Institute.

Mattingly, M.J., K.M. Johnson, and A. Schaefer. 2011. "More Poor Kids in More Poor Places: Children Increasingly Live Where Poverty Persists." Issue Brief No. 18. Durham, NH: Carsey Institute.

McNichol, E., P. Oliff, and N. Johnson. 2012. "States Continue to Feel Recession's Impact." Center on Budget and Policy Priorities. Accessed 12 February 2012. http://www.cbpp.org.

Peck, J., and K. Alexander. 2003. "Maternal, Infant, and Child Health in Rural Areas: A Literature Review." In *Rural Healthy People 2010: A Companion Document to Health People 2010.* Vol. 2. College Station, TX: The Texas A&M University System Health Science Center, School of Rural Public Health, Southwest Rural Health Research Center.

Petrzelka, P., and S. Marquart-Pyatt. 2011. "Land Tenure in the U.S.: Power, Gender, and Consequences for Conservation Decision Making." *Agriculture and Human Values* 28 (4): 549–60. http://dx.doi.org/10.1007/s10460-011-9307-0.

Pilgeram, R. 2007. "'Ass-Kicking' Women: Doing and Undoing Gender in a U.S. Livestock Auction." *Gender, Work and Organization* 14 (6): 572–95. http://dx.doi.org/10.1111/j.1468-0432.2007.00372.x.

Preibisch, K., and E.E. Grez. 2011. "Re-examining the Social Relations of the Canadian 'Family Farm': Migrant Women Farm Workers in Rural Canada." In *Reshaping Gender and Class in Rural Spaces*, ed. B. Pini and B. Leach, 91–112. Surrey, UK: Ashgate Publishing Limited.

Scrivener, K. 2009. "Transnational Advocacy Networks and 'Policymaking from Below' as the New Wave of Social Change: The Experiences of NAFTA and CAFTA." Fifth Summit of the Americas. Accessed 26 February 2013. http://www.summit-americas.org/cs_essay_winners_09.html.

Sherman, J. 2009. *Those Who Work, Those Who Don't: Poverty, Morality, and Family in Rural America.* Minneapolis: University of Minnesota Press.

Sidel, R. 2006. *Unsung Heroines: Single Mothers and the American Dream.* Berkeley: University of California Press.

Snyder, A.R., D.K. McLaughlin, and J. Findeis. 2006. "Household Composition and Poverty among Female-Headed Households with Children: Difference by Race and Residence." *Rural Sociology* 71 (4): 597–624. http://dx.doi.org/10.1526/003601106781262007.

Struthers, C.B., and H. Smith. 2012."The Impact of the State Budget Crisis on Critical Access Hospitals." Paper presented at the annual meeting of the Rural Sociological Society, Chicago, IL, 26–29 July.

Sulzberger, A.G. 2011. "Hispanics Reviving Faded Towns on the Plains." *New York Times*, 14 November, A1.

Tallichet, S. 2006. *Daughters of the Mountain: Coal Miners in Central Appalachia*. College Station: Pennsylvania State University.

Tallichet, S. 2011. "Digging Deeper: Rural Appalachian Women Miners' Reconstruction of Gender in a Class Based Community." In *Reshaping Gender and Class in Rural Spaces*, ed. B. Pini and B. Leach, 145–60. Surrey, UK: Ashgate Publishing Limited.

Tamborini, C.R. 2007. "The Never-Married in Old Age: Projections and Concerns for the Near Future." *Social Security Bulletin* 67 (2): 25–40. Medline:18457083.

Tickamyer, A., and C. Duncan. 1991. "Work and Poverty in Rural America." In *Rural Policies for the 1990s*, ed. C.B. Flora and J.A. Christenson, 102–13. Boulder, CO: Westview Press.

Tickamyer, A., and D. Henderson. 2003. "Rural Women: New Roles for the New Century." In *Challenges for Rural America in the Twenty-First Century*, ed. D.L. Brown and L.E. Swanson, 73–85. University Park: Penn State University Press.

Trauger, A., C. Sachs, M. Barbercheck, K. Braiser, and N.E. Kiernan. 2010. "'Our Market is Our Community': Women Farmers and Civic Agriculture in Pennsylvania, USA." *Agriculture and Human Values* 27 (1): 43–55. http://dx.doi.org/10.1007/s10460-008-9190-5.

Weeks, W.B., A.E. Wallace, S. Wang, A. Lee, and L.E. Kazis. Summer 2006. "Rural-Urban Disparities in Health-Related Quality of Life within Disease Categories of Veterans." *Journal of Rural Health* 22 (3): 204–11. http://dx.doi.org/10.1111/j.1748-0361.2006.00033.x. Medline:16824163.

CHAPTER 26

Rolling in the Hay: The Rural as Sexual Space

Julie C. Keller and Michael M. Bell

Introduction: Where Rurality and Sexuality Meet

Is the rural sexy? In our first imagination of the rural in the word cloud of the mind, sex is likely to be a very small item, if it appears at all. Sex seems somehow more urban, at least in common culture. The rural we tend to imagine is quiet and passive, not a place of passion and action. And, when we do consider the rural and sex, the images are often marginal, bizarre, and even frightening: demeaning jokes about bestiality, slurs about incest and hicks with six fingers, and fears of isolation and sexual violence, as in the "squeal like a pig" scene in the movie *Deliverance*.[1] If we step back just a moment from crude humor and easy images, however, rural sexuality becomes widespread, diverse, "normal," and often just good, clean fun. The rural is both a place of desire and is a prominent basis for the constitution of desire.

Extending from Hugh Campbell and Michael M. Bell's (2000) notion of the *masculine rural* and the *rural masculine*, as well as David Bell's (2003) concepts of the *rural homosexual* and the *homosexual rural*, we argue that there is both the *sexual in the rural* and the *rural in the sexual*—or, in shorter form, the *sexual rural* and the *rural sexual*. In the sexual rural, we focus on the kinds of understandings that M. Bell (2007) terms "first rural": the sexual practices, attitudes, desires, and sexual identities that can be found in the rural as a material place. In the rural sexual, we center the discussion on the kinds of understandings that M. Bell (2007) terms "second rural": the use of the rural in social constructions of sex and sexual identities, wherever these find expression. We then introduce the concept of *rural plural sexualities*, based on what M. Bell (2007) terms the "rural plural," to help us better understand how sexuality and rurality presuppose one another. We conclude with a discussion of various empirical and theoretical areas that could enrich the study of rural sexualities, such as immigration to new destinations, mobilities theory, and sexual fluidity.[2]

Background Literature

Fifteen years ago, it would have been quite a challenge to find any work in the area of rural sexualities in the flagship journals of North American rural sociology, or in many other scholarly journals. But early work on gender by rural studies scholars helped to open a space for later studies on sexualities in rural spaces. Thanks to the pioneering work of Bokemeier (e.g., Bokemeier and Tait 1980), Haney (1982; Haney and Knowles 1988), Sachs (1983; 1996), and Rosenfeld (1985), by the late 1990s gender issues had established a strong foothold in North American rural sociology. In fact, starting in 1982, each decennial volume published by the Rural Studies Series (with the exception of the policy volume) has included a full chapter on women in rural America (Dillman and Hobbs 1982; Flora and Christenson 1991; Brown and Swanson 2003). Judging from the pattern of gender and sexuality studies in general sociology, it was perhaps just a matter of time before sexuality would also find a home in rural sociology. Early on, a few scholars in other disciplines helped to set the wheels in motion, focusing on the lives of rural queers. In the late 1980s, community psychologists drew attention to the lack of services and resources for gays and lesbian in rural areas (D'Augelli and Hart 1987; Poullard and D'Augelli 1989). David Bell and Gill Valentine's (1995) "Queer Country: Rural Lesbian and Gay Lives," although written by geographers in the United Kingdom, introduced several points of engagement for North American rural sociologists, such as the rural idyll, discrimination, and migration. This same year, anthropologist Kath Weston's article on rural-urban gay migration was published in the interdisciplinary *GLQ: A Journal of Lesbian and Gay Studies* (Weston 1995). These scholars helped to build a foundation for scholarly work in the area of sexuality and rural studies. Today, work on rural and small-town sexualities is no longer at the extreme edges of rural studies, and is emerging from a variety of disciplines: legal studies (e.g., Jerke 2011), tourism studies (e.g., Faiman-Silva 2009; Steinberg and Chapman 2009), media studies (e.g., Gray 2009), cultural and gender studies (Morgensen 2009; Herring 2010), psychology (Preston and D'Augelli 2013), geography (e.g., Johnston and Longhurst 2010), and sociology (Annes and Redlin 2012).

Deserving of much more than just a footnote is the point that developing a full understanding of rural sexuality means also investigating rural heterosexuality, much as a full understanding of rural gender means investigating the unnoticed normality that is rural masculinity. Bryant and Pini (2011, 81) point out, "rural places are entrenched, defined, and performed as heterosexual spaces." In fact, several scholars in recent years—mostly from the United Kingdom, Australia, and New Zealand—have gone about documenting this "entrenched" rural heterosexuality. Campbell (2000) shows how pubs in the New Zealand countryside are important venues for not only the construction of masculinity, but heterosexuality as well. And Little (2003) argues persuasively that we cannot fully understand rural sexual minorities without a sure grasp of the hegemonic identities and practices—that is, heterosexualities—located within those rural landscapes. In our conception of rural sexualities, and rural sexual minorities, we include not just rural LGBTQ individuals, but also a focus on rural heterosexuality—or, rather, rural heterosexualities—to illustrate the possibilities for rural sociologists to study diverse sexualities.[3]

What all of these works share—whether focused on queer or heterosexual rural lives—is the resounding message from scholars that when we study sexuality, place matters. And not just any place, but rural places in particular. When it comes to the study of sexual minorities, urban-based research not just tips the scale, but sends it crashing down when weighed against available research on non-urban queers—though, as we note, the recent efforts to counter this tendency are impressive and becoming more numerous. And as we saw above, these calls of metro-centrism are not limited to the study of LGBTQ individuals, as is evident in the relatively slow growth of studies on heterosexuality in rural places. The criticisms of this imbalance are manifold, and the most common is that the emphasis on cities as the singular and exclusive context for sexual minorities' identity and expression assigns the urban gay man with master status, representing all non-heterosexual minority identities (e.g., Brekhus 2003). Related to this criticism of the unflinching gaze on urban sexualities are the practical implications for the lives of nonmetro queers, whose access to resources and support services is often more limited (e.g., Oswald and Culton 2003). A great part of the justification for studying rural sexualities, then, is about spatial and material concerns—for example, capturing the lives of those neglected others in rural places, or better understanding how heterosexuality structures everyday rural life. But the flip side to these justifications is the importance of representations of the rural with respect to sexualities. Works in this latter area tend to come from European, Australian, and New Zealander scholars, but we lean on work in North America in our exploration of both of these understandings.

The Sexual in the Rural

As a context that is so often viewed as incompatible with not only the material lives of queers, but the mere concept of sexual minorities, the rural seems to carry a lot of baggage when it meets up with queerness. Rural studies scholars are then confronted with a pressing question: given this baggage, how do rural sexual minorities manage their lives in rural places? We explore this area of literature in terms of understanding rural sexuality in its material sense, that is, the *sexual in the rural.* In a 1992 review, which is often cited by scholars of rural sexualities, Chris Philo pushes for the study of "neglected rural others," which many have read as an explicit call for more work on the *sexual rural.* Here we will briefly discuss a few recent empirical contributions to this area in North America, then turn to emerging work on rural heterosexualities.

A recent work that challenges the view that the rural is somehow incompatible with sexual minorities is Mary Gray's (2009) book, *Out in the Country: Youth, Media, and Queer Visibility in Rural America.* Drawing from ethnographic observation and in-depth interviews with thirty-four rural queer youth, Gray, a media scholar, examines the impact of the Internet on the construction of rural queer identities and efforts toward social change. Through vivid accounts, Gray challenges the assumption that rural queers are powerless victims, while also questioning the assumption that visibility necessarily leads to a "post-gay" utopia. Conceptually, Gray's work complicates the intersections of sexuality and rurality, while also linking rural studies to emerging studies of the Internet, identity formation, and ongoing debates within media studies about LGBTQ visibility. As such, this study effectively brings together discussions of the impacts of globalization in rural places—in the form of increasing electronic communication—with discussions of rural sexual identities. Legal scholar Bud Jerke recently coined the term *queer ruralism* to refer to a distinct type of discrimination coming from living in a rural place and being LGBTQ (Jerke 2011). Drawing on the concept of heteronormativity, which in part refers to views and practices that uphold heterosexuality and opposite-gender attraction as standard, normal and natural, Jerke describes that queer ruralism stems, in part, from "queer metronormativity," that is, the assumption that all LGBTQ individuals are located exclusively in urban areas. The second component of Jerke's concept is *ruralism,* defined as discrimination based on living in a rural area. He notes that ruralism "uniquely complicates life for queer rural dwellers" (Jerke 2011, 264). He includes narratives from a small sample of rural queers living in South Dakota, and finds that these narratives both align with and challenge popular conceptions of rural queers. In these narratives there are elements of isolation in rural areas and the desire for the perceived freedom of urban queer life, but there is also evidence of community acceptance and rural support networks. So, to understand the sexual rural we must take into account the complex reality of rural queer lives to avoid falling into the extremes of either rural queer idealism or its opposite.

The complexity of rural queer life was recently empirically investigated through focusing on a seldom-studied population: nonmetropolitan LGBTQ parents. Many rural sexual minorities choose to stay in their communities and raise children there, or, due to work or family obligations—particularly with the recent global economic downturn—urban LGBTQ parents may find themselves moving with their children to rural places. Either way, this demographic is not typically included in either studies of rural queers or studies of queer parents. When Holman and Oswald (2011) interviewed nonmetropolitan LGBTQ parents in Illinois about the salience of their sexuality in community social interactions, they found that in many situations, sexuality was not important. And yet, the authors point out that there is a gap between "ignoring sexuality" and "actively accepting these differences" (Holman and Oswald 2011, 451).

Other recent works on rural LGBTQ individuals include Annes and Redlin's (2012) analysis of life narratives of American and French gay men in the countryside, and Gorman-Murray and colleagues' (2012) investigation of a gay and lesbian tourist site in nonmetropolitan Australia. We have noticed in reading such studies of rural LGBTQ individuals a certain philosophy that is associated with rural places—a certain "live and let live" attitude. How might this shape the day-to-day realities of rural queers and their families? And, what is the difference between tolerating queer families, for example, and embracing diverse family forms and by extension diverse sexualities? These are sexual rural questions. Yet if we dig deeper, these questions—which seem so material, so grounded in the everyday—are in some ways intimately connected to the rural sexual. In the following section, we turn our attention to this latter understanding. But for now, we turn to emerging work on rural heterosexualities to see how these expand our vision of the sexual rural.

There is a recent shift toward examining the taken-for-granted sexual in the rural—heterosexualities. An early study in this area centered on the experiences of rural English girls, and how they organized and maintained heterosexual relationships in the countryside (Morris and Fuller 1999). There is also the previously mentioned work on constructions of heterosexuality and rural masculinity in a New Zealand pub (Campbell 2000), along with a later study of men and heterosexuality in pubs in Ireland (Leyshon 2005). Bryant and Pini (2011) provided an extensive overview of the scholarship on gender and heterosexuality, as well as contributed empirical research on the subject in their recent book, *Gender and Rurality*. For example, they find that heteronormativity remains strong in the rural communities in Australia "because growing the business and the family remains one and the same over generations" (Bryant and Pini 2011, 99).

The study of non-hegemonic heterosexualities also adds richness to our understanding of the sexual rural. For example, Little (2003) references Hubbard's (2000) concept of "scary sexualities." These sexualities lie outside of the normative definition of heterosexuality and its core notion that the purpose of sex is procreation. Thus while scary sexualities might include individuals engaged in homosexuality and other queer sexualities, they also encompass a variety of heterosexual practices that challenge notions of sexual modesty, decency, and conventionality. For example, the rural is a common setting for outdoor festivals of sexuality, such as "Miss Nude America," "wet T-shirt," and similar contests, generally oriented toward objectifying women's bodies for the heterosexual male gaze, but also promoting non-procreative sexualities. The rural is also a site for much heterosexual tourism, from weekend getaway cottages to nudist camps to the "adult malls" and "gentlemen's clubs" that can be found along many a rural highway, often offering sites for sexuality that is considered on or even over the borderline of accepted norms. In many instances, these are also sites of homosexual tourism, as the rural provides spatial freedom for a wide range of sexual diversity that is not tolerated in urban and suburban landscapes of normative sexuality. But, too, we need to take note of the "scary heterosexualities" of rural residents, such as rural heterosexuals living single or those viewed as promiscuous (Little 2003, citing Hubbard 2000). As Pini (2003) and Bryant and Pini (2011) point out, there is minimal research on the sexualities of widows or divorced individuals living in rural places. And, we must not forget that there are intentional communities located in rural landscapes that offer spaces for sexualities viewed by many as existing on the fringe. For instance, Aguilar's (2013) recent study of two intentional communities in rural areas reveals how polyamorous relationships are constructed as socially acceptable in that context. Thus, there is a range of possible heterosexualities in rural places and a focus on this diversity would improve our understanding of rural sexual practices and identities, while setting the stage to better informing ourselves of the interplay between the sexual in the rural and the rural in the sexual.

The Rural in the Sexual

Having described the sexual rural, we turn now to explaining in more detail what we mean by the rural in the sexual, or more simply, the rural sexual. We began this chapter with a brief contemplation of what the imagination conjures up with the pairing of sex and rural. But there are quite a few more images we have not yet mentioned. There is, for example, John Steuart Curry's painting, *Our Good Earth*, with its image of the strong American farmer, muscles bulging, standing in a field of wheat, eyebrows furrowed, concentrating on something he sees off in the distance. And then there is the image of the lumberjack, who controls the forest and its creatures, fighting against the natural elements to get the job done (see Brandth and Haugen 2000). Both of these are portraits of hegemonic masculinity to be sure, but just as masculinity is not easily teased apart from heterosexuality, Curry's farmer and the logger can also be viewed as rural sex symbols of sorts. In both we see the rugged, individualistic, aggressive hard man, tested in the wild, and it is undeniable that these qualities are common in our sexual imaginations, whether we live in rural or urban places. We might also consider the sexiness of the tough and rough image of motorcycle gangs in the United States, who frequently roar their way through rural places—clad head to toe in leather—where they have the freedom to ride in wide open spaces. Flipping through a motorcycle magazine at the news stand, for example, it is easy to see that many find sex appeal in motorcycles and rural spaces—in a half-naked woman stretched across a powerful looking "hog," with fields and an open road in the distance.[4] But there is also a softness and cleanliness to the rural—set against the hardness and dirtiness of the rural above—that finds expression in the sexual imagination. This soft and clean image is typically associated with femininity and the tamed, cultivated sense of the rural. For example, there is the farmer's daughter, deployed as a literary stock character in a range of cultural media, from Daisy Mae in *Lil' Abner* comics (see Roddy 2008) to the 1990s television sitcom *Seinfeld*.[5] This young, country girl is often constructed as a naïve and available sex object, always ready and willing to satisfy any male desire. Or there is the mythological sexy green goddess. Or the nymph, a young female spirit creature who is sexually precocious and dwells near brooks, meadows, or woody areas, singing and playing with other nymphs. Just consider the many videogames, adult comic books (e.g. Japanese adult manga), and examples of adult animation that include characters such as these.

Whether masculine and dirty or feminine and clean, these are images that—as suggested in our brief review of media sources above—both urban and rural imaginations alike conjure up when considering sex. We come to see then that sex—that business that happens between the sheets, in the most private and local sphere of our lives—is infused with far-flung geographical meanings, and that these meanings are not purely contingent on sex in situ. As such, we have seen that there are a great many ways in which the rural may be invoked alongside sexuality outside of the physical and material space of the rural.

But these associations are not confined to normative heterosexual imaginaries. There is also rural imagery in non-heteronormative, queer sexual imagination. These constructions are often referred to as the *queer rural idyll.* In an essay on homosexuality in literature, Fone (1983) writes:

> Those who would dwell in Arcadia seek out that secret Eden because of its isolation from the troubled world and its safety from the arrogant demands of those who would deny freedom, curtail human action, and destroy innocence and love. Arcadia can be a happy valley, a blessed isle, a pastoral retreat, or a green forest fastness.

This early work in the area of minority sexualities and rural studies shows us the appeal of the countryside and natural spaces for lesbians, gays, bisexuals, and transgender individuals. And it implies movement. The search for a paradise where one can truly express those sexual desires deemed corrupt by society implies a sense of mobility—in this case, migration from an undesirable place to another place that is full of freedom and natural wonder. But in order to migrate to a more desirable place, one must already construct the countryside as an escape destination, as a zone of safety, free from the fetters of urban life. In fact, previous authors have suggested that this construction of the queer rural idyll is an urban construct (e.g., Gorman-Murray, Waitt, and Gibson 2012). This is rural sexual—the imagined, ideal rural, its images and notions, which operate on the symbolic level.

But the rural sexual, in terms of sexuality but in other ways too, is not always that image of the dreamy escape destination. Images of the rural can also be frightening, as we noted in the opening to this chapter. It is this aspect of rural sexuality—which is sometimes manifested in its material sexual rural sense—that brings many to see as an impossibility the existence of a rural sexual minority. As far as cultural representations of rural sexual minorities, many are quick to point out *Brokeback Mountain* and the violent murder of the character Jack Twist. And for many, considering the idea of rural sexual minorities brings to mind the actual murder of Matthew Shepard in 1998 outside Laramie, Wyoming—or the rape and murder of Brandon Teena, a transgender man, in 1993 in small town Nebraska. Here we are struck by how closely the sexual rural is weaved into the rural sexual when we are scared and frightened of the rural. We are almost unable to decipher which understanding we are invoking. The real? The imagined? From here we turn our attention to both, at once.

Plural Rural Sexualities

Up to this point we have distinguished between the sexual rural and rural sexual, that is, the material understanding of the rural, on the one hand, and the ideal and imaginative, on the other. Taking a *plural rural sexual* approach means seeing the significance of both understandings, and initiating conversations and intersections between the two.[6] We encourage more of a focus on this aspect in sexualities research, and we discuss how interactions between and across sexual rural and rural sexual can lead to new possibilities.

The work of UK geographer David Bell (2003) gives us a vivid understanding of both the rural sexual and the sexual rural as it relates to men in the United States, describing, for example, the rituals of Radical Faeries gatherings in Arizona in the late 1970s. Other scholars focusing on the American context have implicitly employed these two understandings in other ways. Sandilands (2002) investigates lesbian separatist communities in Oregon, showing how women construct queer safe spaces, carve out rural lesbian identities, and experience natural spaces as erotic sites. In a study of the Michigan Womyn's Music Festival, a yearly celebration held on rural land in the upper Midwest, Browne (2011, 21) finds that lesbian utopias challenge "hegemonic heterosexual ruralities." Important aspects of the creation of lesbian utopias include outdoor nudity, rural sex spaces, and spirituality in connection to the land (Browne 2011). The bridge between the imagined and the real is apparent in these instances. In these examples we see the material manifestation of the imaginary rural sexual—in this case, the experience of urban gay migrants arriving to a rural destination and what unfolds thereafter. Considering the plural rural sexual means seeing the communications between the sexual rural and rural sexual, when changes in the actual sex practices and sexual identities of rural places occur in interaction with imagined associations.

Another example that highlights the possibilities of this plural rural sexualities take is a blog on queer farmers that we recently stumbled upon. Titled the *Queer Farmer Film Project*, the blog includes interviews with queer farmers across the country and explores "the dynamic relationships between gender, sexuality, and agriculture, with particular focus on the hearts and hard work of America's queer farmers."[7] One such interview is with a gay farmer, Brandon, who grows organic vegetables and flowers in northeast Arkansas. Of his experience living as a gay man rurally, "Brandon said that he is out to his family and greater community and has experienced very little discrimination based on being gay." Brandon also described dancing to Madonna songs while working in the fields and "his idea for making t-shirts for [his] farm that instead of the John Deere deer, have a unicorn instead and said that his farm is for sure a 'safe space for unicorns.'" Given the cultural symbolic connection between unicorn imagery—as well as rainbows—and LGBTQ individuals, Brandon's Arkansas farm is constructed as a queer sanctuary, a safe space for queer farmers. In this sense, Brandon challenges that typical rural sexual image of the heterosexual farmer by being a queer farmer and, at the same time, he changes the actual sex and sexual identities of rural spaces. He invokes both understandings at once, as well as the interactions between them, showing the possibilities of rural plural sexualities.

Pini (2008) observes that for LGBTQ individuals, rural places are frequently painted as either liberating sanctuaries or their polar opposite. An additional push for more plural rural understandings stems from this critique. So often, rural places are neither utopias nor unequivocally intolerant communities for LGBTQ individuals. They are someplace in between. Some scholars have indicated this rural diversity by highlighting various factors that might shape rural sexual minority experiences: the presence of universities, a history of gays and lesbians in the region (Kirkey and Forsyth 2001), or identification as urban in-migrant versus rural native (Smith and Holt 2005). We should also consider the importance of gender in shaping the experiences of sexual minorities in nonmetropolitan places. Kazyak's (2012) recent article on rural Midwestern gays and lesbians centers on the intersections of place, gender, and sexuality. She concludes that constructions of rurality align with those of female masculinity and lesbian sexuality, while constructions of male femininity and gay sexuality do not align with these same constructions of rurality. Of course, we ought to remember that there are multiple definitions of rural (e.g., Halfacree 1993) and myriad ways rural sexual minorities live life in the countryside (Spurlin 2000). We argue that acknowledging that rural contexts for acceptance of LGBTQ individuals are varied and complex is also part of embracing plural rural sexualities.

Going Forward

To be sure, work on rural sexualities has been on the rise in recent years. Yet there are quite a few avenues that could lead to an improved understanding of this area, and we suggest some of these here.

There tends to be more of a concentration on men in the rural sexualities literature, which mirrors the male-bias in interdisciplinary LGBTQ studies. In this review we have tried to avoid falling into this bias by giving equal emphasis to work on rural women, which helps us better understand how gender hierarchies and sexualities shape one another in rural places. And yet, there is another group that is almost entirely absent from talk of rural gender and sexualities—transgender individuals. Researching this group may present a bit of an empirical challenge, yet we have observed a noticeable increase in both public and academic attention to the "T" in LGBTQ. In fact, the *Atlantic* published a recent article titled "Growing up Gay and Transgendered in Appalachia" (Hannaford 2011). We are confident that rural sociologists will begin to think about how to include this group—as well as other marginalized groups, such as black, Latino, Asian American, and American Indian populations—in studies of gender and sexuality in rural places.

A different possibility to strengthen the study of rural sexualities is the theoretical perspective of *mobilities* that has emerged in recent years (e.g., Urry 2000). In response to this approach, Bell, Lloyd, and Vatovec (2010) note that mobilities research tends to be quite urbanfocused. Often the rural is portrayed as fixed, an unchanging idyll of tradition, a nationwide "nostalgia for our rural past" (Pruitt 2006, 159). But rural areas are dynamic and in flux, just like their urban counterparts. Globalization does not just affect the metropole, but also shapes the countryside as well. The increasing ease with which money, ideas, and people move can be just as easily observed in small town America as it can in the big city. This mobility also has implications for rural sexualities, which is evident in recent work on LGBTQ individuals, migration, and rurality. For example, Waitt and Gorman-Murray (2011) center on the concept of "home," finding important significance in the return stories of LGBTQ individuals who had previously left one regional city for a large urban center, drawing connections between the movement of bodies, meanings of "home," and challenges to homophobia. And in recent work Annes and Redlin (2012) similarly engage with the mobility of LGBTQ individuals in an examination of French and American narratives of bidirectional rural-urban movement.

But there are additional ways that scholars can use mobility perspectives and make global connections to study rural sexualities. One area for exploration here is the impact of neoliberal policies and globalization on the changing demographics of rural areas, specifically, the often hidden demographic of immigrant agricultural workers. For example, in the last ten years Mexican immigrants have increasingly been heading for new destinations in the United States, regions in the South and rural parts of the Midwest where previously little immigration from Mexico occurred (Massey 2008). Following recent calls by rural sociologists to engage with intersectionality perspectives, the study of diverse rural sexualities ought to include groups such as these, who are marginalized by race as well as citizenship. It is clear that mobilities are shaping immigrant experiences in the rural communities where they reside, and sexuality is no doubt part of that experience.

In this review, we have discussed a few examples of studies of rural heterosexualities, but there is much more room in the literature to explore diverse contexts and practices in this area. As rural sociologists, we may assume that there is sex between women and men happening in the rural, but often we are not tuned in to the variety of ways and places it plays out. As we mentioned previously, nudist colonies and other sexual tourism sites, truck stops, and elder care facilities are potential, yet seldom discussed, sites for analyzing rural heterosexuality (as well as rural same-sex encounters). In addition, the ways in which heterosexuality—and for that matter, sexualities generally—is discussed tends not to leave much room for slippage. You are either gay or straight, with no in between. And yet, we have known since the times of Alfred Kinsey that for many Americans, sexual identity, practices, and fantasy do not always line up in a strict either/or. Furthermore, we cannot assume stability of these phenomena over the life course. The term *sexual fluidity* is increasingly used in sex research to describe this slippage (Diamond 2008), and this is one area to which scholars of rural sexualities could contribute.

There are ways in which the sexual rural is also political, and these have consequences for those who wish to study it. In the last decade or so, and most recently in the 2012 battle for the Republican presidential nomination, right-leaning and even moderate politicians attempted to make crystal clear their opposition to same-sex marriage through supporting state bills and constitutional amendments that would limit the definition of marriage to a union between a man and a woman. In 2012, President Obama told Americans that his personal viewpoint on this issue had changed and that he supported same-sex marriage. In a landmark decision in favor of marriage equality, the US Supreme Court in 2013 struck down a key section of the 1996 federal Defense of Marriage Act. But this is all just politics. How do these changes affect the field of rural sociology and the work of rural sociologists? This very question was addressed during the keynote speaker session at the 2008 Rural Sociological Society meeting in Manchester, New Hampshire, when an audience member asked the director of the US Census Bureau why the 2010 census would not be counting same-sex married couples. The director explained that DOMA constrained the bureau's actions, resulting in the recategorization of these marriages into single status. Later, the Census Bureau under the Obama administration reported that DOMA did not pose a constraint, and that gay and lesbian marriages in fact would be counted in the 2010 census after all, thus reversing the decision made under the Bush administration in the summer of 2008 (Associated Press 2009). By way of this example, it is clear that federal policies have affected the ability of rural studies scholars to collect reliable data, in this case, putting a limitation on our understanding of rural queer lives, and thus hemming in research on the sexual rural.

In this chapter we have supplied ample evidence to counter the image of a passive and sexless rural by highlighting the diversity of sexualities in rural spaces. We established a brief history of work on rural sexualities, then turned to sketching out what we mean by the sexual rural and the rural sexual. Seeing the rural combined with the sexual, in both material and imagined ways, and examining how these two understandings interact with each other to create new possibilities, are the defining features of what we have termed plural rural sexualities. This approach means acknowledging the power of the rural in shaping what many, including those living in the metropole, consider sexy, and seeing how this plays out in reality. And yet for all the fun and playfulness that can come with a romp in the hay, embracing plural rural sexualities means seeing that for those who are marginalized, combining sex with the rural is not always that liberating utopia that it is imagined to be. Nor should we assume that same-sex desire and LGBTQ individuals are incompatible with rurality. Balancing these multiple understandings, while also recognizing the political aspects of rural sexuality, is becoming more important. With the increasing use of technology and the easy mobility that come with a globalizing world—the coming together of different groups, and the drawing of boundaries and the tensions that can result—moving past one-sided understandings of how sexuality and rurality relate is crucial to pinning down shifting meanings of identity, community, and place, all of which are prime concerns for rural sociologists in the twenty-first century.

Notes

1 Or so we discovered through a bit of casual ethnography, when we tried out the phrase "rural sexuality" with friends and colleagues and asked them to free associate in response.

2 In this chapter, we use sexuality and sexualities to refer loosely to the realm of the erotic, which in sex research terms may include sexual behavior and practices, desires, fantasies, attractions, or attitudes about sex. As much as possible, we try to use sexual identity—or we use those specific identity terms—to refer to the labeling of an individual's own attractions, practices, and fantasies (e.g., lesbian, gay, heterosexual, bisexual, queer, etc.). We use *sex* as an abbreviation for sexual practices, except in the case of *same-sex*, which in popular lexicon refers to same-gender attraction.

3 We find that the term *LGBTQ* (lesbian, gay, bisexual, transgender, queer, or questioning), rather than the more common variant LGBT, is more inclusive of sexualities that are not heterosexual or normative heterosexual.

4 For example, the August 2012 issue of *Easyriders* magazine features national biker parties, one of which is the Great Southwest Chopper Fest, located in Bizbee, Arizona. The article includes a full-page photo of a woman in a wet T-shirt contest, and other photos depict men riding motorcycles in the desert landscape.

5 *Seinfeld*, "The Bottle Deposit, Part 2," season 7, aired 2 May 1996.

6 Note that we drop here the materialist/idealist distinction implied by the word order *sexual rural* versus *rural sexual*. We take *plural rural sexual* and *plural sexual rural* as equivalent, but plural rural sexual as more linguistically mellifluous.

7 See Lyon (2009) for information on the project's mission. Also see the *Queer Farmer Film Project* website (http://queerfarmer.blogspot.com), and the newly released film *Out Here* (http://outheremovie.com).

References

Aguilar, Jade. 2013. "Situational Sexual Behaviors: The Ideological Work of Moving toward Polyamory in Communal Living Groups." *Journal of Contemporary Ethnography* 42 (1): 104–29. http://dx.doi.org/10.1177/0891241612464886.

Annes, Alexis, and Meredith Redlin. 2012. "Coming Out and Coming Back: Rural Gay Migration and the City." *Journal of Rural Studies* 28 (1): 56–68. http://dx.doi.org/10.1016/j.jrurstud.2011.08.005.

Associated Press. 2009. "Census to Recognize Same-Sex Marriages in '10 Count." *New York Times*, 21 June.

Bell, David. 2003. "Homosexuals in the Heartland: Male Same-Sex Desire in the Rural United States." In *Country Visions*, ed. Paul Cloke, 178–94. London: Prentice Hall.

Bell, David, and Gill Valentine. 1995. "Queer Country: Rural Lesbian and Gay Lives." *Journal of Rural Studies* 11 (2): 113–22. http://dx.doi.org/10.1016/0743-0167(95)00013-D.

Bell, Michael M. 2007. "The Two-ness of Rural Life and the Ends of Rural Scholarship." *Journal of Rural Studies* 23 (4): 402–15. http://dx.doi.org/10.1016/j.jrurstud.2007.03.003.

Bell, Michael M., Sarah E. Lloyd, and Christine Vatovec. 2010. "Activating the Countryside: Rural Power, the Power of the Rural, and the Making of Rural Politics." *Sociologia Ruralis* 50 (3): 205–24. http://dx.doi.org/10.1111/j.1467-9523.2010.00512.x.

Bokemeier, Janet L., and John L. Tait. 1980. "Women as Power Actors: A Comparative Study of Rural Communities." *Rural Sociology* 45: 238–54.

Brandth, Berit, and Marit S. Haugen. 2000. "From Lumberjack to Business Manager: Masculinity in the Norwegian Forestry Press." *Journal of Rural Studies* 16 (3): 343–55. http://dx.doi.org/10.1016/S0743-0167(00)00002-4.

Brekhus, Wayne H. 2003. *Peacocks, Chameleons, Centaurs: Gay Suburbia and the Grammar of Social Identity*. Chicago: University of Chicago Press.

Brown, David L., and Louis E. Swanson. 2003. *Challenges for Rural America in the 21st Century*. University Park: Pennsylvania State University Press.

Browne, Kath. 2011. "Beyond Rural Idylls: Imperfect lesbian Utopias at Michigan Womyn's Music Festival." *Journal of Rural Studies* 27 (1): 13–23. http://dx.doi.org/10.1016/j.jrurstud.2010.08.001.

Bryant, Lia, and Barbara Pini. 2011. *Gender and Rurality*. New York: Routledge.

Campbell, Hugh. 2000. "The Glass Phallus: Pub(lic) Masculinity and Drinking in Rural New Zealand." *Rural Sociology* 65 (4): 562–81. http://dx.doi.org/10.1111/j.1549-0831.2000.tb00044.x.

Campbell, Hugh, and Michael M. Bell. 2000. "The Question of Rural Masculinities." *Rural Sociology* 65 (4): 532–46. http://dx.doi.org/10.1111/j.1549-0831.2000.tb00042.x.

D'Augelli, Anthony R., and Mary M. Hart. February 1987. "Gay Women, Men, and Families in Rural Settings: Toward the Development of Helping Communities." *American Journal of Community Psychology* 15 (1): 79–93. http://dx.doi.org/10.1007/BF00919759. Medline:3604995.

Diamond, Lisa M. 2008. *Sexual Fluidity: Understanding Women's Love and Desire*. Cambridge, MA: Harvard University Press.

Dillman, Don A., and Daryl J. Hobbs. 1982. *Rural Society in the U.S.: Issues for the 1980s*. Boulder, CO: Westview Press.

Faiman-Silva, Sandra L. 2009. "Provincetown Queer: Paradoxes of Identity, Space, and Place." *Journal of Tourism and Cultural Change* 7 (3): 203–20. http://dx.doi.org/10.1080/14766820903267363.

Flora, Cornelia B., and James A. Christenson. 1991. *Rural Policies for the 1990s*. Boulder, CO: Westview Press.

Fone, Byrne R. S. Spring–Summer 1983. "This Other Eden: Arcadia and the Homosexual Imagination." *Journal of Homosexuality* 8 (3–4): 13–34. http://dx.doi.org/10.1300/J082v08n03_02. Medline:6192172.

Gorman-Murray, Andrew, Gordon Waitt, and Chris Gibson. 2012. "Chilling out in 'Cosmopolitan Country': Urban/Rural Hybridity and the Construction of Daylesford as a 'Lesbian and Gay Rural Idyll.'" *Journal of Rural Studies* 28 (1): 69–79. http://dx.doi.org/10.1016/j.jrurstud.2011.07.001.

Gray, Mary. 2009. *Out in the Country: Youth, Media, and Queer Visibility in Rural America*. New York: New York University Press.

Halfacree, Keith H. 1993. "Locality and Social Representation: Space, Discourse, and Alternative Definitions of the Rural." *Journal of Rural Studies* 9 (1): 23–37. http://dx.doi.org/10.1016/0743-0167(93)90003-3.

Haney, Wava G. 1982. "Women in Rural Society." In *Rural Society in the U.S.: Issues for the 1980s*, ed. Don A. Dillman and Daryl J. Hobbs, 124–35. Boulder, CO: Westview Press.

Haney, Wava G., and Jane B. Knowles. 1988. *Women and Farming: Changing Roles, Changing Structures*. Boulder, CO: Westview Press.

Hannaford, Alex. 2011. "Growing up Gay and Transgendered in Appalachia." *Atlantic*, 30 April.

Herring, Scott. 2010. *Another Country: Queer Anti-urbanism*. New York: New York University Press.

Holman, Elizabeth G., and Ramona F. Oswald. 2011. "Nonmetropolitan GLBTQ Parents: When and Where Does Their Sexuality Matter?" *Journal of GLBT Family Studies* 7 (5): 436–56. http://dx.doi.org/10.1080/1550428X.2011.623937.

Hubbard, Philip. 2000. "Desire/Disgust: Mapping the Moral Contours of Heterosexuality." *Progress in Human Geography* 24 (2): 191–217. http://dx.doi.org/10.1191/030913200667195279.

Jerke, Bud W. 2011. "Queer Ruralism." *Harvard Journal of Law and Gender* 34: 259–312.

Johnston, Lynda, and Robyn Longhurst. 2010. *Space, Place, and Sex: Geographies of Sexualities.* Lanham, MD: Rowman and Littlefield.

Kazyak, Emily. 2012. "Midwest or Lesbian? Gender, Rurality, and Sexuality." *Gender & Society* 26 (6): 825–48. http://dx.doi.org/10.1177/0891243212458361.

Kirkey, Kenneth, and Ann Forsyth. 2001. "Men in the Valley: Gay Male Life on the Suburban-Rural Fringe." *Journal of Rural Studies* 17 (4): 421–41. http://dx.doi.org/10.1016/S0743-0167(01)00007-9.

Leyshon, Michael. 2005. "No Place for a Girl: Rural Youth, Pubs, and the Performance of Masculinity." In *Critical Studies in Rural Gender Issues: Perspectives on Rural Policy and Planning*, ed. Jo Little and Carol Morris, 104–22. Aldershot: Ashgate.

Little, Jo. 2003. "'Riding the Rural Love Train': Heterosexuality and the Rural Community." *Sociologia Ruralis* 43 (4): 401–17. http://dx.doi.org/10.1046/j.1467-9523.2003.00252.x.

Lyon, Sammy. 2009. "Queer Farmer Film Project." 4 August. http://www.youtube.com/watch?v=0yJpw0IOaZI.

Massey, Douglas S. 2008. *New Faces in New Places: The Changing Geography of American Immigration.* New York: Sage.

Morgensen, Scott L. 2009. "Arrival at Home: Radical Faerie Configurations of Sexuality and Place." *GLQ: A Journal of Lesbian and Gay Studies* 15 (1): 67–96. http://dx.doi.org/10.1215/10642684-2008-019.

Morris, Karen, and Mary Fuller. 1999. "Heterosexual Relationships of Young Women in a Rural Environment." *British Journal of Sociology of Education* 20 (4): 531–43. http://dx.doi.org/10.1080/01425699995254.

Oswald, Ramona F., and Linda S. Culton. 2003. "Under the Rainbow: Rural Gay Life and its Relevance for Family Providers." *Family Relations* 52 (1): 72–81. http://dx.doi.org/10.1111/j.1741-3729.2003.00072.x.

Philo, Chris. 1992. "Neglected Rural Geographies: A Review." *Journal of Rural Studies* 8 (2): 193–207. http://dx.doi.org/10.1016/0743-0167(92)90077-J.

Pini, Barbara. 2003. "Feminist Methodology and Rural Research: Reflections on a Study of an Australian Agricultural Organization." *Sociologia Ruralis* 43 (4): 418–33. http://dx.doi.org/10.1046/j.1467-9523.2003.00253.x.

Pini, Barbara. 2008. *Masculinities and Management in Agricultural Organizations Worldwide.* Aldershot: Ashgate.

Poullard, Jonathan D., and Anthony R. D'Augelli. 1989. "AIDS Fears and Homophobia among Volunteers in an AIDS Prevention Program." *Journal of Rural Community Psychology* 10: 29–39.

Preston, Deborah Bray, and Anthony R. D'Augelli. 2013. *The Challenges of Being a Rural Gay Man: Coping with Stigma.* New York: Routledge.

Pruitt, Lisa R. 2006. "Rural Rhetoric." *Connecticut Law Review* 39: 159–240.

Roddy, Jan Peterson. 2008. "Country-Queer: Reading and Rewriting Sexuality in Representations of the Hillbilly." In *Negotiating Sexual Idioms: Image, Text, Performance*, ed. Marie-Louise Kohlke and Luisa Orza, 37–52. New York: Rodopi.

Rosenfeld, Rachel A. 1985. *Farm Women: Work, Farm, and Family in the United States.* Chapel Hill: University of North Carolina Press.

Sachs, Carolyn E. 1983. *The Invisible Farmers: Women in Agricultural Production.* Totowa, NJ: Rowman & Allanheld.

Sachs, Carolyn E. 1996. *Gendered Fields: Rural Women, Agriculture, and Environment.* Boulder, CO: Westview Press.

Sandilands, Catriona. 2002. "Lesbian Separatist Communities and the Experience of Nature." *Organization & Environment* 15 (2): 131–63. http://dx.doi.org/10.1177/10826602015002002.

Smith, Darren P., and Louise Holt. 2005. "'Lesbian Migrants in the Gentrified Valley' and 'Other' Geographies of Rural Gentrification." *Journal of Rural Studies* 21 (3): 313–22. http://dx.doi.org/10.1016/j.jrurstud.2005.04.002.

Spurlin, William J. 2000. "Remapping Same-Sex Desire: Queer Writing and Culture in American Heartland." In *De-centering Sexualities: Politics and Representations Beyond the Metropolis*, ed. Richard Phillips, Diane Watt, and David Shuttleton, 182–98. New York: Routledge.

Steinberg, Philip E., and Thomas E. Chapman. 2009. "Key West's Conch Republic: Building Sovereignties of Connection." *Political Geography* 28 (5): 283–95. http://dx.doi.org/10.1016/j.polgeo.2009.08.001.

Urry, John. 2000. *Sociology Beyond Societies: Mobilities for the Twenty-First Century.* New York: Routledge.

Waitt, Gordon, and Andrew Gorman-Murray. 2011. "Journeys and Returns: Home, Life Narratives and Remapping Sexuality in a Regional City." *International Journal of Urban and Regional Research* 35 (6): 1239–55. http://dx.doi.org/10.1111/j.1468-2427.2010.01006.x.

Weston, Kath. 1995. "Get Thee to a Big City: Sexual Imaginary and the Great Gay Migration." *GLQ: A Journal of Lesbian and Gay Studies* 2: 253–77.

CHAPTER 27

Rural Poverty: The Great Recession, Rising Unemployment, and the Under-Utilized Safety Net

Jennifer Sherman

Introduction

In the first decade of the 2000s, rural America, like the rest of the United States, saw its fortunes rise and then fall on the wave of the Great Recession (Grusky, Western, and Wimer 2011), while it continued to struggle with ongoing issues including deindustrialization and the decline of manufacturing and many resource-based industries (Anderson and Weng 2011; Hamilton et al. 2008; Smith and Tickamyer 2011). As in previous decades, poverty has been a persistent problem throughout much of rural America, and overall nonmetropolitan[1] poverty rates have continued to be higher than metropolitan rates throughout the 2000s (Lichter and Graefe 2011, 28; Jensen, Mattingly, and Bean 2011; Farrigan 2010). Rural poverty rates fell in the 1990s, but began rising again in the 2000s, particularly since the 2008 recession and the resulting increase in unemployment (Jensen, Mattingly, and Bean 2011). By the end of the decade nonmetropolitan unemployment rates, which have long been higher than metropolitan rates, reached high levels not seen in more than twenty-five years—9.8 percent in 2009, versus 8.7 percent in metropolitan areas (McBride and Kemper 2009). In 2010, the overall nonmetropolitan poverty rate was 16.5 percent, compared to the metropolitan rate of 14.9 percent. Rural children had even higher poverty rates, at 24.4 percent versus the metropolitan rate of 21.6 percent (USDA Economic Research Service 2011). Children growing up in poverty not only suffer in the short term, but "are less likely to become the productive adult workers, capable parents, and involved citizens," thus contributing to the future disadvantage of rural areas as well (O'Hare 2009, 3).

Poverty is not evenly distributed across rural America, however, and continues to be particularly severe and persistent in the South and West (Farrigan 2010), and to hit rural minority populations the hardest (Anderson and Weng 2011; Kandel et al. 2011; Lichter and Graefe 2011). Nonmetropolitan poverty rates at the end of the decade were over 30 percent for blacks and Native Americans, and 29.5 percent for Hispanics, versus 13.1 percent for whites (USDA Economic Research Service 2011). Factors contributing to rural poverty include economic and industrial restructuring, falling real wages, and increased unemployment, due to both the recession and larger global forces. The continued growth of neoliberal ideologies and policies since the 1980s has been partly responsible for increasing "out-sourcing, privatization, and the growth of part-time and contingent employment" (Clawson and Clawson 1999, 101), and the weakening of worker protections and labor unions (Crow and Albo 2005), all of which have negatively impacted rural American workers and contributed to job losses and falling wages and benefits.

Rural poverty is exacerbated by migration patterns, including the out-migration of young, advantaged, and educated adults from rural communities and the in-migration of low-income populations, often in search of jobs, affordable housing, or lower costs of living (Carr and Kefalas 2009; Crowley, Lichter, and Qian 2006; Lichter and Graefe 2011;). The abilities of families to cope with and survive poverty are impacted by the specific cultural norms and community histories of rural places, which often influence the choices and options available within the context of small, isolated, and often tightly knit communities (Brown and Lichter 2004; Lichter and Graefe 2011; Nelson 2005; Pickering et al. 2006; Sherman 2006; 2009; Tickamyer and Henderson 2011). Academic researchers frequently focus on the structural causes of poverty, including policies, economic shifts, labor markets, and racism (Schiller 2007). However, cultural understandings throughout much of the rural United States, heavily influenced by neoliberal ideologies, tend to portray poverty as an individual shortcoming, thus adding social stigma to the challenges faced by the rural poor (Sherman and Sage 2011; Sherman 2006; 2009). In this chapter, I will examine the causes of and contributors to rural poverty in the 2000s. I will also discuss some of the outcomes of current rural poverty trends, focusing on the impacts of poverty on rural American families and their strategies for survival.

Industrial Restructuring, Employment, and Poverty

Nonmetropolitan poverty rates have been higher than metropolitan rates since the 1960s, when the official US poverty measure was first developed. The bulk of persistent poverty counties in the United States have been, and continue to be, nonmetropolitan (Farrigan 2010). Despite its disproportionate share of US poverty, rural poverty tends to be understudied, and thus both its causes and its dynamics are poorly understood. While many of the main causes of poverty, including deindustrialization, job loss, legacies of racism and discrimination, and lack of educational opportunities, are similar across diverse settings, the impacts and meanings of poverty are often distinct in rural America. In nonmetropolitan America, it has long been common for poor families to include at least one working adult (Shapiro 1989), and the rural poor are more likely to be working than the urban poor (Anderson and Weng 2011). They are also less likely than the metropolitan poor to rely on cash aid, even when they qualify for it (Brown and Lichter 2004; Jensen et al. 2011; Lichter and Graefe 2011; Sherman 2006; 2009). The realities of rural poverty contrast sharply with the common stereotypes of the poor as lazy, immoral, and dependent on "entitlements" (Hays 2003).

In order to understand rural poverty, it is thus important to begin by looking at the labor markets and economies of rural places. According to Pickering et al. (2006, 1), many rural American adults struggle to find or keep jobs, "because local formal economies and labor markets are generally weak, systems of education are poor, transportation is difficult, child care is hard to come by, and levels of human capital are extremely low." Rural America is of course not monolithic, and includes different types of communities with different economic prospects. Hamilton et al. (2008) argue that recent social and economic trends have resulted in the formation of distinct types of rural places, each with a different set of economic trajectories and conditions. These ideal types of rural communities lie on a spectrum, from amenity-rich communities seeing growth in tourism-related industries and in-migration by affluent professionals and retirees, to chronically poor communities with depleted resources, "dysfunctional services, inadequate infrastructure, and ineffective or corrupt leadership" (Hamilton et al. 2008, 6). In the middle are communities with declining resources, many of which have seen their fortunes and economies shrink further over the past decade as the recession increased the pace of industrial losses. Throughout rural America, the last decade has seen the forces of globalization and deindustrialization continue to replace "good jobs" with "bad" ones (Nelson and Smith 1999), as the service sector has come to replace manufacturing and resource-based industries as the main source of employment in most rural American communities (Brown and Schafft 2011; Hamilton et al. 2008; Lichter and Graefe 2011; Smith and Tickamyer 2011).

The growth of the service sector relative to manufacturing and resource-based industries has been one of the largest contributors to working poverty in rural America (Lichter and Graefe 2011; Jensen and Jensen 2011). Other sectors have declined for multiple reasons, most importantly global competition in the form of lower prices or wages overseas. The success of the neoliberal agenda has resulted in decreasing trade restrictions throughout the world and the widespread belief that such deregulation is necessary for capitalist enterprises to flourish (Clawson and Clawson 1999). Loosening regulations have allowed companies to shift manufacturing to less-developed nations where labor and raw materials are cheaper. Much natural resource extraction has also been moved to other countries, where labor and materials are less expensive and environmental regulation weaker. Even agriculture has not been immune to the forces of globalization, as the industry continues to consolidate into fewer and larger farms, due in large degree to national and international policies that favor corporate farming and the globalization of farm commodity markets (Lichter and Graefe 2011). Although these trends predate the recession, the economic downturn hastened the pace of job losses in these industries.

As manufacturing and resource-based jobs have dried up across the rural United States, they have been replaced mostly by service-sector jobs that are more difficult to outsource. However, unlike the work that they often replace, service-sector jobs by and large do not pay living wages, provide full-time employment, or come with benefits such as health care. They are also rarely unionized, thus allowing employers to erode worker protections and other gains made by manufacturing workers over the previous century. The growing popularity of neoliberal doctrines has provided employers with a favorable political environment in which to push for policies that further weaken unions (Albo 2009). Union density in the United States peaked at nearly 32 percent in 1955, but since the early 1980s, "union density declined precipitously, falling to 13.5 percent in 2001" (Crow and Albo 2005, 16). Much of this loss of union power is associated with the growth of the service sector (Albo 2009; Clawson and Clawson 1999; Crow and Albo 2005). While the service sector has grown throughout the United States, the lack of diversity in rural labor markets and economies often means that when a local industry declines, there are few other sources of employment outside of service jobs, and fewer chances for displaced workers to find new jobs that pay as well as those they lost. Compared to metropolitan workers, workers in nonmetropolitan communities are more likely to be concentrated in low-wage service jobs (Brown and Schafft 2011), which contributes heavily to the lower average wages and higher working poverty in rural areas compared to urban and suburban workers (Smith and Tickamyer 2011; Lichter and Graefe 2011).

Deindustrialization and the growth of the service sector have also contributed to changes in the gender makeup of the rural workforce. As Sachs discusses in the framing chapter to this section, rural job losses during the economic downturn have tended to impact men more heavily than women, because men held a disproportionate share of the lost jobs (Jensen and Jensen 2011). This can be particularly difficult for men because rural cultural norms frequently construct masculinity around work in specific types of manual labor (Sherman 2006; 2009), exemplified by the land-based industries upon which a particular community's economy is centered. When jobs in these industries disappear, rural men often struggle to remain in the workforce, as the service sector jobs that remain represent losses both in terms of income and in terms of acceptability and masculinity. Many service sector jobs, including those in care-based industries but also many retail positions, tend to be seen as more appropriate for women, and thus as emasculating for many rural men. To take such jobs can add a level of shame and a loss of both masculine identity and self-esteem for men whose lives have been spent in a traditionally masculine local industry. Thus, many rural men's own cultural norms make it difficult for them to accept jobs in service and care-work industries (Sherman 2009). The result is that many rural communities have experienced not only losses of income, but also changes in the gendered nature of work as deindustrialization occurs.

Even in communities with more traditional and conservative cultural norms, in which men are expected to be the main breadwinners and women the homemakers, it is often the case that women will take on part-time work in service jobs before men will accept feminized positions (Nelson and Smith 1999; Sherman 2009; Smith 2011). Evidence of these trends is seen in the rural workforce participation rates, which are lower for rural men than urban men (Hamilton et al. 2008; Jensen and Jensen 2011; Mattingly, Smith, and Bean 2011). These differences have persisted through the recession, even though unemployment has risen sharply in urban America (McBride and Kemper 2009). Meanwhile, rural women's employment rose until about 2000, and then began declining into the recession along with men's (Smith 2011), but their contributions still grew as a share of total family earnings, particularly since the recession (Smith 2011).

These changes in the gender structures of rural labor markets have several implications that can add to the problems poor rural families face. The emotional struggles that unemployment can create for rural men whose identities have long been tied to their roles as workers and breadwinners can negatively impact families in multiple ways that threaten the stability of romantic partnerships (Sherman 2009). This may contribute to marital instability and the growth of single parenting that is associated with poverty in rural communities (Hamilton et al. 2008). In addition, women's jobs generally tend to be poorly paid relative to men's, and thus the rise in female workforce participation has not been sufficient to make up for the lost male income. Particularly when women are relied on as the main or sole breadwinners, families are more likely to experience poverty and low incomes, and increased reliance on women workers has contributed to the growth of rural poverty (Anderson and Weng 2011; Lichter and Graefe 2011). Given the strain that male job loss puts on families, the recession and continued deindustrialization will likely contribute to even more households relying on women's incomes, putting more rural families at risk for working poverty.

These employment trends, which have been ongoing for decades but were exacerbated by the recession, suggest that rural populations will likely continue to experience hardships into the next decade. Although by 2010 experts believed that the recession had peaked (Grusky et al. 2011), there has not yet been significant recovery in rural America. Research from previous recessions suggests that rural employment may be slower to recover than that in urban and suburban places (Parker, Kusmin, and Marre 2010), and thus it may be years before we see sufficient economic growth and development to replace significant numbers of living wage jobs in rural areas. As I have illustrated in this section, there are not enough jobs to go around, and the work opportunities that do exist are increasingly failing to protect rural families from poverty. Furthermore, changes in the gendered nature of work will continue to influence rural families in new ways, and more research is needed to fully understand their long-term impacts on the structures and survival strategies of rural families.

Regional Differences, Migration, and the Exacerbation of Rural Poverty

Although deindustrialization and its results have been contributing to high unemployment and poverty throughout rural America during the last decade, the severity of problems varies by region and race or ethnic group. Poverty rates tend to be lower in the rural Midwest and Northeast because of the relative stability of the farm economy and the growth of high-tech industries in these regions (Anderson and Weng 2011). Rural communities in the South and West, on the other hand, tend to have the highest poverty rates, and wages and incomes tend to be lowest, particularly for African Americans, Native Americans, and Hispanics (Anderson and Weng 2011). These two regions also have the highest concentrations of minority groups, whose poverty tends to be both persistent and concentrated (Lichter and Graefe 2011). Poverty is an enduring problem for minority populations because their education levels tend to be lower and their unemployment rates tend to be higher (Jensen and Jensen 2011; Kandel et al.

2011; Smith 2011), due to both the dynamics of regional labor markets and the enduring effects of racism that continue to disadvantage minority groups relative to whites. Regional differences in rural poverty rates are due to a complex combination of factors that includes the specific economies of different communities and population dynamics that cause some rural places to have greater or lesser concentrations of people whose race and/or lack of education put them at a disadvantage in the workforce.

Migration patterns and population dynamics have also exacerbated poverty in many rural American communities by contributing to the lack of workers with necessary levels of human capital. Rural communities are often hurt by the out-migration of more advantaged young adults in search of educational and employment opportunities elsewhere, known as the "brain-drain" phenomenon (Carr and Kefalas 2009). Rural areas have experienced slower growth than the rest of the United States—2.9 percent growth in rural counties versus 9.1 percent in the country as a whole between 2000 and 2009—due in large part to the loss of young adults (Gallardo 2010a; 2010b). The brain-drain problem tends to disproportionately impact those communities that are already the most disadvantaged, where lack of employment, education, and training opportunities leave young adults with little chance of finding decent long-term work close to home. The worse off the economy and labor market of a community, the more likely it is to lose its more talented and ambitious young adults. This phenomenon means that many of the most impoverished rural communities are further disadvantaged in that their remaining residents tend to be older and less educated, and their labor pools lack younger and better educated and trained workers. During the past decade, out-migration and brain drain have been particularly severe problems for declining and poor rural communities (Carr and Kefalas 2009; Hamilton et al. 2008).

At the same time, over the past decade in-migration into poor rural communities has often failed to improve their residents' fortunes substantially. Although in some rural communities in-migrants are welcomed for their potential to counteract the impacts of out-migration and brain drain, newcomers frequently differ substantially from the more advantaged residents who have left (Clark 2012). Often in-migrants to poor rural communities are poor themselves, drawn to struggling communities in search of low-cost housing and living (Clark 2012; Sherman 2009). These new low-income residents can be a drain on existing resources, including local schools and social services (Sherman and Sage 2011). Many long-time residents also complain that recent in-migrants, particularly those who are poor, are less likely to actively participate in the community (Sherman and Sage 2011; Sherman 2009), leaving rural communities with growing social problems but declining capacities for addressing them.

Many rural communities, particularly in the Southwest and West, have also attracted substantial numbers of recent immigrants from Latin America and Mexico in search of jobs in agriculture, food processing, construction, and other industries (Crowley et al. 2006; Crowley and Lichter 2009; Lichter and Graefe 2011; Schmalzbauer 2011). As Sachs notes in the introductory chapter to this section, these trends have been accelerated by NAFTA and its negative impacts on Mexican workers. Although they may be attracted to rural communities for the same lifestyle reasons that appeal to both long-standing residents and non-Hispanic newcomers,[2] Latino immigrants are frequently treated as unwelcome outsiders (Crowley and Lichter 2009; Schmalzbauer 2011; Sherman 2009). Often coming with low education levels and cultural and linguistic barriers that set them apart from long-time community residents, these recent immigrants also may contribute to declines in community cohesion, as many long-term residents are reluctant to accept the culturally distinct newcomers (Crowley et al. 2006; Crowley and Lichter 2009). They are also frequently blamed for strains on local services, although researchers have found little evidence that the growth in rural immigrant populations is directly correlated with increased demands on services (Crowley and Lichter 2009). Their propensity for working does not protect immigrant populations from poverty, however, as they are preferred for the lowest paid jobs such as agriculture and service, further contributing to rural working poverty (Crowley et al. 2006). Researchers have expressed concern that the influx of poor immigrants may be turning some rural communities into "rural ghettos," "that impede rather than promote incorporation into American society" (see also Crowley et al. 2006; Lichter and Graefe 2011, 36).

With regard to in- and out-migration, there is still much left unknown, particularly with regard to the long-term impacts of immigrant settlements in rural communities. It is also important to note that with regard to this issue the method of inquiry can influence findings, as rural residents in ethnographic studies have long been found to overstate the negative impacts of in-migration, as well as the degree to which their home communities are attracting low-income newcomers (Crowley and Lichter 2009; Fitchen 1991; Sherman 2009). While there is strong evidence that in- and out-migration trends are exacerbating the poverty of many of the most disadvantaged rural places, and are further contributing to the persistent and concentrated poverty of rural minority groups (Crowley et al. 2006), much additional research is necessary to improve our understandings of the impacts of recent demographic changes.

Surviving Poverty in Rural America

The result of all of the trends discussed above is that many rural families are living close to or below the poverty line and face growing challenges to meeting their own basic needs. Living in poverty is difficult regardless of the setting, but rural communities offer unique barriers to, as well as opportunities for, coping with poverty. When the formal labor market fails to provide either enough jobs or enough income for families to survive, they are faced with a set of tough choices, among them formal aid from government and charitable sources; reliance on social networks including friends, family, and community; and informal work activities that either bring in extra (unreported) income or provide for other basic needs such as food or fuel (Brown and Lichter 2004; Lichter and Graefe 2011; Nelson 2005; Sherman 2006; 2009; Tickamyer and Henderson 2011). The degree to which poor rural families rely on different survival strategies varies according to their circumstances, including local cultural norms and values; size and relative isolation of their communities; available social networks; and constraints of time, knowledge, and physical ability. As I will illustrate in this section, despite the belief in many rural communities that poor in-migrants choose rural settings for the relative ease they provide to those living on restricted incomes, in many ways rural communities come with more challenges and fewer acceptable survival strategies for coping with poverty than do urban communities.

It is often assumed that the poor rely heavily on Temporary Aid to Needy Families (TANF, also known as welfare) in order to survive, and in the United States there is much concern about poor families becoming "dependent" on this aid, which many believe undermines work ethics and moral values (Hays 2003; Sherman 2009). As discussed above, rural poor families are more likely to be working than are non-rural poor families. However, even when they are not working, poor rural families face many barriers to TANF receipt, making them less likely to rely on this form of aid even when they are in need of it. TANF rates are lower in rural areas than in urban (Brown and Lichter 2004; Lichter and Graefe 2011), and have fallen precipitously since welfare reform in 1996 (Jensen et al. 2011). Jensen et al. (2011, 1) find that even the recession has not significantly increased the rate of rural welfare receipt, and "in 2009, just over 11 percent of poor rural families reported receiving any income from TANF, as compared to nearly 14 percent of poor urban families." Thus in rural areas TANF provides less of a safety net for poor families than in other parts of the United States.

The reasons for the lower rural rates of TANF receipt are manifold and difficult to pinpoint. Several researchers have looked in depth at the impact of welfare reform in rural areas, particularly with regard to work requirements in places with very tight labor markets. They find that welfare reform has made the receipt of aid difficult for families in these types of communities, where fulfilling work requirements often requires long commutes to places with jobs. Commutes can be a serious hardship for poor rural families, who often do not have reliable vehicles, and who frequently live in areas without adequate public transportation (Parisi et al. 2011). However, there is evidence that in the past decade there has been greater workforce participation by rural women alongside falling TANF receipt rates, which suggests that TANF's new restrictions may have succeeded to some degree in pushing poor rural women off of aid and into the labor force (Tickamyer and Henderson 2011). Other researchers question whether welfare reform really had much of an impact on rural populations at all however, arguing that even before TANF, welfare generally was inadequate and used "only temporarily to deal with short-term emergencies" (Pickering et al. 2006, 4). Nonetheless, there is some consensus that welfare reform has made it more difficult for rural families to receive and stay on this form of aid, and that the new requirements have resulted in more sanctions and fewer opportunities for education and job training than were available under the previous program (Pickering et al. 2006).

In addition to the bureaucratic and structural constraints to welfare receipt in rural communities, there is also evidence that cultural norms and social stigma play important roles in discouraging rural families from seeking out this form of aid (Brown and Lichter 2004; Lichter and Graefe 2011; Sherman 2006; 2009). Rural cultural norms often stress the importance of hard work, self-sufficiency, and independence (Nelson 2005; Nelson and Smith 1999; Sherman 2006; 2009). Because of welfare's association with laziness, dependency, and moral degeneracy—the antithesis of these values—rural welfare recipients are often judged as undeserving and immoral by others in their communities. High social cohesion and lack of anonymity in rural communities can exacerbate this stigma and its impacts on poor residents, who often refuse this form of aid in order to avoid judgment by community members and exclusion from social networks (Sherman 2006; 2009). The degree to which this stigma applies to other forms of need-based government aid appears to vary by community and cultural norms, as well as by time period. While some research has found a similar tendency for rural families to avoid food stamps in order to minimize stigma (Sherman 2009), there is evidence that Supplemental Nutrition Assistance Program (SNAP, the current version of food stamps) rates have been rising in rural areas since the recession (Bean 2011).

While TANF and SNAP are often highly stigmatized in rural communities, other government aid programs, with either stricter eligibility requirements or clearer ties to prior or current work activity, seem to be preferred. Because of its obvious connection to previous work, aid in the form of unemployment insurance appears to come with less stigma in rural communities, particularly when jobs are scarce or a major local employer suddenly shuts down. In these cases, recipients often see the aid as "earned" or "deserved," and portray themselves as distinctly different from the undeserving recipients of welfare (Sherman 2006; 2009). Disability assistance in the form of Supplemental Security Income (SSI) also is preferred to welfare in many rural communities, often because of the perceived connections between disabilities and prior work activities in dangerous local industries (Pickering et al. 2006; Sherman 2006; 2009). While also less stigmatized because of its tie to labor market activity, the Earned Income Tax Credit is underutilized in rural areas compared to urban (Parisi et al. 2011).

For rural poor families who want to avoid the stigma of welfare and food stamps but do not qualify for less stigmatized forms of aid, options for survival are limited in rural areas. Resources like food banks and homeless shelters are often minimal (or non-existent) in rural communities, as are other types of private, nonprofit support for struggling individuals and families (Whitley 2013). On the other hand, many rural communities offer numerous options for enterprising individuals to enhance their subsistence through informal work and self-provisioning activities such as hunting, fishing, cutting or gathering wood, and growing gardens. Many researchers have noted rural poor families' heavy reliance on these sorts of informal activities as sources of income, as well as well-developed systems of barter with friends, family, and neighbors (Lichter and Graefe 2011; Nelson 2005; Sherman 2006; 2009; Tickamyer and Henderson 2011). Unlike public sources of aid, self-provisioning activities are generally socially and culturally prized in rural communities, and many people who are not poor also engage in significant amounts of informal work as sports or hobbies, or simply as part of a rural lifestyle (Sherman 2006; 2009). These types of informal self-provisioning activities can greatly enhance rural poor families' subsistence while simultaneously helping them to maintain self-respect and social standing within their communities.

Yet, informal work activities are not equally available to all rural poor families, and can be particularly difficult for the elderly and disabled, those who lack social ties, or single parents with young children (Whitley 2013). Nelson (2005) notes that the ability to engage in self-provisioning activities is gendered, and that most of these activities are generally done by men, not women, in rural communities. She finds that single mothers by and large do not engage in self-provisioning activities, despite their disproportionate likelihood of poverty, because they lack skills, time, energy, and help with childcare (Nelson 2005). Left with fewer options for informal subsistence activities, single mothers are more likely to rely heavily on their social networks, which often can create additional stress as they work to manage obligations and avoid conflict (Nelson 2005). The ability to mobilize social networks for support can also be dependent on the level of local community cohesion and an individual's or family's history and social standing, and in some tightly knit communities those who are seen as less morally upstanding are less likely to receive informal help from family and community (Sherman and Sage 2011; Sherman 2006). Unfortunately, often the deepest social divisions are found in the poorest communities, leading to lack of cooperation and support for those at the bottom of the social hierarchy (Hamilton et al. 2008; Sherman 2009). Thus, reliance on both self-provisioning and social networks is generally more common among those poor rural residents who are relatively better off in terms of health, family structure, and social integration. Poor individuals and families who lack these types of advantages are left with few survival options besides the stigma and bureaucratic hurdles of the formal safety net. Receipt of formal aid, which seldom provides enough for poor families' survival, also serves to further diminish their moral worth in the eyes of the larger communities in which recipients reside, and thus often leads to even greater social isolation, which can diminish their options for coping with poverty even further.

Beyond the safety net are illegal activities, which are also often highly stigmatized and generally understudied in the rural context. While it has long been understood that production of certain illegal substances, most notably marijuana and methamphetamines, is common in rural areas (Donnermeyer and Tunnell 2007), their role in the economies of struggling rural communities has rarely been studied, in contrast with the substantial body of literature that investigates illegal activities in urban settings. Most existing rural research on illegal substances has focused on use and abuse rather than production and sales, and thus little is known about the role that illegal drugs play as income generation strategies for the rural poor, despite the high prevalence of both production and use in poor rural communities (Lambert, Gale, and Hartley 2008). With the decriminalization of marijuana in several Western states, there is evidence that this industry is seeing a resurgence in its economic importance to rural communities (Semuels 2009). Meanwhile, growing concern about methamphetamine production and its impact on rural communities (Donnermeyer and Tunnell 2007; Lambert et al. 2008) also begs for more research. Given the sluggishness of the economic recovery, particularly in rural areas (Parker et al. 2010), informal and illegal activities will likely continue to play an important role in the survival strategies of poor rural families, and more research is needed into the social and economic repercussions of illegal drug activity in rural America.

Conclusions

While the 1990s brought hope and some reduction in poverty rates to many rural communities, the first decade of the 2000s has brought renewed struggles and hardships. Poverty has risen again throughout rural America, and persists in many places that have long experienced high poverty and unemployment, as well as lack of infrastructure, educational opportunities, and resources. As in previous decades, rural minorities and single parents are disproportionately likely to be poor and often have fewer resources available for coping with poverty. Given the depth of the recession and its exacerbation of ongoing deindustrialization and globalization trends, it is likely that these problems will not resolve themselves quickly in rural communities. Future research is needed to continue to explore the impact of the recession on rural communities, as well as to expand our knowledge of emerging issues, such as immigrant settlement in rural communities and the growth of rural drug trades and gang activities.

Blanket solutions to the causes and effects of rural poverty are hard to come by, although for many communities investment into economic development and social support would likely help. It is clear that today many rural families need more resources and better options for surviving without sufficient income, and thus investments into both public and private sources of aid are vital. However, as we look past the current crisis into its future recovery, it is important to think about investing into the infrastructure and resources of rural communities in ways that will go beyond short-term solutions to immediate needs. Hamilton et al. (2008) argue that most rural communities would benefit from improvements in telecommunications technology and infrastructure, greater access to affordable health care, better educational facilities and opportunities for both children and adults, improved and expanded public transportation, more affordable housing, and jobs that offer living wages. All of these policies have in common that they will be beneficial to both the working poor and the unemployed poor, and most importantly, to the nonpoor as well. Universality of policies appears to be key to their acceptance by both communities and policymakers, particularly in the current political and economic climate in which the poor are seen as individually responsible for their own poverty, and redistribution policies are widely vilified for undermining economic growth, job creation, and individual work ethics.

As the recession drags on and its recovery is barely perceptible, political agendas across the nation have retrenched rather than questioned the neoliberal agenda, and focused on cutting costs and services, particularly "entitlements" for the poor. As I discussed in the previous section, the rural poor are already using less than their share of publicly available resources, and if the current focus on cutting these programs continues it is likely that the rural safety net will shrink further. Yet it is also clear that in rural America there is even less social acceptance for the stigmatized safety net than in the rest of the nation, and that the best way to protect vulnerable rural families given the current cultural and political climate may be to include them in the larger agenda of rural economic health, rather than treat them as a separate group whose interests are unique from those of their larger communities. While it may not be possible to break down popular stereotypes and images of the poor, we may have more success if we stop thinking of those who live below the (rather arbitrary) poverty line as being fundamentally different from those who hover above it. Investing in the larger economies and infrastructures of rural communities will likely provide more opportunities for better lives for rural Americans, both above and below the poverty line, and eventually contribute to reversing the high rates of poverty in rural America.

Notes

1 Throughout this chapter, I use the terms *rural/nonmetropolitan* and *urban/metropolitan/non-rural* interchangeably, although technically these are somewhat different measures. For detailed information about how rurality is being measured, please see the original sources of data.

2 Schmalzbauer (2011) notes that many of her Latino immigrant subjects in rural Montana chose the location because they felt that rural communities exemplified more traditional gender and family values. This echoes sentiments from long-time white residents in my own rural California case study (Sherman 2009), who similarly describe their rural community as safer and morally superior to urban communities in terms of family values. However, these white subjects also associate Latino immigrants with drugs, gangs, and violence, and resist in-migration by minorities into their mostly white community (Sherman 2009).

References

Albo, Gregory. January 2009. "The Crisis of Neoliberalism and the Impasse of the Union Movement." *Development Dialogue* 51: 119–31.

Anderson, Cynthia D., and Chih-Yuan Weng. 2011. "Regional Variation of Women in Low-Wage Work across Rural Communities." In *Economic Restructuring and Family Well-Being in Rural America*, ed. Kristin E. Smith and Ann R. Tickamyer, 215–30. University Park: The Pennsylvania State University Press.

Bean, Jessica A. 2011. *Reliance on Supplemental Nutrition Assistance Program Continued to Rise Post-Recession.* New Hampshire: Carsey Institute.

Brown, David L., and Kai A. Schafft. 2011. *Rural People and Communities in the 21st Century.* Malden, MA: Polity Press.

Brown, J. Brian, and Daniel T. Lichter. 2004. "Poverty, Welfare, and the Livelihood Strategies of Nonmetropolitan Single Mothers." *Rural Sociology* 69 (2): 282–301.

Carr, Patrick J., and Maria J. Kefalas. 2009. *Hollowing out the Middle: The Rural Brain Drain and What It Means for America.* Boston: Beacon Press.

Clark, Sherri Lawson. 2012. "In Search of Housing: Urban Families in Rural Contexts." *Rural Sociology* 77 (1): 110–34.

Clawson, Dan, and Mary Ann Clawson. 1999. "What Has Happened to the US Labor Movement? Union Decline and Renewal." *Annual Review of Sociology* 25 (1): 95–119.

Crow, Dan, and Gregory Albo. 2005. "Neo-liberalism, NAFTA, and the State of the North American Labour Movements." *Just Labour* 6/7 (Autumn): 12–22.

Crowley, Martha, and Daniel T. Lichter. 2009. "Social Disorganization in New Latino Destinations?" *Rural Sociology* 74 (4): 573–604.

Crowley, Martha, Daniel T. Lichter, and Zhenchao Qian. 2006. "Beyond Gateway Cities: Economic Restructuring and Poverty among Mexican Immigrant Families and Children." *Family Relations* 55 (3): 345–60. http://dx.doi.org/10.1111/j.1741-3729.2006.00407.x.

Donnermeyer, Joseph F., and Ken Tunnell. 2007. "In Our Own Backyard: Methamphetamine Manufacturing, Trafficking, and Abuse in Rural America." *Rural Realities* 2 (2): 1–12.

Farrigan, Tracey. 2010. "Rural Income, Poverty, and Welfare: Poverty Geography." ERS/USDA Briefing Room. Accessed 20 June 2011. http://www.ers.usda.gov/topics/rural-economy-population/rural-poverty-well-being.aspx.

Fitchen, Janet M. 1991. *Endangered Spaces, Enduring Places: Change, Identity, and Survival in Rural America.* Boulder: Westview Press.

Gallardo, Roberto. 2010a. "Rural America in the 2000s: Age." *Daily Yonder*, 21 July. http://www.dailyyonder.com/age-test/2010/07/20/2849.

Gallardo, Roberto. 2010b. "Rural America in the 2000s: Population." *Daily Yonder*, 14 July. http://www.dailyyonder.com/rural-america-2000s-population/2010/07/12/2834.

Grusky, David B., Bruce Western, and Christopher Wimer, eds. 2011. *The Great Recession.* New York: Russell Sage Foundation.

Hamilton, Lawrence C., Leslie R. Hamilton, Cynthia M. Duncan, and Chris R. Colocousis. 2008. "Place Matters: Challenges and Opportunities in Four Rural Americas." *Carsey Institute Reports on Rural America* 1 (4): 2–32.

Hays, Sharon. 2003. *Flat Broke with Children: Women in the Age of Welfare Reform.* Oxford: Oxford University Press.

Jensen, Leif, and Eric B. Jensen. 2011. "Employment Hardship among Rural Men." In *Economic Restructuring and Family Well-Being in Rural America*, ed. Kristin E. Smith and Ann R. Tickamyer, 40–59. University Park: The Pennsylvania State University Press.

Jensen, Leif, Marybeth J. Mattingly, and Jessica A. Bean. 2011. *TANF in Rural America Informing Re-authorization.* New Hampshire: Carsey Institute.

Kandel, William, Jamila Henderson, Heather Koball, and Randy Capps. 2011. "Moving up in Rural America: Economic Attainment of Nonmetro Latino Immigrants." *Rural Sociology* 76 (1): 101–28.

Lambert, David, John A. Gale, and David Hartley. Summer 2008. "Substance Abuse by Youth and Young Adults in Rural America." *Journal of Rural Health* 24 (3): 221–28.

Lichter, Daniel T., and Deboarah Roempke Graefe. 2011. "Rural Economic Restructuring: Implications for Children, Youth, and Families." In *Economic Restructuring and Family Well-Being in Rural America*, ed. Kristin E. Smith and Ann R. Tickamyer, 25–39. University Park: The Pennsylvania State University Press.

Mattingly, Marybeth J., Kristin E. Smith, and Jessica A. Bean. 2011. *Unemployment in the Great Recession: Single Parents and Men Hit Hard.* New Hampshire: Carsey Institute.

McBride, Timothy, and Leah Kemper. 2009. "Impact of the Recession on Rural America: Rising Unemployment Leading to More Uninsured in 2009." RUPRI Center for Rural Health Policy Analysis. Accessed 1 December 2011. http://www.public-health.uiowa.edu/rupri/publications/policybriefs/2009/b2009-6%20Rising%20Unemployment%20Leading%20to%20More%20Uninsured.pdf.

Nelson, Margaret K. 2005. *The Social Economy of Single Motherhood: Raising Children in Rural America.* New York: Routledge.

Nelson, Margaret K., and Joan Smith. 1999. *Working Hard and Making Do: Surviving in Small Town America.* Berkeley: University of California Press.

O'Hare, William P. 2009. "The Forgotten Fifth: Child Poverty in Rural America." New Hampshire: Carsey Institute. Accessed 11 July 2013. http://www.carseyinstitute.unh.edu/publications/Report-OHare-ForgottenFifth.pdf.

Parisi, Domenico, Steven Michael Grice, Guangqing Chi, and Jed Pressgrove. 2011. "Poverty, Work, and the Local Environment: TANF and EITC." In *Economic Restructuring and Family Well-Being in Rural America*, ed. Kristin E. Smith and Ann R. Tickamyer, 320–35. University Park: The Pennsylvania State University Press.

Parker, Timothy S., Lorin D. Kusmin, and Alexander W. Marre. 2010. "Economic Recovery: Lessons Learned from Previous Recessions." United States Department of Agriculture Economic Research Service. Accessed 2 December 2011. http://www.ers.usda.gov/amber-waves/prior-issues-(through-2003).aspx#march20100toc.

Pickering, Kathleen, Mark H. Harvey, Gene F. Summers, and David Mushinkski. 2006. *Welfare Reform in Persistent Rural Poverty: Dreams, Disenchantments, and Diversity. University.* University Park: The Pennsylvania State University Press.

Schiller, Bradley R. 2007. *The Economics of Poverty and Discrimination.* 10th ed. New Jersey: Prentice Hall.

Schmalzbauer, Leah. 2011. "'Doing Gender,' Ensuring Survival: Mexican Migration and Economic Crisis in the Rural Mountain West." *Rural Sociology* 76 (4): 441–60.

Semuels, Alana. 2009. "Marijuana Growers Upend Hard-Luck California Town." *Los Angeles Times*, 1 November. http://articles.latimes.com/2009/nov/01/business/fi-dope-county1.

Shapiro, Isaac. 1989. "Laboring for Less: Working but Poor in Rural America." Washington, DC: Center on Budget and Policy Priorities.

Sherman, Jennifer. 2006. "Coping with Rural Poverty: Economic Survival and Moral Capital in Rural America." *Social Forces* 85 (2): 891–913. http://dx.doi.org/10.1353/sof.2007.0026.

Sherman, Jennifer. 2009. *Those Who Work, Those Who Don't: Poverty, Morality, and Family in Rural America.* Minneapolis: University of Minnesota Press.

Sherman, Jennifer, and Rayna Sage. 2011. "'Sending off All Your Good Treasures': Rural Schools, Brain-Drain, and Community Survival in the Wake of Economic Collapse." *Journal of Research in Rural Education* 26 (11): 1–14.

Smith, Kristin E. 2011. "Changing Roles: Women and Work in Rural America." In *Economic Restructuring and Family Well-Being in Rural America*, ed. Kristin E. Smith and Ann R. Tickamyer, 60–81. University Park: The Pennsylvania State University Press.

Smith, Kristin E., and Ann R. Tickamyer, eds. 2011. *Economic Restructuring and Family Well-Being in Rural America.* University Park: The Pennsylvania State University Press.

Tickamyer, Ann R., and Debra A. Henderson. 2011. "Livelihood Practices in the Shadow of Welfare Reform." In *Economic Restructuring and Family Well-Being in Rural America*, ed. Kristin E. Smith and Ann R. Tickamyer, 294–319. University Park: The Pennsylvania State University Press.

USDA Economic Research Service. 2011. "ERS/USDA Briefing Room—Rural Income, Poverty, and Welfare: Poverty Demographics." Accessed 30 May 2012. http://www.ers.usda.gov/topics/rural-economy-population/rural-poverty-well-being.aspx.

Whitley, Sarah. 2013. "Changing Times in Rural America: Food Assistance and Food Insecurity in Food Deserts." *Journal of Family Social Work* 16 (1): 36–52.

PART V

Rural Economies, Community, and Quality of Life

Economic Change, Structural Forces, and Rural America: Shifting Fortunes across Communities

Linda Lobao

The first decade of the twenty-first century ushered in both continuity and dramatic change in the structural forces influencing the fortunes of rural America. The authors in this section are attentive to these structural forces stemming from the global economy, the state, and society at large, and to their implications for rural people and communities. To synthesize the thematic concerns these authors address, I build from literatures in rural sociology, general sociology, and geography, and particularly from the critical political economy tradition that crosscuts these literatures. The political economy tradition provides a cross-disciplinary approach that solidifies the thematic focus of this section while offering a broad conceptual lens from which to understand structural changes occurring across US society (Falk and Lobao 2003; Harvey 2005; McMichael 2012; Schram 2006).

In this chapter, I frame the thematic attention to economy, community, and quality of life in the following steps. First, I provide an overview of the contours and significance of research spanning these areas. Second, I draw together existing work into a more synthetic framework for addressing structural forces over time and space. I focus particularly on the manner by which long-standing structural relationships are coalescing or unraveling in the twenty-first century. Finally, I outline a series of concerns for social science research aimed at moving forward the study of rural America.

Research on Economy, Community, and Quality of Life: Contours and Significance

Understanding the manner by which structural forces impact rural people and communities is complex, but critical for charting the nation's future. Researchers must generally grapple with four sets of processes pertaining to: (1) economic structure or shifts in industries, firms, and jobs; (2) the state at all levels, important because rural livelihoods derive not only from the private sector but also from government interventions; (3) institutionalized relationships between key social actors, such as relationships between employers and workers, government and citizens, and civic society vis-à-vis government and business, with such relationships reflecting bargaining power for valued societal resources; and (4) finally, spatial or geographic processes, because the previous structural forces wash differentially across regions and communities. These processes, which involve economic structure, the state, social actor relationships, and geography, vary across time and impact populations' quality of life.

Each of the four sets of processes above is addressed in large bodies of social science research. Vast research also exists on different forms of socioeconomic well-being or quality of life outcomes along with their distinct causal determinants and consequences. Yet for the purpose of understanding rural people and places over the past decade, extant research is sorely limited.[1]

Much of the existing research remains aspatial. That is, it little addresses spatial variations in the case of economic structure, government, and social relationships. Moreover, if research is geographically oriented, it tends to be urban biased, focusing on metropolitan areas. This critique of social science research has been leveled previously for the knowledge gap it implies for rural areas. Three decades ago, the Rural Sociological Task Force on Persistent Rural Poverty (1993) sought to extend conventional aspatial and urban-oriented research to the question of rural well-being. Yet despite concerted efforts by rural sociologists (see Lichter and Brown 2011) and some regional scientists (Partridge and Rickman 2006; Weber et al. 2005) and geographers (Glasmeier 2002), it is not clear that things have changed much. Social scientists still overlook the distinctiveness of and diversity within rural areas. For the United States, conventional urban-focused traditions by formal definition exclude nearly all the nation's vast territory, over 60 percent of local (county) governments, and a population that exceeds the size of significant social groups such as the Hispanic, African American, or elderly populations (Brown and Schafft 2011, 11–12).

This long-standing critique of the neglect of rural areas stands particularly with regard to social science theory (Lobao, Hooks, and Tickamyer 2007;

Thomas, Lowe, Fulkerson, and Smith 2011). Most of the invigorating, otherwise-enlightened theory addressing significant structural changes is macro-level or nationally or cross-nationally focused. Within nations, theorizing has been mostly aspatial or, if cognizant of geography, centered on a handful of large, usually global-headquarter cities.

Beyond leaving out rural places and people, existing research suffers from the academic division of labor that provides limited understanding of the new era upon us. The aforementioned bodies of research on structural forces and well-being indicators developed in a manner segmented from one another. In the case of economic structure, researchers specialize in studying manufacturing, different service sectors, farming and the extractive sector, and, more recently, the financial sector, each with separately detailed theoretical conversations and empirical literatures. Researchers do not often study how these sectors overlap or articulate within and across communities. They almost always conceptualize the state as the central or federal-level state, with little recognition that this specialization has crowded out attention to state and local governments. Local governments are increasingly important in an era where population migration has stalled and people are stuck in place. Likewise, a vast academic industry specializes in different markers of quality of life or well-being indicators such as earnings, employment status, poverty, educational attainment, health status, and, more recently, indebtedness. When interrelationship of these indicators is scrutinized, it is mainly at the individual or household level, rather than as a package washing across the nation.

The academic division of labor tends to foster a knowledge base in which theory and empirical research are channeled inward. Scholars typically read only in their home discipline and often confine their efforts to narrow literatures.[2] While offering precise detail in increasingly specialized areas, the academic division of labor runs into limits if the goal is otherwise. It has made it hard to develop an overarching understanding of the fate of the American population and communities over the past few decades. But such comprehensive understanding has become critical as the nation remains marred by a profound downturn—to capture the full force of the reckoning, researchers need to connect the dots.

If scholars are to move in more comprehensive directions, we need to treat structural changes jointly. In turn, we need to clearly identify the mechanisms by which these changes filter down to affect different markers of community, individual, and household well-being, along with the linkages between them. Finally, we need to critically evaluate the degree to which the public and particularly disadvantaged populations today possess meaningful, strategic agency to induce beneficial structural changes—as opposed to putting forth standard Pollyanna-like pronouncements that all people have agency within structure.

In short, the social science understanding of how the four structural processes above work out and their impacts on different forms of well-being for rural communities remains important—more so today than in decades past now gazed upon nostalgically for their relative affluence. It is critical that we document new empirical changes, extend social science theory toward rural sensibility, and seriously take stock of policy and civic society.

Conceptualizing Structural Changes and Well-Being across Time and Place

Although theoretical understanding of the present era is limited, the building blocks are available from the critical political economy perspective (Falk and Lobao 2003; Harvey 2005; McMichael 2012; Schram 2006). This perspective has a number of advantages—it forms a lingua franca across disciplines and captures changes in each of the four structural processes above as well as in general well-being. The limitation of the political economy approach is that it is not well articulated at the subnational scale in a way where it can directly inform changes across rural communities.[3] Drawing from this tradition, I sketch out key trends, taking them down to the case of rural America.

The Seeds of the Present Era

To understand transformations in the economy, state, and social relationships, it is useful to consider how they combined and then unraveled during distinct historical periods since World War II. Various literatures under the political economy banner roughly recognize these same periods: they are formally theorized respectively as regimes (Aglietta 1979) and social structures of accumulation (Kotz 1994), but others treat them more loosely as phases of capitalism (Harvey 2005; Pike, Rodríguez-Pose, and Tomaney 2007). In all these formulations, the character of the economy, the state, and social relationships are seen to coalesce in time at the national or at the cross-national scale, the latter reflected in periodizations of global development (McMichael 2012). Some researchers have also looked at how these structural forces coalesce over time subnationally, or within nations (Brenner 2004). But for the most part, researchers have left direct empirical scrutiny of rural areas out of these conceptualizations.[4] Falk and Lobao (2003) draw from the political economy tradition to understand rural development through the 1990s. Here

I extend their approach, connecting changes in the economy, the state, and social relationships to the well-being of rural people and communities in the twenty-first century.

To analyze present-day rural America, attention needs to be given to the baseline period that forms the touchstone of the political economic literatures above. This is the national growth stage from 1945 to the early 1970s, often termed the Fordist period. This period is characterized by: the global dominance of US manufacturing; the Keynesian welfare state, with its more centralized government structure; social relationships that included greater bargaining power of labor as indicated by union strength; and mass well-being in terms of rising earnings and a growing middle class. In this era, much of urban America prospered, while rural areas experienced a great deal of upheaval that included influx of lower-wage manufacturing industries and movement toward industrialized agriculture and the rapid demise of farming as a livelihood strategy (Lobao and Meyer 2001). Nevertheless, at the subnational scale, Brenner (2004) sees this period as one of "spatial Keynesian"—the most geographically egalitarian of modern eras in which governments across Western nations were concerned with ameliorating regional inequalities. In the United States, for example, Johnson's war on poverty and the formation of the Appalachian Regional Commission occurred in this period.

Attention needs to be given to the stage of Fordist decline that began in the early 1970s as the previous relationships began to fall apart. Changes in industrial structure and institutional relationships disrupted the Fordist system. Manufacturing experienced global competition and national decline. The institutional structure of capital-labor-state relationships that (along with a strong manufacturing sector) assured rising earnings and lower income inequality began to break down, evident in the decline of labor unions and Keynesian social safety net. Downturns appeared first in the urban manufacturing belt, with some rural areas benefitting from the misfortunes of the cities. Industrial restructuring and social upheavals in northern cities partly fueled the 1970s nonmetropolitan population turnaround (Brown and Wardwell 1980). The 1970s energy crisis adversely affected urban manufacturing, while stimulating the rural coal and oil mining industries. Global demand for US agricultural products increased the real values of farmland and created widespread farm prosperity. Thus, US cities tended to stagnate, but the rural economy blossomed and long-standing income and other well-being gaps between metro and nonmetro areas began to close (Falk and Lobao 2003). By the 1980s, however, rural America too faced a reversal of fortunes. The mining and oil industry declined as the energy crisis abated. Deconcentration of manufacturing firms to rural locations slowed. The farm economy went into a protracted debt crisis owing to a world-wide recession and reduced demand for US farm exports.

The seeds of other changes that now reach deeply into the twenty-first century—globalization and its blueprint ideological discourse for state action, neoliberalism—were ushered in. Domestically, Ronald Reagan's 1980 election marks these shifts. While conceptualizations of globalization abound, McMichael's (2012) has proven an influential sociological perspective. He sees globalization as a project led by capitalist elites that creates the institutional infrastructure for deepening the hold of the market over all aspects of human life. McMichael (2012, xiii) notes that its dominant policy discourse is neoliberalism, which proposes "market liberalization, privatization, freedom of capital movement and access, and so on." In the 1980s, the World Bank and International Monetary Fund (IMF) shifted to a free-market focus emphasizing trade over aid. Information and communication technologies and the development of global financial markets further facilitated this project. Globalization redefines the role of the state, pushing it more to elevate private market interests over those of citizens, to respond to the needs of global capital, and to reduce the social safety net. With the events of the 1980s including the imposition of IMF/World Bank structural adjustment policies on developing nations and the later establishment of the WTO in 1995, McMichael (2012) sees neoliberalism as firmly entrenched as the ideology guiding the path of globalization.

The New Decades of the Twenty-First Century

Based on the discussion above, three interrelated trends continue to affect American's well-being: the protracted exhaustion of the Fordist regime and its structure of economic production, state intervention, and social relationships; the acceleration and deepening of globalization; and pro-market neoliberalism as a policy path and hegemonic discourse that squelches public consideration of alternative development paths. While conceptually distinct, researchers stress the interrelationship of these trends and their collateral damage. For example, Wallace, Gauchat, and Fullerton (2012, 377–8) see economic globalization as having direct effects on US communities through increasing the role of majority-owned foreign companies, shifting the nature of exports, and increasing demand for immigrant workers. They note that indirectly, globalization has moved risk away from corporations and toward workers: "major transformations such as deindustrialization, corporate restructuring, bureaucratic burden, and casualization, which are largely products of globalization, have dramatically increased insecurity, flexibility and uncertainty for workers." Schram (2006) attributes the weakening of the social safety net to globalization and its policy influence. However, much like McMichael (2012), he sees globalization less as an economic force and more as discourse capitalists use to reduce wages and exert power over labor. In this view, government actors sponsor neoliberal policies out of acquiescence to business and/or because they believe there is no alternative.

Contemporary communities thus are marked by the remnants of the old Fordist era, increased influence of globalization, and neoliberal policies. As these macro-level processes have unfolded, they have spurred related changes that analysts see as defining in importance for the twenty-first century. Scholars formally recognized the trend toward *financialization*, whereby capital accumulation strategies rest increasingly on investment in financial markets and the overall expanded role of financial actors and institutions in the domestic and global economy (McMichael 2012). The Great Recession and burst of the housing bubble further made serious structural problems such as income inequality more visible, as I will discuss below. All these macro-level processes have spilled over communities' economic structure, government, the character of social relationships, and quality of residents' lives.

Rural communities today thus experience continuity along with change in economic structure, the state, institutional relationships, and well-being. In some sense, rural America lost so much of the prosperity game decades ago that the contemporary downturn may have had less effect than in the past. At a minimum, researchers now need to grapple with a mix of changes that affect rural places in a far less homogeneous manner than in the past.

In terms of economic structure, the future appears mixed. Financialization means that profit-seeking behavior comes increasingly less from investment in production of good and services and more from speculation in financial markets. Large cities have gained as employment and earnings shift toward the financial sector (Scott 2011). Nationally, in 2011, manufacturing recorded its first increase in employment since 1997, but most growth was concentrated in higher wage-durable industries (Norris 2012). Rural areas may not share in this new growth since more of their manufacturing falls into nondurable sectors. Traditional rural industries such as farming and natural resource extraction, however, have boomed, creating benefits for some community segments but serious costs for others. Farmers have benefitted from ethanol production and landowners from the boom in the shale industry and natural gas production. Rural sociologists have long examined the consequences of farm and energy sector development on rural communities (Freudenburg and Gramling 1994; Lobao and Meyer 2001). Though the twenty-first century adds different twists, the tools for studying these sectors are well-honed.

In terms of the state, Brenner (2004) argues that government has been rescaled in the movement away from the Fordist-Keynesian era. Within nations, decentralization has increased the importance of subnational governments in growth and redistribution. In the United States, this has placed additional responsibilities on rural local governments historically disadvantaged by weak fiscal capacity and low tax bases (Warner 2003). More recently, as migration rates drop and populations stay in place, local governments must provide more of the frontline services for needy populations. Though the problems of rural governments are well known, Lobao and Adua (2011) find that over the last decade, metropolitan county governments were more likely to cut services. Metro and nonmetro governments used other austerity policies, such as hiring freezes and layoffs, equally. Because rural governments have provided minimalist services historically, metro governments may have been more affected by the contemporary downturn.

Continuity in social relationships appears evident as labor continues to lose bargaining power, reflected in the decline of industrial unions and the now well-noted trend that productivity growth is occurring without earnings growth (Peet 2011). Private sector interests continue to be elevated over the public good and support of the social safety net. Rural areas have always been relatively disadvantaged along these lines (Glasmeier 2002).

The changes above are inevitably uneven among rural social groups. Persistent poverty among the nation's African American, Native American, Hispanic, and Appalachian rural populations remains. As government is cut back, rural women lose out, insofar as local government employs a higher proportion of women relative to other industries (Glasmeier and Lee-Chuvala 2011). By contrast, rural men's fortunes are likely to have relatively improved as the extractive sector and farming have fared well in the post-Great Recession period.

Conclusions: Studying Rural America Today

What do the changes above mean for researchers studying economic structure, communities, and well-being? In brief, they create complexity, debate, and uncertainty about how to capture contemporary trends, raising concerns we must address as we seek to understand the future.

First, as I note above, the Unites States remains buffeted by: the protracted exhaustion of the Fordist era's structure of economic production, state intervention, and institutionalized social relationships; globalization; and pro-market neoliberalism. The collateral damage of these processes is interrelated and spills over to numerous quality of life indicators. Researchers need to grapple with this complexity.

Second, although economic, state, and social relationships that ensured prosperity in the past period are widely recognized as eroded, the degree of and process behind that erosion is still being sorted out. Most attention has been on movement away from the Fordist-Keynesian period with movement toward some new era usually framed with regard to latter, such as in the "post-Keynesian" or "post-Fordist" state. The present era looks particularly bleak from the standpoint of most political economy theorists. For example, Harvey (2005) sees the development of a new predatory stage of capitalism that is predicated upon elites increasingly dispossessing workers and the public sector by siphoning off economic and other resources. Peck and Tickell (2002) and Hackworth (2007) see a neoliberal roll-out enveloping US communities where the politics of austerity apply to public interests but the politics of largesse apply to the corporate sector. Scott (2011) observes the deepening of stratification across places; communities are becoming more bifurcated with small, elite, well-off populations and large, lower-tier segments whose livelihoods are tied to filling the service needs of the former. Civic society (considered variously as human agency overall, third-sector institutions, and locally existing non-profit entities) is not seen to have the organizational resources and cohesion to stem the tide of these changes. Its promise runs thinner as inequality deepens across the nation. Certainly some scholars keep their fingers crossed for a brighter future. McMichael (2012) notes a global sustainability project might emerge to counter neoliberal globalization. The Occupy Wall Street Movement appeared to be sowing the seeds for such a future.

Third, the time period chosen for study adds complexities. Short-term, temporally specific changes can mask or alternatively uncover long-term profound trends. Even prior to the Great Recession, deeply troubling quality of life trends such as escalating inequality and indebtedness and lack of earnings growth were manifest—but they were masked by the improved economic conditions of the late 1990s and by the housing boom that lasted until 2007 (Bardhan and Walker 2011). Migration rates also had already slowed before the recession period, indicating less geographic mobility of workers and structural problems in national labor market adjustment processes (Partridge and Rickman 2006). But it was not until the 2007 to 2009 recession itself that income inequality, indebtedness, low earnings, lack of residential mobility, and long-term unemployment became a package of quality of life indicators defining the new era (Newman and O'Brien 2011).

Fourth, rurality gives communities different advantages and disadvantages that are not homogeneous across time. As noted above, the degree to which rural communities and people benefit or lose relatively varies in different stages of development. While much of the social science story of rural America is pitched as continual loss of economic opportunities, outmigration, and poverty, the situation at least for some regions is now shifting. Some of the former northern tier states, for instance, have recently gained population (Morrill 2012).

Finally, the issues noted above and others add complexity for research design strategies. Conventional empirical work aimed at determining neat causal linkages runs into barriers when researchers seek to question the manner by which structural forces affect well-being across rural communities. Regional change processes are messy and arrays of factors influence community outcomes. Path dependency is a staple of community development processes. For example, once industries, institutional arrangements, or policies are established in a community, their influence carries forward—they set the stage for future development. Endogeneity, the classic problem of separating cause from effect, permeates any study aimed at assessing community outcomes. For example, communities with weak job growth almost always have higher poverty rates, but at the same time, poor communities have difficulty attracting jobs. The upside with the problems above is the researchers are now charged with thinking out more clearly the variables implicated in causal relationships. But the downside raised by endogeneity and rural complexity is that researchers are increasingly left with two problematic choices: either to not venture into exploring some highly significant research questions, or to explore these questions with imperfect data and methods.

In summary, I have outlined the contours, significance, and barriers scholars face in studying rural America today. The academic division of labor has produced detailed information about structural forces and quality of life indicators, but not the analytical tools to link them well to each other and to the critical problems at hand. The political economy framework that has long informed other rural sociological fields can provide a theoretical foundation for such future work. The Great Recession and its aftermath has put class and inequality squarely back on the research agenda—a transition homeward to sociology's core and contrast from the Reagan era when social scientists began a long-term movement away from these concerns. Lastly, I have noted the complex sets of issues researchers face in addressing economy, community, and quality of life today. The academic division of labor has too-often worked against exploration of compelling societal issues, as scholars confront imperfect data and methodologies and conceptual questions that can be framed only in broad brushstrokes. Nevertheless, if rural sociologists are to have an impact on the future of rural America, we need to continually ask the big questions of our time.

Notes

1 The themes authors address in this section cover extensive research ground. To condense the discussion, my points are made primarily along rural-urban (nonmetro-metro) differences and for economic well-being outcomes such as poverty and income inequality. The direct consequences of shifts in rural economic structure, government, and social relationships tend to be manifest foremost on economic well-being indicators. The points made here must be situated in light of the extensive diversity among rural populations, but to do justice to this diversity is not possible in a short chapter. Such diversity includes region of the country and distance from metro centers where long-standing relationships such as poorer conditions in more remote areas and the rural south persist. Like elsewhere globally, those higher in the stratification order based on gender, race/ethnicity, and class fare still relatively better. Finally, it is important to note that people living in the urban core and in remote rural areas have relatively similar levels of economic well-being (Brown and Schafft 2011).

2 I am not advocating abandoning disciplines and moving toward kitchen-sink interdisciplinary work. Rather in the case of sociology, premiere among the social sciences for its concern with inequality, impact would be greater if we started from the sensitivities of the home discipline but branched out with inquiry and accorded greater value to theory and research from other disciplines.

3 By contrast, the political economy tradition has a strong presence in other areas of rural sociology, such as the sociology of agriculture and globalization/development studies.

4 For some exceptions, see Falk and Lobao (2003) and Page and Walker (1991).

References

Aglietta, Michael. 1979. *A Theory of Capitalist Regulation: The U.S. Experience.* London: Verso.

Bardhan, Ashok, and Richard Walker. 2011. "California Shrugged: Fountainhead of the Great Recession." *Cambridge Journal of Regions, Economy, and Society* 4 (3): 303–22. http://dx.doi.org/10.1093/cjres/rsr005.

Brenner, Neil. 2004. *New State Spaces: Urban Governance and the Rescaling of Statehood.* Oxford: Oxford University Press. http://dx.doi.org/10.1093/acprof:oso/9780199270057.001.0001.

Brown, David L., and Kai A. Schafft. 2011. *Rural People and Communities in the 21st Century.* Cambridge, UK: Polity Press.

Brown, David L., and John M. Wardwell. 1980. *New Directions in Urban-Rural Migration: The Population Turnaround in Rural America.* New York: Academic Press.

Falk, William, and Linda M. Lobao. 2003. "Who Benefits from Economic Restructuring? Who is Worse Off? Lessons from the Past and Challenges for the Future." In *Challenges for Rural America in the Twenty-First Century,* ed. David L. Brown and Louis E. Swanson, 152–65. University Park: The Pennsylvania State University Press.

Freudenburg, William R., and Robert Gramling. 1994. "Natural Resources and Rural Poverty: A Closer Look." *Society & Natural Resources* 7 (1): 5–22. http://dx.doi.org/10.1080/08941929409380841.

Glasmeier, Amy K. 2002. "One Nation Pulling Apart: The Basis of Persistent Poverty in the USA." *Progress in Human Geography* 26 (2): 155–73. http://dx.doi.org/10.1191/0309132502ph362ra.

Glasmeier, Amy K., and Christa R. Lee-Chuvala. 2011. "Austerity in America: Gender and Community Consequences of Restructuring the Public Sector." *Cambridge Journal of Regions, Economy, and Society* 4 (3): 457–74. http://dx.doi.org/10.1093/cjres/rsr029.

Hackworth, Jason. 2007. *The Neoliberal City: Governance Ideology, and Development in American Urbanism.* Ithaca: Cornell University Press.

Harvey, David. 2005. *A Brief History of Neoliberalism.* Oxford: Oxford University Press.

Kotz, David M. 1994. "Interpreting the Social Structure of Accumulation Theory." In *Social Structures of Accumulation*, ed. D.M. Kotz, T. McDonough, and M. Reich, 50–71. Cambridge: Cambridge University Press. http://dx.doi.org/10.1017/CBO9780511559501.004.

Lichter, Daniel T., and David L. Brown. 2011. "Rural America in an Urban Society: Changing Spatial and Social Boundaries." *Annual Review of Sociology* 37 (1): 565–92. http://dx.doi.org/10.1146/annurev-soc-081309-150208.

Lobao, Linda, and Lazarus Adua. 2011. "State Rescaling and Local Governments Austerity Policies across the USA, 2001–2008." *Cambridge Journal of Regions, Economy, and Society* 4 (3): 419–35. http://dx.doi.org/10.1093/cjres/rsr022.

Lobao, Linda, and Katherine Meyer. 2001. "The Great Agricultural Transition: Crisis, Change, and Social Consequences of Twentieth Century Farming." *Annual Review of Sociology* 27 (1): 103–24. http://dx.doi.org/10.1146/annurev.soc.27.1.103.

Lobao, Linda, Gregory Hooks, and Ann Tickamyer. 2007. "Introduction: Advancing the Sociology of Spatial Inequality." In *The Sociology of Spatial Inequality*, ed. Linda Lobao, Gregory Hooks, and Ann Tickamyer, 1–25. Albany: The State University of New York Press.

McMichael, Phillip. 2012. *Development and Social Change: A Global Perspective.* Thousand Oaks, CA: Sage.

Morrill, Dick. 2012. "Washington: The Growth State?" *Crosscut.com*, 3 January. http://crosscut.com/2012/01/03/crosscut-blog/20728/Washington-growth-state.

Newman, Katherine S., and Rourke L. O'Brien. 2011. *Taxing the Poor: Doing Damage to the Truly Disadvantaged.* Berkeley: University of California Press.

Norris, Floyd. 2012. "Making More Things in the U.S.A." *New York Times*, 6 January, B1, B7.

Page, Brian, and Richard Walker. 1991. "From Settlement to Fordism: The Agro-industrial Revolution in the American Midwest." *Economic Geography* 67 (4): 281–315. http://dx.doi.org/10.2307/143975.

Partridge, M.D., and D.S. Rickman. 2006. *The Geography of American Poverty: Is There a Need for Place-Based Policies?* Kalmazoo, MI: Upjohn.

Peck, Jamie, and Adam Tickell. 2002. "Neoliberalizing Space." *Antipode* 34 (3): 380–404. http://dx.doi.org/10.1111/1467-8330.00247.

Peet, Richard. 2011. "Inequality, Crisis, and Austerity in Finance Capitalism." *Cambridge Journal of Regions, Economy, and Society* 4 (3): 383–99. http://dx.doi.org/10.1093/cjres/rsr025.

Pike, Andy, Andrés Rodríguez-Pose, and John Tomaney. 2007. "What Kind of Local and Regional Development and for Whom?" *Regional Studies* 41 (9): 1253–69. http://dx.doi.org/10.1080/00343400701543355.

Rural Sociological Society Task Force on Persistent Rural Poverty. 1993. *Persistent Poverty in Rural America*. Boulder, CO: Westview Press.

Schram, Sanford F. 2006. *Welfare Discipline: Discourse, Governance, and Globalization*. Philadelphia: Temple University Press.

Scott, Allen. 2011. "A World in Emergence: Notes toward a Resynthesis of Urban-Economic Geography for the 21st Century." *Urban Geography* 32 (6): 845–70. http://dx.doi.org/10.2747/0272-3638.32.6.845.

Thomas, Alexander R., Brian M. Lowe, Gregory M. Fulkerson, and Polly J. Smith. 2011. *Rural Theory: Structure, Space, Culture*. Lanham, MD: Lexington Books.

Wallace, Michael, Gordon Gauchat, and Andrew S. Fullerton. 2012. "Globalization and Earnings Inequality in Metropolitan Areas: Evidence from the USA." *Cambridge Journal of Regions, Economy, and Society* 5 (3): 377–96. http://dx.doi.org/10.1093/cjres/rss001.

Warner, Mildred. 2003. "Competition, Cooperation, and Local Government." In *Challenges for Rural America in the Twenty-First Century*, ed. David L. Brown and Louis E. Swanson, 252–61. University Park: The Pennsylvania State University Press.

Weber, Bruce, Leif Jensen, Kathy Miller, Jane M. Mosely, and Monica Fisher. 2005. "A Critical Review of Rural Poverty Literature: Is There Truly a Rural Effect?" *International Regional Science Review* 28 (4): 381–414. http://dx.doi.org/10.1177/0160017605278996.

CHAPTER 28

Education and Schooling in Rural America

Kai A. Schafft and Catharine Biddle

Introduction

During the 2010 to 2011 school year, twelve million children attended public schools in rural school districts, accounting for approximately 24 percent of the total public school enrollment in the United States, an increase of over four million rural students from the 1999 to 2000 academic year (Aud et al. 2013; Strange, Johnson, Showalter, and Klein 2012). Furthermore, fully 57 percent of school districts and about one third of schools are located in rural areas (Aud et al. 2013). However, rural schools and rural education seldom receive serious attention within policy arenas or academic scholarship (Sipple and Brent 2008). This would seem to represent a significant oversight, not only given rural schools' statistical representation, but also because of the challenges, as well as the unique social and educational assets, many of them contain.

A major obstacle facing both rural education research and public policy in addressing rural education is the wide diversity of rural school and community contexts. For example, while rurality in the United States is often popularly imagined as a relatively undifferentiated "white" space, with rural places as repositories of tradition and stability in a rapidly changing and globalizing society (Brown and Schafft 2011; Vanderbeck 2008), there are four states (New Mexico, Alaska, Arizona, and California) in which more than half of all rural students are non-white, and many other states that have seen significant changes in rural racial and ethnic diversity over the last decade or so (Strange et al. 2012). Rural areas in America are starkly differentiated by regional location, economic and industrial activity, and deep historical and cultural legacies. Some rural areas have faced long-term concentrated poverty and economic

Table 28.1
State-level educational characteristics of states with the highest percentage of rural students, 2008 to 2009

							Percent change, 1999–2000 to 2008–9		
	Percent rural students	Total rural students	Percent rural minority students	Instructional expenditures per rural pupil	Percent rural student poverty	Rural HS graduation rate	Total number rural students	Total number rural Hispanic students	Percent rural student poverty
Mississippi	54.7	268,862	40.6	$4,578	62.9	63.1	34.1	530.2	-1.7
Vermont	54.6	47,784	4.2	$8,651	29.9	84.1	-17.3	78.5	4.7
Maine	52.7	99,185	7.8	$6.827	38.8	n/a	-14.1	67.7	8.2
N. Carolina	47.2	685,409	40.5	$5,010	31.5	75.1	46.6	292.7	-6.0
S. Dakota	42.5	53, 760	20.8	$5,375	38.2	95.3	-7.3	124.8	4.6
S. Carolina	40.0	285,442	40.5	$5,238	57.1	†	79.0	446.9	5.8
Alabama	39.7	295,906	28.1	$5,207	52.3	67.5	57.7	397.0	5.1
Tennessee	38.7	375,453	11.6	$4,518	46.8	86.9	114.4	†	†
N. Dakota	38.6	36,508	17.9	$5,707	36.5	88.3	-21.7	45.9	-0.9
Kentucky	38.5	157,637	6.5	$5,114	57.1	72.8	24.2	366.9	4.0

Note: † Data not available. Source: Strange, Johnson, Showalter, and Klein (2012).

stagnation along with aging populations and rural out-migration, while others have found themselves remade by the arrival of new immigrant populations or transformed into high amenity retirement destination communities (Brown and Schafft 2011).

In short, as Shucksmith, Brown, and Vergunst (2012, 298) argue, contemporary rural society is not only widely varied, but is "constructed by a broad range of demographic, economic, social and political transformations that result in a highly interactive social space joining rural and urban areas." These transformations and diverse social and historical contexts directly affect the provision of education as well as the relationship between the well-being of rural schools and communities. Table 28.1, for example, shows data from the ten states with the largest percentages of rural students.[1] Even these basic descriptive data illustrate some of the stark differences across multiple rural contexts in region, student demographics, school spending, socioeconomic conditions, and educational attainment.

The wide-ranging diversity within rural areas is one of the main reasons that some rural scholars advocate for regional development approaches that are more responsive to local conditions (Brown and Schafft 2011; Falk, Schulman, and Tickamyer 2003). By the same logic, rural education advocates similarly argue that in order to avoid inadvertently reinforcing or creating new inequities for rural youth, educational policies need to be deeply cognizant of the extent to which community characteristics and educational needs, as well as local resources and constraints, can vary significantly across different rural areas (Strange 2011). However, just as Lobao points out in the introduction to this section that social scientists more broadly "still overlook the distinctiveness and diversity within rural areas," within the field of education, serious attention to the people and places occupying the spatial peripheries has also tended to remain relegated to the scholarly peripheries. A search for the keywords "urban" and "rural" in the titles and abstracts of all articles published between January 2004 and January 2014 in the top three US educational research journals ranked by impact factor (*Review of Educational Research*, *American Educational Research Journal*, and *Academy of Management, Learning and Education*) revealed forty-seven published articles with an urban focus but only five with a rural focus.

The Rural School-Community Connection

As local social institutions, schools play critical community roles. While they prepare young people for participation in a variety of social, economic and civic spheres, they are also one of the main social institutions that help to define and provide coherence to the communities where people live. Scholars have suggested the multiple ways in which the increasing globalization of economic and cultural forces has undermined the meaning and integrity of local places (Bauman 1998; Brown and Schafft 2011; Gruenewald and Smith 2008; Shucksmith, Brown, and Vergunst 2012). Yet, people still reside in and interact with other people within localities. As Groenke and Nespor (2010, 52) argue, "how such large-scale economic and cultural shifts play out in rural settings depends on a complex politics of articulation in which different groups struggle to define themselves in terms of particular versions of 'rural' or 'local' life." Patterns of local social interaction continue to inscribe the boundaries of localities, in the process creating, reproducing, and sometimes contesting a variety of place-based identities (Brown and Schafft 2011; Corbett 2007; Gray 2009; Wilkinson 1991). Schools are institutions of the state and therefore necessarily must be responsive to state and national-level interests, reforms, and

Table 28.2
Percent distribution of public schools and students by locale, 2010 to 2011

Schools by size (enrollment)	City	Suburb	Town	Rural			
				Fringe	Distant	Remote	All
< 400 students	37.8	29.3	48.4	35.7	72.8	92.2	61.7
400–799	44.0	48.1	42.1	43.9	24.2	7.4	28.6
800–1,999	15.8	19.9	9.3	18.9	3.0	0.4	9.0
2,000+	2.4	2.7	0.2	1.6	0.1	0.0	0.7
Percent of students attending school by size (enrollment)							
< 400 students	15.2	10.9	24.5	13.8	47.9	75.8	29.5
400–799	43.0	42.9	51.8	43.3	41.7	22.1	40.8
800–1,999	31.1	35.5	22.6	36.1	10.0	2.1	25.3
2,000+	10.7	10.7	1.1	6.8	0.4	0.0	4.3
NAEP Reading achievement levels; percent at or above proficient							
Grade 4	26.2	37.3	28.9	37.6	30.8	28.1	34.5
Grade 8	26.0	35.8	29.5	35.3	30.7	29.0	33.2
NAEP Mathematics achievement levels; Percent at or above proficient							
Grade 4	33.2	45.0	34.7	45.6	38.4	36.2	42.4
Grade 8	28.6	37.2	31.5	38.3	30.2	31.9	33.2
Percent distribution of residents age 25+ by highest level of educational attainment							
Less than HS	16.7	11.8	16.5	†	†	†	13.2
HS or equivalent	24.7	26.6	33.4	†	†	†	33.4
Some college	27.5	29.1	30.2				30.1
Bachelor's degree or greater	31.0	32.5	19.9	†	†	†	23.3

Note: † Data not available. Sources: US Department of Education, National Center for Education Statistics, Schools and Staffing Survey, "Public School and BIA School Data Files," 2010–11; US Department of Education, National Center for Education Statistics, National Assessment of Educational Progress (NAEP), 2011 Reading Assessment, 2011 Mathematics Assessment (see http://nces.ed.gov/surveys/ruraled/students.asp).

agendas. However, as public institutions mandated with providing services to all eligible local residents, schools also remain one of the primary enduring *local* institutions, run by locally elected school boards, providing a context for collective identity and association, a site for shared intergenerational identity, and an important context for community interaction, social solidarity, and collective action (Schafft 2010; Schafft and Harmon 2011; Zekeri, Wilkinson, and Humphrey 1994).

The school-community relationship is arguably accentuated in rural areas. First, rural schools are characterized by their relatively smaller size. Nearly 62 percent of schools in rural areas have 400 or fewer students, but the same is true for only 38 percent of city schools. Similarly, while only about 15 percent of students in cities attend schools with 400 or fewer students, in rural areas overall nearly one-third of students attend schools that size. In the most remote rural areas,[2] over 75 percent of students attend schools with 400 or fewer students (see Table 28.2). Parents of rural students are more likely to attend school events or volunteer on school committees than their non-rural counterparts. In comparison to urban settings, teachers in rural schools also report fewer problems with students and higher levels of job satisfaction (Provasnik et al. 2007). In many rural places the school is often the largest local employer. Because of these characteristics, rural schools are often described as fostering especially strong social ties given their smaller size and the close linkages to the communities they serve (Bauch 2001; Elder and Conger 2000).

The presence of a school within a community can also be strongly related to elevated indicators of broader social and economic welfare, including housing values and local employment (Brasington 2004; Lyson 2002; Sell and Leistritz 1997). This means that those in positions of leadership within a rural school district, including the superintendent and school board members, necessarily assume not only educational leadership roles, but also local economic development roles (Lyson 2002; Schafft and Harmon 2011). In comparison to other areas, the public visibility and scrutiny of teachers, and especially administrators, within smaller and rural communities is heightened, which can, as Lamkin (2006, 22) notes, "preclude many opportunities for privacy and for confidentiality" that exist in urban areas where social relationships are less dense. Moreover, rural school leaders are far more frequently required to assume community outreach roles and hone community relationship-building skills in ways that are less common within urban settings (Harmon, Gordanier, Henry, and George 2007). Despite the complex set of skills needed to address the multiple responsibilities facing rural educators, rural school districts have disproportionate difficulty in attracting, retaining, and offering competitive salaries to teachers and other employees, challenges only increased by the lower professional status associated with practice within rural schools and districts (Lamkin 2006; Monk 2007).

Academic Achievement among Rural Students

While evidence supports the social and academic benefits of smaller school environments (Howley 1996; Kahne, Sporte, de la Torre, and Easton 2008), others argue that rural schools, by virtue of their decreased size and capacity, are less able to offer a breadth of curricular options in comparison to urban and suburban schools. In recent years, many rural schools have attempted to mitigate this challenge by using technology for distance education. While connectivity is no longer as significant of an issue for rural schools as it was even a decade ago, many rural schools still face challenges in distance education due to other barriers including funding for technology, scheduling, and implementation (Hannum, Irvin, Banks, and Farmer 2009).

Overall, however, recent data show that rural schools tend to perform relatively well in academic assessments in comparison to their urban and suburban counterparts (Fan and Chen 1999; Provasnik et al. 2007). The National Assessment of Educational Progress (NAEP) is the foremost nationally representative academic assessment at the primary and secondary levels, and provides a uniform metric of student achievement. In both reading and mathematics assessments at fourth and eighth grade levels, rural students on average outperform their counterparts in both cities and towns. Dropout and graduation rates show similar patterns: dropout rates are highest and graduation rates lowest in city schools, while suburban schools yield the lowest dropout rates and share the highest graduation rates along with schools in rural remote areas (Provasnik et al. 2007).

While rural schools overall compare favorably with their counterparts elsewhere, rural student achievement and academic outcomes vary widely across different rural places. In Table 28.1 for example, among the ten states with the highest proportions of rural students, graduation rates range from over 95 percent in South Dakota to slightly over 63 percent in Mississippi. Johnson and colleagues (2010), in a study of the 616 most economically disadvantaged school districts across fifteen southern states, note that within these disadvantaged districts the graduation rate is only about 60 percent and the lowest performing schools are disproportionately likely to serve children of color. However, they also find that the school districts with the highest academic outcomes tend to be the smallest in size, consistent with other research suggesting the social and academic benefits of smaller school environments for economically disadvantaged students (Howley 1996).

Although rural schools as a whole do comparatively well in fostering academic achievement, a body of work has suggested the ways in which a number of factors tend to depress the postsecondary educational aspirations of rural youth, including local place attachment, family background, limited proximity to higher education institutions, and the perceived limited rural use-value of postsecondary degrees (Gibbs 1998; Hektner 1995; Howley, Harmon, and Leopold 1996; McGrath, Swisher, Elder, and Conger 2001; Sherman and Sage 2011; Turley 2011). In an analysis of rural-non-rural differences in postsecondary enrollment and college degree completion using data from the National Educational Longitudinal Study (NELS), Byun, Meece, and Irvin (2012) found that suburban students were 61 percent more likely than rural students to earn a bachelor's degree and students from urban backgrounds were 106 percent more likely to earn a bachelor's degree. Only 23.3 percent of rural residents aged twenty-five and older have a bachelor's degree or higher as compared with nearly a third of adults in city and suburban areas (Table 28.2).

Schooling can easily be perceived ambivalently by rural youth, but also by educators and community members who recognize the ways in which "successful" schooling may result in siphoning off their best and brightest for life beyond the rural home community (Hektner 1995; Sherman and Sage 2011), a process by which local human and fiscal resources end up, in effect, subsidizing the development of places elsewhere. As Michael Corbett (2007, 18) notes, "continued schooling in rural communities is a different order of decision for the young people who live there, and it represents taking the first steps toward severing important ties to place, community and family."

While these are dilemmas that are not easily overcome, rural community colleges, where they exist, provide one possibility for rural postsecondary attainment, offering more cost-effective educational alternatives that are closer to home, are more flexibly responsive to local community contexts and employment opportunities, and are therefore more likely to engage as active partners in creating and sustaining rural communities. Others have suggested ways in which postsecondary institutions can engage more effectively and deliberately in rural high school student outreach (McDonough and Gildersleeve 2010). More broadly, increasing rural student postsecondary access and attainment and simultaneously strengthening rural communities will require strategic partnerships at local and regional levels. Connections between higher education institutions and, at the local level, partnerships between school districts, career and technical institutes, businesses, and local governments will better align affordable postsecondary training and education with existing and emerging economic opportunities in rural America (Eppley 2009; Harmon and Schafft 2009), thereby lessening the extent to which higher education represents a permanent one-way ticket out of home communities for rural students.

Rural Education and Poverty

Nonmetropolitan poverty rates have consistently been higher than those in metropolitan areas (Brown and Schafft 2011; Jensen, McLaughlin, and Slack 2003), and therefore many rural schools are disproportionately likely to educate children from economically disadvantaged backgrounds. Streams and colleagues (2011) note that among the ten states with the highest incidence of poverty, 36 percent of students and 57 percent of school districts were located in rural areas. Many rural schools serving the highest percentages of disadvantaged students are located in areas with historical legacies of discrimination and exclusion. High-poverty rural schools often have especially limited administrative capacity, and typically face particularly pronounced problems with teacher recruitment and retention. Poverty directly affects student academic outcomes, but high-need students from poverty backgrounds can also represent unmanageably high costs if they require mandated special services, adding additional burdens to resource-strapped schools.

Title 1 of the Elementary and Secondary Education Act is the primary federal program designed to provide additional resources to schools serving economically disadvantaged students, with funds dedicated toward improving student academic achievement. However, many rural education advocates have protested that the formula governing the disbursement of Title 1 funds is weighted in ways that significantly disadvantage rural schools. Through Title 1, district disadvantage is assessed through poverty concentration as measured by either the percentage of students in poverty or by the total numbers of poor students. This bifurcated assessment system, however, systematically works to the benefit of very large districts while it disadvantages small and rural districts, in addition to many small city high poverty districts. Marty Strange (2011, 15) notes, for example, that in Virginia, "Fairfax County, with a 6 percent poverty rate, gets more Title 1 money for each disadvantaged student than rural Virginia's Lee County Public Schools with its 33 percent poverty rate." Because of this, organizations such as the Rural School and Community Trust and the Children's Defense Fund have strongly advocated for changes to the Title 1 funding formula. They suggest that funds be either (a) distributed according to a formula that only takes into account the percentage of disadvantaged students rather than total numbers, or (b) selectively uses the existing formula in large districts with concentrated numbers of disadvantaged students (Rural School and Community Trust 2011)

The Rural and Low Income School program (RLIS) is another federal initiative that provides support to efforts within rural schools to meet adequate yearly progress (AYP) goals as specified under No Child Left Behind (NCLB). RLIS funds can be allocated in a number of different ways, including teacher recruitment and retention, professional development, and technology support. RLIS funds target rural school districts[3] in which 20 percent or more of the children served by the district come from families with incomes below the poverty line. In the 2009 to 2010 fiscal year, $86 million was disbursed to nearly 1,500 school districts in forty-one states, averaging about $57,000 per district (Magill, Hallberg, Hinojosa, and Reeves 2010).

Between 1999 to 2000 and 2008 to 2009, poverty in rural schools (as measured by student eligibility for the federally subsidized school meal program) rose nearly ten percentage points to 41 percent, with rural poverty rates rising in all but six states, the most significant increases concentrated particularly in the South and Southwest (Strange et al. 2012). While federal programs such as Title 1 and the RLIS provide critically important resources to support rural schools, poverty has been a particularly pernicious challenge for many rural schools and communities. Because of this, it is particularly important to take funding equity and access seriously, ensuring not only that resources flow to where they are most needed, but also that low capacity schools and districts are not further disadvantaged because of their relatively diminished administrative capacity to secure competitive grant funding from federal and other sources.

Federal Policy Issues in Rural Education

The last three decades have witnessed subtle but major discursive shifts regarding the purpose of schooling in America, with increasing emphases on school choice, privatization, standardization of curricula and assessment, student testing outcomes, and the creation of human capital in the form of a labor force able to flexibly and effectively respond to the shifting needs of a global economy (Garrison 2012; Ravitch 2010; Theobald, 2009). It is almost impossible to discuss the status of current education policy without referencing *A Nation at Risk*, the 1983 report that successfully reframed the educational policy debate in economic terms around the failure of America's schools to adequately prepare the nation's youth to compete with their counterparts in the rest of the world (Labaree 2011). Using language that positioned the alleged failings of the US educational system as nothing less than a national security issue, the report issued by the National Commission on Excellence in Education (1983, 7) stated, "if an unfriendly foreign power had attempted to impose on America the mediocre educational performance that exists today, we might as well have viewed it as an act of war." By intertwining the fate of the economy with the success of

America's youth, *A Nation at Risk* traced a direct line from the classroom to the global economy, setting the stage for future educational initiatives emphasizing privatization, accountability through standardized assessments, and business models of education. These included influential federal legislation and reports such as 1994's *Goals 2000*, the Reading Excellence Act of 1998, and the Education Sciences Reform Act of 2001, all of which to varying degrees emphasized standardization and accountability measures in education as critical components of securing national economic prosperity (Eppley 2009).

Scholars have pointed to the crucial role that the introduction of the most recent re-authorization of the Elementary and Secondary Education Act of 1965, the NCLB Act of 2002, has had on still further aligning the organization of education with neoliberal priorities (Hursh 2007; Labaree 2011; Schafft, Killeen, and Morrissey 2010). The passage of NCLB represented an unprecedented shift in the formal relationship of the federal government to state-run education systems, tying the federal funds upon which states had come to depend since the inception of ESEA to new proficiency benchmarks that states were to create and measure through their own standardized assessments. These benchmarks were designed for all schools to reach 100 percent proficiency by 2014 (US Department of Education 2001). The "highly qualified teacher" provision originating with NCLB requires that all teachers have licensure and a bachelor's degree in every subject that they teach, a requirement creating particular difficulties for rural schools, where teachers often are responsible for teaching multiple subjects or grade levels (Eppley 2009).[4] While the receipt of federal dollars served as the incentive for state compliance with these new requirements, NCLB accountability measures were accompanied by punishments for schools failing to meet the appropriate yearly proficiency benchmarks. These punishments created the opportunity for "choice" for students in the nation's lowest performing schools through allowing them to transfer to other, higher performing schools (US Department of Education 2001).

A key feature of neoliberalism is the belief that social goods are most effectively attained through market mechanisms supported by the systematic development of databases supporting decision-making within that marketplace (Engel 2000; Harvey 2005). The increasingly favorable reception of value-added scores that purport to measure the unique contributions of individual teachers to student test scores as a new kind of public accountability tool represent a concrete step in the direction of such an educational marketplace. In small schools with small class sizes, such value-added measures of teacher performance based, in part or in whole, on test scores may be more sensitive to random variation due to factors the teacher is unable to control (Brown and Schafft 2011; Goetz 2005).

Therefore, their publication in newspapers, recently ruled constitutional in New York, has many implications for teachers in small communities who already face heightened levels of personal scrutiny as compared to their suburban and urban peers (McClelland 1997). Worrisome also is the prospect that impoverished students may be doubly disadvantaged if teachers attempt to avoid formal responsibility for students with ascribed characteristics known to be associated with lower achievement scores (Nichols and Berliner 2007; Schafft, Killeen, and Morrissey 2010).

Just as NCLB "disciplines" schools to enforce compliance with federal policies and priorities, Schafft, Killeen, and Morrissey (2010) draw comparisons between NCLB and the imposition of Structural Adjustment Policies (SAPs) by the World Bank and the International Monetary Fund on debt-burdened developing countries. Introducing a series of structural changes in exchange for debt relief, in most cases, these policy measures have included extreme austerity for public institutions, the privatization of nationalized industry, and tax breaks and other subsidies to encourage and enforce neoliberal reform (Harvey 2005; McMichael 2012). "Similar to structural adjustment policies imposed on developing countries by global lending institutions," Schafft and colleagues (2010, 109) write:

> NCLB imposes market logic and disciplinary measures to reduce or eliminate "inefficiencies" that threaten academic achievement. With achievement as the "bottom line," the operating assumption is that educational improvement can be attained through regulative and normative measures designed to increase accountability and, by extension, improve institutional and academic performance. Schools failing to make AYP receive technical assistance and must provide school choice for those students who opt to attend other "non-failing" schools. Continued failure to reach AYP results in increased sanctions and threat of further "structural adjustment," which may ultimately involve school closure and privatization through the reconstitution of public schools as charter schools.

Ten years into life under NCLB, the implications of this "structural adjustment" to public education continue to unfold. In 2010, the Obama administration introduced its plan for the long overdue reauthorization of NCLB. The Blueprint for Reform, as the plan is called, is touted by the administration as introducing increased flexibility and using inducements for success rather than punishments for failure (Duncan 2012). However, the punitive measures that are laid out for low-performing schools are left intact, and in many ways the proposed plans deepen and extend the neoliberal underpinnings first introduced in NCLB. The Blueprint for Reform calls for even greater dependence on standardized assessments to measure student (and increasingly teacher and principal) performance, the adoption of nation-wide curricular standards, and greater inducements for the introduction of private-public partnerships at the local level (US Department of Education 2010).

Rural areas, with fewer people, geographically dispersed populations, and more limited political influence, have unique difficulties when the provision of public services is left to market choice (Brown and Schafft 2011). Federal education dollars under the Blueprint for Reform are to be allocated to states who will then be allowed to reserve certain levels of these funds for low-income districts; the remaining funds will be open for competitive grant proposals from individual districts (US Department of Education 2010). However, states with large rural areas note the difficulty of building state-wide education policy around the other Blueprint for Reform criteria, which seem to assume densely settled populations able to support these measures. Under-developed municipal and administrative capacity disadvantages rural districts left to compete with more densely populated areas for resources (Lamkin 2006). For all of these reasons, the trend toward privatized solutions for educational inequities over the strengthening of schools as civic institutions within a democratic society contains a number of particularly worrisome aspects for rural schools.

Conclusions

Building collaborations and forging new connections between rural community development and local educational provision will be critical for meeting the multiple social and economic challenges that will undoubtedly be faced by rural people, their schools, and their communities as the twenty-first century unfolds. This will be no small task given current national-level education policy environments, which tend to favor one-size-fits-all solutions based principally around national and global, rather than local and regional, priorities.

Within such a policy environment, research on the diverse particularities of rural districts, schools, and communities itself becomes an act of advocacy. Understanding the strengths, constraints, and connections between local vitality and schooling across the full breadth of rural settings does not necessarily lend itself to the intervention-based research designs focused on scale or to the creation of more accurate measures of educational effectiveness currently favored by federal education policy informed by neoliberal principles. However, moving away from a focus on scale in order to better understand the strengths and constraints of partnerships within local contexts will better help both educators and policy makers to create more responsive policies and programs that go beyond "a singular focus on student achievement to a blended community and educational leadership strategy that takes as a fundamental assumption that ensuring the academic success of students, on the one hand, and the social and economic vitality of the rural community, on the other, are not mutually *exclusive* priorities, but are indeed deeply and inextricably connected" (Harmon and Schafft 2009, 8).

We have discussed some of the particular dilemmas of accountability for those rural educators who intuitively understand the fundamentally entwined relationship between the well-being of rural schools and the communities they serve (Schafft 2010), including consolidation in the face of state and federal budget austerity, out-migration and the recent institution of "college and career-ready" standards, and measures of success or benchmarks of teacher effectiveness that remain insensitive to small schools, class sizes, and community demographics. The issues presented suggest the question of how educators should interpret the meaning of "accountability" as they attempt to strike a balance between state and national policy mandates versus community needs, priorities and lived experiences. As Lobao notes in the introduction to this section, understanding the complexities of the relationships between institutionalized forces and local well-being is critical for informing policy and thus sensitivity to these struggles of accountability should be addressed. Furthermore, state- and national-level policy makers who are seriously interested in enhancing the vitality of rural communities would do well to similarly recognize the rural school-community connection, understanding the complex role education and schooling might play in a broader policy vision for people and communities across rural America.

Notes

1 Some of the most urbanized states with the lowest percentages of rural students also have some of the largest *total* populations of rural students. For example, California, with only 4.5 percent of its students enrolled in rural schools, nonetheless has nearly 279,000 rural students. Texas similarly falls below the national average with 18 percent rural students. Yet, that 18 percent accounts for over 834,000 students in total (Strange et al. 2012).

2 Since 2006, the National Center for Education Statistics (NCES) has used a twelve-category classification system to identify the location of schools and school districts along the urban-rural continuum, using city, suburban, town, and rural classifications, each with three sub-classifications to denote relative size. For more information on definitions and classifications, see http://nces.ed.gov/ccd/rural_locales.asp.

3 Under the RLIS program, "rural" school districts are those that receive an NCES locale code of six (small town), seven (rural), or eight (rural area near an urban area).

4 "Rural flexibility" provisions give teachers in school districts qualifying for the US Department of Education's Small Rural Schools Achievement (SRSA) program extra time to attain

highly qualified status. However, SRSA districts are those with fewer than 600 students or located in counties with less than ten persons per square mile. Further, all schools in the qualified districts must be located in communities with less than 2,500 residents. These criteria effectively exclude nearly three-quarters of all rural school districts. Those qualified are located mostly within the Midwest and Great Plains regions.

References

Aud, Susan, Sidney Wilkinson-Flicker, Paul Kristapovich, Amy Rathbun, Xiaolei Wang, and Jijun Zhang. 2013. *The Condition of Education 2013.* Washington, DC: National Center for Education Statistics.

Bauch, Patricia. 2001. "School-Community Partnerships in Rural Schools: Leadership, Renewal, and a Sense of Place." *Peabody Journal of Education* 76 (2): 204–21. http://dx.doi.org/10.1207/S15327930pje7602_9.

Bauman, Zygmunt. 1998. *Globalization: The Human Consequences.* New York: Columbia University Press.

Brasington, David M. 2004. "House Prices and the Structure of Local Government: An Application of Spatial Statistics." *Journal of Real Estate Finance and Economics* 29 (2): 211–31. http://dx.doi.org/10.1023/B:REAL.0000035311.59920.74.

Brown, David L., and Kai A. Schafft. 2011. *Rural People and Communities in the 21st Century: Resilience and Transformation.* Malden, MA: Polity Press.

Byun, Soo-yong, Judith L. Meece, and Matthew J. Irvin. 1 June 2012. "Rural-Nonrural Disparities in Postsecondary Educational Attainment Revisited." *American Educational Research Journal* 49 (3): 412–37. http://dx.doi.org/10.3102/0002831211416344. Medline:24285873.

Corbett, Michael. 2007. *Learning to Leave: The Irony of Schooling in a Coastal Community.* Halifax: Fernwood Publishing.

Duncan, Arne. 2012. "Escaping the Constraints of No Child Left Behind." *Washington Post,* 8 January. http://www.ed.gov/blog/2012/01/after-10-years-it's-time-for-a-new-nclb.

Elder, Glen H., Jr., and Rand D. Conger. 2000. *Children of the Land: Adversity and Success in Rural America.* Chicago: University of Chicago Press.

Engel, Michael. 2000. *The Struggle for the Control of Public Education: Market Ideology vs. Democratic Values.* Philadelphia: Temple University Press.

Eppley, Karen. 2009. "Rural Schools and the Highly Qualified Teacher Provision: A Critical Policy Analysis." *Journal of Research in Rural Education* 24: 1–11.

Falk, William W., Michael D. Schulman, and Ann R. Tickamyer. 2003. "Empirical Realities, Theoretical Lessons, and Political Implications." In *Communities of Work,* ed. William W. Falk, Michael D. Schulman, and Ann R. Tickamyer, 419–29. Athens: Ohio University Press.

Fan, Xitao, and Michael J. Chen. 1999. "Academic Achievement of Rural School Students: A Multi-Year Comparison with their Peers in Suburban and Urban Schools." *Journal of Research in Rural Education* 15 (1): 31–46.

Garrison, Jim. 2012. "Individuality, Equality, and Creative Democracy—The Task before Us." *American Journal of Education* 118 (3): 369–79. http://dx.doi.org/10.1086/664739.

Gibbs, Robert. 1998. "College Completion and Return Migration among Rural Youth." In *Rural Education and Training in the New Economy: The Myth of the Rural Skills Gap*, ed. R.M. Gibbs, P.L. Swaim, and R. Teixeira, 61–80. Ames: Iowa State University Press.

Goetz, Stephan. 2005. "Random Variation in Student Performance by Class Size: Implications of NCLB in Pennsylvania." *Journal of Research in Rural Education* 20: 1–8.

Gray, Mary L. 2009. *Out in the Country: Youth, Media, and Queer Visibility in Rural America*. New York: New York University Press.

Groenke, Susan L., and Jan Nespor. 2010. "'The Drama of Their Daily Lives': Racist Language and Struggles over the Local in a Rural High School." In *Rural Education for the Twenty-First Century: Identity, Place, and Community in a Globalizing World*, ed. Kai A. Schafft and Alecia Youngblood Jackson, 51–71. University Park: Penn State University Press.

Gruenewald, David A., and Gregory A. Smith. 2008. "Making Room for the Local." In *Place-Based Education in the Global Age*, ed. David A. Gruenewald and Gregory A. Smith, xiii–xxiii. New York: Lawrence Erlbaum Associates.

Hannum, Wallace H., Matthew J. Irvin, Jonathan B. Banks, and Thomas W. Farmer. 2009. "Distance Education Use in Rural Schools." *Journal of Research in Rural Education* 24 (3): 1–15.

Harmon, Hobart L., Janna Gordanier, Lana Henry, and Ann George. 2007. "Changing Teacher Practices in Rural Schools." *Rural Educator* 28 (2): 8–12.

Harmon, Hobart L., and Kai A. Schafft. 2009. "Rural School Leadership for Collaborative Community Development." *Rural Educator* 30 (3): 4–9.

Harvey, David. 2005. *A Brief History of Neoliberalism*. New York: Oxford University Press.

Hektner, Joel M. 1995. "When Moving up Implies Moving Out: Rural Adolescent Conflict in the Transition to Adulthood." *Journal of Research in Rural Education* 11: 3–14.

Howley, Craig B. 1996. "Compounding Disadvantage: The Effects of School and District Size on Student Achievement in West Virginia." *Journal of Research in Rural Education* 12: 25–32.

Howley, C.B., Hobart L. Harmon, and Gregory D. Leopold. 1996. "Rural Scholars or Bright Rednecks? Aspirations for a Sense of Place among Rural Youth in Appalachia." *Journal of Research in Rural Education* 12 (3): 150–60.

Hursh, David. 2007. "Assessing No Child Left Behind and the Rise of Neoliberal Education Policies." *American Educational Research Journal* 44 (3): 493–518. http://dx.doi.org/10.3102/0002831207306764.

Jensen, Leif, Diane K. McLaughlin, and Tim Slack. 2003. "Rural Poverty: The Persisting Challenge." In *Challenges for Rural America in the Twenty-First Century*, ed. David L. Brown and Louis E. Swanson, 118–31. University Park: The Pennsylvania State University Press.

Johnson, Jerry, Marty Strange, and Karen Madden. 2010. *The Rural Dropout Problem: An Invisible Achievement Gap*. Arlington, VA: The Rural School and Community Trust.

Kahne, Joseph E., Susan E. Sporte, Marisa de la Torre, and John Q. Easton. 2008. "Small High Schools on a Larger Scale: The Impact of School Conversions in Chicago." *Educational Evaluation and Policy Analysis* 30 (3): 281–315. http://dx.doi.org/10.3102/0162373708319184.

Labaree, David. 2011. "Consuming the Public School." *Educational Theory* 61 (4): 381–94. http://dx.doi.org/10.1111/j.1741-5446.2011.00410.x.

Lamkin, Marcia L. 2006. "Challenges and Changes Faced by Rural Superintendents." *Rural Educator* 28 (1): 17–24.

Lyson, Thomas A. 2002. "What Does a School Mean to a Community? Assessing the Social and Economic Benefits of Schools to Rural Villages in New York." *Journal of Research in Rural Education* 17 (3): 131–7.

Magill, Kathleen, Kelly Hallberg, Trisha Hinojosa, and Cynthia Reeves. 2010. *Evaluation of the Implementation of the Rural and Low Income School Program: Final Report.* Washington, DC: US Department of Education.

McClelland, Jerry. 1997. "Knowing and Being Known: Parent's Experiences with Rural Schools." *Journal of Research in Rural Education* 13: 108–16.

McDonough, Patricia M., and R. Evely Gildersleeve. 2010. "The Golden Cage of Rural College Access: How Higher Education Can Respond to Rural Life." In *Rural Education for the Twenty-First Century: Identity, Place and Community in a Globalizing World*, ed. Kai A. Schafft and Alecia Youngblood Jackson, 191–209. University Park: The Pennsylvania State University Press.

McGrath, Daniel J., Raymond R. Swisher, Glen H. Elder, Jr., and Rand D. Conger. 2001. "Breaking New Ground: Diverse Routes to College in Rural America." *Rural Sociology* 66 (2): 244–67. http://dx.doi.org/10.1111/j.1549-0831.2001.tb00066.x.

McMichael, Phillip. 2012. *Development and Social Change: A Global Perspective.* London: Pine Forge Press.

Monk, David. Spring 2007. "Recruiting and Retaining High-Quality Teachers in Rural Areas." *Future of Children* 17 (1): 155–74. http://dx.doi.org/10.1353/foc.2007.0009. Medline:17407927.

National Commission on Excellence in Education. 1983. *A Nation at Risk.* Washington, DC: Government Printing Office.

Nichols, Sharon L., and David C. Berliner. 2007. *How High-Stakes Testing Corrupts America's Schools.* Cambridge, MA: Harvard Education Press.

Provasnik, Stephen, Angelina KewalRamani, Mary McLaughlin Coleman, Lauren Gilbertson, Will Herring, and Qingshu Xie. 2007. *The Status of Education in Rural America.* Washington, DC: US Department of Education. http://dx.doi.org/10.1037/e665642007-001.

Ravitch, Diane. 2010. *The Death and Life of the Great American School System.* New York: Basic Books.

Rural School and Community Trust. 2011. "Formula Fairness Campaign: Number Weighting Remedies." Accessed 13 June 2012. http://www.formulafairness.com/number_weighting_remedies.

Schafft, Kai A. 2010. "Economics, Community and Rural Education: Rethinking the Nature of Accountability in the Twenty-First Century." *Rural Education for the Twenty-First Century: Identity, Place and Community in a Globalizing World*, ed. Kai A. Schafft and Alecia Youngblood Jackson, 275–90. University Park: The Pennsylvania State University Press.

Schafft, Kai A., and Hobart L. Harmon. 2011. "Schools and Community Development." In *Introduction to Community Development: Theory, Practice and Service-Learning*, ed. Jerry W. Robinson and Gary Paul Green, 245–60. Los Angeles: Sage.

Schafft, Kai A., Kieran M. Killeen, and John Morrissey. 2010. "The Challenges of Student Transiency for Rural Schools and Communities in the Era of No Child Left Behind." In *Rural Education for the Twenty-First Century*, ed. Kai A. Schafft and Alecia Youngblood-Jackson, 95–114. University Park: The Pennsylvania State University Press.

Sell, Randall S., and F. Larry Leistritz. 1997. "Socioeconomic Impacts of School Consolidation on Host and Vacated Communities." *Journal of the Community Development Society* 28 (2): 186–205. http://dx.doi.org/10.1080/15575339709489782.

Sherman, Jennifer, and Rayna Sage. 2011. "Sending off All Your Good Treasures: Rural Schools, Brain Drain, and Community Survival in the Wake of Economic Collapse." *Journal of Research in Rural Education* 26: 1–14.

Shucksmith, Mark, David L. Brown, and Jo Vergunst. 2012. "Constructing the Rural-Urban Interface: Place Still Matters in a Highly Mobile Society." In *Rural Transformations and Rural Policies in the US and UK*, ed. Mark Shucksmith, David L. Brown, Sally Shortall, Jo Vergunst, and Mildred E. Warner, 287–303. New York: Routledge.

Sipple, John W., and Brian O. Brent. 2008. "Challenges and Strategies Associated with Rural School Settings." In *Handbook of Research in Education Finance and Policy*, ed. H.F. Ladd and E.B. Fiske, 612–30. New York: Routledge.

Strange, Marty. 2011. "Finding Fairness for Rural Students." *Phi Delta Kappan* 92 (6): 8–15.

Strange, Marty, Jerry Johnson, Daniel Showalter, and Robert Klein. 2012. *Why Rural Matters 2011–12*. Washington, DC: Rural School and Community Trust.

Streams, Meg, J.S. Butler, Joshua Cowen, Jacob Fowles, and Eugenia F. Toma. 2011. "School Finance Reform: Do Equalized Expenditures Imply Equalized Teacher Salaries?" *Education Finance and Policy* 6 (4): 508–36. http://dx.doi.org/10.1162/EDFP_a_00046.

Theobald, Paul. 2009. *Education Now: How Rethinking America's Past Can Change Its Future*. Boulder, CO: Paradigm Publishers.

Turley, Ruth N. Lopez. 2011. "College Proximity: Mapping Access to Opportunity." *Sociology of Education* 82 (2): 116–46.

US Department of Education. 2001. No Child Left Behind Act. Washington, DC: Government Printing Office.

US Department of Education. 2010. *Blueprint for Reform*. Washington, DC: Government Printing Office.

Vanderbeck, Robert M. 2008. "Inner-City Children, Country Summers: Narrating American Childhood and the Geographies of Whiteness." *Environment & Planning A* 40 (5): 1132–50. http://dx.doi.org/10.1068/a39192.

Wilkinson, Kenneth P. 1991. *The Community in Rural America*. Middleton, WI: Social Ecology Press.

Zekeri, Andrew A., Kenneth P. Wilkinson, and Craig R. Humphrey. 1994. "Past Activeness, Solidarity, and Local Development Efforts." *Rural Sociology* 59 (2): 216–35. http://dx.doi.org/10.1111/j.1549-0831.1994.tb00530.x.

CHAPTER 29

Work in Rural America in the Era of Globalization

Tim Slack

Introduction

The guiding theme of this volume is the need to understand the lives of rural Americans in the context of a globalizing world. Despite nostalgic notions to the contrary, small town and rural America has never been somehow isolated and/or disconnected from the larger social and economic forces shaping broader society. For example, in the late nineteenth and early twentieth century, when the industrial revolution drove great social change, rural areas played a prominent role by providing much of the labor and raw materials that fueled industrialization. As labor demand shifted from farms to factories, people migrated from the countryside to cities in search of work, ultimately tipping the population balance of the nation from rural to urban. The intertwined processes of industrialization and urbanization led to changes in the national character of work and residence that transformed rural and urban life alike (Falk, Schulman, and Tickamyer 2003). Today, the lives and livelihoods of rural Americans are very much embedded in the process of globalization, the dominant force of social change in the current era.

In this chapter, I provide a comparative treatment of issues facing those who work and earn a living in small town and rural America at the outset of the twenty-first century, contextualized within the broader process of globalization. I begin with an overview of structural changes in employment across time and space from the mid-twentieth century to the present. I then provide an original descriptive analysis that carries the statistical record on employment and employment hardship forward through the first decade of the twenty-first century, comparing the circumstances of metropolitan and nonmetropolitan workers. I conclude with attention to the importance of informal work as a rural livelihood strategy.

Structural Changes in Employment across Time and Space

In setting the context for this section of the volume, Lobao argues that understanding the interrelationships between economy, community, and quality of life requires researchers to wrestle with the interrelated issues of: (1) economic structure and changes in industries, firms, and jobs; (2) the state at all levels; and (3) institutionalized relationships linking key social actors and their implications for power over societal resources. Her essay underscores the importance of conceptualizing social change processes as unfolding over time and space. Related to this point are calls for attention to comparative inequality between relational spatial structures (e.g., rural versus urban) characterized by variable degrees of power and opportunity (Lobao, Hooks, and Tickamyer 2007; Tickamyer 2000). The long tradition in rural sociology of comparative regional research and attention to middle-range territorial units positions the discipline to make unique contributions to the social-scientific understanding of spatial inequality in the emerging era (Lobao 2004). This includes addressing questions related to uneven development and the spatial division of labor (Lobao et al. 2007).

Change in the National Labor Market Context

In her framing essay to this section of the volume, Lobao suggests that the critical political economy perspective provides an important framework for conceptualizing linkages between structural change and well-being across time and place. The touchstone of the political economic literatures is the historical stage spanning from 1945 to the early 1970s, termed the Fordist period. This stage of development saw US manufacturing rise to global dominance; expansion of the centralized Keynesian welfare state; a strong organized labor movement; dramatic improvements in the average standard of living; and declining inequality. But in the early 1970s, the nation's economic trajectory took a radical change of course in what has been dubbed the Great U-Turn (Harrison and Bluestone 1988). Inequality began to increase as the incomes of the very rich rose dramatically, while the incomes of the vast majority of Americans stagnated (Harrison and Bluestone 1988; Massey 2007; Morris and Western 1999). These trends have not gone unnoticed by the American public, as evidenced by the recent Occupy Movement with its slogan "We Are the 99%."

Trends in income inequality can be linked in part to globalization and attendant industrial restructuring in the latter decades of the twentieth century (Harrison and Bluestone 1988; Massey 2007; Morris and Western 1999). Restructuring changed the landscape of employment opportunities facing American workers in two key respects: by shifting from a goods-producing to a service-based economy (i.e., deindustrialization) and by increasing reliance on non-standard employment (i.e., temporary and contingent work) (Morris and Western 1999). While the manufacturing sector dominated in the decades that followed World War II, the service sector surpassed manufacturing in its employment share in the 1980s, and by the 1990s accounted for nearly all (more than 97 percent) of US job growth (Goodman and Steadman 2002). These changes have not only had implications for the kind of jobs American workers are performing, but also have contributed to bifurcation in terms of job quality (i.e., "good jobs" versus "bad jobs") given the displacement of manufacturing workers and polarized job quality within the service sector (e.g., healthcare versus food services) (Harrison and Bluestone 1988; Morris and Western 1999). Moreover, while some workers have benefited from more flexible employment relations (e.g., freelance professionals), most non-standard workers indicate they would prefer standard employment, a preference no doubt related to the fact that such workers are much more likely to earn low wages and lack fringe benefits (Kalleberg, Reskin, and Hudson 2000).

A hallmark of the Fordist era was strong labor unions, which provided a key institutional mechanism for protecting and promoting the economic interests of workers. However, union density fell steadily from a height of about 40 percent of the labor force in the mid-1950s to only about 10 percent by the turn of the century (Clawson and Clawson 1999). The processes of globalization and industrial restructuring have contributed to this decline due to the loss of manufacturing sector jobs where unions have traditionally been strongest. Other reasons lie within the labor movement itself, including a disproportionate focus on protecting industrial unionists in the face of deindustrialization, and less focus on organizing new members in emerging sectors (i.e., services). The United States is also unique among industrialized democracies for its level of employer hostility to organized labor, especially in the post-Fordist era (Clawson and Clawson 1999). The net result is that the fastest growing sectors of the economy, particularly the low-wage service sector, while ripe for organizing, are still largely nonunion (Bernstein 2004). That the Service Employees International Union (SEIU) is currently one of the largest and fastest growing unions in the country shows that the labor movement is doing better to capitalize on organizing opportunities in the service sector. However, contemporary battles between public sector unions and their detractors in states like Wisconsin and Ohio, and recent legislation in the union stronghold of Michigan to make it a Right to Work state, also demonstrate the persistent hostility to unionization.

These changes in the structure of the US economy have had especially detrimental consequences for workers with a high school education or less, and men with little education in particular (Bianchi 1995; Morris and Western 1999). In fact, the real earnings of all male workers has fallen since the 1970s, a trend that has led families to increase their labor supply in order to maintain their standard of living (Danziger and Gottschalk 1995). Coupled with evolving gender norms, this reality has played a major role in the tremendous increase in female labor force participation over the last fifty years (Danziger and Gottschalk 1995; Juhn and Potter 2006). In fact, by 2000, approximately two thirds of married couples with children were dual-earner households (Bureau of Labor Statistics 2002).

The policy discourse concerning social welfare programs also did an about-face with the onset of the post-Fordist era, shifting from a federal agenda aimed at eradicating poverty through government intervention (i.e., the War on Poverty) to one centered on reducing welfare dependency (Ellwood 1989; Mead 1992; Murray 1984). Analysts point to the ideologies of neoliberalism and market fundamentalism as being central in shifting the debate on poverty away from state intervention and toward the private market as the proper mechanism for dealing with poverty, sentiments that culminated in the welfare reform bill of 1996 (Somers and Block 2005). The guiding ideas behind this legislation were that the welfare system fostered dependency and that the best way to reduce poverty was to move people from "welfare to work." Welfare reform ended cash assistance as a federal entitlement and replaced it with a state block-grant program that imposes strict time limits on receipt and requires "work effort" in exchange for aid. In the wake of welfare reform, cash assistance caseloads have precipitously decreased and become a much less prominent component of the social safety net, while "work supports" (e.g., the Earned Income Tax Credit) have become increasingly important (Brookings Institution 2013).

Bringing the focus to the first decade of the twenty-first century, it is notable that this period has been characterized by both significant macroeconomic growth and decline. We began the 2000s in the midst of the longest continuous economic expansion in the post–World War II era (1991 to 2001, 120 months), and ended the decade with the worst downturn in the US economy since the Great Depression (2007 to 2009, eighteen months) (National Bureau of Economic Research 2012). Research demonstrates a clear counter-cyclical relationship between the state of the macroeconomy and economic well-being, but also shows that the benefits of growth can be offset by inequality if its rewards are disproportionately accrued by a few (Iceland 2003). The Great Recession stands out from others since World War II in its severity, including major labor market dislocations and wealth destruction (e.g., the housing bubble) (Grusky,

Western, and Wimer 2011). The magnitude of this contraction raises pressing questions about how the crisis has influenced social and economic cleavages across the country.

Importantly, none of the aforementioned processes are aspatial. Economic restructuring is fundamentally spatial, with jobs lost in some places and gained in others, as the regional identification of places like the Rust Belt and Silicon Valley well illustrates. Relatedly, union density is not spatially random. Rather, it has traditionally been greatest in industrial metro areas and in states where the legal framework is more conducive to labor organizing (i.e., Fair Share states) versus states where the law makes it is more difficult (i.e., Right to Work states). Devolution too is inherently spatial, as decision making transitions from centralized federal authorities to more local levels. And finally, economic growth and decline are spatial in nature, with prime examples being the uneven geography of job losses and the housing crisis during the Great Recession.

The Nonmetro Labor Market

The spatial nature of the processes outlined above lead to important questions concerning the circumstances of nonmetro workers in comparative perspective. Employment in rural America has long offered workers less protection from economic hardship compared to their urban counterparts (Brown and Hirschl 1995; Jensen, McLaughlin, and Slack 2003; Jensen et al. 1999; Lichter, Johnston, and McLaughlin 1994; Slack 2010; Slack and Jensen 2002; 2008). Impacts of economic restructuring are evidenced here, as research has shown rural workers to be more likely to be employed in non-standard jobs, where wages tend to be lower and fringe benefits meager or absent (McLaughlin and Coleman-Jensen 2008). Moreover, 86 percent of the counties in the United States characterized by very "low-employment"—places where less than 65 percent of prime working age adults are employed—are nonmetro (Economic Research Service 2005). Despite these labor market disadvantages, however, the nonmetro poor have also been shown to rely more heavily on income generated from employment and less on public assistance compared to the metro poor (Jensen and Eggebeen 1994; Lichter and Jensen 2002).

Many factors contribute to the disadvantages of nonmetro workers. For example, lower average educational levels put nonmetro workers at a disadvantage in the modern labor market, given the increasing premium being placed on credentialed human capital (Beaulieu and Mulkey 1995; Provasnik et al. 2007). But research also shows that nonmetro workers receive lower returns to the human capital endowments they possess, a factor that has been linked to selective out-migration (to metro locales) among more highly educated nonmetro residents (Domina 2006; McLaughlin and Perman 1991). Physical isolation, low population density, and the absence of economies of agglomeration can be location deterrents for firms, leading to a lack of economic diversification in many nonmetro labor markets. Less diverse local economies in turn limit employment options and opportunities for workers. According to the USDA's Economic Research Service (2008), 92 percent of the counties identified as "farming-dependent," 88 percent of the counties identified as "mining-dependent," 65 percent of the counties identified as "manufacturing-dependent," and 58 percent of the counties identified as "federal/state government-dependent" are nonmetro. In areas where the local economy is dependent on a specific industry, the impacts of economic restructuring can be devastating. This is underscored by research that shows nonmetro workers face a lower probability of finding a new job after being laid off (Hamrick 2001).

The research summarized above helps to illustrate how the social, political, and economic changes wrought by globalization intersect with space and other axes of inequality in the American labor market. In the following section, I provide an original comparative account of employment and employment hardship in nonmetro and metro areas during the first decade of the twenty-first century, bringing the statistical record forward to the current period.

Employment and Employment Hardship in Nonmetro Areas, 1999 to 2009

In this section, I compare the circumstances of nonmetro and metro workers over the years spanning 1999 to 2009. I draw on data from the country's most comprehensive national labor force survey, the March Current Population Survey (CPS). I analyze concatenated (linked) data files from the March CPS from 1999 to 2009 and examine the employment circumstances of all individuals aged eighteen to sixty-four years—those in the prime of their working years living in sampled households. The stratified cluster sampling design of the CPS necessitates the use of weights to produce reliable population estimates. In this analysis, I use the person weights divided by their means to yield weighted case sizes that are approximately equal to the CPS sample size.

Data for the share of employment across major industrial sectors in nonmetro and metro areas from 1999 to 2009 (available on request) indicate that employment in extractive industries and manufacturing and construction are disproportionately represented in nonmetro areas, while other sectors, most notably services, represent a greater share of jobs among metro workers. In light of the trends in economic restructuring being driven by globalization, it is notable that sectors that are more highly represented in nonmetro areas (extraction and manufacturing) are those in which the United States has witnessed steep declines in employment in the post–World War II era. In contrast, metro employment is more weighted toward sectors in which the nation has seen the most employment growth (i.e., services). There are exceptions within sectors, of course, but on balance this suggests one respect in which the employment prospects of nonmetro workers are being squeezed in the age of globalization.

An important aspect of worker well-being has to do with the types of economic hardship people face on the job. A key way to conceptualize employment hardship is as *underemployment*—the degree to which workers are *not* employed full-time (or at least the number of hours they wish to be working) at jobs that pay above-poverty-level wages. One of the most prominent methods used to measure underemployment is the Labor Utilization Framework (LUF). Drawing on the LUF measure developed by Clogg and Sullivan (Clogg 1979; Clogg and Sullivan 1983; Sullivan 1978), the operational states of underemployment that I utilize here are:

> *Discouraged* includes individuals who would like to be employed but are currently not working and did not look for work in the past four weeks due to discouragement with their job prospects (official measures do not define these workers as "in the labor force," as they are neither employed nor looking for work);
>
> *Unemployed* is consistent with the official definition and includes those not employed but who (a) have looked for work during the previous four weeks, or (b) are currently on lay off but expect to be called back to work;
>
> *Low hours* (or involuntary part-time) is consistent with the official definition of those who are working "part-time for economic reasons" (i.e., those employed less than thirty-five hours or more per week only because they cannot find full-time employment); and
>
> *Low income* (or working poor) includes full-time workers (i.e., those employed thirty-five or more hours per week) whose average weekly earnings in the previous year were less than 125 percent of the individual poverty threshold;

All other workers are defined as *adequately employed*, while those who are not employed and do not indicate a desire to be so are defined as *not in the labor force*. I do not include the latter group in my analysis.

Figure 29.1 shows the percentage of workers underemployed in nonmetro and metro areas from 1999 to 2009. These data reveal two important points. The first is that nonmetro underemployment has remained higher than metro

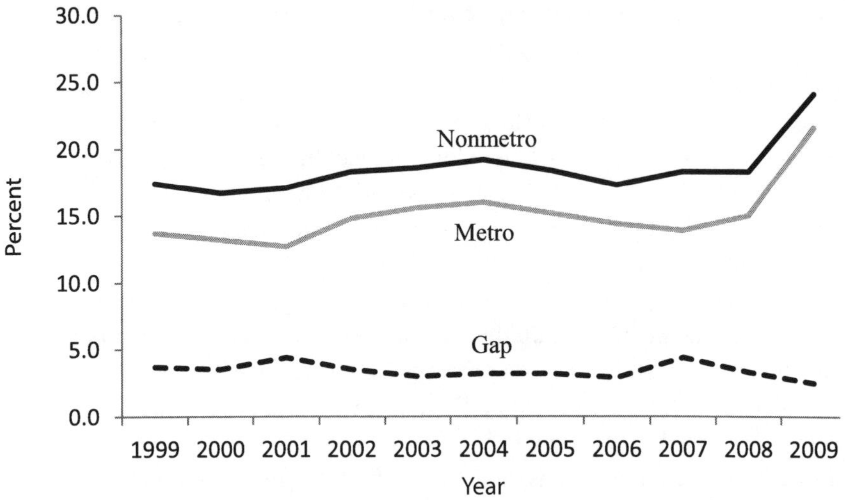

Figure 29.1. Underemployment by residence, 1999 to 2009. Source: March Current Population Surveys, 1999–2009.

underemployment in every single year of the last decade. Over this period, underemployment has averaged 18.5 percent in nonmetro areas compared to 15.1 percent in metro contexts, an average gap of 3.4 percent. The consistent disadvantage of nonmetro workers in terms of underemployment is in keeping with a trend that dates back to the 1960s when the government first began tracking these data (Slack and Jensen 2002). A second takeaway from Figure 29.1 is that underemployment is counter-cyclical—it climbs when the economy is weak and declines when the economy is strong. The impact of the Great Recession is clearly evident in this respect. Between 2008 and 2009, underemployment jumped by about six percentage points in both residential settings. By decade's end, nearly one quarter (24.1 percent) of all nonmetro workers and over one fifth (21.6 percent) of metro workers were underemployed.

Ancillary analyses (available on request) unpack underemployment by type for nonmetro and metro areas, respectively, for each year between 1999 and 2009. In nearly all years (exceptions being 2009 in nonmetro areas, and 2002 and 2009 in metro areas), those underemployed by low income comprise the largest share of the underemployed. Over the decade, underemployment by low income averaged 8.2 percent in nonmetro areas and 6.0 percent in metro areas. Unemployment is shown to be the second most common form of underemployment on average, centering around 5.8 percent and 5.3 percent in nonmetro and metro areas, respectively. In both residential contexts unemployment jumped to capture the largest share of the underemployed in 2009, reflecting the profound impact of the Great Recession on job loss. Underemployment by low hours is the third most common type of underemployment, averaging 3.9 percent in nonmetro areas and 3.1 percent in metro contexts. The only exception to this relative ranking is in metro areas in 2009, when involuntary part-time work jumped higher than low-income work during the downturn. Last, discouraged workers represent the smallest share of the underemployed, averaging 0.7 percent in both settings over the decade.

Again, the counter-cyclical nature of underemployment and the particular impact of the Great Recession are evident in these numbers. Notably, in 2009 in both residential settings, unemployment, low hours, and discouragement all rose, while low-income work actually ticked down. This no doubt reflects the impacts of layoffs and hour cutbacks across the American labor market during the downturn, including cutbacks among the working poor. A key point to note given the focus of this chapter is that underemployment for the three largest types of underemployment (low income, unemployment, and low hours) are higher in nonmetro than metro areas in every single year examined.

Table 29.1 describes the prevalence of underemployment in nonmetro and metro areas across key socio-demographic groups as well as the difference between residential settings on each indicator. The data here are pooled for the decade spanning 1999 to 2009. Overall, the same general pattern is evident across variables in each setting. The risk of underemployment varies greatly by age, with young workers facing the highest levels of underemployment, its prevalence falling as people enter the middle of their working years, and then ticking up again among those in the oldest age bracket. The numbers provide evidence of the continued advantages of men relative to women in the US labor market. Stark differences are observed between whites and non-whites, with major disadvantages realized among blacks and Hispanics, the nation's two largest minority groups. The data also show that immigrant status matters, with foreign-born noncitizens being subject to disproportionately high underemployment in comparison to other groups. The economic advantage of marriage (no doubt also somewhat a function of the relationship with age) is also evident in the data, with those who are married subject to lower underemployment than those who are not. Great differences exist across educational groups, underscoring the importance of educational attainment and credentials as arbiters of opportunity in the modern labor market. Labor union membership also clearly provides workers a significant form of protection from underemployment. There are notable differences across industrial sectors as well, with those in extractive industries (farming, forestry, fishing, mining) and trade

Table 29.1
Underemployment by residence and selected characteristics, 1999 to 2009

	Nonmetro	Metro	Gap
Total	18.6%	15.3%	3.3%
Age			
18–24	35.7	31.2	4.5
25–34	19.0	15.3	3.7
35–44	15.6	12.1	3.5
45–54	14.0	11.4	2.6
55–64	15.5	11.8	3.7
Gender			
Male	17.0	14.6	2.4
Female	20.4	16.2	4.2
Race/ethnicity			
Non-Hispanic white	16.9	12.4	4.5
Non-Hispanic black	29.7	22.1	7.6
Hispanic	25.6	23.2	2.4
Other	25.7	15.1	10.6
Nativity			
Third generation or higher	18.4	14.2	4.2
Second generation	18.4	16.0	2.4
Foreign-born, citizen	18.2	13.4	4.8
Foreign-born, noncitizen	25.9	24.3	1.6
Marital status			
Married	13.2	10.4	2.8
Never married	31.5	24.2	7.3
Divorced/separated	21.9	16.2	5.7
Widowed	22.5	17.8	4.7
Education			
Less than high school	33.7	32.6	1.1
High school	20.9	18.9	2.0
Some college	18.3	15.7	2.6
College degree or more	9.6	8.0	1.6
Labor union			
Union	4.7	4.7	0.0
Non-union	18.9	15.6	3.3
Industry			
Extractive	20.8	25.0	-4.2
Manufacturing and construction	17.5	15.0	2.5
Transportation and utilities	12.3	11.1	1.2
Wholesale and retail trade	21.7	18.2	3.5
Finance, insurance, and real estate	10.0	8.3	1.7
Services	18.0	14.5	3.5
Region			
Northeast	17.7	14.5	3.2
Midwest	17.4	15.2	2.2
South	19.3	15.0	4.3
West	20.3	16.5	3.8

Source: March Current Population Surveys, 1999–2009.

having particularly high rates of underemployment (among the former, those employed in agriculture, forestry, and fishing have been shown to be especially susceptible to underemployment, and among the latter, retail trade is known for low wages and hours) (McLaughlin, Gardner, and Lichter 1999; Slack and Jensen 2004). Finally, while regional differences in underemployment are not substantial, residents of the South and the West do appear to be at a slight disadvantage.

Given the comparative focus of this chapter, it is noteworthy that nonmetro workers are subject to higher underemployment than metro workers across nearly every indicator. Indeed, there are only two exceptions: (1) union membership appears to provide workers with equal protection from employment hardship in both settings; and (2) extractive workers realize a disadvantage in metro areas (this small number of workers likely faces a spatial mismatch).

In sum, the data presented here demonstrate that the long-run trend of more pronounced employment hardship among nonmetro workers has clearly carried through the first decade of the twenty-first century. The traditional challenges faced in small town and rural America in terms of returns to investments in human capital (i.e., lower returns and out-migration among educated youth) and obstacles to economic diversification stand to grow increasingly salient as globalization and related processes continue to play out in the new century.

Informal Work

While my primary focus in this chapter has been on work in the "formal economy"—economic production and exchange that takes place within the institutional and regulatory framework of the state—it is important to recognize that a great deal of work, that is for the most part licit, occurs outside of the boundaries of state governance in the "informal economy." The traditional Western discourse on economic development assumed that the informal economy was primarily a characteristic of less-developed nations, and that its importance would wane with the advance of capitalist development. However, research has shown that informal work continues to coexist alongside formal employment, even in advanced capitalist economies with highly formalized labor and consumption markets (Pahl 1984; Portes 1994; Portes, Castells, and Benton 1989). In fact, some analysts argue that the related processes of globalization, economic restructuring, and market deregulation are leading to a casualization of labor, and thus actually *increasing* the salience of informal work in the post-Fordist era (Castells and Portes 1989; Sassen 1991). To underscore this point, note that the definition of informal work hinges on the formalized institutional and regulatory frameworks that characterize the economy in a given historical moment, and neoliberal advocates have been busy scaling back the scope of state regulation and other formal institutional mechanisms (e.g., unions) viewed as restraining "free" and "open" markets.

Rural sociologists have made substantial contributions to a literature that elucidates the prominence of informal work across a wide range of contemporary rural contexts (Campbell, Spencer, and Amonker 1993; Duncan 1992; Edgcomb and Thetford 2004; Fitchen 1981; Jensen, Cornwell, and Findeis 1995; Levitan and Feldman 1991; Nelson 1999; Nelson and Smith 1999; Pickering 2000; Slack 2007a; 2007b; Slack and Jensen 2010; Tickamyer and Wood 1998; 2003; Ziebarth and Tigges 2003). While informal work is undertaken in both rural and urban settings, Slack and Jensen (2010) highlight a number of reasons that such activities may be unique in rural areas. For example, the lack of economic diversity in many rural areas, outlined earlier in this chapter, may motivate people to seek and provide informal alternatives for production and exchange not available in the formal market. In addition, some types of informal economic activities require access to natural resources that are only available, or at least more abundant, in the countryside (e.g., goods produced from hunting and fishing, or foraging for natural goods). Further, in light of the more restricted formal sector opportunities that rural workers face, informal work may be used as a substitute for or complement to formal sector employment. And, finally, because social networks and *enforceable trust* (norms of trust and reciprocity that are enforced by the threat of network exclusion for violators) are key factors undergirding participation in the informal economy, the strong bonds of kin, friends, and community often assumed to characterize rural social relations should facilitate engagement in informal work.

Nonetheless, despite the scholarly attention informal work has received to date, significant gaps continue to exist in our understanding of the patterns and dynamics that shape participation in the informal sector, including its relationship to formal labor supply and conventional predictors of formal labor market stratification, as well as how it varies across the rural-urban continuum. To the degree that globalization and neoliberalism are increasing the salience of the informal economy in the post-Fordist era, a challenge for rural sociologists in the coming decades will be to help fill the gaps in what is understood about the dynamics of informal work.

Conclusions

In this chapter, I provided a comparative treatment of issues facing those who work and earn a living in rural America. I began by outlining structural changes in employment across time and space, with attention to the transition from the Fordist era's structure of economic production, state intervention, and institutionalized social relationships to a post-Fordist era dominated by the forces of globalization and its attendant processes. I then provided new analysis that carries the statistical record on employment and employment hardship forward through the first decade of the twenty-first century. This descriptive account clearly demonstrated that the long-standing employment disadvantage of nonmetro workers relative to their metro counterparts has persisted through the century's first decade. Finally, I closed with attention to the importance of informal work as a rural livelihood strategy.

As Lobao outlines in her introductory essay for this section of the volume, a key challenge for stratification scholars in the era of globalization will be monitoring the manner in which economic, state, and institutionalized social actor relationships of the previous era erode, identifying new structures emerge in their wake, and deciphering the implications for existing social cleavages and new forms of inequality. For rural sociologists in particular, a pivotal task will be to articulate the way these processes play out in a comparative spatial perspective. As the structural changes brought on by globalization continue to unfold, gaining a critical understanding of the comparative advantages and disadvantages realized by rural people and places stands as a significant challenge, especially given the increasing interconnectedness and interdependence of rural and urban life (Lichter and Brown 2011).

Stepping up to this challenge will require staying true to rural sociology's long tradition of comparative regional research and attention to middle-range territorial units (Lobao 2004; Lobao et al. 2007), while simultaneously looking forward by applying cutting-edge theory and methods and, most importantly, asking timely questions. In terms of future research on rural work and workers, questions that probe at the intersection of uneven development, the spatial division of labor, and territorial inequality on the one hand, and issues including economic restructuring, devolution, technological change, the Great Recession, and informal work on the other hand, represent important lines of inquiry. In addition, multi-level research that does better to capture the embeddedness of workers and communities in broader social-spatial contexts is called for. Ultimately, globalization is driving an increasingly rapid pace of social change, meaning relevant directions for future research are emerging and evolving on a continual basis.

References

Beaulieu, Lionel J., and David Mulkey. 1995. *Investing in People: The Human Capital Needs of Rural America.* Boulder, CO: Westview Press.

Bernstein, Jared. 2004. "The Low-Wage Labor Market: Trends and Policy Implications." In *Work-Family Challenges for Low-Income Parents and Their Children*, ed. Ann C. Crouter and Alan Booth, 3–34. Mahwah, NJ: Lawrence Erlbaum.

Bianchi, Suzanne M. 1995. "Changing Economic Roles of Men and Women." In *State of the Union*, ed. Reynolds Farley, 107–54. New York: Russell Sage.

Brown, David L., and Thomas A. Hirschl. 1995. "Household Poverty in Rural and Metropolitan-Core Areas of the United States." *Rural Sociology* 60 (1): 44–66. http://dx.doi.org/10.1111/j.1549-0831.1995.tb00562.x.

Bureau of Labor Statistics. 2002. "Both Spouses Work in Most Married-Couple Families." US Department of Labor, Washington, DC. Accessed 16 July 2009. http://www.bls.gov/opub/ted/2001/apr/wk4/art02.htm.

Campbell, Rex R., J.C. Spencer, and R.G. Amonker. 1993. "The Reported and Unreported Missouri Ozarks: Adaptive Strategies of the People Left Behind." In *Forgotten Places: Uneven Development in Rural America*, ed. Thomas Lyson and William Falk, 30–52. Lawrence: University of Kansas Press.

Castells, Manuel, and Alejandro Portes. 1989. "World Underneath: The Origins, Dynamics, and Effects of the Informal Economy." In *The Informal Economy: Studies in Advanced and Less Developed Countries*, ed. Alejandro Portes, Manuel Castells, and Lauren A. Benton, 11–37. Baltimore: Johns Hopkins University Press.

Clawson, Dan, and Mary Ann Clawson. 1999. "What Has Happened to the U.S. Labor Movement? Union Decline and Renewal." *Annual Review of Sociology* 25 (1): 95–119. http://dx.doi.org/10.1146/annurev.soc.25.1.95.

Clogg, Clifford C. 1979. *Measuring Underemployment: Demographic Indicators for the United States.* New York: Academic Press. http://dx.doi.org/10.1016/B978-0-12-176560-6.50007-0.

Clogg, Clifford C., and Teresa A. Sullivan. 1983. "Labor Force Composition and Underemployment Trends, 1969–1980." *Social Indicators Research* 12 (2): 117–52. http://dx.doi.org/10.1007/BF00318232.

Danziger, Sheldon, and Peter Gottschalk. 1995. *America Unequal.* New York: Russell Sage.

Domina, Thurston. 2006. "What Clean Break?: Education and Nonmetropolitan Migration Patterns, 1989–2004." *Rural Sociology* 71 (3): 373–98. http://dx.doi.org/10.1526/003601106778070626.

Duncan, Cynthia M. 1992. "Persistent Poverty in Appalachia: Scarce Work and Rigid Stratification." In *Rural Poverty in America*, ed. Cynthia M. Duncan, 111–33. New York: Auburn House.

Economic Research Service. 2005. "County Typology Codes: Description and Maps." US Department of Agriculture, Washington, DC. Accessed 16 March 2012. http://www.ers.usda.gov/data-products/county-typology-codes/descriptions-and-maps.aspx#.UsrRMPRDvz8.

Edgcomb, Elaine L., and Tamra Thetford. 2004. "The Informal Economy: Making it in Rural America." Microenterprise Fund for Innovation, Effectiveness, Learning and Dissemination

(FIELD), The Aspen Institute, Washington, DC. Accessed 18 May 2006. http://www.fieldus.org/Publications/IE_Rural.pdf.

Ellwood, David T. 1989. "The Origins of 'Dependency': Choices, Confidence, or Culture?" *Focus (San Francisco, Calif.)* 120: 6–13.

Falk, William W., Michael D. Schulman, and Ann R. Tickamyer. 2003. "Introduction." In *Communities of Work: Rural Restructuring in Local and Global Contexts*, ed. William W. Falk, Michael D. Schulman, and Ann R. Tickamyer, xi–xxiii. Athens: Ohio University Press.

Fitchen, Janet M. 1981. *Poverty in Rural America: A Case Study*. Boulder, CO: Westview Press.

Goodman, B., and R. Steadman. 2002. "Services: Business Demand Rivals Consumer Demand in Driving Job Growth." *Monthly Labor Review* 125: 3–16.

Grusky, David B., Bruce Western, and Christopher Wimer. 2011. "The Consequences of the Great Recession." In *The Great Recession*, ed. David B. Grusky, Bruce Western, and Christopher Wimer, 3–20. New York: Russell Sage.

Hamrick, Karen. S. 2001. "Displaced Workers: Differences in Nonmetro and Metro Experience in the Mid-1990s." *Rural Development Research Report*, No. 92. Economic Research Service, US Department of Agriculture, Washington, DC.

Harrison, Bennet, and Barry Bluestone. 1988. *The Great U-Turn: Corporate Restructuring and the Polarizing of America*. New York: Basic Books.

Iceland, John. August 2003. "Why Poverty Remains High: The Role of Income Growth, Economic Inequality, and Changes in Family Structure, 1949–1999." *Demography* 40 (3): 499–519. http://dx.doi.org/10.1353/dem.2003.0025. Medline:12962060.

Institution, Brookings. 2013. "The Earned Income Tax Credit Series." Accessed 8 July 2013. http://www.brookings.edu/about/programs/metro/eitc/eitc-homepage.

Jensen, Leif, Gretchen T. Cornwell, and Jill L. Findeis. 1995. "Informal Work in Nonmetropolitan Pennsylvania." *Rural Sociology* 60 (1): 91–107. http://dx.doi.org/10.1111/j.1549-0831.1995.tb00564.x.

Jensen, Leif, and David Eggebeen. 1994. "Nonmetropolitan Poor Children and Reliance on Public Assistance." *Rural Sociology* 59 (1): 45–65. http://dx.doi.org/10.1111/j.1549-0831.1994.tb00521.x.

Jensen, Leif, Jill L. Findeis, Wan-Ling Hsu, and Jason P. Schachter. 1999. "Slipping into and out of Underemployment: Another Disadvantage for Nonmetropolitan Workers?" *Rural Sociology* 64 (3): 417–38. http://dx.doi.org/10.1111/j.1549-0831.1999.tb00360.x.

Jensen, Leif, Diane K. McLaughlin, and Tim Slack. 2003. "Rural Poverty: The Persisting Challenge." In *Challenges for Rural America in the Twenty-First Century*, ed. David L. Brown and Louis E. Swanson, 118–31. University Park: The Pennsylvania State University Press.

Juhn, Chinhui, and Simon Potter. 2006. "Changes in Labor Force Participation in the United States." *Journal of Economic Perspectives* 20 (3): 27–46. http://dx.doi.org/10.1257/jep.20.3.27.

Kalleberg, Arne L., Barbara F. Reskin, and Ken Hudson. 2000. "Bad Jobs in America: Standard and Nonstandard Employment Relations and Job Quality in the United States." *American Sociological Review* 65 (2): 256–78. http://dx.doi.org/10.2307/2657440.

Levitan, L., and S. Feldman. 1991. "For Love or Money: Nonmonetary Economic Arrangements among Rural Households in Central New York." *Research in Rural Sociology and Development* 5: 149–72.

Lichter, Daniel T., and David L. Brown. 2011. "Rural America in an Urban Society: Changing Spatial and Social Boundaries." *American Review of Sociology* 37 (1): 565–92. http://dx.doi.org/10.1146/annurev-soc-081309-150208.

Lichter, Daniel T., and Leif Jensen. 2002. "Rural America in Transition: Poverty and Welfare at the Turn of the Twenty-First Century." In *Rural Dimensions of Welfare Reform*, ed. Bruce A. Weber, Greg J. Duncan, and Leslie A. Whitener, 77–110. Kalamazoo, MI: W.E. Upjohn Institute.

Lichter, Daniel T., Gail M. Johnston, and Diane K. McLaughlin. 1994. "Changing Linkages between Work and Poverty in Rural America." *Rural Sociology* 59 (3): 395–415. http://dx.doi.org/10.1111/j.1549-0831.1994.tb00539.x.

Lobao, Linda M. 2004. "Continuity and Change in Place Stratification: Spatial Inequality and Middle-Range Territorial Units." *Rural Sociology* 69 (1): 1–30. http://dx.doi.org/10.1526/003601104322919883.

Lobao, Linda M., Greg Hooks, and Ann R. Tickamyer. 2007. *The Sociology of Spatial Inequality*. Albany: State University of New York Press.

Massey, Dougles S. 2007. *Categorically Unequal: The American Stratification System*. New York: Russell Sage.

McLaughlin, Diane K., and Alisha J. Coleman-Jensen. 2008. "Nonstandard Employment in the Nonmetropolitan United States." *Rural Sociology* 73 (4): 631–59. http://dx.doi.org/10.1526/003601108786471558.

McLaughlin, Diane K., Erica L. Gardner, and Daniel T. Lichter. 1999. "Economic Restructuring and Changing Prevalence of Female-Headed Families in America." *Rural Sociology* 64 (3): 394–416. http://dx.doi.org/10.1111/j.1549-0831.1999.tb00359.x.

McLaughlin, Diane K., and Lauri Perman. 1991. "Returns vs. Endowments in the Earnings Attainment Process for Metropolitan and Nonmetropolitan Men and Women." *Rural Sociology* 56 (3): 339–65. http://dx.doi.org/10.1111/j.1549-0831.1991.tb00438.x.

Mead, Lawrence M. 1992. *The New Politics of Poverty: The Nonworking Poor in America*. New York: Basic Books.

Morris, Martina, and Bruce Western. 1999. "Inequality in Earnings at the Close of the Twentieth Century." *Annual Review of Sociology* 25 (1): 623–57. http://dx.doi.org/10.1146/annurev.soc.25.1.623.

Murray, Charles. 1984. *Losing Ground: American Social Policy, 1950–1980*. New York: Basic Books.

National Bureau of Economic Research. 2012. "U.S. Business Cycle Expansions and Contractions." Accessed 16 January 2012. http://www.nber.org/cycles.html.

Nelson, Margaret K. 1999. "Economic Restructuring, Gender, and Informal Work: A Case Study of a Rural County." *Rural Sociology* 64: 26–35.

Nelson, Margaret K., and Joan Smith. 1999. *Working Hard and Making Do: Surviving in Small Town America*. Berkeley: University of California Press.

Pahl, R.E. 1984. *Divisions of Labour.* Oxford: Basil Blackwell.

Pickering, Kathleen. 2000. "Alternative Economic Strategies in Low-Income Rural Communities: TANF, Labor Migration, and the Case of the Pine Ridge Indian Reservation." *Rural Sociology* 65 (1): 148–67. http://dx.doi.org/10.1111/j.1549-0831.2000.tb00347.x.

Portes, Alejandro. 1994. "The Informal Economy and Its Paradoxes." In *The Handbook of Economic Sociology*, ed. Neil J. Smelser and Richard Swedberg, 426–49. Princeton, NJ: Princeton University Press.

Portes, Alejandro, Manuel Castells, and Lauren A. Benton. 1989. *The Informal Economy: Studies in Advanced and Less Developed Countries.* Baltimore: Johns Hopkins University Press.

Provasnik, Stephen, Angelina KewalRamani, Mary McLaughlin Coleman, Lauren Gilbertson, Will Herring, and Qinghsu Xie. 2007. *Status of Education in Rural America.* National Center for Education Statistics, US Department of Education, Washington, DC.

Sassen, Saskia. 1991. *The Global City: New York, London, Tokyo.* Princeton, NJ: Princeton University Press.

Slack, Tim. 2007a. "The Contours and Correlates of Informal Work in Rural Pennsylvania." *Rural Sociology* 72 (1): 69–89. http://dx.doi.org/10.1526/003601107781147392.

Slack, Tim. 2007b. "Work, Welfare, and the Informal Economy: Toward an Understanding of Household Livelihood Strategies." *Community Development* 38 (1): 26–42. http://dx.doi.org/10.1080/15575330709490183.

Slack, Tim. 2010. "Working Poverty across the Metro-Nonmetro Divide: A Quarter-Century in Perspective, 1979–2003." *Rural Sociology* 75 (3): 363–87. http://dx.doi.org/10.1111/j.1549-0831.2010.00020.x.

Slack, Tim, and Leif Jensen. 2002. "Race, Ethnicity, and Underemployment in Nonmetropolitan America: A 30-Year Profile." *Rural Sociology* 67 (2): 208–33. http://dx.doi.org/10.1111/j.1549-0831.2002.tb00101.x.

Slack, Tim, and Leif Jensen. 2004. "Employment Adequacy in Extractive Industries: An Analysis of Underemployment, 1974–1998." *Society & Natural Resources* 17 (2): 129–46. http://dx.doi.org/10.1080/08941920490261258.

Slack, Tim, and Leif Jensen. January 2008. "Employment Hardship among Older Workers: Does Residential and Gender Inequality Extend into Older Age?" *Journals of Gerontology. Series B, Psychological Sciences and Social Sciences* 63 (1): S15–24. http://dx.doi.org/10.1093/geronb/63.1.S15. Medline:18332197.

Slack, Tim, and Leif Jensen. 2010. "Informal Work in Rural America: Theory and Evidence." In *Informal Work in Developed Nations*, ed. Enrico A. Marcelli, Colin C. Williams, and Pascale Joassart, 175–91. New York: Routledge.

Somers, Margaret R., and Fred Block. 2005. "From Poverty to Perversity: Ideas, Markets and Institutions over 200 Years of Welfare Debate." *American Sociological Review* 70 (2): 260–87. http://dx.doi.org/10.1177/000312240507000204.

Sullivan, Teresa A. 1978. *Marginal Workers, Marginal Jobs: Underutilization of the U.S. Work Force.* Austin: University of Texas Press.

Tickamyer, Ann R. 2000. "Space Matters! Spatial Inequality in Future Sociology." *Contemporary Sociology* 29 (6): 805–13. http://dx.doi.org/10.2307/2654088.

Tickamyer, Ann R., and Teresa A. Wood. 1998. "Identifying Participation in the Informal Economy Using Survey Research Methods." *Rural Sociology* 63 (2): 323–39. http://dx.doi.org/10.1111/j.1549-0831.1998.tb00677.x.

Tickamyer, Ann R., and Teresa A. Wood. 2003. "The Social and Economic Context of Informal Work." In *Communities of Work: Rural Restructuring in Local and Global Contexts*, ed. William W. Falk, Michael D. Schulman, and Ann R. Tickamyer, 394–418. Athens: Ohio University Press.

Ziebarth, Ann, and Leann Tigges. 2003. "Earning a Living and Building a Life: Income-Generating and Income Saving Strategies of Rural Wisconsin Families." In *Communities of Work: Rural Restructuring in Local and Global Contexts*, ed. William W. Falk, Michael D. Schulman, and Ann R. Tickamyer, 316–38. Athens: Ohio University Press.

CHAPTER 30

Rural Entrepreneurship

Lori A. Dickes and Kenneth L. Robinson

Introduction

Over recent decades, rural economies have experienced structural shifts in their economic profiles that have had substantial impacts on livelihoods and quality of life. Historical drivers of economic development focused on improving a region's export base; strategies focused on financial incentives, industrial consolidation, industrial parks, and other forms of cost reduction. By the 1970s and 1980s, economic development policy largely emphasized "tax abatements, investment credits, low-interest loans, land write-downs, and labor-training grants to reduce labor and operating costs and lure manufacturing plants" (Turner 2003, 272). Bradshaw and Blakely (1999) call this period of "smokestack chasing" the first wave of industrial recruitment efforts. As the 1980s wore on, second wave development strategies, including business creation support, development of business incubators, increasing investment capital, and providing other types of technical assistance, increased in popularity (Bradshaw and Blakely 1999).

Prior to the 1980s, these economic development policies paralleled what is often referred to as the Fordist period of national growth (Lobao and Meyer 2001). There were structural economic changes across the nation, but Brenner (2004) argues this period was focused on reducing regional and geographic inequalities. However, as the 1990s began, the forces of industrial restructuring and globalization precipitated a new wave of economic development, the so-called third wave of economic development, and a post-Fordist new industrial order. Turner (2003) argues that to be successful in today's third wave of economic development all communities must create and maintain a competitive advantage in the face of dynamic, persistent change. Turner (2003), Dabson

(2007), and others uphold innovation and entrepreneurship as the major drivers of regional economic growth and development. The keys to success in this new era of development highlight the importance of leveraging unique regional assets, including human capital, educational resources, and natural amenities (Dabson 2007).

While definitions vary, *entrepreneurship* frequently refers to the rapid growth of new and innovative businesses and is associated with individuals who create or seize business opportunities and pursue them without regard for resources under their control (Kayne 1999). Many states today have a variety of entrepreneurial initiatives, networks, and centers to promote this development strategy (NGA 2004; Williams 2004). However, one ongoing area of concern is that local development practitioners and community activists may view entrepreneurial strategies as too difficult or out of reach for their community. Furthermore, there is increasing confirmation that many communities, especially small and rural communities, continue to engage in traditional economic development practices even in the face of mounting evidence that these approaches may not provide the assumed benefits (Chi 1997; ICMA 2004).

In response to the challenges presented in today's global economy, community activists and rural policy makers are beginning to call for development strategies that focus attention on small firms, regional trade associations, industrial districts, and local entrepreneurs. Others argue that if policy makers and program planners expect to foster economic development in underserved, low-income communities, a policy of endogenous self-development for sustainable economic growth is needed. This notion is backed by a growing body of theory and research that reexamines the bigger-is-better model and emphasizes the organizational embedded nature of small-scale, locally controlled economic enterprises (Robinson, Lyson, and Christy 2002). Moreover, such research suggests that the establishment of more entrepreneurship-centered economic development, by enhancing the strategic agency of rural and economically disadvantaged communities, could provide opportunities to reverse stagnant local and regional economic conditions.

In this chapter, we place the practice of rural entrepreneurial development in a wider theoretical context, and review of the state of research on rural entrepreneurship. We then offer a case study emphasizing unique aspects of the barriers and opportunities for rural entrepreneurship, and conclude with theoretical and practical implications.

A Theoretical Lens of Rural Entrepreneurship

An Institutional Perspective on Entrepreneurial Development

In *General Theory of Entrepreneurship*, Shane (2003) recognizes that entrepreneurship does not occur in a vacuum. Entrepreneurship can be viewed as a nexus between individual entrepreneurs and diverse external influences and opportunities. Related to this, regional economists have long recognized that entrepreneurial/small business development is, along with business recruitment and business retention, one component of a three-legged economic development stool (Pulver 1986). Thus the development of local entrepreneurs and a climate that supports them is a critical component of any community's economic development strategic plan. While entrepreneurs differ in their infrastructure and support needs, many new and emerging firms depend on local economic development organizations to provide local organizational and structural capacity to help facilitate their success.

Busenitz et al. (2003) were the first to introduce the idea of moving beyond a unitary model of entrepreneurship to one that viewed the diverse sources of opportunities that impact successful entrepreneurship across communities. Shane (2003) extends this by describing entrepreneurship as a nexus between the individual efforts of the entrepreneur and a diverse set of cultural, institutional, personal, and social factors. Fortunato and Alter (2011) advance this model as a framework, placing entrepreneurship "at the three-way nexus between individual entrepreneurs, institutions supporting entrepreneurship, and sources of opportunity, all bounded by an environmental space" (Fortunato and McLaughlin 2012, 4). In this framework, institutions play an equally important role in identifying entrepreneurial opportunity and supporting individual entrepreneurs. The field of entrepreneurship increasingly recognizes that research focused exclusively on the individual entrepreneur provides only a partial perspective on the diverse influences that impact entrepreneurial processes and outcomes (Fortunato and McLaughlin 2012).

Institutions in this framework can be formal or informal, and are defined as "human relationships that structure opportunity via constraints and enablement" (Schmid 2004, 1). It is evident that there are local and regional features that impact entrepreneurial opportunities, local opinions and perceptions of entrepreneurship, and even the success rate of entrepreneurial firms (Fritsch and Schmude 2006). Similarly, Granovetter (1985) argues that the social and economic institutions of economies incorporate individual decisions and actions that make up these broader institutions. As such, individual entrepreneurial activity is not the sole mechanism that will result in successful entrepreneurial enterprises or high entrepreneurial regions. Instead, this individual action, in coordination and collaboration with both formal and informal institutions, is critical to the success of entrepreneurial development efforts and individual entrepreneurial success.

Related to this, public choice theory, and more broadly institutional economics, inform the relationships between institutions, economic and social activity, and the nexus of individual decision making within institutional settings. The rational choice model explains the institutional environment as a set of "stable" procedures and constraints that dictate the rules of the game. The formal and informal institutional environment in a public organization can significantly influence the policy agenda, policy outcomes, as well as the implementation of policy. Within the public policy environment, formal institutions (state/federal government, local/regional governments, constitutions, laws, and courts) can be equally as important as informal institutions (family, friends, social norms, or codes of behavior) in influencing an individual's decision-making set (Schmid 2004).

All economic developers are constrained by an array of formal institutions that influence their policy objectives. For example, the state and local legal environment can make a substantive impact on the ability of economic developers to accomplish their development goals. If a county or state has a strong policy bias toward business recruitment or retention, local development officials may have little incentive to encourage entrepreneurial development. Informal institutions can be equally formidable. For example, in communities where the informal power structures are exclusive and rigid, economic developers, especially those from outside the community, may have difficulty accomplishing their objectives.

Networks and Entrepreneurship

An alternative approach seeks to place entrepreneurship within the wider context of community development, where individuals and organizations transcend their individual self-interest for the wider benefit of the community (Wilkinson 1991). Wilkinson (1991) argues that when individuals and organizations are engaged in a broad and purposive approach to community development, local entrepreneurial conditions and results will improve. We further theorize that individuals and organizations can perceive it being in their individual self-interest to view decisions in a wider community context and, equally, to realize the individual and community benefits from these. Using this framework, individuals and organizations may have a strong incentive to interact across a diverse set of community networks with types of engagement that seek to improve community well-being through local and regional entrepreneurial development.

The practice of entrepreneurial development in rural communities is further complicated by potential gaps in the formal institutional environment across rural areas. For local and regional communities to effectively support small business development, a diverse network of institutional infrastructure and community and business partnerships must be in place. Fortunato and McLaughlin (2012) argue that communities with a strong small business sector have support mechanisms in place for local entrepreneurs and examples of successful entrepreneurship. These assets may include small business and technology training, access to local business incubators, information on and access to business financing and capital, networks of local entrepreneurs, and networks of specialized human capital resources (e.g., accountants, patent attorneys, and supply chain specialists). With the appropriate institutional infrastructure, rural community institutions can impact entrepreneurial development and the identification of entrepreneurial opportunities.

Many communities, especially rural communities, may not be endowed with a broad network of this type of entrepreneurial support. To facilitate entrepreneurial success, it is important that obstacles to entrepreneurship are removed and entrepreneurial development support is improved (Fortunato and McLaughlin 2012). Using a public choice lens, institutional weaknesses in rural communities may be accompanied by weak incentives for local economic development officials to support entrepreneurial economic development strategies. This is especially true in states or regions where alternative economic development policies are strongly supported with financial incentives and diverse networks of programming and infrastructure. In addition, these institutional gaps in entrepreneurial development programming, role models, or culture may also discourage individuals from choosing entrepreneurship as a career path. With weak supporting institutions and incentives for individual entrepreneurs, there is the potential for a vicious cycle of low levels of entrepreneurship and a correspondingly low level of entrepreneurial institutions and culture.

A rich research stream documents the importance of networks and interaction for successful entrepreneurship and general economic decision making (Granovetter 1973; Aldrich and Zimmer 1986; Larson 1992; Burt 1995; Bruderl and Preisendorfer 1998; Witt 2004). However, in many low-income and rural communities, small business development seems to be complicated by the very circumstances that it aims to eradicate. A weak state of socioeconomic welfare coincides, and most likely contributes to, a dismal state of enterprise development. This is exacerbated by the remoteness of rural communities and limited local demand (Dabson 2001). Increasingly, however, small enterprise development is purported to be more sustainable as compared to traditional business attraction approaches that tend to be more costly (Henderson 2002; Shaffer et al. 2004). Walzer et al. (2007) also argue it is a more sustainable strategy when key stakeholders, entrepreneurs, local business owners, local economic developers, and politicians, among others, are local.

Entrepreneurship as Economic Development

Walzer et al. (2007) document the increasing use of entrepreneurial strategies as an economic development tool as many rural communities continue to suffer from the effects of industrial restructuring, globalization, and more recent recessionary effects. From an applied perspective, it is not difficult to frame entrepreneurship in a positive light. Entrepreneurship improves community welfare through the creation of new jobs and the generation of additional income as new firms start and existing ones grow. It can also be argued that developing local entrepreneurs diversifies the local economic base into areas from which new and existing firms may be attracted. Moreover, local entrepreneurs are more likely to be committed to supporting and enhancing overall community and economic development, engaged in community leadership, and building civic infrastructure when compared to their nonlocal industrially recruited counterparts. As local entrepreneurship grows, in theory, the overall competitiveness of the local economy increases and creates spillover employment and innovation from this entrepreneurial climate.

Given these arguments, entrepreneurship as a rural development strategy has continued to gain credibility (Gittell and Thompson 1999; Porter 1995). This has prompted government and donor agencies to expand funding for entrepreneurship development programs, and more articles now appear in both the scholarly and popular media about the success of this "new approach" in terms of incomes, employment generation, and social empowerment (Kayne 1999; Henderson 2002; Adkins 2006). As of 1999, the majority of US states had higher education programs in entrepreneurship (Kayne 1999). Henderson (2002) reports that in 1997, over 370 business schools offered some type of entrepreneurial development coursework. Another example of this institutional support is at the kindergarten to Grade 12 level. Thirteen states provide K–12 educational funding for entrepreneurial programming (Adkins 2006). While education is only one part of entrepreneurial development, these examples provide evidence of the growing trend of public involvement in growing and developing entrepreneurs.

While developing and growing entrepreneurial economies is theoretically defensible and popular, the evidence on rural entrepreneurship policy shows little impact and the barriers to rural entrepreneurship are well documented (Aziz 1984; Bryant 1989; Dabson 2001; Dabson et al. 2003). These results may in part be understood from the public choice model described here. Local officials understand these are longer-term development strategies that—even with a firm-by-firm sales pitch—may generate fewer jobs when compared against industrial recruitment. In addition, local officials understand their communities are competing against other towns and regions for residents and businesses. Entrepreneurial development may not be as attractive as luring a new business with proof positive of new employment.

However, hope is not lost. Research on the wide variation across rural communities in entrepreneurship and entrepreneurial development confirms the importance of the institutional environment for supporting entrepreneurs and identifying opportunities. Fortunato and McLaughlin (2012) find that high entrepreneurship communities are marked by greater levels of, frequency of, and value placed on interactions among entrepreneurs and their supporting institutions. These results ultimately provide evidence that when individual and institutional interests align or are mutually advantageous, purposive collaboration and engagement can enhance entrepreneurial development and success in rural areas. The next section of this research provides background on the institutional and policy environment surrounding entrepreneurial development across the United States. While specific entrepreneurial development policy remains nascent in many communities, there is positive evidence coming from those states and regions with targeted entrepreneurial policy efforts.

The State of Entrepreneurship

Research reveals that states, regions, and localities continue to actively practice industrial recruitment and do not appear to be making substantial reductions in industrial recruitment efforts or significant improvements to alternative development programs (ICMA 2004). Moreover, twenty-five states reported no state funding specifically toward entrepreneurial development (NASDA 1998). The National Association of State Development Agencies (NASDA) 1998 survey of state economic development agencies reports that only $19 million of the $26.7 billion spent on economic development was targeted toward entrepreneurial development. Entrepreneurial development efforts are an increasingly important part of state policy, but the scope and breadth of these efforts remain quite mixed (Kayne 1999). State policy and programs generally fall into two categories: states with well-defined objectives for the development and success of entrepreneurs, versus states that encourage entrepreneurship under a general umbrella of economic development programming.

The Kauffman Foundation's (Kayne 1999) research indicates that states that have a better understanding of the unique contribution of entrepreneurs to state economic growth are more likely to have policy measures in place that support the specific needs of entrepreneurs. Evidence (Pages and Poole 2003) also indicates that organizations that rate entrepreneurship as their highest priority are more likely to have entrepreneurial development programs and invest in them at higher levels. As well, states and organizations with a longer and more substantial commitment to entrepreneurial development programs are more likely to rate these efforts as a top priority compared to business attraction or business retention policies. Moreover, Pages and Poole (2003) classify the majority of entrepreneurial development programs across states as "adolescent" in their development.

A criticism of entrepreneurial policy is that it is often piecemeal and ignores important components of the entrepreneurial process (Lichtenstein, Lyons, and Kutzhanova 2004). However, a considerable body of research confirms the types of strategies that may facilitate entrepreneurial development success across communities. One strategy is attracting and sustaining "creative class" workers within rural communities. Developing a climate of entrepreneurship and innovation often rests, in part, on the effectiveness of business support networks (Dabson 2001; NCOE 2001; Malecki 1993). Malecki (1993) argues that, while development policy may not be able to create these networks, public policy can help facilitate and support them. Firms that operate in dense, agglomerative environments are more likely to receive the benefits of information spillovers and network economies, but regions without these benefits can use community and economic development policy to improve external networks and related agglomeration economies (Malecki 1993).

A number of states and regions have developed their own organizations in an effort to enhance internal and external business networks. The Appalachian Regional Council (ARC) developed the Entrepreneurial Initiative, which focuses in part on the development of entrepreneurial networks and clusters (Dabson 2001). Research on this initiative (Brandow Company, Inc. 2001) reveals that business retention rates have improved and survival rates of new firms are higher than the national average. Minnesota has created several network-building programs that may be important models for enhancing statewide entrepreneurship. The Minnesota Rural Angel Investor Networks (RAIN) seeks to find and encourage angel investors—individuals who invest in young firms in exchange for equity holdings—in rural areas of the state. The Minnesota Rural

Partners created a Virtual Entrepreneurial Network that provides online access to advanced technology and communication tools (Henderson 2002).

Rural entrepreneurial development may be especially dependent on the creation of external networks. Ács (2001) reports that Farmington, New Mexico, generated the third-highest share of high-growth entrepreneurs in the nation in the early 1990s owing largely to the cooperation of surrounding community and business leaders who were able to collaborate to overcome labor market challenges and business obstacles to rural economic development. Rural communities that work together to create and enhance networks improve economies of scale, access to resources and technology, and local and regional cooperation and communication (Anesi et al. 2002).

The ARC has also been investing heavily to improve the entrepreneurial climate. It views entrepreneurship as "a critical element in the establishment of self-sustaining communities that create jobs, build wealth, and contribute broadly to economic and community development" (Markley et al. 2008, 3). Since 1997, the ARC has invested $43 million toward 340 unique entrepreneurial policy efforts (Goetz et al. 2010), including youth entrepreneurial education, business incubators, capital access, small business, and technical training for adults and targeted sector activities, including network facilitation. Philosophically, this effort sought to build a pipeline of entrepreneurs throughout the region by implementing programming across a range of sectors, communities, and individuals.

Markley et al. (2008) finds that these programs have increased the number of firms and jobs in the region. By 2005, the Entrepreneurship Initiative had created at least 9,156 jobs, retained another 3,022 jobs, helped create 1,787 new businesses, and served 8,242 businesses. The approximate public cost per job created or retained ranged from $579 to $3,994. These initial investments also helped to generate another $73 million in private investment in the region. Overall, new business sectors have emerged and the entrepreneurial pipeline has improved and expanded.

The ARC's Entrepreneurial Initiative highlights several important lessons. Projects were more successful if project and community leaders recognized the long-term nature of entrepreneurial development and if these leaders were flexible in adapting project goals and objectives throughout the process. In addition, communities with existing local champions and organizational capacity in place were able to realize a "catalytic" effect in leveraging these resources. The ARC's efforts also underscore the importance of a region's entrepreneurial climate and point to potential challenges that regions may have in improving the entrepreneurial climate (Markley et al. 2008).

This broad-based effort also points to challenges in the implementation of rural entrepreneurial development. Delivering these resources to communities is often dependent on state leadership and local partners, which can vary substantially. In addition, the funds available, even in this case, were relatively small for such a large region. Markley et al. (2008) revealed that the size of investments were not large enough to provide transformative regional economic development. Moreover, changing attitudes toward entrepreneurship requires a persistent commitment to promoting the value of this strategy to community and state leadership.

Despite challenges, rural communities across the nation have achieved measures of success across a range of rural settings. Lichtenstein and Lyons (2010) acknowledge that entrepreneurship takes place in a diversity of settings, with entrepreneurial talent unevenly distributed across regions. Ács and Armington (2005) argue that entrepreneurial activity is influenced by specific local and regional characteristics, and Malecki (1993) upholds that entrepreneurship is greatly influenced by local culture, history, and infrastructure, among other variables. Successful entrepreneurship policy must therefore consider the unique strengths and weaknesses of each community and may thus necessitate the development of a unique set of policy measures for each community.

A Case Study in Entrepreneurial Development

In 1999, Phillips County, Arkansas, was one of the twenty poorest counties in the United States and had also experienced a consistent decrease in population of about 18 percent since 1990, signaling a local economic decline. Agriculture was the largest economic sector in the county, with cotton being the main crop. Government subsidies for traditional row crops, like cotton, soybeans, and rice, had until the late 1990s allowed local farmers to survive. However, with the expansion of the World Trade Organization and the inevitability of subsidy reduction that characterizes the neoliberal era, Southern farmers have begun to shift from row to vegetable crops. In 2003, a small group of six traditional row-crop farmers came together to form the Arkansas Delta Produce Marketing Association, LLC (ADPMA), which represented an innovative organizational form for newly emerging, small-scale farm enterprises (Robinson et al. 2011). They were among only 543 African American farmers in Arkansas who had farming as their primary occupation, of which only sixty-three were producing vegetables and melons (USDA 2007). As rural entrepreneurs, ADPMA's founding members maintained that the future of Arkansas farming is in sweet potatoes and greens, not cotton and soybeans. These farmers also recognized that without reorganizing their operations and organization their farms would not survive. They viewed ADPMA as a way to confront the challenges of the Delta.

ADPMA is as much a business venture as it is a project among six friends. The entity's structure was established with equality between members. Each farmer contributed $250 to the LLC's capital account and has equal voting privileges within the group. The profits, liabilities, and expenses of the LLC are to be allocated to each member pro rata and the proportions are to be calculated based on the amount of acreage each individual dedicates to production. There is a high level of cooperation, synergy, and sharing of equipment and information. For example, all members of the LLC share the two $20,000 sweet potato unearthing machines and two refrigerated trucks.

While African American farmers in the Delta often do little more than subsist, there appears to be some hope for farmers looking to move into sweet potato and vegetable production. The United States is a net exporter of sweet potatoes (USDA Economic Research Service 2011), and there is increasing demand domestically for healthy vegetables and greens, including sweet potatoes. Determined to be a step ahead, ADPMA made plans to build its own cold storage facility, which would prevent farmers from having to sell all their crops at harvest time when supply is highest and prices are lowest. Instead, it would allow the LLC to capitalize on the heightened price levels of the winter seasons (approximately $20 to $26 per bushel) and limit the selling of crops "green" (at a highly discounted price of approximately $6 to $10 per bushel). The storage facility is able to ship and receive crops, and contain equipment needed to grade, wash, and package the potatoes. The facility will help control market supply and provide farmers with the ability to streamline their revenue. In addition, the storage facility will provide ADPMA with the option to further expand its operations by processing the sweet potatoes into value-added products. An expansion toward value-added production could increase profit margins and potentially make a positive impact on local employment.

The sweet potato storage facility in Phillips County is an example of how a diverse network of institutional infrastructure and community and business partnerships can provide effective support for small business and entrepreneurship development. ADPMA entered into a partnership with the Central Arkansas Resource Conservation and Development Council, Inc. (CARCDC), a 501(c)(3) non-profit organization, in an effort to create jobs and to allow local growers to supply distributors year-round (USDA 2010). The ADPMA-CARCDC partnership is part of a larger collaboration called the Delta Bridge Project (DBP), which is a public-private partnership between dozens of local organizations and hundreds of area individuals that intends to coordinate community and economic development efforts in Phillips County (CARDC 2004). A major component of the economic development goals in the Delta Bridge Project centers on supporting sweet potato production in the Delta by building the sweet potato cold storage facility to ensure optimal distribution.

The US Department of Agriculture's Arkansas Natural Resources Conservation Service suggests that the concept is a new generation business model, where one nonprofit with expertise in infrastructure projects raises capital, constructs, and operates infrastructure needed to help provide meaningful assistance to the underserved public within the Delta region of Arkansas (USDA 2010). The facility is owned by CARCDC and employs an agronomist–sweet potato expert to manage the facility and provide technical assistance to members of the ADPMA. The leasing agreement allows CARCDC to lease the facility to ADPMA and gives permission for the LLC to further sublease any extra space. There are no cash requirements upfront to store produce until sales are made for such items. Essentially, it is a "pay as you sell" agreement, with rents charged based only on the operational cost of the storage facility fee (of $3.50 to $4.00 per bushel). It is also agreed that ADPMA will eventually take over ownership and management of the facility (Leggett 2007).

The ADPMA case speaks to earlier theoretical issues and their implications for rural entrepreneurship. Issues such as appropriate organizational structure, financing options, and contractual arrangements are obstacles that the ADMPA experienced. This case study further highlights the importance of supporting collective or cooperative strategies that have the potential to improve the competitiveness of local communities. Addressing issues such as public consensus and collective action are vital to enhancing the strategic agency of these communities and their local businesses.

Facilitating economic development is increasingly embraced by policy makers at local, state, and regional levels. However, as public choice theory and the entrepreneurial policy environment suggest, there are often inadequate resources or inappropriate incentives in place for the development and implementation of these types of policy efforts. The survey results we present in the next section provide evidence related to the support and implementation of specific entrepreneurial policy at the state and local level across South Carolina.

Support for Entrepreneurial Development in South Carolina

Clemson University researchers administered a statewide survey in 2008 in an effort to gain a more comprehensive understanding of the local and regional institutional commitment to entrepreneurship policy efforts across South Carolina (see Dickes 2011 for methodological details). Evidence was sought on entrepreneurship and other economic development policy priorities for a wide range of community and economic development practitioners across the state. For reasons noted at the outset of this chapter, it was hypothesized that local and regional level economic development officials across the state continue to practice incentive-based industrial recruitment at the expense of entrepreneurial and other economic development policy alternatives. It was expected that any organization with a functional role in economic development would be involved in entrepreneurial policy efforts, or at least have relevant knowledge and insight. Only 27 percent of the ninety-nine respondents to an online survey operate any type of entrepreneurial development program, even though over half felt that their communities recognized the importance of entrepreneurship. Only one respondent mentioned entrepreneurial development as their community's most important future development issue (thirty-nine placed it in their top five). In contrast, thirty-nine respondents indicated job creation was their number one future development issue, while sixteen indicated that business attraction was. Clearly, job creation through business attraction, as opposed to entrepreneurship development, was the strongly preferred approach.

Communities may have weak entrepreneurial development programming due to barriers in supporting and implementing entrepreneurial focused economic development policy. Indeed, the majority of respondents rated a lack of funding as their biggest barrier in implementing entrepreneurial oriented development policy. Moreover, respondents evaluated the quality of a range of potential entrepreneurial services and programs in their communities, including a local business incubator; access to venture capital or angel investors; access to start up or seed capital; advertising/marketing assistance; an organized by local program; local hiring initiatives; local infrastructure assistance (e.g., buildings, broadband); micro-lending programs; networking and mentoring opportunities for community businesses; and small business and entrepreneurial training. Virtually none of these were ranked as above average or excellent. Well over half of respondents ranked access to five of these entrepreneurial service areas—local business incubator, venture capital or angel investors, seed capital, advertising or marketing assistance, and micro-lending programs—as poor or extremely poor. While respondents were a little less pessimistic about local infrastructure assistance, networking and mentoring opportunities, and small business training, overall these results paint a weak picture of entrepreneurial service access and support in South Carolina.

This case study provides support for both of the theoretical approaches outlined earlier. The institutional incentive structure for state and local economic development agents can serve as a barrier to the implementation of entrepreneurial development strategies. In addition, policy perceptions impact the policy practice of local development institutions. The case study also highlights that with a strong foundation of entrepreneurial institutional support and engagement there is a greater likelihood that communities will embrace these types of development initiatives. The evidence reveals that many of these communities see the value in entrepreneurial development but have a diverse set of barriers that prevent the implementation of these strategies.

Conclusions

Some rural communities have long relied on a development model that emphasizes free trade, minimal regulation, low taxes, and heightened competition as the best prescription for economic growth. This model has resulted in ongoing efforts to recruit new business based on a business-friendly environment but not necessarily an entrepreneurial climate with corresponding levels of entrepreneurial infrastructure. However, the OECD (2003) and the US Census Bureau (Edmiston 2007) report that the majority of new jobs created in the United States and around the world are in small- and/or medium-sized firms. The dynamic nature of entrepreneurial activity allows for the creation of local jobs, wealth, the innovative use of local assets and resources, and enhanced local and regional economic growth. Thus, research continues to verify that entrepreneurial focused economic development is a critical driver for regional economic growth, while industrial recruitment policy remains the most popular development approach for many communities.

In many rural communities, traditional industrial recruitment and business retention efforts are easier policy choices than developing local entrepreneurs and assisting local business. Realigning these incentives could begin with a focused and concerted entrepreneurial policy effort from the state. If local and regional community leaders witness a concerted policy effort from the state, accompanied with resources and support to facilitate this effort, communities might begin to embrace entrepreneurial development policy within their own local and regional economies. Theory and case studies provide evidence that, with effective institutional and infrastructure support, entrepreneurial development programs can be successful in rural communities. However, until the incentive structure is altered such that enhancing entrepreneurship and developing local business takes priority as a broader community development strategy benefitting individual entrepreneurs and the community at large, other development strategies may continue to take precedence and rural entrepreneurs may struggle to gain a foothold in many of these regions.

References

Ács, Zoltan J. 2001. "Endogenous Technological Change, Entrepreneurship and Regional Growth." In *Knowledge, Complexity, and Innovation Systems*, ed. Manfred M. Fisher and Josef Frohlich, 228–47. Heidelberg and New York: Springer. http://dx.doi.org/10.1007/978-3-662-04546-6_12.

Ács, Zoltan J., and Catherine Armington. 2005. "Using Census Bits to Explore Entrepreneurship, Geography, and Economic Growth." Small Business Research Summary 248. Washington, DC: Small Business Administration, Office of Advocacy.

Adkins, Jasmine. 2006. Study: Entrepreneurship Programs Continue to Expand. Inc.com, 2 June. http://www.inc.com/news/articles/200606/colleges.html .

Aldrich, Howard, and Catherine Zimmer. 1986. "The Entrepreneurship through Social Networks." In *The Art and Science of Entrepreneurship*, ed. Donald Sexton and Raymond Smiler, 3–23. New York: Ballinger.

Anesi, Greg, David Eppich, and Thomas Taylor. 2002. "Lines in the Sand: Four Corners Regional Cooperation." In *The New Power of Regions: A Policy Focus for Rural America.* Proceedings of a conference sponsored by Federal Reserve Bank of Kansas City, Center for the Study of Rural America, 9–10 May.

Aziz, Sartaj. 1984. "Rural Development—Some Essential Prerequisites." *International Labour Review* 123: 277–85.

Bradshaw, Ted K., and Edward J. Blakely. 1999. "What are the "Third-Wave" State Economic Development Efforts? From Incentives to Industrial Policy." *Economic Development Quarterly* 13 (3): 229–44. http://dx.doi.org/10.1177/089124249901300303.

Brandow Company, Inc. 2001. Analysis of Business Formation, Survival, and Attrition Rates of New and Existing Firms and Related Job Flows in Appalachia. Appalachian Regional Commission. http://www.arc.gov/assets/research_reports/AnalysisBusinessFormationSurvivalandAttritionRatesofNewExistingFirms1.pdf.

Brenner, Neil. 2004. *New State Spaces: Urban Governance and the Rescaling of Statehood.* Oxford: Oxford University Press. http://dx.doi.org/10.1093/acprof:oso/9780199270057.001.0001.

Bruderl, Josef, and Peter Preisendorfer. 1998. "Network Support and Success of Newly Founded Businesses." *Small Business Economics* 10: 213–25. http://dx.doi.org/10.1016/0743-0167(89)90060-0.

Bryant, Christopher R. 1989. "Entrepreneurs in the Rural Environment." *Journal of Rural Studies* 5 (4): 337–48. http://dx.doi.org/10.1016/0743-0167(89)90060-0.

Burt, Ronald S. 1995. *Structural Holes: The Social Structure of Competition*. Cambridge, MA: Harvard University Press.

Busenitz, Lowell W., G. Page West III, Dean Shepherd, Teresa Nelson, Gaylen N. Chandler, and Andrew Zacharakis. 2003. "Entrepreneurship Research in Emergence: Past Trends and Future Directions." *Journal of Management* 29: 285–308.

Central Arkansas Rural Development Corporation (CARDC). 2004. "The Tri-county Sweet Potato Storage Facility." 15 October.

Chi, Keon. 1997. State Business Incentives: Trends and Options for the Future. Council of State Governments. Council of State Governments, Lexington, KY: 1–6.

Dabson, Brian. 2001. "Supporting Rural Entrepreneurship." In Exploring Policy Options for a New Rural America. Conference proceedings. Center for the Study of Rural America, Federal Reserve Bank of Kansas City: 35–48. http://wrdc.usu.edu/files/publications/publication/pub__2858626.pdf.

Dabson, Brian. 2007. "Entrepreneurship as a Rural Economic Development Policy: A Changing Paradigm." In *Entrepreneurship and Local Economic Development*, ed. Norman Walzer, 21–38. Plymouth, UK: Lexington Books.

Dabson, Brian, Jennifer Malkin, Amy Mathews, Kimberly Pate, and Stickle Sean. 2003. *Mapping Rural Entrepreneurship*. Battle Creek, MI: W.K. Kellogg Foundation; Washington, DC: CFED.

Dickes, Lori A. 2011. "The Theory and Practice of Third Wave Regional Development Strategies." PhD dissertation, Clemson University.

Edmiston, Kelly. 2007. "The Role of Small and Large Businesses in Economic Development." Kansas City, MO: The Federal Reserve Bank of Kansas City. http://www.kc.frb.org/publicat/econrev/pdf/2q07edmi.pdf. http://dx.doi.org/10.2139/ssrn.993821.

Fortunato, Michael, and Theodore R. Alter. 2011. "The Individual-Institutional Opportunity Nexus: An Integrated Framework for Analyzing Entrepreneurship Development." *Entrepreneurship Research Journal* 1 (1): 1–34. http://dx.doi.org/10.2202/2157-5665.1002.

Fortunato, Michael, and Diane K. McLaughlin. 2012. "Interaction and Purpose in Highly Entrepreneurial Communities." *Entrepreneurship Research Journal* 2 (1): 1–34. http://dx.doi.org/10.2202/2157-5665.1049.

Fritsch, Michael, and Jürgen Schmude. 2006. *Entrepreneurship in the Region*. New York: Springer Science and Business Media Inc.

Gittell, Ross, and Phillip J. Thompson. 1999. "Inner City Business Development and Entrepreneurship: New Frontiers for Policy and Research." In *Urban Problems and Community Development*, ed. Ronald F. Ferguson and William T. Dickens, 473–520. Washington, DC: Brookings Institution Press.

Goetz, Stephan J., Mark Partridge, Steven C. Deller, and David A. Fleming. 2010. "Evaluating U.S. Rural Entrepreneurship Policy." *Journal of Regional Analysis and Policy* 40: 20–33.

Granovetter, Mark. 1973. "The Strength of Weak Ties." *American Journal of Sociology* 78 (6): 1360–80. http://dx.doi.org/10.1086/225469.

Granovetter, Mark. 1985. "Economic Action and Social Structure: The Problem of Embeddedness." *American Journal of Sociology* 91 (3): 481–510. http://dx.doi.org/10.1086/228311.

Henderson, Jason. 2002. "Building the Rural Economy with High Growth Entrepreneurs." Economic Review Third Quarter. Federal Reserve Bank of Kansas City. http://www.kc.frb.org/publicat/econrev/Pdf/3q02hend.pdf.

International City/County Management Association (ICMA). 2004. "2004 Economic Development Survey." http://icma.org.

Kayne, Jay. 1999. "State Entrepreneurship Policies and Programs." Kauffman Center for Entrepreneurial Leadership. The Ewing Marion Kauffman Foundation, Kansas City, Missouri.

Larson, Andrea. 1992. "Network Dyads in Entrepreneurial Settings: A Study of the Governance of Exchange Relations." *Administrative Science Quarterly* 15: 3–20.

Leggett, Bruce. 2007. Central Arkansas Resource Conservation and Development Council, Executive Director. Telephone interview, October.

Lichtenstein, Gregg A., and Thomas S. Lyons. 2010. *Investing in Entrepreneurs; A Strategic Approach for Strengthening Your Regional and Community Economy.* New York: Praeger Press.

Lichtenstein, Gregg A., Thomas S. Lyons, and Nailya Kutzhanova. 2004. "Building Entrepreneurial Communities: The Appropriate Role of Enterprise Development Activities." *Journal of the Community Development Society* 35 (1): 5–24. http://dx.doi.org/10.1080/15575330409490119.

Lobao, Linda H., and Katherine Meyer. 2001. "The Great Agricultural Transition: Crisis, Change, and Social Consequences of Twentieth Century Farming." *Annual Review of Sociology* 27 (1): 103–24. http://dx.doi.org/10.1146/annurev.soc.27.1.103.

Malecki, Edward J. 1993. "Entrepreneurship in Regional and Local Development." *International Regional Science Review* 16 (1–2): 119–53. http://dx.doi.org/10.1177/016001769401600107.

Markley, Deborah, Erik Pages, Brian Dabson, Thomas Johnson, Sara Lawrence, Sara Yanosy, and Karen Dabson. 2008. *Creating an Entrepreneurial Appalachian Region: Findings and Lessons from an Evaluation of the Appalachian Regional Commission's Entrepreneurship Initiative: 1997–2005.* RUPRI: Center for Rural Entrepreneurship.

National Association of State Development Agencies. 1998. *State Economic Development Expenditure Survey.* Washington, DC: NASDA.

National Commission on Entrepreneurship (NCOE). 2001. Building Entrepreneurial Networks.

National Governors Association. 2004. A Governors Guide to Strengthening State Entrepreneurship Policy. Washington, DC: NGA.

Organisation for Economic Co-operation and Development. 2003. *Entrepreneurship and Local Economic Development: Programme and Policy Recommendations.* Paris: OECD.

Pages, Erik R., and Kenneth Poole. 2003. Understanding Entrepreneurship as an Economic Development Strategy: A Three State Survey. A Joint Project of the National Commission on Entrepreneurship and the Center for Regional Competitiveness, Washington, DC.

Porter, M.E. 1995. "The Competitive Advantage of the Inner City." *Harvard Business Review* 73: 55–71.

Pulver, Glen. C. 1986. Community Economic Development Strategies. Madison, WI: Department of Agricultural Journalism, University of Wisconsin-Madison.

Robinson, Kenneth L., Edward Abrokwah, Iris Liang, Scott Sanders, Michael Wang, and Kytson McNeil. 2011. "The Arkansas Delta Produce Marketing Association: Rural Entrepreneurship in the US Delta Region." In *The Handbook of Research on Entrepreneurship in Agriculture and Rural Development*, ed. Gry Alsos, Sara Carter, Elisabet Ljunggren, and Friederike Welter, 180–98. Northampton, MA: Edward Elgar Publishing, Inc. http://dx.doi.org/10.4337/9780857933249.00017.

Robinson, Kenneth L., Thomas A. Lyson, and Ralph D. Christy. 2002. "Civic Community Approaches to Rural Development in the South: Economic Growth with Prosperity." *Journal of Applied Econometrics* 34: 327–38.

Schmid, A.A. 2004. *Conflict and Cooperation: Institutional and Behavioral Economics.* Malden, MA: Blackwell Publishing.

Shaffer, R., S. Deller, and D. Marcouiller. 2004. *Community Economics: Linking Theory and Practice.* Ames, IA: Blackwell Publishing.

Shane, Scott. 2003. *A General Theory of Entrepreneurship: The Individual-Opportunity Nexus.* Cheltenham, England: Edward Elgar Publishing.. http://dx.doi.org/10.4337/9781781007990.

Turner, Robert C. 2003. "The Political Economy of Gubernatorial Smokestack Chasing: Bad Policy and Bad Politics." *State Politics & Policy Quarterly* 3 (3): 270–93. http://dx.doi.org/10.1177/153244000300300303.

US Department of Agriculture (USDA). Census of Agriculture 2007. http://www.agcensus.usda.gov/publications/2007/full_report/census_by_state/arkansas/index.asp.

US Department of Agriculture. 2010. Central Arkansas Resource Conservation and Development projects, Natural Resources Conservation Service. Last modified 28 March. http://www.nrcs.usda.gov/wps/portal/nrcs/site/ar/home/.

USDA Economic Research Service. 2011. "U.S. Sweet Potato Statistics." http://usda.mannlib.cornell.edu/MannUsda/viewDocumentInfo.do?documentID=1492.

Walzer, Norman, Adde Athiyaman, and Gisele F. Hamm. 2007. "Entrepreneurship and Small Business Growth." In *Entrepreneurship and Local Economic Development*, ed. Norman Walzer, 59–80. Plymouth, UK: Lexington Books.

Wilkinson, Kenneth P. 1991. *The Community in Rural America.* Appleton, WI: Social Ecology Press.

Williams, Lori E. 2004. "Entrepreneurial Education: Creating a Usable Economic Base." *Rural Research Report* 15 (8). Macomb: Illinois Institute for Rural Affairs.

Witt, Peter. 2004. "Entrepreneurs' Networks and the Success of Startups." *Entrepreneurship and Regional Development* 16 (5): 391–412. http://dx.doi.org/10.1080/0898562042000188423.

CHAPTER 31

Community Organization and Mobilization in Rural America

Cornelia Butler Flora and Jan L. Flora

Introduction

There are many structural forces over which rural communities have little control. These include global economic shifts and international, federal, and state policies. As social contracts between capital-labor and state-citizen have eroded, rural communities are in a position to fill the void by creating new relationships and enhancing old ones (Jaffe and Quark 2005). Those actions can in part mitigate the impacts of larger structural forces.

Structural forces in the twenty-first century are negatively impacting community well-being. High rates of economic growth without strong policies of redistribution dramatically increase inequality and social exclusion (Kuznets 1955; Stiglitz 2012). When an absentee firm, whether an oil or coal company, a national meatpacker, a recreational conglomerate, or a transnational manufacturing company, promotes economic growth, the small portion of the wealth generated that remains in the community tends to be concentrated in a few hands, resulting in serious community dysfunctions (Wilkinson and Pickett 2009a; 2009b). The market by itself does a poor job of reducing poverty or inequality (Sen 2000). It is also singularly inept at protecting the ecosystem (Daly 1996). Local governments and local civil society have a limited, but important, role in striving to curb potential market excesses.

The Community Capitals Framework (CCF; Flora and Flora 2013) is a tool to identify and analyze relative stocks and flows of community resources to mobilize for the common good. These include natural capital (Jansson et al. 1994), cultural capital (Bourdieu 1986), human capital (Becker 1975), social capital (Putnam 1993; Portes 1998; Woolcock 1998), political capital (Boltanski and Thévenot 2006), financial capital (Foster and McChesney 2009), and built capital (Grübler 1990). These capitals are heuristic devices that allow identification of the entire range of community assets, which, when invested to create new resources, become capital.

Macro trends have made it more difficult for local governments to respond as they did in past recessions by investing in themselves (Cox 2009). State and federal laws increasingly limit what can be taxed at the county and community level and how much it can be taxed, while generous tax breaks for corporate interests have changed governance strategies in rural communities (Cox 2009). Local governments have increased burdens in terms of schools, highways, and health and police protection, as federal and state governments shed functions (Hutchinson and Osborne 2004; Hawkins, Bingham, and Hedge 1982). Local governments have less access to the capitals necessary to respond to large influxes of contingent workers and their families. The different historical, cultural, political, and economic contexts in which each community acts provide the impetus and the limitations to community organization and mobilization.

We examine the mobilization of community capitals in the face of what seems to be overwhelming structural forces: the current boom in petrochemical extraction facilitated by the technology of hydraulic fracturing, a major economic force, and the lack of comprehensive immigration reform, a state (as in government) force, through two community case studies. The major issues addressed by each community center around social relations.

Community Response to External Forces

We present two studies of community responses to population changes threatening their existing institutional relations in the Great Plains and Midwest, regions that historically stressed the need for local communities to take charge of their own futures (Wunthrow 2011). We began our studies of these communities in 2005 and 2008. These communities confronted structural change with relatively high degrees of entrepreneurial social infrastructure (Flora and Flora 1990; Flora et al. 1997) that facilitated their collective responses in the face of financialization of the economy (Tomaskovic-Devey and Lin 2011) and the shrinking of the state (except for law enforcement institutions, e.g., Immigration and Customs Enforcement) (Smith and Tickamyer 2011).

One community we examined responded to the out-migration of the local rural labor force and the influx of immigrants from Mexico and Central America (Sioux County, Iowa) and the other to the rapid in-migration of petroleum workers as new technologies increased the extraction of natural gas and oil in a major shale deposit (McKenzie County, North Dakota). Both cases required civic engagement of local enterprises (market), local governments (state), and voluntary association (civil society) actors to utilize local assets to maintain and enhance local communities.

In McKenzie County and its county seat and largest town, Watford City, change was market led by private sector oil and gas drilling and their service companies. Civil society and local government mediated the disruption caused by the rapid influx of workers. The president's inability to build consensus in Congress on a balanced and reasoned energy and resource taxation policy has accelerated domestic resource extraction beyond the market-based incentives for exploration and extraction generated by an expanding world demand for energy.

In Sioux County, the state was the primary actor to which the market and civil society felt obligated to respond. The county sheriff took advantage of a political vacuum created by the failure of the federal government to act on comprehensive immigration reform; as we shall see, civil society and market-based firms responded. Despite recognition of the need for comprehensive immigration reform by both the George W. Bush and Barack Obama administrations, no resolution to the increasing reliance of American industry on undocumented immigrant labor has emerged from Congress (Donato and Armenta 2011). As immigrants are increasingly targeted by groups seeking political advantage through encouraging nativist sentiments (Massey and Sanchez 2010), hopes of a federal or even state solutions fade (Rosenblum 2010; Terrazas 2011).

Natural Resource-Based Boomtown: McKenzie County and Watford City, North Dakota

The Setting

The Little Missouri National Grasslands, the Theodore Roosevelt National Park (North Unit), Lake Sakakawea, Fort Berthold Indian Reservation, the Missouri River, and the Little Missouri Rivers are part of McKenzie County. Underneath the varied ecosystem lies the Bakken rock formation containing substantial reserves of oil that traditional petroleum extraction techniques could not reach.

In 2000, over 24 percent of Watford City's population was more than sixty-five years old. Watford's population fell by about 19.6 percent in the 1990s, but grew by 21.5 percent in the succeeding decade (US Census Bureau 2010). Many of the younger folks that moved away during the 1990s moved back in the early 2000s to raise families, viewing a small town as a safer, more nurturing environment. In 2000, just over 77 percent of McKenzie County residents had a high school diploma and perhaps some college. An additional 17 percent of the population had a bachelor's degree or higher (US Census Bureau 2000).

Entrepreneurial Social Infrastructure

Trust and interdependence pervaded Watford City and McKenzie County from at least the 1930s through the first decade of the twenty-first century. That ability to work together and with the outside to innovate is evident from the grazing association that negotiated to manage Bureau of Land Management land to the employee-furnished coffee area at the county courthouse, where the sign on the wall reads that you're welcome to anything, just please contribute to the pot. Local store owners knew and trusted their customers. As one woman said in our 2005 community meeting, "If you forget your checkbook [while you're out shopping] and you say, 'Can I take it?' there's no question that it's OK." This trust reciprocates back to store owners; several residents said that for hard-to-find items they'd rather patronize local stores and ask them to special order the items rather than drive out of town to find the item immediately.

In August 2006, a "Fabulous Western Fantasy Playground" was erected in downtown Watford City. Six women organized the project, with Rene Johnson at the head. Johnson designed the project as part of NDSU Extension's Rural Leadership North Dakota program. Various groups entirely within the community, including children going door to door with red wagons collecting change, raised $200,000. Once the ground had been prepared and all the equipment received, an all-volunteer crew erected the playground in three days. Over 7,500 person hours were donated. Free childcare was provided for volunteers. All the local and regional news articles covering the projects mentioned the tremendous sense of community felt by all involved. People from all walks of life came to help and many made new friends.

The Long-X Bottle Shop liquor store, long the only non-restaurant licensed to sell liquor in Watford City due to a city ordinance limiting the city to one license per 3,000 residents based on census population, is an interesting example of social entrepreneurship. All profits go to community grants, but particularly to the county health facilities. The Watford City Community Benefit Association originally opened the shop to support the improvements at the local hospital and later the nursing home. That holistic approach to serving the community in a variety of ways was manifest in the social entrepreneurship in Watford City. In a community meeting with us as part of an action research project with North Dakota State Cooperative Extension, a resident emphasized how the community seeks to be politically integrative and why: "You bring in the naysayers, because if they have a better idea, you want to do it." This political capital would not be possible without the strong base of social capital that Watford City possesses.

The First International Bank and Trust, headquartered in Watford City, has helped politically and financially spearhead many development initiatives. The "get it done" ethic of Watford City is leveraged by First International to help the community. As a bank representative told us, "When we call the Bank of North Dakota, they listen because they know we'll do what we say."

In the mid-1990s, First International Bank and Trust moved to in-house check processing and bought two banks in Arizona, complementing their several other in-state branches. To manage their dispersed banks, they invested heavily in information technology, including video conferencing with which to conduct meetings and interview new employees.

A community-wide high-speed Internet push followed the bank's lead. Community Internet and computer training courses were widely offered by various groups including the Community Technology Center in Watford City, the North Dakota State University Extension Service (both local and state staff), and the McKenzie County IT coordinator. Participation in these courses was high. Local businesses benefited from the human and built capital of this technology. An example is e-pharmacist Larry Larsen who owns two drugstores, one in Watford City and another fifty miles away. He keeps an (electronic) eye on the latter, helping customers remotely via video over the Internet.

The McKenzie County Health Care System consists of faith-affiliated and public institutions. The hospital, the clinic, the Good Shepard retirement home, and the local wellness center are locally controlled and co-located. This allows all the facilities to share resources and personnel and contributes to the cohesiveness of the community.

Of the city's $1.3 million 2005 budget (not including utilities, which are self-financing), about $500,000 came from oil and gas revenue. The city was debt free, with no bonds or loans to service. City taxable sales have been steadily climbing since the mid-2000s. Watford City has a 1 percent sales tax called the Roughrider Fund, which goes entirely to fund citywide improvements as stated in the City Plan.

Watford City and McKenzie County provide a social and cultural setting where local residents can work together and where business formation, success, and failure are considered part of community life. Many of the local businesses support financial and human capital formation, including a locally started financial institution and a large number of health enhancement services. The community also understands its dependence on natural resources.

The Disruption

Commercial development of the hydraulic fracturing process (popularly known as fracking) fueled the recent boom in shale oil production, setting the stage for an invasion of oil rigs and massive crews to install them. The first horizontal well was drilled in in North Dakota in 2006. (Seifert n.d.; see also Kinchy et al. in this volume). The new phase of oil and gas expansion using this new drilling technology began in in McKenzie County in 2010 (SafeTech Solutions 2011, 9).

There is a rich literature on boomtowns that demonstrates the impacts of huge investments of financial capital to create the built capital to extract natural capital. Changes in human capital, social capital, and political capital are dramatic, although some communities can mediate those shocks to a degree (Albrecht 1978; Freudenburg 1981; 1992; Kiefer and Miller 1984; Smith, Krannich, and Hunter 2001; Brown, Dorius, and Krannich 2005; Kinchy et al. in this volume). Generally, there are huge disruptions as population and financial capital flow to the community to extract the resource, followed by increases in social dislocation and in social problems, including crime, substance abuse, and interpersonal violence. Inequality rises, as those who do not have access to the mineral rights or the high paying jobs associated with wealth extraction find it difficult to access housing or services, and all prices rise. Public services, such as police, health care, and fire departments, are stretched by huge increases in emergencies that require their services. Infrastructure deteriorates, as renters do not care for their living space and heavily loaded construction vehicles pulverize the roads. As extraction of natural capital often requires a great deal of water, water and sewage systems experience overload and failure. Recovery does occur, but there is little chance of the earlier equilibrium of local businesses and institutions reestablishing themselves. Better-organized communities with high degrees of the entrepreneurial social infrastructure prior to the boom appear to recover better.

McKenzie County had 6,360 residents in April 2010 before extensive fracking reached its part of the Bakken Shale Formation later that year. Twelve months later, the population had increased by 10.4 percent, equal to the growth over the entire previous decade (US Census Bureau 2000). In 2012, Watford City, which in 2010 had a population of 1,744 (US Census Bureau 2012a), redid its strategic plan to accommodate fifteen thousand residents. It did so building on its record of progressive participation. We argue that progressive participation, in which a community makes decisions for the common good, is an outcome of high bridging and high bonding social capital. This, in turn, fosters entrepreneurial social infrastructure (Flora and Flora 2013, 128, 132–8). With the rapid influx of newcomers, the critical question is whether the "soft" capitals can be maintained in the face of the current energy boom.

The Response

The proposed county budget for the 2013 fiscal year was $95.8 million, double that of the 2012 budget. Oil and gas revenues provided a large portion of the increase. McKenzie County also experienced the largest increase in sales tax revenue in the state in 2012. In addition, revenue from heavy vehicle fees increased dramatically.

Oil development, particularly fracking, is a huge drain on groundwater. Plans for water procurement had to be completely revamped. The McKenzie County Water Resource District developed plans for a $12 million systems expansion ("Oil in North Dakota Brings Big Opportunity, Big Challenges" 2008).

The greatest immediate problem was lack of affordable housing for this booming population. By mid-2012, there were plans for nine different housing developments near Watford City, which annexed three adjacent areas to accommodate growth. In total, these annexations and development plans encompass more than 800 acres.

Civil society and its market partnerships have worked hard to respond, but have faced setbacks in their ability to mobilize local resources for the public good. Under pressure from developers, the City Council, despite opposition from the Watford City Community Benefit Association (WCCBA), voted to change the city ordinance limiting the number of off-site liquor licenses (City of Watford City Council Meeting, 4 June 2012). The Oppidan Investment Company of the Twin Cities in Minnesota promoted the change. The ability of the WCCBA to contribute to the city's common good has greatly decreased as outside investors gain influence. This will have particular impact on the hard-pressed health care facilities.

The community has mobilized a series of activities to make it convenient for the families of the workers to move to town, through such efforts as Mothers of Preschoolers (MOPS). MOPS organizes activities for preschoolers and their families that integrates them quickly into the community by providing the opportunity to contribute to the group through working with the children and well as to receive needed childcare.

The inequalities generated by the boom have not yet been fully appreciated, but have implications for social, human, financial, and even cultural capital. Because of the external origin and control of the oil and gas extraction enterprise (externally based financial and political capital), Watford City and McKenzie County are likely to be pushed in the direction of clientelism (high-bridging but low-bonding social capital; see Flora and Flora 2013, 128). There is already a tendency for ambitious local leaders to ally themselves with the oil companies, developers, and other external agents, rather than continuing to strengthen bonding social capital in the face of external pressure and growing inequalities. Whether or not the community can continue to exhibit entrepreneurial social infrastructure remains to be seen, and much depends on proactive local efforts to maintain bonding social capital by reaching out to new residents. At the same time, it is important to diversify external contacts (bridging social capital), enlisting outside resources to ameliorate the negative social, cultural, and financial features of the externally based growth machine (Logan and Molotch 1987).

New Immigrants and Rural Communities: Local and Federal Policy Clashes

The Setting

Located in the fertile river-crossed plain immediately east of the Missouri River, Sioux County provided the Sioux (Lakota) with a good living combining hunting, gathering, and migratory farming. The oak savannah was well-suited to the large buffalo herds that roamed the prairie.

Dutch immigrants settled the county beginning in 1869. They maintain many of the customs that were prevalent in the Dutch Reformed areas of the Netherlands in the nineteenth century. As of 2011, 80 percent of Sioux County residents were descendants of Dutch immigrants ("Sioux County, Iowa" 2012).

Sioux County is prosperous and conservative. In 2007, the county ranked first in Iowa in sales of beef cattle, dairy products, hogs, and sheep; first in broiler inventory; and second in number of acres of corn in production (US Department of Agriculture 2012). Agriculture in Sioux County employs the latest farm machinery and biotechnology.

Sioux County's median income is higher than that of the state of Iowa, while its cost of living is lower. There are the usual government jobs with schools, hospitals, and other government services, but most of the employment is with small- and medium-sized private sector enterprises. Taxable valuation is higher than that of other rural Iowa counties. Well-manicured golf courses are surrounded by McMansions, although in the countryside the homes are solid but modest from the outside. Building permits continued high throughout the Great Recession that started in 2008.

Unemployment in Sioux County was less than 3 percent in 2008 and only 3.9 percent in 2012, according to the economic data of the Federal Reserve Bank of St. Louis. Persons below the poverty level made up 6.4 percent of the population, well below the 11.6 percent of the Iowa population so classified (average 2006 to 2010; US Census Bureau 2012b). Most young people from Sioux County seek higher education after high school. Those who complete their college education tend not to return to the county.

Entrepreneurial Social Infrastructure

Sioux County is noteworthy for its large number of locally owned businesses, particularly light manufacturing and agriculture. There is support for economic innovation, stemming in part from the strong Calvinist background of most of the residents.

Members of the two branches of the Dutch Reformed church established colleges in Sioux County. Northwestern College is affiliated with the Reformed Church in America, the North American branch of the Dutch Reformed Church. Dordt College is affiliated with the Christian Reformed Church, an even more Calvinist offshoot of the Dutch Reformed Church. Dutch ethnic solidarity and its work ethic and communal cooperation fostered strong entrepreneurs, strong families, and educated youths. Faith is an important component of the county's cultural capital. According to the Glenmary Research Center, at the turn of the twenty-first century, 96.4 percent of the Sioux County population claimed a religious congregation, compared to 50.2 percent of the US population as a whole (Jones et al. 2002). Further, a very large portion of K–12 education is provided by church-based schools.

In 1998, service professional in hospitals, schools, local governments, and churches founded CASA (Center for Assistance, Service and Advocacy), an all-volunteer non-profit organization that seeks to meet immediate needs of the county's immigrant residents and cultivate community support by sponsoring education and outreach initiatives and engaging community leadership. Its mission is "to justly assist, serve and advocate for people of all races, creeds, and cultures by building bridges that strengthen the whole person, family, and community" (CASA Sioux County 2012). CASA provides or brokers resources for Sioux County immigrants and area advocacy and faith groups working with immigrants.

CASA partners with diverse area and state groups (bridging social capital) to ensure seamless service provision and ample community education opportunities. Active members include retirees and college students, Anglos, American Indians and Hispanics/Latinos, priests, nurses, and stay-at-home parents. For most CASA members, actions and attitudes toward their immigrant neighbors are informed primarily by their respective faith traditions. Diverse in their political views, they agree that "welcoming the stranger" is a Biblical mandate.

CASA as an organization is acutely aware that without regional government and law enforcement support, documented and undocumented immigrants as well as native-born Latinos in Sioux County will continue to face significant challenges to integration in the community.

The Disruption

The wave of immigration to the United States that began in the 1980s and continued until the Great Recession was a response to globalizing forces and, in particular, the imposition of neoliberal policies implemented in the wake of the world economic slowdown in developing countries during the early 1980s. Those policies were designed to ensure repayment of loans transferred to developing countries to pay for increased energy costs in the 1970s and to oblige those countries to integrate more fully in the international trade regime created by the World Trade Organization and multilateral and bilateral trade agreements designed to promote expansion of international trade (Flora 1990). The flood of subsidized US agricultural products that resulted from the rapid elimination of tariffs between the United States and Mexico with the implementation of North American Free Trade Agreement set up a situation in which corn was traded for people as people in rural Mexico lost their livelihoods. Because no international migration regime was developed to parallel the trade regime, the bulk of North American migration per force was extralegal.

In the United States, weakening trade unions and expanding wage and income inequality contributed to a substantial numbers of jobs that the US-born population was reluctant to take. Many of those jobs in rural parts of the United States have an impact on labor and ethnic dynamics in industrial agricultural and manufacturing communities throughout the rural Midwest and South, including Sioux County, Iowa.

Sioux County's population increased 6.7 percent to 33,700 between 2000 and 2010 ("Sioux County, Iowa" 2012), in part through the immigration of workers employed by the major livestock industries in the county, as well as a number of small manufacturing firms in the county. In 2011, Hispanics were 9.2 percent of the population (US Census Bureau 2012b) compared to 2.6 percent in 2000 ("Sioux County, Iowa" 2012). Both farm and nonfarm employment increased with the expansion of dairies and hog confined animal feeding operations. These jobs are overwhelmingly low-wage and require little formal education. The Latino population tends to live in the less expensive neighborhoods of the outlying towns.

Employers in Sioux County found that their Latino workers were not coming to work in the last months of 2007. The local sheriff's department was stopping vehicles driven by immigrants on their way to work. Cell phones are the major communication tool among immigrants, and once one immigrant worker was stopped, other workers were notified by their colleagues and did not even attempt to go to work. Some immigrant families permanently left the area out of fear.

For Sioux County meat processors and dairies, as well as beef, swine, and poultry producers, no workers meant no production and hence no income. Others in the community were concerned because of the broken families that resulted when a parent was deported.

The Response

The business owners and school and medical community representatives got together with the help of Cooperative Extension, which was viewed as a neutral convener with both production and social concerns. They asked for a meeting with the Sioux County Board of Supervisors to combat what they perceived as racial harassment (Heronemus 2009).

Approximately one hundred people attended the meeting on 26 February 2008. Much to the group's surprise, the county sheriff and the county attorney were there. All agreed that something needed to be done at the local level. That meeting established a planning committee with representatives from the board of supervisors, Iowa State University Extension, Social Services, and the president of CASA Sioux County. The group met regularly from March through May 2008, and then launched a focus group discussion series on immigration issues in order to provide a venue for community and business leaders to learn, share information, and communicate candidly with each other in a safe environment. When federal Immigration and Customs Enforcement authorities appeared after the meeting in the workplace of one of those on the panel who had explained the value of immigrants for his business, the wariness of Anglo employers began to match those of their Latino employees.

The Focus Group Discussion Series examined immigration topics from multiple perspectives, looking specifically at how immigration affects Sioux County. Based on this, participating community and business leaders would make recommendations to the county supervisors for addressing immigration locally. Nineteen local leaders and two facilitators met from mid-June through mid-September to learn all they could about the issue. They dealt with the myths about immigrants—and discovered the facts of the matter. They learned about the complexities of immigration law, as well as the limits of current immigration laws to respond to the needs of Sioux County because of the limited number of visas available to unskilled workers. The group was dismayed to learn that there is no practical way for immigrants seeking unskilled labor positions in Sioux County to do so legally.

The public forum discussing the economic impact of immigrants on Sioux County included an egg production manager, a dairy manager, the local economic development director, a construction company owner, and a local retail business manager. Pointing to the positive economic position of Sioux County in terms of business and population growth and the low local unemployment rate, they explained why they needed immigrant labor to fill their unskilled positions. They found Hispanic workers dependable, hardworking, pleasant, and genuinely grateful for a chance to work. Rather than taking away jobs from the local labor force, the employers judged that immigrants were filling a strongly felt shortage of unskilled labor. They came up with three action steps:

1. Hold politicians accountable for practical solutions.
2. Develop a media campaign to provide the public with thoughtful consideration of issues regarding our immigrant population
3. Provide learning opportunities for the public regarding immigration and its impact on our communities.

These activities have been implemented throughout the county.

The Sioux County 100 formed in the spring of 2012 following an eight-week community education workshop at the American Reformed Church in Orange City, Iowa. The group crafted a petition calling for immigration reform at the federal level as well as humane and welcoming policy and social changes at the local and regional levels (Helping Our Iowa Neighbors 2012). The group collaborates with the Iowa Compact, a statewide effort to get local and state agencies to institute more immigrant-friendly rules and regulations and to stop capturing individuals of suspect documentation and turning them over to Immigration and Customs Enforcement, to be detained in private prisons without access to relatives or legal recourse. The Sioux County 100 also has devised an effort to encourage influential Iowans to push on the national scene for comprehensive immigration reform.

While there were 803 signers of the petition as of 9 November 2012, there seems to be little political impact. The recently reelected congressional representative for the area, Steve King, announced he was filing a suit to reinstate the deportation of young people without documentation brought to the United States as children by their parents.

Sioux County has a historic reputation—largely deserved—of being a tight knit community where bonding social capital, based on the dominant ethnicity (cultural capital), is high. It is also well connected. The communities of Sioux County are able to solve their own problems, but are also not afraid to reach out for information and resources. The rapid growth of the Latino population that accompanied the latest phase of the industrialization of agriculture threatened the progressive participation consensus, by throwing up potential boundaries among factions of its inhabitants as they struggled with the question of unauthorized immigration. Collective agency has strengthened relationships so that the new, hard-working inhabitants whose work ethic and strong familism resemble that the values of the dominant culture will be accepted into the community and that the differences among factions of the long-term residents smoothed over, if not resolved.

Conclusions

The two cases studied above illustrate the difficulty local communities have in overcoming and moderating globalizing forces that affect them. The communities studied showed strength in all the capitals prior to the outside forces impinging on them. Partly because of their strong social, cultural, and political capital, they were both relatively well-off with respect to financial, built, and human capital. In McKenzie County and Watford City, the particular combination of capitals provides a degree of resilience as they face the typical issues boomtowns face. However, there is the real possibility that the community will be overwhelmed by the issues it must confront in relation to rapid growth—housing, social services, etc.—but also by the disproportionate power held by the oil and gas companies and related service companies compared with the local governments and civic organizations. The sheer difficulty the communities had in obtaining information on the effect of fracking on water quality means that they operate from an information deficit vis-à-vis the powerful outside economic forces. Similarly, in Sioux County the challenges of creating a welcoming environment for new immigrants in the context of archaic immigration laws, rules, and regulations limits the ability of each community to enhance social inclusion and ecosystem health.

The alternatives available in McKenzie County were limited by federal policies that decreased the power of labor to negotiate stable working conditions and of the state to regulate damage to natural capital as a result of hydraulic fractionation. Even fewer options were available in Sioux County without comprehensive immigration reform and in the face of increased local-national collaboration on enforcement. Both communities had a strong sense of local identity and had experience in developing collective effort to deal with controversial issues in the past. Both developed innovative ways to welcome strangers—in one case, documented workers (although often without benefits or long-term contracts) that came in vast numbers. The city and county governments combined their assets to create an orderly mechanism to deal with the housing, the most visible disrupter of relationships, through creating new mixed-income developments. A high level of community capacity was mobilized and key local actors from the banks and local firms, civil society, and county and city governments made the arrival of new workers and their families less disruptive than it might otherwise have been. In Sioux County, strong ethnic and religious values provided the convention around which pragmatists and pluralists could organize for local and national policy change and immigrant support.

McKenzie County mobilized its assets to resolve at least partially the disruption from the shifting economic, policy, and technological trends. They are much less aware of the role of federal policies than are the people of Sioux County, even as concern for water quality and quantity increases. In Sioux County, local assets were mobilized to increase social inclusion by drawing on local cultural capital to influence political capital to respond to local, rather than national, conventions regarding the treatment of immigrants. Given relative local prosperity, it was easier for these two communities to act to repair the social fabric, but, given the larger forces, such efforts were incomplete in achieving the desired goals of a healthy ecosystem, economic security for all, and social inclusion.

References

Albrecht, Stan L. 1978. "Socio-cultural Factors and Energy Resource Development in Rural Areas in the West." *Journal of Environmental Management* 7: 73–90.

Becker, Gary S. 1975. *Human Capital.* 2nd ed. New York: Columbia University Pres.

Boltanski, Luc, and Laurent Thévenot. 2006. *On Justification: The Economies of Worth.* Princeton, NJ: Princeton University Press.

Bourdieu, Pierre. 1986. "The Forms of Capital." In *Handbook of Theory and Research for the Sociology of Education*, ed. John C. Richardson, 241–58. New York: Greenwood Press.

Brown, Ralph B., Shawn F. Dorius, and Richard S. Krannich. 2005. "The Boom-Bust Recovery Cycle: Dynamics of Change in Community Satisfaction and Social Integration in Delta, Utah." *Rural Sociology* 70 (1): 28–49. http://dx.doi.org/10.1526/0036011053294673.

CASA Sioux County. 2012. "Mission." Accessed 29 September 2012. http://www.casasiouxcounty.org/.

City of Watford City Council Meeting, 4 June 2012. Watford City, North Dakota.

Cox, Raymond W. 2009. "Seeding the Clouds for the Perfect Storm: A Commentary on the Current Fiscal Crisis." *State and Local Government Review* 41 (3): 216–22. http://dx.doi.org/10.1177/0160323X0904100307.

Daly, Herman E. 1996. *Beyond Growth: The Economics of Sustainable Development.* Boston: Beacon Press.

Donato, Katharine M., and Amada Armenta. 2011. "What We Know about Unauthorized Migration." *Annual Review of Sociology* 37 (1): 529–43. http://dx.doi.org/10.1146/annurev-soc-081309-150216.

Flora, Cornelia B. 1990. "Presidential Address: Rural Peoples in a Global Economy." *Rural Sociology* 55 (2): 157–77. http://dx.doi.org/10.1111/j.1549-0831.1990.tb00678.x.

Flora, Cornelia B., and Jan L. Flora. 1990. "Developing Entrepreneurial Rural Communities." *Sociological Practice* 8: 197–207.

Flora, Cornelia B., and Jan L. Flora. 2013. *Rural Communities: Legacy and Change.* 4th ed. Boulder, CO: Westview Press.

Flora, Jan L., Jeff S. Sharp, Cornelia Butler Flora, and Bonnie Newlon. 1997. "Entrepreneurial Social Infrastructure and Locally-Initiated Economic Development." *Sociological Quarterly* 38 (4): 623–45. http://dx.doi.org/10.1111/j.1533-8525.1997.tb00757.x.

Foster, John B., and Robert W. McChesney. 2009. "Monopoly Finance Capital and the Paradox of Accumulation." *Monthly Review (New York, N.Y.)* 61 (5): 1–28. http://dx.doi.org/10.14452/MR-061-05-2009-09_1.

Freudenburg, William R. 1981. "Women and Men in an Energy Boomtown: Adjustment, Alienation, and Adaptation." *Rural Sociology* 46: 220–44.

Freudenburg, William R. 1992. "Addictive Economies: Extractive Industries and Vulnerable Localities in a Changing World Economy." *Rural Sociology* 57 (3): 305–32. http://dx.doi.org/10.1111/j.1549-0831.1992.tb00467.x.

Grübler, Arnold. 1990. *The Rise and Fall of Infrastructures: Dynamics of Evolution and Technological Change in Transport.* New York: Springer-Verlag.

Hawkins, Brett W., Richard D. Bingham, and David M. Hedge. 1982. "A Note on the Local Effects of State Revenue Centralization." *State and Local Government Review* 14 (2): 91–93.

Helping Our Iowa Neighbors. 2012. Accessed 29 September. http://ouriowaneighbors.com/contact.

Heronemus, Cheryl. 2009. "Immigration Focus Group: Sioux County, Iowa." Presented at the 2009 meeting of the National Association of Community Development Extension Professionals, San Diego, CA.

Hutchinson, Peter, and David Osborne. 2004. *Price of Government: Getting the Results We Need in an Age of Permanent Fiscal Crisis.* New York: Basic Books.

Jaffe, JoAnn, and Amy Quark. 2005. "Social Cohesion: Theory or Politics? Evidence from Studies of Saskatchewan Rural Communities under Neoliberalism." *Prairie Forum* 30: 229–52.

Jansson, Ann M., Monica Hammer, Carl Folke, and Robert Costanza, eds. 1994. *Investing in Natural Capital: The Ecological Economics Approach to Sustainability.* Covelo, CA: Island Press.

Jones, Dale E., Sherri Doty, Clifford Grammich, James E. Horsch, Richard Houseal, Mac Lynn, John P. Marcum, Kenneth M. Sanchagrin, and Richard H. Taylor. 2002. *Religious Congregations and Membership in the United States 2000: An Enumeration by Region, State and County Based on Data Reported for 149 Religious Bodies.* Fairfield, OH: Glenmary Research Institute.

Kiefer, David, and Jan Miller. 1984. "Public Budgets and Public Capital in Boom Towns." *Policy Sciences* 16 (4): 349–69. http://dx.doi.org/10.1007/BF00135954.

Kuznets, Simon. 1955. "Economic Growth and Income Inequality." *American Economic Review* 45: 1–28.

Logan, John R., and Harvey L. Molotch. 1987. *Urban Fortunes: The Political Economy of Place.* Berkeley: University of California Press.

Massey, Douglas, and Magaly R. Sanchez. 2010. *Brokered Boundaries: Creating Immigrant Identity in Anti-Immigrant Times.* New York: Russell Sage Foundation.

"Oil in North Dakota Brings Big Opportunity, Big Challenges." 2008. North Dakota Water, December.

Portes, Alejandro. 1998. "Social Capital: Its Origins and Applications in Modern Sociology." *Annual Review of Sociology* 24 (1): 1–24. http://dx.doi.org/10.1146/annurev.soc.24.1.1.

Putnam, Robert D. 1993. *Making Democracy Work: Civic Traditions in Modern Italy.* Princeton, NJ: Princeton University Press. http://dx.doi.org/10.1002/ncr.4100820204.

Rosenblum, Marc R. 2010. "Immigrant Legalization in the United States and the European Union: Policy Goals and Program Design." Policy brief. Washington, DC: Migration Policy Institute.

SafeTech Solutions. 2011. "The Impact of Oil and Energy Development on out-of-Hospital Emergency Medical Services: Dunn, Williams, Mountrail, and McKenzie Counties," Conducted for the North Dakota Department of Health, June. Accessed 4 November 2012. http://ndhealth.gov/ems/pdfs/oil-impact-final-report.pdf.

Seifert, Laura. n.d. "A Basic Analysis of the Bakken Oil Boom: Precautions and Planning." University of Minnesota, unpublished manuscript. Accessed 4 November 2012. http://www.ndoil.org/image/cache/bakken_precautions_and_planning_-_seifert.pdf.

Sen, Amartya K. 2000. *Social Exclusion: Concept, Application, and Scrutiny.* Manila, Philippines: Asian Development Bank.

"Sioux County, Iowa." 2012. *Wikipedia: The Free Encyclopedia.* Accessed 11 November 2012. http://en.wikipedia.org/wiki/sioux_county,_iowa.

Smith, Kristin E., and Ann R. Tickamyer. 2011. *Economic Restructuring and Family Well-Being in Rural America.* University Park: The Pennsylvania State University Press.

Smith, Michael D., Richard S. Krannich, and Lori M. Hunter. 2001. "Growth, Decline, Stability and Disruption: A Longitudinal Analysis of Social Well-Being in Four Western Rural Communities." *Rural Sociology* 66 (3): 425–50. http://dx.doi.org/10.1111/j.1549-0831.2001.tb00075.x.

Stiglitz, Joseph E. 2012. *The Price of Inequality.* New York: W.W. Norton.

Terrazas, Aaron. 2011. *Migration and Development: Policy Perspectives from the United States.* Washington, DC: Migration Policy Institute.

Tomaskovic-Devey, Donald, and Ken-Hou Lin. 2011. "Income Dynamics, Economic Rents, and the Financialization of the U.S. Economy." *American Sociological Review* 76 (4): 538–59. http://dx.doi.org/10.1177/0003122411414827.

US Census Bureau. 2000. Demographic Profiles. Accessed 5 November 2012. http://censtats.census.gov/pub/Profiles.shtml.

US Census Bureau. 2010. "Interactive Population Search." Accessed 4 January 2014. http://www.census.gov/2010census/popmap.

US Census Bureau. 2012a. "State and County Quick-Facts: McKenzie County, North Dakota." Last modified 24 September. http://quickfacts.census.gov/qfd/states/19000.html.

US Census Bureau. 2012b. "State and County Quick-Facts: Sioux County, Iowa." Last modified 24 September. http://quickfacts.census.gov/qfd/states/19000.html.

US Department of Agriculture. 2012. "County Profile: Sioux County, Iowa," 2007 Census of Agriculture. Last modified 10 April. http://www.agcensus.usda.gov/Publications/2007/Online_Highlights/County_Profiles/Iowa/cp19167.pdf.

Wilkinson, R.G., and K.E. Pickett. 2009a. "Income Inequality and Social Dysfunction." *Annual Review of Sociology* 35 (1): 493–511. http://dx.doi.org/10.1146/annurev-soc-070308-115926.

Wilkinson, R.G., and K.E. Pickett. 2009b. *The Spirit Level: Why Greater Equality Makes Societies Stronger*. New York: Bloomsbury Press.

Woolcock, Michael. 1998. "Social Capital and Economic Development: Toward a Theoretical Synthesis and Policy Framework." *Theory and Society* 27 (2): 151–208. http://dx.doi.org/10.1023/A:1006884930135.

Wunthrow, Robert. 2011. *Remaking the Heartland: Middle America Since the 1950s*. Princeton, NJ: Princeton University Press.

CHAPTER 32

Community as Moral Proximity: Theorizing Community in a Global Economy

Todd L. Goodsell, Jeremy Flaherty, and Ralph B. Brown

Introduction

In this chapter we contribute to the discussion about how morality and community are related to each other. Specifically, we propose that community is defined by moral proximity; in other words, our community is the sphere of individuals, institutions, and activities for which a person feels responsible. When community is local, a concept long accepted with axiomatic fervor in rural sociology, people often feel a greater sense of responsibility for and are immediately confronted by the consequences of their actions. However, under conditions of globalization—the increased global interconnectedness of social and economic life brought about by rapid changes in information and transportation technologies (Bailey, Jensen, and Ransom in this volume; Lechner and Boli 2012)—this sense of community is thrown into question and makes the relationship between the decision makers' actions and the consequences of these actions unclear, distant, and often indirect. Therefore, we believe it is important to promote community as responsibility in a globalizing world. We build this theory in the following section by exploring the intersection of globalization with the work of Ulrich Beck and Zygmunt Bauman, two contemporary theorists who explore the consequences of modernity and its effects on community. We then highlight the need to define community by moral proximity: a community is the sphere of individuals, institutions, and activities for which a person feels responsible. We believe that the global challenges residents of rural communities face can only be addressed by a community built on moral proximity that takes responsibility for neighbors both local and global.

Community is a form of social organization wherein the social interactions necessary for the reproduction of daily life occur within the boundaries of moral proximity. The overriding problem of modernity—the loss of community—allows for the removal of these interactions from that proximity. In late-modern life, this problem has only been exacerbated, as the globalization of economics has provided a context in which individuals' mundane daily actions sometimes result in singularly immoral consequences on a global level for which the individuals feel no responsibility.

Theories that define community as local solidarities or networks of primary ties help perpetuate the problem of modernity by placing essential social ties and interactions beyond the boundaries of moral concern. Such theories are no longer viable approaches to community or community development. These theories are trapped in an ahistorical and overly romantic view that fails to address the primary issues facing communities today. Following the work of Beck and Bauman, we argue that community—understood as moral proximity—is brought into question because of globalization and that the consequences of the separation of responsibility from essential aspects of everyday life have potentially disastrous consequences. In the context of globalization, community must be reimagined to include, once again, *all* the ties and interactions necessary to individuals' daily lives—whether they occur locally or not—so that communities can begin to address the problems associated with the removal of these ties and interactions from our moral proximity.

Linking Morality and Community

Scholars have linked morality and community for centuries. Nineteenth-century political historian Alexis de Tocqueville gives two reasons that morality and community are linked. First, he argues that citizens in democratic nations are "independent and feeble," without any way of obliging others to help them: "They all, therefore, fall into a state of incapacity, if they do not learn voluntarily to help each other" (de Tocqueville 2000, 629). Second, beyond this basic, functional need for voluntary cooperation, de Tocqueville observes that citizens in democratic societies need moral judgment and that this moral sense is only developed through human associations and relationships (631). Scholars in various disciplines have since continued to explore this relationship between morality and community. In geography, for example, Smith (1999) notes that community has a normative component; it is not just locality (cf. Goodsell et al. 2011). Radical geography of the 1970s foregrounded moral concerns, and morality enjoyed a resurgence in geography during the 1990s (Smith 2000). In sociology, moral questions have always been central to the discipline (Levine 1995, 100), and sociological community studies often address moral problems such as inequality, mobility, and social and economic exclusion (e.g., Anderson 1967; Anderson 1990; Banfield 1958; Baumgartner 1988; Brown-Saracino 2009; Dollard 1988; DuBois 1996; Erikson 1976; Goodsell 2013; Pérez 2004; Wirth 1998; Zorbaugh 1976).

Three Approaches to Morality and Community

The relationship between morality and community is complex and there are several ways in which scholars have explored it; however, such studies tend to fall within one of three general categories: (1) those that take a framework of rationality, (2) those that focus on subjectivity and the communicative processes that create it, and (3) those that focus on responsibility as the defining feature of moral community. Our purpose in reviewing this literature is to situate our work within the larger field of theory and research on morality and community, and specifically to extend the scholarship on the third category of community as responsibility. The literature here is quite large, so we only provide a sampling of relevant research, but this sample is sufficient to provide the foundation for our argument.

Rationality

The first approach to the relationship between morality and community uses a framework of rationality. Within this broader approach, some studies use a conflict framework that claims the rational approach to community is one that gains an advantage (such as belonging or security) for the individual and the members of the individual's own group while excluding others who are not members of that group (Bauman 2001; Baumgartner 1988; Reed 2004, 228; Ryle and Robinson 2006; Sherman 2006; Sherman 2009). Exclusion, inequality, and social justice are key concerns. Other studies in this approach examine the perceived tension between autonomy and community, particularly the conflict between a moral code that values autonomy (emphasizing harm, rights, and justice) and one that values community (emphasizing duty, hierarchy, and interdependence). Some scholars have found that Western cultures place more emphasis on the former (Haidt, Koller, and Dias 1993; Shweder et al. 1997), while others maintain that autonomy and community can flourish together (Beauchamp and Childress 2009, 102; Bellah et al. 1996, 162). A final set of studies begins with the rationalist framework for morality and community and then questions whether the bases for making moral judgments are rational (e.g., Jones and Ryan 1997) or emotional/intuitive (e.g., Haidt 2001; Haidt and Hersh 2001; Shilling and

Mellor 1998). The latter presupposes a more extensive and meaningful connection between the individual and community than does the former. While studies in this approach differ, with some questioning the role of rationality itself, they are all engaged in a common debate about the status of rationality in the relationship between morality and community.

Communication

A second approach to the relationship between morality and community involves the exploration of subjectivity and the communicative processes that create it. This approach is theoretically framed by arguments that draw upon particular conceptions of space in order to exercise moral leverage that justifies certain actions or ideas (Goodsell 2005; Lefebvre 1991). Community studies in this tradition note how people draw moral lessons from their environment (Bell 1994) and conceptualize places in ways that justify certain behaviors (Enticott 2003; Reed 2004). Other scholars focus on community as "constructed in communicative processes" (Delanty 2010, 152) and research how that process works (Haste and Abrahams 2008; Patterson et al. 2011). Thus, this approach differs from the first in its focus on subjectivity and communication, rather than on a (however debatable) rational basis for morality and community.

Responsibility

The third approach to morality and community emphasizes responsibility as foundational to community. Some scholars, such as Etzioni (1993; 1996), suggest that communitarianism is a precursor to this discussion, that responsibilities are as important as rights, and that a community practicing responsibility is a positive alternative to state intervention or compulsion. Within and across such communities, he explains, people should build cross-cultural dialogue, develop their own moral standards, and encourage moral behavior through persuasion. Other scholars, such as Selznick (1992), argue that a community adequately promoting moral development (and thus encouraging social responsibility) *presumes* diversity and pluralism in addition to social integration and that a healthy community is diverse and flexible (Gregg 2002; Haidt and Hersh 2001). Current scholars (e.g., Beauchamp and Childress 2009) increasingly accept an alternative ethical framework, as MacIntyre (2007) develops. While sometimes grouped with the communitarians, MacIntyre (2007) forms his own sophisticated, theoretical foundation for his argument that the creation of communities of practice fosters the development of moral virtues in the lives of community members. This current line of thinking focuses on responsibility as the essence of community (Dyck 2005; Gombay 2010; Prus 2011), where people's fundamental relation to the world is one of concern (Sayer 2011). This discussion focuses on how responsibility is understood and practiced in community and how it can be further developed in the lives of community members (e.g., individuals taking responsibility for the well-being of their neighbors; see Crow, Allan, and Summers 2002; Kusenbach 2006; Lofland 1998).

Globalization and Communal Responsibility

One branch of scholarship using this third approach focuses on the moral problems that communities face when they must deal with globalization. Bellah and colleagues (1996, 39) saw a precursor of this in de Tocqueville's observations that moral tensions in American society result from the difficulties in sustaining community "while navigating the flood of geographical, demographic, and economic expansion." Under conditions of globalization, the people affected by changes—especially those being harmed by these changes—are not always the ones making decisions (Kirkpatrick 2001, 165; Smith 1999, 27). Further, globalization multiplies the problems of managing diversity. Modernist ideals of a universal moral standard are increasingly challenged, and many scholars are falling back on the idea, articulated by Walzer (1983), that morality must be community-based and historical. Several scholars suggest that we must accept cultural and moral pluralism (Beauchamp and Childress 2009; Haste and Abrahams 2008; Herman 2007; Kirkpatrick 2001). For example, Kirkpatrick (2001, 164) argues that "any adequate ethics of community must acknowledge the rise of the internationalization of world commerce" and concludes that the crucial issue is how communities accommodate or respond to globalization. He suggests that moral communities should "inform a good society about its responsibilities and help prepare and morally ground its citizens for their work in the polis" and that a good society can "provide the empowering conditions for communities to flourish" and, when necessary, can extend "principles of justice to historically marginalized people" (Kirkpatrick 2001, 120).

Ultimately, Kirkpatrick and other scholars argue that societies (whether national or global) can benefit from healthy communities and vice versa. However, the current intellectual climate tends to be unfavorable toward those who promote a universal moral standard (whether religious or secular), and instead supports the exploration of how community-based moralities can continue and even thrive under conditions of globalization, even in rural localities. We begin by exploring what Beck and Bauman consider to be universal moral issues facing modernity.

Modernity and the Loss of Community

Beck, Risk, and Individualization

Risk has come to define contemporary social life. Earlier modernization efforts were, in large part, about knowing, predicting, and controlling problems, so some may assume that the presence of risk indicates the failure of modernization. However, Beck (1992, 21) argues that risk actually results from successful modernization. Modernization introduces hazards, insecurities, threats, and doubts, and this evokes a mindset focused on risk: "Risk society means precisely a constellation in which the *idea* of the controllability of decision-based side effects and dangers which is guiding for modernity has become questionable" (Beck 2009, 15). Importantly, while catastrophes are real and do happen, people's lives have become organized around threats. Since risk is about future potential (Beck 1992, 33), it cannot be reduced "to mere statements of fact" (27). Further, because of its "perceptual and cognitive" basis, risk is necessarily controversial: "Risks count as urgent, threatening or real or as negligible and unreal only as a result of particular cultural perceptions and evaluations" (Beck 2009, 13). As a consequence, people can expect controversy as various groups attempt to move certain understandings of potential consequences into public awareness and others seek to downplay the same.

The other side of risk society is individualization, "a structural characteristic of highly differentiated societies" that "does not endanger their integration but actually makes it possible" by releasing "individual creativity" (Beck and Beck-Gernsheim 2002, xxi). People are compelled to manage their own lives in response to changing conditions (4). Thus, modernity is not exactly the freeing of individuals from structural constraints; while many of the old constraints fade, there are new structures (e.g., the state, bureaucracies, the labor market) that create new rules for action. Institutionalized individualism means that individuals must lead independent lives unbounded by old institutions (e.g., family, religion, social class, race), but "within the new guidelines and rules," which institutions like the state, the labor market, and bureaucracies create (11). It requires that individuals face these new structures as individuals rather than as members of groups. This creates new elements of risk, such as constraining individual knowledge, weakening the individual's ability to respond, and requiring that the individual adapt to a rapidly shifting environment despite this limited knowledge and limited ability to respond.

Despite these risks, this individualism also creates a potential for action, as people in a risk society have new ways of thinking, even when compared to people in mid-twentieth-century modernity. They are separated from old categorical memberships and are given the responsibility of making something of their lives as individuals. They can see new connections and new possibilities. All of this creates an obligation for the individual to act. The failure of the "risk contract," as Beck (2009, 9) calls it, necessitates action. To take action under these circumstances, individuals must adopt a cosmopolitan stance, the ability to see how vulnerable they are but also how they can "overcome boundaries" in their former ways of thinking and acting (Beck 2009, 61). With this stance, individuals can "realize a resilient diversity and a postnational order" (66). Cosmopolitan individuals discover their own abilities, as well as new methods and new forums in which to take action (96–7). All of this was made possible and required by large-scale shifts—detraditionalization, globalization, the rise of new logics and new moralities, and individualization (Beck 2009; Beck and Beck-Gernsheim 2002).

Globalization heightens both the risk environment and the individualization that permits and requires individual action. Under conditions of globalization, decision makers are separated from the effects of their actions (Beck 1992, 22; Beck and Beck-Gernsheim 2002, 25); however, they are never fully removed from them. Examples include pollution in the air, waste in oceans, and chemicals in food, all of which can travel back to and otherwise affect the original offenders (Beck 1992). Thus, global risks require that we "confront the apparently excluded other" (Beck 2009, 15). Of course, when problems become global, they become much more complex. Local problems may have both causes and solutions located far away. Causes and consequences are often non-linear, and problems become "unpredictable, almost incomprehensible and even less 'manageable'" (Beck 2009, 177). In addition, the risks are not distributed equally, as those with the fewest resources tend to be exposed to the greatest risks (Beck 1992). Still, globalization has made risk a universal daily experience. In this light, the greatest resistance to cosmopolitan thinking will come from those who still think in terms of the nation and of local place: "In this way, the nationally fixed social categories of industrial society are culturally dissolved or transformed. They become 'zombie categories,' which have died yet live on" (Beck and Beck-Gernsheim 2002, 27). In this famous passage, Beck and Beck-Gernsheim urge individuals to think in terms of new categories, not dead ones that have lingered in our ways of thinking. These new categories will help people to grapple with the significant threats that confront the population in a global era.

Bauman and Liquid Modern Community

Where Beck suggests "risk" as the means to describe contemporary social life and to emphasize the dangers of modernization, Bauman selects the metaphor of "liquidity" to describe social life today, emphasizing the processes of social life itself. A society becomes liquid when "the conditions under which its members act change faster than it takes the ways of acting to consolidate into habits and routines" (Bauman 2005, 1). Rapid change, then, requires that people develop new ways of thinking and acting to manage the new social environment. Most important to these new ways of thinking and acting is avoiding any commitment or constraint, because being caught in any binding or lasting relationships means that an individual risks being left out of new opportunities or being left with old burdens: "The prime technique of power is now escape, slippage, elision and avoidance, the effective rejection of any territorial confinement with its cumbersome corollaries of order-building, order-maintenance and the responsibility for the consequences of it all as well as of the necessity to bear their costs" (Bauman 2000a, 11). Indeed, it is those with power who are able to avoid constraints and commitments. They can move on, not having to pay the price of maintaining relationships or facing the consequences of their own choices. One by one, modernity has "melted down" the various institutions that provided stable contexts and frames of reference (6). This is a critical juncture in liquid modernity, because if individual lives can be effectively separated from political and collective action, the ability of individuals to act for the good of the whole, democratic participation in political processes, and the human capacity for concern for the good of the other are all in doubt.

Bauman suggests that for much of human history, community has been fundamental to individuals' development of social awareness and participation in social spheres. Three elements composed the "epistemological foundation" (Bauman 2001, 47–8) of community. The first is the existence of "a social setting that [is] more durable, more secure and more reliable than the timespan of an individual life." The second is "the certainty . . . that we will be meeting repeatedly and for a very long time to come—and that therefore society can be presumed to have a long memory and what we do to each other today will come to comfort us or grieve us in the future." The third is the belief that "the consequences of our actions will stay with us long after the actions have apparently ended." These three elements—(1) a social setting that extends beyond individual lives, (2) ongoing relationships with other people, and (3) the need to take responsibility for the consequences of actions—form the foundation of community. All three have also been brought into question in the current age, where settings, relationships, and responsibilities are all becoming temporary, flexible, open to interpretation, negotiable, and even revocable at will. However, while everyone has lost or is losing these "orientation points" (47), it is those who are in positions of power who can *choose* to lose their orientation points: "The 'secession of the successful' is, first and foremost, escape from community" (57). Removing themselves from such connections and responsibilities allows such individuals the freedom to move on to other opportunities and to avoid paying the price of remaining in relationships.

Globalization is simply an extension of this process. The breakdown of community under conditions of globalization leads to a reduction in obligation:

> Near, close to hand, is primarily what is usual, familiar and known to the point of obviousness; someone or something seen, met, dealt or interacted with daily, intertwined with habitual routine and day-to-day activities . . . "Far away," on the other hand, is a space which one enters only occasionally or not at all, in which things happen which one cannot anticipate or comprehend, and would not know how to react to once they occurred: a space containing things one knows little about, from which one does not expect much and regarding which one does not feel obliged to care. (Bauman 1998, 13)

While obviously events that happen on the other side of the world are more easily "far away," the social aspects of distance actually become more important here. Indeed, issues that are physically far away can be made close if there is familiarity, comprehension, and an obligation to care; without these qualities, even that which is physically close can become far away.

Globalization's effect of connecting people across great physical distances carries significant risk when it is not accompanied by processes that increase familiarity, comprehension, and obligation, and when it provides the means with which to deny commitment. When commitment is denied, dangers seem less threatening or can be set aside as someone else's responsibility. This can seem comforting, but when the damaging effects of an individual's consumption are felt by others, there is the potential for a serious moral breach (Bauman 2005, 107):

> The mobility acquired by "people who invest"—those with capital, with money which the investment requires—means the new, indeed unprecedented in its radical unconditionality, disconnection of power from obligations: duties towards employees, but also towards the younger and weaker, towards yet unborn generations and towards the self-reproduction of the living conditions of all; in short, freedom from the duty to contribute to daily life and the perpetuation of the community. (Bauman 1998, 9)

In other words, the individuals most likely to engage in behaviors that threaten others (including those they have not met or those they have not even thought about) are those who have more resources.

Community as Moral Proximity

Both Beck and Bauman identify, albeit in different terminology, universal moral issues resulting from globalization. We represent these universal commonalities as "community as moral proximity." Ultimately, community requires that its members care about other people. This is why community can be defined by the sphere for which individuals feel responsible. Community means *moral proximity*. It involves seeing others as neighbors, regardless of where those neighbors happen to be located geographically. Thus, to better understand rural community and rural communities in the first few decades of the twenty-first century, we must first see them not as isolated and insular, but as the opposite. Bauman (2001, 149–50) writes, "If there is to be a community in the world of the individuals, it can only be (and it needs to be) a community woven together from sharing and mutual care; a community of concern and responsibility for the equal right to be human and the equal ability to act on that right." By displacing the consequences of an action from the individuals doing the acting, globalization problematizes community. Community is problematized further when envisioned as isolated or insular. Rural community sociologists must better envision the global nature of rural locations by envisioning community as moral proximity.

This thinking in no way discounts the importance of local communities. Empirically and practically, global and local communities are still connected to each other. It is only in theory that the abstract space of global decision makers can be separated from the immediate and tangible worlds of locals where lines "can be easily drawn" (Bauman 2007, 79). In material effect, globalization creates problems that individuals and localities must manage: "Risks and contradictions go on being socially produced; it is just the duty and the necessity to cope with them which are being individualized" (Bauman 2000a, 34). However, Bauman (2003, 115) emphasizes that there can be "no local solutions to globally generated problems," as the magnitude of globally produced problems overloads the capacity of local politics and local action (Bauman 2007, 84).

Local is also still important because it provides a context for human thought, relationships, and action. Even "global operators" inhabit local, physical spaces:

> It is around *places* that human experience tends to be formed and gleaned, that life-sharing is attempted to be managed, that life meanings are conceived, absorbed and negotiated. And it is *in* places that human urges and desires are

> gestated and incubated, that they live in the hope of fulfillment, run the risk of frustration—and are indeed, more often than not, frustrated and strangled. (Bauman 2007, 80–1; italics in original)

Community requires shared experiences, and shared experiences require—at least to some degree—shared space: "The 'fusion' that mutual understanding requires may only be the outcome of *shared* experience; and sharing experience is inconceivable without shared space" (Bauman 2003, 114; italics in original). Bauman then takes this idea one step further: he argues not only that mutual understanding requires the shared experience that comes from shared space, but also that a sense of moral responsibility rests upon physical proximity. Citing the philosopher Emmanuel Levinas, Bauman (2003, 94) suggests that individuals are challenged in physical proximity by "the immediate presence of the other human being" who needs their help. Community requires moral concern for the other, and when the other who is affected by individuals' actions is at great physical remove, their sense of responsibility for that other is less likely to be activated (Beck 2009, 51; cf. Bauman 2000b).

Conclusions

"As regards global risks," sociological theory "must accord central importance to the temporal, spatial and social uncoupling of the 'we' of the decision-makers from the 'we' of the side effects" (Beck 2009, 163). Community scholars in an era of globalization must articulate new narratives that identify and create moral proximity where it has been undermined or where it never existed on a global scale. This requires taking some of the strongest elements of rural community scholarship—high feelings of solidarity, densities of acquaintanceship, etc.—and extending them beyond the traditionally bounded concept of rural isolation and insularity. Community in our individualized, liquid-modern risk society can only be one of "concern and responsibility" (Bauman 2001, 150). For much of human history, immediate presence overlapped with immediate action (Bauman 2003, 96), making moral proximity relatively unproblematic to individuals. Yet the separation of individuals from cause and consequence of their actions opened up the probability of amoral humanity. People tend to see their actions and the consequences of their daily decisions as morally irrelevant—for instance, how many individuals consider the simple act of eating to be a moral act? Yet as conscientious individual consumers seek to maximize their personal choice of food options, they also perpetuate contemporary "food deserts" and destruction of the biosphere, and create global-level problems for which no one individual or group of individuals feel personally responsible, though all help perpetuate the immoral outcome. Thus, some of the most persistent and sticky problems in contemporary rural sociological research fall directly under this purview.

The processes of globalization have the potential of opening a whole new era of morally based community research. For in a global era, "nothing is truly, or can remain for long, indifferent to anything else—untouched and untouching. No well-being of one place is innocent of the misery of another" (Bauman 2000b, 6). This is, of course, one of the many ironies of liquid modernity. Now we are all connected more than ever, but we live as if we are not because being human means having a limited moral capacity. Furthermore, contemporary social organization has increasingly privatized responsibility, but has done so in a context where the individual lacks any real power. Thus, the individual must act but does not have the knowledge or capacity to do so; today, the ubiquitous result of collective action ironically becomes the "class action" law suit that only brings attention to how a class of individuals may have been "wronged" but fails to bring attention to how the everyday actions of individuals can wrong others on a collective and often distant scale. When the individual's moral capacity does not function in a global environment (i.e., within the individual's moral proximity), the individual assumption of responsibility leads to immoral outcomes. Indeed, the global separation of consequences from actions means that it is difficult for individuals to feel morally responsible.

If we conceive of community as the group that enjoys moral proximity with the individual and to which the individual feels responsibility, globalization affects community in several ways. By bringing different groups into contact with each other—groups that have fundamentally different frameworks for social and moral life—globalization requires that communities reassess the adequacy of their narratives, whether by undercutting or by directly challenging community. The primary task of the community scholar in the new millennium is to understand the development of and interplay between moral visions and their implications for human action and institutions. Indeed, in the contemporary global era, there will be ample raw material for such a research agenda, as groups are coming into proximity (physical, communicative, cultural, and otherwise) at a rate unseen in human history. (That such intergroup proximity might not—at least at first—include moral proximity is exactly the problem.) Individuals in this social context will necessarily pursue a reconstruction or re-narrating of their lives (both individually and collectively), for without this reconstruction, they may fail to see the other presented to them. The elements of a sociological analysis of this reconstruction would include individual practices, life narratives, and community (MacIntyre 2007). All of these, we argue, would be in flux under conditions of globalization, and as they change, they require changes in each other and in the outcomes—namely, revised moral conceptions that can only come into being through socio-cultural globalization. Narrative becomes a vehicle through which a meaningful moral connection is articulated between the local and the global. Practices are the means through which those moral conceptions are both developed and realized in the lives of individuals and others in the communities to which they belong.

Community research in this line should focus on the everyday practices and narratives that develop conceptions of responsibility in the context of global flows and transitions. While much of this research would be qualitative, another line of research should be aimed at quantifying the consequences of local social life, identifying the non-local aspects of community that have been removed as part of the process of modernity, and highlighting examples where moral proximity is effectively extended in an effort to build community across space and time. This would be a particularly important and fruitful line of research for rural community scholars. In addition, "community" development will almost inevitably have to occur across geographic levels. The essential factor for it to be community development is that it must involve the consequences of actions, even when those consequences are extra-local or mediated in some way that makes them easy to ignore. In the new millennium, the only thing keeping rural communities isolated and insular are the same moral universals at play in their urban counterparts—not physical isolation, but ignorance of people's responsibility to others far removed but still within their moral proximity.

References

Anderson, Elijah. 1990. *StreetWise: Race, Class, and Change in an Urban Community.* Chicago: University of Chicago Press.

Anderson, Nels. 1967. *The Hobo: The Sociology of the Homeless Man.* Chicago: University of Chicago Press.

Banfield, Edward C. 1958. *The Moral Basis of a Backward Society.* New York: Free Press.

Bauman, Zygmunt. 1998. *Globalization: The Human Consequences.* New York: Columbia University Press.

Bauman, Zygmunt. 2000a. *Liquid Modernity.* Cambridge, UK: Polity.

Bauman, Zygmunt. 2000b. "The Deficiencies of Community." *Responsive Community* 10 (3): 74–9.

Bauman, Zygmunt. 2001. *Community: Seeking Safety in an Insecure World.* Cambridge, UK: Polity.

Bauman, Zygmunt. 2003. *Liquid Love: On the Frailty of Human Bonds.* Cambridge, UK: Polity.

Bauman, Zygmunt. 2005. *Liquid Life.* Cambridge, UK: Polity.

Bauman, Zygmunt. 2007. *Liquid Times: Living in an Age of Uncertainty.* Cambridge, UK: Polity.

Baumgartner, M.P. 1988. *The Moral Order of a Suburb.* New York: Oxford University Press.

Beauchamp, Tom L., and James F. Childress. 2009. *Principles of Biomedical Ethics.* 6th ed. New York: Oxford University Press.

Beck, Ulrich. 1992. *Risk Society: Towards a New Modernity.* Trans. Mark Ritter. Los Angeles: Sage.

Beck, Ulrich. 2009. *World at Risk.* Trans. Ciaran Cronin. Cambridge, UK: Polity.

Beck, Ulrich, and Elisabeth Beck-Gernsheim. 2002. *Individualization: Institutionalized Individualism and Its Social and Political Consequences.* Los Angeles: Sage.

Bell, Michael M. 1994. *Childerley: Nature and Morality in a Country Village.* Chicago: University of Chicago Press.

Bellah, Robert N., Richard Madsen, William M. Sullivan, Ann Swidler, and Steven M. Tipton. 1996. *Habits of the Heart: Individualism and Commitment in American Life.* Berkeley: University of California Press.

Brown-Saracino, Japonica. 2009. *A Neighborhood that Never Changes: Gentrification, Social Preservation, and the Search for Authenticity.* Chicago: University of Chicago Press. http://dx.doi.org/10.7208/chicago/9780226076645.001.0001.

Crow, Graham, Graham Allan, and Marcia Summers. 2002. "Neither Busybodies nor Nobodies: Managing Proximity and Distance in Neighbourly Relations." *Sociology* 36 (1): 127–45. http://dx.doi.org/10.1177/0038038502036001007.

de Tocqueville, Alexis. 2000. *Democracy in America.* Trans. Henry Reeve. New York: Bantam Dell. First published 1840 by Saunders and Otley.

Delanty, Gerard. 2010. *Community.* 2nd ed. London: Routledge.

Dollard, John. 1988. *Caste and Class in a Southern Town.* Madison: University of Wisconsin Press.

DuBois, W.E.B. 1996. *The Philadelphia Negro: A Social Study.* Philadelphia: University of Pennsylvania Press. First published 1899 by University of Pennsylvania.

Dyck, Arthur J. 2005. *Rethinking Rights and Responsibilities: The Moral Bounds of Community.* Revised edition. Washington, DC: Georgetown University Press.

Enticott, Gareth. 2003. "Risking the Rural: Nature, Morality and the Consumption of Unpasteurised Milk." *Journal of Rural Studies* 19 (4): 411–24. http://dx.doi.org/10.1016/S0743-0167(03)00023-8.

Erikson, Kai T. 1976. *Everything in Its Path: Destruction of Community in the Buffalo Creek Flood.* New York: Touchstone.

Etzioni, Amitai. 1993. *The Spirit of Community: Rights, Responsibilities, and The Communitarian Agenda.* New York: Crown.

Etzioni, Amitai. 1996. *The New Golden Rule: Community and Morality in a Democratic Society.* New York: BasicBooks.

Gombay, Nicole. 2010. "Community, Obligation, and Food: Lessons from the Moral Geography of Inuit." *Geografiska Annaler. Series B, Human Geography* 92 (3): 237–50. http://dx.doi.org/10.1111/j.1468-0467.2010.00350.x.

Goodsell, Todd L. 2005. "Fatherhood and the Social Organization of Space: An Essay in Subjective Geography." In *Situated Fathering: A Focus on Physical and Social Spaces*, ed. William Marsiglio, Kevin Roy, and Greer Litton Fox, 27–47. Lanham, MD: Rowman & Littlefield.

Goodsell, Todd L. 2013. "Familification: Family, Neighborhood Change, and Housing Policy." *Housing Studies* 28 (6): 845–68. http://dx.doi.org/10.1080/02673037.2013.768334.

Goodsell, Todd L., Matthew Colling, Ralph B. Brown, and J. Lynn England. 2011. "On Past and Future of Community: A Pragmatic Analysis." *American Sociologist* 42 (4): 277–87. http://dx.doi.org/10.1007/s12108-011-9137-y.

Gregg, Benjamin. 2002. "The Law and Courts of Enlightened Localism." *Polity* 35 (2): 283–309.

Haidt, Jonathan. October 2001. "The Emotional Dog and its Rational Tail: A Social Intuitionist Approach to Moral Judgment." *Psychological Review* 108 (4): 814–34. http://dx.doi.org/10.1037/0033-295X.108.4.814. Medline:11699120.

Haidt, Jonathan, and Matthew A. Hersh. 2001. "Sexual Morality: The Cultures and Emotions of Conservatives and Liberals." *Journal of Applied Social Psychology* 31 (1): 191–221. http://dx.doi.org/10.1111/j.1559-1816.2001.tb02489.x.

Haidt, Jonathan, Silvia Helena Koller, and Maria G. Dias. October 1993. "Affect, Culture, and Morality, or Is It Wrong to Eat Your Dog?" *Journal of Personality and Social Psychology* 65 (4): 613–28. http://dx.doi.org/10.1037/0022-3514.65.4.613. Medline:8229648.

Haste, Helen, and Salie Abrahams. 2008. "Morality, Culture and the Dialogic Self: Taking Cultural Pluralism Seriously." *Journal of Moral Education* 37 (3): 377–94. http://dx.doi.org/10.1080/03057240802227502.

Herman, Barbara. 2007. *Moral Literacy*. Cambridge, MA: Harvard University Press.

Jones, Thomas M., and Lori Verstegen Ryan. 1997. "The Link between Ethical Judgment and Action in Organizations: A Moral Approbation Approach." *Organization Science* 8 (6): 663–80. http://dx.doi.org/10.1287/orsc.8.6.663.

Kirkpatrick, Frank G. 2001. *The Ethics of Community*. Oxford, UK: Blackwell.

Kusenbach, Margarethe. 2006. "Patterns of Neighboring: Practicing Community in the Parochial Realm." *Symbolic Interaction* 29 (3): 279–306. http://dx.doi.org/10.1525/si.2006.29.3.279.

Lechner, Frank J., and John Boli. 2012. *General Introduction to the Globalization Reader*. 4th ed. Ed. Frank J. Lechner and John Boli, 1–5. Chichester, UK: Wiley-Blackwell.

Lefebvre, Henri. 1991. *The Production of Space*. Trans. Donald Nicholson-Smith. Malden, MA: Blackwell.

Levine, Donald N. 1995. *Visions of the Sociological Tradition*. Chicago: University of Chicago Press.

Lofland, Lyn H. 1998. *The Public Realm: Exploring the City's Quintessential Social Territory*. New York: Aldine de Gruyter.

MacIntyre, Alasdair. 2007. *After Virtue: A Study in Moral Theory*. 3rd ed. Notre Dame, IN: University of Notre Dame Press.

Patterson, Anne, John Cromby, Steven D. Brown, Harriet Gross, and Abigail Locke. 2011. "'It All Boils down to Respect Doesn't It?': Enacting a Sense of Community in a Deprived Inner-City Area." *Journal of Community & Applied Social Psychology* 21 (4): 342–57. http://dx.doi.org/10.1002/casp.1078.

Pérez, Gina M. 2004. *The Near Northwest Side Story: Migration, Displacement, and Puerto Rican Families*. Berkeley: University of California Press.

Prus, Robert. 2011. "Examining Community Life 'In the Making': Emile Durkheim's *Moral Education*." *American Sociologist* 42 (1): 56–111. http://dx.doi.org/10.1007/s12108-010-9119-5.

Reed, Maureen G. 2004. "Moral Exclusion and the Hardening of Difference: Explaining Women's Protection of Industrial Forestry on Canada's West Coast." *Women's Studies International Forum* 27 (3): 223–42. http://dx.doi.org/10.1016/j.wsif.2004.05.001.

Ryle, Robyn R., and Robert V. Robinson. 2006. "Ideology, Moral Cosmology, and Community in the United States." *City & Community* 5 (1): 53–69. http://dx.doi.org/10.1111/j.1540-6040.2006.00155.x.

Sayer, Andrew. 2011. *Why Things Matter to People: Social Science, Values and Ethical Life*. Cambridge, UK: Cambridge University Press. http://dx.doi.org/10.1017/CBO9780511734779.

Selznick, Philip. 1992. *The Moral Commonwealth: Social Theory and the Promise of Community*. Berkeley: University of California Press.

Sherman, Jennifer. 2006. "Coping with Rural Poverty: Economic Survival and Moral Capital in Rural America." *Social Forces* 85 (2): 891–913. http://dx.doi.org/10.1353/sof.2007.0026.

Sherman, Jennifer. 2009. *Those Who Work, Those Who Don't: Poverty, Morality, and Family in Rural America*. Minneapolis: University of Minnesota Press.

Shilling, Chris, and Philip A. Mellor. 1998. "Durkheim, Morality and Modernity: Collective Effervescence, *Homo Duplex* and the Sources of Moral Action." *British Journal of Sociology* 49 (2): 193–209. http://dx.doi.org/10.2307/591309.

Shweder, Richard A., Nancy C. Muirch, Manamohan Mahapatra, and Lawrence Park. 1997. "The 'Big Three' of Morality (Autonomy, Community, Divinity) and the 'Big Three' Explanations of Suffering." In *Morality and Health*, ed. Allan M. Brandt and Paul Rosin, 119–69. New York: Routledge.

Smith, D.M. 1999. "Geography, Community, and Morality." *Environment & Planning* 31 (1): 19–35. http://dx.doi.org/10.1068/a310019.

Smith, D.M. 2000. *Moral Geographies: Ethics in a World of Difference*. Edinburgh, UK: Edinburgh University Press. http://dx.doi.org/10.1191/030913200671792325.

Walzer, Michael. 1983. *Spheres of Justice: A Defense of Pluralism and Equality*. New York: Basic Books.

Wirth, Louis. 1998. *The Ghetto*. New Brunswick, NJ: Transaction.

Zorbaugh, Harvey Warren. 1976. *The Gold Coast and the Slum: A Sociological Study of Chicago's Near North Side*. Chicago: University of Chicago Press.

CHAPTER 33

Food Insecurity and Obesity in Rural America: Paradoxes of the Modern Agrifood System[1]

Keiko Tanaka, Patrick H. Mooney, and Brett Wolff

Introduction

How can food insecurity, often synonymous with hunger and "obesity," generally considered a sign of overconsumption, co-exist in places that make the United States the breadbasket of the world? The issue of food security is riddled with contradictions. When the United States entered the Great Recession in December 2007, food became more expensive as unemployment increased (US Bureau of Labor Statistics 2012a; 2012b). Meanwhile, more "food" and cropland was diverted to the production of biofuels. Increased economic uncertainty forced more urban households to make difficult spending choices. But what about rural Americans?

For the approximately 80 percent of Americans who live in suburban and urban areas (US Census Bureau 2012), rural America is a mysterious place where farmers supposedly reside and work. They hardly fathom the impact of the Great Recession on rural residents, such as increased rates of food insecurity, obesity, and higher health care costs. In the crevices of the contradiction between food insecurity and obesity we begin to uncover the complexity of food security.

In this chapter, we examine two sets of contradictions surrounding food security. First, in the United States, more people are becoming both hungry and obese. The second contradiction deals with rural areas as places of both food production and food insecurity. We argue that these apparent contradictions lie in a misunderstanding of material reality. In the modern globalized world, gone are the simplistic connections among poverty, economic disadvantage, and hunger.

To be food insecure no longer implies going hungry. Obesity is no longer only a problem of the rich, but also of the poor. There is growing evidence that obesity in America is not just a health issue, but also a serious economic and political issue (Carolan 2011; Guthman 2011). The productive capacity of modern agriculture creates large volumes of inexpensive calories, but as Carolan (2011, 58) argues, "cheap food rests upon a cheapened understanding of food . . . In terms of maximizing calorie production, today's food system has been an unqualified success. The global obesity epidemic is testament to this fact."

We contend that the existing literature on rural food insecurity and obesity is insufficient. Odd and often contradictory findings reflect this inadequacy. "Rural" must be treated as more than just a geographical variable. The importance of place and history in shaping key social relationships must be recognized by social scientists in addressing the paradox of food insecurity and obesity in rural America.

The Paradox of Hunger and Obesity in America

Hunger in the United States

The US Department of Agriculture (USDA) broadly defines a food insecure household as one that, at some point during the last year, could not claim to have "access at all times to enough food for active, healthy life" (Coleman-Jensen et al. 2012, 4). Since 1995, the USDA has collected annual data on household-level food security through a US Census Bureau survey that supplements the Current Population Survey (CPS). The USDA further breaks food insecurity down into "low food security" and "very low food security." Households with low food security reported three to five food insecure conditions on an eighteen-item questionnaire. Households with very low food security reported six or more food insecure conditions.

Since 1995, the overall household food insecurity rate was lowest in 1999 at 10.1 percent (Coleman-Jensen et al. 2012). Between 1998 and 2011, the prevalence of household food insecurity in the United States increased from 11.8 percent to 14.9 percent, or by 5.7 million households. Over the same period, the number of individuals in food insecure households increased from thirty-six million (13.5 percent) to fifty million (16.5 percent), including two million additional children living in food insecure households (Coleman-Jensen et al. 2012). Among food insecure households, the proportion of households with very low food security rose from 29.7 percent in 1999 to 32.8 percent in 2004 and to 35.5 percent in 2005. By 2008, the proportion of very low food security among the overall food insecure population was 39 percent. This indicates that both the overall prevalence of food insecurity has increased, as has its relative severity among food insecure households.

Most food insecure households tend to be food insecure temporarily, say during spates of unemployment or illness when family budgets are constrained (Coleman-Jensen et al. 2012). Other households tend to suffer temporary but recurrent hunger, such as at the end of each month, or annually due to regular seasonal fluctuations in employment and household expenses (e.g., utility bills, medical bills). As Table 33.1 shows, household food insecurity rates vary by household demographics. We summarize the key characteristics of vulnerable groups.

Low-Income Households

Low-income households are at greater risk for food insecurity. Approximately one-third of all households with income below 185 percent of the official poverty threshold are food insecure. Each year since 2008, over 40 percent of households with income under the official poverty threshold experience food insecurity at some point of the year. Among households with children, vulnerability is higher.

Households with Children, Particularly Those Headed by Single Mothers

In 2011, one of every five households with children were food insecure at some point in the year, and one of every four children resided in food insecure households (Coleman-Jensen et al. 2012). Both Table 33.1 and Figure 33.1 show a significant rise in food insecurity among households with children after 2008. High vulnerability among children living in single-parent households, particularly those headed by single women, is alarming.

Black and Hispanic Households

Non-Hispanic black and Hispanic households, especially those with children, are distinctly more likely to experience food insecurity than those of non-Hispanic whites. Between 2005 and 2011, the rate of food insecurity among Hispanic households increased by nearly 50 percent. In 2008, the Hispanic population had become the racial and ethnic group most vulnerable to overall food insecurity. However, a higher proportion of non-Hispanic black households continue to experience very low food security.

Households in the South and West

Food insecurity prevalence rates vary among regions and among states within regions (Coleman-Jensen et al. 2012). The South and the West have consistently

Table 33.1
Selected characteristics of food insecure households, 2004 to 2011

	2004	2005	2006	2007	2008	2009	2010	2011
All households	11.9	11	10.9	11.1	14.6	14.7	14.5	14.9
Household composition:								
With children < 18 yrs	17.6	15.6	15.6	15.8	21	21.3	20.2	20.6
Married couple	11.6	9.9	10.1	10.5	14.3	14.7	13.8	13.9
Female head, no spouse	33	30.8	30.4	30.2	37.2	36.6	35.1	36.8
Male head, no spouse	22.2	17.9	16.9	18	27.6	27.8	25.4	24.8
Other household with child	17.7	18.9	17.4	16	29.2	32.6	20.8	19
Without children < 18 yrs	8.9	8.5	8.5	8.7	11.3	11.4	11.7	12.2
More than one adult	6.7	6.7	6.5	6.7	9.1	9.2	9.9	9.9
Women living alone	11.8	11	11.3	11.7	14.9	14.7	13.7	15.6
Men living alone	12.3	11.5	11.4	11.2	14	14.5	15	15.5
With elderly	6.5	6	6	6.5	8.1	7.5	7.9	8.4
Elderly living alone	7.3	6.4	5.9	7.3	8.8	7.8	8	8.8
Race/ethnicity:								
White	8.6	8.2	7.8	7.9	10.7	11	10.8	11.4
Black	23.7	22.4	21.8	22.2	25.7	24.9	25.1	25.1
Hispanic	21.7	17.9	19.5	20.1	26.9	26.9	26.2	26.2
Other	11.1	9.6	9.6	9.6	13.7	13.2	12.7	8.4
With children:								
White	12.7	11.8	11.3	11.7	15.5	15.7	14.4	15.5
Black	29.2	27.4	26.4	25.9	31.9	32.6	32.9	29.2
Hispanic	26.8	21.6	23.8	23.8	32.1	32.7	30.6	32.3
Other	15.3	12.2	11.3	10.5	17.5	16.8	16.6	15.2
Household income-to-poverty ratio:								
Under 1	36.8	36	36.3	37.7	42.2	43	40.2	41.1
1.85 and over	5.4	6.7	5.3	5.5	13.7	7.6	9.3	7

Sources: Nord, Andrews, and Carlson (2005, 2006, 2007, 2008, 2009); Nord et al. (2010); Coleman-Jensen et al. (2011, 2012).

higher rates of household food insecurity than the Midwest and Northeast. Between 2004 and 2011, regional gaps in food insecurity rates shifted unevenly, reflecting regional differences in the rates of economic growth and contraction.

Households in Inner Cities and outside Metropolitan Areas

With few exceptions, the prevalence of food insecurity has been consistently higher among rural (or nonmetro) than urban and suburban (or metro) households. Among households with children, the gap between these two residential areas is greater and more consistent (Figure 33.1). Within metropolitan areas, households in principal cities[2] are more vulnerable than those in more prosperous suburbs.

Obesity in America

Overweight and obesity contribute to serious illnesses such as coronary heart disease, hypertension, and Type 2 diabetes. The economic impact of overweight and obesity and associated health problems include high medical costs,[3] as well as lost income, decreased productivity, and absenteeism (CDC 2012a).

CDC monitors the data on obesity and overweight through a series of surveys including the Behavioral Risk Factor Surveillance System (BRFSS), National Health and Nutrition Examination Survey (NHANES), and Youth Risk Behavior Surveillance System (YRBS). CDC (2012c) defines overweight and obesity based on body mass index (BMI), which is calculated from one's weight and height (CDC 2013).

Obesity data are difficult to interpret in order to identify vulnerable groups. Unlike household food insecurity, which tends to be an outcome of low household income, obesity is a result of multiple factors at the individual, family, and community levels, from one's genetics and lifestyle to the available infrastructure for recreation, health care, and food access.

Rising Obesity Rates

Approximately 35.7 percent of adults and 17 percent of children and adolescents aged two to nineteen are considered obese (Ogden et al. 2012). Between 1985 and 2010, the prevalence of obesity in the United States dramatically increased. Until 1991, no state had a prevalence of obesity more than 20 percent. In 2010, no state had a prevalence of obesity less than 20 percent (CDC 2012b).

Higher Rural Obesity Rates

In 2005 to 2006, 27.4 percent of rural[4] adult residents were classified as obese compared to 23.9 percent of their urban counterparts (Bennett, Olatoshi, and Probst 2008). In 2003, among children between ten and seventeen years of age, urban children were slightly more likely to be overweight (16 percent) than rural children (15 percent), while more rural children were considered obese (16.5 percent) than urban children (14.5 percent) (Liu et al. 2007).

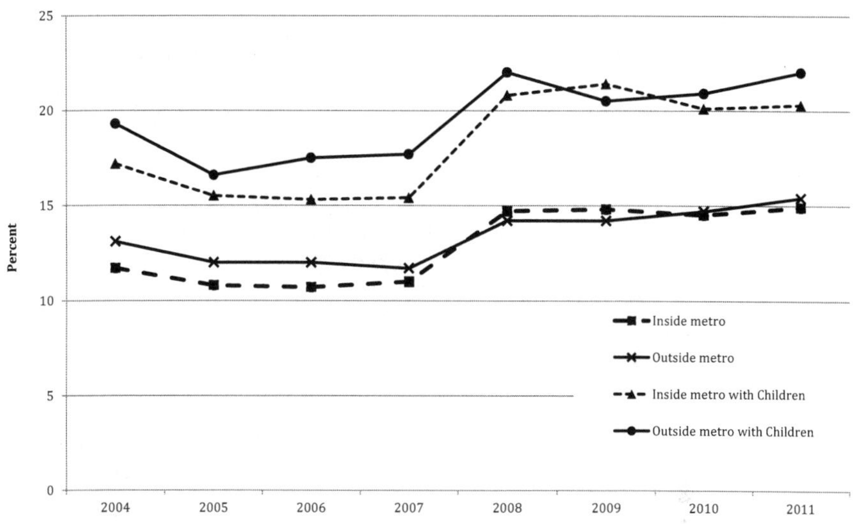

Figure 33.1. Food insecure households, rural versus urban, 2004 to 2011. Sources: Nord, Andrews, and Carlson (2005, 2006, 2007, 2008, 2009); Nord et al. (2010); Coleman-Jensen et al. (2011, 2012)

Obesity Rates affect Socioeconomic Groups Differently

Obesity rates vary among regions and states. By 2011, thirty-nine states had a prevalence of 25 percent or more and twelve had a prevalence of 30 percent or more. The analysis of the NHANES data for 2005 to 2008 paints a complex relationship between obesity and socioeconomic status in adults (Ogden et al. 2010). Most obese male and female adults (approximately forty-two million) are white non-Hispanic with income at or above 130 percent of the poverty level. About fifteen million obese adults are low income at or below 130 percent of the poverty level. Although obesity prevalence among non-Hispanic white men is similar at all income and educational levels, among non-Hispanic black and Mexican American men, obesity prevalence increases as income increases. However, obesity among women decreases as income and education increase. The intersection of gender and race/ethnicity with obesity prevalence is an interesting issue that requires further investigation.

Keep in mind that food insecurity and obesity are neither necessary nor sufficient conditions for causing each other. Although certain groups are at higher risk of both, other groups are at higher risk for one, but not for the other. Variations in the prevalence of household food insecurity and obesity among socioeconomic groups indicate that larger social transformations differentially affect their vulnerability. In the next section, we discuss how key transformations in rural America have contributed to creating paradoxical problems of food insecurity and obesity.

Paradox of Rural America

Food insecurity and obesity trends clearly indicate that geography does matter. Rural Americans are vulnerable to both food insecurity and obesity. Many rural communities and states with large rural populations are increasingly burdened by the rapidly growing costs of providing adequate services to rural residents experiencing hunger and obesity. Recent rural health literature indicates a growing sense of urgency to understand and address rural hunger and obesity (e.g., NACRHHS 2011; NACo 2008). Unfortunately, many findings from the existing literature are puzzling and sometimes raise more questions than they answer. More importantly, there is an urgent need for good data on rural children.

Following Busch and Lacy (1984), as well as others, we identify four distinct dimensions: *availability*, *accessibility*, *affordability*, and *adequacy*. At the empirical level, these four dimensions of food security closely interact, affecting socioeconomic groups differently. High food insecurity and obesity rates in rural America reflect the unequal spatial distribution of economic, political, social, and cultural capital. We discuss these four dimensions of food security to better understand growing food insecurity and obesity rates in rural America in relation to four interrelated social processes (see Lobao's introduction to this section of this volume).

Rural Americans Depend on Global Food Economy for Food Availability

Over the last century, rapid transformations in the structure of agriculture and food economies have dramatically altered food availability. Today, technological advances as well as neoliberal trade agreements have enabled easier flow of capital, goods, services, and labor in agricultural and food systems across national borders.

Government policies and programs, particularly subsidization of certain crops, and rapid concentration of food markets among a few corporations facilitated domination by fewer, bigger farms; regional specialization; and our high dependence on an energy intensive distribution system that moves food long distances (Brown and Shaft 2011). Much of our farmland is used to produce raw ingredients for processed food at very low cost or biofuel, rather than nutrient-rich fresh vegetables and fruits. Cheap food becomes a culprit for increasing obesity prevalence in this country and the world. In this food system, only a small portion of the value generated from food production stays in the hands of farmers and the rural communities (Gereffi, Lee, and Christian 2009). Rural Americans are as dependent on grocery stores to purchase food as urban Americans.

Yet, food availability is still geographically determined because the global agricultural and food economy varies enormously between and within most nations. Improved food availability has contributed to the paradox of hunger and obesity in this country, including for rural Americans. To understand this paradox as a geographically situated social process, *community food security* is a useful concept. Community food security expands the measurement of household food security that "concerns the underlying social, economic, and institutional factors within a community that affect the quantity and quality of available food and its affordability or price relative to the sufficiency of financial resources available to acquire it" (Cohen, Andrews, and Kanter 2002, 3). Community food security is a critical element of the environment that shapes individuals' health behaviors and outcomes.

County-based analysis of community food security highlights the complexity of hunger as a spatially and temporally grounded public problem. High rates of food insecure households in rural areas, particularly in the South, alone do not necessarily demonstrate that food availability, per se, in these geographical areas is more limited. Existing work on food accessibility (e.g., Morton and Blanchard 2007) and affordability (e.g., Zimmerman, Ham, and Frank 2008) confirms that readily available foods for urban Americans are surprisingly less available to rural Americans. Accessibility, affordability, and adequacy of available food are important components in assessing community food security.

Food Access is Limited in Rural America

Accessibility refers to all members of society being able to obtain the food they need. A *food desert* illustrates the lack of large food retailers within close proximity, and low food accessibility in a given community. Measuring food deserts usually involves spatial identification of urban neighborhoods that are more than one mile, or "walkable distance," from supermarkets and grocery stores. In rural areas, a distance of more than ten miles from a supermarket or grocery store has been used to measure rural food deserts (Morton et al. 2005).

This latter measure reveals 418 food desert counties in the United States. When the unit of analysis for food deserts is at the county level, nearly all food deserts are nonmetro counties, mostly counties with no towns or cities with a population of more than 10,000. Morton and Blanchard (2007) identify common characteristics of these counties, including lower educational attainment, higher poverty, lower median family incomes, higher concentrations of elders, more convenience stores per capita, and smaller grocery stores.

According to Feeding America (2009), communities of color tend to face a higher likelihood of community food insecurity. Most of these high food insecure counties with large percentages of ethnic minorities are located in rural areas.

Food is Less Affordable in Rural America

As Busch and Lacy (1984, 2) note, "simply making food available is not enough; one must also be able to purchase it." The Cost of Living Index grocery survey, published by the Council for Community and Economic Research or ACCRA-COLI, is an instrument used to assess food affordability (C2ER 2012). For SNAP (Supplemental Nutrition Assistance Program; the erstwhile food stamp program) allotments, the USDA's Thrifty Food Plan (TFP) is used as a national standard for a nutritious diet at a minimal cost. This TFP is another useful instrument for market basket surveys in documenting geographical variations in the availability of basic goods and services as well as the cost of living.

According to the Current Population Survey (CPS), food secure individuals spend $2.54 per meal on average[5] (Feeding America 2009). Among the 313 counties with the most expensive food costs, the average meal costs $3.12, or 23 percent higher than the national average. Many high-cost meal counties were located in rural areas.

Zimmerman, Ham, and Frank (2008) in Kentucky and Morton and colleagues (2005; 2008) in Iowa suggest that the relationships among poverty, food insecurity, hunger, and obesity in rural America are not directly comparable with those in urban America. Zimmerman, Ham, and Frank (2008) point out that the ACCRA-COLI is based on urban-biased market baskets and neglects expenditures needed to make up for the lack of some basic services such as public water and municipal sewer services in rural Kentucky. Rural residents from eight case study counties in rural Kentucky, on average, needed to drive 28.2 miles round trip to access the items listed in the ACCRA-COLI survey.[6] In their study of rural communities in Iowa, Morton et al. (2004) found that open-country rural residents[7] shop at more stores for groceries and shop more often at superstores or wholesale/discount stores outside their county than in-town rural residents.

Spatial differences in the cost of living also lead to a variation between rural and urban households in their use of nonmarket food exchanges to mitigate food insecurity. The study of two rural and two urban low-income counties in

Iowa shows that low-income urban Americans may be more likely to use food redistribution mechanisms organized by government and community groups such as the SNAP, WIC, food pantries, and elder meal programs, while their rural counterparts are more likely to use reciprocal exchange of food with family, friends, and neighbors through gardening, fishing, and/or hunting (Morton et al. 2008). The same study suggests that rural Americans may be more likely to donate foods through these redistribution mechanisms than urban Americans. While food insecure households in urban areas can use cheap public transportation to frequent food redistribution services, many rural households may need to travel long distances, incurring significant costs, to access foods through such institutions.

Residential differences in the use of nonmarket mechanisms to access food illustrate the different ways that family, neighborhood, churches, and communities mitigate hunger among low-income households (Duncan 1999; Lee, Coward, and Netzer 1994; Meert 2000). Morton et al. (2008, 114) point out that "urban density may contribute to the community of strangers providing and depending on public redistribution programs rather than reciprocity relations of friends and kin found in smaller rural places." While a stronger cultural norm of giving (Hofferth and Iceland 1998; Lee, Coward, and Netzer 1994; Meert 2000) may encourage rural Americans to contribute to food banks and meal programs, the lack of anonymity, which encourages food-giving behavior, may also discourage rural low-income households' reception of food through food assistance programs for fear of social stigma. The Feeding America study (2009) finds rural Americans to be less knowledgeable about benefit eligibility. In short, geo-spatial factors such as density and distance continue to reproduce differential socio-spatial patterns of interaction (e.g., anonymity, cohesion) that influence food security (Hofferth and Iceland 1998).

One of the critical findings in the Iowa study is that those who are older, more educated, and have home gardens are more likely to maintain nutritionally adequate diets through consumption of fruits and vegetables. This suggests that participation in the reciprocity economy requires a set of life skills to make gardening a financially and nutritionally effective way for mitigating food insecurity. The attainment and use of such life skills needs further investigation in relation to food adequacy. Long-term approaches to mitigating food insecurity must include not only the facilitation of reciprocal economic mechanisms at the community level, but also transmission of these life skills as cultural capital across generations.

Food Adequacy Reflects Unique Institutionalized Relationships in Rural America

Adequacy refers to balanced diets for the nutritional needs of various segments of the population and implies that food is safe. It may also include a number of cultural, or personal, preferences in an adequate diet. Even among experts, there is considerable disagreement over what constitutes an adequate diet and which foods are safe (Guthman 2011; Nestle 2003).

At the macro level, FAO (2012) uses total availability of calories in a particular nation to estimate food adequacy. That is, whether the total caloric requirements for the entire population, while accounting for varied caloric requirements for diverse population groups (e.g., pregnant women, children, elderly), can be met through that country's food supply. Under this measurement, the United States appears to have plenty of available food and should not be facing food insecurity as a public policy issue.

At the micro level, such measures can be problematic. In measures of per capita consumption, many Americans' extremely high levels of calorie consumption statistically obscure populations that might be deprived of an adequate number of calories. Household surveys, which include food intake indicators, are often used to measure the amount of food actually consumed at the individual or household level. Nutritional status, measured by anthropometric measures (e.g., BMI), is also used to assess dietary deficiencies (Migotto et al. 2005). In many industrialized countries, a somewhat invisible form of food insecurity or malnutrition is constituted not by low caloric intake, but by a high intake of nutritionally inadequate calories.

In community food security assessments, food adequacy is rarely evaluated at both macro and micro levels. If measured, food adequacy is often estimated with a combination of food availability, accessibility, and affordability variables. Health researchers often rely on prevalence rates of obesity and obesity-associated health outcomes (e.g., Type 2 diabetes, hypertension) among residents as an indicator of food adequacy in the community (Dabney and Gosschalk 2003; Drewnowski and Darmon 2005; Liu et al. 2008). Not only do food insecurity and obesity co-exist in rural America, the breadbasket, but also the prevalence of obesity is treated as a sign of food insecurity.

Understanding Obesity in Rural America

The existing literature consistently shows that obesity rates are higher in rural America, particularly in the South. Henderson and Low (2006, 3) point out, "at the state level, per capita spending on obesity-related healthcare was not only higher in rural states, but also accounted for a greater share of the states' total spending on healthcare." Obesity rates among children and adolescents tend to be higher in rural areas, indicating "a reversal of the situation in the United States prior to 1980, when, in general, obesity was more common in children in large metropolitan areas" (Tai-Seale and Chandler 2003, 116).

Yet, comparative analysis of obesity rates between urban and rural adults and children by different social demographic groups depicts a complex picture of how structural changes in the agricultural and food economy affect these groups differently. For example, in 2005, non-Hispanic white, non-Hispanic black, and Hispanic adults in rural areas were significantly more obese than their urban counterparts. However, this was not the case among Asian, Native American, and other ethnic adults (Bennett, Olatoshi, and Probst 2008). Rural residence is correlated with obesity and overweight among white adult men and women, but not among black men and women when controlling for demographic and other mediating variables. However, extremely obese black men are more prevalent in rural areas and large cities (Liu et al. 2008; Tai-Seale and Chandler 2003).

According to Liu et al. (2007), among those aged ten to seventeen, rural children are more likely to be obese than urban children. Among rural children, younger children (aged ten to fourteen), boys, and children in households below the 200 percent poverty threshold and in relatively poor health are at a greater risk of obesity. Rural African American children (23.8 percent) are almost twice as likely to be obese as rural white children (14.5 percent). Significantly higher overweight and obesity rates were found in rural areas among white children, male children, children with family incomes at 200 to 400 percent above the poverty line, and children with self-perceptions of "excellent/very good" health status. This study found no significant residential differences in the impact of race, ethnicity, or poverty level on the risk of obesity among children.

One possible explanation for these differences is that obesity and food insecurity may interact differently for diverse social groups across geographical space. Whether in urban or rural areas, certain institutionalized relationships such as race, ethnicity, and household income appear to consistently play a critical role. In rural areas, however, obesity may not necessarily be an outcome of poverty, particularly for white residents. Other environmental factors may play a role in moderating the interaction, as discussed below.

Environmental Factors

Health researchers use various institutional and environmental factors to examine obesity and overweight rates among rural residents: including physical activity levels (Ahern, Brown, and Dukas 2011; Bennett, Olatoshi, and Probst 2008; Joens-Matre et al. 2008; Liu et al. 2007, 2008); access to health care

(Bennett, Olatoshi, and Probst 2008; Liu et al. 2007; 2008); the number of total restaurants, fast food restaurants, and convenience stores (Ahern, Brown, and Dukas 2011); and the frequency of family meals (Liu et al. 2007). According to Bennett, Olatoshi, and Probst (2008), in 2005 rural adults were significantly less physically active while rural children were significantly more physically active; and rural children ate family meals less frequently than urban children. The same study reports that one primary care physician was available to every 1,461 persons in rural counties, in contrast to one physician to every 880 persons in urban counties.

Ahern et al. (2011) examine health outcomes (total age-adjusted mortality rates, adult obesity rates, and adult diabetes rates) of food availability and access variables to infer food adequacy among adults in metro and nonmetro counties. In nonmetro counties, more fast food restaurants per capita were unexpectedly associated with greater diabetes rates but lower obesity rates. These researchers confirmed previous findings that the availability of grocery stores was associated with better health outcomes. Surprisingly, in nonmetro counties, a higher number of grocery stores per capita was associated with higher mortality. In metro counties, direct farm sales per capita were negatively associated with both mortality and diabetes rates. In nonmetro counties, direct farm sales per capita were negatively associated with mortality and obesity rates but positively associated with diabetes rates.

Rather than offering possible explanations, we emphasize that these seemingly anomalous findings in urban-rural comparisons reveal challenges in conceptualizing and measuring the difference of food adequacy in rural areas. These findings require rigorous scrutiny for explanation through collaborative research between health scientists and rural social scientists. Designing instruments to effectively assess food adequacy, both quantitatively and qualitatively, either at the individual and household level or at the community level, is not an easy task because numerous variables (e.g., age, gender, ethnicity, religion, geography, health status) need to be taken into account.

First, these unexpected results in rural counties indicate the limitation of focusing solely on formal market mechanisms, or even formal redistribution mechanisms, for understanding food access and availability. Some of the assumptions about the relationships between food consumption behaviors and health outcomes, taken for granted among urban Americans, may not be applicable to the rural population. A second problem concerns the use of obesity and health outcomes as indicators of food adequacy. Health measures oversimplify how the quality of our individual and family lives is shaped over a lifetime. These limitations often lead to policy and program recommendations that only address temporary challenges of food insecurity. As Morton et al. (2008, 116) emphasize, "neither redistribution nor reciprocity solve the problem of rural food insecurity" because they are insufficient in addressing challenges of attaining nutritionally, culturally, and socially adequate foods at reasonable costs. We must consider the livelihood strategies of households and individuals in a given community for mitigating periodic hunger and malnutrition over time. In this way, we can address structural problems that continuously reproduce food insecurity among the same social groups, if not the same individuals, in the same geographical areas. A concerted effort is necessary among government agencies at different levels, the food industry, community organizations, activist groups, and scholars to revise and/or create new policies and programs such as agricultural subsidies, price supports, regulatory action, institutional feeding, and consumer education.

Conclusions

The root of the apparent contradictions between food insecurity and obesity and between the rural as a place of both food production and food insecurity comes from a simplistic and anachronistic understanding of food insecurity's relationship to production, distribution, hunger, and poverty. That same outdated vision of what it means to be poor or hungry or food insecure obscures the ways that structural forces and individual choices intertwine in the modern complex of US food inequality. Prevalent popular discourses aimed at helping the hungry and blaming the obese are tragic evidence of this short-sightedness.

The rise of obesity is also, in part, an outcome of macro-structural transformations that limit access, availability, and adequacy in food deserts. This is not a private but a public issue, insofar as the market is inadequate to serve those neighborhoods or communities, who, even collectively, cannot effectively participate in it. Thus we can observe the uneven effects of these unhealthy trends across racial, gender, and class lines, and again across geographical space.

In 2008, total US expenditures on all foods and beverages were estimated at $1,204 billion (USDA-ERS 2012), while obesity-related medical expenditures that same year were estimated at $147 billion (Finkelstein et al. 2009). At the micro level, consumers are encouraged to choose healthier and more nutritious diets and maintain regular physical exercise in order to save on medical costs. At the macro level, how this smart lifestyle by individual residents will eventually translate into actual savings in medical expenditures at the community, state, and federal levels is not very clear. Both food insecurity and obesity are public policy issues tied to the declining minimum wage; the lack of health insurance and family benefits; government subsidization of calorie-dense but nutritionally inadequate crops; the subsequent over-promotion of high-calorie, nutrition-poor diets; and declining neighborhood resources. These issues need to be addressed through a concerted program of environmental and policy interventions.

Existing research on food insecurity and obesity tends to focus on food access and affordability by using spatial and economic data such as the distance that food travels (or food miles), or the distance that people must travel to geographically concentrated food stores and restaurants. Each rural place and area is unique in a more subtle way. The democratization of food policy and economies can provide solutions to those unique local circumstances and many communities are experimenting (e.g., local food policy councils) with diverse efforts to resolve the constellation of problems specific to their community (Mooney, Ciciurkaite, and Tanaka 2012).

More collaborative research is needed between health scientists and rural social scientists to examine the qualitative features of food consumption, particularly surrounding the adequacy of food, and the economics of food choices. Health scientists recognize obesity as an outcome of food environments, but do not always investigate the socioeconomic environment of obese people. Rural sociologists and social scientists examine the socioeconomic environment of obese people, but do not quite find effective ways to incorporate obesity and other health outcomes, as well as other socio-cultural variables, in assessing the qualitative variation of food (in)security. Fruitful collaborations between these two groups of scientists will provide a more nuanced understanding of food insecurity and obesity, highlighting the implications of variable gender, racial, and ethnic dynamics in a diverse rural America.

Notes

1 The authors thank anonymous reviewers and editors for constructive comments on earlier versions of this chapter. This project was partially funded by the Dr. & Mrs. C. Milton Coughenour Sociology Professorship in Agriculture & Natural Resources in the College of Agriculture at the University of Kentucky.

2 The USDA defines households "in principal cities" as those "within incorporated areas of the largest cities in each metropolitan area" (Nord, Andrews, and Carlson 2005, 9).

3 In 2008, the total medical cost was estimated to be $147 billion (Finkelstein et al. 2009).

4 National health surveillance data collected by the CDC use the USDA-ERS's 2003 Urban Influence Codes (UICs) to categorize rural and urban counties. In the obesity literature under our review, UICs of one and two, or metropolitan areas, were classified as urban. While all other UICs were classified as rural, this is further divided into "micropolitan" rural (UICs three, five and eight), "small rural adjacent to a metro area" (UICs four, six, and seven), and "remote rural" (UICs nine, ten, eleven, and twelve).

5 Based on the assumption of three meals per day, seven days per week, an average cost per meal was calculated by dividing the average dollar amount of weekly food expenditures that food secure individuals reported by twenty-one.

6 In order to determine distances needed to access the goods and services listed in the ACCRA-COI inventory, for each case county Zimmerman, Ham, and Frank (2008) measured the miles driven to access each item from the population center of that county as the starting point. They coded any business located in the population center as zero miles. Then, they calculated the average mileage.

7 Open counties, or noncore, rural counties, are those statistical areas without an urban cluster of at least 10,000 people. In-town rural countries are micropolitan areas, centered on urban clusters of 10,000 or more people.

References

Ahern, M., C. Brown, and S. Dukas. Winter 2011. "A National Study of the Association between Food Environments and County-Level Health Outcomes." *Journal of Rural Health* 27 (4): 367–79. http://dx.doi.org/10.1111/j.1748-0361.2011.00378.x. Medline:21967380.

Bennett, Kevin J., Bankole Olatoshi, and Janice C. Probst. 2008. *Health Disparities: A Rural—Urban Chartbook*. Columbia, SC: South Carolina Rural Research Center.

Brown, D., and K. Shaft. 2011. *Rural People and Communities in the 21st Century: Resilience and Transformation*. Malden, MA: Polity Press.

Busch, L., and W.B. Lacy. 1984. *Food Security in the United States*. Boulder, CO: Westview Press.

C2ER. 2012. "Cost of Living Index Manual." Accessed 2 September. http://www.coli.org/surveyforms/colimanual.pdf.

Carolan, Michael. 2011. *The Real Cost of Cheap Food*. London, New York: Routledge.

CDC (Center for Disease Control). 2012a. "Adult Obesity Facts." Accessed 15 March. http://www.cdc.gov/obesity/data/adult.html.

CDC. 2012b. "Obesity Trends among U.S. Adults between 1985 and 2010." PowerPoint presentation. Accessed 10 August. http://www.cdc.gov/obesity/data/adult.html.

CDC. 2012c. "Defining Overweight and Obesity." Accessed 10 August. http://www.cdc.gov/obesity/adult/defining.html.

CDC. 2013. "Body Mass Index." Accessed 11 July. http://www.cdc.gov/healthyweight/assessing/bmi/index.html.

Cohen, B., M. Andrews, and L.S. Kanter. 2002. "Community Food Security Assessment Toolkit." Electronic Publications from the Food Assistance & Nutrition Research Program. Washington DC: USDA Economic Research Service. Accessed 14 February 2012. http://www.ers.usda.gov/publications/efan-electronic-publications-from-the-food-assistance-nutrition-research-program/efan02013.aspx.

Coleman-Jensen, A., M. Nord, M. Andrews, and S. Carison. 2011. *Household Food Security in the United States in 2010*. USDA Economic Research Report Number 125. Washington, DC: USDA. Accessed 15 February 2012. http://ers.usda.gov/publications/err-economic-research-report/err125.aspx.

Coleman-Jensen, A., M. Nord, M. Andrews, and S. Carison. 2012. *Household Food Security in the United States in 2011*. USDA Economic Research Report Number 141. Washington, DC:

USDA. Accessed 20 September. http://www.ers.usda.gov/publications/ap-administrative-publication/ap-058.aspx.

Dabney, Betty, and Annie Gosschalk. 2003. "Diabetes in Rural America: A Literature Review." In *Rural Healthy People 2010: A Companion Document to Healthy People 2010*, ed. Larry D. Gamm, Linnae L. Hutchison, Betty J. Dabney, and Alicia Dorsey, 57–72. College Station, TX: The Texas A&M University System Health Science Center, School of Rural Public Health, Southwest Rural Health Research Center. Accessed 3 September 2012. http://www.srph.tamhsc.edu/centers/rhp2010/05Volume1diabetes.pdf.

Drewnowski, A., and N. Darmon. July 2005. "The Economics of Obesity: Dietary Energy Density and Energy Cost." *American Journal of Clinical Nutrition* 82 (1 Suppl): 265S–73S. Medline:16002835.

Duncan, C. 1999. *Worlds Apart: Why Poverty Persists in Rural America*. New Haven, CT: Yale University Press.

FAO. 2012. "Hunger." Accessed 27 September. http://www.fao.org/hunger/en/.

Feeding America. 2009. *Map the Meal Gap 2011. Highlights of Findings*. Chicago, IL: Feeding America.

Finkelstein, Eric A., Justin G. Trogdon, Joel W. Cohen, and William Dietz. September–October 2009. "Annual Medical Spending Attributable to Obesity: Payer-and Service-Specific Estimates." *Health Affairs (Project Hope)* 28 (5): w822–31. http://dx.doi.org/10.1377/hlthaff.28.5.w822. Medline:19635784.

Gereffi, Gary, Joonkoo Lee, and Michelle Christian. July 2009. "US-Based Food and Agricultural Value Chains and Their Relevance to Healthy Diets." *Journal of Hunger & Environmental Nutrition* 4 (3–4): 357–74. http://dx.doi.org/10.1080/19320240903321276. Medline:23144675.

Guthman, Julie. 2011. *Weighing In: Obesity, Food Justice, and the Limits of Capitalism*. Berkeley: University of California Press.

Henderson, J., and S. Low. 2006. "Obesity: America's Economic Epidemic. The Main Street Economist: Commentary on the Rural Economy." *Center for the Study of Rural America* 1 (11): 1–4.

Hofferth, S., and J. Iceland. 1998. "Social Capital in Rural and Urban Communities." *Rural Sociology* 63 (4): 574–98. http://dx.doi.org/10.1111/j.1549-0831.1998.tb00693.x.

Joens-Matre, R.R., G.J. Welk, M.A. Calabro, D.W. Russell, E. Nicklay, and L.D. Hensley. Winter 2008. "Rural-Urban Differences in Physical Activity, Physical Fitness, and Overweight Prevalence of Children." *Journal of Rural Health* 24 (1): 49–54. http://dx.doi.org/10.1111/j.1748-0361.2008.00136.x. Medline:18257870.

Lee, G., R. Coward, and J. Netzer. 1994. "Residential Differences in Filial Responsibility Expectations among Older Persons." *Rural Sociology* 59 (1): 100–9. http://dx.doi.org/10.1111/j.1549-0831.1994.tb00524.x.

Liu, J., K.J. Bennett, N. Harun, and J.C. Probst. Fall 2008. "Urban-Rural Differences in Overweight Status and Physical Inactivity among US Children Aged 10–17 Years." *Journal of Rural Health* 24 (4): 407–15. http://dx.doi.org/10.1111/j.1748-0361.2008.00188.x. Medline:19007396.

Liu, J., K.J. Bennett, N. Harun, J.C. Probst, and R.R. Pate. 2007. *Overweight and Physical Inactivity among Rural Children Aged 10–17: A National and State Portrait*. Columbia, SC: South Carolina Rural Health Research Center.

Meert, H. 2000. "Rural Community Life and the Importance of Reciprocal Survival Strategies." *Sociologia Ruralis* 40 (3): 319–38. http://dx.doi.org/10.1111/1467-9523.00151.

Migotto, Mauro, Benjamin Davis, Gero Carletto, and Kathleen Beegle. 2005. *Measuring Food Security Using Respondents' Perception of Food Consumption Adequacy*. ESA Working Paper No. 05-10. Agricultural and Development Economics Division, the Food and Agriculture Organization of the United Nations. Accessed 15 September 2012. http://www.fao.org/economic/esa/en.

Mooney, Patrick, Gabriele Ciciurkaite, and Keiko Tanaka. 2012. "The Food Policy Council Movement in North America: A Convergence of Alternative Local Agrifood Interests?" Presented at the 13th World Congress for Rural Sociology, Lisbon, Portugal, August.

Morton, L.W., E. Bitto, M. Oakland, and M. Sand. 2004. "Rural Food Access Patterns: Elderly Open-Country and in-Town Residents." *Iowa Food Security, Insecurity, and Hunger*. SP 236. Iowa State University, University Extension. Accessed 20 February 2012. http://www.foodshedproject.ca/pdf/postingtowebsitejanuary2011/grocery%20stores%20and%20hunger.pdf.

Morton, L.W., E. Bitto, M. Oakland, and M. Sand. 2005. "Solving the Problems of Iowa Food Deserts: Food Insecurity and Civic Structure." *Rural Sociology* 70 (1): 94–112. http://dx.doi.org/10.1526/0036011053294628.

Morton, L.W., E. Bitto, M. Oakland, and M. Sand. 2008. "Accessing Food Resources: Rural and Urban Patterns of Giving and Getting Food." *Agriculture and Human Values* 25 (1): 107–19. http://dx.doi.org/10.1007/s10460-007-9095-8.

Morton, L.W., and T.C. Blanchard. 2007. "Starved for Access: Life in Rural America's Food Deserts." *Rural Realities* 1 (4): 1–10.

National Advisory Committee on Rural Health and Human Services (NACRHHS). 2011. *The 2011 Report to the Secretary: Rural Health and Human Services Issues*. Accessed 10 September 2012. http://www.hrsa.gov/advisorycommittees/rural/publications/index.html.

National Association of Counties (NACo). 2008. *Rural Obesity: Strategies to Support Rural Counties in Building Capacity*. Accessed 10 August 2012. http://www.leadershipforhealthycommunities.org/resources-mainmenu-40/reports/235-report98.

Nestle, M. 2003. *Safe Food: Bacteria, Biotechnology, and Bioterrorism*. Berkeley, Los Angeles: University of California Press.

Nord, M., M. Andrews, and S. Carlson. 2005. *Household Food Security in the United States, 2004. Measuring Food Security in the United States*. Washington, DC: USDA Economic Research Service.

Nord, M., M. Andrews, and S. Carlson. 2006. *Household Food Security in the United States, 2005. Measuring Food Security in the United States*. Washington, DC: USDA Economic Research Service.

Nord, M., M. Andrews, and S. Carlson. 2007. *Household Food Security in the United States, 2006. Measuring Food Security in the United States*. Washington, DC: USDA Economic Research Service.

Nord, M., M. Andrews, and S. Carlson. 2008. *Household Food Security in the United States, 2007. Measuring Food Security in the United States*. Washington, DC: USDA Economic Research Service.

Nord, M., M. Andrews, and S. Carlson. 2009. *Household Food Security in the United States, 2008. Measuring Food Security in the United States.* Washington, DC: USDA Economic Research Service.

Nord, M., A. Coleman-Jensen, M. Andrews, and S. Carlson. 2010. *Household Food Security in the United States, 2009.* Washington, DC: United States Department of Agriculture.

Ogden, Cynthia L., Margaret D. Carroll, Brian K. Kit, and Katherine M. Flegal. 1 February 2012. "Prevalence of Obesity and Trends in Body Mass Index among US Children and Adolescents, 1999–2010." *JAMA: Journal of the American Medical Association* 307 (5): 483–90. http://dx.doi.org/10.1001/jama.2012.40. Medline:22253364.

Ogden, Cynthia L., Molly M. Lamb, Margaret D. Caroll, and Katherine M. Flegal. 2010. *Obesity and Socioeconomic Status in Adults: United States, 2005–2008. NCHS Data Brief No. 50.* Washington, DC: US Department of Health and Human Services, Center for Disease Control and Prevention.

Tai-Seale, T., and C. Chandler. 2003. "Nutrition and Overweight Concerns in Rural Areas: A Literature Review." In *Rural Healthy People 2010: A Companion Document to Healthy People 2010*, vol. 2. ed. Larry D. Gamm, Linnae L. Hutchison, Betty J. Dabney, and Alicia Dorsey, 115–30. College Station, TX: The Texas A&M University System Health Science Center, School of Rural Public Health, Southwest Rural Health Research Center.

US Bureau of Labor Statistics. 2012a. "Labor Force Statistics from the Current Population Survey." Unemployment Rate. Accessed 18 July. http://bls.gov/data.

US Bureau of Labor Statistics. 2012b. "Consumer Food Price Index." Accessed 18 July. http://bls.gov/data/.

US Census Bureau. 2012. "Growth in Urban Population Outpaces Rest of Nation, Census Bureau Reports." 26 March press release. http://www.census.gov/newsroom/releases/archives/2010_census/cb12-50.html.

USDA-ERS. 2012. "Food Expenditure." Accessed 20 September. http://ers.usda.gov/data-products/food-expenditures.aspx.

Zimmerman, J.N., S. Ham, and S.M. Frank. 2008. "Does It or Doesn't It? Geographic Difference and the Costs of Living." *Rural Sociology* 73 (3): 463–86. http://dx.doi.org/10.1526/003601108785766561.

CHAPTER 34

Thinking about Rural Health[1]

E. Helen Berry

Rural Health: Contours and Significance

For quality of life, little is more important than health, and on average rural health in the United States is surprisingly good. When measured at the aggregated level of mortality rates by age, sex, and race, rural residents are healthier than urban dwellers (Geronimus et al. 2001; McLaughlin, Stokes, and Nonoyama 2001; Sparks 2012). Controlling for lower overall incomes, lower average educational levels, older age structure, lower rates of health insurance, and residence at greater distance from health care services, rural mortality rates are lower than that of urban dwellers (Sparks 2012). In other words, in the face of globalization, associated economic restructuring, and the decline in the social safety net that Lobao (in this volume) describes, health in rural areas is, paradoxically, similar to or even better than that in non-rural areas.

Yet discussions of rural health invariably begin with a litany of disparities. First, there is lesser availability of services for people resident in geographically peripheral regions as opposed to core or urban centers. Small populations do not easily sustain the expensive infrastructure that underlies the modern medical care system (Glasgow, Morton, and Johnson 2004). For patients, travel to urban centers is burdensome, expensive, and thus they tend to get less preventive health care (Glasgow, Morton, and Johnson 2004).

Added to the disparities between urban and rural medical care has been the restructuring and increasing institutionalization of the health care industry. Medical providers are increasingly consolidating their businesses, within the context of the economic restructuring described by Lobao (in this volume) and McMichael (2012). Changing business practices include incorporation of individual medical practices, hospitals, and insurance providers into regional or nationwide conglomerates, a process exacerbated in some states by the passage of the Affordable Health Care Act (AHCA, also known as Obamacare).

To understand rural health, it must be situated within local, national, and global healthcare regimes. Health is influenced by the individual's situation; the local environment, insurance or state-provided care; access to networks of nurses, physician's assistants, doctors, hospitals, dental and mental health professionals, and emergency care facilities; and access to multinational resources like vaccines and pharmaceuticals. An infant's first vaccinations are dependent on availability of vaccines from pharmaceutical companies and the distance to the local health department or pediatrician's office; dental health is influenced by the presence of fluoride in the water and thus by local politics; and tendencies toward asthma, cancer, or other dose-influenced illnesses are associated with environmental conditions correlated with automobile use, environmental regulations, and local manufacturing (Davenhall and Kinabrew 2003). In other words, while individual health is undoubtedly affected by personal circumstances and health behaviors, these circumstances and behaviors are affected in important ways by environmental context, state actors, and economic institutions that operate at all levels, from the local to the global.

What Does "Health" Mean?

Health is measured in various ways, dependent on whether one is speaking of illness (also called morbidity) for individuals; rates of morbidity or mortality for groups; or life expectancies for a population. Health includes individual well-being as well as public health features like sanitation, accident prevention, or inoculation against disease. To limit the scope of this discussion, I will use rates to define health and health differentials.

To appreciate the relationship between health and rurality, it is useful to think of rural health as having several overlapping components. The first is the geographic, referring to residents' relative isolation from, or lesser access, to services. Related to this form of isolation is the challenge of economic access to services: rural areas have fewer employers that provide insurance, have lower paying jobs, and have local governments that have historically provided fewer services for lower income people than metro governments. A second component of rurality describes the behavioral aspect of rural life that takes into account both economic and spatial isolation and behaviors associated with spatial isolation. That is, if getting to care requires a long commute, then distance produces health-related behaviors that include being less likely to schedule visits to health care professionals and/or being more likely to use alternative strategies to maintain health.

Why is Rural Health Important?

The answer to this question is economic, demographic, and social, with the three variables interacting with one another. First, the distribution of health care services in North America is a direct function of market forces (Hart et al. 2002; Probst et al. 2007). To repeat, smaller and less dense populations do not support much infrastructure. It should be obvious that when a medical specialist is needed is when rural individuals experience their greatest challenges (Probst et al. 2007; Glasgow, Morton, and Johnson 2004).

Market forces are exacerbated by rural demography. Rural communities and regions are aging faster than urban places (Johnson 2011; Berry 2012), and rural doctors are older, on average, than urban ones (Leonardson et al. 2009). Rural physicians are retiring at higher rates than metro-based health care providers (Leonardson et al. 2009). Health Professional Shortage Areas (HPSAs) are federally designated communities where one or more medical service including dental, mental, or other medical health care services are unavailable (Redlener and Grant 2009), and 60 percent of rural areas in the Midwest, 40 percent in the South, 37 percent in the Northeast, and 31 percent in the West are classified as HPSAs (Redlener and Grant 2009).

Rural communities have difficulty attracting or keeping trained medical personnel for a variety of reasons: few medical schools are in rural settings and few physicians are educated in rural regions. Nonmetro medical infrastructure is rarely similar to that in urban settings and networks of other health specialists with whom to confer and provide social support are, by definition, at greater distance (Ricketts 2000). No less important, cultural amenities are often scarce near rural practices.

Medical schools increasingly try to assist by providing clinical placements in rural areas (Deaville and Grant 2011) or building social networks for students before placing them in rural practices (Toomey et al. 2011). Communities leverage state and federal medical school loan repayment programs to lure physicians or dentists into setting up practice (Pathman et al. 2012). A number of states have medical/dental school loan forgiveness programs for providers who agree to practice in underserved areas (Hegeman 2012).

Income Inequality and Health Insurance

Health care affordability is of particular concern in rural areas where populations are less likely to be employed by institutions with health insurance benefits (Glasgow, Morton, and Johnson 2004). As a result, rural residents tend to forgo preventive care, placing them at greater risk for chronic illnesses. The Affordable Health Care Act was designed to both assist individuals whose health care access was limited as well as provide insurance for those who did not have it. Thus, the AHCA is likely to benefit a greater proportion of people in rural areas than urban ones (Pam 2011).

Furthermore, rural hospitals are generally critical access hospitals (CAHs) with limited equipment and capabilities. Most CAHs have limited funding, in part because many patients have little or no insurance. The AHCA is seen as one way for rural clinics to improve their finances and thereby improve patient care. Should the AHCA be restricted, financial strains on rural hospitals will not only remain (and may remain even if the AHCA is not restricted), but are predicted to worsen (Pam 2011).

The explicit tension between economic and geographic variables is the key to allocation of limited resources in decisions to place medical facilities in rural places and in choices by individuals to place their medical practices in rural spaces (Gardent and Reeves 2009). The economic advantage of being in more central, larger catchment areas for patients, as well as the progressively more market-driven nature of medical practice, places care provision in urban and not rural arenas (Ricketts 2000). The overall effect of the AHCA is that rural health care institutions may be better off, but the state, as insurance provider of last resort, becomes more embedded in rural life.

Regional Differentials Tied to Poverty, Minority Status, and Culture

Urban and rural health differentials also exist regionally. The southern and western United States have higher infant mortality rates and lower infant birth weights, particularly among American Indian and African American populations, even with socioeconomic status controlled (Eberhardt and Pamuk 2004). When minority status and region are tied together as Murray et al. (2006) do in their "Eight Americas" research, connections between rurality, region, and minority status appear. They show that rural, northern low-income whites and low-income Appalachian and Mississippi Valley whites have poor health experiences. Western Native Americans, low-income southern rural blacks, and the most urban African Americans also have poor health. In contrast, residents of suburbia and the middle class are best off. The quality of health within and between the various regional and racial groups varies somewhat based on gender and insurance status. But the story that should be clear is that interactions between rurality, socioeconomic, race/ethnic, and other dimensions of status are important.

Murray et al. (2006) do not, however, take into account proximity to urban places, as do Morton (2004) and Monnat and Beeler Pickett (2011). Using the

USDA's urban-influence categories, Morton illustrates that nonmetro, nonadjacent communities that are isolated, and suburban communities that are adjacent to metro areas, have worse age-adjusted health than metro places. She finds one anomaly: that those in adjacent nonmetro counties with medium size populations (between 10,000 and 49,999), have overall better health than those living in other nonmetro areas. Monnat and Beeler Pickett (2011) show that the health differential is explainable by rural structural disadvantages, specifically, higher rates of unemployment and population loss, and the lower levels of educational attainment.

Behavioral Differences Associated with Rural Life

Residential variation in the prevalence of some diseases is suggestive of rural-urban differences in health behaviors. For example, the quintessential behavioral health risk, smoking, is manifest in trends and differences in smoking-related mortality. Age-adjusted rates of lung cancer were lower for persons living in nonmetro areas in 1950 and stayed lower until the early 1990s, when they become higher than those for metro areas (Singh, Siahpush, and Williams 2012). Similarly, cervical cancer mortality, which is twice as high for smokers, has remained high in nonmetro areas despite steep declines in metro areas (Singh 2012). In both cases, lung and cervical cancer, the reason metro residents began to fare better over time seems correlated with decreased smoking prevalence. Although rates of smoking in urban places continue to be higher than in rural areas, Singh, Siahpush, and Williams (2012) conclude that smoking reduction efforts ought to be more focused in rural places because of the close association with cancer.

Another risky health behavior, obesity, also varies by rural/urban residence (see Tanaka, Mooney, and Wolff in this volume). The usual measure of obesity is the body mass index or BMI (weight in kilograms divided by height in meters squared). Wang and Beydoun (2007) document that, by 2005, the more rural states in the US South (Louisiana and Mississippi) had the highest BMIs. Similarly, Patterson and colleagues (2004) show that obesity was more likely in rural than urban residents in every racial and ethnic group when controlling for other variables, a result attributed, at least partially, to inactivity. Examining obesity prevalence by type of rural county, the most rural counties in the most rural states tended to have more obesity, although African Americans had their highest BMIs if they lived in counties adjacent to urban places (Jackson et al. 2005). In studies that have received much attention, Lopez (2004) and James et al. (2012) show that the built environment is at least correlated with obesity.

Specifically, residents in less dense neighborhoods, rural places, or areas of urban sprawl have higher BMIs than those living in more densely built and populated environments like central cities (Lopez 2004; James et al. 2012).

Lufiyya and colleagues (2007) find that rural overweight children tend to be poor and to have had no preventive health care in the past twelve months. Tai-Seale and Chandler (2003) add that lack of access to preventive care, such as nutritionists or hospitals, is another likely culprit for rural obesity. These researchers also emphasize that prevention is made more difficult by built environments in rural places that have limited sidewalks and few exercise facilities. Tai-Seale and Chandler (2003) indicate that there may be cultural limitations or at least changes in rural places that have resulted in behavioral changes for children. Historically, physically active lifestyles kept rural children healthier, but more recently, higher dietary fat and calorie consumption plus sedentary lifestyles have resulted in rural children becoming overweight and obese (Tai-Seale and Chandler 2003). On the other hand, in two rural Wisconsin counties, Kaiser and Baumann (2010) show that Mexican-background families were more likely to meet exercise guidelines (and not be overweight) because their occupations required more physical activity, not unlike rural residents in a more farm-oriented economy.

For individuals for whom barriers to exercise are posed by sedentary occupations and who also experience barriers to accessing fruits and vegetables, both exercise and healthy dietary intake is limited (Kaiser and Baumann 2010). Researchers have shown that distance to supermarkets and grocery stores, and thus distance to healthy foods, as opposed to fast food sources, is associated with increased odds of obesity (Michimi and Wimberly 2010). Hawkes (2006), in her review of the globalization of the retail and wholesale marketing of food, comments on the way that marketing of food is focused on consumption habits: as supermarkets take the place of local grocers, there is also a greater focus on foods that are more easily shipped and have longer shelf lives. The resultant poorer diet quality has been correlated with obesity in both rural and urban places (Hawkes 2006).

Other behavioral variations may simply be a response to rural living. For example, older rural residents tend to use over-the-counter medicines and home remedies for self-care more than do their urban counterparts (Grzywacz et al. 2012), implying that when no care provider is at hand over-the-counter medicine is simply more convenient. In research on access to health care, Leonardson et al. (2009) find that emergency rooms are sometimes used as the usual source of care for rural residents, that is, it is a place where the staff knows the patient. Taken together, that over-the-counter medicine/home remedies and emergency rooms are used more often in rural areas, mastery of the health setting in rural places seems to require a sort of muddling through via the use of what is at hand.

Rural Health Paradox

Research on a worldwide level shows health differentials between rural and urban places. Where rural health is worse, in both more and less developed countries, the reason seems to be associated with less education and more poverty, resulting in a complex interaction between health and socioeconomic variables. Yet the relationship of health to geography is not simplistic as documented by the rural health paradox. When examining variables beyond those measured at the individual level, rural areas are often actually advantaged. Sparks (2012) cites the correlation between sex, age, race, and adjusted mortality rates for rural places. Her work on infant mortality suggests the paradox may be a function of where on the rural-urban continuum one lives: those in the most rural places have less access to health care infrastructure, while those closer to urban places do better (Sparks 2012).

Yang, Jensen, and Haran (2011) comment that the paradox can be partially explained by controlling for the social relations individuals have within their communities. The benefits of these social relationships, called social capital, come from cooperation between individuals and groups within the community. Taking into account the affluence, ethnicity, and spatial contiguity of places to urban areas, Yang and associates argue that the personal and social connections that individuals have in their communities, their social capital, may explain the rural health paradox (Yang, Jensen, and Haran 2011). However, one must keep in mind that not all rural peoples live in small villages or towns: some live on widely spread isolated ranches or farmsteads where they may still have social capital but where that capital may be less immediately accessible.

Is the Physical Environment in Rural Places Better or Worse?

Exposure to environmental hazards is known to differ in urban and rural places but evidence does not favor rural over urban areas. Rather, there tend to be stronger correlations between disadvantaged populations and health hazards than with geography (Brulle and Pellow 2006). For developed nations, Smith, Humphreys, and Wilson (2008) propose that it is being in a hazardous environment or having a hazardous occupation that leads to greater individual risk. Prevailing health disparities that are associated with exposure to hazards (e.g., environmental pollutants) are bound up with issues tied to environmental justice. Paul Mohai et al. (2009) confirm that racial and socioeconomic disadvantages are closely associated with proximity to industrial facilities, which is not limited to rural or urban space.

Certainly one aspect of rural living appears to be exceptionally dangerous. Recent research has shown that injury-related mortality is higher in the most rural counties and lower in urban ones. Death rates for automobile and machinery accidents, drowning, poisoning, falling, and other accident-associated death rates are higher in the most rural places and are less risky as one moves across the rural-urban continuum toward urban places (Myers et al. 2013). The differential injury death rate appears to be a function of differential behaviors in rural areas associated with driving, work behaviors, and possibly distance to trauma centers (Myers et al. 2013).

Mental Health in Rural Places

Mental health is also of concern and in both higher and lower income nations. Rural places are known to have higher rates of suicide (Vijayakumar et al. 2005; Stark, Riordan, and O'Connor 2011; Hirsch 2006), although the odds of depression and mental health difficulties do not appear to differ substantially between rural and urban places once poverty, education, age, and other variables are controlled (Probst et al. 2006). Of course, if mental health in rural areas is worse when socioeconomic variables are not controlled, then it is likely that deprivation itself explains the higher rates of suicide in rural areas. Mental health providers are less available in rural places, and patients in the most rural places are least likely to receive mental health services (Hauenstein et al. 2007).

The argument has already been made that social capital may be greater in rural than urban places, which should make for better mental health. Yet in examples like those from Australia, where restructuring of the agricultural economy is resulting in fewer employment opportunities and greater out-migration, there is more negative mental health, and where rural employment opportunities are expanding mental health is better (Fraser et al. 2005).

Is there something about rural life, beyond job losses, that produces a difference in mental health? Some researchers suggest that for minorities rural places are doubly isolating because of the impact of being both a minority and geographically isolated (Vijayakumar et al. 2005). The double isolation produces a "weathering" effect that results in shorter life expectancy and overall worse health (Lee and Singelmann 2013). In the end, Kelly et al. (2010) indicate that evidence of an impact of rurality on mental health is inconsistent, even with sex, socioeconomic status, population change, and migration held constant.

Clearly focused research is needed on residential disparities in mental health and health care.

Globalization and Health

Health may be among the most globalized spheres of rural life. The globalization is of technology, corporatized health care systems, and research. First, there is the brain drain of youth with high aspirations for medical, nursing, or other schooling opportunities to cities (Brooks et al. 2010). The phenomenon is even more obvious when it involves already accredited medical personnel moving out of more rural, more peripheral countries and toward medical practices in urban or more central economies (Groenhout 2012; Clark, Stewart, and Clark 2006). In the United States, for example, one fourth of physicians have degrees from non-US institutions, whether those physicians are US nationals or not. Telemedicine supplements, urbanizes, and ultimately globalizes rural medicine by providing services that would not otherwise be available. This might include analyses of CAT scans at nearby metro hospitals or a midnight reading of a radiograph from Pennsylvania by a doctor in India (Wachter 2006). The outcome is a more international flow of health care professionals and health care knowledge and greater centralization of medical care itself into large, urban, establishments.

Second, health care is increasingly corporatized (Crone 2008). By corporatization, I mean the organization of doctors and health providers, including clinics and hospitals, into corporations that bureaucratize the provision of care. The effect is to bring what was once the independent physician/clinic into a routinized legal entity or partnership that responds to market pressures. The logic of organizing care in a systematized format is that bureaucratization will control health care costs; improve delivery of services; provide better coordination among specialists, hospitals, and patients; and better manage government interactions with care providers (Burns, Bradley, and Weiner 2012; Crone 2008). Whether this rationalization of health care has improved the quality of care for individuals is unclear. Regardless, the cost of health care has continued to increase.

Third, pharmaceutical research has moved from the global North to the global South and both clinical and medical device trials now take place in middle and poorer income countries (Glickman et al. 2009; Berndt, Cockburn, and Thiers 2007). Reasons for this particular move vary but include larger populations available for the trials and lower costs per patient. The manufacture of medical equipment and medications also now occurs worldwide, although increasingly larger proportions of each come from countries with lower manufacturing and labor costs (Glickman et al. 2009; Berndt, Cockburn, and Thiers 2007).

Globalization of health means that care is globalized for both rural and urban residents. The point can be made from a very different angle by examining how rapidly illnesses can and do spread in the age of easy cross-border travel. During the H1N1 (swine) influenza epidemic of 2009, the governments of China and Japan screened every international airplane passenger for any sign of infection. Travelers arriving in the United States from Asia, Europe, Canada, and elsewhere are met at the border with questions regarding any visits to farming areas with the assumption that proximity to farming areas might impact the health of farm animals, crops, or US residents.

Conclusions

Lobao (in this volume) sees four trends influencing rural life and by implication, rural health. The first is the continuation of economic restructuring that has shifted the United States from a manufacturing to an information and service-industry oriented nation. The second is an acceleration of the importance of the state. The third is the related institutionalization of relationships between employers and workers, government and citizens, and a related globalization of many industries and service relationships. The fourth is that spatial and geographic processes differ depending on the region or community under discussion.

In my review of the rural health and healthcare literature in this chapter, I address these trends implicitly and explicitly. First, economic restructuring of the United States economy is reflected in the types of employment available in rural areas, which are less likely to provide health insurance and more likely to be in the low-paying service sector. The economic restructuring also means that rural places are less likely to be served by "full-service" hospitals, and more likely to be HPSAs—places where health professionals are in short supply. The increasing corporatization of the health industry adds to the challenge.

Second, the importance of the state to health care provision has been made exceedingly clear by the lack of universal health insurance, a deficit that is to be ameliorated by the Obama administration's Affordable Health Care Act. The AHCA insures preventive health screenings, results in state and federal insurance exchanges, and includes a number of other provisions. Rural care facilities have generally championed the AHCA because it has meant that many of their charity patients will finally be insured, but the act also clearly illustrates the intervention of the state into individual relationships, again, as Lobao describes.

Another example of the increasing influence of the state on individual relationships are several recently passed abortion bills, like one in Texas, that bans abortions after twenty weeks of pregnancy, requires clinics to meet the standards of care of hospital surgery centers, and requires physicians who perform abortions to have admitting privileges at a hospital within thirty miles of the clinic. Such moves will certainly be subject to constitutional scrutiny but threaten to greatly curtail the availability of health services to women in rural areas especially. Further, these bills specifically place the state within the relationship between clinicians and patients.

At the same time that the state is having a greater influence on individual relationships, the healthcare industry is corporatizing and globalizing, moving outside the constraints of the state. The example of medical device and pharmaceutical trials being moved overseas has already been given. Another example is the increasing incorporation of groups of doctors into specialty hospitals that are wholly owned by the physicians and are sometimes merged into national or international corporations.

That spatial processes differ depending on the communities or regions under discussion is patently obvious yet often neglected. Both Myers et al. (2013) and Morton (2004) explicitly illustrate that where individuals live along the rural-urban continuum, adjacent to or farther from a metropolitan center, make a difference in their health. Murray and colleagues' (2006) research similarly illustrates this point as they make clear that region, e.g., being in the rural northern Midwest versus Appalachia or the Mississippi, is associated with differential health for whites as is being in the Deep South for African Americans. But geography influences health in other ways as well. As rural youth migrate out of rural areas in the Great Plains and elsewhere and populations age in place, natural decrease becomes almost inevitable (Johnson 2011). Natural decrease is associated with the loss of rural health care infrastructure due to fewer and fewer patients. On the other hand, where there is in-migration of retirees to high-amenity retirement destinations, the new in-migrants demand higher levels of medical services (Brown et al. 2010), thereby improving infrastructures.

In sum, rural health and healthcare are each subject to the same sets of restructuring, institutionalization, globalization, and geographic differentials that influence other aspects of rural life. Future research needs to unpack this complex nexus of relationships with an eye toward identifying and prioritizing problem areas and informing the development of ameliorative policies and programs. Focused study is urgently needed given the sheer pace of change. Also, that some developments (e.g., the increasing need for a "good job" to ensure adequate health insurance) work to the disadvantage of rural Americans, while others (e.g., the spread of telemedicine that stands to relieve the costs of distance) may disproportionately benefit those in the countryside underscores the need for future research to be attentive to rural-urban differences.

The rural paradox is manifest in lower standardized mortality rates and suggests that there are health advantages to rural residence. However, persisting inequities in health care access require that rural health remain a focus of research and policy attention. The research needs to be attentive to the social and economic forces of a rapidly changing world as it influences rural life.

Notes

1 I prepared this chapter with the support of the W2001: Population Dynamics and Change: Aging, Ethnicity and Land Use Change in Rural Communities, CSREES, USDA; the Utah Experiment Station Projects 0835 and 1124; two thoughtful anonymous reviewers; and the guidance and support of this volume's editors.

References

Berndt, Ernst R., Iain M. Cockburn, and Fabio A. Thiers. 2007. "The Globalization of Clinical Trials for New Medicines: Where are the Trials Going and Why?" Paper presented at iHea 6th World Congress: Explorations in Health Economics, Maastricht, the Netherlands, June.

Berry, E. Helen. 2012. "Rural Aging in International Context." In *International Handbook of Rural Demography*, ed. Laszlo J. Kulcsar and Katherine J. Curtis, 67–79. Dordrecht: Springer. http://dx.doi.org/10.1007/978-94-007-1842-5_6.

Brooks, Trevor, Sang-Lim Lee, E. Helen Berry, and Michael B. Toney. 2010. "The Effects of Occupational Aspirations and Other Factors on the out-Migration of Rural Youth." *Journal of Rural and Community Development* 5: 19–36.

Brown, David L., Benjamin C. Bolender, Laszlo J. Kulcsar, Nina Glasgow, and Scott Sanders. 2010. "Intercounty Variability of Net Migration at Older Ages as a Path Dependent Process." *Rural Sociology* 76 (1): 44–73. http://dx.doi.org/10.1111/j.1549-0831.2010.00034.x.

Brulle, R.J., and David N. Pellow. 2006. "Environmental Justice: Human Health and Environmental Inequalities." *Annual Review of Public Health* 27 (1): 103–24. http://dx.doi.org/10.1146/annurev.publhealth.27.021405.102124. Medline:16533111.

Burns, Lawton Robert, Elizabeth H. Bradley, and Bryan Jeffrey Weiner. 2012. *Shortell & Kaluzny's Health Care Management Organization Design & Behavior.* Clifton Park: Delmar Cengage Learning.

Clark, Paul F., James B. Stewart, and Darlene A. Clark. 2006. "The Globalization of the Labour Market for Health-Care Professionals." *International Labour Review* 145 (1–2): 37–64. http://dx.doi.org/10.1111/j.1564-913X.2006.tb00009.x.

Crone, Robert K. February 2008. "Flat Medicine? Exploring Trends in the Globalization of Health Care." *Academic Medicine* 83 (2): 117–21. http://dx.doi.org/10.1097/ACM.0b013e318160965c. Medline:18303354.

Davenhall, William F., and Christopher Kinabrew. 2003. "Redefining Quality of Patient Care and Patient Safety Using GIS." In HIC 2003 RACGP12CC [combined conference]:

Proceedings, ed. Stephen Chu and Carmel Simpson, 337–42. Brunswick East, Victoria: Royal Australian College of General Practitioners.

Deaville, Jennifer, and Andrew Grant. 2011. "Overcoming the Pull Factor of Convenient Urban Living—Perceptions of Rural General Practice Placements." *Medical Teacher* 33 (4): e211–7. http://dx.doi.org/10.3109/0142159X.2011.557409. Medline:21456980.

Eberhardt, M.S., and Elsie R. Pamuk. October 2004. "The Importance of Place of Residence: Examining Health in Rural and Nonrural Areas." *American Journal of Public Health* 94 (10): 1682–86. http://dx.doi.org/10.2105/AJPH.94.10.1682. Medline:15451731.

Fraser, Cait, Henry Jackson, Fiona Judd, Angela Komiti, Garry Robins, Gret Murray, John Humphreys, Pip Pattison, and Gene Hodgins. June 2005. "Changing Places: The Impact of Rural Restructuring on Mental Health in Australia." *Health & Place* 11 (2): 157–71. http://dx.doi.org/10.1016/j.healthplace.2004.03.003. Medline:15629683.

Gardent, Paul B., and Susan A. Reeves. 2009. "Ethics Conflicts in Rural Communities: Allocation of Scarce Resources." In *Handbook for Rural Health Care Ethics: A Practical Guide for Professionals*, ed. William A. Nelson, 165–85. Lebanon: University Press of New England.

Geronimus, Arline T., John Bound, Timothy A. Waidmann, Cynthia G. Colen, and Dianne Steffick. May 2001. "Inequality in Life Expectancy, Functional Status, and Active Life Expectancy across Selected Black and White Populations in the United States." *Demography* 38 (2): 227–51. http://dx.doi.org/10.1353/dem.2001.0015. Medline:11392910.

Glasgow, Nina, Lois Wright Morton, and Nan E. Johnson. 2004. *Critical Issues in Rural Health*. Oxford: Blackwell.

Glickman, Seth W., John G. McHutchison, Eric D. Peterson, Charles B. Cairns, Robert A. Harrington, Robert M. Califf, and Kevin A. Schulman. 19 February 2009. "Ethical and Scientific Implications of the Globalization of Clinical Research." *New England Journal of Medicine* 360 (8): 816–23. http://dx.doi.org/10.1056/NEJMsb0803929. Medline:19228627.

Groenhout, Ruth. 2012. "The 'Brain Drain' Problem: Migrating Medical Professionals and Global Health Care." *International Journal of Feminist Approaches to Bioethics* 5 (1): 1–24. http://dx.doi.org/10.2979/intjfemappbio.5.1.1.

Grzywacz, Joseph G, Eleanor Palo Stoller, A. Nichol Brewer-Lowry, Ronny A. Bell, Sara A. Quandt, and Thomas A. Arcury. June 2012. "Gender and Health Lifestyle: An in-Depth Exploration of Self-Care Activities in Later Life." *Health Education & Behavior* 39 (3): 332–40. http://dx.doi.org/10.1177/1090198111405195. Medline:21632439.

Hart, Gary L., Edward Salsberg, Debra M. Phillips, and Denise M. Lishner. 2002. "Rural Health Care Providers in the United States." *Journal of Rural Health* 18 (5 Suppl): 211–31. http://dx.doi.org/10.1111/j.1748-0361.2002.tb00932.x. Medline:12061515.

Hauenstein, Emily J., Stephen Petterson, Virginia Rovnyak, Elizabeth Merwin, B. Heise, and D. Wagner. May 2007. "Rurality and Mental Health Treatment." *Administration and Policy in Mental Health* 34 (3): 255–67. http://dx.doi.org/10.1007/s10488-006-0105-8. Medline:17165139.

Hawkes, Corinna. 2006. "Uneven Dietary Development: Linking the Policies and Processes of Globalization with the Nutrition Transition, Obesity and Diet-Related Chronic Diseases." *Globalization and Health* 2: 4. http://dx.doi.org/10.1186/1744-8603-2-4. Medline:16569239.

Hegeman, Roxana. 2012. "Rural Hospital Attracts Mission-Minded Doctors." *Washington Times*, 5 January.

Hirsch, Jameson K. 2006. "A Review of the Literature on Rural Suicide: Risk and Protective Factors, Incidence, and Prevention." *Crisis* 27 (4): 189–99. http://dx.doi.org/10.1027/0227-5910.27.4.189. Medline:17219751.

Jackson, J. Elizabeth, Mark P. Doescher, Anthony F. Jerant, and L. Gary Hart. Spring 2005. "A National Study of Obesity Prevalence and Trends by Type of Rural County." *Journal of Rural Health* 21 (2): 140–48. http://dx.doi.org/10.1111/j.1748-0361.2005.tb00074.x. Medline:15859051.

James, Peter, Philip J. Troped, Jaime E. Hart, Corinne E. Joshu, Graham A. Colditz, Ross C. Brownson, Reid Ewing, and Francine Laden. 2012. "Urban Sprawl, Physical Activity, and Body Mass Index: Nurses' Health Study and Nurses' Health Study II." *American Journal of Public Health* 103 (2): 369–75. http://ajph.aphapublications.org/doi/abs/10.2105/AJPH.2011.300449. Medline:22698015.

Johnson, Kenneth M. 2011. "The Continuing Incidence of Natural Decrease in American Counties." *Rural Sociology* 76 (1): 74–100. http://dx.doi.org/10.1111/j.1549-0831.2010.00036.x.

Kaiser, Betty L., and Linda C. Baumann. November–December 2010. "Perspectives on Healthy Behaviors among Low-Income Latino and Non-Latino Adults in Two Rural Counties." *Public Health Nursing (Boston, Mass.)* 27 (6): 528–36. http://dx.doi.org/10.1111/j.1525-1446.2010.00893.x. Medline:21087306.

Kelly, Brian J., Helen J. Stain, Clare Coleman, David Perkins, Lyn Fragar, Jeffrey Fuller, Terry J. Lewin, David Lyle, Vaughan J.U. Carr, Jacqueline M. Wilson, et al. February 2010. "Mental Health and Well-Being within Rural Communities: The Australian Rural Mental Health Study." *Australian Journal of Rural Health* 18 (1): 16–24. http://dx.doi.org/10.1111/j.1440-1584.2009.01118.x. Medline:20136810.

Lee, Marlene, and Joachim Singelmann. 2013. "Place and Race: Health of African Americans in Nonmetropolitan Areas." In *Rural Aging in 21st Century America*, ed. Nina Glasgow and E. Helen Berry, 99–113. Dordrecht: Springer. http://dx.doi.org/10.1007/978-94-007-5567-3_6.

Leonardson, J.D., E.C. Ziller, A.F. Coburn, and N. Anderson. 2009. *Profile of Rural Health Insurance Coverage: A Chartbook.* Portland: University of Southern Maine, Maine Rural Health Research Service.

Lopez, Russ. September 2004. "Urban Sprawl and Risk for Being Overweight or Obese." *American Journal of Public Health* 94 (9): 1574–79. http://dx.doi.org/10.2105/AJPH.94.9.1574. Medline:15333317.

Lufiyya, May Nawal, Martin S. Lipsky, Jennifer Wisdom-Behounek, and Melissa Inpanbutr-Martinkus. 2007. "Is Rural Residency a Risk Factor for Overweight and Obesity for US Children?" *Obesity: A Research Journal* 15 (9): 2348–56. http://dx.doi.org/10.1038/oby.2007.278.

McLaughlin, Diane, C.S. Stokes, and A. Nonoyama. 2001. "Residence and Income Inequality: Effects on Mortality among U.S. Counties." *Rural Sociology* 66 (4): 579–98. http://dx.doi.org/10.1111/j.1549-0831.2001.tb00085.x.

McMichael, Phillip. 2012. *Development and Social Change: A Global Perspective.* Thousand Oaks, CA: Sage.

Michimi, Akihiko, and Michael C. Wimberly. 2010. "Associations of Supermarket Accessibility with Obesity and Fruit and Vegetable Consumption in the Conterminous

United States." *International Journal of Health Geographics* 9 (1): 49. http://dx.doi.org/10.1186/1476-072X-9-49. Medline:20932312.

Mohai, Paul, Paula M. Lantz, Jeffrey Morenoff, James S. House, and Richard P. Mero. November 2009. "Racial and Socioeconomic Disparities in Residential Proximity to Polluting Industrial Facilities: Evidence from the Americans' Changing Lives Study." *American Journal of Public Health* 99 (S3 Suppl 3): S649–56. http://dx.doi.org/10.2105/AJPH.2007.131383. Medline:19890171.

Monnat, Shannon M, and C. Beeler Pickett. January 2011. "Rural/Urban Differences in Self-Rated Health: Examining the Roles of County Size and Metropolitan Adjacency." *Health & Place* 17 (1): 311–9. http://dx.doi.org/10.1016/j.healthplace.2010.11.008. Medline:21159541.

Morton, Lois Wright. 2004. "Spatial Patterns of Rural Mortality." In *In e Critical Issues in Rural Health*, ed. Nina Glasgow, Lois Wright Morton, and Nan E. Johnson, 37–45. Oxford: Blackwell.

Murray, Christopher J.L., Sandeep C. Kulkarni, Catherine Michaud, Niels Tomijima, Maria T. Bulzacchelli, Terrell J. Iandiorio, and Majid Ezzati. September 2006. "Eight Americas: Investigating Mortality Disparities across Races, Counties, and Race-Counties in the United States." *PLoS Medicine* 3 (9): e260. http://dx.doi.org/10.1371/journal.pmed.0030260. Medline:16968116.

Myers, Sage R., Charles C. Branas, Benjamin C. French, Michael L. Nance, Michael J. Kallan, Douglas J. Wiebe, and Grendan G. Carr. October 2013. "Safety in Numbers: Are Major Cities the Safest Places in the United States?" *Annals of Emergency Medicine* 62 (4): 408, e3. http://dx.doi.org/10.1016/j.annemergmed.2013.05.030. Medline:23886781.

Pam, Robyn. 2011. "High Stakes for Rural Health in Fight over Affordable Health Act." The Bill Lane Center for the American West. 8 September. Accessed 12 September 2012. http://www.stanford.edu/group/ruralwest/cgi-bin/drupal/content/health/affordable-care-fight.

Pathman, Donald E., Jennifer Craft Morgan, Thomas R. Konrad, and Lynda Goldberg. Fall 2012. "States' Experiences with Loan Repayment Programs for Health Care Professionals in a Time of State Budget Cuts and NHSC Expansion." *Journal of Rural Health* 28 (4): 408–15. http://dx.doi.org/10.1111/j.1748-0361.2012.00409.x. Medline:23083087.

Patterson, Paul Daniel, Charity G. Moore, Janice C. Probst, and J.A. Shinogle. Spring 2004. "Obesity and Physical Inactivity in Rural America." *Journal of Rural Health* 20 (2): 151–59. http://dx.doi.org/10.1111/j.1748-0361.2004.tb00022.x. Medline:15085629.

Probst, Janice C., Sarah B. Laditka, Charity G. Moore, Nusrat Harun, M. Paige Powell, and Elizabeth G. Baxley. October 2006. "Rural-Urban Differences in Depression Prevalence: Implications for Family Medicine." *Family Medicine* 38 (9): 653–60. Medline:17009190.

Probst, Janice C., Sarah B. Laditka, Jong-Yi Wang, and Andrew O. Johnson. 2007. "Effects of Residence and Race on Burden of Travel for Care: Cross Sectional Analysis of the 2001 US National Household Travel Survey." *BMC Health Services Research* 7 (1): 40. http://dx.doi.org/10.1186/1472-6963-7-40. Medline:17349050.

Redlener, Irwin, and Roy Grant. 3 December 2009. "America's Safety Net and Health Care Reform—What Lies Ahead?" *New England Journal of Medicine* 361 (23): 2201–4. http://dx.doi.org/10.1056/NEJMp0910597. Medline:19955523.

Ricketts, Thomas C. 2000. "The Changing Nature of Rural Health Care." *Annual Review of Public Health* 21 (1): 639–57. http://dx.doi.org/10.1146/annurev.publhealth.21.1.639. Medline:10884968.

Singh, Gopal K. February 2012. "Rural-Urban Trends and Patterns in Cervical Cancer Mortality, Incidence, Stage, and Survival in the United States, 1950–2008." *Journal of Community Health* 37 (1): 217–23. http://dx.doi.org/10.1007/s10900-011-9439-6. Medline:21773819.

Singh, Gopal K., Mohammad Siahpush, and Shanita D. Williams. April 2012. "Changing Urbanization Patterns in US Lung Cancer Mortality, 1950–2007." *Journal of Community Health* 37 (2): 412–20. http://dx.doi.org/10.1007/s10900-011-9458-3. Medline:21858690.

Smith, Karly B., John S. Humphreys, and Murray G.A. Wilson. April 2008. "Addressing the Health Disadvantage of Rural Populations: How Does Epidemiological Evidence Inform Rural Health Policies and Research?" *Australian Journal of Rural Health* 16 (2): 56–66. http://dx.doi.org/10.1111/j.1440-1584.2008.00953.x. Medline:18318846.

Sparks, P. Johnelle. 2012. "Rural Health Disparities." In *International Handbook of Rural Demography*, ed. Laszlo J. Kulcsar and Katherine J. Curtis, 255–71. Dordrecht: Springer. http://dx.doi.org/10.1007/978-94-007-1842-5_18.

Stark, C.R., V. Riordan, and R. O'Connor. 2011. "A Conceptual Model of Suicide in Rural Areas." *Rural and Remote Health* 11 (2): 1622. Medline:21702640.

Tai-Seale, Tom, and Coleman Chandler. 2003. "Nutrition and Overweight Concerns in Rural Areas: A Literature Review." In *Rural Healthy People 2010: A Companion Document to Healthy People 2010*, vol. 2, ed. Rural Healthy People 2010, 115–29. College Station: The Texas A&M University Systems Health Sciences Center, School of Rural Public Health, Southwest Rural Health Research Center.

Toomey, P., N. Hanlon, J. Bates, G. Poole, and Chris Y. Lovato. 2011. "Exploring the Role of Social Capital in Supporting a Regional Medical Education Campus." *Rural and Remote Health* 11 (4): 1774. Medline:22087512.

Vijayakumar, L., S. John, J. Pirkis, and H. Whiteford. 2005. "Suicide in Developing Countries (2): Risk Factors." *Crisis* 26 (3): 112–19. http://dx.doi.org/10.1027/0227-5910.26.3.112. Medline:16276753.

Wachter, Robert M. 16 February 2006. "The "Dis-location" of U.S. Medicine—The Implications of Medical Outsourcing." *New England Journal of Medicine* 354 (7): 661–65. http://dx.doi.org/10.1056/NEJMp058258. Medline:16481632.

Wang, Youfa, and May A. Beydoun. 2007. "The Obesity Epidemic in the United States—Gender, Age, Socioeconomic, Racial/Ethnic, and Geographic Characteristics: A Systematic Review and Meta-Regression Analysis." *Epidemiologic Reviews* 29 (1): 6–28. http://dx.doi.org/10.1093/epirev/mxm007. Medline:17510091.

Yang, Tse-Chuan, Leif Jensen, and Murali Haran. 2011. "Social Capital and Human Mortality: Explaining the Rural Paradox with County-Level Mortality Data." *Rural Sociology* 76 (3): 347–74. http://dx.doi.org/10.1111/j.1549-0831.2011.00055.x.

CHAPTER 35

Housing in Rural America

Katherine A. MacTavish, Ann Ziebarth, and Lance George

Introduction

Housing is more than shelter. It is critical to the quality of life for individuals and families and core to the social and economic well-being of communities. Housing relates to opportunities to earn a living, access healthy food, obtain an education, and engage in civic life. As a community asset, housing affects the kind of population a community is able to attract and hold onto, thus contributing deeply to social and economic vitality (Ziebarth 2000).

In 2010, there were just over thirty million housing units in rural and small-town America making up 23 percent of the nation's housing stock (Housing Assistance Council 2012). By many measures, rural Americans appear well housed within these units. More rural Americans, in both relative and absolute terms, live in safe, decent, high quality housing than ever before in our nation's history. Rural homeownership rates continue to exceed national rates, with a significant portion of rural homeowners owning their home "free and clear" of a mortgage (Housing Assistance Council 2012). Further, rural homeowners pay substantially less for housing than do their urban and more suburban counterparts; a trend that holds for rural renters as well (Housing Assistance Council 2012). Yet serious inequalities by geography and socio-cultural categories continue to affect housing in rural and small-town areas. Such inequalities leave an unacceptable proportion of the rural population without access to the goal that "every American family be able to afford a decent home in a suitable living environment" established originally in 1949 by the National Affordable Housing Act.

The Current State of Housing in Rural America

As a nation, we recently experienced one of the most extensive and painful economic crises of an entire generation with housing markets believed to be at the center of that crisis. Millions of Americans struggle to meet their mortgage payments as others face foreclosure or eviction. A lack of reliable information makes it difficult to determine the full extent of foreclosure in rural communities. However, with 432,000 rural homeowners either losing or being on the way to losing their homes between June 2009 and July 2010, it is safe to assume that a significant proportion of rural homeowners have been affected by the mortgage crisis and that the effects will be significant in an already depressed rural economy (Housing Assistance Council 2012).

Ownership

Homeownership is culturally ingrained in the national dream of a good life defined by financial security, social prestige, and residential stability (Cullen 2004). Despite a slight decline from the all-time high ownership rates in 2000, close to 72 percent of rural housing units are currently owner-occupied; a figure that exceeds the national average of some 67 percent (Housing Assistance Council 2012). Nonetheless, the anticipated benefits of a comparative advantage in rural homeownership rates are compromised in several ways.

First, the significant contribution of manufactured housing to rural markets explains much of the rural advantage in ownership rates (Housing Assistance Council 2005). Nationally, manufactured housing accounts for only 7 percent of the housing stock; in rural America, it makes up almost 17 percent. Close to three-fourths of rural manufactured homes are owner-occupied. During the 1990s, manufactured housing emerged as the leading pathway to "affordable" homeownership for rural households. Yet despite efforts to advance today's manufactured housing beyond the "trailers" of earlier eras, a host of structural, financial, and social insecurities continue to erode the ownership benefits of manufactured housing (MacTavish, Eley, and Salamon 2006). Concerns about tornadoes and fire danger, leeching toxins, and a relatively limited useful life span persist and compromise any long-term sense of security despite federal government attempts to ensure structural integrity. Rapid depreciation, high-pressure sales tactics, and high cost or even predatory financing severely limit the economic benefits of manufactured homeownership (Housing Assistance Council 2005). Social stigmatization of manufactured home residents as "trailer trash" along with their marginalization to the edge of town restrict the life chances of young people in ways similar to urban ghetto neighborhoods (MacTavish 2007; MacTavish and Salamon 2006). These insecurities are especially pronounced when a manufactured home is located on rented land in a mobile home or trailer park, as is the case for 2.6 million rural households (MacTavish, Eley, and Salamon 2006). Thus, while a manufactured home purchase has emerged as a favored pathway to ownership among rural families of modest means, many of these rural homeowners never realize the full benefits of their investment.

Second, as is the trend across the nation as a whole, ethnic and racial minority groups do not realize equitable opportunities for homeownership in rural and small-town America. Homeownership rates among rural minorities, although higher than those in urban areas, fall a full twenty percentage points below those of rural non-Hispanic whites (Housing Assistance Council 2012). Further, rural minorities experienced some of the most significant declines in homeownership rates during the recent recession. Among rural African American headed households, ownership rates fell by more than five percentage points as compared to declines of less than two percentage points among the white, non-Hispanic rural population (Housing Assistance Council 2012).

Finally, an almost singular focus on homeownership as the rural ideal leaves out the needs of the over seven million rural renters for whom homeownership remains out of reach or not of interest (Housing Assistance Council 2012). Rural renters, who have lower incomes and are often racial or ethnic minorities, experience some of the greatest challenges and most limited opportunities for finding decent and affordable housing.

Quality

Despite dramatic progress during the last half century in addressing quality issues, unacceptable numbers of rural Americans continue to live in "substandard" housing. A home is designated as substandard when it lacks such basics as a complete kitchen or plumbing, or when features like a leaking roof, broken windows, or sagging porch indicate structural concerns (Housing Assistance Council 2012). Data from the American Housing Survey indicate that in 2009, 6 percent or 1.5 million homes outside of metropolitan areas were either moderately or severely substandard. While not alarmingly high, these levels are higher than those found in suburban areas of the United States. Among rural minorities, problems of housing quality are pronounced. Rural minority households are twice as likely to live in substandard housing as rural non-Hispanic whites, while rural African American headed households are three times as likely to live in substandard housing as rural households of all races (Housing Assistance Council 2012).

Crowding provides another indicator of housing inadequacy. Defined as more than one person per room, crowding is most pronounced in our nation's cities, where close to 6 percent of the housing is crowded (Housing Assistance Council 2012). Yet, crowding among specific rural populations exceeds even these proportions. Hispanics in rural and small-town America have crowding rates ten times the national and three times the national rural rate. On Native American lands, just shy of 9 percent of the housing is crowded. Among farm workers, even with dorms and barracks excluded, almost 31 percent of housing is crowded. In rural areas, crowding is often an invisible form of homelessness (Fitchen 1994). Pressed by social and economic situations, households "double up" with family or friends. Beyond compromising quality of life in more general ways, substandard and overcrowded housing are associated with a range of public health issues including the spread of close-contact diseases like tuberculosis, pneumonia, and conjunctivitis, and with social concerns like domestic violence, child abuse, and alcoholism (Bashir 2002; Krieger and Higgins 2002).

Affordability

Rural housing has long been assumed more affordable than housing in other geographic areas. Indeed, rural homeowners pay 40 percent less on average per month for housing than do their urban and suburban counterparts. Yet comparative costs tell only so much about affordability. Housing-cost burden—a ratio of income to housing costs—is a better indicator of affordability. A household is housing-cost burdened if it spends more than 30 percent of its monthly income on housing; a severely cost-burdened household spends more than half its income on housing. Three-in-ten or approximately seven million rural households are cost burdened; for close to three million, cost burden is severe (Housing Assistance Council 2012). At 47 percent, cost burden hits rural renters hardest, and nearly half are severely cost burdened.

Housing cost burden provides a good approximation of material hardship. When a household spends an inordinate amount of its income on housing, it experiences what Stone (1993) terms *shelter poverty*, with little left for essentials like food, clothing, transportation, or health care. Unaffordable housing is linked to rural residential instability where moves from place to place disrupt children's educational experiences (Schafft 2006) and reinforce the persistence of rural poverty (Fitchen 1994).

Contemporary Issues and Rural Housing Inequalities

While housing inequalities identified above are a physical manifestation of historical processes, they also reflect more contemporary processes (Barcus 2011). The continued diversification of rural economies over recent decades, for example, has reinforced already diverging trajectories among sub-regions of the rural United States. The housing issues emerging in places of rapid growth contrast greatly with those in areas of economic and population decline and stagnation. Alongside uneven patterns of growth and change, recent trends in home mortgage finance coupled with the foreclosure crisis bring new economic realities that heighten vulnerability, particularly for specific rural populations and places (Dickstein et al. 2006). Finally, shifts in federal supports to rural housing add additional layers of complexity to contemporary rural housing opportunities.

Rural Development and Housing

Amenity and exurban development that have characterized rural growth in recent decades have significant impacts on rural housing opportunities (Marcouiller, Lapping, and Furuseth 2011; Stedman, Goetz, and Weagraff 2006). Much of the 11 percent growth (three million units) in rural housing between 2000 and 2010 happened in high-amenity and exurban areas where private sector-led development responded to emerging markets. Parts of the Rocky Mountain West, the Upper Great Lakes, and scenic areas of the Northeast are hot spots for amenity and exurban growth (Housing Assistance Council 2012).

Advances in technology and transportation make it increasingly possible to live (and work) in a place of one's choosing. A desire for a lifestyle offering access to scenic beauty and outdoor recreation fueled housing development in amenity-rich rural communities (Esparza 2011). Between 1990 and 2000, recreation counties in the United States grew at a rate of 20 percent, or three times the rates found across other nonmetro areas (Johnson 2006; Johnson and Beale 2002).

New construction and the gentrification of existing housing stock typical of amenity growth naturally increase local housing quality (Barcus 2011). Furthermore, such development opens up ownership opportunities as reflected in the 77 percent growth between 1970 and 2000 in the nation's stock of seasonal or second homes in high amenity places (Esparza 2011). Yet such market-driven development profoundly affects the housing opportunities for those of lesser means (Hammer and Winkler 2006). While tourism-based economic growth creates jobs, they seldom pay a wage adequate to afford housing let alone homeownership. In a story not unlike that of urban gentrification, lower-income residents, families with children, and young households least able to afford the escalating land and home prices are either pressed into a situation of shelter poverty or pushed toward other options. Some turn to cheaper and insecure mobile homes (Lapping, Furuseth, and Marcouiller 2011). Others double up or relocate to nearby towns. All such choices potentially compromise quality of life.

Amenity-driven development slowed amidst the recent recession but is predicted to persist. Esparza asserts (2011, 36) that "the lure of open spaces will not be denied those with the wherewithal." High-end housing in high-amenity places is thus likely to proliferate in the years to come. A key task here is finding ways to keep housing opportunities open not only for hotel housekeepers but also for schoolteachers, main-street business owners, and even young doctors. Without some kind of balance, high amenity places face balkanization into the rural "served" and their "servants" with all the attendant inequalities inferred (Lapping et al. 2011, 274–6).

In a similar way, rural regions in close proximity to metro areas have experienced dramatic growth and subsequent changes in housing opportunities (Marcouiller et. al 2011). Between 2000 and 2010, exurban development emerged as the leading form of land use in the United States (Esparza 2011). A recent estimate indicates some 38 percent of homes in the lower forty-eight states are found within the so-called wildland-urban interface (Stewart, Radeloff, and Hammer 2006). For many urbanites, the draw was a single-family home on a large lot made affordable by lower than metro land prices. Rich ethnographic accounts (Salamon 2003; MacGregor 2010) illustrate how small towns are transformed by the arrival of newcomers seeking access to good schools, a safe community, and a home worthy of their status, but who have little interest in broader community life. Tensions emerge as old-timers feel their hometown become a *non-town*—a place where civic engagement among newcomers is limited and differing priorities and allegiances essentially bifurcate community (Bradshaw 1993).

The loss of affordable housing in some areas has resulted from exurban development. The rampant sale and closure of mobile home parks has made headline news across rural America (Killgannon 2007). As growth and development progress and land pressures increase, mobile home parks and other affordable but "less desirable" kinds of development become targets of redevelopment toward "higher and better use." Low-income elderly and young families are most vulnerable to displacement. Because moving a manufactured home is costly, the closure of a park often means the loss of hard-won homeownership status among rural households of modest means.

Outside these areas of amenity and exurban growth lie rural pockets of social and economic decline. Population loss in these areas impacts the local housing stock (Housing Assistance Council 2012). Absentee ownership becomes commonplace, and older residents are unable to maintain their homes. House values also decline, making mortgages and home rehabilitation loans more difficult to obtain. Meeting housing and other needs becomes even more difficult when low population densities spread populations out over large expanses of territory far from any centralized resources.

In some declining rural communities, the availability of low-cost housing attracts newcomers who are often disproportionately non-white and/or low income (Burton, Garrett-Peters, and Eason 2011; Fitchen 1994; Salamon 2003). Burton et al. (2011) and Clark (2012) document the experience of poor urban blacks in search of housing in rural Pennsylvania, drawn by readily available (often subsidized) rental housing and a chance to leave the troubles of the city behind. Once relocated, such families often struggle to find work and meet resistance from long-term residents. In Salamon's (2003) declining Midwestern community of Splitville, the chance to own even a "shabby" home without a down payment drew formerly residentially mobile poor and working poor families to town. Differing norms and values about property upkeep and life ways created serious antagonism and made community life a "contested territory." In a desperate attempt to hold onto a sense of place, long-time residents turn to local ordinances and exclusionary policies such as limitations on the number of cars or people per home (Burton et al. 2011; Salamon 2003).

The spatial concentration of poor and working poor families in declining rural places creates the potential for the emergence of rural ghettos where compromised quality of life becomes intractable (Burton et al. 2011; Eason 2012; Fitchen 1994). The relocation of low-income families to dying towns where work is hard to find perpetuates poverty. Social exclusion creates stubborn barriers with serious implications for the life chance of children and youth (Fitchen 1994; MacTavish 2007; Salamon 2003). Thus, housing opportunities seemingly made available in declining rural areas are not without complications.

In other economically declining places, industrial restructuring stems population loss. Meat packing plants and large agricultural operations often draw ethnic minorities (Broadway 2000), largely Hispanics, willing to accept low wages and difficult working conditions (Ziebarth 2000). This can quickly outpace a small town's housing stock (Prochaska-Cue, Ziebarth, and Shrewsbury 1997; Whitener 2001; Broadway 2000). Further complicating things, long-term residents often frown on doubling up and other coping strategies (Salamon 2003), and property owners often raise rents and reduce investments in upkeep. Nationally, Hispanics in rural America experience some of the largest challenges in finding access to decent, affordable housing (Housing Assistance Council 2012).

Rural Home Finance and Mortgage Access

In recent decades, quality (or prime) home mortgage finance has become both harder to come by and costlier, especially in rural America (Housing Assistance Council 2012). Rural homeowners are more prone to have high-cost mortgage loans, those with an interest rate at least 1.5 percentage points higher than the annual percentage rate offered on prime mortgage loans of comparable type.

In 2010, 11 percent of rural home origination loans were high cost, a proportion twice that found nationally (Housing Assistance Council 2012). High-cost lending increased considerably in recent years, particularly in areas of persistent poverty where one-third or more of all new mortgage loans were high-cost loans (Dickstein et al. 2006). Declining competition as the number of rural lending institutions diminishes and the additional cost of doing business remotely make rural mortgages more costly for borrowers (Dickstein et al. 2006). However, the increasingly active nature of sub-prime and predatory lenders in nonmetro areas contributes as well.

Sub-prime lending has made significant inroads in nonmetro markets. Sub-prime loans, typically for smaller amounts, carry higher interest rates, greater origination fees, and shorter terms. Higher interest rates are justified by the additional risk of lending to a borrower assumed to be at greater risk of defaulting on a loan. However, by some estimates as many as half who take out sub-prime or high-cost loans would have qualified for prime rate loans (Dickstein et al. 2006; Crump 2011). These borrowers, never offered more affordable options, were steered toward higher cost (and higher profit) loans—a practice associated with *predatory lending*. Although sub-prime loan demand remains lower in rural than in urban areas, the use of such mortgages seems to be on the rise (Housing Assistance Council 2012).

Subprime rural mortgage markets are strongly associated with the finance of manufactured home purchases. Personal property (or *chattel*) loans are used for most manufactured homes. In the 1990s, when manufactured home sales were at their peak, manufactured home purchases accounted for 27 percent of all sub-prime loans nationally with more than 40 percent of these loans included interest rates upwards of 10 percent (Housing Assistance Council 2004). Record foreclosures in the late 1990s were linked to egregious practices of over-extending credit to low-income buyers and left a glut of manufactured home on the market. Such practices thus precipitated the manufactured home foreclosure crisis—a crisis from which the manufactured housing industry is still recovering. Given the ubiquitous presence of manufactured housing in rural America, the effects of the manufactured housing crisis can be assumed to have had widespread implications for rural housing markets.

There is clear evidence as well of subprime and predatory lenders disproportionately targeting low income and minority rural populations (Dickstein et al. 2006). Essentially redlining in reverse, subprime and predatory lending opens avenues for credit to rural populations previously denied a chance at the American dream of homeownership (Crump 2011). This chance, however, comes with significant costs. In addition to higher interest rates, predatory mortgages include abusive conditions such as prepayment penalties in the thousands of dollars that trap borrowers in an expensive loan contract. With little consideration given to the borrower's capacity to repay the loan, the loss of a job or other crisis can spell disaster to a homeowner with a sub-prime or predatory loan. At least one recent study has established a link between high-cost loans and rural home foreclosures (Crump 2011). While rural evidence is limited, urban studies find that when subprime lending and foreclosures are spatially clustered, the impacts are magnified (Crump 2011). Activist groups like ACORN have documented how economically distressed urban communities are stripped of equity, how home values decline, and how hard won gains in minority homeownership are lost through predatory lending.

In a depressed economic climate, applications for rural home loans declined by 59 percent between 2003 and 2010 (Housing Assistance Council 2012). Most recent mortgage loan activity in rural areas and nationwide has been around refinancing as owners seek to lower their mortgage interest rates (Housing Assistance Council 2012). Higher rates of credit denial, with more than 18 percent of rural applicants denied compared to just over 14 percent nationally, have further constrained rural housing markets in recent years (Housing Assistance Council 2012). Bank mergers driven by the need to be "too big to fail" will likely make finding and accessing equitable credit even tougher for rural and small-town residents.

Diminishing Public Investment

Two trends in the public investment in rural housing emerge as significant to current housing opportunities. Both are well detailed in the Housing Assistance Council's 2012 *Taking Stock* report. First, federal support for rural housing has been on a diminishing trajectory for decades. For example, direct lending for single-family homeownership through the US Department of Agriculture (USDA) 502 loan programs declined from $1,121 million in 2011 to $900 million in 2012. These declines began before the Great Recession. In the mid-1990s, the direct lending program regularly funded more than 20,000 affordable mortgages a year, and as of writing that number is cut in half at about 10,000 per year (and dropping). Programs to assist very low-income households, primarily elderly homeowners, repair their homes saw funding in the same one-year time frame decline from over $57 million in 2011 to $39 million in 2012.

Second, administrative processes around accessing federal support create an inherent rural disadvantage. State governments serve as gatekeepers for access to federal funding to rural areas and small towns. While major cities can apply directly to the US Department of Housing and Urban Development for funding to address critical housing needs in their jurisdictions, small towns and local governments in rural places must compete with funding that is allocated to states. Local governments can apply to regional USDA offices for loans and grants to improve public utilities and community facilities. Individual households must make their own requests for support for homeownership or home improvements through mortgage lenders or directly to regional USDA offices. Contractors and developers must apply to state housing agencies for highly competitive low-income housing tax credit project capital. Local housing authorities managing low-income, farmworker, or senior housing seek financial assistance for maintaining and operating affordable rental housing through state agencies or USDA regional offices. Tenants seeking rent assistance through local housing authorities often face limited choices as well. The complex chain of command to access rural housing supports becomes another form of rural disadvantage.

Economic recession leaves governments pulled in many directions. The focus in recent years, in particular, has not been on rural nor affordable housing. Some policy analysis thus concludes, "Federal rural housing policy—especially in the critical areas of affordability, rental markets, subsidies, as well as construction and preservation aids, and homelessness—is narrowing and it has largely been left to the non-profits sector to address these concerns" (Lapping et al. 2011, 273).

Rural Housing into the 2010s

By the numbers and the stories emerging from rural America, the promise of our national housing act put into place more than half a century ago remains unrealized. Private sector-led development and free market home finance approaches have failed to ensure the provision of affordable housing in a decent environment for every American family. Yet housing is not only a private sector commodity but also a public good, essential to successful economic development and the public health and well-being of the nation. Public policy has been critiqued recently as operating from an "ethos of individualism and competition" wherein the state falls short of fulfilling its obligations to ensure equitable opportunities (Padt and Luloff 2009, 239). Under such an approach, it is said that rural housing has come to "serve as a visual proxy for underlying economic disparities that exist across rural America" (Lapping et al. 2011, 275).

The challenges in addressing housing inequality loom large as the integration of rural America into the global economy persists. Our assessment of the challenges suggests a set of tensions that will have to be dealt with if we are to move forward. First among these is defining the role of the state or government in balancing housing opportunities. Certainly there is a role for the state in reforming home mortgage finance. The Dodd-Frank Wall Street Reform Consumer Protection Act is a bold yet contested mechanism to protect low-income rural people from predatory subprime lending practices and provide relief from high-cost loans. These protections, however, need to come with other alternatives for home finance. The USDA's Section 502 Homeownership Loan Program is an example of "sub-prime lending done right" (Housing Assistance Council 2012, 31). Since the 1950s, that program has helped more than 2.5 million low-income households become homeowners. A redirection of the program away from direct lending toward loan guarantees that serve more moderate income households has, however, narrowed support for the program's lowest income applicants. A reversal of that trend seems necessary.

In the wake of declining governmental investment, the growing efforts of non-profits to meet the housing needs of low-income rural populations prove vital. Rural housing developers often meet difficulty in trying to provide affordable alternatives. Local policies that seek to preserve the rural small-town character by banning mobile homes and erecting barriers to multi-family housing reduce the housing options of lower income residents (Ziebarth 2000). Such practices need to be evaluated. Nonprofits can help inform local governments about the economics of affordable housing and community vitality. They can leverage the public and private funding needed to upgrade local infrastructure and level the additional costs that come with rural distances.

Given the shortage of affordable and rental housing in rural America, strategies need to be put into place to preserve and improve what is there. Many of the affordable rental units developed under the USDA's Section 515 program are poised to convert to market-rate housing in the next few years as owners of the project prepay loans. Well over 250,000 units of affordable housing could be lost with that conversion. Manufactured housing, already a significant part of the rural housing landscape, offers a potential alternative *if* the long list of challenges associated with it can be addressed. One approach that promises to alleviate many of the financial and social issues associated with manufactured housing is the conversion of land lease mobile home parks to Resident-Owned Communities or ROCs (Bradley 2000). The New Hampshire Community Loan Fund has become a leader in the ROC conversion movement (Bradley 2000). The conversion of land-lease parks to ROCs has begun to spread, particularly in states like Vermont, New Hampshire, and Oregon.

Increasing pressures from energy-driven development present emerging tensions in housing rural America into the 2010s. Boom-bust economic development has impacted rural places for decades, but recent trends around energy-driven development point to increasing difficulties for rural communities. The shale gas boom across Pennsylvania resulted in dramatic changes to the rural landscape with lasting implication for quality of life. One homeowner discovered that her dream home now sits "780 feet downwind of three enormous gas compressors;" other residents have been "beset by eye-watering fumes and noxious drinking water" (Humes 2012, 52).

In the North Dakota Bakken oil field, new drilling has created severe housing shortages. To meet the demand, companies and private developers have built temporary housing including "man camps" of low-slung modular dormitory-style buildings. Two of these built on either side of the highway house up to 3,700 residents (Sulzberger 2011). The labor demand of drilling has made local housing prices soar to the point that previous renters are displaced and communities have difficulty in attracting school teachers, police, and firemen, while other businesses cannot compete to hire waitresses or store clerks at wages that can allow them to find affordable housing (Davey 2010; Donovan 2011). Even the construction companies doing highway work are discovering that "housing is the one thing money can't buy in the oil patch" (Donovan 2012).

Finally is the tension of housing an aging rural population. Rural America is "older" than the nation as a whole (see Nelson in this volume). Most seniors' primary wish is to remain in their homes as long as possible. However, rural elders are increasingly challenged with housing affordability, and many seniors do not have the physical or financial resources to improve their housing conditions and maintain their quality of life. Rural communities will need to develop a range of housing options such as rental housing, rehab and repair programs, housing with services, and assisted living to adequately house rural seniors.

Conclusions

Housing of rural Americans is largely similar to the nation as a whole. There are, however, some substantial and important issues unique to rural housing. Among these, as we have described, are the dynamics of manufactured housing, the persistence of quality issues, and the challenges emerging for particular areas and populations. Our ability to respond to the challenges we have identified will rest in no small part on developing an adequate research-based focus on rural housing. That the two preceding "decennial volumes" lacked chapters on rural housing underscores its neglect as a pressing and imperative issue. While researchers in natural resources, poverty, and community development have been bumping into housing for decades, they have not given it much direct focus. In the absence of more complete body of literature on rural housing, we leaned heavily on the work of the Housing Assistance Council and the Carsey Institute in the preparation of this chapter. Indeed, the recent publication of an edited volume by Marcouiller and colleagues (2011) in our view represents the first focused and comprehensive effort to look at rural housing issues through an academic lens. That work, and hopefully this chapter, will inspire future rural housing research.

There was much attention to the recent housing crisis, namely because it reached up into middle and higher income areas and into the suburbs. However, the housing crisis impacted rural America too. A lack of economic diversification and dynamism in many rural areas may mean that the housing crisis will lag and last longer in rural places. Further, we know virtually nothing about rural foreclosure and what happened in rural markets during the foreclosure crisis. To assess, build and return to healthy housing markets we need improvements in housing data and reporting.

There are areas such as the Lower Mississippi Delta region, Border Colonias areas, and Native American lands and related populations—namely Native Americans, Hispanics, African Americans, farm workers, and the rural white poor—in housing crisis long before 2008. These populations, often "hidden" from mainstream America, will continue to experience housing problems after the larger market has recovered. While we have tried to highlight some of the inequalities experienced by these populations, much more thoughtful focus is needed if we are to craft strategies for better balancing housing opportunities.

If anything, the last few years have affirmed the importance of housing to our national economy and to community and family well-being. Public investment in housing is diminishing at a time when it is perhaps needed most. A focus on understanding the implications of our current policy approach for the quality of life among all rural residents is critical.

References

Barcus, Holly. 2011. "The Nature of Rural Housing Markets." In *Rural Housing, Exurbanization, and Amenity-Driven Development: Contrasting the "Haves" and the "Have Nots,"* ed. David Marcouiller, Mark Lapping, and Owen Furuseth, 51–74. Burlington, VT: Ashgate Publishing.

Bashir, Samiya A. May 2002. "Home is Where the Harm Is: Inadequate Housing as a Public Health Crisis." *American Journal of Public Health* 92 (5): 733–8. http://dx.doi.org/10.2105/AJPH.92.5.733. Medline:11988437.

Bradley, Paul. 2000. "Manufactured Housing Park Cooperatives in New Hampshire: An Enterprising Solution to the Complex Problems of Owning a Home on Rented Land." *Cooperative Housing Journal*: 22–32. http://www.coophousing.org/uploadedfiles/nahc_site/resources/nahc%20manufactured%20bradley.pdf.

Bradshaw, Ted. 1993. "In the Shadow of Urban Growth: Bifurcation in Rural California Communities." In *Forgotten Places: Uneven Development in Rural America*, ed. Thomas Lyson and William Falk, 218–56. Lawrence: University of Kansas Press.

Broadway, Michael. 2000. "Planning for Change in Small Towns or Trying to Avoid the Slaughter House Blues." *Journal of Rural Studies* 16 (1): 37–46. http://dx.doi.org/10.1016/S0743-0167(99)00038-8.

Burton, Linda, Raymond Garrett-Peters, and John Major Eason. 2011. "Morality, Identity, and Mental Health in Rural Ghettos." In *Communities, Neighborhoods, and Health: Social Disparities in Health and Health Care*, ed. Linda M. Burton, Susan P. Kemp, Leung ManChui, Stephen A. Matthews, and David T. Takeuchi, 91–110. New York: Springer Publishing. http://dx.doi.org/10.1007/978-1-4419-7482-2_6.

Clark, Sherry L. 2012. "In Search of Housing: Urban Families in Rural Contexts." *Rural Sociology* 77 (1): 110–34. http://dx.doi.org/10.1111/j.1549-0831.2011.00069.x.

Crump, Jeffrey. 2011. "Subprime Lending and Foreclosure in Rural Minnesota." In *Rural Housing, Exurbanization, and Amenity-Driven Development: Contrasting the "Haves" and the "Have Nots,"* ed. David Marcouiller, Mark Lapping, and Owen Furuseth, 207–23. Burlington, VT: Ashgate Publishing.

Cullen, Jim. 2004. *The American Dream: A Short History of the Idea That Shaped a Nation.* New York: Oxford University Press.

Davey, Monica. 2010. "A State with Plenty of Jobs but Few Places to Live." *New York Times*, 20 April.

Dickstein, Carla, Lance George, Theresa Singleton, and Hannah Jones. 2006. "Subprime and Predatory Lending in Rural America: Mortgage Lending Practices that Can Trap Low-Income Rural People." *Carsey Institute Policy Brief* 4: 1–10.

Donovan, Lauren. 2011. "With Housing Shortages in Western ND, Some Look to Make a Buck." *Bismarck Tribune*, 2 July. http://bismarcktribune.com/news/state-and-regional/with-housing-shortage-in-western-nd-some-look-to-make/article_12f53694-a348-11e0-8727-001cc4c002e0.html.

Donovan, Lauren. 2012. "N.D. Housing Shortage Extends to Highway Workers." *Bismarck Tribune*, 12 August. http://bismarcktribune.com/bakken/n-d-housing-shortage-extends-to-highway-workers/article_33bb2bda-e42f-11e1-91d5-0019bb2963f4.html.

Eason, John. 2012. "Extending the Hyperghetto: Toward a Theory of Punishment, Race, and Rural Disadvantage." *Journal of Poverty* 16 (3): 274–95. http://dx.doi.org/10.1080/10875549.2012.695534.

Esparza, Adrian. 2011. "The Exurbanization Process and Rural Housing Markets." In *Rural Housing, Exurbanization, and Amenity-Driven Development: Contrasting the "Haves" and the "Have Nots,"* ed. David Marcouiller, Mark Lapping, and Owen Furuseth, 27–50. Burlington, VT: Ashgate Publishing.

Fitchen, Janet. 1994. "Residential Mobility among the Rural Poor." *Rural Sociology* 59 (3): 416–36. http://dx.doi.org/10.1111/j.1549-0831.1994.tb00540.x.

Hammer, Roger, and Richelle Winkler. 2006. "Housing Affordability and Population Change in the Upper Midwestern North Woods." In *Population Change and Rural Society*, ed. William A. Kandel and David L. Brown, 293–309. Netherlands: Springer. http://dx.doi.org/10.1007/1-4020-3902-6_14.

Housing Assistance Council. 2004. *Run While You Still Can: Subprime and Predatory Lending in Rural America*. Washington, DC: Housing Assistance Council.

Housing Assistance Council. 2005. *Moving Home: Manufactured Housing in Rural America*. Washington, DC: Housing Assistance Council.

Housing Assistance Council. 2012. *Taking Stock: Rural People, Poverty, and Housing in the 21st Century*. Washington, DC: Housing Assistance Council.

Humes, Edward. 2012. "Fractured Lives: Detritus of Pennsylvania's Shale Gas Boom." *Sierra Magazine*, August. http://www.sierraclub.org/sierra/201207/pennsylvania-fracking-shale-gas-199.aspx.

Johnson, Kenneth. 2006. *Demographic Trends in Rural and Small Town America*. University of New Hampshire: Carsey Institute. http://www.carseyinstitute.unh.edu/publications/Report_Demographics.pdf.

Johnson, Kenneth, and Calvin Beale. 2002. "Nonmetro Recreation Counties: Their Identification and Rapid Growth." *Rural America* 17: 12–19.

Killgannon, Corey. 2007. "Trailer-Park Sales Leave Residents with Single-Wides and Few Options." *New York Times*, 18 April.

Krieger, James, and Donna L. Higgins. May 2002. "Housing and Health: Time Again for Public Health Action." *American Journal of Public Health* 92 (5): 758–68. http://dx.doi.org/10.2105/AJPH.92.5.758. Medline:11988443.

Lapping, Mark, Owen Furuseth, and David Marcouiller. 2011. "Conclusions and Integrative Thoughts on Rural Housing Policy." In *Rural Housing, Exurbanization, and Amenity-Driven Development: Contrasting the "Haves" and the "Have Nots,"* ed. David Marcouiller, Mark Lapping, and Owen Furuseth, 273–76. Burlington, VT: Ashgate Publishing.

MacGregor, Lynn. 2010. *Habits of the Heartland: Small-Town Life in Modern America*. Ithaca, NY: Cornell University Press.

MacTavish, Katherine. 2007. "The *Wrong Side of the Tracks*: Social Inequality and Mobile Home Park Residence." *Community Development* 38 (1): 74–91. http://dx.doi.org/10.1080/15575330709490186.

MacTavish, Katherine, Michelle L. Eley, and Sonya Salamon. 2006. "Housing Vulnerability among Rural Trailer Park Households." *Georgetown Journal of Poverty Law & Policy* 13: 95–117.

MacTavish, Katherine, and Sonya Salamon. 2006. "Pathways of Youth Development in a Rural Trailer Park." *Family Relations* 55 (2): 163–74. http://dx.doi.org/10.1111/j.1741-3729.2006.00367.x.

Marcouiller, David, Mark Lapping, and Owen Furuseth. 2011. *Rural Housing, Exurbanization, and Amenity-Driven Development: Contrasting the "Haves" and the "Have Nots."* Burlington, VT: Ashgate Publishing.

Padt, F.J.G., and A.E. Luloff. 2009. "An Institutional Analysis of Rural Policy in the United States." *Community Development* 40 (3): 232–46. http://dx.doi.org/10.1080/15575330903091696.

Prochaska-Cue, Kathleen, Ann Ziebarth, and Bonnie Shrewsbury. 1997. "Where One Size Does Not Fit All." *Great Plains Research* 7: 209–23.

Salamon, Sonya. 2003. *Newcomers to Old Towns: Suburbanization of the Heartland*. Chicago: University of Chicago Press. http://dx.doi.org/10.7208/chicago/9780226734118.001.0001.

Schafft, Kai A. 2006. "Poverty, Residential Mobility and Student Transiency within a Rural New York School District." *Rural Sociology* 71 (2): 212–31. http://dx.doi.org/10.1526/003601106777789710.

Stedman, Richard, Stephan Goetz, and Benjamin Weagraff. 2006. "Does Second Home Development Adversely Affect Rural Life?" In *Population Change and Rural Society*, ed. William A. Kandel and David L. Brown, 277–92. Netherlands: Springer. http://dx.doi.org/10.1007/1-4020-3902-6_13.

Stewart, Susan I., Volker C. Radeloff, and Roger B. Hammer. 2006. "The Wildland-Urban Interface in the United States." In *The Public and Wildland Fire Management: Social Science Findings for Managers*, ed. S.M. McCaffrey, 197–202. Gen. Tech. Rep. NRS-1. Newtown Square, PA: US Department of Agriculture, Forest Service, Northern Research Station.

Stone, Michael. 1993. *Shelter Poverty: New Ideas on Housing Affordability*. Philadelphia, PA: Temple University Press.

Sulzberger, A.G. 2011. "Oil Rigs Bring Camps of Men to the Prairie." *New York Times*, 25 November 25. http://www.nytimes.com/2011/11/26/us/north-dakota-oil-boom-creates-camps-of-men.html?pagewanted=all&_r=0.

Tilly, Charles. 1999. *Durable Inequalities*. Berkeley: University of California Press.

Whitener, L.A. 2001. "Housing Poverty in Rural Areas Greater for Racial and Ethnic Minorities." *Rural America* 15: 2–7.

Ziebarth, Ann. 2000. "Local Housing Policy: The Small-Town Myth and Economic Development." *Rural America* 15: 18–22.

Contributors

Conner Bailey is a professor of rural sociology at Auburn University. He is a past president of the Rural Sociological Society. His primary research interests are in natural resources and the environment as well as questions of poverty and power in the southeastern United States. He received his PhD from Cornell University in 1980.

Carmen Bain is an associate professor of sociology at Iowa State University. Her primary research interests are in international development, the political economy of agrifood systems, and the social dimensions of the bioeconomy. She received her PhD from Michigan State University in 2007.

Merrill Baker-Médard is a doctoral student at the University of California, Berkeley. Her primary research interests are on human dimensions of natural resource management, including the political ecology of marine conservation, gendered property relations, and resource use conflict arising from political upheaval.

Michael M. Bell is a Vilas Distinguished Achievement Professor of community and environmental sociology at the University of Wisconsin-Madison, where he is also director of the Center for Integrated Agricultural Systems. His scholarship has three central foci: dialogics, the sociology of nature, and social justice.

Leigh A. Bernacchi currently researches rural sociology and regional approaches to climate change in Pacific Northwest agriculture at the University of Idaho. She focuses primarily on environmental communication and sociology of climate change. She completed her MS in environmental humanities at the University of Utah and is completing a PhD in wildlife and fisheries sciences at Texas A&M University.

E. Helen Berry received her PhD from Ohio State University in 1983 and is now a professor of sociology at Utah State University and president-elect of the Rural Sociological Society. Her research focuses on the ways that changing population processes influence the economic and social life of rural and urban environments.

Catharine Biddle is a doctoral candidate in educational leadership at the Pennsylvania State University. Her work examines the intersections of space, schooling, and education policy in the United States, with a particular focus on grassroots-led educational reform.

Alessandro Bonanno is a Texas State University System Regents' professor and distinguished professor of sociology at Sam Houston State University. He focuses on the globalization of agriculture and food, the impact that globalization has on the state, democracy, labor relations, and the emancipatory options of subordinate groups. He received his PhD from the University of Kentucky in 1985 and currently serves as editor of the journal *Rural Sociology*.

Kathryn Brasier is an associate professor of rural sociology in the department of agricultural economics, sociology, and education at the Pennsylvania State University. Her research and extension programs focus on environment-society interactions at the community level and collective action related to agricultural and environmental issues. She received her PhD in sociology from the University of Wisconsin-Madison in 2002.

David L. Brown is professor and chair of development sociology and co-director of the Community and Regional Development Institute at Cornell University, and a past president of the Rural Sociological Society. His research focuses on migration and population redistribution in the United States and Europe, with emphasis on their interaction with local community organization. He also studies the production and reproduction of social and economic inequalities between regions and rural versus urban areas. He received his PhD in 1974 from the University of Wisconsin.

Ralph B. Brown is a professor of sociology and director of the international development minor at Brigham Young University, and serves as the executive director and treasurer of the Rural Sociological Society. His research has centered on applied research and assessment, the sociology of community, and social change and rural development in the United States and Southeast Asia. He received his PhD from the University of Missouri-Columbia in 1992.

Jessica A. Carson is a research scientist at the Carsey Institute and a doctoral student in the sociology department at the University of New Hampshire. Her primary research interests are in the intersections of health, gender, poverty, and the family.

Douglas H. Constance is a professor of sociology at Sam Houston State University. His research focuses on the relationship between the globalization of the agrifood system and the quality of life in rural communities. He received his PhD in rural sociology from the University of Missouri-Columbia and served as vice president of the Rural Sociological Society.

John Cromartie is senior demographer at the Economic Research Service, USDA, and visiting lecturer at the George Washington University. He conducts research on rural migration, population distribution, and the effects of demographic change on rural well-being. He received a PhD in geography from the University of North Carolina in 1989.

Martha Crowley is an associate professor of sociology at North Carolina State University. Her research addresses social stratification, with emphasis on work, education, and spatial inequality. She received her PhD from Ohio State University in 2006.

Erinn Cruz is a research assistant in the Office of Community Partnerships at the University of Idaho. Originally from eastern Washington, her work focuses on food systems and broadband in rural Idaho. She received her BS in agricultural economics in 2011 from the University of Idaho.

Dani Deemer is a graduate student at Ohio State University and a visiting assistant professor of sociology at Juniata College. Her research interests include inequality, development, and the sociology of food and agriculture.

Sarah Dewees is the senior director of research, policy, and asset-building programs at First Nations Development Institute, a national non-profit focused on economic development on Indian reservations. She received her PhD from the University of Kentucky in 1998.

Lori A. Dickes is assistant director of the South Carolina Water Resources Center and a faculty member in the masters in public administration program at Clemson University. Her research interests are economic and community development, rural entrepreneurship, and natural resources economics. She received her PhD from Clemson University in 2011.

Kim Ebert is an assistant professor at North Carolina State University. Her research focuses on the maintenance of ethnoracial inequalities and emergent collective action among immigrant newcomers. She received her PhD from the University of California Davis in 2009.

John Eshleman is a dual-title PhD candidate in rural sociology and the human dimensions of natural resources and the environment at the Pennsylvania State University. His dissertation explores the role of national-level non-profit organizations in agrifood social movements, particularly analyzing areas of convergence, divergence, and change among these organizations.

Jeremy Flaherty is a stay-at-home dad living in Northern Indiana. He received his PhD in sociology from Brigham Young University in 2012.

Courtney G. Flint is an associate professor of natural resource sociology at Utah State University. Her research focuses on community-environment interactions along rural to urban gradients; environmental decision making in the face of disturbance, risk, and uncertainty; and alignment issues within transdisciplinary efforts. She received her PhD from the Pennsylvania State University in 2004.

Cornelia Butler Flora is the Charles F. Curtiss distinguished professor emerita of sociology, agriculture, and life sciences at Iowa State University and research professor of sociology at Kansas State University. Her primary research interests are community and food, agriculture, and natural resources, both nationally and internationally. She received her PhD from Cornell University in 1970 and is a past president of the Rural Sociological Society.

Jan L. Flora is a professor emeritus of sociology and a community extension specialist at Iowa State University and a research professor of sociology at Kansas State University. His primary research interests include community, immigration, and social justice with particular emphasis on Latin America and the United States. He received his PhD from Cornell University in 1971 and is a past president of the Rural Sociological Society.

Louise Fortmann is a professor of natural resource sociology and Rudy Grah Chair in forestry and sustainable development in the department of environmental science, policy, and management at the University of California, Berkeley. She received her PhD in rural sociology from Cornell University in 1973.

Lance George is the director of research and information at the Housing Assistance Council (HAC). George's research and policy analysis at HAC encompasses a wide array of issues and topics related to rural housing, including manufactured housing, poverty and high need rural areas, rural definitions and classifications, mortgage access and finance, and general demography, mapping, and data analysis of rural people and their housing conditions.

Brian Gentry is a doctoral student in the sociology graduate program at Utah State University. His dissertation research focuses on reactions to natural gas development in the Intermountain West, Texas, and the Northeast. His most recent work includes a report on the barriers to and drivers of "environmentally friendly" drilling techniques used in the production of natural gas in Utah.

Leland L. Glenna is an associate professor of rural sociology and science, technology, and society at the Pennsylvania State University. His research interests are in agricultural, food, and environmental science and technology. He received his PhD from the University of Missouri-Columbia in 1997.

Todd L. Goodsell is on the faculty of sociology at the University of Utah. His research interests are in community, family, and the culture of everyday life. He received his PhD from the University of Michigan in 2004.

Robert Gramling is an emeritus professor of sociology at the University of Louisiana at Lafayette. His primary research interests are in environmental sociology particularly related to natural resources in coastal areas. He earned his PhD from Florida State University in 1975.

John J. Green is the director of the Center for Population Studies and an associate professor of sociology at the University of Mississippi. His primary research interests concern socioeconomic and health disparities and development in community and regional contexts. He received his PhD in rural sociology from the University of Missouri-Columbia in 2002.

Amy Guptill is an associate professor of sociology at the College at Brockport, State University of New York. Her research focuses on spatial and structural shifts in agrifood systems and local food marketing. She received her PhD from Cornell University in 2004.

William D. Heffernan is a professor emeritus of rural sociology at the University of Missouri. His primary research focused on the causes and social consequences of the changing structure of the agrifood system. He received his PhD in 1968 from the University of Wisconsin-Madison and was elected president of the Rural Sociological Society in 1987.

Mary Hendrickson is an assistant professor of rural sociology at the University of Missouri. Her research programs focus on understanding the changes taking place in the global food system in order for farmers, eaters, and communities to create profitable alternatives. She received her PhD from the University of Missouri-Columbia in 1997.

Christopher R. Henke is an associate professor of sociology and chair of the department of sociology and anthropology at Colgate University. He is the author of *Cultivating Science, Harvesting Power: Science and Industrial Agriculture in California* (MIT Press, 2008). He earned his PhD from the University of California, San Diego in 2000.

Clare Hinrichs is a professor of rural sociology at the Pennsylvania State University. Her research interests center broadly on social, political, and cultural aspects of transitions to sustainable food and agricultural systems. She served as editor of the Rural Sociological Society's Rural Studies Series from 2004 to 2008. She received her PhD from Cornell University in 1993.

Phillip H. Howard is an associate professor in the department of community sustainability at Michigan State University. His research focuses on visualizing structural changes in the food system, and characterizing consumer interests in food ecolabels. He received his PhD in rural sociology from the University of Missouri-Columbia.

Douglas Jackson-Smith is a professor of sociology at Utah State University. His primary research interests are in the sociology of agriculture and food, community, environment, and natural resources. He received his PhD from the University of Wisconsin-Madison in 1995 and served as a vice president of the Rural Sociological Society.

Jeffrey Jacquet is an assistant professor of sociology and rural studies at South Dakota State University. His research and teaching interests are in natural resource sociology and rural industrialization. He received his PhD from Cornell University in 2012.

Eric B. Jensen is a demographer in the population division of the US Census Bureau. His research interests are in the areas of international migration, Mexican migration, and farm labor. He received his PhD in rural sociology and demography from the Pennsylvania State University in 2010.

Leif Jensen is a distinguished professor of rural sociology and demography at the Pennsylvania State University. His primary interests are in rural sociology, social stratification, demography, and international development. He received his PhD in sociology from the University of Wisconsin-Madison in 1987.

Kenneth M. Johnson is a professor of sociology and senior demographer at the Carsey Institute at the University of New Hampshire. His primary research interest is demography with a focus on US population redistribution trends, population diversity, and the relationship between demographic and environmental change. He received his PhD from the University of North Carolina in 1980.

Stephanie L. Kane is an administrative planning specialist and student data analyst working in the Office of Institutional Research at Washington State University. As such, she specializes in survey sampling and estimation, and analyzing institutional data for trends in student enrollment. She holds master's degrees in zoology and statistics from Washington State University.

Julie C. Keller is a visiting assistant professor of sociology at Oberlin College. She received her PhD from the University of Wisconsin-Madison in 2013. Her research interests center on new immigrant destinations, as well as gender and sexuality in rural places.

Alice Kelly is a doctoral candidate of environmental science, policy, and management at the University of California, Berkeley. Her primary research interests are in protected area management and issues of security within them.

Abby Kinchy is an assistant professor in the science and technology studies department at Rensselaer Polytechnic Institute. She received her PhD in sociology from the University of Wisconsin-Madison in 2007, and specializes in the study of political controversies surrounding changes in the systems that produce food and energy.

Richard S. Krannich is a professor of sociology and director of the Center for Society, Economy and the Environment at Utah State University. His research has focused broadly on the effects of changing environmental and natural resource conditions on rural people and communities. He was co-founder and executive director of the International Association for Society and Natural Resources, and served as president of the Rural Sociological Society. He received his PhD from the Pennsylvania State University in 1980.

Naomi Krogman is a professor in environmental sociology at the University of Alberta and also the academic director of the Office of Sustainability. Her primary research interests are the future of the sustainability sciences, sustainable consumption, and environmental policy implementation. She received her PhD from Colorado State University in 1995.

Shirley Laska is an environmental sociologist and long-term community recovery specialist. She is a professor emerita of sociology at the University of New Orleans and the founding director emerita of the UNO Center for Hazards Assessment, Response and Technology. Her research interests include environmental sociology and community recovery from disaster. She received her PhD from Tulane University in 1972.

Linda Lobao is a professor of rural sociology, sociology, and geography at Ohio State University. Her primary research interests are spatial inequality and the role of state and market changes in regional and community well-being. She received her PhD from North Carolina State University in 1986 and is a past president of the Rural Sociological Society.

A.E. Luloff is a professor of rural sociology and co-chair of the human dimensions of natural resources and the environment intercollege graduate degree program at the Pennsylvania State University. Luloff is the co-founder, current executive director, and previous secretary-treasurer of the International Association for Society and Natural Resources. He received his PhD from the Pennsylvania State University in 1977.

Katherine A. MacTavish is an associate professor in human development and family sciences at Oregon State University. For more than a decade she has been engaged in ethnographic work examining the community effect of rural mobile home park residence on child and family well-being. MacTavish received her PhD from University of Illinois Champaign Urbana in 2001.

Marybeth J. Mattingly is the director of research on vulnerable families and a research assistant professor of sociology at the University of New Hampshire. Her primary research interests are in patterns and consequences of child poverty, family, the social safety net, and the intersections of work, family, and gender. She received her PhD from the University of Maryland in 2005.

Diane K. McLaughlin is a professor of rural sociology and demography at the Pennsylvania State University. Her primary research interests are in the ways that community conditions and change influence family and individual well-being with an emphasis on work, income and poverty, and rural youth. She received her PhD from the Pennsylvania State University in 1990.

Patrick H. Mooney is a professor of sociology at the University of Kentucky. His primary research interests are in the sociology of food and agriculture, especially issues of political and economic organization. He received his PhD from the University of Wisconsin-Madison in 1985.

Lois Wright Morton is a professor of rural sociology at Iowa State University. Her primary research interests are civic structure, how place-based communities address natural resource and environmental vulnerabilities, performance-based environmental agricultural management, water quality, and agricultural adaptation to changing climate conditions. She received her PhD from Cornell University in 1998.

Peter B. Nelson is a professor of geography at Middlebury College. His research focuses on migration and community change in the rural United States with a particular interest in the migration patterns of the postwar baby boom. He received his PhD from the University of Washington in 1999.

Timothy S. Parker is a sociologist in the farm and rural household well-being branch of the resources and rural economics division at USDA's Economic Research Service. His research focuses on rural labor markets, poverty, and measures of rurality. He received his MA from the University of Maryland in 1986.

Simona Perry is the research director at c.a.s.e. Consulting Services. She is an ethnographic practitioner focused on energy and natural resource policy, disaster preparedness and response strategies, and the intersection of psychological and cultural change processes. She received her PhD from University of Massachusetts-Amherst in 2009.

Peggy Petrzelka is an associate professor of sociology at Utah State University. Her primary research interests are on the social, political, and environmental impacts of varying land uses, ranging from absentee landownership in the United States to industrialized strawberry agriculture in southern Spain. She received her PhD from Iowa State University in 1999.

Elizabeth Ransom is an associate professor of sociology at the University of Richmond. Her primary research interests are in international development, global agriculture, and food systems with an emphasis on Southern Africa, and science and technology studies especially in relation to agriculture and food. She received her PhD from Michigan State University in 2003.

Danielle Rhubart is a graduate student of rural sociology and demography at the Pennsylvania State University. Her primary research interests are in stratification and poverty in the United States as well as dilemmas of development and political economy in East Africa. She has conducted field research on street children in Kenya. She received her MS from the Pennsylvania State University in 2013.

Kenneth L. Robinson is an associate professor of rural sociology at Clemson University. His primary research interests are in rural entrepreneurship, social impact analysis, and community and economic development. He received his PhD from Cornell University in 2001.

Peter G. Robertson is a doctoral student in the sociology graduate program at Utah State University, specializing in environment and community sociology. His current research activities seek to understand the effects of rapid development of utility-scale renewable energy on nearby communities and examine the varied responses of both local and non-local residents to such developments.

Tom Rudel is a professor in the department of human ecology and sociology at Rutgers University and studies the social dimensions of landscape changes in the Americas, both North and South. His research has focused on metropolitan expansion in the United States and forest losses in the Ecuadorian Amazon. He is currently carrying out field research on the social dimensions of changing pastures in the Amazon. He received his PhD from Yale University in 1977.

Carolyn Sachs is a professor of rural sociology and women's studies at the Pennsylvania State University. Her research interests are in women in agriculture and food systems, gender and environment, sustainable agriculture, and international development. She received her PhD from the University of Kentucky and is a past president of the Rural Sociological Society.

Priscilla Salant directs the Office of Community Partnerships at the University of Idaho. Her work is guided by a core belief that by engaging with statewide constituents, universities produce more useful research and students have better learning outcomes. She received her BS in economics from the University of California Berkeley and her MS from University of Arizona.

Kai A. Schafft is an associate professor of education in the department of education policy studies at the Pennsylvania State University. He directs the Center on Rural Education and Communities and edits the *Journal of Research in Rural Education*. He received his PhD in development sociology from Cornell University in 2003.

Theresa Selfa is an associate professor of environmental studies at the State University of New York, College of Environmental Science and Forestry. Her primary research areas are the politics and governance of agriculture and natural resources, with a regional focus on the United States and Latin America. She received her PhD in development sociology from Cornell University in 2001.

Jeff Sharp is a professor of rural sociology in the School of Environment and Natural Resources at Ohio State University. His primary research interests focus on agricultural and community change at the rural-urban interface. He received his PhD from Iowa State University in 1998.

Jennifer Sherman is an assistant professor of sociology at Washington State University. Her research focuses on the ways in which structural conditions including industrial decline and restructuring impact rural families and communities. Sherman received her BA in sociology and South Asian studies from the University of Wisconsin-Madison in 1995, and her PhD in sociology from the University of California, Berkeley in 2006.

Carla Shoff is a research associate in the Population Research Institute and the Social Science Research Institute at the Pennsylvania State University. Her primary research interests focus on spatial disparities in population health and health-related behaviors between rural and urban areas in the United States. Carla received her PhD in rural sociology and demography from the Pennsylvania State University in 2012.

Tim Slack is an associate professor of sociology at Louisiana State University. His primary research interests are in the areas of social stratification and social demography, with emphasis on forms of economic and spatial inequality. He received his PhD from the Pennsylvania State University in 2004.

Richard Stedman is an associate professor and director of the Human Dimensions Research Unit in the department of natural resources at Cornell University. His primary research and teaching interests are in sense of place and the well-being of natural resource dependent communities. He received his PhD from the University of Wisconsin-Madison in 2000.

Diana Stewart is an assistant professor with a joint position in sociology and the Kellogg Biological Station at Michigan State University. Her work focuses on issues related to food, agriculture, and the environment while theoretically engaging with concepts from environmental sociology, political economy, and science and technology studies. She received her PhD in Environmental Studies from the University of California Santa Cruz in 2009.

Cynthia B. Struthers is an associate professor of sociology and the health and housing program manager for the Illinois Institute for Rural Affairs at Western Illinois University. Her primary research interests are community, family, and poverty in Illinois and the rural Midwest. She received her PhD from Michigan State University in 1999.

Suzanne E. Tallichet is a professor of sociology at Morehead State University where she teaches courses in rural and environmental sociology and seminars in Appalachian studies. Her primary research interests are in environmental issues, economic transition, and grassroots movements. She received her PhD in rural sociology from the Pennsylvania State University in 1991.

Keiko Tanaka is the Dr. & Mrs. C. Milton Coughenour sociology professor in agriculture and natural resources at the University of Kentucky. Her research primarily focuses on the role of agricultural science and technology. Her geographical specialization is in Asia with extensive fieldwork experience in Japan and China. She received her PhD in sociology from Michigan State University in 1997.

Philip Watson is an assistant professor of natural resource and regional development economics. His research focuses on the role of natural resources in the economic health of communities and evidence based economic development planning. He received his PhD in regional economic development and natural resource economics from Colorado State University.

Rick Welsh is a professor of food studies in the department of public health, food studies, and nutrition. His research interests are in the sociology of agrifood systems, science and technology studies, and environmental sociology. He received his PhD in development sociology from Cornell University in 1995.

Brett Wolff received his MA in sociology from the University of Kentucky in 2012. He currently works in the department of horticulture at the University of Kentucky. His research interests are the politics of food security and the role of food security measurement in the United States.

Michelle R. Worosz is an associate professor of rural sociology and core faculty member of the Food Systems Institute at Auburn University. Her research focuses on agrifood system governance, particularly the impact of formal and informal rules on small-scale supply chain actors. She received her PhD from Michigan State University in 2006.

J.D. Wulfhorst is a professor of rural sociology at the University of Idaho. His primary research interests include natural resources management, climate effects in agricultural production, and environmental risk policy in the western United States. He received his PhD from Utah State University in 1997.

Ann Ziebarth is a professor in the housing studies program at the University of Minnesota, College of Design. As a rural sociologist, she studies the impact of economic, social, and political change on people living in small towns and rural areas. She holds a master's of public administration from Harvard University Kennedy School of Government and a PhD in sociology/rural sociology from Louisiana State University.